The United States in the World Economy

D1225582

A National Bureau
of Economic Research
Conference Report

The
United States
in the World
Economy

Edited and with an Introduction by

Martin Feldstein

The University of Chicago Press

Chicago and London

MARTIN FELDSTEIN is the George F. Baker Professor of Economics at Harvard University and president of the National Bureau of Economic Research. He is the author of *Inflation, Tax Rules, and Capital Formation* (1983) and the editor of *The American Economy in Transition* (1980), *Behavioral Simulation Methods in Tax Policy Analysis* (1983), *The Effects of Taxation on Capital Accumulation* (1987), and *Taxes and Capital Formation* (1987), all published by the University of Chicago Press for the National Bureau of Economic Research.

The University of Chicago Press, Chicago 60637
The University of Chicago Press, Ltd., London

97 96 95 94 93 92 91 90 89 88   5 4 3 2 1

Library of Congress Cataloging-in-Publication Data

The United States in the world economy/edited and with an
  introduction by Martin Feldstein.
      p. cm.—(A National Bureau of Economic Research conference
  report)
   These papers are the results of a conference organized by the NBER
in March 1987.
   Includes bibliographies and indexes.
   ISBN 0-226-24077-0. ISBN 0-226-24078-9 (pbk.)
   1. United States—Commercial policy—Congresses. 2. United
States—Foreign economic relations—Congresses. 3. Investments,
American—Congresses. 4. Competition, International—Congresses.
I. Feldstein, Martin S. II. National Bureau of Economic Research.
III. Series: Conference report (National Bureau of Economic
Research)
HF1456.U55 1988
337.73—dc19   87-27718
                                               CIP

Contents

Preface   ix

The United States in the World Economy:
  Introduction   1
Martin Feldstein

1.   **The United States and Foreign Competition**
    in Latin America
    1. Sebastian Edwards   9
    2. Thomas O. Enders   64
    3. Jesus Silva-Herzog   69

2.   **U.S. and Foreign Competition in the**
    Developing Countries of the Asian
    Pacific Rim
    1. Robert E. Baldwin   79
    2. Robert S. Ingersoll   141
    3. Woo-choong Kim   152

3.   * **Our LCD Debts**
    1. Rudiger Dornbusch   161
    2. Thomas S. Johnson   196
    3. Anne O. Krueger   201

4.   * **Financial Innovations in International**
    Financial Markets
    1. Richard M. Levich   215
    2. E. Gerald Corrigan   257
    3. Charles S. Sanford, Jr., and George J. Votja   264

5.   **International Competition in the Products of**
      U.S. Basic Industries
      1. Barry Eichengreen   279
      2. Charles W. Parry   354
      3. Philip Caldwell   358

6.   **International Competition in Services**
      1. Rachel McCulloch   367
      2. Maurice R. Greenberg   407
      3. Lionel H. Olmer   413

7.   **International Competition in Agriculture and**
      U.S. Farm Policy
      1. Bruce L. Gardner   423
      2. H. B. Atwater, Jr.   460
      3. John R. Block   468

8.   **Changing Patterns of International**
      Investment in and by the United States
      1. Robert E. Lipsey   475
      2. Mario Schimberni   545
      3. Robert V. Lindsay   550

9.   **International Capital Flows and Domestic**
      Economic Policies
      1. Jeffrey A. Frankel   559
      2. Saburo Okita   627
      3. Peter G. Peterson   633
      4. James R. Schlesinger   644

      Biographies   659

      List of Contributors   663

      Author Index   667

      Subject Index   00

Preface

This volume brings together the results of a very unusual conference organized by the NBER in March 1987. As a background for this conference, nine academic economists prepared nontechnical background papers on different aspects of the changing role of the United States in the world economy. At the conference itself, the discussion of each of these subjects was launched by prepared personal statements by individuals who have played leading roles in government or business in either the United States or a foreign country. A detailed summary of the discussion at the conference is also included in the volume.

Eight of the nine background papers were written by research associates of the NBER. Their analyses reflect ongoing work in the bureau's International Studies program. William Branson, director of that program, played a key role at an early stage in planning the subjects of this conference.

The authors of the background papers met as a group on two occasions before the final conference to discuss the approach to be taken in each paper and to review critically the preliminary drafts. Each of the authors also benefited from the comments of an outside reviewer who examined his or her paper.

The nineteen individuals who prepared the remarks that launched the individual sessions included several former cabinet members from the United States, Japan, and Mexico, two former U.S. ambassadors, and the chief executive officers of leading businesses in the United States, Europe, and Korea. Their willingness to share their experiences and to participate throughout the conference made for a uniquely interesting series of discussions. The summaries of the discussions were prepared by Andrew Berg.

I am grateful to the Andrew Mellon Foundation for financial support of this conference and of the research presented in the background papers. I am grateful also to the members of the NBER staff for their assistance with all of the details involved in the planning and execution of the meeting and this volume, particularly to Kirsten Foss Davis, Ilana Hardesty, Mark Fitz-Patrick, and Carolyn Terry.

Martin Feldstein

The United States in the World Economy: Introduction

Martin Feldstein

Until the decade of the 1980s it was common for Americans to ignore the international role of our economy. Imports and exports accounted for less than 10 percent of our gross national product, trade was approximately in balance, and international capital flows financed a very small portion of the net investment in the United States. In this environment, government officials, businessmen, and academic economists could safely think about the American economy with little attention to its international linkages.

The events of the 1980s changed all of that. The dollar rose more than 75 percent between 1980 and 1985, leading to a massive trade deficit and a correspondingly large capital inflow. By 1986, the trade deficit exceeded $170 billion or 4 percent of GNP and was inflicting substantial pain on those firms that exported to the rest of the world or that competed with imports from abroad. In addition, the international debt crisis that began in the fall of 1982 drew attention to the links between U.S. banks and the performance of foreign debtor nations. It was no longer possible to ignore the international environment within which the U.S. economy operated.

The NBER conference presented in this volume was held in March 1987. By then the dollar had been declining from its peak for two years and was back within 10 percent of its initial trade-weighted real value. There was, however, no clear evidence that the U.S. trade deficit had begun to shrink. Although the Commerce Department had recently estimated a small decline in the real trade deficit in the final quarter of 1986, the volume of imports was still rising. Congress was debating new trade legislation that would close American markets to foreign products, and the finance ministers of the major industrial countries were discussing ways to stabilize the exchange rates.

Despite the very slow adjustment of the U.S. trade deficit, most economists believed that the reversal of the dollar's rise would soon cause a significant rise in exports and decline in imports. I and several others had predicted that the dollar would go on declining and would fall enough so that the United States would actually have a trade surplus by the early 1990s. This shift from massive trade deficit to trade surplus will occur because the world financial markets will not finance the flow of capital to the United States that would be required if the United States continued to have a trade deficit.

More specifically, past experience implies that if the dollar remained at its level of early 1987, the U.S. trade deficit would shrink from $170 billion to about $90 billion but would then stop declining. Financing that trade deficit would therefore require a capital inflow of $90 billion a year from the rest of the world. But in addition to this capital inflow, the United States would also require additional credit from the rest of the world to finance the interest and dividends that accrued on the foreign investments in the United States. By the end of 1986, the net foreign investment in the United States was $200 billion. That total was growing at an annual rate of $140 billion and could be expected to exceed $800 billion within five years. The interest and dividends on this amount would be about $60 billion. Thus the total capital inflow required by the early 1990s would be $150 billion a year and rising.

Foreign investors are very unlikely to be willing to devote so much of their own saving to investments in U.S. assets. Even if they are willing to go on lending the full amount of the interest and dividends that accrues each year, the United States would still have to export an amount equal to our imports, that is, to be in trade balance. If foreign investors want to provide less credit and get some net interest and dividend income on the funds that they have already provided, the United States will have to run a trade surplus. Indeed, a shift to trade surplus must eventually begin since otherwise the United States will have enjoyed a monumental capital inflow without ever giving anything in return. (For a more complete but non-technical discussion, see Feldstein 1987.)

The challenge to the United States is to achieve this rebalancing of trade without a reduction in net investment in the United States and without a recession. The current level of U.S. investment in plant and equipment and in housing has been sustained by the capital inflow from the rest of the world. As the trade deficit and the current account deficit shrink, the capital inflow from the rest of the world will also decline. Unless saving in the United States increases substantially, our domestic investment will inevitably fall.

The key to increasing the national saving rate is to reduce the deficit in the federal budget. A government budget deficit in 1987 of $180 billion would absorb about half of all the net saving of households, businesses, and state and local governments. If the capital inflow from the rest of the world declines without a corresponding fall in government borrowing, real interest rates in the United States would have to rise to induce a substantial enough fall in net investment in plant and equipment and in housing. The fact that real long-term interest rates are currently nearly twice their historic average reflects the market's concern that this clash between the government's borrowing needs and private investment demand will soon be exacerbated by a decline in the inflow of foreign capital.

The requirement for avoiding a decline in domestic investment while the economy returns to a trade balance is easier to specify than it is to achieve politically. The goal of shrinking the budget deficit has been accepted by both political parties since the beginning of the decade, but they have not been able to find a consensus on the composition of the deficit reduction.

The challenge of avoiding a recession while the United States returns to a trade balance is equally difficult, but the problem is technical as well as political because it is not clear what steps, if any, need to be taken. The most obvious direct effect of the decline in the trade deficit is expansionary since exports rise and imports fall. But the decline in the trade deficit also brings with it contractionary side effects: the rise in interest rates and fall in investment, the decline in the fiscal stimulus if the budget deficit is reduced in order to limit the interest rate increase, and the fall in consumption that occurs because American households become poorer as the decline in the dollar reduces their purchasing power in world markets and therefore reduces the real income that they have to spend at home. No one can know the relative speeds with which these positive and negative forces will affect overall demand and production in the United States. If the direct effect on net exports comes sooner and is stronger, a recession will automatically be avoided. But if the adverse effects on investment and consumption occur sooner, the economy could fall into a temporary recession.

A monetary policy aimed at stabilizing nominal GNP might dampen these effects but could not be certain to prevent a recession. A more expansionary monetary policy could lead to rising inflation that would create even greater problems in the future. And discretionary fiscal policies aimed at offsetting a potential but uncertain economic downturn could actually exacerbate cyclical instability if the timing of their effects are inappropriate. The risk of an economic downturn in the process of returning to a trade balance is the price that the American economy must pay for not dealing sooner with the fiscal imbalances that caused the trade deficit.

Changes Abroad

The shift of the United States from a massive trade deficit to a trade surplus will bring substantial gains to many American firms and their employees. But the nature and magnitude of those gains will depend on developments in the rest of the world. Much of the conference dealt with the potential for such changes abroad.

A central issue in this context is the extent to which foreign countries will give American firms greater access to their markets. Although the financial forces in world capital markets will eventually cause the dollar to decline by enough to lead to a U.S. trade surplus regardless of whether or not foreign markets are opened, the gains for both Americans and foreigners will be greater if foreign markets are more open as this occurs. If foreign markets are open, U.S. firms will be able to produce those products and services in which we are relatively more efficient. This allows American workers and firms to benefit from doing more of what they do best and permits foreign buyers to take advantage of the relatively low cost of U.S. production.

If however foreign markets are closed to an increased volume of American products, the shift from the current trade deficit to a trade surplus will be achieved by reducing imports into the United States. This reduction in imports could be obtained by either an even greater fall in the dollar than would otherwise be necessary or by explicit protectionist policies of quotas and tariffs. The fall in the dollar would be the least harmful of these while the quotas would be the most harmful. In either case, American firms and workers would lose the opportunity to sell more of the products in which they have a comparative advantage. Moreover, American consumers would be denied the opportunity to buy the foreign goods that they would have been able to purchase if foreigners were buying more of U.S. products.

There is a clear risk that the falling dollar will lead the major trading partners of the United States to become more protectionist in order to avoid competition at home from American producers. This would not stop the shifting trade balance but it would hurt foreign consumers and foreign exporters and would encourage protectionist retaliation by the United States.

It is not surprising, therefore, that the problem of access to foreign markets came up repeatedly in the conference. Much of this discussion focused on the special problems of access to the markets of Japan and the newly industrialized countries of the Asian Pacific rim. There was also substantial attention to the problem of selling in Latin America now that the international debt situation has required those countries to reduce their imports.

Access to foreign markets involves access for the sale of services and for investments as well as for the sale of goods. This point was emphasized in two of the sessions of the conference and has been recognized in the new round of GATT negotiations. Access for services is more complex in many ways than access for goods since access for services generally involves being able to produce the service in the foreign country as well as to sell it there. Effective access means providing the same "national" treatment to foreign suppliers of a service as to domestic suppliers so that the two can compete equally. Because there are so many special features in the markets for services and in foreign investment, it appears that progress will be slow and will have to be made on a bilateral case-by-case basis as well as under the umbrella of an expanded multilateral GATT (General Agreement on Tariffs and Trade).

Restricting the imports of goods and services and excluding foreign investment are not the only barriers to free international commerce. The other major problem discussed at the conference was the provision of government subsidies to exports and to domestic producers. This has been a problem in a number of industries but has been particularly acute in agriculture.

The dramatic reduction of U.S. agricultural exports in recent years can also be traced to technological changes abroad, to trends in foreign income and population, and to the introduction of effective production incentives in China, Latin America, and elsewhere. But the growing volume of agricultural subsidies in Europe, Japan, and the United States is extremely wasteful. They cause a serious misallocation of productive resources to low-value activities, contribute significantly to government budget deficits, and raise the cost of food to European and Japanese consumers.

Latin American Debtors

The increased agricultural exports from Latin America have helped those countries adjust to the drying up of new foreign capital after 1982. The sessions at the conference on Latin America and on the international debt problem emphasized the progress being made in those countries as well as the seriousness of the current situation for both the debtors and the creditor institutions.

The fundamental problem in achieving the successful management of the debt problem in the major middle-income debtor countries is achieving a cooperation between creditors and debtors that neither has a compelling incentive to offer. The debtors need to limit their debt service payments in order to achieve an acceptable rate of economic growth, while the creditors need to limit their exposure in order to raise funds at a cost that permits them to compete in world credit markets. It is tempting, therefore, for each side to unilaterally abandon the effort at a cooperative solution.

Fortunately, it is in principle possible to permit the debt to grow at a rate that is fast enough to support acceptable growth in the debtor countries while still shrinking the ratio of the debt to the GNPs and exports of those countries and to the overall size of the banks' capital and earnings. The problem is to convince both creditors and debtors that such a cooperative solution is more in their interest than a de facto unilateral repudiation of debt by the debtors or an unwillingness to provide any additional credit by the creditors. And as the conference presentations emphasized, any additional credit will be more effective if it is combined with reforms in the debtor countries that lead to higher growth and better resource use.

Changing World Capital Markets

The dramatic fluctuations in the relative value of the dollar and the unprecedented growth in the size of the U.S. trade deficit captured the headlines in the 1980s. But the more fundamental and persistent changes in the world economy that happened during those years were the structural innovations in international financial markets. New technologies and regulatory reforms have combined to create global financial markets that did not exist a decade ago. The pace of change was accelerated when the sharp fluctuations in exchange rates and interest rates spurred the demand for new instruments that could protect investors from unwanted speculation.

The new financial instruments and their new uses have permitted individual investors to achieve a better allocation of credit and of risks around the world. But while protecting individual investors, they may also have increased the overall risks to the banking and financial systems. Neither the banks and other financial institutions that use the new domestic and international instruments nor the government agencies that regulate those banks can be fully confident that they know the effects of the new instruments and new investment strategies. Only substantially more study and time will tell the significance of their increasing role.

The conference discussion highlighted some of the risks of the changing financial marketplace and the impact of international competition as a driving force in this change. Moreover, because American investors and borrowers can use foreign capital markets and foreign institutions that do business in the United States, the traditional bank regulations may significantly reduce the competitiveness of American banks and weaken the American banking system. This is accelerating the deterioration of the old role of banks and hastening their shift to the development of new and riskier products and services.

In an integrated world capital market, regulatory provisions must be uniform across countries and competing institutions in order to avoid weakening those institutions and markets that are more tightly regulated. Some steps have already been taken by the Federal Reserve and the Bank of England to coordinate bank capital requirements. Over time, this type of coordination of banking rules is likely to spread to other countries and other issues. Ultimately it may become a principal that extends to other financial service industries.

The impact of our integrated world capital markets may reach much further. If long-term capital comes to flow very freely among major industrial countries, it will no longer be possible to develop tax systems without taking such capital flows into account. A country with higher tax rates will drive away profitable businesses, while a country with generous investment allowances will attract more investments in plant and equipment. At the level of macroeconomic policy, the availability of foreign capital postponed the rise in U.S. interest rates and may therefore have given U.S. officials the political luxury of ignoring the deficit for a longer time than would otherwise have been possible. Similarly, the current fall in the dollar and corresponding rise in interest rates may force political action to reduce the deficit sooner than would otherwise have happened.

The falling dollar may also have an important impact on national security decisions and American strategic policies. The substantial decline of the dollar makes it more expensive for the United States to maintain troops abroad, to provide foreign aid, and to do anything that requires purchasing goods and services in foreign markets. The government may respond to this higher price by cutting back on such overseas activities, changing the volume and nature of the American presence abroad.

In the years ahead the role of the United States in the world economy is likely to change fundamentally as foreign companies play a larger direct role inside the American economy. The United States is of course fundamentally attractive to foreign investors because of its massive $5 trillion market place, its political stability, its continuing flow of technological and product innovations, and its relatively flexible labor and product markets. The recent tax changes increase the appeal of location in the United States to businesses that produce substantial taxable profits or high professional incomes. The sharp decline in the dollar also makes American assets more attractive to foreign buyers and lowers the relative cost of production in the United States. The next decade is therefore likely to see an increase in the volume and range of foreign businesses investing in American facilities.

The papers in this volume indicate the diversity of the ways in which the American economy influences and is influenced by economic events and conditions around the world. The experience of the 1980s has dramatically demonstrated the power and extent of this interdependence. American businessmen must become increasingly global in their activities and in their vision of the market environment within which they operate. Policy officials in the United States must recognize that the response of the American economy to changes in American economic policies is very much influenced by the impact of those policies on trade and capital flows. This conference and the resulting book will have been a success if they increase the awareness of corporate leaders, policymakers, and economic analysts to this changing role of the United States in the world economy.

Reference

Feldstein, Martin. 1987. Correcting the trade deficit. *Foreign Affairs,* Spring.

1 The United States and Foreign Competition in Latin America

1. Sebastian Edwards
2. Thomas O. Enders
3. Jesus Silva-Herzog

1. Sebastian Edwards

1.1 Introduction

This paper analyzes the role of the United States in the development of Latin America's international trade relations. In particular the paper investigates the behavior of trade flows between the United States and the Latin American nations in the last fifteen years or so, and analyzes the possible path these trade relations will take in the future. In doing this, I place special emphasis on any possible changes in the directions of trade in Latin America, scrutinizing whether there has been, or will possibly be, a significant increase in south-south trade, and if new trade partners such as Japan and the newly industrialized countries of Southeast Asia have displaced the more traditional Latin American trade partners (i.e., the United States). The paper also deals with issues related to direct investment in Latin America, comparing the importance of the United States and other nations. Finally, I also discuss the role of international trade in the solution to the current Latin American debt crisis and in the resumption of sustained growth in the region. An important, indeed crucial, issue relates to the future evolution of the current protectionist mood in the United States and much of the developed world.

As we enter the final years of the 1980s, policy issues related to the volume and direction of U.S. international trade have become increasingly important. In particular, a number of special interest lobbies have argued with alarming insistence that the "increased competition" by other countries to capture foreign markets and unfair trade practices, such as dumping and export subsidy schemes not sanctioned by the GATT (General Agreement on Tariffs and Trade), have been responsible for the mounting trade deficits and for the "loss of jobs" in the United States. Several important questions emerge here: First, what is meant exactly by "loss of U.S. international competitiveness"? Second, given an answer to the first question, has the United States indeed lost competitiveness? Third, what are the future prospects for U.S. trade relations? And finally, what and to whom will the United States export in the future, and from which countries will U.S. imports come? The present paper deals with these questions from the perspective of the U.S. trade relations with Latin America.

The evolution of the volume and direction of trade is also of paramount importance for the Latin American countries. In the early 1980s, after two decades of sustained economic growth averaging approximately 6 percent per annum, Latin America entered a period of severe adjustment. The need for this adjustment resulted, to a large extent, from a series of major shocks—both exogenous and policy induced—that greatly disturbed the region's economy. The principal exogenous shocks were the oil price increases of 1973–74 and 1979–80, the drastic deterioration of the terms of trade experienced after 1980, and the steep rise of world interest rates in 1980–82 which provoked a major increase in the debt service burden. At the policy level, the substantial increases in government expenditure and fiscal deficits and the economic liberalization reforms attempted by some of these countries, as well as general and very significant increases in external indebtedness, constituted the most important events. Some countries went from being highly praised "economic miracles" to "international pariahs." Others, which in the mid- to late 1970s were flooded with abundant foreign exchange—obtained mainly through the exportation of petroleum—have experienced severe difficulties servicing their foreign debt. The region is at this moment still struggling to overcome its worst recession since the 1930s. As it slowly emerges from the crisis, it finds a substantial portion of its export earnings mortgaged for the foreseeable future to service the accumulated external debt and a general scarcity of additional external funds.

There is little doubt that a permanent solution to Latin America's current crisis and the resumption of sustained growth will require a major effort to increase exports and to enhance the role of the external sector as a source of foreign exchange earnings. In that regard, it is especially important to determine whether the Latin American countries' efforts to increase their exports will be frustrated by protectionist policies implemented by the industrialized nations. Indeed, the Latin American countries' efforts to adjust and put the crisis behind them would receive a severe blow if the current protectionist lobby scores victories in the United States and European countries. Increased protectionism could take two forms: the enactment of protective legislation or the stepping up of the already significant nontariff barriers existing in these countries.

Some of the sections of this paper are largely descriptive; this has been deliberate since an important purpose of this study is to scrutinize the data and to document and interpret the recent history of the Latin American trade relations with the United States. In spite of the descriptive tone of some sections, the paper as a whole makes a number of analytical points related to the nature of these external relations. Section 1.2 discusses some of the main current characteristics of the Latin American economies as well as the way in which the region's external sector policies have evolved. Section 1.3 deals with Latin American imports; it investigates the recent behavior of the region's degree of openness, aggregate imports, and origin of imports at the disaggregated level. In this section I show that much of the region's effort to cope with the debt crisis has been translated into a substantial drop in the real value of imports. This section contains massive amounts of data on how much, what, and from whom sixteen Latin American countries import. Emphasis is placed on analyzing the evolution of the U.S. share of the value of Latin America's imports and the changing composition of the region's imports from the United States. I show here that when the constant-market-share criterion is used, there is no support for the contention of a recent loss of aggregate U.S. competitiveness in Latin America. The data, however, do show that there has been a change in the composition of Latin America's imports from the United States. The share of traditional manufacturing has declined, while primary products and technology-intensive manufactures have experienced an increased presence among the region's imports.

Section 1.4 deals with Latin America's exports and investigates their recent behavior and composition. It shows that in spite of a series of corrective measures taken by these countries since the debt crisis, for the region as a whole the recent evolution of the (real) value of exports has been very disappointing. An important issue analyzed in this section is related to the role of protectionism in the industrialized countries on the possible access of Latin American products to those markets. Using recent data on nontariff barriers, I show that the extent of these nontariff impediments to trade is much more generalized than previously thought. I then argue that only to the extent that a drastic change occurs in the protectionist mood in the industrial world will it be possible for Latin America's trade to gain in prominence.

Section 1.5 deals with commercial policy and protectionism in Latin America. Here I show how in the late 1960s and 1970s, after the heyday of the import substitution development strategy, most of the Latin

American countries slowly began to reduce their impediments to trade. This trend, which was particularly marked in the Southern Cone countries in the late 1970s, was reversed in the 1980s when, as a consequence of the debt crisis, most of these countries resorted to the imposition of controls to reduce imports. In this section I also discuss the role of nontariff barriers in Latin America. Section 1.6 deals with exchange rate policies. Here two main issues are addressed. First, I look at the behavior of real exchange rates in these nations and argue that the fairly generalized tendency toward overvaluation in the late 1970s and early 1980s greatly contributed to the poor behavior of the region's external sector. Second, I point out how the existence of multiple nominal exchange rates and of pervasive parallel markets for foreign exchange have played an important protective role in these countries. Section 1.7 deals with direct investment. Here I analyze the historical evidence and argue that in the next few years direct investment will probably be one of the more important sources of external financing that these countries will have. This, of course, will require some creative rethinking of the current regional policy on direct foreign investment and related issues. Finally, section 1.8 deals with the possible future evolution of U.S.–Latin American trade relations and contains the concluding remarks.

1.2 The Latin American Economies: A Brief Overview

Table 1.1 contains data on a number of economic indicators for sixteen Latin American countries.[1] There are very marked differences across the countries of the region in terms of income per capita, recent growth performance, and inflation, which of course makes generalizations difficult. In fact there is no such thing as "the representative" Latin American country. Therefore my analysis generally provides data on only these sixteen countries.

Although today the countries of Latin America are economically diverse and stand at different junctions of their development paths, they share a common evolution of their policies toward the external sector. In the rest of this section, and to put things in perspective, I provide a brief description of the role of the external sector in the development of the Latin American countries.

1.2.1 Latin American Development and External Sector Policies

Until the 1930s the external sector in the great majority of the Latin American countries was highly opened; exchange controls were almost nonexistent, import tariffs were low, and the "rules of the game" were strictly followed. The Great Depression, with its devastating effect on

Table 1.1 **Basic Indicators for Selected Latin American Countries**

	GNP per Capita 1984 (1984 US$)	Average Rate Growth GDP (%)		Average Yearly Inflation 1973–84 (%)	1984 Total Long-Term Gross Foreign Debt as % GNP	Manufacturing Production as % GDP 1984
		1965–73	1973–84			
Upper middle income						
Argentina	2,230	4.3	0.4	180.8	46.8	30
Brazil	1,720	9.8	4.4	71.4	44.0	27
Chile	1,700	3.4	2.7	75.4	100.2	21
Mexico	2,040	7.9	5.1	31.5	54.2	24
Uruguay	1,980	1.2	2.0	50.0	54.5	n.a.
Venezuela	3,410	5.1	1.9	11.7	52.7	18
Middle income						
Colombia	1,390	6.4	3.7	23.8	25.7	18
Paraguay	1,240	5.1	7.5	12.9	36.2	17
Costa Rica	1,190	7.1	2.8	24.1	114.0	n.a.
Guatemala	1,160	6.0	3.1	9.4	7.0	n.a.
Ecuador	1,150	7.2	4.8	17.8	75.1	19
Peru	1,000	3.5	1.5	56.7	162.0	25
Lower income						
Nicaragua	860	3.9	−1.1	13.0	7.0	25
El Salvador	710	4.4	−0.3	11.3	9.0	16
Honduras	700	4.5	3.8	8.6	4.0	15
Bolivia	540	4.4	0.8	54.5	n.a	20

Source: World Bank.

the region's economies, put an end to all of that; it marked the beginning of an epoch of import substitution and protectionism.[2]

During the 1950s and 1960s, under the intellectual leadership of the United Nations Economic Commission for Latin America (ECLA), and its charismatic secretary general Raul Prebisch, most of the Latin American countries embarked on ambitious industrialization programs based on import substitution. This strategy was based on the idea that high import tariffs and other impediments to international trade would provide temporary protection to the local industries and help them develop. In theory, after some time the domestic firms would have "learned" and protection would no longer be necessary (Prebisch 1984). Things did not work out as predicted by the theory, however, and protection became a permanent feature in the region. As a result, in most of these countries the industrial sector that was developed under the barriers of protection was largely inefficient, using highly capital-intensive techniques (Krueger 1983).

During the 1950s and first half of the 1960s it became apparent that the import substitution strategy was losing dynamism. Although the easier and more obvious imports had already been substituted, these countries remained highly "dependent" on imported intermediate inputs and capital goods. At the same time the highly overvalued domestic currencies conspired against the development of a dynamic export sector, with the consequent scarcity of foreign exchange.[3]

During the late 1960s a reaction against excessive protectionism started to take place, and a number of countries—Colombia being the premier example—moved toward export promotion schemes (Diaz-Alejandro 1976). Also during this period some serious efforts were made to create common markets comprising subgroups of Latin American countries. In that respect the creation of the Andean group and the Central American Common Market were particularly important. Although in some regards these integrationist schemes were successful, they did not turn around the region's economies, and in many cases the external sector—and the excessive protectionism—was still seen as the "weak link" by most analysts (see Blejer 1984).

During the second half of the 1970s a fairly generalized recognition of the benefits of export promotion had developed, and most countries tended to rationalize their external sector. In the countries of the Southern Cone (Argentina, Chile, and Uruguay), massive reforms aimed at opening up these economies were implemented: tariffs were reduced, and exchange controls disappeared. After an initial successful period, these opening reforms faltered, and in the early 1980s these countries entered into a major recession, as did the rest of Latin America.[4] The 1980 crisis forced the Latin American countries to greatly reduce their imports and to improve their current account balances. As discussed in section 1.5, most countries resorted to increased import controls in their attempts to improve their foreign accounts.

1.3   The Structure and Evolution of Imports in Latin America

This section analyzes the recent evolution of imports in Latin America, placing special emphasis on the role of the United States as a trade partner. An important question addressed here is whether the available data show any trend in the value of Latin America's imports from the United States. The analysis focuses on three important aspects of this problem. We first look at the historical evaluation of the dollar value of international trade (imports and exports) in Latin America. Second, we analyze the evolution of the degree of openness of the countries in the region, and we also look in detail at the behavior of the trade and current account balances. And third, we analyze the distribution of Latin American imports both across countries and across productive sectors, looking in detail at the United States' and other countries' shares of the value of Latin American imports.

1.3.1   Imports, Exports, and the Degree of Openness

Tables 1.2 and 1.3 contain data on the dollar value of imports and exports for fourteen Latin American countries between 1965 and 1985. In table 1.4 the current account balances for these countries are presented. Table 1.5 presents the evolution of indicators of openness defined as the ratio of total trade—imports *plus* exports—to GDP.

Table 1.2 on imports is extremely revealing, showing that for most countries the (nominal) dollar value of imports peaked between 1980 and 1982, only to experience a dramatic fall in the years following the eruption of the debt crisis. In every single country the (nominal) dollar value of imports in 1985 was well below its 1980 level. For these fourteen countries as a whole the (nominal) dollar value of imports was, in 1985, 36 percent below its 1980 value. Moreover, when expressed in real dollar terms, 1985 total imports are 45 percent below their 1980 value.[5] Of course, this mainly reflects the reduction in imports required by the adjustment programs implemented by these countries after the 1982 debt crisis.[6] Table 1.3 on the value of exports also reflects the effects of the adjustment programs. In a number of these countries— Argentina, Brazil, Ecuador, and Mexico—the value of exports was in 1985 significantly above its 1980 value. This was achieved in spite of the fact that for most of the countries in the region the international prices of their exports declined substantially during the period (see section 1.4).

Table 1.2 Evolution of Imports in Selected Latin American Countries, 1965–85 (millions of U.S. dollars)

	1965	1970	1975	1980	1982	1983	1984	1985
Argentina	1,199	1,694	3,946	10,541	5,337	4,504	4,585	3,814
Bolivia	134	159	575	678	578	545	474	582
Brazil	1,096	2,849	13,592	24,961	21,069	16,801	15,210	14,346
Chile	604	941	1,338	5,123	3,528	2,968	3,191	2,742
Columbia	454	843	1,495	4,663	5,478	4,968	4,498	4,141
Costa Rica	178	317	694	1,540	889	988	1,094	1,098
Dominican Republic	97	304	889	1,640	1,444	1,471	1,446	1,487
Ecuador	151	274	987	2,253	1,989	1,465	1,716	1,606
Guatemala	229	284	733	1,598	1,388	1,135	1,277	1,175
Mexico	1,560	2,461	6,571	19,460	15,127	8,023	11,788	13,994
Panama	208	357	892	1,449	1,569	1,412	1,984	1,423
Peru	729	622	2,551	2,500	3,601	2,548	2,212	1,835
Uruguay	151	231	557	1,680	1,110	788	777	788
Venezuela	1,393	1,869	6,004	11,827	12,944	8,709	7,594	8,178

Source: International Monetary Fund.

Table 1.3   Evolution of Exports in Selected Latin American Countries, 1965–85 (millions of U.S. dollars)

	1965	1970	1975	1980	1982	1983	1984	1985
Argentina	1,493	1,773	2,961	8,021	7,624	7,836	8,107	8,396
Bolivia	n.a.	190	444	942	828	755	725	673
Brazil	1,596	2,739	8,670	20,132	20,175	21,899	27,005	25,639
Chile	637	1,248	1,552	4,671	3,710	3,836	3,657	3,797
Colombia	539	736	1,465	3,945	3,095	3,080	3,461	3,551
Costa Rica	112	231	493	1,002	870	882	1,006	962
Dominican Republic	126	249	894	961	767	785	868	735
Ecuador	164	190	974	2,481	2,128	2,224	2,583	2,905
Guatemala	187	298	641	1,557	1,153	1,180	1,127	—
Mexico	1,120	1,403	2,904	15,570	21,214	21,818	24,407	22,108
Panama	79	110	286	361	375	321	276	335
Peru	685	1,034	1,291	3,898	3,293	3,015	3,147	2,966
Uruguay	191	233	384	1,059	1,023	1,045	925	855
Venezuela	2,455	2,627	8,800	19,221	16,499	15,159	13,971	12,272

Source: International Monetary Fund.

Table 1.4 Current Account Balance in Selected Latin American Countries, 1965–85 (millions of U.S. dollars)

	1965	1970	1975	1980	1982	1983	1984	1985
Argentina	222	-163	-1,287	-4,774	-2,353	-2,436	-2,495	-954
Bolivia	-24	4	-130	-118	-94	-151	-179	-282
Brazil	284	-837	-7,008	-12,806	-16,312	-6,837	42	-273
Chile	-43	-91	-490	-1,971	-2,304	-1,117	-2,060	-1,307
Colombia	-21	-293	-172	-206	-3,054	-3,003	-1,401	-1,390
Costa Rica	-68	-74	-218	-664	-278	-317	-253	-374
Dominican Republic	43	-102	-73	-671	-443	-418	-163	n.a.
Ecuador	-19	-113	-220	-642	-1,195	-104	-248	-85
Guatemala	-35	-8	-66	-163	-399	-224	-377	-246
Mexico	-352	-1,068	-4,042	-8,162	-6,218	5,328	3,966	540
Panama	-100	-64	-169	-311	-51	247	-70	21
Peru	—	-22	-1,541	62	-1,612	-875	-223	53
Uruguay	72	-45	-190	-709	-235	-60	-124	-108.1
Venezuela	35	-104	2,171	4,728	-4,246	4,427	5,418	2,923

Source: International Monetary Fund.

Table 1.4 on the current account balances also vividly portrays the impact of the crisis on the region's external sector and the substantial efforts the region has made to adjust to the new post-1982 reality. In eleven of the fourteen countries, the current account balance experienced a substantial improvement between 1980 and 1985. Moreover, five of these countries—Argentina, Brazil, Chile, Mexico, and Uruguay—turned trade deficits into fairly large trade surpluses during this period.

Table 1.5 contains data on an indicator of these economies' degree of openness: the ratio of total trade (imports *plus* exports) to GDP. Although the behavior of this index differs from country to country, it is still possible to draw some general pattern of behavior. According to this index there was a fairly significant increase in the degree of openness in the 1970s. This general move toward greater openness is revealed both when 1975 is compared with 1970 and when 1980 is compared with 1970. For example, between 1970 and 1975 the index of total trade to GDP experienced significant increases in twelve of the thirteen countries that have data. During this period, in nine out of the thirteen countries that have data the ratio of total trade to GDP increased by at least five percentage points, and in two other countries it increased by more than two percentage points. Only in the cases of Bolivia and Costa Rica did this index decline. Moreover, the ratio of

Table 1.5   **Openness Index in Selected Latin American Countries, 1965–85**

	1965	1970	1975	1980	1985
Argentina	—	—	33.8	12.8	18.4[a]
Bolivia	40.2	33.6	41.4	30.9	14.6[b]
Brazil	12.5	13.7	19.3	21.0	20.2[b]
Chile	18.6	29.2	61.1	35.5	38.0
Colombia	22.0	22.5	23.8	27.2	21.0
Costa Rica	48.9	55.6	60.5	52.6	56.8
Dominican Republic	23.3	37.2	49.5	39.2	47.7
Ecuador	28.6	33.1	45.5	40.3	33.4[b]
Guatemala	31.3	30.6	37.1	40.0	25.6[b]
Mexico	13.0	10.9	10.81	18.9	13.3
Panama	43.6	45.7	64.0	50.8	37.4
Peru	33.0	26.6	31.4	41.9	31.6[b]
Uruguay	34.8	19.3	29.3	29.0	34.8[b]
Venezuela	45.2	38.3	53.7	52.4	51.6[b]

Note: This index was constructed as the ratio of total trade (imports plus exports) to GDP.

Source: Constructed from data from the International Monetary Fund.

[a]1983.

[b]1984.

imports to GDP tells very much the same story. Only for the cases of
Bolivia, Costa Rica, and Ecuador did it decline between 1970 and 1980.[7]
Generally speaking the available evidence strongly indicates that the
1970s was a decade where most of the nations of Latin America became
more open to the rest of the world. In fact, as shown in section 1.5,
this openness is reflected in the evolution of the level of import tariffs
and other impediments to trade during this period.

As table 1.5 clearly shows, during the first half of the 1980s the trend
toward greater openness was drastically reversed, with the openness
index exhibiting a sharp drop for most countries. This, of course, was
partially the consequence of the crisis and adjustment policies that
required a significant cut in imports. Table 1.5 shows that in the case
of the total trade ratio, in nine of the fourteen countries there was a
decline between 1980 and 1985.[8] The imports ratios also experienced
significant declines in twelve of the fourteen countries; in most of these
countries the 1985 imports ratios were significantly below their 1970
and 1975 values.

1.3.2   The Composition of Imports

In this section we look at the evolution of different countries' shares
of the value of Latin America's imports both at an aggregate and dis-
aggregate level. This analysis is particularly important to assess whether
the United States has experienced a loss in its competitive position in
the region. In fact, according to the so-called constant-market-share
criterion, a country's degree of competitiveness in a particular market
will remain constant (decrease) if its share of that region's imports
remains constant (decreases).[9] However, the discussion that follows
should be interpreted with some caution, since these are shares of the
U.S. dollar value of imports and are thus influenced by changes in the
real value of the dollar. In particular, a real appreciation of the dollar
will result in an increase in these market shares, even if the *quantities*
imported from the United States and other countries remain constant.
Naturally, a real depreciation of the dollar will have the opposite effect:
it will decrease the market shares even if quantities imported are not
affected.[10] In spite of this shortcoming, however, the analysis of the
evolution of market shares is revealing. Moreover, these shares are the
only indicators on the distribution of Latin American imports that can
be constructed with the available data.

Aggregate Trends

Tables 1.6, 1.7, and 1.8 contain data on the percentage distribution
of the value of imports for sixteen Latin American countries for 1977–
85. These data give us information on what fraction of the U.S. dollar
value of each of these countries' imports came from industrialized

Table 1.6 **Upper-Income Latin American Countries: Distribution of Total Imports by Origin, 1977–85 (percentage)**

	1977	1978	1979	1980	1981	1982	1983	1984	1985
Argentina									
From:									
Industrialized	65.8	67.5	65.0	68.2	69.1	62.8	65.0	58.1	62.7
U.S.	18.8	18.6	21.1	22.6	22.2	35.1	20.2	18.5	17.5
Japan	—	—	—	—	—	12.8	6.7	8.2	6.6
Oil exporting	5.9	2.4	3.0	5.6	4.5	3.3	.7	n.a.	n.a.
Non-oil LDCs	26.5	27.1	30.2	24.6	24.4	32.2	33.2	n.a.	n.a.
Brazil									
From:									
Industrialized	53.4	56.1	48.9	46.6	41.8	38.6	38.5	39.7	46.7
U.S.	19.6	21.1	18.3	18.6	16.3	15.0	15.6	16.6	21.2
Japan	7.1	8.9	6.0	4.8	5.7	4.6	3.7	4.0	4.4
Oil exporting	30.2	29.1	33.1	36.4	41.4	41.9	40.9	n.a.	n.a.
Non-oil LDCs	14.8	13.4	16.9	16.0	15.8	17.2	17.4	n.a.	n.a.
Chile									
From:									
Industrialized	53.4	57.4	54.2	60.1	60.7	57.0	50.1	52.2	52.1
U.S.	20.5	27.0	22.6	28.5	25.6	26.0	25.5	21.5	21.1
Japan	11.0	7.5	7.6	7.2	10.6	6.5	5.9	9.0	6.0
Oil exporting	13.7	10.3	12.7	5.2	7.6	7.7	11.3	n.a.	n.a.
Non-oil LDCs	31.8	28.5	28.9	30.9	26.0	21.8	38.5	n.a.	n.a.
Mexico									
From:									
Industrialized	92.8	93.1	92.0	85.8	87.1	88.2	84.1	84.9	89.9
U.S.	63.7	60.4	62.6	61.6	63.8	59.9	60.3	62.2	68.5
Japan	5.4	8.1	6.5	5.1	5.0	5.7	4.4	4.2	5.6
Oil exporting	0.3	0.4	0.4	0.2	0.2	0.3	0.2	n.a.	n.a.
Non-oil LDCs	6.6	6.2	6.9	5.6	6.6	6.6	15.3	n.a	n.a
Uruguay									
From:									
Industrialized	38.5	36.8	34.9	35.9	35.8	34.7	29.8	31.8	36.8
U.S.	9.6	8.7	9.3	9.8	9.7	12.3	8.3	8.5	9.3
Japan	2.4	2.0	2.5	4.1	4.9	2.8	2.4	1.8	2.4
Oil exporting	25.5	26.0	22.0	25.4	21.4	27.8	29.7	n.a.	n.a.
Non-oil LDCs	34.8	31.0	41.5	36.4	41.4	36.5	38.2	n.a.	n.a.
Venezuela									
From:									
Industrialized	85.5	86.2	85.3	86.3	86.1	84.6	85.2	84.7	86.9
U.S.	39.6	41.5	46.1	47.8	48.3	43.5	46.0	50.1	49.5
Japan	11.0	9.6	8.2	8.0	8.0	9.8	5.7	5.2	5.2
Oil exporting	—	0.1	—	0.4	0.1	—	—	n.a.	n.a.
Non-oil LDCs	12.7	12.7	13.7	12.6	13.1	14.2	n.a.	n.a.	n.a.

Source: Constructed from data reported by the International Monetary Fund.

Note: These indexes were constructed as the ratio of the dollar value of each year's imports from a particular country (or group of countries) to total imports.

Table 1.7 **Middle-Income Latin American Countries: Distribution of Total Imports by Origin, 1977–85 (percentage)**

	1977	1978	1979	1980	1981	1982	1983	1984	1985
Columbia									
From:									
Industrialized	76.2	75.7	75.4	75.3	70.7	70.4	71.4	71.6	78.9
U.S.	35.2	35.2	39.6	39.5	34.4	34.6	34.5	34.2	39.3
Japan	10.4	9.9	9.1	9.3	9.6	11.1	11.3	9.6	11.5
Oil exporting	4.6	3.9	3.3	4.2	7.9	6.5	7.2	n.a.	n.a.
Non-oil LDCs	17.5	19.0	19.5	18.4	19.7	21.7	19.3	n.a.	n.a.
Paraguay									
From:									
Industrialized	44.1	44.9	40.3	36.8	38.9	34.5	34.0	38.8	30.4
U.S.	12.2	11.0	11.5	9.9	9.9	9.0	6.4	8.7	7.9
Japan	9.0	7.9	8.2	8.1	8.3	5.5	4.2	11.9	4.6
Oil exporting	9.3	10.9	12.0	7.4	7.4	13.0	13.7	n.a.	n.a.
Non-oil LDCs	45.4	42.4	46.2	54.3	52.0	51.3	52.1	n.a.	n.a.
Costa Rica									
From:									
Industrialized	65.6	68.0	62.4	63.7	60.9	56.3	58.8	61.7	65.1
U.S.	33.7	34.3	30.4	34.3	33.3	35.6	40.2	36.3	37.2
Japan	13.4	14.4	12.4	11.6	9.8	4.2	5.6	7.5	8.7
Oil exporting	3.5	1.0	3.8	5.8	7.6	12.1	6.8	n.a.	n.a.
Non-oil LDCs	30.2	30.2	32.9	29.4	30.6	30.8	34.2	n.a.	n.a.
Guatemala									
From:									
Industrialized	67.4	63.3	60.3	59.4	60.6	57.6	53.6	52.7	55.4
U.S.	34.5	30.0	32.2	34.5	33.8	31.1	32.9	32.5	35.3
Japan	11.4	10.6	8.2	8.0	7.7	5.2	4.6	5.1	4.5
Oil exporting	8.2	7.4	7.3	9.9	6.8	5.9	7.0	n.a.	n.a.
Non-oil LDCs	22.2	27.9	29.1	29.0	30.4	34.7	37.2	n.a.	n.a.
Ecuador									
From:									
Industrialized	83.1	83.1	79.1	73.8	73.5	78.8	74.3	69.9	76.3
U.S.	37.9	38.3	38.8	35.5	33.7	37.3	39.7	29.9	33.1
Japan	18.4	16.1	11.3	11.8	11.7	12.4	6.9	13.6	11.9
Oil exporting	0.6	0.4	0.6	1.1	1.1	1.0	0.8	n.a.	n.a.
Non-oil LDCs	14.4	13.9	16.6	22.2	22.3	17.2	23.6	n.a.	n.a.
Peru									
From:									
Industrialized	67.0	74.9	63.7	62.0	66.7	67.7	64.8	61.5	57.4
U.S.	28.9	36.3	31.0	29.7	33.1	32.0	34.1	29.5	24.6
Japan	7.4	7.2	6.0	8.0	8.6	8.8	6.9	6.3	7.0
Oil exporting	9.4	3.4	1.4	1.1	1.1	0.9	1.1	n.a.	—
Non-oil LDCs	23.0	14.8	12.5	12.7	15.2	17.2	33.7	n.a.	n.a.

Source: See table 1.6.

Table 1.8   **Lower-Income Latin American Countries: Distribution of Total Imports by Origin, 1977–85 (percentage)**

	1977	1978	1979	1980	1981	1982	1983	1984	1985
Nicaragua									
From:									
Industrialized	58.9	56.4	43.7	42.0	40.2	39.9	37.0	44.4	42.3
U.S.	28.8	31.4	25.3	27.4	25.2	18.9	20.8	17.1	7.3
Japan	10.1	6.9	3.8	3.2	1.6	1.4	1.4	2.0	4.1
Oil exporting	11.4	11.6	18.5	16.7	11.4	11.3	10.0	n.a.	n.a.
Non-oil LDCs	29.3	31.3	37.5	40.7	47.7	47.7	49.5	n.a.	n.a.
El Salvador									
From:									
Industrialized	60.2	60.6	54.9	35.9	46.9	49.3	50.8	50.0	59.0
U.S.	29.3	30.8	28.4	19.9	25.5	33.6	38.5	36.0	42.8
Japan	11.0	11.8	7.9	3.9	3.4	2.8	3.3	4.3	4.2
Oil exporting	9.3	7.6	11.1	25.2	4.1	3.6	3.0	n.a.	n.a.
Non-oil LDCs	29.6	31.2	32.9	37.8	40.4	35.4	46.1	n.a.	n.a.
Honduras									
From:									
Industrialized	67.7	66.5	66.0	67.0	64.8	60.2	69.3	65.0	68.3
U.S.	42.9	41.9	43.3	42.4	41.5	39.5	47.5	40.6	43.3
Japan	11.0	8.8	7.7	9.9	6.7	6.5	6.2	4.6	6.6
Oil exporting	5.4	6.2	8.4	10.4	4.4	1.9	1.8	n.a.	n.a.
Non-oil LDCs	25.6	25.8	24.3	21.3	29.7	36.7	28.8	n.a.	n.a.
Bolivia									
From:									
Industrialized	58.7	66.2	61.0	61.1	57.9	59.8	55.7	38.2	47.5
U.S.	23.0	27.2	28.4	28.5	22.9	28.9	26.4	16.9	22.0
Japan	13.4	13.3	9.7	9.7	11.9	11.0	3.6	3.4	8.7
Oil exporting	0.1	0.1	0.1	0.1	0.1	—	—	—	—
Non-oil LDCs	35.9	28.9	33.2	32.6	38.6	36.1	44.2	n.a.	n.a.

Source: See table 1.6.

countries, what share came from oil-exporting LDCs (less developed countries) and what share from non-oil-exporting LDCs. For the case of industrialized countries an additional refinement has been made by explicitly identifying the U.S. and the Japanese shares. Since a few minor trade partners—mainly from the Soviet bloc—have been excluded, the sum of these shares does not necessarily add up to one hundred. Figures 1.1, 1.2, and 1.3 depict the U.S. share of these countries' imports for the same period.

Several facts emerge from these tables and figures. First, the distribution of imports varies significantly across countries. For example, while in some of them the U.S. share in total imports is in the 20 percent to 25 percent range (i.e., Argentina, Chile, Bolivia), in others it is approximately 40 percent to 50 percent (or more), while in still

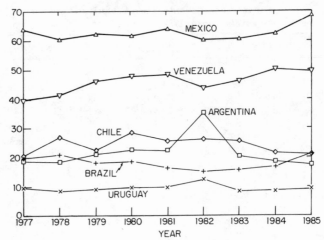

Fig. 1.1   U.S. share of Latin American imports, upper-income countries.

others it is below 10 percent (i.e., Uruguay). Second, and more important, these tables—and in particular these figures—show clearly that for the great majority of the Latin American countries there have been no perceptible changes in the proportion of imports coming from the United States.[11] Third, even a very detailed analysis at the country level reveals that there is no clear common pattern in the shares behavior during the years immediately following the debt crisis. However, in 1982 or 1983 in some of the large- and medium-size countries there

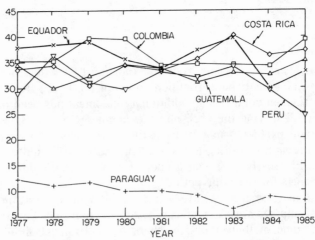

Fig. 1.2   U.S. share of Latin American imports, middle-income countries.

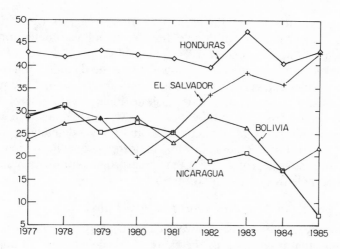

Fig. 1.3   U.S. share of Latin American imports, lower-income countries.

is a slight drop in the share of imports coming from the industrialized countries (Argentina, 1982; Brazil, 1982; Chile, 1982 and 1983; Mexico, 1983). In Argentina, Mexico, and Venezuela there is also a decline in the U.S. share in either 1982 and 1983. Finally, eleven of these countries experienced a slight increase in the industrialized countries' market share in 1985 (Argentina, Brazil, Mexico, Uruguay, Venezuela, Colombia, Costa Rica, Ecuador, El Salvador, Honduras, and Bolivia). Moreover, in the cases of Brazil, Mexico, Colombia, Ecuador, El Salvador, Honduras, and Bolivia, the U.S. share of imports experienced some increase between 1984 and 1985.

An important question is whether this lack of trend in the U.S. share of the Latin American imports market is only a recent phenomenon (i.e., post-1977) or if it reflects a longer-run phenomenon. To investigate this issue, trend regressions for 1970–83 were estimated both for the region as a whole and for each of the fourteen countries in table 1.1. The results obtained were definitive, showing that for the region as a whole there has been no statistically significant change in the U.S. market share of aggregate Latin American imports. At the individual country level there were no changes in nine cases, while in two countries (Mexico and Peru) there has been an increase in the U.S. share; five countries show a decline (Brazil, Colombia, Paraguay, Honduras, and Nicaragua). Naturally, the Nicaraguan trend responded mainly to political reasons.[12] Surprisingly perhaps, according to this statistical analysis the U.S. market share of these sixteen Latin American countries was not sensitive to contemporaneous or lagged fluctuations in the real value of the dollar. In the appendix we present the detailed results from this regression analysis.

This aggregate market share analysis, then, suggests categorically that for the vast majority of these countries the popular contention that the United States has experienced a major loss of its degree of competitiveness in the region is not supported by the data. What has happened is something very different: the value—both nominal and real—of U.S. exports to Latin America has declined severely since 1980. This, however, has little to do with loss of aggregate competitiveness; it is simply the result of the debt crisis and the accompanying monumental fall in Latin America's *total* imports during the period. The region still gets (approximately) the same proportion of its much reduced imports from the United States.

What Does Latin America Import from the United States?

In the preceding subsection we looked at aggregate import shares and found that in most cases the share of the dollar value of imports coming from the United States has not exhibited a trend. In this subsection we ask What do these countries import from the United States? Tables 1.9–1.14 show, for six of the larger Latin American countries, how their imports from the United States were distributed across ten "categories," or sections numbered from 0 to 9, for the years 1970– 83.[13] Each cell in each of these tables indicates what proportion of that particular country's *imports from the United States* corresponds to that specific "category." Consequently, except for rounding errors, these percentages add up to 100 across each category for each year.

Table 1.9   Argentina: Imports from the United States as a Fraction of Total U.S. Imports

	Total $ World	Total $ U.S.	Category									
Year			0	1	2	3	4	5	6	7	8	9
1970	1,688.8	420.4	.006	.001	.041	.045	0	.173	.262	.408	.062	0
1971	1,844.7	416.2	.008	.001	.057	.069	.008	.207	.13	.462	.059	0
1972	1,903.6	388.2	.007	0	.075	.037	.001	.23	.12	.489	.042	0
1973	2,234.7	479.9	.19	0	.078	.058	0	.206	.14	.284	.043	0
1974	3,634.3	616.6	.008	0	.108	.065	0	.331	.148	.293	.046	0
1975	3,942.3	643.8	.012	0	.159	.111	0	.294	.107	.274	.042	0
1976	3,027.6	544.1	.003	.001	.083	.09	0	.315	.109	.365	.034	0
1978	3,831.7	712.2	.009	.002	.036	.058	0	.246	.077	.503	.067	0
1979	6,691.7	1,413.7	.01	.001	.042	.074	0	.208	.079	.52	.065	0
1980	10,535.2	2,378.1	.016	.003	.031	.034	0	.179	.106	.521	.11	0
1981	9,426.0	2,092.4	.014	.004	.028	.04	0	.188	.112	.498	.114	0
1982	5,335.2	1,176.3	.008	.003	.037	.07	.001	.269	.089	.456	.068	0
1983	4,503.0	986.2	.005	.001	.046	.038	.001	.328	.101	.413	.068	0

Source: CEPAL.
Note: Data for 1977 not available.

Table 1.10   **Brazil: Imports from the United States as a Fraction of Total U.S. Imports**

Year	Total $ World	Total $ U.S.	0	1	2	3	4	5	6	7	8	9
1970	2,829.5	915.9	.075	0	.036	.08	.003	.196	.129	.43	.05	0
1971	3,657.7	1,040.6	.093	0	.044	.064	.007	.2	.106	.435	.05	0
1972	4,715.1	1,320.4	.049	0	.044	.0457	.003	.223	.095	.463	.063	.002
1973	6,917.4	1,982.4	.137	.001	.038	.039	.004	.191	.128	.408	.053	.001
1974	14,061.5	3,401.6	.081	.001	.047	.038	.011	.237	.179	.364	.042	0
1975	13,575.8	3,379.1	.093	0	.039	.056	.004	.234	.108	.42	.045	0
1976	13,748.2	3,102.7	.088	0	.039	.057	.002	.266	.081	.42	.047	0
1977	13,567.3	2,758.5	.041	0	.042	.067	.001	.286	.09	.422	.051	0
1978	15,630.9	3,423.5	.161	0	.037	.043	0	.262	.079	.369	.048	0
1979	20,568.0	3,994.3	.123	0	.044	.062	.007	.279	.084	.35	.05	0
1980	25,601.2	4,922.9	.141	0	.034	.06	.006	.294	.084	.334	.047	0
1981	24,768.5	4,362.9	.215	0	.033	.056	0	.195	.079	.386	.045	0
1982	21,958.5	3,719.7	.149	0	.038	.088	.001	.188	.084	.398	.052	0
1983	17,293.1	2,834.9	.179	0	.032	.099	0	.192	.068	.371	.058	0

Source: CEPAL.

Table 1.11   **Chile: Imports from the United States as a Fraction of Total U.S. Imports**

Year	Total $ World	Total $ U.S.	0	1	2	3	4	5	6	7	8	9
1970	930.5	344.4	.051	.01	.019	.034	.018	.117	.163	.547	.041	.001
1971	979.4	267.2	.029	.014	.03	.04	.021	.136	.135	.537	.058	0
1972	944.8	165.3	.069	.007	.103	.04	.006	.189	.118	.421	.048	0
1973	1,102.0	183.8	.13	.003	.056	.068	.004	.209	.102	.388	.039	.0
1974	1,910.0	415.6	.307	.005	.056	.065	.052	.163	.067	.255	.03	0
1975	1,533.2	446.7	.265	.001	.032	.022	.006	.155	.084	.406	.031	0
1976	1,642.6	522.7	.316	.003	.038	.036	.005	.091	.095	.376	.041	0
1977	2,034.1	468.3	.14	.013	.045	.051	.022	.145	.1	.407	.075	0
1978	2,594.9	698.1	.28	.012	.026	.031	.024	.121	.098	.342	.064	0
1979	4,229.1	955.4	.236	.014	.026	.012	.025	.152	.114	.355	.067	0
1980	5,122.7	1,302.0	.227	.016	.023	.041	.006	.15	.118	.354	.066	0
1981	6,276.7	1,530.3	.222	.012	.027	.017	.011	.148	.123	.358	.082	0
1982	3,526.5	898.7	.273	.028	.024	.033	.005	.138	.105	.308	.086	0
1983	2,694.6	689.1	.269	.003	.032	.03	.01	.206	.096	.266	.068	0

Source: CEPAL.

Table 1.12   **Mexico: Imports from the United States as a Fraction of Total U.S. Imports**

Year	Total $ World	Total $ U.S.	Category 0	1	2	3	4	5	6	7	8	9
1970	2,461.2	1,567.8	.053	.001	.1	.04	.005	.117	.115	.494	.075	0
1971	2,406.1	1,479.0	.045	0	.09	.048	.003	.133	.103	.495	.083	0
1972	2,934.0	1,774.3	.084	.002	.07	.045	.001	.127	.107	.477	.088	0
1973	4,144.5	2,609.2	.098	.001	.087	.045	.013	.114	.117	.453	.072	0
1974	6,051.8	3,778.6	.154	.001	.109	.042	.023	.143	.130	.357	.041	0
1975	6,571.8	4,131.9	.116	.001	.081	.051	.007	.125	.119	.46	.041	0
1976	5,885.3	3,686.4	.043	.001	.09	.042	.005	.139	.132	.5	.048	0
1977	5,525.2	3,505.3	.111	.001	.107	.035	.009	.153	.118	.421	.044	0
1978	8,048.2	4,864.3	.092	.001	.111	.034	.013	.143	.125	.437	.044	0
1979	12,196.4	7,681.9	.086	.002	.097	.025	.006	.126	.144	.464	.051	0
1980	17,788.7	12,004.6	.144	.001	.074	.027	.008	.115	.158	.420	.044	0
1981	23,743.5	15,668.3	.133	.001	.067	.034	.003	.102	.165	.454	.05	0
1982	14,420.2	9,312.1	.089	.003	.078	.043	.012	.123	.134	.468	.05	0
1983	10,651.4	7,808.0	.2	.002	.103	.026	.011	.133	.107	.368	.05	0

Source: CEPAL.

Table 1.13   **Colombia: Imports from the United States as a Fraction of Total U.S. Imports**

Year	Total $ World	Total $ U.S.	Category 0	1	2	3	4	5	6	7	8	9
1970	836.4	397.3	.042	.023	.05	.013	.01	.182	.12	.515	.042	.002
1971	917.0	390.2	.092	.009	.054	.01	.02	.167	.093	.51	.038	.006
1972	853.1	333.9	.09	.002	.058	.005	.019	.19	.09	.504	.04	.002
1973	1,059.4	430.4	.156	.005	.077	.004	.021	.223	.084	.376	.052	.002
1974	1,593.8	640.4	.141	.004	.064	.003	.028	.266	.11	.334	.048	.002
1975	1,494.5	644.8	.114	.003	.05	.007	.022	.225	.106	.431	.04	.002
1976	1,707.7	725.1	.117	.002	.046	.006	.049	.168	.119	.451	.041	.002
1977	2,028.0	753.1	.107	.009	.041	.006	.058	.22	.085	.428	.043	.003
1978	2,836.0	999.3	.149	.011	.033	.01	.048	.207	.09	.41	.04	.003
1979	3,232.9	1,278.7	.103	.012	.039	.093	.065	.174	.081	.386	.043	.003
1980	4,662.3	1,839.8	.133	.014	.036	.081	.046	.186	.085	.374	.04	.004
1981	5,198.8	1,787.4	.087	.013	.028	.051	.054	.193	.109	.399	.052	.014
1982	5,477.3	1,884.9	.112	.012	.039	.033	.041	.181	.103	.424	.047	.008
1983	4,950.6	1,761.8	.131	.011	.046	.018	.04	.182	.099	.413	.051	.009

Source: CEPAL.

Table 1.14   **Venezuela: Imports from the United States as a Fraction of Total U.S. Imports**

Year	Total $ World	Total $ U.S.	Category 0	1	2	3	4	5	6	7	8	9
1970	1,902.6	924.8	.1	0	.058	.021	.009	.12	.119	.509	.063	.001
1971	2,124.9	945.3	.104	0	.053	.011	.016	.119	.115	.52	.059	.003
1972	2,485.4	1,107.6	.112	0	.047	.005	.011	.109	.119	.534	.062	.001
1973	2,844.2	1,194.1	.123	0	.041	.004	.017	.106	.132	.516	.06	.001
1974	4,307.6	2,448.2	.11	0	.073	.003	.016	.128	.156	.464	.049	.001
1975	5,806.7	2,821.8	.097	0	.043	.004	.021	.093	.146	.542	.053	.001
1976	6,905.2	3,098.9	.086	.001	.036	.004	.009	.099	.118	.595	.051	.001
1977	11,200.0	4,340.5	.091	0	.032	.009	.012	.101	.135	.572	.048	0
1978	11,667.9	4,829.4	.077	.001	.037	.007	.017	.094	.125	.581	.061	0
1979	11,037.0	5,085.7	.094	0	.044	.009	.02	.108	.131	.53	.062	.001
1980	12,257.7	5,898.3	.125	.001	.047	.014	.023	.122	.13	.474	.036	0
1981	13,555.9	6,555.0	.142	.001	.033	.012	.028	.104	.123	.494	.063	0
1982	13,389.8	6,128.8	.106	.001	.038	.009	.017	.108	.131	.515	.076	0
1983	6,146.5	2,849.6	.202	.001	.048	.012	.037	.157	.104	.385	.054	0

Source: CEPAL.

These tables, constructed from data provided by the U.N.'s Economic Commission for Latin America (ECLA), also contain the dollar value of total yearly imports for each country (column 1) as well as total yearly imports from the United States (column 2).[14] Categories 0 through 9 correspond to the SITC one-digit classification and are defined in the following way:

Category 0: Food stuffs and live animals
Category 1: Beverages and tobacco
Category 2: Raw nonfood materials, except fuel
Category 3: Fuel and related products
Category 4: Oil, greases, and waxes of vegetable and animal origins
Category 5: Chemical products
Category 6: Manufactured products
Category 7: Machinery and transport equipment
Category 8: Other manufactured goods
Category 9: Other commodities

Two important patterns emerge from these tables. First, with almost no exceptions, the bulk of these countrys' imports from the United States have been concentrated throughout the period on the manufacturing sector (categories 5–8), with capital goods (category 7) the most important single item in almost every country.

Second, in spite of the dominating role of manufacturing, there is a clear decline through time in the relative importance of category 7 in almost every country. At the same time, categories 0 (foodstuffs and live animals) and 5 (chemical) have increased their relative shares. This change in the composition of Latin American imports from the United States, away from traditional labor-intensive manufacturing industries and into natural resources and capital-intensive (including human capital) products (including food, farm products, and chemicals), reflects a change in the U.S. pattern of comparative advantage, which has been observed for some years now. In fact, Leamer (1984) has recently shown that, according to the predictions of the Heckscher-Ohlin theory of international trade, the U.S. exports have shifted from being concentrated on relatively more labor-abundant commodities to more capital- and resources-abundant products.[15]

U.S. and Foreign Competition: Disaggregated Trends

This section tackles the important question of how the Latin American import shares of different categories of imports are distributed among the United States and other countries. Tables 1.15–1.18 provide disaggregated information on the distribution of imports for the twelve upper-middle-income and middle-income Latin American countries for which these data are available. The disaggregation used here distinguishes between primary products and manufactured goods. These tables contain data for the years 1970, 1975, 1980, and 1983 on the shares of each of these categories that have been imported from (*a*) the rest of Latin America and the Caribbean; (*b*) the United States; (*c*) Japan; (*d*) the rest (i.e., other than the United States or Japan) of the OECD; (*e*) the Soviet bloc (CAME); and (*f*) the rest of the world. To know whether a given share represents a low or high dollar value, on each of these tables data on the dollar value of imports of each category is also included (first column). These tables contain the most recent data available and have been constructed from raw information obtained from the U.N.'s Economic Commission for Latin America (ECLA) (see CEPAL 1986d).

The two commodities categories in these tables are defined in the following way:[16] (1) primary products—foodstuffs; live animals; beverages; tobacco; raw nonfood materials except fuel; oil, greases, and waxes of vegetable and animal origins (that is, categories 0, 1, 2, and 4 as defined above); and (2) manufactured goods—categories 5, 6, 7, and 8.

From these tables we detect some common patterns across countries. First, perhaps with the exception of intra–Latin American imports of manufactured goods, there are no drastic changes in the distribution of imports between 1970 and 1983. A second interesting pattern is that

Table 1.15   **Upper-Middle-Income Countries: Imports of Primary Products, Selected Years, 1970–83**

	Total $	L.A. and Caribbean	U.S.	Japan	Rest of OECD	CAME	Rest of World
Argentina							
1970	287.4	0.693	0.071	0.002	0.166	0.001	0.067
1975	600.1	0.616	0.185	0.004	0.14	0.004	0.051
1980	499.0	0.181	0.319	0.011	0.462	0.015	0.012
1983	530.5	0.646	0.113	0.007	0.133	0.001	0.1
Brazil							
1970	391.8	0.38	0.267	0.009	0.302	0.006	0.036
1975	1,209.3	0.243	0.381	0.019	0.267	0.008	0.082
1980	3,141.3	0.333	0.283	0.003	0.317	0.003	0.061
1983	1,857.7	0.252	0.323	0.004	0.33	0.031	0.06
Chile							
1970	188.3	0.628	0.178	0.002	0.169	0.011	0.012
1975	353.8	0.418	0.383	0.005	0.158	0.023	0.013
1980	1,080	0.412	0.327	0.011	0.212	0	0.038
1983	611.6	0.451	0.377	0.002	0.129	0.002	0.039
Mexico							
1970	374.7	0.082	0.661	0.002	0.222	0	0.033
1975	1,286.1	0.191	0.657	0.001	0.098	0.002	0.051
1980	3,528	0.041	0.775	0.001	0.112	0.036	0.035
1983	2,816.7	0.029	0.876	0.001	0.06	0.009	0.025
Uruguay							
1970	51.5	0.671	0.071	0.005	0.164	0.003	0.086
1975	90.7	0.463	0.181	0.006	0.207	0.001	0.142
1980	208.9	0.642	0.097	0.009	0.159	0.002	0.091
1983	99.4	0.655	0.087	0.002	0.197	0.002	0.057
Venezuela							
1970	281.3	0.079	0.549	0.014	0.294	0.011	0.053
1975	879.6	0.098	0.515	0.012	0.282	0.005	0.088
1980	2,182.3	0.089	0.529	0.006	0.246	0.006	0.124
1983	1,514.1	0.21	0.542	0.001	0.191	0.005	0.051

Source: CEPAL.

in Argentina, Chile, and Uruguay a majority of imports of primary products came, for all these years, from other Latin American countries. Third, the increased importance of imports of primary products from the United States has been such that in Brazil, Mexico, Colombia, Peru, Nicaragua, El Salvador, and Honduras the United States has displaced other Latin American and Caribbean countries as the main providers of this type of good. Moreover, by 1983 most of these countries imported almost half of their primary products from the United States.

The distribution of the imports of fuels has not been shown in these tables, but behaves as expected: the majority of the region's non-oil-

Table 1.16   Middle-Income Countries: Imports of Primary Products Selected
                    Years, 1970–83

	Total $	L.A. and Caribbean	U.S.	Japan	Rest of OECD	CAME	Rest of World
Colombia							
1970	105	0.321	0.472	0.006	0.167	0.001	0.033
1975	224.9	0.241	0.539	0.041	0.13	0.002	0.047
1980	733.3	0.218	0.578	0.009	0.151	0.003	0.041
1983	705.5	0.218	0.568	0.008	0.17	0.001	0.035
Paraguay							
1970	17.1	0.313	0.426	0.004	0.246	0	0.011
1975	32.2	0.237	0.198	0.004	0.552	0	0.009
1980	75.7	0.333	0.216	0.004	0.436	0	0.011
1983	55.1	0.635	0.084	0.004	0.27	0.003	0.004
Costa Rica							
1970	40.2	0.546	0.331	0.003	0.093	0	0.027
1975	80.9	0.437	0.394	0.015	0.122	0.001	0.031
1980	172.4	0.313	0.457	0.003	0.142	0	0.085
1983	123.5	0.262	0.553	0	0.093	0	0.092
Guatemala							
1970	37.1	0.341	0.463	0.026	0.142	0	0.028
1975	80.1	0.262	0.555	0.028	0.137	0	0.018
1980	160.7	0.219	0.556	0.035	0.16	0.001	0.029
1983	129.9	0.299	0.545	0.008	0.122	0	0.026
Ecuador							
1970	29.5	0.113	0.565	0.124	0.166	0.002	0.03
1975	102.1	0.059	0.688	0.041	0.182	0.001	0.029
1980	227.5	0.1	0.631	0.008	0.208	0.008	0.045
1983	204.9	0.221	0.555	0.012	0.184	0.001	0.027
Peru							
1970	151.2	0.496	0.183	0.013	0.271	0.012	0.025
1975	452.7	0.101	0.479	0.01	0.313	0.003	0.094
1980	670.3	0.217	0.52	0.015	0.162	0.001	0.085
1983	613	0.246	0.527	0.002	0.174	0.016	0.035

Source: CEPAL.

producing countries import most of the fuel from oil producer Latin
American countries, with the rest of the world (mainly OPEC countries
in this instance) also being important.

The data on manufacturing imports are particularly revealing. They
show that in the majority of cases the OECD as a whole (United States,
Japan, and the rest of OECD) lost ground to competitors from the
south, and in particular to other Latin American suppliers.[17] As can
be seen from tables 1.17 and 1.18, imports from other Latin American
and Caribbean countries have increased significantly. Although Japan
has in many cases made some progress, its presence in the region is
far from overwhelming. Moreover, in many countries the share of Japanese manufactured imports in 1983 was substantially lower than its

Table 1.17   Upper-Middle-Income Countries: Imports of Manufactured Goods, Selected Years, 1970–83

	Total $	L.A. and Caribbean	U.S.	Japan	Rest of OECD	CAME	Rest of World
Argentina							
1970	1,320.7	0.108	0.288	0.064	0.499	0.011	0.03
1975	2,822.9	0.12	0.164	0.170	0.517	0.029	0.00
1980	8,311.4	0.132	0.262	0.117	0.424	0.011	0.054
1983	3,509	0.2	0.249	0.097	0.41	0.018	0.026
Brazil							
1970	2,058.5	0.047	0.358	0.084	0.463	0.027	0.021
1975	8,812.4	0.042	0.31	0.14	0.472	0.016	0.02
1980	11,659.7	0.093	0.32	0.099	0.421	0.018	0.049
1983	6,020.3	0.083	0.325	0.109	0.426	0.036	0.021
Chile							
1970	682.8	0.069	0.438	0.04	0.441	0.003	0.009
1975	875.8	0.16	0.344	0.085	0.396	0.005	0.01
1980	3,097.6	0.156	0.289	0.124	0.311	0.002	0.118
1983	1,503.5	0.155	0.291	0.103	0.368	0.002	0.081
Mexico							
1970	2,007.1	0.017	0.626	0.042	0.301	0.003	0.011
1975	4,923.4	0.026	0.625	0.062	0.274	0.012	0.001
1980	13,898.3	0.042	0.644	0.064	0.229	0.004	0.017
1983	7,585.9	0.013	0.677	0.052	0.21	0.002	0.046
Uruguay							
1970	147.2	0.254	0.168	0.022	0.471	0.055	0.03
1975	264.6	0.298	0.136	0.044	0.481	0.018	0.023
1980	932.8	0.362	0.14	0.066	0.349	0.031	0.052
1983	323.9	0.361	0.134	0.046	0.368	0.044	0.047
Venezuela							
1970	1,597.5	0.034	0.47	0.092	0.378	0.011	0.015
1975	4,871.4	0.052	0.483	0.09	0.35	0.003	0.022
1980	9,871.7	0.071	0.472	0.097	0.313	0.002	0.045
1983	4,454.5	0.085	0.448	0.077	0.35	0	0.04

Source: CEPAL.

1980 or even 1975 share (i.e., Argentina, Chile, Mexico, Uruguay, Venezuela, Paraguay, Gautemala, Ecuador, Nicaragua, El Salvador, Honduras, and Bolivia). With regard to the United States, in many of the countries there is a decline in the share of manufactured imports, with Mexico being the major exception.

1.4 Latin American Exports and Protectionism in the Industrialized Countries

In this section we deal with the behavior of exports in Latin America during the last fifteen years or so. As already noted, after the 1982 debt crisis most Latin American countries implemented major adjustment

Table 1.18   Middle-Income Countries: Imports of Manufactured Goods, Selected Years, 1970–83

	Total $	L.A. and Caribbean	U.S.	Japan	Rest of OECD	CAME	Rest of World
Columbia							
1970	720.8	0.063	0.474	0.072	0.355	0.023	0.013
1975	1,249	0.084	0.414	0.096	0.375	0.012	0.019
1980	3,338.1	0.107	0.378	0.128	0.329	0.024	0.034
1983	3,562.9	0.111	0.299	0.153	0.368	0.034	0.035
Paraguay							
1970	47.2	0.226	0.195	0.106	0.439	0.006	0.028
1975	134.8	0.494	0.133	0.082	0.268	0.005	0.018
1980	367.9	0.472	0.113	0.15	0.215	0.008	0.042
1983	341.4	0.486	0.315	0.077	0.091	0.003	0.028
Costa Rica							
1970	263.8	0.218	0.36	0.108	0.292	0.004	0.018
1975	534.9	0.223	0.376	0.112	0.246	0.01	0.033
1980	1,094.2	0.227	0.369	0.153	0.21	0.007	0.034
1983	670.3	0.228	0.211	0.078	0.425	0.003	0.055
Guatemala							
1970	240.5	0.265	0.332	0.117	0.277	0.002	0.007
1975	553.9	0.223	0.372	0.115	0.277	0.003	0.01
1980	1,020.5	0.188	0.416	0.121	0.238	0.004	0.033
1983	828.7	0.305	0.21	0.071	0.38	0.005	0.029
Eduador							
1970	224.1	0.079	0.444	0.097	0.348	0.021	0.011
1975	859.1	0.122	0.363	0.167	0.316	0.009	0.023
1980	1,790.3	0.119	0.362	0.147	0.295	0.024	0.053
1983	1,267.7	0.172	0.314	0.108	0.336	0.017	0.053
Peru							
1970	456.4	0.06	0.369	0.102	0.448	0.004	0.017
1975	1,638.6	0.103	0.314	0.109	0.444	0.018	0.012
1980	1,948.6	0.122	0.339	0.125	0.362	0.021	0.031
1983	1,545.4	0.14	0.375	0.133	0.316	0.003	0.033

Source: CEPAL.

programs aimed at reducing the magnitude of their balance of payments problems. In the majority of cases these adjustment efforts have been largely successful; in fact, as documented in section 1.3, in most countries both the current account and trade balances have experienced drastic improvements between 1980 and 1985. However, a fact many times overlooked is that for the region as a whole more than 100 percent of the improved external situation has been the consequence of the decline in imports; in many cases exports have even declined in real terms between 1980 and 1985. For example, for the fourteen countries in table 1.2, *real* value of imports declined 45 percent between 1980 and 1985 when the U.S. WPI is used as the relevant price index. On the other hand, for the thirteen countries for which there are data, the total real value of exports *declined* by almost 10 percent during the same period.[18] Of course, in those countries where the real value of exports dropped, this was mainly the result of the fall in price of many of their countries' principle exports. The extent of this decline in relative export prices is captured in table 1.19 on the evolution of the terms of trade.

There is little doubt that a definitive solution to Latin America's pressing economic problems and the resumption of growth in the region will require a significant increase in exports.[19] Moreover, only to the extent that exports exhibit significant growth in the next few years will the region be able to increase its imports.[20] A crucial question, then, is what and to whom will Latin America export in the next decade or so. The analysis that follows helps answer this important question.

1.4.1 The Destination of Latin American Exports

Table 1.20 contains data on the regional distribution of aggregate exports for our sixteen countries for 1970 through 1983. Tables 1.21 and 1.22, on the other hand, contain more disaggregated data on the sectoral distribution of exports destination for the sixteen countries. Finally, tables 1.23 and 1.24 provide information for the upper-middle-income countries on the distribution of exports destination of primary products and manufactured goods.[21]

A number of interesting facts emerge from these tables. First, at the aggregate level for the region as a whole (i.e., the sixteen countries) there is a decline in the proportion of exports going to the OECD. Exports to the United States, however, have not exhibited much of a trend. It is also clear from these tables that intra–Latin American ex-

Table 1.19   Terms of Trade Index: Selected Latin American Countries (1970 = 100)

	1975	1980	1982	1984
Argentina	100.7	94.2	82.0	86.4
Bolivia	111.0	143.6	132.1	138.1
Brazil	85.4	67.4	54.2	59.5
Chile	53.2	49.0	35.4	34.5
Colombia	81.5	126.3	109.9	115.4
Costa Rica	85.5	97.3	90.0	84.7
Ecuador	159.0	237.6	196.9	177.7
Guatemala	70.8	94.2	72.1	70.1
Mexico	105.7	164.3	134.7	127.7
Peru	104.0	131.1	93.8	93.0
Uruguay	75.4	81.4	71.6	74.7
Venezuela	335.3	509.9	492.1	500.5

Source: CEPAL 1986a.

Table 1.20　Destination of Exports: Sixteen Latin American Countries, 1970–83 (percentage)

	1970	1975	1976	1977	1978	1979	1980	1981	1982	1983
Latin American and Carribbean	13.4	16.5	15.8	16.1	15.6	16.4	16.2	15.9	14.3	10.5
ALADI	9.3	12.5	12.1	12.7	12.1	13.4	13.2	12.8	11.8	8.2
OECD	75.0	63.6	66.1	66.4	67.5	66.2	63.6	58.4	62.8	69.0
U.S.	30.4	28.5	28.9	29.8	32.3	31.1	29.4	26.8	29.5	37.1
Japan	5.8	4.8	4.8	4.5	4.4	4.5	4.9	4.6	6.0	5.5
CAME	2.5	5.2	4.9	4.6	3.9	3.3	4.6	6.1	4.3	4.5
Rest of Asia	1.1	2.9	2.1	3.4	3.6	3.8	3.7	3.1	4.8	7.1
Rest of World	8.0	11.8	11.1	9.5	9.4	10.3	11.9	16.5	12.0	8.9
Total	100.0	100.0	100.0	100.0	100.0	100.0	100.0	100.0	100.0	100.0

Source: United Nations Economic Commission for Latin America.
Note: The countries included here are Argentina, Bolivia, Brazil, Colombia, Costa Rica, Chile, Ecuador, El Salvador, Guatemala, Honduras, Mexico, Nicaragua, Paraguay, Peru, Uruguay, and Venezuela.

ports declined substantially in 1982 and 1983. Finally, another interesting trend captured in table 1.20 is the steady increase in Latin American exports going to the rest (i.e., non-Japan) of Asia and the Soviet bloc countries.

The data in table 1.21 describe the evolution of the composition of regional exports. Several facts emerge from this table. First, exports of foodstuffs and agricultural products (category 0) have declined steadily throughout the period. Second, exports of fuel increased in importance as a result of both the increases in the price of oil and the increased gas and oil production in the region. Third, manufactured exports corresponding to categories 5 (chemicals), 8 (various manufactured products), and 7 (machinery and transportation equipment) experienced an important increase. This trend is captured in an even cleaner way in table 1.22, which excludes full fuel: whereas in 1970 categories 5, 7, and 8 represented no more than 8 percent of nonfuel exports, in 1983 they accounted for 23 percent. Fourth, these data also show that category 6 (manufactures) has approximately retained its relative importance, accounting for around 19 percent of nonfuel exports. The disaggregated information on the destination of exports in tables 1.23 and 1.24 shows that in the majority of the cases, exports of primary products go to the OECD.

Table 1.24 shows that the proportion of the larger countries' exports of manufactured goods that go to the United States has increased through time. In most cases this higher share of exports to the United States has come out of declining shares of exports to the rest of Latin America.

Table 1.25 contains data at an even more disaggregated level on the percentage distribution of the sixteen countries' exports to the United States. For each year this table gives information on how Latin American exports to the United States are distributed across the ten one-digit sections of the SITC (see section 1.3 for a detailed definition of these categories). By and large, this table confirms the patterns observed for total disaggregated exports reported in table 1.22. First, the relative importance of food product exports (category 0) has declined steadily during the period. This, of course, is but another reflection of the changing pattern of comparative advantages discussed above. As the production of food has become more capital intensive, the industrial countries, and in particular the United States, have tended to produce and export more and more food, while the poorer countries have exported less and less of it (Leamer 1984).[22]

1.4.2   Protectionism in the Industrial Nations and the Future Evolution of Latin American Exports

While most Latin American nations have been going through serious efforts aimed at improving their external balance, the industrial coun-

Table 1.21   Sectoral Composition of Exports for Sixteen Latin American Countries, 1970–83 (percentage)

Category	1970	1975	1976	1977	1978	1979	1980	1981	1982	1983
0	38.9	30.9	34.0	38.0	35.4	30.2	26.0	23.4	22.3	25.6
1	0.6	0.9	0.9	0.9	1.0	0.9	0.7	0.8	1.0	0.9
2	15.1	14.0	13.3	11.8	11.9	11.4	10.6	10.1	9.1	8.5
3	22.5	31.6	28.4	25.5	24.7	30.2	37.9	42.6	45.0	40.3
4	1.7	1.3	1.6	2.0	2.0	1.9	1.5	1.5	1.3	1.4
5	2.2	2.8	2.6	2.5	2.8	2.8	2.9	3.0	3.1	3.4
6	15.2	10.5	11.8	11.3	12.1	13.8	11.4	9.7	9.8	11.5
7	2.4	5.3	4.7	5.2	6.8	6.0	6.2	6.5	6.1	7.8
8	1.4	2.6	2.6	2.9	3.4	3.0	2.7	2.5	2.4	2.8
9	0.0	0.0	0.0	0.0	0.0	0.0	0.0	0.0	0.0	0.0
Total[a]	13.648	32,124	37,398	44,732	48,744	65,454	83,096	89,718	81,893	85,828

Source: CEPAL.

[a]Millions of U.S. dollars.

Table 1.22   **Sectoral Composition of Nonfuel Exports of Sixteen Latin American Countries, 1970–83 (percentage)**

Category	1970	1975	1980	1983
0	50.1	45.2	41.9	39.6
1	0.7	1.4	1.1	1.5
2	19.5	20.1	17.4	14.2
4	2.2	2.0	2.5	2.3
5	2.8	4.0	4.7	5.7
6	19.7	15.4	18.4	19.3
7	3.1	7.7	10.0	13.0
8	1.8	3.8	4.3	4.4
9	0.0	0.0	0.0	0.0

Source: CEPAL.

Note: Due to rounding, the sum across sections may not add up to 100.

Table 1.23   **Upper-Middle-Income Countries: Exports of Primary Products, Selected Years, 1970–83**

	Total $	L.A. and Caribbean	U.S.	Japan	Rest of OECD	CAME	Rest of World
Argentina							
1970	1,517.2	0.16	0.07	0.07	0.61	0.044	0.045
1975	2,223	0.17	0.06	0.05	0.43	0.15	0.14
1980	5,737	0.176	0.074	0.02	0.34	0.3	0.09
1983	6,136.1	0.094	0.05	0.054	0.257	0.292	0.253
Brazil							
1970	2,329	0.062	0.261	0.055	0.507	0.054	0.061
1975	6,068	0.051	0.137	0.096	0.448	0.119	0.149
1980	11,906	0.047	0.174	0.079	0.45	0.098	0.152
1983	11,465.3	0.042	0.15	0.079	0.477	0.113	0.139
Chile							
1970	214.7	0.196	0.133	0.306	0.33	0.014	0.018
1975	454	0.305	0.133	0.202	0.255	0.008	0.097
1980	1,713	0.237	0.057	0.226	0.302	0.014	0.164
1983	1,548.8	0.119	0.159	0.182	0.336	0.024	0.18
Mexico							
1970	682	0.021	0.77	0.085	0.1	0.003	0.021
1975	1,337	0.025	0.72	0.078	0.118	0.008	0.051
1980	2,688	0.022	0.667	0.064	0.176	0.02	0.051
1983	2,579.2	0.02	0.744	0.052	0.122	0.022	0.04
Uruguay							
1970	192	0.098	0.057	0.001	0.583	0.145	0.116
1975	265	0.228	0.012	0.021	0.509	0.088	0.142
1980	657	0.317	0.043	0.014	0.328	0.11	0.188
1983	253	0.058	0.032	0.031	0.334	0.198	0.347
Venezuela							
1970	231.4	0.006	0.588	0.021	0.337	0.007	0.041
1975	378.4	0.016	0.621	0.004	0.286	0.03	0.043
1980	423.8	0.034	0.413	0.009	0.459	0.019	0.066
1983	97.5	0.026	0.189	0.047	0.219	0.064	0.455

Source: CEPAL.

Table 1.24   Upper-Middle-Income Countries: Exports of Manufactured Goods,
                    Selected Years, 1970–83

	Total $	L.A. and Caribbean	U.S.	Japan	Rest of OECD	CAME	Rest of World
Argentina							
1970	248	0.499	0.205	0.003	0.231	0.031	0.031
1975	722.3	0.546	0.084	0.022	0.157	0.185	0.006
1980	1,995.3	0.415	0.155	0.042	0.248	0.058	0.082
1983	1,363.8	0.281	0.276	0.024	0.204	0.049	0.166
Brazil							
1970	368.5	0.403	0.169	0.04	0.279	0.014	0.095
1975	2,209.9	0.369	0.201	0.036	0.263	0.019	0.112
1980	7,546.7	0.377	0.182	0.038	0.227	0.019	0.157
1983	8,987.3	0.173	0.222	0.059	0.258	0.016	0.272
Chile							
1970	1,104.1	0.143	0.137	0.074	0.622	0	0.024
1975	1,180.4	0.204	0.069	0.081	0.601	0.004	0.041
1980	2,807	0.244	0.129	0.041	0.527	0	0.059
1983	2,010.1	0.132	0.343	0.021	0.457	0.012	0.035
Mexico							
1970	454.1	0.213	0.596	0.022	0.126	0.005	0.038
1975	1,062.2	0.297	0.416	0.01	0.2	0.027	0.05
1980	2,156.9	0.231	0.541	0.026	0.153	0.007	0.042
1983	6,194.9	0.067	0.782	0.022	0.086	0.006	0.037
Uruguay							
1970	41	0.259	0.22	0	0.466	0.014	0.041
1975	114.2	0.424	0.198	0.001	0.292	0.05	0.035
1980	401.8	0.463	0.135	0.001	0.34	0.02	0.041
1983	313.3	0.319	0.236	0.006	0.279	0.069	0.091
Venezuela							
1970	39	0.623	0.126	0.001	0.09	0	0.16
1975	103.4	0.428	0.32	0	0.118	0	0.134
1980	692.8	0.213	0.124	0.375	0.177	0.003	0.108
1983	564.5	0.128	0.244	0.371	0.18	0.004	0.073

Source: CEPAL.

tries have been invaded with protectionist sentiments. In fact, already in the past few years the industrial countries have used a series of nontariff mechanisms to impede a freer flow of Latin American goods. According to the GATT (1984), industrial countries currently use more than forty nontariff measures to impede international flows of commodities.

A few authors have dealt with the issue of nontariff barriers, analyzing the extent of these practices, their coverage across countries and products, and their evolution through time.[23] For example, in a comprehensive recent study, Nogues, Olechowski, and Winters (1986b)

Table 1.25   Sectoral Distribution of Sixteen Latin American Exports to the
                    United States, 1970–83 (percentage)

Category	1970	1975	1976	1977	1978	1979	1980	1981	1982	1983
0	44.3	30.1	36.4	36.5	35.7	30.8	26.2	22.1	19.7	17.3
1	0.4	1.0	0.9	0.9	0.9	0.9	0.8	1.1	1.4	0.6
2	10.9	9.5	8.0	5.4	5.9	5.2	4.7	5.4	4.0	4.0
3	25.6	44.3	37.6	39.4	36.0	44.6	52.0	51.5	55.0	48.5
4	0.6	0.4	0.4	0.5	0.3	0.2	0.2	0.2	0.1	0.1
5	1.6	1.8	1.8	1.8	1.7	1.8	2.1	3.3	2.4	2.4
6	12.5	6.6	8.6	8.9	10.2	9.0	6.9	16.2	8.5	11.5
7	2.8	2.7	2.9	3.1	5.0	4.4	4.3	2.5	5.4	11.4
8	1.4	3.4	3.4	3.5	4.3	3.2	2.8	0.2	3.3	4.4
9	0.0	0.0	0.0	0.0	0.0	0.0	0.0	0.0	0.0	0.0

Source: United Nations Economic Commission for Latin America.

analyzed the use of nontariff barriers in sixteen industrialized countries.[24] For the purpose of their analysis they defined the following
practices as nontariff barriers: prohibitions, quotas, discretionary import authorizations, conditional import authorizations, "voluntary"
export restraints, variable levies, minimum price systems, "voluntary"
price restraints, tariff quotas, seasonal tariffs, price and volume investigations, and antidumping and countervailing duties. Table 1.26
contains data on an index of the coverage of these nontariff barriers,
defined as the proportion of these countries' imports of a particular
product that are subject to the NTBs (nontrade barriers).[25] As can be

Table 1.26   Coverage of Nontariff Barriers in Sixteen Developed Countries,
                    1983 (percentage)

	Coverage %
All Products	27.1
Fuel	43.0
Agriculture	36.1
Manufactures	16.1
Textiles	44.8
Footwear	12.6
Iron and steel	35.4
Electrical machinery	10.0
Vehicles	30.4
Other manufactures	8.8

Source: Nogues, Olechowski, and Winters 1986b.

Note: This coverage index is defined as the proportion of these countries' imports subject
to the following nontariff barriers: prohibitions, quotas, discretionary import authori-
zation, conditional import authorizations, "voluntary" export restraints, variable levies,
minimum price systems, "voluntary" price restraints, tariff quotas, seasonal tariffs, price
and volume investigations, and antidumping and countervailing duties.

seen, coverage of this type of impediments is quite broad, affecting more than one-fourth of all these countries' imports, with textiles being the industry most severely affected. An important question is whether imports from all countries or regions are affected in the same way by the NTBs. Nogues, Olechowski, and Winters (1986a, 1986b) have shown that this is not the case; imports from the developing world are more severely affected by this type of "semidisguised" protectionism than those from the industrialized world.

Once the effects of the NTBs are taken into account, the degree of protection the industrialized countries grant to some products can be remarkable. Table 1.27, for example, estimates the total average rate of protection to which some Argentinian and Brazilian exports to the EEC, Japan, and the United States were subject in 1980. These figures are in many ways staggering, indicating that in many cases the NTBs more than double the tariff protection.

What is even more serious is that the existing evidence clearly indicates a slow but steady increase in the degree of coverage of the NTBs. For example Nogues, Olechowski, and Winters (1986a) found that the NTBs' coverage for all goods in the sixteen industrial countries increased by 1.5 percentage points between 1981 and 1983. To the extent that these NTBs increase, or even are maintained at their current levels, it will become very difficult, if not impossible, for Latin American countries to increase their exports at the rate required to solve

Table 1.27   **Estimated Total Rates of Protection for Some Argentinian and Brazilian Exports, 1980 (percentage)**

	EEC	Japan	USA
Argentina			
Fresh meat (011)	118	328	46
Wheat (041)	120	145	0
Corn (044)	63	n.a.	10
Textile fibers (26)	59	13	68
Hides (611)	18	25	5
Steel (67)	43	8	35
Garments (84)	59	18	79
Brazil			
Fresh meat (011)	118	328	46
Sugar and honey (061)	160	44	27
Coffee and derivatives (071)	93	161	39
Cocoa (072)	12	173	4
Textiles (65)	59	13	68
Footwear (851)	27	16	9

Source: CEPAL 1986e.

Note: The numbers in parentheses refer to the SITC classification. Total rate of protection is defined as tariff rate plus tariff equivalent of NTBs.

the current debt crisis. While the main responsibility for increasing exports rests with the Latin American countries, their efforts, no matter how serious, can be easily frustrated by the protectionist policies of the industrialized world.[26]

1.5   Commercial Policies, Protectionism, and Latin American Trade

1.5.1   Historical Perspective

As noted in section 1.2, during the 1940s most of the Latin American countries embarked on ambitious industrialization programs based on an import substitution development strategy. This inward-looking development program was based on the idea that small developing economies would only grow sufficiently rapidly if they were able to develop a large and diversified industrial sector. This, in turn, could only be achieved if sufficiently high protection in the form of import tariffs or quotas was granted to the incipient domestic industries. Most proponents of the import substitution strategy also pointed out that the high degree of protection would only be necessary as a temporary measure; after an initial learning period these "infant industries" would move into their "adolescence" and would not require tariffs (Prebisch 1984). Reality, however, showed this view to be wrong. In a way, protectionism became a semipermanent feature of the Latin American economies.

During the first years of the industrialization process, a number of the larger countries' important heavy industries were created, as the bases for a manufacturing sector were set. However, alongside the industrialization process, an impressive array of restrictions, controls, and often contradictory regulations evolved. In fact, thanks to these import restrictions many of the domestic industries were able to survive. For example, a number of comparative studies have indicated that some of the Latin American countries (e.g., Chile) had for a long time one of the highest, and more variable, structures of protection in the developing world. As a consequence, many (if not most) of the industries created under the import substitution strategy were quite inefficient. In an empirical study directed by Krueger (1980), it was found that in Colombia, Chile, and Uruguay this inward-looking strategy resulted in the use of very capital intensive techniques, which hampered the creation of employment, among other inefficiencies.

As in most historical cases, the Latin American import substitution strategy was accompanied by an acutely overvalued domestic currency which precluded the development of a vigorous nontraditional export sector. In particular, in many of these countries the agricultural sector was seriously harmed by the real exchange rate overvaluation. In fact in many cases the lagging of agriculture became one of the most noticeable symptoms of Latin America's economic problems of the 1960s.

During the early and mid-1960s the import substitution strategy began to run out of steam. At that time, most of the easy and obvious substitutions of imported goods had already taken place, and the process was rapidly becoming less dynamic (Furtado 1969).

Starting in the late 1960s, and during most of the 1970s, most countries made some movements toward rationalizing their external sectors via the reduction in coverage of quantitative restrictions and reduction in the average level of tariffs. In many cases these liberalization efforts were accompanied by active policies aimed at promoting exports. In a number of countries these export promotion schemes were based on an active management of the nominal exchange rate, aimed at avoiding overvaluation, and thus helped maintain a steady growth in exports.

The Colombian experience is particularly interesting. After decades of an almost chaotic external sector policy—where exchange rate crises were the norm rather than the exception—in 1967 the Colombian government implemented a series of measures aimed at encouraging exports and at reducing the extent of protectionism. The exchange rate was devalued significantly, and a crawling peg system based on periodic adjustments of the nominal exchange rate was adopted. At the same time the percentage of commodities subject to prior import licensing was drastically reduced, as were the average levels of tariffs. The exchange rate and import liberalization policies were supplemented with a dynamic export subsidies scheme (the so-called CATs). The Colombian experience was in many ways a big success. Exports soared, new efficient industries were developed, and the external sector stayed extremely healthy, to the extent that Colombia was the only country among the large and medium Latin American nations not affected in a traumatic way by the debt crisis.[27]

Undoubtedly, the most ambitious attempts to liberalize the external sector took place in the Southern Cone during the late 1970s. Starting around 1975, Argentina, Chile, and Uruguay embarked on major programs to reform their economies. These cases were particularly interesting since the reforms implemented corresponded closely to what many economists have been advocating for a long time: quantitative restrictions on trade were eliminated, tariff levels and dispersion were reduced, domestic capital markets were developed, and restrictions on international capital movements were lifted. The main objective of these reforms was to transform these countries into open export-oriented economies.

A decade after these reforms were first implemented, the evidence indicates that they were to a large extent failures. In all three countries the liberalization reforms have been partially reversed. Tariffs have been raised, so that these economies are tending once again to become less integrated with the rest of the world. Severe financial crises resulted in the collapse and virtual nationalization of the banking sectors.

Although this is still an area of debate, it is possible to argue that the failure of these liberalizations was, to a large extent (but not exclusively), due to the implementation of inappropriate macroeconomic policies, including wage rate and exchange rate policies. Also, the way in which the financial reforms were implemented—with little or no supervision on behalf of the authorities—played an important role in the final disappointing outcome.

A major indirect negative effect of the failure of the Southern Cone experiences is that they have generated a bad press for import liberalization and market-oriented policies in the rest of the region. The collapse of these economies, the financial scandals, and the reversal of the policies have given ammunition to those who, on political or other grounds, oppose economic liberalization and tariff reform as a development strategy.

1.5.2 Tariffs and "True Protection"

Table 1.28 contains data on nominal and effective rates of protection for selected Latin American countries.[28] Although these data refer to only a handful of countries, and in some cases to quite a few years back, they give a flavor of the extent and evolution of protectionism in the region. First, the effective rates of protection (or protection to value-added) are extremely high. This is especially the case in the 1960s and 1970s. Second, for the cases of Argentina, Chile, Colombia, Peru, and Uruguay, these figures reflect vividly the move toward tariff liberalization that took place in the late 1970s and early 1980s.

What is not reflected in this table, however, is the post-debt-crisis (i.e., post-1982) generalized movement toward greater protection in the region. As these countries were forced to reduce imports and improve their external balance, they hiked their tariffs fairly significantly and imposed other forms of import controls. Even Chile, under the super-open-economy approach of Pinochet, responded to the crisis by (temporarily?) increasing tariffs by more than 50 percent in 1983 (see Edwards and Edwards 1987, 126–29).

Tariffs, of course, constitute only one form of protection, and countries in fact use many other mechanisms to introduce de facto wedges between domestic and world prices. As discussed in section 1.3, nontariff barriers (NTBs) can take many different forms ranging from prior deposits to outright quotas. The history of nontariff barriers in Latin America is long. As a number of authors have pointed out, import licenses, prior import deposits, and quotas have been generalized in these countries. Not surprisingly, use of nontariff barrier mechanisms increased significantly after the debt crisis (Cepal 1986f). In Colombia, for example, the proportion of imports subject to an import license increased from 47 percent in 1980 to 66 percent in 1983 (see Edwards 1983).

Table 1.28   Nominal and Effective Rates of Protection in Selective Latin American Countries

	Year	Nominal Rate of Protection	Effective Rate of Protection
Argentina			
Manufacturing	1969	51.5	97.4
All industries	1969	35.5	46.9
Manufacturing	1976	94.0	n.a.
Manufacturing	1980	53.4	n.a.
Brazil			
Consumer goods (manufactured)	1967	n.a.	66
Capital goods	1967	n.a.	52
Chile			
Manufacturing	1974	n.a.	10.1
Manufacturing	1979	n.a.	13.6
Colombia			
All industries	1979	n.a.	47.6
All industries	1981	n.a.	38.7
Peru			
All industries	1973	80.1	n.a.
Manufacturing	1975	n.a.	198
All industries	1980	37.0	n.a.
Uruguay			
All industries	1974	452	n.a.
All industries	1982	53	n.a.

Sources: Argentina: Cavallo and Cotani 1986; Brazil: Carvalho and Haddad 1981; Chile: Edwards and Edwards 1987; Colombia: Edwards 1983; Peru: Nogues 1986; Uruguay: Favaro and Spiller 1986.

Unfortunately the data available on NTBs in the developing countries, and in particular in Latin America, are exceedingly sketchy. In fact, as far as I know it is not possible to find, for Latin America, data on the coverage of NTBs which would be equivalent to the data presented in section 1.4. However, a recent study by ALADI (1984) provides some indication of the coverage of two forms of NTBs: outright prohibitions and prior import licenses. Table 1.29 summarizes these data. As can be seen from this table, NTBs are as prevalent in Latin America as in the developed countries, if not more so.

Multiple exchange rates are another mechanism used extensively by the Latin American nations to impede trade flows. Interestingly, studies on NTBs have not focused on this protective tool. In section 1.6, however, we look into this problem in more detail.

The lack of reliable data on NTBs has generally frustrated analysts trying to assess with some rigor the extent of protection in the developing world. For this reason, in a recent massive cross-country study

Table 1.29   **Coverage of Some Nontariff Barriers in Selected Latin American Countries, 1983**

	Percent of Import Items Subject to Outright Prohibition	Percent of Import Items Subject to Import Licenses
Argentina		
All products	23	29
Brazil		
All products	42	n.a.
Textiles	93	n.a.
Agriculture	86	n.a.
Wood	80	n.a.
Chile		
All products	0	0
Colombia		
All products	n.a.	60
Ecuador		
All products	30	n.a.
Agriculture	71	n.a.
Mexico		
All products	n.a.	82

Source: ALADI 1984.

undertaken at the World Bank, an effort to construct subjective "indexes of liberalization" was made. These indexes are supposed to capture the extent of trade impediments, including tariffs and other NTBs. They are *subjective* in the sense that they do not combine actual objective measures. Although there are some shortcomings related to this subjectivity, including the nonverifiability and noncomparability across countries, their construction has been extremely useful in helping to understand the evolution of "true protectionism" in some of these countries. For the five Latin American nations included among the eighteen countries covered by the study, the indexes reflect the protectionist history of these countries as well as the efforts toward liberalization implemented in the late 1970s and early 1980s (see Michaely, Papageorgiou, and Choksi 1986).

1.6 Latin America's Exchange Rate Policies and the External Sector

This section briefly analyzes the exchange rate policies of the Latin American countries, placing special emphasis on two issues: (*a*) real exchange rate overvaluation, and (*b*) the protective role of multiple and parallel (or black) market exchange rates. The evolution of the external sector can be affected in several ways by the evolution of the real exchange rate.[29] For example, real exchange rate misalignment, and especially an overvalued real exchange rate, greatly harms export performance (and in particular nontraditional exports) and encourages capital flight. On the other hand a highly volatile real exchange rate enhances uncertainty, tending to reduce and even mislocate investment.[30]

1.6.1   Exchange Rate Policies, the Dollar, and Real Exchange Rates

During the last thirteen years or so, the Latin American countries have followed the most diverse nominal exchange rate policies, including fixed to the dollar, crawling peg (i.e., periodic adjustments approximately determined by the differential between domestic and world inflation), periodic devaluations, preannounced declining rate of nominal devaluation, and so on. Surprisingly perhaps, in spite of these different policies, during the late 1970s and early 1980s a large number of countries experienced significant real appreciations, which led to acute overvaluation of their currencies.[31]

In general, it is possible to single out three main causes of these fairly generalized movements toward real overvaluation: Many of these countries pursued expansive monetary and fiscal policies that became incompatible with the nominal exchange rate regime chosen (i.e., Mexico, Peru, Argentina). In this case, the loose macropolicies resulted in expansions of aggregate demand, which exercised upward pressure on domestic prices. As prices increased at a rate higher than the nominal rate of devaluation (which under fixed nominal rates is zero), the real exchange rate appreciated and the country's exports became less competitive in international markets. A second cause of real appreciation, which affected mainly the Southern Cone countries, was the adoption of preannounced declining devaluation schedules, which started at rates below the ongoing rate of inflation (i.e., the *tablitas*). The combination of these *tablitas* with other policies, such as backward wage indexation in Chile and relaxation of capital controls in Argentina, Chile, and Uruguay, conspired to generate significant real appreciations in these three countries (Edwards 1984). A final and important factor that contributed to the loss in the region's competitiveness was the significant appreciation of the dollar in international financial markets between 1980 and 1985. Most of the Latin American countries either peg their nominal exchange rate to the U.S. dollar or use the dollar as a term of reference to conduct their exchange rate policy. Consequently, as the dollar appreciated in the international financial markets with respect to other industrial countries' currencies, so did most of the Latin American currencies.[32]

Figures 1.4–1.7 depict the behavior of two indexes of the real exchange rate for Brazil, Chile, El Salvador, Paraguay, Peru, and Mexico. These indexes were constructed using quarterly data and in most cases

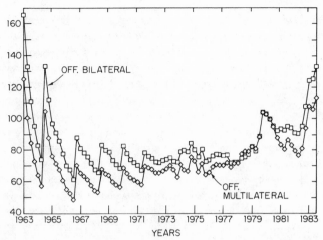

Fig. 1.4   Brazil. Real exchange rate: $e = E^*CP1(\text{world})/CP1(\text{home})$
(1980 = 100).

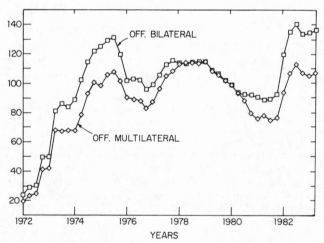

Fig. 1.5   Chile. Real exchange rate: $e = E^*CP1(\text{world})/CP1(\text{home})$
(1980 = 100).

cover up to mid-1983 or early 1984. The average for 1980 is equal to
100.[33] In these diagrams an increase in the indexes reflects real depreciation, while a decline in the index denotes real appreciation or loss
of international competitiveness. The first index is the traditional bilateral real exchange rate computed with respect to the U.S. dollar and
is called "off bilateral" in the diagrams. The second index, called "off
multilateral," was constructed taking into account, for each country,

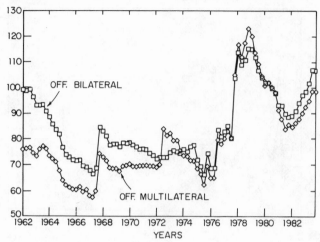

Fig. 1.6   Peru. Real exchange rate: $e = E^*CP1(\text{world})/CP1(\text{home})$ (1980 = 100).

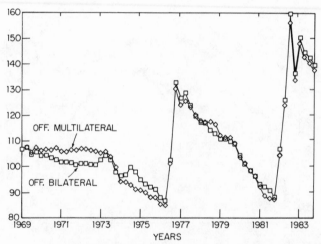

Fig. 1.7   Mexico. Real exchange rate: $e = E^*CP1(\text{world})/CP1(\text{home})$ (1980 = 100).

the changes in international competitiveness relative to a group of its ten most important trade partners. In this way this multilateral real exchange rate index is able to take into account the way in which fluctuations among the partners' exchange rates affect international competitiveness.

These diagrams neatly reflect some of the features of real exchange behavior discussed earlier. First, in all countries we observe that in the mid- to late 1970s a process of real appreciation, which entailed a reduction in the countries' degree of international competitiveness, took place. While in some cases this declining trend in the RER was reversed in the early 1980s (Brazil, Chile, Peru, Mexico) via nominal devaluations, in others (Paraguay, El Salvador) it continued until at least 1984. These diagrams also reflect in a nice way the differences between bilateral and multilateral real exchange rates, as well as the effects of the dollar appreciation in the first half of the 1980s. Notice that in all countries after 1980 the multilateral index declines (i.e., appreciates) much faster than the bilateral rate, indicating that the degree of "true" overvaluation—which takes into account changes in the degree of competitiveness relative to all trade partners—was much greater than that computed with respect to the U.S. dollar only.

1.6.2 Multiple Exchange Rates, Parallel Markets, and Protectionism in Latin America

In many cases nonunified exchange rates play an important protective role. To the extent that two types of international transactions are subject to different rates of exchange, a wedge between their prices that acts in the same way as a tax will be imposed.[34] Moreover, multiple exchange rates for commercial transactions will have an effect equivalent to import tariffs (or export taxes), since the domestic public will have to pay a higher price for those imports subject to a higher exchange rate.

For the exchange rate system to play a protective role, the authorities need not officially adopt multiple rates. In fact, a parallel market for foreign exchange will usually also have a protective effect. Generally speaking, in many cases marginal imports will be brought into the country at the higher parallel market (or free) exchange rate.[35]

The Latin American countries have had a long tradition with multiple exchange rates. In many cases—as in Argentina and Colombia for example—a lower rate has been applied to traditional exports as an implicit way of taxing them. Also, in many countries, and for long periods of time, different rates have been applied to commercial and financial transactions. Perhaps the most extreme case is that of Chile in 1972, when fifteen different "official" exchange rates were in effect.

In fact in the 1980s multiple rates have become such a commonplace that in 1983 all but three of the Latin American countries for which there are data had two or more official exchange rates. While in many of these countries multiple rates have been a long-term feature (Argentina, Colombia, Paraguay, Ecuador), in many others they have only made an appearance (or reappearance) in the early 1980s, usually as part of the packages aimed at dealing with the debt and economic crisis (i.e., Chile, Venezuela, Dominican Republic). This profusion of multiple official rates as well as the significant parallel market premiums observed in many of these countries indicate that the extent of protection in Latin America is generally higher than what data on tariffs, or even import licenses and quotas, would suggest.

1.7 Direct Foreign Investment in Latin America

For many years, direct foreign investment has been a controversial issue in Latin America. Most countries in the region have carefully regulated the conditions under which direct foreign investment can take place, and have determined with even greater care regulations that govern profits repatriation, reinvestment, transfer pricing, and so on. Moreover, in a number of countries regulations establish a time limit after which any foreign investment should be "nationalized," with at least 51 percent of the equity belonging to locals. Perhaps the most severe of these regulations regarding direct foreign investment was contained in article 24 of the Cartegena Agreement which governed the functioning of the Andean Pact.[36] According to this regulation, any foreign investment had to be nationalized before fifteen years had elapsed.

Latin America's attitude toward foreign investment has in many instances been discriminatory and sector-specific; while direct foreign investment is welcomed in some sectors, it is completely kept out of other so-called strategic areas. Good examples of this type of policy are the Brazilian and Mexican rejections of recent proposals to develop U.S.-owned computer manufactures in those countries.[37] Also the incorporation in the Chilean constitution of state *ownership* of all major copper (and other) mines is striking.[38]

In spite of the "suspicious" attitude with which many of the Latin American countries have faced the subject, direct foreign investment in the region has continued to be substantial, with the United States as the principal actor. Table 1.30 contains the latest available data on the *accumulated value* of direct foreign investment in Latin America by country of origin. Although these data—as is much of the information on direct foreign investment in the region—are highly incomplete, they reflect two interesting facts. First, the United States plays a very dominant role in the area. Second, as far as this information shows, the relative importance of the United States declined between 1976 and 1981. In fact, according to the data the U.S. share in the accumulated value of foreign direct investment fluctuated around 63–64 percent between 1967 and 1978; in 1981, the last year for which there are data, this share was only 54 percent.

Betwen 1982 and 1984 there was no change in the value of U.S. investments in the region. However, 1983 was a year of a fairly important net disinvestment, concentrated almost exclusively in Vene-

Table 1.30   Accumulated Value of Direct Foreign Investment in Latin America by Country of Origin (millions of U.S. dollars)

	1967	1976	1977	1978	1979	1980	1981	1984
U.S.	11,777	23,934	27,514	32,662	35,056	38,882	38,864	28,094
Japan	403	3,301	3,757	4,373	5,000	6,168	n.a.	n.a.
Germany (FR)	753	3,494	4,381	4,674	n.a.	n.a.	n.a.	n.a.
U.K.	1,228	n.a.	n.a.	1,995	n.a.	n.a.	n.a.	n.a.
Canada	1,093	2,287	n.a.	n.a.	n.a.	n.a.	n.a.	n.a.
OECD Total	18,453	37,740	43,293	50,550	n.a.	n.a.	71,800	n.a.
ALADI	n.a.	n.a.	n.a.	n.a.	n.a.	590	654	n.a.

Source: CEPAL 1986b.

zuela. In 1984 there was a net positive investment of almost the same value as the drop of 1983. However, the geographical as well as the sector composition changed drastically. While investments in Venezuela were minimal in 1984, they surged in Brazil. Also, oil saw a big dip in 1984, with manufactures and commerce experiencing important increases.

Undoubtedly, the economic and political uncertainties of the last few years in Latin America have dictated the relative stagnation of U.S. investment flows into the region. On the other hand, abundant natural resources and substantial labor cost differentials still make the region a very attractive place for U.S. and other multinationals to locate. For example, the data in figure 1.8 suggest that the relative differential between U.S. and local labor costs has widened since the mid-1970s.[39]

In the aftermath of the debt crisis, direct foreign investment will probably become very important for the Latin American countries. For a number of years to come the region will not be able to obtain abundant (or even meager) funds from the international banking community, or from the flotation of bonds. Consequently, additional funds to finance increased capital accumulation and the resumption of growth will have to come from other sources. Of course, the natural alternative sources of funds to finance investment are (a) increased domestic savings (both private and public), (b) reversal of the massive capital flight that took place in the early 1980s,[40] (c) increased funds obtained from multilateral organizations such as the World Bank and the Interamerican Development Bank, and (d) increased direct investment.

Whether these potential sources of additional foreign funds will actually become available will depend on a series of factors, including

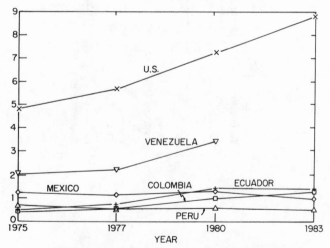

Fig. 1.8   Wages in manufacturing for the United States and five Latin American countries, selected years, 1975–83.

the countries' domestic policies. However, with respect to direct foreign investment, substantial increases in the flow of funds will require fairly creative policies by the Latin American countries that would encourage these additional funds from abroad, while at the same time would allow these countries to maintain their main development and "national objectives." An interesting possibility would be to link any efforts to attract new direct foreign investment to the opening up of the "services sector." For example, in 1984 the United States' accumulated direct investment in the commercial banks, finance, insurance, and real estate sectors was only 11.9 percent of the total of these investments.[41]

1.8   Concluding Remarks

In this paper I have analyzed in detail a number of different aspects related to the evolution and recent behavior of U.S. trade relations with the Latin American countries. In this section I wrap up the analysis by summarizing the findings and by discussing the possible future evolution of U.S.–Latin American trade relations. The main conclusions of this study are the following:

1. When market import shares (computed using U.S. dollar values of imports) are used as an indicator of competitiveness, there is no evidence of a loss in the U.S. degree of competitiveness in Latin America in the last fifteen years or so. In fact, the statistical analysis of the existing empirical evidence shows that there has been no significant change in the U.S. share of the aggregate Latin American import market since 1970.

2. At the individual country level, however, there have been some changes. In nine countries, the U.S. share of imports has not changed significantly; in two it has increased; and in five, including Nicaragua, there has been a decline.

3. Although at the *overall aggregate* level there have been no significant changes in the degree of U.S. competitiveness in Latin America, there have been substantial changes in what the United States exports to these countries. There has been a very important increase in Latin American imports of primary products and of chemicals from the United States, with a decline in imports of other (traditional) manufactured goods. Thus, there has been an increase in the "degree of competitiveness" of U.S. primary products and chemicals in Latin America, accompanied with a loss in competitiveness of traditional manufacturing sectors.

4. Although the share of the United States in total Latin American imports has not changed, the (real) dollar value of U.S. exports to the region has declined very significantly in the last three or four years. This is because, as a result of the debt crisis, every country in the

region has gone through major—and in some cases highly innovative—adjustment programs, which have resulted in important reductions in total imports. For the region as a whole, the *real* value of aggregate imports declined by more than 45 percent between 1980 and 1985.

5. The reduction in the real value of Latin America's imports in the last years was a result of the contractionary demand policies implemented in many countries, of important (real) exchange rate adjustments, and of the imposition in many cases of fairly massive import controls. These import controls—which take many forms, including higher tariffs, more generalized NTBs, multiple exchange rates, and parallel exchange rates—mark an important turn from a liberalizing trend observed, since the mid-1970s, in most countries in the region. It is clear that this mode of Latin American adjustment is not sustainable in the long run. The resumption of growth will require a rationalization of the external sector and an increase in imports and in exports.

6. In terms of foreign competition, Japan has not experienced any significant increases in its presence in the Latin American import market. At the manufactured goods level, the drop in the U.S. share has been picked up by other NICs (i.e., Korea, Taiwan) and especially by intra–Latin American trade. In fact, CEPAL/ECLA projects a substantial increase in overall intraregional trade for the next years (CEPAL 1986c). For example, in July 1986 CEPAL/ECLA projected that the share of intra-ALADI imports would increase from 16 percent in 1985 to 18.6 percent in 1990 and to 22.2 percent in 1994. Naturally, if this happens, other countries' shares, including the United States', would decline. Although we cannot discard ECLA's projections casually, their numbers are possibly on the high side, since they are based on the (fairly unlikely) assumption of "dedollarization" of the interregional trade.

7. A remarkable fact, surprisingly not widely known, is that practically all of the recent adjustment has come through a reduction in imports, with the *real value* of exports having declined in many of these countries, mainly as a result of the reduction of prices of commodity exports.

8. The recovery of the Latin American economy will require an increase in exports and a rationalization of these nations' import sector, via reduced protection and increased efficiency. This rationalization and easing of the current high levels of import restrictions will probably come about slowly. It is highly likely that these countries will proceed cautiously, avoiding this time around the errors and mistakes of the recent Southern Cone liberalization. Special care will be placed on avoiding exchange rate overvaluation.

9. A sustained increase in Latin America's exports—which is, of course, a prerequisite for an increase in its imports—requires a number of conditions. First, there has to be a steady increase in the demand

for these goods by the developed world. In fact, it has been recently estimated that an average increase in industrial countries' GDP of approximately 3 percent per annum will be "required" during the next years (Balassa et al. 1986). Second, increased efficiency in the regional productive process must occur; this could be achieved via a generalized increase in efficiency, including the rationalization of the external sector. Also, real exchange rate overvaluation must be avoided. More important, the current protectionist trend in the industrial countries must be reversed.

10. The data presented in this paper indicate that at this time the extent of nontariff barriers, as a form of protection in the industrial countries, is very significant. Moreover, the data show that these NTBs are particularly important for goods originating in the developing nations and that their tariff equivalents are in many cases very significant.

11. Although the United States is still the most important country regarding direct investment in Latin America, its relative importance has declined in recent years. Since 1981 the accumulated value of U.S. investment in Latin America has not changed. However, its sectoral and geographical composition has changed, with oil and commerce being negatively affected. Both because of its resources and labor costs, Latin America continues to be an attractive region for foreign investors. Moreover, in the aftermath of the debt crisis, direct foreign investment has become one of the few possible sources of foreign funds to finance capital accumulation and growth in the region. Whether significant investments will materialize will depend on expected economic and political stability and on innovative changes in local regulations.

The evidence examined in this paper suggests that the United States' overall competitive position in Latin America has not changed significantly in the last fifteen years or so. At the sectoral level, however, the composition of U.S. exports to Latin America has changed, reflecting a changing pattern of U.S. comparative advantage: chemicals and primary products have increased their shares, with traditional manufactures hurting. Foreign competition in Latin America is not coming from Japan but from other NICs, and, more important, from intra–Latin American trade. As a result of the debt crisis the value of Latin American imports has greatly declined, bringing down with it the value of U.S. exports to the region. As imports recover and move toward their peak (real) value, the United States will also increase its exports to the region. How will the recovery of imports be financed? Possibly, in part by higher exports—this in turn requires steady growth in the industrial world and an end to the protectionist mood—and in part through new funds made available by increased direct foreign investment.

Appendix

Table 1.A.1   **Regressions Results for U.S. Import Market Shares in Sixteen Latin American Countries; 1970–83**

Country	Constant	Time Trend	Log U.S. Real Exchange Rate	Log U.S. RER Lagged	D.W.	R^2
Argentina	0.626 (0.292)	0.013 1.088	−0.044 (−0.066)	−0.439 (−0.571)	1.229	0.222
Brazil	3.061Q* (4.678)	−0.046* (−12.469)	0.387 (1.824)	−0.470 (−1.890)	2.572	0.975
Chile	1.487 (0.398)	−0.009 (−0.442)	−1.383 (−1.143)	1.003 (0.706)	1.238	0.132
Mexico	2.999* (4.973)	0.009* (2.603)	−0.171 (−0.877)	−0.059 (−0.258)	2.173	0.598
Uruguay	0.613 (0.246)	−0.009 (−0.677)	−0.232 (0.281)	0.131 (0.971)	2.010	0.159
Venezuela	4.271* (3.798)	−0.005 (−0.887)	−0.569 (−1.564)	0.657 (1.537)	1.521	0.211
Colombia	4.354* (4.008)	0.021* (−3.462)	−0.176 (−0.501)	0.287 (−0.696)	1.805	0.647
Paraguay	−1.659 (−0.557)	−0.061* (−3.608)	0.354 (0.367)	−1.331 (1.175)	1.377	0.814
Costa Rica	1.984* (2.521)	0.001 (0.305)	−0.389 (1.525)	0.065 (0.219)	1.475	0.388
Guatemala	3.453 (3.742)	−0.004 (−0.676)	−0.577 (−1.929)	0.560 (1.598)	1.749	0.278
Ecuador	3.023* (2.758)	−0.005 (−0.757)	−0.179 (0.505)	0.043 (0.103)	1.041	0.144
Peru	3.480* (2.521)	0.027* (3.469)	0.395 (0.882)	−0.359 (0.684)	1.254	0.658
Nicaragua	7.534 (6.311)	−0.045* (−6.680)	0.063 (1.627)	0.182 (0.402)	2.674	0.901
El Salvador	3.017 (2.334)	−0.002 (−0.232)	0.680 (1.625)	−0.753 (−1.532)	1.091	0.378
Honduras	5.211 (5.816)	−0.011* (−2.147)	0.067 (0.237)	0.277 (0.665)	1.539	0.435
Bolivia	−1.365 (−0.760)	0.009 (0.904)	0.274 (0.470)	−1.238 (−1.813)	1.940	0.428

Notes: The regression run was the following log share$_t$ = a_0 + a_1 TIME + a_2 log USRER$_t$ + a_3 log USRER$_{t-1}$ + μ_t. The data on real exchange rates correspond to (the inverse) of the IMF MERM indexes.

The numbers in parentheses are t-statistics; D.W. is the Durbin-Watson statistic; R^2 is the coefficient of determination. All asterisks mean that the coefficient is significant.

Notes

Comments on this paper by Alejandra Cox Edwards, Arye Hillman, and the participants of the preconference meeting held in Cambridge, Massachusetts, December 1986, have been very useful. The help obtained from Dr. Rolando Sanchez during the author's visit to CEPAL (Santiago, Chile) to gather data for this paper is gratefully acknowledged. David Gould provided able research assistance. This research was supported by the NSF (Grant SAS 84 19932) and by UCLA's Academic Senate.

1. These are the countries for which disaggregated data on directions of trade are available.

2. On the evolution of Latin America's external sector see, for example, Furtado 1969. On Latin America and the Great Depression see Diaz-Alejandro 1982 and 1983, and Maddison 1985. On the development strategies in Latin America, see Corbo 1986.

3. See, for example, the discussion in Furtado 1969.

4. On the Southern Cone see, for example, Calvo 1986; Corbo 1985; Hanson and de Melo 1985; Edwards 1985; and Edwards and Edwards 1987.

5. An important issue concerns to which external price index should be used to compute the evolution of the real value of imports and exports. The figure quoted earlier was calculated using the U.S. CPI. If the wholesale price index for the industrialized countries as a whole, as computed by the IMF, is used instead, Latin American imports declined by 49 percent on real terms between 1980 and 1985.

6. In some of these countries imports had also grown at a fantastically high pace between 1975 and 1980 (i.e., the Southern Cone countries). Notice, however, that for the fourteen countries as a whole, the real value of imports grew at a slower rate during 1975–80 than in the period 1965–75.

7. However, both the trade-GDP and the import-GDP ratios exhibit quite a bit of fluctuation from year to year. To get a sense of the general trend in the degree of openness, regressions of the log of both of these indexes on time were run for the period 1960–83. The results show that in the great majority of these countries, openness increased during this period.

8. The decline of the trade ratio, however, is less marked than that of the imports ratio. The reason is that as a result of the adjustment program in some of these countries, exports increased during the period.

9. On the constant-market-share criterion for assessing the degree of international competitiveness, see Leamer and Stern 1970.

10. This can be illustrated using the following example. Assume that a particular Latin American country imports goods from the United States and the rest of the world. The *quantities* imported are M^{US} amd M^R respectively. The price of imports from the United States is P^{US}, while the price of imports from R, expressed in U.S. dollars, is EP^R, where E is the nominal exchange rate between the United States and the rest, and P^R is the price of M^R in the rest of the world currency. Our market share then is equal to $s = [P^{US}M^{US}/(P^{US}M^{US} + P^REM^R)]$. This can be rewritten as $s = [M^{US}/(M^{US} + (EP^R/P^{US})M^R)]$. Notice that $[(EP^RP^{US})]$ is the real value of the dollar. Clearly, then, even if M^{US} and M^R—the quantities imported—remain constant, changes in (ER^R/P^{US}) will affect s.

11. In Argentina, Chile, Venezuela, Peru, and El Salvador the U.S. share exhibited a slight increase between 1977 and 1982; in Brazil, Paraguay, and Nicaragua there was somewhat of a decline during the same period. In the

other countries the U.S. share fluctuated around a fairly stable value during 1977–81.

12. The coefficient for the time trend turned out to be -0.004 with a t-statistic of -1.2. In fact, Nicaragua is the only country with a significant increase in imports from the Soviet bloc during the 1980s.

13. Due to space considerations, detailed data for the rest of the countries are not provided here. However, these data are available from the author on request.

14. Given the different sources (IMF and ECLA) there are some (minor) divergences between these figures and those in tables 2.1–2.4. See CEPAL 1985 and 1986d.

15. The Heckscher-Ohlin theory predicts that, in general, a country will tend to export those goods whose production process is intensive in the factor that the country has in relative abundance (see Leamer 1984). Notice that Leamer's study covers only up to 1975. The data presented here, then, confirms that Leamer's results are also valid for the more recent period.

16. This classification corresponds to ECLA.

17. This of course is consistent with the shift in the U.S. comparative advantage detected above and documented in the previous subsection.

18. In not all countries, however, did the real value of exports decline during this period. In Brazil, Ecuador, and Mexico, for example, the real value of exports was significantly higher in 1985 than in 1980. In both cases the real value of imports and exports were computed using the data in tables 1.2 and 1.3 and the U.S. WPI as a price deflator for the nominal dollar values. If, however, the wholesale price index for the industrialized countries as a whole is used as the deflator, real exports of these thirteen countries have declined by almost 18 percent.

19. For a comprehensive discussion on the role of exports in the recovery of Latin America, see the analysis in Balassa et al. 1986. Even in those quarters where traditionally there has been skepticism regarding the role of trade, there is now agreement on the importance of exports expansion in the next decade or so.

20. See, however, section 1.7 for a discussion on alternative sources of financing of new imports.

21. As in the case of imports, these shares have been computed by dividing the dollar value of exports to a particular country by the total dollar value of exports.

22. Another interesting regularity is that the relative importance of fuel exports (category 3) increased dramatically during the period. This rapid growth, of course, reflects increases in both oil prices (notice, for example, the jump of this share in 1979) and oil production. Naturally, the recent decline in the price of oil has had the opposite effect on these shares.

23. See Balassa and Balassa 1984; Cline 1985; Jones 1983; and Nogues, Olechowski, and Winters 1986a and 1986b.

24. Denmark, France, Germany, Greece, Ireland, Italy, the Netherlands, the United Kingdom, Australia, Austria, Finland, Japan, Norway, Switzerland, and the United States.

25. Since the numerator in this index is *actual* imports, its value will tend to be biased downward. For this reason Nogues, Olechowski, and Winters construct alternative indexes, which is pretty much the same story as that presented here.

26. In fact, in their recent blueprint for Latin American recovery, Balassa et al. 1986 stress that it is crucial that the industrialized countries avoid any

new import protection or export subsidization, "indeed [what is required is] a renewal of trade liberalization" (p. 34). In that regard, the U.S. 1984 Trade and Tariff Act allows for the possibility of implementing a series of protectionist measures. For an analysis of the act from a Latin American perspective, see Rodriguez-Mendoz 1986.

27. Of course, the coffee boom of 1975–79 and the boom in illegal drug-related trade also helped. On coffee and the Colombian economy see Edwards 1983. On the Colombian external sector see Diaz-Alejandro 1976 and Thomas 1986.

28. The effective rate of protection is a measure of the relative degree of inefficiency of domestic production relative to international production. A positive value means that domestic value-added for that particular activity exceeds value-added at international prices. The effective tariff for good i (τ_i) is computed as $\tau_i = (t_i - \Sigma_{ij} t_j)/(1 - \Sigma_{aij})$, where t_i is the nominal tariff, a_{ij} is the input/output coefficient between input j and good i, and t_j is the nominal tariff on input j. Notice that if the good and *all* inputs have the same nominal tariff, then the effective and nominal rates of protection are the same ($\tau_i = t_i$).

29. The real exchange rate is a measure of the international competitiveness of a country and is defined as $RER = EP^*/P$, where E is the nominal exchange rate, and P^* and P are foreign and domestic price levels. An increase in RER represents a real depreciation and reflects an increase in competitiveness.

30. On the effects of real exchange rate overvaluation in the developing countries, see, for example, Pfefferman 1985. On overvaluation and capital flight, see Cuddington 1986. A series of essays on exchange rates in developing countries can be found in Edwards and Ahamed 1986.

31. Notice that since overvaluation is defined as a (significant) discrepancy between the actual and equilibrium real exchange rate, not all real appreciation necessarily reflects a situation of overvaluation. It is possible that the equilibrium real exchange rate appreciates. For a fuller discussion see Edwards 1987.

32. Balassa et al. 1986, for example, considers the dollar appreciation episode of 1982–85 as an important determinant of the debt crisis.

33. For a detailed discussion on the construction of these indexes, see Edwards and Ng 1985.

34. This is an extensive technical literature on multiple exchange rates. See, for example, Dornbusch 1986a.

35. For a general discussion on the role of multiple and parallel rates in the developing countries, see Dornbusch 1986a and 1986b, and Edwards 1987.

36. Even the ultra-free-market-oriented Pinochet government in Chile showed apprehension regarding direct foreign investment when the Mining Law was enacted. See *Estudios Publicos,* Summer 1986.

37. On the Brazilian computer industry see Evans 1986.

38. The constitution allowed the state to grant concessions to foreign firms. The nature of these concessions was regulated by the Mining Law of 1979, which included an ingenious system for calculating indemnization in case of early termination of the concessions. See Pinera 1986.

39. Of course these comparisons are highly sensitive to the exchange rate used. To the extent that the Latin American countries succeed in avoiding real overvaluation, their real wages will remain relatively low by international comparisons.

40. On the extent of capital flight see, for example, Cuddington 1986.

41. This is significantly below its 1977 share of 25 percent.

References

ALADI. 1984. Elementos de juicio para el establecimiento de un programa para la eliminacion de restricciones no arancelarias. Caracas, Venezuela.

Balassa, B., and C. Balassa. 1984. Industrial protection in the developing countries. *World Economy* (June): 179–96.

Balassa, B., G. M. Bueno, P. P. Kuczynski, and M. H. Simoensen. 1986. *Toward renewed economic growth in Latin America*. Washington, D.C.: Institute of International Economics.

Blejer, M. 1984. Economic integration: An analytical overview. In *Economic and social progress in Latin America*. Interamerica Development Bank.

Calvo, G. 1986. Fractured liberalism: Argentina under Martinez de Hoz. *Economic Development and Cultural Change,* April.

Carvalho, J., and C. Haddad. 1981. Foreign trade strategies and employment in Brazil. In A. O. Krueger, H. B. Lary, T. Monson, and N. Akrasanee, eds., *Trade and Employment in Developing Countries*. Chicago: University of Chicago Press.

Cavallo, D., and J. Cotani. 1986. The timing and sequencing of economic liberalization: The case of Argentina. World Bank Typescript.

CEPAL. 1985. *Origen y destino del comercio exterior de los paises de la Asociación Latinoamericana de Integracion y del Mercado Comun Centroamericano*. Cuadernos Estadisticos de la Cepal 9. Santiago, Chile.

———. 1986a. *Anuario estadistico de la cepal*. Santiago, Chile.

———. 1986b. Banco de datos sobre inversiones extranjeras directa en America Latina y el Caribe. September.

———. 1986c. Cooperación comercial y negociaciones regionales. Santiago, Chile. July.

———. 1986d. Origen y destino de comercio exterior en 1983. Santiago, Chile. August.

———. 1986e. Relaciones economicas internacionales y cooperación de America Latina y el Caribe. Santiago, Chile. May.

———. 1986f. Reorientacion del comercio exterior de productos basicos hacia America Latina. Santiago, Chile. June.

Cline, W. 1985. *Imports of manufactures from developing countries: Performance and prospects for market access*. Washington, D.C.: Brookings Institution.

Corbo, V. 1985. Chilean economic policy and international economic relations since 1970. In G. M. Walton, ed., *The national economic policies of Chile*. Greenwich, Conn.: JAI Press.

———. 1986. Problems, development theory and strategies of Latin America. DRD Working Paper No. 190. World Bank.

Cuddington, J. 1986. Capital flight from the developing countries. World Bank Typescript.

Diaz-Alejandro, C. F. 1976. *Colombia*. New York: Columbia University Press.

———. 1982. Latin America in depression, 1929–1939. In M. Gersovitz et al., eds., *The theory and experience of economic development*. London: Allen and Unwin.

———. 1983. Stories of the 1930s for the 1980s. In P. Aspe Armella et al., eds., *Financial policies and the world capital market*. Chicago: University of Chicago Press.

Dornbusch, R. 1986a. Multiple exchange rates for commercial transactions. In S. Edwards and L. Ahamed, eds., *Economic Adjustment and Exchange Rates in Developing Countries*. Chicago: University of Chicago Press.

———. 1986b. Special exchange rates for capital account transactions. *World Bank Economic Review* (September): 3–34.

Edwards. S. 1983. The external sector in Columbia. Paper prepared for the World Bank.

———. 1984. *The order of liberalization of the external sector in developing countries*. Princeton Essays in International Finance No. 156.

———. 1985. Stabilization with liberalization: An evaluation of the years of Chile's experience with free market policies, 1973–1983. *Economic Development and Cultural Change,* January.

———. 1987. Exchange rate misalignment in developing countries. NBER Working Paper.

Edwards, S., and L. Ahamed, eds. 1986. *Economic adjustment and exchange rates in developing countries*. Chicago: University of Chicago Press.

Edwards, S., and A. Cox Edwards. 1987. *Monetarism and liberalization: The Chilean experiment*. Cambridge, Mass.: Ballinger.

Edwards. S., and F. Ng. 1985. Trends in real exchange rate behavior in selected developing countries. CPD Working Paper. World Bank.

Evans, P. B. 1986. State, capital, and the transformation of dependence: The Brazilian computer case. *World Development* (July): 791–800.

Favaro, E., and P. Spiller. 1986. The timing and sequencing of economic liberalization: The case of Uruguay. World Bank Typescript.

Furtado, C. 1969. *La economia latinoamericana*. Santiago, Ed. Universitaria.

GATT. 1984. Report of the group of quantitative restrictions and other non tariff barriers. Geneva.

Hanson, J., and J. de Melo. 1985. External shocks, financial reforms, and stabilization attempts in Uruguay during 1974–1983. *World Development* (August): 134–46.

International Monetary Fund. Various issues. *Directions of trade.*

———. Various issues. *International financial statistics.*

Jones, C. D. 1983. Visible imports subject to restraint. Government Economic Services WP No. 62.

Krueger, A. O. 1983. *Trade and employment in developing countries: Synthesis and conclusions*. Chicago: University of Chicago Press.

Krueger, A. O., H. B. Lary, T. Monson, and N. Akrasanee, eds. 1980. *Trade and employment in developing countries*. Vol. 1. Chicago: University of Chicago Press.

Leamer, E. E. 1984. *Sources of international comparative advantage*. Cambridge, Mass.: MIT Press.

Leamer, E., and R. Stern. 1970. *Quantitative international economics*. Boston: Bycon Press.

Maddison, A. 1985. *Two crises: Latin American and Asia, 1929–38 and 1973–1983*. Paris: OECD.

Michaely, M., D. Papageorgiou, and A. Choksi. 1986. The phasing of a trade liberalization policy: Preliminary evidence. Paper presented at AEA Meeting, New Orleans.

Nogues, J. 1986. The timing and sequencing of liberalization: Peru. World Bank Typescript.

Nogues, J., A. Olechowski, and L. A. Winters. 1986a. The extent of non tariff barriers to imports of developing countries. World Bank Staff Working Paper 789.

———. 1986b. The extent of non tariff barriers to industrial countries' imports. *World Bank Economic Review* (September): 181–99.

Pfefferman, G. 1985. Overvalued exchange rates and development. *Finance and Development* 22 (March): 17–19.

Pinera, J. 1986. La ley minera. *Estudios Publicos* 21 (Summer).
Prebisch, R. 1984. Five stages in my thinking on development. In G. M. Meier and D. Seers, eds., *Pioneers in development*. Oxford: Oxford University Press.
Rodriguez-Mendoza, M. 1986. Latin America and the U.S. Trade and Tariff Act. *Journal of World Trade Law* (February): 47–60.
Thomas, V. 1986. *Linking macroeconomic and agricultural policies for adjustment with growth*. Baltimore: Johns Hopkins University Press.
World Bank. 1986. *World development report*. Washington, D.C.
World currency yearbook. Various issues.

2. Thomas O. Enders
The Latin Debt Problem Can Be Downsized, but Growth Will Be Long in Coming Back

Why is it that after nearly five years of sacrifice—per capita income in Latin America has fallen by perhaps 8 percent in the 1980s and will fall again this year—the debt crisis appears no nearer to solution now than when it started?

The current crisis in Brazil—the product of a weak and divided government reacting to its own loss of control over the economy—throws a sharper light on that question; it puts the focus on the enduring domestic weaknesses that so exacerbate the impact of the debt.

Theoretically, when Latin America reached its borrowing limits in 1982, it could have gone on growing by sacrificing a couple of years' increases in consumption, increasing savings, switching those resources into exports, and running a trade surplus, in order to be able to service the debt without net new capital imports. Indeed, that is exactly what Korea did.

Latin America did swing from a trade deficit in 1981 to surpluses ranging from $27 billion to $37 billion in the last four years. But it has done so only to a small extent by diverting to export goods that could have been consumed at home. After decades of attempting to industrialize by building protected and often highly subsidized import substitution industries, Latin America—Brazil is the only significant partial exception—has had little to sell on the world market other than commodities and less experience in selling it. As a result, most of the burden of achieving a trade surplus has fallen on imports, which in the 1980s have fallen by no less than 45 percent in real terms.

This brutal cut has been achieved by restrictions at the frontier rather than by reductions in spending at home. But that in turn has left massive unsatisfied demand. The result: a sharp continentwide surge in inflation. And, as prices accelerated, governments that in better times already had only limited ability to raise revenue found themselves falling further and further behind. Ballooning *domestic* debts have become a central preoccupation of every government in the hemisphere, with *domestic* interest payments taking a bigger and bigger share of national income. As fiscal deficits widened and foreign balances swung to surplus, less and less of savings has been available for investment, which has fallen from nearly a quarter of GNP to about a sixth. Dramatic programs to control inflation—the Austral and Cruzado Price Freeze plans—have been tried, have worked for a while beyond their authors' wildest dreams, and then, in at least one case, failed beyond their wildest dreams. Ironically, the country most capable of switching resources from consumption to exports—Brazil—is also the country that has most spectacularly lost control of domestic demand and watches as its normally strong exports are sucked inexorably back into the country.

As a result of these internal mechanisms, it has cost Latin America enormously in income and employment to generate the trade surplus required to service a constant or slowly growing debt. Already, half a decade of growth has been lost. And the social consequences—growing disorder and violence in many of the hemisphere's main centers—are evident. Latin America shows no particular inclination to revert to the old populist dictators, who after all caused a lot of the economic problems from which the continent now suffers. But some Latin American societies do show signs of becoming ungovernable.

If it costs so much in lost income and jobs just to maintain the existing debt, why not do something about the debt itself?

One alternative—the Baker Plan—was to ease the burden of the debt by seeking additional commercial bank lending conditioned on market-oriented policy reforms. Some reforms are in fact occurring, but it is now clear that no matter what their scope, creditors are and will remain reluctant to see their Latin American exposure increase. Although new money has been obtained in individual cases—Mexico and Chile— private lenders continue overall to take out of Latin America more than official lenders put in.

Another alternative—the Bradley Plan and countless variations—is debt relief. In light of the current Brazilian impasse, new calls are being made for adoption of this solution, even though other major debtors are going in the opposite direction and conducting new deals with creditors—Mexico, Chile, Argentina, and Venezuela. While there are clearly good reasons for the banks to make provision for, write down, or write off Latin American loans, they are unlikely to abandon claims for principal or interest without strong inducements or pressure.

Given high, if much reduced, exposure—Latin debt was still about 90 percent of the combined equity of U.S. money center and major regional banks at the end of 1985 and much higher for the former— there is no disposition on the part of the United States or other governments to pressure their banks to grant relief. And the borrower's interest in at least rolling over the existing debt gives the creditor banks bargaining power.

A third alternative—payments moratoriums—has a following in every country and of course keeps coming back as an option or bargaining tactic. Brazil has suspended payments pending a new restructuring. Peru has limited payments to 10 percent of foreign earnings. Both creditors and debtors are well aware that repudiation might be a political opportunity for some thrusting leader to make a breakthough, as it was for Perón a couple of generations ago. But after decades of import substitution, more autarky is unlikely to work very well. And the immediate costs can be high as countries try to get on without trade credit or insurance. It will be interesting to see how Peru develops. Its partial moratorium was accompanied by a consumption boom.

But now the party's over and the question is whether Peru can grow without regularizing its participation in the world economy. That question applies even more strongly to Brazil. It is of course possible—and would be very damaging for all concerned—for Brazil's stalemated government to fail to find a timely compromise with the creditors. Argentina—struggling with the erosion of the Austral Plan—could go into crisis at the same time. But even if both those events occur, it would be a country-specific failure, not the start of a systemic failure and one not likely to last forever. Such moratoriums are unlikely to become the dominant phenomenon, unless there is a new, deep worldwide recession. At that point everything could start snapping.

A final option is the return of Latin money that has fled abroad. There may be $100 billion or more of it. The usual fix on this is that if Latin countries adopt reliable market-oriented policies, some of the flight capital will go back. But recent experiments with tight money in Mexico and elsewhere suggest that some reflows can be induced if businesses find they have no alternative source of working capital. And governments are beginning to incentivize reflows by offering some variant of the debt-for-equity swaps many countries now offer to foreign nationals.

By themselves none of these options offers a systemic solution. That said, there are plainly trends under way that will eventually—in this decade—substantially downsize the debt problem.

One is the use of incentives to lessen the amount of debt outstanding. Many countries permit foreign nationals to buy debt in the open market (at a discount) and exchange it at par for equity. This is a form of subsidizing foreign investment. Clearly there are limits to it, given the small capital base for Latin American companies and concerns about foreign control and inflation. But there is a steady flow of transactions. Most of the open market purchases and sales of Latin American bank debt (perhaps $3 billion or $4 billion in a year) are related to debt-for-equity swaps.

The same concept can be applied to company debt—a much larger universe. Indeed, the new Mexican rescheduling agreement signed on March 20 does just that.

These mechanisms can also be used to attract flight capital back. Governments have an understandable concern about round-tripping, but the process is already starting. Mexico has just informed its creditors that such transactions will be authorized. The potential scope here is also very large.

A second trend is toward more write-offs. European banks are the most advanced in this regard and many have either fully provisioned or sold off their Latin portfolios. U.S. banks will have more scope for such actions in the next few years. As a simple matter of arithmetic, should present earning trends continue, exposure of U.S. money center and major regional banks could fall to half its present level as a percentage of capital by the end of the decade. Japanese banks are getting together to sell their Latin loans (at market discounts) to a sort of debt collection company.

The problem here is to develop a mechanism by which write-downs and write-offs can be translated into an actual reduction in debt outstanding—the interest of debtor—and into reflief from participating in the next forced rollover—the interest of the creditor. Work is now underway on exchanges of existing debt for lower face value debt bearing the same interest, but which would not be subject to refinancing at maturity. Debtors could write down the debt, but give up the quasi-automatic roll-over option. Creditors would take a hit on their balance sheet, but could get out of the next forced loan. The point would be to give more options to both creditors and debtors to find a mutually convenient way to recognize, loan by loan, country by country, that a lot of money has been invested at a loss and cannot be fully recovered.

The third trend is toward more participation in the world economy. Mexico, once the most autarkic of all, is discovering the export market; at last it is keeping the exchange rate realistic and has made the historic decision to join GATT. If you go to Monterrey now, you find that companies that never made a dollar in the United States are suddenly seeing their sales here take off. Last year, Mexico made more money exporting non-oil goods than petroleum. The collapsing price of oil contributed powerfully to the swing. But so did non-oil exports with growth of 34 percent. One finds similar trends in Chile and many of the smaller countries. Simultaneously, attitudes toward foreign investment are changing, and there is a continentwide move to privatize or at least subject state enterprise to better economic discipline.

Finally, the cost of the debt itself is coming down. Recent deals— Mexico, Chile, Venezuela—have saved almost a full percentage point on earlier spreads. No doubt Brazil, when it finally comes to terms, will also succeed in comprising its spread.

We swing from pessimism to optimism back to pessimism. Last year we were extolling Brazil and excoriating Mexico, with well-known figures predicting Mexican collapse into anarchy or revolution. Today it is Brazil we agonize about. Actually, behind the stop/go so characteristic of the hemisphere, the basic situation is changing only with soul-trying slowness.

Few Latin American countries have sufficient capacity to govern expenditures and to raise revenue to control internal demand. That defeated the Cruzado Plan, is defeating the Austral Plan, and could easily bring the currently improved performance of Mexico to grief. There is no evidence of any real institutional or political change in this crucial respect.

Without adequate demand control and still with few internationally tradable goods, it is painfully difficult and astonishingly costly to divert domestic resources to the creation of foreign trade surpluses. That leaves Latin America clawing away at the problem: borrowing a few dollars more where it can, trying to compress the cost of each new forced loan, using incentives to extinguish what debt it can, and just beginning to invent a capability to export goods other than commodities. The cumulative effect of each of these small changes will accelerate. But it will be the end of the decade before most of the countries can come back to the market—perhaps the most operational of definitions of the conclusion of the crisis.

Per capita income at the start of the 1990s will still be below that of 1980. And nothing we know about Latin America permits us to believe that it can find its way back to the sustained 6 percent growth of the last generation that made it one of the important engines of U.S. exports in the 1960s and 1970s.

3. Jesus Silva-Herzog
A Latin American Perspective

Latin America is probably going through the most severe economic and social crisis in more than fifty years. This is a well-known fact. After enjoying a period a relatively fast growth, Latin America began to see a profound change in its economic environment in the early 1980s.

Today's per capita income is 10 percent lower than in 1980. A number of social indicators are showing a serious deterioration that will affect potential growth. Investment has diminished; unemployment is on the rise, exports are sluggish, and the region has been a net exporter of capital since 1983.

On the other hand, around 94 percent of the population of the region are now living under democratic regimes.

The problem is not only the present situation, but the immediate prospects, which do not look very promising. It is possible that the 1980s will be remembered as a lost decade for the Latin American region as a whole. The basic reasons are complex and vary from country to country, even though there are some common elements. However, the explanation cannot rely on negative external factors or erroneous domestic policies alone. The basic causes of the process include both external and domestic factors.

The essential responsibility, however, lies on the domestic front. We, the Latin Americans, are the ones mainly responsible for what happened in Latin America. But we must recognize that there were a number of important unfavorable external factors that contributed significantly to the origin and permanence of the crisis.

The sudden and abrupt upward change in the level of interest rates in 1981, from low or negative real levels in the previous years, the deterioration of the terms of trade, and the interruption of financial flows to the region after the summer of 1982 were very destabilizing elements in the Latin American picture. On the other hand, inward-oriented trade policies, heavy foreign borrowing, overvaluation of the currencies, huge government deficits, and a more generalized inflationary atmosphere were domestic factors that have also contributed to the crisis.

Given that it will be difficult to change the negative transfer of resources in the short run, because of the very high level of external indebtedness, and that the prices of the main export commodities look unfavorable over the next few years, we might conclude that there are difficult times ahead for Latin America. And there is a real menace to the well-being of the majority of the population and to the democratic process that has been so welcome in different countries. Austerity and democracy cannot live together for too long.

Latin America has faced the crisis in a serious and responsible manner. Basic economic attitudes that had been sustained for a long period of time are changing, and a closer perception of the necessary changes is more evident all over the region. Recent efforts to bring down inflation through the so-called heterodox approach are good examples.

In the basic challenge that lies ahead there is one essential element: resumption of economic growth. Growth needs to be stimulated as the only way to come out of the crisis. And growth will not come by itself. It will need the proper doses of domestic economic policies, with a favorable external environment.

The essential responsibility for growth lies with the Latin Americans. No one will do for us what we do not do for ourselves. One thing must be stressed: the emphasis on growth cannot be interpreted as forgetting about control of inflation. Avoiding rapid rates of inflation is a precondition for sustained economic growth.

Given the economic constraints that we are facing and that we will face in the coming years, the resumption of growth, with greater importance attached to equity considerations, will require profound changes in the economic policy of Latin America. Many of the traditional ways things have been done in the region will have to be altered— from the essential orientation of trade policies to the basic attitude toward the mobilization of internal savings and the role of the state.

In the next few years it is reasonable to expect that the region will not have net external financing comparable to the levels of the past decade. This necessarily implies that greater reliance on domestic savings will be absolutely necessary. We will have to learn, as we have on several past occasions, to live more closely linked with our own means and to do more with less.

On the other hand, an expansion of the export capacity will be the only way to earn the necessary foreign exchange to pay for imports and the service on the debt. If exports have always been a priority, at least in the official statements, today they have reached an indispensable precondition level for the coming years.

In the near future the options open to the Latin American countries will depend, perhaps to a greater degree than in the past, on a number of domestic determinants. This is not to say that we do not require an ample effort of international economic cooperation but only that we will depend more on our decisions and actions.

The resumption of economic growth in Latin America will require, in my opinion, four basic elements: (1) in the trade field, a more clearly export-oriented approach; (2) in the savings field, a mobilizaiton of a higher level of domestic savings and its improved allocation; (3) in relation to the external debt problem, a more clear and definite solution; and (4) a sustained effort to control inflation.

After some brief comments on each element, the possible role of the United States in this region will be self-evident.

Trade

The Latin American region has been, in general, inward oriented during the last decades. The import substitution model followed after the Second World War, which was useful for a certain period of time, has produced some important domestic distortions that need to be corrected.

Protectionism was translated in many cases into a barrier to improved efficiency and productivity, resulting in a significant loss of international competitiveness. As the Economic Commission for Latin America has recently recognized, protectionism was "excessive, too general, and too prolonged."

The only way Latin America will obtain the foreign exchange needed to pay for imports and to service its external debt is through an expansion of exports, both of raw materials and of manufactured products. This implies a needed change in the mentality of government, business, and labor. It will not be easy, nor will it be obtained in the short run. But it is absolutely necessary. We already see some encouraging signs, especially in Brazil and Mexico. Two things are essential to this objective. One, a lowering of the highly protectionist trade policies the majority of the Latin American countries have followed. And two, the maintenance of adequate exchange rate policies, avoiding a common phenomenon of overvaluation, which so deters the expansion of exports.

There is enormous room for an expanded export of manufactured products from Latin America. Latin American exports of manufactured products are less than one percent of total consumption in the industrial countries. A very small increase in market share in the United States or in other industrial countries, at the expense of East Asian or western European reductions, could mean a tremendous difference for the region as a whole.

However, we must recognize that we face a protectionist mood in the industrial countries and in the United States. As Sebastian Edwards' paper mentions, to the extent that these nontariff barriers increase, or are maintained at the current level, it will become very difficult, if not plainly impossible, for the Latin American countries to increase their exports at the rate required to solve their current debt crisis.

While the main responsibility for increasing exports rests within the Latin American countries, their efforts, no matter how serious, can be easily frustrated by the protectionist policies of the industrialized world.

The reciprocal trade between the Latin American countries has diminished during the years of the crisis. We now have a special opportunity to foster in a more aggressive way the efforts for economic integration. It could be a way that better utilizes existing capacity and scarce foreign exchange resources.

Savings

The reduction in foreign borrowing necessarily implies the need to rely more on domestic resources. Thus we need to foster domestic savings, including savings in the public sector, where they have been negative. A positive real interest rate, a tax policy directed at stimulating savings, a decisive effort to reduce public sector deficits, the possible establishment of mechanisms to attract the repatriation of capital invested abroad, and new flows of foreign investments are essential elements for the fulfillment of this objective.

In this connection, a healthy trend has been the selling back to the private sector of a number of government companies in different countries. The process has begun; now it needs further acceleration.

Debt

The difficult and very tiresome yearly restructuring exercises and the obtaining of fresh money on a forced lending basis has given the Latin American debtors time and breathing space, but the debt problem is not solved. More debt to solve the debt problem is not the solution. The issue is becoming more and more politicized. In industrial countries the problem is still of a financial nature. In the debtor countries it is a highly political issue. Latin America and its creditors are beginning to feel so-called debt fatigue.

The problem needs to be recognized as one that impedes the resumption of growth. A new, more farsighted attitude needs to be adopted, and the closer interrelationship between trade and debt should be recognized.

Different approaches, so far considered unorthodox, will increasingly take the place of the more business-as-usual arrangements. In this connection, the adjustment of payments to a debtor country's real capacity to pay will also be increasingly observed. The concept of debt relief, a reduction of the debt burden, is growing in acceptance in different circles.

Any economic projection exercise for the region as a whole makes impossible the maintenance of the present debt burden and an adequate rate of economic growth in the coming years. On the other hand, the basic situation of the three main Latin debtors—Argentina, Brazil, and Mexico—may become more similar in 1987 than in any of the previous years since the debt crisis began.

It is not an exaggeration to say that Latin America has been neglected by the United States. The region has not been given proper attention. We do not represent a great risk. Nor do we represent a great economic or security advantage.

In the recent past, Washington's interest in Latin America has been overshadowed by its obsession with Central America. However, what the United States will or will not do will affect Latin America in a very direct manner. One important U.S. contribution would be to give greater attention to the repercussions of its own national economic decisions.

Finally, the United States has a long tradition of pragmatism, while Latin America has been under the influence of ideological considerations for many years. But now it seems the roles have changed: we are pragmatic, and the United States is now religious.

The external presence has been too dominant in recent years, and we require more indigenous solutions of our own. They are essential for successful implementation and for the society in general. Latin America has an enormous potential for economic and social growth. Important changes are taking place within democratic regimes that are in essence stimulating the possibility of change. They require a better climate in the international world, and I think it can be provided.

Summary of Discussion

The discussion centered around the opportunities and climate for direct investment in Latin America and the need for a global solution to the problems of the region.

Peter Peterson was struck by the apparent contradiction between the need for the Latin American debtors to increase manufacturing exports and the fact that a correction in the U.S. trade balance implies that the U.S. role as the market for manufacturing imports will have to change. The United States will have to become a manufactured goods exporter to pay the interest on the debt and eventually the principal; this suggests a roughly $200 billion swing in the U.S. manufactured goods trade balance.

Thomas Enders pointed out that the current Latin American trade surplus with the United States is probably sufficient to sustain the debt service with growth, but agreed that in the face of a large swing in Latin America's trade balance with the United States, the debts would be written off.

Sebastian Edwards agreed that there is no way for the debtor countries to service their debt and run trade deficits with the United States. He noted that the aggregate U.S. share in Latin American manufacturing imports has been about the same since 1970. The composition has shifted significantly, he noted, especially from manufactured goods to food. Most strikingly, total imports of the region fell by about 50 percent in real terms. For Latin American imports from the United States to increase, exports will have to increase. The adjustment to the debt problems has come more than entirely in imports, since declining terms of trade have caused the value of exports to decline since 1982.

Jesus Silva-Herzog agreed that everyone wants to export, but argued that the United States could increase manufacturing imports from Latin America and correct its own trade imbalances by focusing on the regions of the world where its trade deficit is more important and where the primary problem lies. Latin American problems are not independent of other problems, agreed Saburo Okita. The solution to the need of both the United States and Latin America to increase exports will indeed require increased imports in other parts of the world, such as Japan, Taiwan, and other emerging countries.

Attention shifted to the possibilities for direct investment and their role in a resolution of the problems of the region. Philip Caldwell argued that, Silva-Herzog to the contrary, he has not seen any fundamental change in policy toward direct investment in Latin America. The key word is profit, and he has not seen any encouragement there. He expressed doubt about the idea of investing during the downslide, as he has tried that four or five times without getting close to any upswing; more and more of his colleagues say they are giving up unless and until opportunities for profit improve.

George Vojta concurred and wondered how far the political endorsement of equity investment had come. He suggested that the policy orientation has moved but that the essential doctrines are fundamentally intact.

The Andean Pact discourages investment, reported Maurice Greenberg, who claimed that bilateral treaties are needed to encourage investment. Enders suggested that this type of treaty will be negotiable and proposed that, while the climate will be spotty for a while, the situation will become more reliable. He pointed out that many automakers are investing in Mexico, where the number of controlled domestic prices has been reduced substantially. Automobile investments—primarily for export—were mandated by decree for those who wished to continue a domestic presence in Mexico. Such investments have been the source of more recent profit problems for investors.

Rudiger Dornbusch disagreed with Caldwell's characterization of the lack of political change in the region. He pointed out that the area is in a major depression, worse than the depression of the 1930s. The upswings were there quite recently, he argued, noting that the main source of profits for Ford in 1981 was Argentinean income, as overvaluation made repatriation very profitable. The profit aberrations of the early 1980s have been largely dissipated by later economic and political upheavals which have caused the more current unsatisfactory investment environment.

There has been a move to a more liberal trade regime, argued Silva-Herzog. In Mexico in 1982, for example, all manufactured imports required permits, but by 1985 such quantitative restrictions were beginning to decrease, and now only a third of imports are under such restrictions. Thus, while official prices have been established as compensation, the picture has completely changed. Furthermore, Mexico has joined GATT. A basic change is taking place in the orientation of production and marketing outward, after four decades of looking inward. The situation is similar in other countries, but it may be too early after the basic decisions for Caldwell to see the change.

On the foreign investment question, Silva-Herzog conceded that recently the situation has not been very favorable. There are indications, however, that some investment is coming in to take advantage of the approaching upswing. There are indications that the regulations on direct investment are being applied in a more flexible manner than before. There are serious misunderstandings in industrialized countries about the degree to which Mexico, for example, still restricts foreign investment. In the highly publicized IBM case, the problem was that IBM's terms could not be better than those given to Hewlett-Packard and Apple. After all, IBM has been in Mexico for forty years. The rules on foreign investment are clear and decreasingly discretionary. Ten years ago there was the same legislation and large foreign inflows, so the problem is not the legislation.

Several people commented on capital flight and its possible repatriation. The foreign money will come in when capital flight money is repatriated, suggested Robert Ingersoll.

Silva-Herzog explained that the most important cause of capital flight was speculation against overvalued currencies in 1981. People expected a devaluation and they were right. Eventually general economic prospects determine capital flight. In Mexico in 1984 and 1985, for example, a search for safety provoked capital flight. There can be other reasons for capital flight, or reflow. In the second half of 1986 a credit squeeze forced domestic businesses to resort to repatriation as a source of working capital. Contributing factors were a high real interest rate and an exchange rate that was undervalued by 20 percent to 25 percent.

Special incentives for repatriation are politically difficult to sustain, Silva-Herzog pointed out. For this reason, subsidized debt-equity swaps do not have a bright future, he believes. In response to a suggestion by Bruce Atwater that the amount of the capital flight was roughly proportional to the external debt, Silva-Herzog argued that some of the higher estimates of the amount of capital flight are highly exaggerated. He brought the discussion around to broader issues by arguing that confidence is the key to capital reflow and that no simple policy of high real interest rates and exchange rate undervaluation will bring the capital back; the answer is a longer-term solution to the debt problem itself.

Thomas Johnson and Rudiger Dornbusch agreed with this analysis from two different points of view. Johnson contended that a policy of focusing on getting foreign or repatriated capital will be self-defeating if it only treats the symptoms. Dornbusch alluded to recent developments in the economic literature on the option value of time which suggest that in a highly uncertain environment it will always pay for capital that has flown to wait until the incentives for repatriation are entirely frontloaded so as to compensate for the risk of getting stuck. This type of program is self-defeating, as the level of profits required is impossible to sustain politically, especially since the economies have shrunk so much that there is not that much incentive available.

Focus then shifted to the broad outlines of a resolution to the debt crisis. John Block argued that there is a double standard in the treatment of the large money-center banks and banks in rural America, where no one is bailing out anybody. The cloud of the interest burden hangs over the debtor economies, discouraging investment because the future is so uncertain. It is time, he believes, that people accept that the money just is not coming back with interest.

Gerald Corrigan made several summary points. First, there is no magic plan that will solve all the problems. Second, sovereign debt is more difficult to deal with than private debt, partly because every decision requires a consensus of hundreds of partners, private, governmental, and multinational, not to mention the lawyers. Third, the Latin American countries have, all things considered, done a good job of policy adjustment. The nature and direction of change is correct.

Corrigan recommended taking the long view in the search for a solution. Growth is key. We are in the fifth year of worldwide growth, and it may be difficult to sustain this growth for five more years, but we have to do it. This requires, among other things, keeping inflation under control. A second key is a flow of savings into these developing countries, as development always requires external financing. Whatever form the solution takes, it will involve positive net capital flows. Third, the creditworthiness of countries cannot be undercut or everyone is worse off. Finally new techniques and instruments, such as the debt-equity swap, can be useful, but not as a generalized approach.

Enders agreed about the need for growth. He added a note of caution, however, adding that it used to be said that if the price of oil and interest rates would fall and U.S. growth sustain itself, the debt problem would go away. These conditions prevailed, yet the problem is still with us. Policy reform received his emphasis as well. He suggested that even more emphasis is needed on the fundamentals within the debtor countries. These countries still cannot tax income, and without taxes these shocks are difficult to solve. In this area there is less room for optimism than elsewhere. More generally, the issue of continuity in policy reform remains; investors wonder how long policy changes will last. In summary, Enders believes that a variety of individual instruments and partial solutions will be needed. The creditors and debtors must realize that much money has been invested nonprofitably.

Silva-Herzog echoed the need for consistency in policy and proposed that the approach be long term. Closer links between debt and trade are needed but not clearly accepted.

2   U.S. and Foreign Competition in the Developing Countries of the Asian Pacific Rim

1. Robert E. Baldwin
2. Robert S. Ingersoll
3. Woo-choong Kim

1. Robert E. Baldwin

2.1 Introduction

The ability of the major developing countries of the Asian Pacific rim (APR)—Hong Kong, the Republic of Korea (henceforth referred to as Korea), the Republic of China (henceforth referred to as Taiwan), the Philippines, Malaysia, Singapore, Thailand, Indonesia, and the Peoples's Republic of China (henceforth referred to as China)—to compete in the markets of the United States is well known and frequently cited by many domestic industries as a matter for national concern. Much less is known about the competitive performance and potential of American industries in the markets of the major developing countries of the APR, and interest in this matter is only beginning to develop;[1] it is the focus of this paper.

Section 2.2 provides an economic overview of the APR by comparing the main economic characteristics of the countries in the region and those of the region as a whole with other major groupings of countries. Since the prospects for exporting goods and services to the countries of the region depend on the policies these countries follow in such matters as promoting economic growth and the opening of domestic markets, section 2.3 briefly describes the economic policies pursued by each APR country in the recent past. This section also analyzes the success of major trading partners in penetrating the market for imports

79

in each country and the success of each country in exporting to major foreign markets. Finally, the trade and development policies likely to be followed in the future in each country are briefly discussed.

Section 2.4 analyzes the competitive performance of the United States and its major competitors in the markets for imports in three groups of APR countries, namely, the advanced developing countries (ADCs) of the region—Hong Kong, Korea, Taiwan, and Singapore; the resource-rich countries (RRCs) of the region—the Philippines, Malaysia, Thailand, and Indonesia; and China. It also examines changes since the early 1960s in the shares of the import markets in these APR country groups captured by the United States, Canada, Japan, the European Community, Australia and New Zealand, and other countries within the region, together with changes in the commodity composition of exports to the APR groups from these countries and country-groups. A technique for revealing the sources of a country's comparative advantage is used to determine the relative factor-price advantages and disadvantages the United States has in its trade with the countries of the region.

Section 2.5 briefly looks at the performance of the three APR country-groups in exporting to the United States and other major foreign markets and examines changes since the early 1960s in the share of their exports absorbed by the United States and other countries and shifts in the commodity composition of their exports.

Because trade and investment are closely linked, it is necessary to take foreign investment into account in evaluating U.S. competitive prospects in the region. Section 2.6 examines the volume and country distribution of direct foreign investment in the region by the United States and its main competitor in the area, Japan. Changes in the relative importance of U.S. direct investment in different sectors in the APR countries are also studied. The final section summarizes the main conclusions of the paper.

2.2 An Overview of Economic Characteristics and Performance

2.2.1 The Developing Countries of APR Compared to Other Regions

The tremendous market potential in the developing countries of the Asian Pacific rim lies simply in their being not only the most populous but the fastest-growing region of the world. The population of the nine countries totals 1.33 billion, whereas that of the next most populous region, South Asia, amounts to 0.87 billion. Gross national product (GNP) per capital in the nine countries grew at a remarkable average rate of 5.75 percent between 1965 and 1984. In contrast, GNP per capital in the industrial market-economy countries increased at an average rate of only 2.5 percent during this period and at average rates of 1.9 percent in both South Asia and the countries of South America (*World Development Report 1986,* annex table 1).

Table 2.1 compares the APR countries with a selected group of countries outside of the area in terms of basic economic characteristics and performance indicators. Except for the Philippines, per capita income grew much more rapidly in the developing countries of the Asian Pacific rim than in mature developed countries such as the United States and West Germany and, in most cases, even Japan, the newest and most dynamic developed country. Yet, although per capita income levels in the APR countries rank among the highest for all developing nations, there is still a wide per capita income gap between the advanced industrial market economies and these countries. West Germany's 1984 per capita income, for example, is more than five times as large as South Korea's and almost seventeen times as large as the Philippines' per capita income in that year.

The magnitude of the APR's output and imports is also small when compared to that of the developed countries. The total of all nine countries' gross domestic product in 1984 was $656 billion, only slightly more than one-half of Japan's and not much greater than West Germany's GDP. The difference in imports is less striking due to the high degree of dependence on trade of most countries in the region. Their total 1984 imports of $181 billion are roughly equal to those of Japan and of West Germany in that year. Thus, the major market opportunities for the United States are still in other developed countries; the major developing countries of Southeast Asia and East Asia represent an important potential market rather than a major current one.

Compared with other developing regions, however, the developing countries of the Asian Pacific rim already rank as the largest market. The 1984 $656 billion GDP level of the region compares with GDP levels of $623 billion for all of South America, Central America, and the Caribbean and of $406 billion for South Asia, for example. Moreover, the 1984 $181 billion import level of the region compares with only $64 billion for South America, Central America, and the Caribbean and $25 billion for South Asia. This market-size advantage is likely to widen during the rest of the century, given the currently higher growth rates in the Pacific rim countries.

Table 2.2 indicates the growth and trade experience of APR and selected other countries before and after the first oil crisis. The general slowdown in growth in both the developing and developed countries after the first oil shock is evident from the table. However, the relative decline in growth rates has been less in the APR countries than in such developed countries as the United States, Japan, and Germany. In the

Table 2.1   Basic Economic Indicators

	Area	Population		Income			Goods Trade			
	(thousands Km²)	Size (million)	Growth Rate 1973–84 (%)	GDP 1984 (billions of $)	GNP per Capita Growth 1965–84 (average annual % rate)	GNP per Capita 1984 ($)	Exports 1984 (billion $)	Imports 1984 (billion $)	Exports Share in GDP, 1984 (%)	Imports Share in GDP, 1984 (%)
Singapore	1	3	1.3	18	7.8	7,260	24	29	133	161
Hong Kong	1	5	2.4	31	6.2	6,330	28	29	90	94
Taiwan	35	19	1.6	57	7.0	3,050	30	26	56	45
South Korea	98	40	1.5	83	6.6	2,110	29	31	35	37
Malaysia	330	15	2.4	29	4.5	1,980	16	14	55	48
Thailand	514	50	2.2	42	4.2	860	7	11	17	26
Philippines	300	53	2.7	33	2.6	660	5	6	15	18
Indonesia	1,919	159	2.3	81	4.9	540	22	14	27	17
China	9,561	1,029	1.4	281	4.5	310	25	26	9	9
United States	9,363	237	1.0	3,635	1.7	15,390	216	338	6	9
Japan	372	120	1.0	1,255	4.7	10,360	170	134	14	11
West Germany	249	61	0	613	2.7	11,130	171	153	28	25
Australia	7,687	16	1.3	182	1.7	11,740	23	23	13	13
India	3,288	749	2.3	162	1.6	260	9	15	6	9

Source: World Development Report, 1986.

Table 2.2 **Savings and Investment Rates**

	Gross Domestic Investment as Share of GDP (%)		Gross Domestic Savings as Share of GDP (%)		Resource Gap (%)	
	1960	1984	1960	1984	1960	1984
Singapore	11	47	3	43	−8	−4
Hong Kong	19	24	1	29	−18	5
Taiwan	20	22	13	33	−7	12
South Korea	11	29	1	30	−10	1
Malaysia	14	31	27	32	13	1
Thailand	16	23	17	21	1	−2
Philippines	16	18	16	18	0	0
Indonesia	8	21	8	20	0	−1
China	25[a]	30	25[a]	30	0	0
United States	18	19	19	16	1	−3
Japan	34	28	34	31	0	3
West Germany	27	21	29	23	2	2
Australia	29	21	25	19	−4	−2
India	17	24	14	22	−3	−2

Sources: *World Development Report*, 1979 and 1986; Asian Development Bank, *Key Indicators of Developing Country Member Countries of ADB*, 1984, and *ADB Annual Report, 1985*.
[a]1965.

United States, the percentage decline in the average annual growth rate of GDP between 1965–73 and 1973–84 was 28 percent; in Japan, 56 percent; and in Germany, 57 percent. The average annual GDP growth rate actually increased in Hong Kong and Malaysia (also India) and declined by only 18 percent on the average in the other seven developing countries in the Asian Pacific rim.

2.2.2 Diversity among the APR Countries

As shown in table 2.1, there are significant economic differences among the developing countries of the Asian Pacific rim. It is usual to divide the countries into three groups, the first comprising South Korea, Taiwan, Hong Kong, and Singapore; the second consisting of the Philippines, Malaysia, Thailand, and Indonesia; and the third being China. The first group is usually designated the newly industrializing countries (NICs) of Asia, a term indicating their relatively early emphasis on export-oriented industrialization. While the words *newly industrializing* were appropriate in the 1960s and early 1970s when these countries first adopted policies aimed at significantly increasing the exports of manufactures, it seems more appropriate to use Hong and Krause's

(1981) term, "advanced developing countries" (ADCs), especially since other countries of the region later also adopted policies aimed at export-oriented industrialization. Per capita income in all of the ADCs is higher than in the countries of the other two groups, though if per capita income alone is the basis of the classification, it seems reasonable to include Malaysia in the first group. There is also a significant gap between income levels in Singapore and Hong Kong and in Taiwan and South Korea.

The second group of four nations is usually described as the four resource-rich countries (RRCs) that are ASEAN members to indicate the much greater share of primary products in their exports compared to the ADCs (see table 2.3).[2] The greater share of production devoted to agriculture is an indication of their greater land resources as well as their lower per capita income levels. Except for Malaysia, the RRCs are less open than the ADCs of Asia in terms of trade's share of GDP; these countries have pursued import-substitution policies more vigorously than the ADCs. Another difference is the higher natural rate of population growth in the RRCs than in the ADCs.[3]

China is unique in several respects. It is by far the most populous country in the world, and it ranks third in area. Although it has become much more outward-looking in recent years, it remains, as the export and import shares presented in table 2.1 indicate, a very closed econ-

Table 2.3   **External Public and Private Debt**

| | Total Long-Term Debt Disbursed and Outstanding (millions of $) | | Total Long-Term Debt Service as Percentage of Exports of Goods and Services | |
	1970	1984	1970	1984
Singapore	152[a]	1,911[a]	.6	.8[d]
Hong Kong	2[a]	270[a]	0[a]	0[a]
Taiwan	1,195[b]	6,147[c]	—	4.3[c]
South Korea	1,972	29,990	20.3	15.8
Malaysia	390[a]	11,846[a]	3.6[a]	5.1[d]
Thailand	726	10,936	14.0	21.5
Philippines	1,494	14,135	7.5[e]	17.9
Indonesia	2,904	26,683	13.8	19.0

Sources: *World Development Report*, 1984 and 1986; Asian Development Bank, *Key Indicators of Developing Member Countries of ADB*, April 1984.

[a]Long-term public and publicly guaranteed debt.

[b]External public debt outstanding, 1971.

[c]External public debt outstanding, 1981.

[d]Long-term public and publicly guaranteed debt, 1982.

[e]External public debt outstanding.

omy compared to other countries in the region, although not in comparison to such countries as India and the United States. While its GDP growth rate since 1965 compares favorably with the RRCs, China's low per capita income level makes the country more similar to the countries of South Asia than to those of the Asian Pacific rim.

2.2.3   Savings-Investment, Foreign Debt, and Trade Adjustment

A necessary, though not sufficient, requirement for a country to raise its growth rate is to increase its investment and savings rates significantly. As table 2.4 shows, such an increase has occurred in the ADCs, the RRCs, and China. In five of the nine countries, investment as a share of GDP rose by more than ten percentage points between 1960 and 1984, and in three others the increase was at least five percentage points. The investment ratio in Singapore in 1984 was an incredible 47 percent, and it was 30 percent or more in Taiwan, Malaysia, and China. The increase in domestic savings has been even more impressive, especially in Singapore, Hong Kong, Taiwan, South Korea, and Indonesia. Gross domestic savings is now about 30 percent or more in six of the nine countries. The only developed countries that can match these savings rates are Japan (31 percent) and Norway (35 percent).

An excess of domestic investment over domestic savings indicates that savings by foreigners are financing part of a country's investment activities. Such was the case for the ADCs in the initial phases of their takeoff to high rates of growth, as the figures in table 2.4 on the resource gap indicate. The large positive number for Hong Kong in 1984 indicates that domestic savers were investing some of their savings abroad, probably because of their uncertainty about the political future of the city-state.

A more direct indication of the extent to which a country has relied on external sources of finance is the magnitude of its external debt and the ratio of the external debt to the country's GNP. The debt service share of exports of goods and services is a rough indicator of the degree of difficulty the country has in meeting its external obligations. Table 2.5 presents information on these various debt indicators for the APR countries, except for China, on which debt data are unavailable. As with developing countries generally, the data show a very rapid increase in external borrowing for APR countries over the last fifteen years. This ability to draw upon external sources, especially private capital markets, has been an important factor in enabling growth to continue at high rates. It has, however, also led to serious debt-servicing problems for some nations that borrowed heavily and then around 1980 were suddenly faced with both much higher real interest rates and falling prices for their export products. Four APR countries—South Korea, Thailand, the Philippines, and Indonesia—are on most lists of

Table 2.4 Growth Rates of GDP and Foreign Trade

	GDP (%)		Exports (%)		Imports (%)		Terms of Trade (1980 = 100)	
	1965–73	1973–84	1965–73	1973–84	1965–73	1973–84	1982	1984
Singapore	13.0	8.2	11.0	7.1	9.8	7.1	100	101
Hong Kong	7.9	9.1	11.7	12.9	10.6	9.3	110	109
Taiwan	7.9	9.3[a]	23.7[b]	16.7[c]	17.9[b]	13.5[a]	—	—
South Korea	10.0	7.2	31.7	15.1	22.4	9.7	100	100
Malaysia	6.7	7.3	8.0	7.5	4.4	8.9	85	93
Thailand	7.8	6.8	6.9	10.4	4.4	5.9	77	81
Philippines	5.4	4.8	4.2	5.6	3.0	2.3	89	101
Indonesia	8.1	6.8	11.1	1.4	14.0	10.5	105	101
China	7.8	6.6	—	10.1	—	10.2	106	101
United States	3.2	2.3	6.8	2.3	9.4	3.8	106	112
Japan	9.8	4.3	14.7	7.5	14.9	1.6	103	109
West Germany	4.6	2.0	10.7	4.5	11.3	3.9	97	96
Australia	5.6	2.4	9.3	3.0	6.8	3.4	98	95
India	3.9	4.1	2.4	3.3	−5.7	5.4	104	107

Sources: World Development Report, 1979 and 1986; Asian Development Bank, Key Indicators of Developing Member Countries of ADB, 1984.

[a]1973–83.
[b]1960–70.
[c]1970–77.

Table 2.5   Commodity Structure of Production and Trade (percentage shares)

	Production, 1984			Exports, 1983		Imports	
	Agriculture	Industry	Services	Primary Goods	Manufactures	Primary Goods	Manufactures
Singapore	1	39	60	44	56	44	56
Hong Kong	1	22	78	8	92	25	75
Taiwan	—	—	—	6[a]	94[a]	—	—
South Korea	14	40	47	9	91	49	51
Malaysia	21	35	44	78	22	28	72
Thailand	20	28	52	68	32	36	64
Philippines	25	34	41	49	51	40	60
Indonesia	26	40	34	92	8	38	62
China	36	44	23	43	57	34	66
United States	4	43	54	30	70	37	63
Japan	3	41	56	3	97	77	23
West Germany	2	46	52	13	87	42	58
Australia	—	—	—	77	23	20	80
India	35	27	38	47	53	50	50

Source: World Development Report, 1986.
[a]1982.

countries faced with significant debt-servicing problems; debt-servicing charges in 1984 claimed more than 15 percent of the foreign exchange they earned from exporting goods and services. The drain of debt servicing on the foreign exchange earnings of Singapore and Hong Kong is negligible and only about 5 percent for Taiwan and Malaysia.

To cope with increased debt-servicing charges, a country must generate additional foreign exchange by improving its balance of trade. Table 2.6 shows that the trade balance of the four main indebted countries—South Korea, Thailand, the Philippines, and Indonesia—improved between 1983 and 1985. Korea, whose balance of trade has improved steadily since 1981, achieved the most desirable type of trade adjustment between these years—an expansion of imports and exports. Thailand's improved trade balance between 1983 and 1985 came about through an expansion of exports and contraction of imports, whereas the recent trade adjustment in the Philippines and Indonesia occurred by reducing both exports and imports.

Table 2.6   **Merchandise Trade of Four Indebted Countries in the Asian Pacific Rim, 1981–85 (billions of dollars, exports [f.o.b.], imports [c.i.f.])**

	Korea	Philippines	Thailand	Indonesia
1980				
Exports	21.1	5.7	7.0	22.3
Imports	26.1	8.5	9.9	13.3
Balance	4.9	−2.8	−2.9	9.0
1982				
Exports	21.9	5.0	7.0	22.3
Imports	24.3	8.3	8.6	16.9
Balance	−2.4	−3.3	−1.6	5.4
1983				
Exports	24.5	4.9	6.4	21.1
Imports	26.2	8.0	10.3	16.3
Balance	−1.7	−3.1	−3.9	4.8
1984				
Exports	29.2	5.3	7.4	21.9
Imports	30.6	6.4	10.4	13.9
Balance	−1.4	−1.1	−3.0	8.0
1985				
Exports	30.3	4.6	7.1	19.7
Imports	31.1	5.5	9.2	10.2
Balance	−.8	−.9	−2.1	9.5

Sources: International Trade, 1984–85, table A-4; and *International Trade, 1985–86*, table A-14, both from General Agreement on Tariffs and Trade (GATT).

2.3 Development Policy and Trade Performance

As with most developing countries in the world, the major economic goal of those in the Asian Pacific rim over the last forty years has been to increase the rate of economic development. Their success in achieving this goal and the extent to which their development policies involve a willingness to open their own markets to the products of other countries largely determine the trading opportunities of the United States and others in the region. This section briefly describes the nature of the development strategies pursued by the individual APR countries and analyzes the shifts that have taken place in the commodity composition and geographical distribution of their exports and imports. It also speculates as to each country's likely future trade and development policies.

2.3.1 The Advanced Developing Countries

Hong Kong

Trade and development policy. The British colony of Hong Kong is unique among developing economies in that it has achieved its remarkable post–World War II growth under a policy of "positive nonintervention."[4] Imports and exports of both goods and capital were completely free from government taxes, subsidies, or other controls, and no effort was made to direct investment into particular sectors. The standard tax rate on earnings and profit was also the lowest of any industrial state, being set at the level of 12.5 percent from 1951–66.

Until the early 1950s, Hong Kong's prosperity was based on reexporting products from South China throughout the world and serving as an entry port for foreign products destined for the mainland. Two external events in the 1950s disrupted this entrepôt role. The first was the change of government as the Communists took control of the mainland. The inward-looking policies of the Communist government resulted in a significant diminution in China's trade with Hong Kong. In addition, dissatisfaction with the new form of government led to massive immigration from China, which increased Hong Kong's population by almost 50 percent in a few years. The second event that reduced Hong Kong's role as a trade facilitator was the United Nations embargo imposed on China because of its role in the Korean War.

Fortunately, the immigrants included entrepreneurs who had both industrial experience, especially in textiles, and the capital necessary to establish manufacturing activities. Utilizing the abundant supply of low-wage workers who also became available through immigration, these individuals spearheaded the shift in Hong Kong's economic structure from that of entrepôt to exporter of labor-intensive manufactured products. The industrialization effort was also helped by the existence of an excellent infrastructure of port, banking, insurance, and shipping facilities and a long history of commercial ties with overseas traders. Manufacturing employment increased from 82,000 in 1950 to 216,000 in 1960, while the share of reexports in total exports declined from 88 percent to 27 percent in that decade.

Trade performance. As can be seen from table 2.7, which indicates the colony's pattern of exports and imports in 1960, 1978, and 1983, Hong Kong has gradually diversified its manufacturing activities and, in particular, reduced its dependence on textiles and clothing. Exports in the machinery and transport equipment category have become significant. This diversification has been due in part to the efforts of the government, which, beginning in the late 1970s, backed away somewhat from its hands-off policy and began to arrange industrial support facilities and technical services to facilitate the shift toward more capital-intensive, high-skill manufacturing sectors.

A more detailed breakdown of the composition of Hong Kong's trade with its major trading partners is presented in table 2.8. Between 1963 and 1980, both the United States and Japan moderately increased their share of the combined exports to Hong Kong by the United States, Canada, Japan, Australia and New Zealand, the European Community, other ADCs, the RRCs in the region, and China. The U.S. share in-

Table 2.7   **Structure of Hong Kong's Merchandise Trade, 1960, 1978, and 1983 (percentage distribution)**

			Exports		
	Fuels, Minerals, and Metals	Other Primary Commodities	Textiles and Clothing	Machinery and Transport Equipment	Other Manufactures
1960	5	15	45	4	31
1978	1	2	46	15	36
1983	2	6	33	22	36
			Imports		
	Food	Fuel	Other Primary Commodities	Machinery and Transport Equipment	Other Manufactures
1960	27	3	16	10	44
1978	15	5	7	19	54
1983	12	7	6	21	54

Sources: World Development Report, 1981 and 1986.

Table 2.8   Distribution of Singapore's Imports from and Exports to Selected Countries or Regions, 1963, 1970, 1980, and 1984 (in percentages)

	1963		1970		1980		1984	
	Imports	Exports	Imports	Exports	Imports	Exports	Imports	Exports
U.S.	16.5	35.0	19.4	50.3	18.3	40.7	12.1	50.1
Canada	1.9	3.0	1.0	3.7	1.0	3.2	0.6	3.6
Japan	29.3	4.3	34.2	4.7	33.8	4.2	28.0	4.2
Australia and New Zealand	0.0	4.9	3.6	4.4	2.7	3.9	1.8	3.5
European Community	31.2	43.9	25.6	29.2	21.3	36.3	13.4	22.9
ADCs	8.4	0.4	11.1	4.3	16.5	5.1	11.8	3.7
RRCs	8.4	7.8	4.8	2.3	6.1	3.4	2.2	2.6
China	—	0.2	—	0.2	—	2.8	29.7	9.0
Total	100.0	100.0	100.0	100.0	100.0	100.0	100.0	100.0

Source: UNCTAD trade data tape.

creased from 16 percent to 18 percent. The countries that increased their export share the most, however, were the other ADCs, that is, Taiwan, Korea, and Singapore; their share rose from 8 percent to sixteen percent between these years, despite the exclusion from the figures of exports from Taiwan to Hong Kong in 1980 (and 1984). The European Community and the four resource-rich countries, namely, the Philippines, Malaysia, Thailand, and Indonesia, were the losers in terms of export shares between 1963 and 1980.

The major change between 1980 and 1984 was the emergence of China as a major supplier to the Hong Kong market. In 1984 almost 30 percent of exports to Hong Kong came from China. Of course, much of this reflects the reemergence of entrepôt trade for Hong Kong as China became more open. The U.S. market share declined about a third between 1980 and 1984 (from 18 percent to 12 percent), due no doubt in part to the appreciation of the dollar relative to other major currencies after 1980. Japan's share also declined between these years but less in relative terms than the U.S. share.

Table 2.8 also shows the country-region distribution of Hong Kong's own exports between 1963 and 1984. The share of exports to the United States increased from 35 percent in 1963 to 50 percent in 1970 and then declined to 41 percent by the end of the 1970s, a decade in which the dollar depreciated. As the dollar appreciated in the early 1980s, the share of Hong Kong's exports absorbed by the United States again rose to 50 percent. The value of Hong Kong's exports to the United States in 1984 was $7.8 billion compared to $2.8 billion of imports from the United States. Remarkably, the share of exports absorbed by Japan remained at about 4 percent over the entire period. In contrast, the trend in the EC share was downward over the period, with an especially sharp fall evident after 1980.

The main factor in Hong Kong's long-term economic outlook is the coming return of sovereignty over Hong Kong to China in 1997. The agreement reached in 1984 between the United Kingdom and China called for the maintenance of Hong Kong's market-oriented economy for at least fifty years after 1997, but, despite this provision, there is understandably a great deal of uncertainty about the future.

Singapore

Trade and development policies. The economy of Singapore, like that of Hong Kong, was for many years based on entrepôt trade, specifically, the processing, repackaging, and reexporting of the primary products of Southeast Asia to other areas and the reexporting of imported industrial goods to other parts of Asia.[5] Following the attainment of self-government in 1959, Singapore adopted an industrialization strategy that has passed through three stages: an import substitution phase from 1960 to 1966; a labor-intensive, export-oriented phase from 1966 to 1970; and since 1970 a higher-technology, skill-intensive phase that is also export oriented (Yue 1980).

The first phase, which involved the use of tariffs and quotas to stimulate domestic manufacturing, was closely tied to the prospect of a Malaysian common market. Government officials thought that this market would be of sufficient size for Singapore to become an efficient supplier of manufactured products, given temporary protection. But the political union of Malaya, Sabah, Sarawak, and Singapore lasted only from 1963 to 1965, and with Singapore's withdrawal from the federation, the proposal for a Malaysian common market collapsed.

Although import protection was increased to ease the domestic adjustments related to the country's withdrawal from the federation, the development strategy shifted around 1966 to one of attracting foreign investment to expanding exports of labor-intensive manufactures. In addition to establishing new tax incentives to attract foreign investors, the government introduced restrictive labor legislation to restrain wage increases and maintain stable labor relations, restructured the educational system to provide more technical workers, and provided a wide range of facilities and services to industrialists. The outcome was a rapid decrease in unemployment, an increase in the share of domestic exports in total exports from 25 percent in 1965 to 38 percent in 1970, and a marked acceleration of the growth rate.

As the upward pressure on wages increased due to the success of these measures, Singapore began to shift to a new development strategy in the early 1970s, emphasizing exports of skill-intensive, higher-technology products. To stimulate the export of these products, the government provided equity and loan assistance to firms producing them, expanded training facilities and gave financial support to private sector training activities, allocated funds for financing export bills below the prime rate, subsidized the insurance of export activities, and undertook extensive export-promotion programs. Beginning in 1969, most tariffs and quotas also were reduced or abolished to enable exporting firms to obtain needed inputs at competitive world prices, and by the mid-1970s, Singapore's level of protection was very low.

The extent to which Singapore has relied on foreign investment to increase its exports of manufactured goods is indicated by the fact that, in 1980, export sales by wholly foreign-owned firms constituted 72 percent of the economy's total exports of manufactured goods, export sales by joint ventures 21 percent, and export sales by wholly locally owned firms only 7 percent. Another notable feature of the country's development policy is the high rate of domestic savings achieved by compulsory retirement contributions by employers and employees. By 1978 the contribution rate reached 38.5 percent of wages and salaries and contributed 22 percent of total national savings. The government has used these funds to provide an infrastructure that is conducive to development.

Trade performance. Unlike Hong Kong, Singapore never relied on textiles and clothing as an important export product, as table 2.9 shows. Instead, its industrialization via the export route has been based mainly on oil refining and, to an increasing extent, on skill-intensive machinery and other manufactures. Industrialization has also expanded the market within Singapore for high-skill, high-technology products, as the changes in the country's import pattern indicate.

The United States has done very well in the Singapore market (table 2.10), increasing its export share from 7 percent in 1963 to 21 percent in 1984—a performance that outdid the Japanese export share increase. The other ADCs also gained in market share, while the EC and, especially, the RCCs lost in relative terms. On the export side, the figures show that the shares of Singapore's exports taken by both the United States and Japan rose between 1963 and 1984, the United States from 13 percent to 27 percent, and Japan from 8 percent to 12 percent. As would be expected from exchange rate developments, the increase in the share of exports going to the United States was especially large between 1980 and 1984. Export to the United States in 1984 totaled $4.7 billion, while imports from the United States in that year amounted

Table 2.9   **Structure of Singapore's Merchandise Trade, 1960, 1978, and 1983 (percentage distribution)**

	Exports				
	Fuels, Minerals, and Metals	Other Primary Commodities	Textiles and Clothing	Machinery and Transport Equipment	Other Manufactures
1960	1	73	5	7	14
1978	31	23	5	25	16
1980	31	13	4	31	22
	Imports				
	Food	Fuels	Other Primary Commodities	Machinery and Transport Equipment	Other Manufactures
1960	21	15	38	7	21
1978	10	24	9	29	23
1983	7	31	6	30	26

Sources: *World Development Report*, 1981 and 1986.

Table 2.10   Distribution of Singapore's Imports from and Exports to Selected Countries or Regions, 1963, 1970, 1980, and 1984 (in percentages)

	1963 Imports	1963 Exports	1970 Imports	1970 Exports	1980 Imports	1980 Exports	1984 Imports	1984 Exports
U.S.	7.3	13.3	12.9	18.9	18.2	17.8	21.7	26.9
Canada	—	1.8	0.6	2.0	1.0	0.9	0.6	1.0
Japan	16.0	7.7	24.3	13.0	24.0	10.8	28.1	11.8
Australia and New Zealand	5.7	6.9	5.5	5.1	3.6	7.9	4.2	5.3
European Community	25.0	29.9	17.7	29.6	15.0	15.5	16.0	11.9
ADCs	1.6	6.3	5.3	9.6	3.9	15.1	5.1	12.3
RRCs	44.2	32.8	33.3	18.8	34.1	29.5	16.2	29.2
China	—	0.9	—	2.5	—	2.0	7.7	1.2
Total	100.0	100.0	100.0	100.0	100.0	100.0	100.0	100.0

to $3.5 billion. Shipments to other ADCs also increased in relative terms over the twenty-one-year period. In contrast, the share of Singapore's exports received by the EC fell from 29 percent to 12 percent from 1963 to 1984.

There is no alternative for Singapore, if it is to continue to raise its living standard, but to remain an open, export-oriented economy. At the same time, one can expect to see a continued shift in the composition of its exports toward higher-labor-skill products, while importing high-technology goods as well as products where scale economies are important.

Korea

Trade and development policies. From 1945 to 1960, Korea followed an import-substitution development policy, using high protective tariffs, quantitative import restrictions, and a multiple exchange rate system with a generally overvalued currency to stimulate domestic production for local markets.[6] While growth was fairly impressive during the 1950s, it was largely induced by substantial U.S. aid following the Korean War. For example, 74 percent of Korean investment was financed by foreign aid between 1953 and 1960. The growth rate began to decline in the late 1950s as the easy import substitution opportunities were exploited and U.S. economic aid was reduced. The degree of inwardness of the economy at that time is indicated by the fact that exports of goods and services were only 3 percent of GDP in 1960, whereas they had climbed to 36 percent by 1980.

A significant shift in Korean development policy toward an outward-looking strategy occurred following the student revolution in 1960 and the military coup in 1961. The won was devalued and a unitary exchange rate system established, the interest rate was permitted to rise to encourage domestic savings, and a stabilization program was implemented. A number of export incentives were introduced, including exemption from tariffs on imported inputs and capital equipment for use in export production, accelerated depreciation on capital facilities employed in export production, and a lowering of direct taxes on income earned from exporting. Exporters also had access to credit below the market rate of interest, received preferential electricity and transportation rates, and were granted generous wastage allowances on imported inputs.

In the late 1970s another change in development policy occurred as government leaders, fearing that Korea was losing its competitive advantage in labor-intensive manufactures due to rising real wages, began to encourage the production of capital-intensive intermediate products. This policy shift was reversed in the early 1980s and priority again given to export expansion as the major engine of growth.

The rate of growth that followed the shift in development strategy toward export promotion can only be described as phenomenal. Per capita incomes rose at an average annual rate of 7 percent between 1960 and 1980. During the export-led industrial transformation, the share of manufactures in total exports increased from 14 percent in 1960 to 91 percent in 1983 (table 2.11), and domestic savings as a fraction of GDP rose from 1 percent to 30 percent between 1960 and 1984 (table 2.4).

A feature of Korean policy of considerable concern to the United States and other industrial countries with which Korea has a large export surplus is the continuing high levels of protection in both the agricultural and industrial sectors that make it difficult for foreign suppliers to sell in the Korean market.

Trade performance. As table 2.12 indicates, the United States' export share in the Korean import market, after falling sharply from 49 percent to 31 percent between 1963 and 1970, increased slightly to 34 percent between 1970 and 1980 and then remained constant thereafter. Japan was the main gainer at U.S. expense between 1963 and 1970, with its share rising from 35 percent to 49 percent, but this share had fallen back to about 41 percent by 1984. Australia and New Zealand, Canada, and the RRCs have all gained steadily in market share throughout the twenty-one-year period.

Table 2.11   **Structure of Korea's Merchandise Trade, 1960, 1978, and 1983 (percentage distribution)**

			Exports		
	Fuels, Minerals, and Metals	Other Primary Commodities	Textiles and Clothing	Machinery and Transport Equipment	Other Manufactures
1960	30	56	8	—	6
1978	1	10	32	21	36
1983	3	6	25	32	34
			Imports		
	Food	Fuels	Other Primary Commodities	Machinery and Transport Equipment	Other Manufactures
1960	10	7	25	12	46
1978	8	16	17	33	26
1983	8	27	14	29	22

Sources: World Development Report, 1981 and 1986.

Table 2.12 Country Distribution of Korea's Imports from and Exports to Selected Countries or Regions, 1963, 1970, 1980, and 1984 (in percentages)

	1963		1970		1980		1984	
	Imports	Exports	Imports	Exports	Imports	Exports	Imports	Exports
U.S.	49.5	32.5	31.1	50.7	33.7	35.2	33.5	46.4
Canada	0.7	0.3	1.1	2.5	3.3	2.6	3.2	3.8
Japan	34.7	34.5	49.4	29.8	40.4	23.0	41.2	20.2
Australia and New Zealand	1.8	0.3	0.9	1.0	3.9	1.9	5.3	1.9
European Community	7.1	9.3	9.4	8.6	10.0	20.8	10.1	14.5
ADCs	4.0	18.4	2.5	5.9	2.3	9.9	2.2	8.9
RRCs	1.8	4.5	5.2	1.3	6.0	6.3	4.1	3.9
China	—	—	—	—	—	—	—	—
Total	100.0	100.0	100.0	100.0	100.0	100.0	100.0	100.0

Source: UNCTAD trade data tape.

The distribution of Korean exports exhibits considerable volatility. Exports to the United States, for example, constituted 50 percent of all exports to the regions listed in the first column in 1970, rising from 32 percent in 1963, then dropping to 35 percent in 1980, only to rise again to 46 percent during the period of dollar appreciation in the early 1980s. In value terms, Korean exports to the United States in 1984 came to $10.5 billion compared to imports of $5.8 billion. The share of exports sent to Japan shows a steady decline over the entire period. In contrast, exports to the European Community display an upward trend.

Because the country's poor endowment of natural resource and comparatively small size leave no alternative for achieving continued rapid growth but to retain the emphasis on exporting manufactured goods, Korea is likely to remain an outward-looking economy. Like Singapore, it can be expected to move into higher-skill, more capital-intensive export production, however. At the same time, with some prodding it should become a better market for high-technology goods and agricultural products.

As regards international political relations, the Republic of Korea's relations with North Korea are of major concern to the United States. Because of the perceived threat of aggression from the north, the United States still maintains military forces in South Korea and has a treaty commitment to the country's security. The U.S. government favors gradual reunification between North and South Korea, but there seems little prospect for that to take place in the short term. Yet the prospect for reasonably peaceful relations between the two countries in the short term seems favorable.

Taiwan

Trade and development policies. There was great political and economic turmoil in Taiwan in the period immediately after World War II.[7] The end of fifty years of Japanese rule and thus the loss of the country's traditional export market was followed by the Communists' takeover of mainland China, the Nationalists' assumption of power in Taiwan with a large immigration from the mainland, and the loss of another important market in China.

The government's first response to the economic problems it faced was to undertake a land reform program in the agricultural sector and an import substitution policy with high levels of protection for the manufacturing sector. The country's adjustment efforts were assisted by a substantial inflow of foreign aid, mainly from the United States. Between 1951 and 1959, 37 percent of total investment was financed by foreign aid.

Beginning in the late 1950s and continuing into the early 1960s, the government introduced policies that changed Taiwan's development strategy from one of import substitution to one that emphasized the export of labor-intensive manufactures. The multiple exchange rate system was abolished and the overvaluation of the country's currency corrected by a series of devaluations. Import controls were eased and tariffs reduced on many manufactured goods. (As in Korea, the Taiwanese government still highly protects some domestic industries with import controls and tariffs.) Investment by foreigners and local residents was encouraged by such measures as a five-year income tax holiday for certain new industrial establishments, a sharp reduction in the maximum business income tax, and tax exemption for undistributed profits retained for investment purposes. Exporting was also encouraged directly by rebating customs duties on imported inputs, permitting the deduction from taxable income of an amount equal to 2 percent of annual export earnings, and allowing a 10 percent tax deduction for manufacturing, mining, and handicraft firms that exported more than 50 percent of their output. In addition, some industries received direct export subsidies that were financed by levies on domestic sales. Low-interest loans and government assistance in the form of marketing, managerial, and technical services were also available for exporting activities. Beginning in the mid-1960s, the government also established duty- and tax-free export-processing zones.

Trade performance. As in the Korean case, the post–World War II development policies of Taiwan transformed the country from an agricultural to an industrial economy within a comparatively short period. In the period 1952–54, industrial exports made up only 9 percent of total exports, but in 1970 the share of industrial exports in total exports was up to a level of 78 percent; by 1982, this figure had risen to 88 percent.

As table 2.13 shows, changes in the country or regional distribution of Taiwan's imports between 1963 and 1984 are similar to those of Korea. The U.S. share of imports into Taiwan declined sharply from 43 percent to 26 percent between 1963 and 1970, then increased to 33 percent in 1980 and remained constant thereafter. As in the Korean case, Japan's export share rose considerably between the first two years (from 35 percent to 52 percent), then declined to 40 percent by 1980 and remained there over the next four years. The EC's export share also rose over the entire period. In contrast to the Korean case, however, the export share of the other ADCs rose, whereas that of the RRCs fell.

Since the UNCTAD trade data tape does not contain exports from Taiwan for 1980 and 1984, the country-region composition of Taiwanese

Table 2.13   Distribution of Taiwan's Imports from and Exports to Selected Countries or Regions, 1963, 1970, 1980, and 1984 (in percentages)

	1963		1970		1980		1984	
	Imports	Exports	Imports	Exports	Imports	Exports	Imports	Exports
U.S.	43.1	19.9	25.7	44.2	33.0	—	31.7	—
Canada	1.1	2.1	1.3	3.9	1.6	—	3.5	—
Japan	34.7	38.4	51.7	16.7	40.4	—	40.7	—
Australia and New Zealand	5.0	1.2	3.0	1.6	3.4	—	4.9	—
European Community	7.1	10.2	8.7	11.0	9.8	—	10.4	—
ADCs	2.4	20.5	3.3	15.6	5.3	—	5.6	—
RRCs	6.4	7.3	6.0	6.6	6.1	—	2.8	—
China	0.0	0.0	0.0	0.0	0.0	—	0.0	—
Total	100.0	100.0	100.0	100.0	100.0	—	100.0	—

Source: UNCTAD trade data tape.

exports is given for 1963 and 1970 only. These years show the marked shift in the direction of Taiwanese exports toward the United States. From accounting for only 20 percent of these exports in 1963, the U.S. share had increased to 44 percent by 1970. U.S. trade data indicate that in 1982, Taiwanese exports to the United States amounted to $8.8 billion, whereas imports from the United States totaled $3.9 billion. The European community's share rose slightly. The most significant other shift between these years was the fall in Japan's share from 38 percent to 17 percent.

Like Korea, to achieve continued rapid growth, Taiwan has no alternative but to concentrate on exporting manufactured goods, but it can be expected to shift toward higher-skill-requiring, more-capital-intensive products. As it is pressured to liberalize its own trade barriers, Taiwan should improve as a market for high-technology manufactures and agricultural products.

There is, of course, considerable uncertainty about the political future of Taiwan. In proposing unification, China has offered to make Taiwan a special administrative region, following the Hong Kong approach, and allow it to maintain its economic and social system. Thus far, however, no visible progress has been made toward reunification, despite Taiwan's increasing political isolation in the world. The official position of the U.S. government seems to be that a gradual and natural process of unification is the best solution and that other countries should neither speed up or slow down this process.

2.3.2   The Resource-Rich Countries

The Philippines

Trade and development policies. The development policy of the Philippines since the late 1940s can be characterized as initially one of import substitution, followed by a series of modest and short-lived efforts to liberalize the trade and exchange-rate regimes.[8] Exchange controls were first introduced in late 1949 as a consequence of a balance of payments crisis caused immediately by the election-related easy credit and liberal spending policies of the government and more basically by the country's overvalued currency and pent-up demand for consumption goods. Rather than lifting the controls after the crisis passed, the government used them during the 1950s to promote the development of domestic manufacturing activities. As often happened in developing countries that follow this strategy, growth rates initially were quite high, but by the late 1950s, as the easy stage of import substitution had passed, they had fallen significantly.

Devaluation, the elimination of most exchange controls, and the establishment of a unified exchange rate system occurred in the early 1960s, but these changes were in response to charges of maladministration of the controls and pressures from traditional exporters rather than to a conscious decision to promote exports of manufactures. High tariffs still protected the manufacturing sector, although its growth rate fell even further in the early 1960s. An effort in the late 1960s to stimulate growth through credit and fiscal expansion led to a new balance of payments crisis and the reintroduction of exchange controls.

The 1970s began with the floating of the peso and the passage of legislation aimed directly at stimulating exports of nontraditional agricultural and manufactured goods. Firms exporting more than 50 percent of their output were exempt from sales or customs taxes on materials used in export production and permitted to deduct part of their export revenue from taxable income. The government also constructed the first export-processing zone. Partly in response to these measures but probably due more importantly to the 50 percent decline in real wage costs in manufcturing between 1969 and 1974, there was sustained growth in manufacturing exports until 1981 (Alburo and Shepherd 1986). The share of manufacturing exports in total exports rose from 12 percent in 1970 to 44 percent in 1980.

Further liberalization efforts were undertaken in the early 1980s, the most important of which was the reduction of tariffs under a new, more rational system of import protection, but the exchange crisis of 1983, related to the country's external debt problems, prevented the full implementation of the measures as exchange controls were introduced once again. Since 1984 the cutoff of foreign capital, the austerity measures the government was forced to adopt, and the political crisis in the country have brought about a decline in real GNP.

Trade performance. The commodity distribution of the Philippines' exports and imports is given in table 2.14. Primary product exports other than minerals have declined significantly between 1960 and 1983 as the share taken by manufactured goods rose from 4 percent to 50 percent. In contrast, due to the greater importance of fuel imports, the share of imports of manufactured goods fell from 75 percent to 65 percent between 1960 and 1983.

The Philippines is another case where the U.S. share of the country's import market decreased significantly between 1963 and 1970, while Japan's share increased significantly (table 2.15). The U.S. export share rose in the 1970s and, despite the exchange rate developments, rose again in the 1980s. The other major gainers were the ADCs, whose share of the Philippines' imports went up from 2 percent to 11 percent between 1963 and 1984. In contrast, the Japanese and EC export shares of the Philippine market fell in both of these periods.

The country-region distribution of Philippine exports shows a decreasing dependence on the United States as a trading partner. The share of the country's exports sent to the United States declined from

Table 2.14   Structure of the Philippine's Merchandise Trade, 1960, 1978, and 1983 (percentage distribution)

	Exports				
	Fuels, Minerals, and Metals	Other Primary Commodities	Textiles and Clothing	Machinery and Transport Equipment	Other Manufactures
1960	10	86	1	0	3
1978	14	52	6	2	26
1983	13	36	7	5	38

	Imports				
	Food	Fuels	Other Primary Commodities	Machinery & Transport Equipment	Other Manufactures
1960	15	10	5	36	34
1978	8	21	7	27	37
1983	8	27	5	21	39

Sources: *World Development Report*, 1981 and 1986.

47 percent in 1963 to 27 percent by 1980.[9] In absolute terms, Philippine exports to the United States amounted to $1.8 billion in 1982, while imports from the United States were also valued at $1.8 billion in that year. The share of exports taken by Japan rose somewhat from 1963 to 1980; the EC share remained about the same. The most important shift was the increase from 3 percent to 11 percent in the relative importance of the ADCs as an export market between these years. This may be due to trade diversion associated with the establishment of the Association of Southeast Asian Nations (ASEAN), since ADC Singapore is an ASEAN member. Export shares of the other ASEAN members, the RRCs, remained roughly the same, however.

The economic history of the Philippines over the last forty years and the present political turmoil do not give reason to expect the country to shift its development strategy in the foreseeable future and focus on becoming an outward-looking exporter of manufactured goods. Periodic attempts to liberalize can be expected, but the conflicting economic and political pressures within the country seem likely to result in the same pattern of on-again, off-again government controls on trade and development that has been seen over the last forty years. Yet, because of the richness of its human and physical resources, the Philippines is likely to continue to grow at a respectable rate.

U.S. concerns with the Philippines go beyond the historically close political and economic relationships between the two countries. Clark Air Force Base and Subic Bay Naval Base are the largest overseas

Table 2.15 Distribution of the Philippine's Imports from and Exports to Selected Countries or Regions, 1963, 1970, 1980, and 1984 (in percentages)

	1963		1970		1980		1984	
	Imports	Exports	Imports	Exports	Imports	Exports	Imports	Exports
U.S.	46.4	46.6	30.3	42.7	34.3	26.6	38.6	—
Canada	2.9	0.1	2.4	0.2	1.6	1.0	1.0	—
Japan	22.1	28.0	38.0	40.5	29.1	32.7	24.5	—
Australia and New Zealand	2.8	0.3	4.5	0.4	4.2	2.1	3.2	—
European Community	17.4	21.7	17.7	8.7	14.0	20.6	11.8	—
ADCs	2.4	2.9	2.2	6.7	9.6	11.0	10.9	—
RRCs	5.6	0.0	4.6	0.4	6.9	4.6	4.3	—
China	—	—	—	—	—	1.0	5.4	—
Total	100.0	100.0	100.0	100.0	100.0	100.0	100.0	100.0

Source: UNCTAD trade data tape.

American air and naval facilities, and they are generally regarded as vital to a U.S. military presence not only in the Pacific but also in the Indian Ocean and Persian Gulf. It would be a severe blow to U.S. military strategy if a Philippine government forced the United States to relinquish control over these bases. Since poor economic performance in the Philippine economy contributes to the possibility of such an outcome, the United States may wish to consider establishing closer economic ties with the Philippines, for example, by granting the country more favorable treatment under the Generalized System of Preferences or perhaps by negotiating a free trade arrangement with the country.

Malaysia

Trade and development policies. Peninsular Malaysia achieved political independence in 1957; Sabah and Sarawak gained their independence and became part of Malaysia in 1963.[10] Fortunately, Malaysia already had a per capita income that was considerably above the other three resource-rich countries. As in most developing countries, the Malaysian government began its industrialization endeavors with import substitution fostered by moderate levels of protection and generous fiscal incentives, such as were provided in the Pioneer Industries Ordinance in 1958 and the broader Investment Incentive Act in 1968. In the late 1960s and early 1970s, a deliberate effort was made to promote exports. This included permitting a double deduction from taxable income for export expenses and a further tax deduction based on Malaysian raw material and wage costs. Free-trade and export-processing zones, in which firms can freely import materials and capital goods used in export production, were also established in various parts of the country. Furthermore, the government provided low-cost export insurance, helped keep shipping rates low, and engaged in the promotion of Malaysian exports throughout the world.

The country's development efforts have been successful in achieving an impressive degree of diversification of both primary product and manufacturing activities. For example, palm oil and timber production has increased to the point that these sectors are now as important as the rubber and tin industries as earners of foreign exchange. Impressive processing activities have been established in the palm oil and rubber sectors. The oil and natural gas industries have also become major export-earning industries. In addition, textiles and apparel, electrical machinery, and, especially, electronics products have become important export items. As can be seen from table 2.16, exports of manufactured products increased from 6 percent of total exports in 1960 to 22 percent in 1983.

Trade performance. The Malaysian import figures for 1963 seem unreliable, due perhaps to its political union with Singapore in that year.

Table 2.16   **Structure of Malaysia's Merchandise Trade, 1960, 1978, and 1983 (percentage distribution)**

	Exports				
	Fuels, Minerals, and Metals	Other Primary Commodities	Textiles and Clothing	Machinery and Transport Equipment	Other Manufactures
1960	20	74	—	—	6
1978	27	52	2	11	8
1983	35	43	2	14	6

	Imports				
	Food	Fuels	Other Primary Commodities	Machinery and Transport Equipment	Other Manufactures
1960	29	16	13	14	28
1978	17	13	7	34	29
1983	9	14	5	44	28

Sources: *World Development Report*, 1981 and 1986.

Subsequent data show a steady increase in the share of the Malaysian import market captured by the United States, this share rising from 11 percent in 1970 to 16 percent by 1984 (table 2.17). Japan's share increased significantly between these years, from 4 percent to 25 percent, while the EC's share decreased significantly. Import trade with the ADCs also rose appreciably but dropped with the other RRCs.

The country-region distribution of Malaysian exports indicates that the United States gradually increased its share between 1963 and 1980.[11] In 1982, Malaysia exported $1.8 billion worth of goods to the United States and imported $1.7 billion. Shipments to Japan, the ADCs, and the other RRCs remained about the same in share terms over the time period; those to the EC fell in relative importance.

Malaysia has been successful in achieving an export-oriented industrialization strategy that is based on processing its abundant natural resources and on utilizing its abundant supply of low-cost labor. There seem to be no major reasons why this pattern will not continue, at least in the medium term.

Thailand

Trade and development policies. The modern industrialization efforts of the government of Thailand can be dated as beginning around 1960 when a board of investment, set up to promote domestic investment with the use of tax incentives, was established (1959) and a new, mildly protective customs schedule put into effect (1960).[12] The government

Table 2.17   Distribution of Malaysia's Imports from and Exports to Selected Countries or Regions, 1963, 1970, 1980, and 1984 (in percentages)

	1963		1970		1980		1984	
	Imports	Exports	Imports	Exports	Imports	Exports	Imports	Exports
U.S.	—	12.6	10.7	14.9	14.4	18.3	15.6	—
Canada	0.4	2.0	2.3	2.2	0.9	0.5	1.2	—
Japan	4.4	24.7	3.6	21.0	23.1	25.7	24.8	—
Australia and New Zealand	2.6	2.5	11.6	3.0	6.2	2.0	4.3	—
European Community	16.7	24.8	42.4	23.2	15.7	19.8	11.8	—
ADCs	66.4	28.8	22.6	30.3	35.2	27.9	36.6	—
RRCs	9.2	4.1	6.6	3.6	4.3	3.6	3.7	—
China	—	0.1	—	1.4	—	1.8	1.7	—
Total	100.0	100.0	100.0	100.0	100.0	100.0	100.0	—

Source: UNCTAD trade data tape.

also influenced industrial expansion by means of entry controls and the use of preferential credit arrangements. The net effect was a development policy that to some extent favored manufacturing industries producing for the domestic market.

With the passage of the Export Promotion Act in 1972, greater attention was given to the promotion of manufactured exports. Its provisions included exemption from paying import duties on imported materials used in production for export, exemption from business taxes on export-producing activities, and a Bank of Thailand discount facility at below-market rates for short-term export loans made by commercial banks. Since 1972, exporters are also eligible for a 20 percent rebate on electricity charges incurred in export production. The Department of Commerce began export-promoting activities in 1975.

Beginning in 1974, as the sharp increase in the price of oil caused a deterioration in the country's balance of payments, there was an increase in industrial import protection. Nominal protection on import-competing manufactured goods increased from 35 percent to 50 percent between 1974 and 1978 (World Bank 1980). Greater increases in business taxes on imports than on comparable domestic products, the imposition of import surcharges on certain products, and the increased use of import controls were other policies favoring import-substituting activities. The debt crisis of the early 1980s and a sharp deterioration in Thailand's terms of trade brought about further import restrictions.

Trade performance. Despite the somewhat contradictory nature of Thailand's recent development policies, export growth has been very high in the last decade (table 2.2), with exports of textiles and apparel, machinery and equipment, and other manufactures continuing to make up an increasing share of the country's total exports (table 2.18).

As in a number of the other APR countries, the U.S. share of Thailand's imports from its major trading partners decreased between 1963 and 1970 as Japan's share increased (table 2.19). In the Thai case, however, these share changes were not as great as in the other cases. The pattern of a U.S. share gain and a Japanese loss in the 1970s, as the dollar depreciated, and the reverse of these changes in the 1980s, as the dollar appreciated, also took place in Thailand. The EC share in Thailand's imports fell steadily throughout the period. The other important change in export shares was the increase in the ADCs' share from 11 percent in 1963 to 22 percent in 1984. The share of the other RCCs in exports to Thailand remained about the same over the period.

The share of Thailand's exports absorbed by the United States rose significantly from 10 percent to 22 percent between 1963 and 1984. Shipments to the EC also increased between these years but only from 23 percent to 27 percent. Thailand's exports to the United States in

Table 2.18   Structure of Thailand's Merchandise Trade, 1960, 1978, and 1983
               (percentage distribution)

			Exports		
	Fuels, Minerals, and Metals	Other Primary Commodities	Textiles and Clothing	Machinery and Transport Equipment	Other Manufactures
1960	7	91	0	0	2
1978	11	64	10	3	12
1983	6	62	11	6	15
			Imports		
	Food	Fuels	Other Primary Commodities	Machinery and Transport Equipment	Other Manufactures
1960	10	11	11	25	43
1978	4	21	9	31	35
1983	4	24	8	29	35

Sources: *World Development Report*, 1981 and 1986.

1984 amounted to $1.2 billion and its imports from the United States to $1.0 billion. Japan's share fell after 1970 from 30 percent to 17 percent. Interestingly, Thai exports to other RRCs and the ADCs diminished in relative importance over the entire period.

The Thai government's policy of modest intervention in the market economy seems likely to continue into the foreseeable future and result in high growth rates and a growing degree of export-oriented industrial diversification.

Indonesia

Trade and development policies. Indonesia has been the least successful of the resource-rich countries in shifting from an inward-looking policy that protects domestic producers of manufactured products from foreign competition to a strategy of promoting exports of manufactures.[13] The 8 percent share of manufactures in total exports in 1983 (table 2.3) is much lower than that for the other three resource-rich countries. The unusual richness of its resources and especially its ability to take advantage in export markets of the sharp oil price increase in the 1970s may in part be responsible for this low manufacturing share by reducing the balance of payments pressures for the expansion of manufactured exports.

Four separate periods can be distinguished since Indonesia achieved its independence in 1949: the period of constitutional democracy (1950–

Table 2.19   **Distribution of Thailand's Imports from and Exports to Selected Countries or Regions, 1963, 1970, 1980, and 1984 (in percentages)**

	1963		1970		1980		1984	
	Imports	Exports	Imports	Exports	Imports	Exports	Imports	Exports
U.S	18.7	9.6	14.8	15.0	19.1	15.3	15.7	22.4
Canada	0.5	0.0	0.7	0.1	2.1	0.4	1.2	1.5
Japan	34.6	25.6	44.9	29.5	33.6	18.9	36.7	17.0
Australia and New Zealand	1.9	0.3	3.6	0.5	3.2	1.3	2.6	2.3
European Community	28.7	22.9	24.3	22.2	18.0	32.6	15.9	26.9
ADCs	11.6	26.3	9.6	23.1	18.8	18.0	22.2	19.2
RRCs	1.5	14.9	1.7	9.3	4.9	10.7	1.4	7.1
China	—	—	—	—	—	2.4	3.8	3.1
Total	100.0	100.0	100.0	100.0	100.0	100.0	100.0	100.0

Source: UNCTAD trade data tape.

57); the "guided democracy" of 1958–65; the liberalization of the "new order" (1966–71); and developments up to the present after the period of liberalization (Pitt 1985). The first period saw sporadic attempts to dismantle the elaborate system of foreign exchange controls and import quotas that had existed under Dutch rule. But lobbying pressures on the government to grant preferential import privileges to the new class of indigenous importers and to monopolistic organizations of domestic industrial firms formed to import a common raw material tended to undermine these liberalization efforts.

The second period, 1958–65, was marked by President Sukarno's implementation of his concept of "guided democracy" under which there was an aversion to free markets and foreign capital. The traditional Dutch trading houses were nationalized so that by 1959 only 20 percent of the import trade remained in private hands. The government allocated all foreign exchange and, in doing so, favored inward-oriented state enterprises. Moreover, the government's policy of allocating raw materials on the basis of a firm's existing productive capacity encouraged the expansion of capacity, though this capacity was underutilized; in 1965, manufacturing as a whole operated at only between 20 percent and 30 percent of capacity.

The period 1966–71 was one of sweeping liberalization in Indonesia, beginning with a scheme to encourage exports that permitted exporters to sell a portion of their foreign exchange earnings at free market prices. The government ended the direct allocation of foreign exchange to manufacturing firms, and importers were permitted to buy almost any good they wished. Subsidies and preferential credit rates to state enterprises were cut sharply. Another important change was the enactment of a law to encourage foreign investment by exempting firms that undertook priority investments from taxes on as much as 60 percent of their profits for up to six years. A unified exchange rate system was established in 1970.

In the period immediately after the liberalization phase, the new government shifted back toward import substitution with the increased use of quantitative import controls, including the banning of imports of many consumer goods, an increase in tariffs, and the introduction of numerous regulations covering investment activities. In 1978, however, the currency was devalued and an export certificate scheme was introduced that tended to subsidize exports of manufactured goods. This led to a significant percentage increase in such exports, though starting from a very low level. Nevertheless, the government's policies are still biased toward capital-intensive, import-substituting activities and include cumbersome regulations that discourage exports of labor-intensive manufactures.

Trade performance. Unlike in the other countries analyzed, Indonesia's structure of production has not shifted significantly toward export-oriented manufacturing. Only 7 percent of the country's exports were manufactured goods in 1983 (table 2.20), while the share of fuels, minerals, and metals in exports rose from 33 percent to 80 percent between 1960 and 1983.

The country-region composition of Indonesian imports (table 2.21) shows a rise in shares from both the United States and Japan between 1963 and 1970 and a decline in the export shares of the ADCs, the RRCs, and the EC. In the 1970s the U.S. share fell and Japan's increased, while in the 1980s their shares remained unchanged. In contrast, the share of imports from the European community increased in the 1980s. Imports from the ADCs dropped sharply from 19 percent to 5 percent between 1963 and 1970 but remained roughly constant thereafter.

Indonesian exports to both the United States and Japan rose significantly in the 1970s, while exports to the EC and the ADCs fell appreciably during this period. Indonesian exports to the United States in 1984 amounted to $4.5 billion compared to imports of only $1.2 billion. In the period of the 1980s covered in table 2.21, the pattern of Indonesian exports by country destination remained roughly the same.

As in the Philippines, there seem to be no strong reasons to expect that Indonesia will change its development strategy from that of recent

Table 2.20   **Structure of Indonesia's Merchandise Trade, 1960, 1978, and 1983 (percentage distribution)**

	Exports				
	Fuels, Minerals, and Metals	Other Primary Commodities	Textiles and Clothing	Machinery and Transport Equipment	Other Manufactures
1960	33	67	0	—	—
1978	72	26	—	1	1
1983	80	12	1	1	6

	Imports				
	Food	Fuels	Other Primary Commodities	Machinery and Transport Equipment	Other Manufactures
1960	23	5	10	17	45
1978	18	9	6	36	31
1983	8	25	5	35	28

Sources: World Development Report, 1981 and 1986.

Table 2.21 Distribution of Indonesia's Imports from and Exports to Selected Countries or Regions, 1963, 1970, 1980, and 1984 (in percentages)

	1963		1970		1980		1984	
	Imports	Exports	Imports	Exports	Imports	Exports	Imports	Exports
U.S.	21.8	—	28.2	15.9	17.3	20.9	16.8	22.4
Canada	0.2	—	1.7	0.0	2.2	0.1	3.1	0.2
Japan	20.7	—	34.5	37.9	42.8	52.5	43.0	51.7
Australia and New Zealand	0.8	—	3.9	3.9	5.3	2.1	4.0	2.4
European Community	29.2	—	23.2	18.4	22.3	6.9	26.8	5.3
ADCs	19.3	—	5.2	20.8	5.2	15.9	4.3	15.9
RRCs	7.6	—	3.0	2.8	4.6	1.3	0.6	1.8
China	—	—	—	0.0	—	—	0.9	0.0
Total	100.0	—	100.0	100.0	100.0	100.0	100.0	100.0

Source: UNCTAD trade data tape.

years. Strong vested interests have been created that favor an inward-looking industrialization strategy, and they are likely to continue to prevail in the political decision-making process determining development policy into the foreseeable future.

2.3.3 China

Trade and Development Policies

Undoubtedly, the developing country in the APR whose policies are of greatest potential significance to the United States and other competitors in the region is China.[14] The modernization reforms initiated in the late 1970s could eventually transform the Chinese economy into both a major competitor and market in the area and the world. But the possibility of a return to Maoist economic policies, involving autarky and a deemphasis on the acquisition of Western technology, cannot be ruled out.

China's current trade policies are aimed at increasing exports in order to pay for the capital equipment, intermediate inputs, and advanced technology needed for industrial and agricultural modernization. One means of stimulating exports has been the establishment of Special Export Zones in which Western know-how, managerial skills, and capital can be combined in joint ventures with low-wage Chinese labor. As table 2.22 indicates, the share of exports of manufactures in total exports equaled 57 percent in 1983, with textiles and clothing being the most important export category. Among the country's primary

Table 2.22   **Structure of China's Merchandise Trade, 1978 and 1983 (percentage distribution)**

			Exports		
	Fuels, Minerals, and Metals	Other Primary Commodities	Textiles and Clothing	Machinery and Transport Equipment	Other Manufactures
1978	13	38	24	3	22
1983	22	21	19	6	32
			Imports		
	Food	Fuels	Other Primary Commodities	Machinery and Transport Equipment	Other Manufactures
1978	17	0	43	18	22
1983	15	1	18	19	47

Sources: *World Development Report*, 1981 and 1986.

product exports, crude petroleum and petroleum products have become increasingly important.

Encouraged by government policy, foreign investment in China exceeded $3.5 billion by 1985, but firms doing business in China face many difficulties, including arbitrary tax and tariff charges, inadequate supplies of skilled labor, poor transportation and communication facilities, and the resistance of vested interests to the economic reforms.

Trade Performance

After U.S. trade with China opened up, the United States quickly became an important supplier, furnishing by 1980 about a quarter of China's imports from its major market-oriented trading partners (table 2.23). The U.S. share dropped to 18 percent by 1984, perhaps reflecting the overvalued dollar. Japan's share rose from 11 percent in 1963 to 43 percent by 1984, and the ADCs became more important as exporters to China over the period, whereas the shares of exports supplied by the EC and Australia and New Zealand declined between these years.

Chinese export figures are only available for 1984 on the UNCTAD data tape. The 42 percent share going to Hong Kong indicates the importance of that colony as an entrepôt for China. Japan is the next largest recipient of Chinese goods at 27 percent, while the United States and the European Community each absorbed about 12 percent in 1984. In value terms, Chinese exports to and imports from the United States were $2.3 billion and $3.0 billion, respectively, in 1984.

It seems much too early to predict, even in the medium term, what China's future role in the world trading and foreign investment system will be.

2.4   The Competitive Performance of the United States and Its Major Competitors in the APR Market

In the preceding section the major country-region distribution of the imports and exports of each of the nine developing countries in the Asian Pacific rim was examined. As is apparent from this analysis, no single pattern emerges as to how well the United States has competed in the area. In three markets, Singapore, Malaysia, and China, the share of U.S. exports in total exports from the countries' major trading partners was greater in 1984 than in 1963. In four countries, the Philippines, Hong Kong, Indonesia, and Thailand, this export share declined but by six percentage points or less. In two countries, Korea and Taiwan, the U.S. share of exports dropped by more than ten percentage points over the period. Interestingly, except for Hong Kong, Korea and Taiwan ship a larger proportion of their exports to the United States than do any other countries in the group.

Table 2.23   Distribution of China's Imports from and Exports to Selected Countries or Regions, 1963, 1970, 1980, and 1984 (in percentages)

	1963		1970		1980		1984	
	Imports	Exports	Imports	Exports	Imports	Exports	Imports	Exports
U.S.	0.0	—	—	—	26.5	—	17.9	12.1
Canada	18.5	—	10.1	—	5.2	—	5.5	1.3
Japan	11.9	—	42.3	—	35.5	—	43.0	26.9
Australia and New Zealand	38.6	—	9.9	—	6.5	—	5.1	1.3
European Community	29.1	—	33.8	—	19.0	—	17.4	11.5
ADCs	1.2	—	2.0	—	4.2	—	9.7	42.7
RRCs	0.3	—	1.6	—	2.7	—	1.1	3.9
China	—	—	—	—	—	—	—	—
Total	100.0	—	100.0	—	100.0	—	100.0	100.0

Source: UNCTAD trade data tape.

In only two countries, Hong Kong and China, is there a more than 5 percent decline in the U.S. export share between 1980 and 1984, when the dollar appreciated significantly. Indeed, the U.S. export share rose between these years in the Philippines, Singapore, and Malaysia. During the 1970s, however, when the dollar depreciated against the major currencies, the U.S. share of the export market increased in Korea, Taiwan, Thailand, Malaysia, Singapore, and the Philippines. Furthermore, in all of these countries the share of exports supplied by the United States was higher in 1984 than in 1970. In four countries, Thailand, Korea, the Philippines, and Taiwan, the U.S. competitive position worsened between 1963 and 1970. (Data are not available for these two years for China and Malaysia.)

Table 2.24 indicates the importance of developing countries of the APR as an export market for the United States. The shares of total U.S. exports going to the ADCs, the RRCs, and China all increased between 1968 and 1982, the combined share for all three rising from 6.5 percent in 1968 to 13.1 percent in 1982. If one adds Japan's share of U.S. exports to these figures, which increased between 1968 and 1982 from 8.5 percent to 9.9 percent, the combined exports of the United States to the major developing and developed countries of the APR constituted 15.0 percent of all U.S. exports in 1968 and 23.0 percent in 1982. There is no doubt that the Asian Pacific rim is becoming a major area of export interest to the United States.

Table 2.24   **Distribution of U.S. Exports to and Imports from Selected Regions, 1968, 1975, and 1982 (in percentages)**

| | All Goods | | | | | |
| | 1968 | | 1975 | | 1982 | |
	Exports	Imports	Exports	Imports	Exports	Imports
ADCs	3.7	3.4	4.6	5.7	7.1	9.3
RRCs	2.8	3.1	3.1	4.8	4.6	4.5
China	—	—	0.3	0.2	1.4	0.9
South Asia	3.1	1.2	2.0	0.7	1.1	0.7
European Community	27.0	25.7	23.5	18.0	24.2	17.8
Other Western Europe	4.6	4.2	3.6	3.1	3.4	3.2
Japan	8.5	12.6	8.8	12.0	9.9	15.8
Australia and New Zealand	2.9	1.4	2.1	1.4	2.6	1.2
Canada	23.5	26.8	20.1	22.5	15.4	18.8
Rest of world	23.9	21.6	31.9	31.6	30.3	27.8

Source: Trade data bank of author.

Table 2.25 examines the success in trade of the United States relative to its major competitors in the import markets of developing countries of the APR, not on an individual-country basis but in the ADCs and the RRCs, as groups of countries, and in China. The competitive record of the United States is shown to be a mixed one. The U.S. export share in the import market of the ADCs in the area remained at around 20 percent between 1963 and 1984, being 20 percent in 1963, 18 percent in 1970, and 21 percent in both 1980 and 1984, whereas its share of the goods exported by the major suppliers to the four RRCs dropped steadily from 24 percent in 1963 to 16 percent in 1984.[15] In contrast, after U.S. trade with China was opened, the U.S. share of the Chinese market rose to 27 percent by 1980, then declined to 18 percent in 1984. For the region as a whole, the trend in the U.S. export share was slightly upward, moving down from 21.6 percent in 1963 to 19.0 percent in 1970 but then rising to 23.5 percent in 1980 and remaining almost unchanged at 23.2 percent in 1984, despite the sharp appreciation of the dollar. The significance of this upward trend in export performance in the APR market can be appreciated by noting that the U.S. share in world exports declined between 1963 and 1984, falling from 14.6 percent in 1963 to 13.6 percent in 1970 and 11.0 percent in 1980 and then rising slightly to 11.2 percent in 1984.

The most successful competitor in the APR market was Japan. Its shares of total exports to the ADCs, the RRCs, and China from the countries listed in the first column of table 2.25 rose for all three between 1963 and 1984. By 1984, Japan was their largest supplier, supplying 30 percent of the ADCs' import market, 26 percent of the RRCs' import market, and 43 percent of China's imports from the countries listed. The main loser in competition for sales in these markets was the European Community; its export shares declined steadily in all three parts of the APR market over the twenty-one-year period.

An important change in the markets of developing countries that is only beginning to be appreciated (e.g., see Ahmad 1985) is that the more advanced developing countries are beginning to be important suppliers of manufactured goods to other developing countries. This is occurring in the APR market. As table 2.25 shows, the export share of the ADCs in their own import market increased from 8 percent in 1963 to 12 percent by 1984, while their export share in the RRCs' market rose from 1 percent to 10 percent between these years. The less industrially advanced RRCs did not participate in this trend, however; their shares to the ADCs and to other RRCs declined over the period.

Another aspect of the growing importance of the market for international goods in the developing countries of the APR is that total exports to these countries by the United States, Canada, Japan, Aus-

Table 2.25 Shares of the United States and Selected Foreign Competitors in Exports to APR Countries (in percentages)

	1963			1970			1980[a]			1984[a]		
	ADCs	RRCs	China	ADCs	RRCs	China	ADCs	RRCs	China	ADCs	RRCs	China
	Total Exports From All Row Countries											
U.S.	20	24	0	18	20	0	21	16	27	21	16	18
Canada	1	1	18	1	2	10	1	1	5	2	1	6
Japan	22	21	12	33	30	42	28	26	36	30	26	43
Australia and New Zealand	3	2	39	3	5	10	3	4	7	3	3	5
EC	17	20	29	14	22	39	12	14	19	11	13	17
ADCs[b]	8	23	1	10	15	2	12	30	4	12	35	10
RRCs[b]	29	9	0	21	7	2	23	8	3	11	4	1
China	0	0	—	0	0	—	0	0	—	10	2	—
	Natural Resource-Intensive Exports from All Row Countries[c]											
U.S.	21	22	0	20	27	0	20	13	52	23	13	28
Canada	1	3	26	1	2	28	2	3	12	4	3	20
Japan	7	7	2	13	13	9	8	7	7	10	6	11
Australia and New Zealand	6	3	55	5	9	27	5	10	15	9	8	19
EC	7	8	14	7	10	26	5	5	4	6	5	11
ADCs[b]	9	34	2	8	19	5	13	40	3	13	47	7
RRCs[b]	49	23	0	46	20	4	50	22	6	24	12	4
China	0	0	—	0	0	—	0	0	—	11	6	—

Labor-Intensive Exports from All Row Countries[c]

U.S.	11	20	0	0	13	0	7	7	22	5	7	6
Canada	0	0	0	0	0	0	0	1	0	0	1	0
Japan	49	33	35	53	37	40	42	23	47	31	24	37
Australia and New Zealand	1	0	0	1	1	0	1	1	1	1	1	0
EC	21	8	59	12	13	60	12	8	8	9	8	4
ADCs[b]	13	37	6	26	33	2	27	56	21	18	54	51
RRCs[b]	5	2	0	2	3	0	10	4	2	4	4	1
China	0	0	—	0	0	—	0	0	—	32	2	—

Technology-Intensive Exports from All Row Countries[c]

U.S.	23	30	0	24	20	0	27	22	15	25	20	22
Canada	1	0	0	0	2	0	1	1	1	1	1	1
Japan	35	23	32	43	34	56	39	32	50	40	32	44
Australia and New Zealand	1	1	0	1	2	0	1	1	0	1	1	0
EC	33	32	68	23	33	44	17	20	30	15	17	23
ADCs[b]	2	12	0	6	8	0	8	22	5	11	28	9
RRCs[b]	5	1	0	2	1	0	7	2	0	4	1	0
China	0	0	—	0	0	—	0	0	—	3	0	—

Table 2.25 (continued)

	1963			1970			1980[a]			1984[a]		
	ADCs	RRCs	China	ADCs	RRCs	China	ADCs	RRCs	China	ADCs	RRCs	China
Human-Capital-Intensive Exports from All Row Countries[c]												
U.S.	14	17	0	9	9	0	9	4	4	9	3	1
Canada	0	1	0	0	0	0	1	1	2	0	1	0
Japan	47	41	43	59	50	71	63	51	70	59	47	79
Australia and New Zealand	2	1	6	3	6	0	3	3	5	1	2	2
EC	26	24	51	16	18	29	13	11	17	16	13	15
ADCs[b]	4	16	0	9	16	0	8	28	1	7	32	2
RRCs[b]	7	1	0	3	1	0	3	2	1	2	1	0
China	0	0	—	0	0	—	0	0	—	4	1	—

Source: UNCTAD trade data tape.

Note: Figures represent shares of total exports of countries listed.

[a] Data for Taiwan are not included in the 1980 and 1984 figures since the United Nations no longer recognizes Taiwan as a separate country; therefore U.N. agencies no longer collect data on Taiwan.

[b] The shares of the ADCs and RRCs in their own regions measure trade within these regions.

[c] The commodity breakdown into goods that are natural-resource-intensive, unskilled-labor-intensive, technology-intensive, and human-capital-intensive is adapted from Krause 1982.

tralia, New Zealand, the European Community, as well as by the countries of the region to each other amounted to 2.97 percent of world exports in 1963, 3.56 percent in 1970, 4.74 percent in 1980, and 5.85 percent in 1984.

Changes in the commodity composition of U.S. exports to the ADCs, the RRCs, and China between 1968 and 1982 are indicated in the first part of table 2.26. The comparative advantage of the United States in agricultural products and high-technology goods is evident. As would be expected, agricultural imports are more important for the resource-scarce ADCs and China than for the RRCs. For both the ADCs and the RRCs, exports of machinery have grown significantly in relative importance over the period, from 21 percent for the ADCs in 1963 to 34 percent in 1982 and from 30 percent to 49 percent for the RRCs between these years. The relative decline in exports to China of machinery between 1975 and 1982 may reflect special circumstances. Another commodity class that gained somewhat in relative importance over the period is chemicals, whereas transportation equipment declined.

Further insight into which categories of goods the competitors in the APR market have been successful in exporting can be gained by utilizing Krause's (1982) breakdown of goods into four groups: natural-resource-intensive, unskilled-labor-intensive, technology-intensive, and human-capital-intensive. Table 2.25 divides the exports to the APR region of the United States and its competitors to the region into these four categories. As would be predicted under the factor-proportion theory of international trade, the commodity groups in which the United States has the largest market share are natural-resource-intensive and technology-intensive goods. In trade with the ADCs, the U.S. export share increased modestly over the 1963–84 period for both types of goods. For the RRCs, the U.S. export share declined for natural resource products—a not unexpected result—and also for technology-intensive products, though less than in the other product categories. U.S. performance in the import market of the APR countries declined, as expected, for labor-intensive products and also, rather surprisingly, for human-capital-intensive products. As table 2.27 indicates, the fastest growing category of exports to ADCs and RRCs was, except for the 1980–84 period, technology-intensive goods. The United States is in the fortunate position of specializing in commodities for which market demand is growing rapidly.

Another picture of the nature of the U.S. exports, utilizing the U.S. Department of Commerce (1976) breakdown of all goods into those that are technology-intensive and non-technology-intensive, is presented in table 2.28. The analytical framework behind this division emphasizes temporary differences among countries in developing and introducing new technological knowledge as the basis for differences

Table 2.26 Distribution of Major U.S. Exports to and Imports from APR Countries, 1968, 1975, and 1982 (in percentages)

SIC Industries	1968			1975			1982		
	ADCs	RRCs	China	ADCs	RRCs	China	ADCs	RRCs	China
Exports									
Agricultural-crops (1)	23	14	—	26	11	28	18	10	51
Food and kindred products (20)	9	13	—	7	2	0	5	3	1
Lumber and wood products (24)	1	0	—	0	0	0	1	0	7
Chemicals	8	8	—	7	12	2	10	11	22
Primary metal industries (33)	2	2	—	3	5	19	2	2	3
Fabricated metal products (34)	7	4	—	4	4	13	5	4	0
Machinery, exc. electrical (35)	13	24	—	16	29	30	18	22	5
Electrical and electronic machinery (36)	9	6	—	14	17	1	16	27	2
Transportation equipment (37)	13	13	—	10	9	1	7	9	1
All other products	15	16	—	13	11	6	18	22	8
Imports									
Agricultural-crops (1)	0	15	—	0	2	5	0	3	1

Industry									
Agricultural-livestock (2)	1	0	—	0	0	6	0	0	1
Forestry (8)	1	16	—	0	7	0	0	5	0
Oil and gas (13)	0	5	—	0	41	0	0	30	8
Food and kindred products (20)	4	27	—	4	17	4	1	7	5
Textile products (22)	10	1	—	8	1	22	3	1	10
Apparel (23)	26	3	—	24	3	7	22	6	28
Lumber and wood products (24)	10	6	—	5	2	3	2	2	3
Chemicals (28)	0	0	—	0	0	12	0	0	6
Petroleum products (29)	0	0	—	1	5	0	1	3	18
Rubber and misc. plastic products (30)	6	0	—	6	0	0	4	0	1
Leather and leather products (31)	2	0	—	3	0	1	10	1	3
Primary metal industries (33)	0	18	—	3	6	29	4	3	3
Electrical and electronic machinery (36)	16	0	0	23	10	1	23	30	1
Miscellaneous mfg. (39)	7	1	3	9	1	3	11	2	3
All other products	7	8	3	14	5	7	19	7	8

Source: Trade data bank of author.

Note: An industry is included if the export or import share of the industry is at least 5 percent in any region in any of the three years.

Table 2.27   Comparative Growth Rates by Factor-Intensity Breakdowns of
                  Exports to APR Countries, 1963–70, 1970–80, and 1980–84
                  (average annual growth rates in percentages)

	ADCs	RRCs	China
1963–1970			
Natural-resource-intensive	18.6	9.8	4.9
Unskilled-labor-intensive	35.2	4.8	17.3
Technology-intensive	36.8	18.3	45.1
Human-capital-intensive	27.7	17.9	15.6
1970–80			
Natural-resource-intensive	72.5	74.8	97.3
Unskilled-labor-intensive	37.9	43.3	168.3
Technology-intensive	91.6	82.7	107.0
Human-capital-intensive	76.5	62.0	56.6
1980–84			
Natural-resource-intensive	−1.3	−0.5	−5.7
Unskilled-labor-intensive	21.6	4.3	17.4
Technology-intensive	7.8	2.7	11.5
Human-capital-intensive	0.5	−2.2	12.7

Source: UNCTAD trade data tape.

Note: Exports are from the United States, Canada, Japan, Australia and New Zealand, the European community, the ADCs, the RRCs, and China.

among countries in the commodity composition of trade. Though not always explicit, the ability to create new technology and undertake innovation depends, in turn, on there being high levels of research and managerial skills. The table shows that over the 1968–82 period, the United States has shifted the composition of its exports to every country or region toward high-tech goods. Imports from every region have also moved in this direction, but the percentage by which technology-intensive exports to the world by the United States exceed technology-intensive imports was still about the same in 1982 as in 1968.

Consistent with the factor-proportion theory, table 2.25 shows that the main U.S. competitor in the APR, Japan, gained market-share position over the period in the ADCs, the RRCs, and China in technology-intensive and human-capital-intensive goods, while it lost in the labor-intensive category. The EC lost in every category between 1963 and 1984. In contrast, the ADCs gained in export shares within their own market in every category, registering an especially impressive gain in the high-technology group.

A technique developed by Hilton (1983) provides still another means of revealing the comparative cost position of the United States vis-à-vis the countries of the Asian Pacific rim. It involves regressing the ratio of U.S. exports to U.S. imports to a country by commodity on

Table 2.28   **Composition of U.S. Exports to and Imports from Selected Regions by Technology Intensity, 1968, 1975, and 1982 (in percentages)**

	1968		1975		1982	
	Exports	Imports	Exports	Imports	Exports	Imports
Technology-intensive goods						
ADCs	38	15	41	26	42	27
RRCs	24	0	40	25	52	54
China	—	—	86	94	47	96
South Asia	30	0	42	1	42	4
European Community	42	13	51	17	47	20
Japan	32	26	33	25	37	30
Australia and New Zealand	41	11	40	21	41	29
Canada	19	4	16	5	23	11
World	31	13	31	16	37	20
Non-technology-intensive goods						
ADCs	62	85	59	74	58	73
RRCs	76	100	60	75	48	46
China	—	—	86	94	47	96
South Asia	70	100	58	99	58	96
European Community	58	87	59	83	53	80
Japan	68	74	67	75	63	70
Australia and New Zealand	59	89	59	79	59	71
Canada	81	96	85	95	77	89
World	69	87	69	84	63	80

Source: Trade data bank of author.

the cost shares of capital, unskilled labor, skilled labor, land, and other natural resources in the individual commodities. The coefficients on the various factor shares are a measure of the differences in relative factor prices between the United States and the other country. If, for example, the coefficient on a particular factor is positive, this implies that the relative price of the factor is lower in the United States than in the other country. A negative sign means that the factor is relatively cheaper in the other country and, thus, that the other country has a comparative advantage in producing goods in which that factor constitutes a relatively large proportion of production costs.

The results of regressing bilateral export-import ratios for the United States and the countries of the APR for (in most cases) over two hundred commodities on a fivefold division of factor shares for these commodities are presented in table 2.29. For all the countries listed, the United States has a relative factor-price advantage in skilled labor and a disadvantage in unskilled labor. Furthermore, for all countries except Indonesia (and that coefficient is not significant at the 10 percent level or better), the United States has a comparative factor-price ad-

Table 2.29   **Estimated Order of Relative Factor-Price Differences between the United States and Selected Countries or Regions, 1978**

	Capital	Unskilled Labor	Skilled Labor	Land	Natural Resources	# Observations
Singapore	4.23	−3.50	4.81	−.96	−89.61	203
	(2.88)	(−2.97)	(3.11)	(−.22)	(−2.02)	
Hong Kong	4.39	−5.39	4.63	14.88	9.71	240
	(3.07)	(−5.02)	(3.12)	(3.47)	(.13)	
Taiwan	3.10	−9.40	6.99	10.74	121.80	240
	(2.07)	(−8.25)	(4.68)	(3.15)	(2.55)	
Korea	3.76	−8.52	7.63	4.05	116.26	236
	(2.42)	(−6.98)	(4.86)	(1.03)	(2.37)	
Malaysia	7.56	−6.36	4.44	−9.36	−128.82	139
	(2.92)	(−3.31)	(1.81)	(−1.70)	(−1.48)	
Thailand	2.49	−6.33	10.29	−4.34	14.50	157
	(1.19)	(−4.03)	(4.82)	(−.96)	(−.14)	
Phillippines	2.39	−5.36	10.03	−2.97	−.04	193
	(1.25)	(−3.71)	(4.78)	(−.61)	(.02)	
Indonesia	−.05	−4.92	13.27	−12.52	−201.86	109
	(−.02)	(−2.86)	(4.77)	(−2.75)	(−2.27)	
All	4.26	−6.81	5.67	8.45	−7.50	274
	(3.30)	(−6.55)	(4.07)	(2.64)	(−.18)	
ASEAN	3.35	−4.30	6.69	−5.51	−92.68	242
	(2.26)	(−3.68)	(4.26)	(−1.36)	(−2.00)	
China	.47	−6.45	10.84	5.45	−183.90	89
	(.11)	(−1.96)	(2.82)	(.89)	(−1.22)	
Japan	5.42	−4.12	−1.92	18.29	130.50	281
	(4.57)	(−4.30)	(−1.51)	(6.04)	(3.18)	

Source: Trade data bank of author.

Note: The t-statistic is in parentheses under each coefficient. A t-statistic of 1.67 is significant at 10 percent.

vantage in physical capital. As expected, the United States has a comparative advantage in land-intensive and natural-resource-intensive products vis-à-vis Hong Kong, Taiwan, and Korea. The land coefficient has the wrong (but not significant) sign for Singapore, while the negative sign on the natural resource coefficient reflects Singapore exports of refined petroleum.

The four resource-rich countries, Malaysia, Thailand, the Philippines, and Indonesia, all have a factor-price advantage in both land and natural resources relative to the United States. The U.S. trade pattern with Japan reveals that the United States has a relative factor-price advantage in natural resources, land, and capital and a disadvantage in unskilled labor. Interestingly, though not quite significant at the 10 percent level, the coefficient on skilled labor indicates that Japan has a comparative price advantage in this factor, too.

2.5 Export Performance of the Developing Countries of the APR

Although this paper is primarily concerned with the performance of the United States and its competitors in the APR market, data have also been collected on the performance of the developing countries of the region in the markets of the United States, Canada, Japan, Australia and New Zealand, the European Community, and in the region itself. Analysis of the trade of the individual countries in section 2.3 revealed that every country except the Philippines shipped a larger proportion of its exports to the United States at the end of the period covered (usually 1984) than in the beginning (usually 1963). In most cases the increase was very significant. In contrast, the share of exports from Korea, Taiwan, the Philippines, and Thailand to Japan declined over the period, while the export shares from Hong Kong and Malaysia to Japan remained unchanged. Only the export shares of Indonesia and Singapore to Japan rose. The share of exports taken by the EC declined for Malaysia, Indonesia, and Hong Kong, remained about the same for Singapore, Taiwan, and the Philippines, and increased for Korea and Thailand.

In value terms, the ADCs had a very large trade surplus with the United States in 1984, with exports of $23.1 billion and imports of only $16.7 billion. In contrast, the RRCs' exports to and imports from the United States in 1984 both equaled $5.7 billion.

The relative position of the APR countries as sources of imports for the United States is given in table 2.24. The developing countries of the region supplied 6.5 percent of all U.S. imports in 1968, 10.7 percent in 1968, and 14.7 percent in 1982. The share of the ADCs in these figures rose from 53 percent in 1975 to 63 percent in 1982. Adding Japan's import share to the shares of the developing countries brings the figures to 19.1 percent, 22.7 percent, and 30.5 percent, respectively, in the three years. However, as table 2.30 indicates, although the developing countries of the APR (excluding China) significantly increased their share of total exports directed to the United States between 1963 and 1970, this proportion decreased slightly between 1970 and 1984.

The U.S. export share to the developing countries of the APR rose 6.5 percentage points between 1968 and 1982, while the U.S. import share from these countries increased 8.2 percentage points. The U.S. export share to Japan rose 1.2 percentage points, and the U.S. import share from Japan rose 3.2 percentage points in the same period.

The most important category of imports into the United States from the ADCs and China is textiles and apparel (table 2.26). The proportion that these goods make up of total U.S. imports from the ADCs is declining, but textiles and apparel have become more important in U.S. imports from China. Oil and gas was the main import from the RRCs

Table 2.30   Distribution of Total Exports of APR Countries to the United States and Other Selected Countries and Regions, 1963, 1970, 1980, and 1984 (in percentages)

	1963			1970		
	ADCs	RRCs	China	ADCs	RRCs	China
United States	18.5	19.0	—	37.0	17.9	—
Canada	1.7	0.8	—	2.8	0.7	—
Japan	11.2	20.9	—	11.9	25.0	—
Australia and New Zealand	3.8	1.1	—	2.8	1.7	—
EC	23.8	18.9	—	18.2	14.6	—
ADCs	12.3	31.6	—	15.1	33.8	—
RRCs	28.1	7.2	—	11.3	5.5	—
China	0.3	0.0	—	0.5	0.4	—
Total	100.0	100.0		100.0	100.0	

	1980			1984		
	ADCs	RRCs	China	ADCs	RRCs	China
United States	24.6	16.4	—	34.4	18.7	12.1
Canada	1.7	0.3	—	2.4	0.4	1.3
Japan	10.5	31.8	—	10.9	36.8	26.9
Australia and New Zealand	3.7	1.6	—	2.8	2.0	1.3
EC	18.9	12.3	—	13.4	8.4	11.5
ADCs	16.7	31.0	—	14.2	27.9	42.7
RRCs	22.1	5.6	—	19.2	4.9	3.9
Total	100.0	100.0		100.0	100.0	100.0

Source: UNCTAD trade data tape.

in the early part of the period covered, but by 1982 the 30 percent share for this category was matched by a 30 percent share for imports of electrical and electronic machinery. Electrical and electronic products are also an important category of imports from the ADCs.

The change in composition of U.S. imports from the APR developing countries toward more complex products such as electrical and electronic machinery is also apparent from table 2.28, which divides all imports into technology-intensive and non-technology-intensive goods. As this table indicates, imports from all the countries or regions listed are becoming more technology-intensive.

2.6 Direct Investment in the APR Countries

Achieving a market position abroad by means of direct foreign investment, in addition to exporting goods, has become an increasingly important element in corporate strategy over the last twenty-five years. Table 2.31 indicates the extent to which U.S. and Japanese companies

Table 2.31   Outstanding Direct Investment, 1980 (millions of dollars)

Country of Investment	Investment by United States	Investment by Japan
Japan	6,274	—
United States	—	8,878
South Korea	587	1,137
Taiwan	510	370
Hong Kong	1,969	1,095
Indonesia	1,334	4,424
Malaysia	618	650
Philippines	1,244	615
Singapore	1,196	936
Thailand	360	396
ASEAN: Subtotal	4,752	7,021
ADME[a] Subtotal	7,818	9,623
World Total	213,460	36,497

Source: Patrick, 1983.
[a]Advanced developing market economies.

have pursued this strategy in the APR countries. Although total Japanese direct investment in the ADCs and RRCs combined is nearly $2 billion more than U.S. investment, American investment in the ADCs is greater than Japan's, $4.2 billion versus $3.5 billion. In view of Japan's lack of natural resources, it is to be expected that Japanese direct investment in the RRCs is greater. Japanese investment in oil-rich Indonesia alone amounted to 46 percent of its total investment in the region. Korea and Hong Kong were Japan's next most important direct investment markets. Hong Kong, followed by Indonesia and the Philippines, was the most important U.S. investment market in the area.

Tables 2.32–2.35 provide additional information on U.S. direct investment. Tables 2.32 and 2.33 indicate the share of total U.S. direct investment received by individual APR countries and industries in these countries. U.S. direct investment in the APR is a small but rapidly growing proportion of total U.S. direct investment, with the share of total U.S. direct investment rising from 3.6 percent in 1977 to 6.7 percent in 1984. The shares in each country except the Philippines increased between these years. The most important APR countries for U.S. foreign direct investment in 1977 (and, as seen from table 2.31, also in 1980) were, in order of relative importance, Hong Kong, Indonesia, and the Philippines; in 1984 the rank order was Indonesia, Hong Kong, and the Philippines/Malaysia.

U.S. investment in the region is focused more on the primary and service sectors than on manufacturing, which absorbed only 3.6 percent of total U.S. manufacturing investment abroad in 1984, whereas the

Table 2.32   Country Shares of All U.S. Foreign Direct Investment in an
Industry, 1977 (percentage)

Country	All Industries	Mining	Petr.	Total Mfg.	Food	Chem.	Prim. Metal Fab.	Mach. exc. Elect. Eqpt.	Elect. Eqpt.
Indonesia	0.7	a	2.6	0.2	0.0	0.3	a	b	0.2
Malaysia	0.3	0.1	a	0.1	0.1	0.1	0.0	0.0	0.8
Philippines	0.6	b	1.0	0.5	1.8	0.7	0.3	0.0	0.6
Singapore	0.4	0.0	0.8	0.2	0.1	0.0	0.6	0.1	0.8
Thailand	0.2	0.1	a	0.1	0.2	0.1	0.0	0.0	0.2
Korea	0.3	0.0	a	0.3	0.1	0.8	0.0	a	0.3
Taiwan	0.2	0.0	0.1	0.3	0.2	0.4	0.0	0.0	1.6
Hong Kong	0.9	0.0	1.0	0.3	0.1	0.4	a	0.1	1.1

	Transp. Eqpt.	Other Mfg.	Trade	Bank- ing	Finance exc. Banking	Other Industries
Indonesia	b	a	0.1	0.2	0.0	a
Malaysia	b	0.1	a	0.2	0.0	0.2
Philippines	a	a	0.5	2.1	0.1	0.7
Singapore	0.0	0.1	0.4	1.1	0.1	0.5
Thailand	b	0.1	a	0.6	0.0	0.1
Korea	a	0.0	a	0.4	0.1	0.1
Taiwan	0.1	0.1	0.1	0.8	0.0	0.0
Hong Kong	b	a	2.2	3.0	0.8	2.5

Source: U.S. Department of Commerce, 1981.
aSuppressed to avoid disclosure of data on individual companies.
bIndicates an amount between-$500,000 and + $500,000.

shares were 8.7 percent for petroleum, 10.7 percent for banking, 6.4
percent for trade, and 4.7 percent for banking. Indonesia and Malaysia
were the major countries in which petroleum investments were undertaken. Hong Kong, Singapore, and the Philippines were important
as host countries for U.S. investment in service activities.

Table 2.34 and 2.35 show the industry distribution of U.S. direct
investment in each country in 1977 and 1984. Except for Indonesia,
there has been a relative shift away from investment in primary-product
sectors and toward manufacturing and/or service activities. In Korea
and Taiwan the relative importance of U.S. manufacturing investment
declined between 1977 and 1984, perhaps reflecting their advancing
industrialization. The share of investment in manufacturing increased
significantly in Malaysia and Singapore and remained about the same
in Hong Kong and the Philippines. Service activities investment increased in relative terms in Korea, Hong Kong, and the Philippines.

Table 2.33   **Country Shares of All U.S. Foreign Direct Investment in an Industry, 1984 (percentage)**

Country	All Industries	Mining	Petr.	Total Mfg.	Food	Chem.	Prim. Metal Fab.	Mach. exc. Elect. Eqpt.	Elect. Eqpt.
Indonesia	1.9	a	6.1	0.2	0.1	0.2	a	0.0	0.3
Malaysia	0.5	0.0	1.1	0.4	a	0.1	0.1	a	3.1
Philippines	0.5	0.0	a	0.5	1.1	0.8	0.4	0.0	a
Singapore	1.0	0.0	0.8	1.1	a	0.5	1.2	a	5.2
Thailand	0.4	0.2	a	a	0.0	0.2	a	0.0	a
Korea	0.4	0.0	a	0.2	0.5	0.0	a	a	1.0
Taiwan	0.4	0.0	0.2	0.5	0.2	0.6	a	a	1.8
Hong Kong	1.6	0.0	0.5	0.7	0.2	0.7	0.9	a	2.0

Country	Transp. Eqpt.	Other Mfg.	Trade	Banking	Finance exc. Banking	Other Industries
Indonesia	0.0	a	0.2	0.2	0.0	a
Malaysia	a	0.2	0.3	0.1	a	a
Philippines	a	a	0.2	2.0	a	a
Singapore	a	a	1.0	1.6	0.5	0.8
Thailand	a	a	0.2	0.4	0.0	a
Korea	0.3	0.1	0.4	1.6	a	a
Taiwan	0.2	a	0.4	0.9	0.0	0.1
Hong Kong	0.0	a	3.7	3.9	4.2	4.7

Source: U.S. Department of Commerce 1981.

aSuppressed to avoid disclosure of data on individual companies.

2.7 Conclusion

A number of conclusions can be drawn from this analysis of the economic performance of the United States and its competitors in the developing countries of the Asian Pacific rim, defined to include Singapore, Hong Kong, Taiwan, Korea, the Philippines, Malaysia, Thailand, Indonesia, and China. First, and perhaps most important, is that the APR is a rapidly growing, though still small, international market for goods and services and foreign direct investment. Exports to the countries of the region by their major trading partners, defined as the United States, Canada, Japan, the European community, Australia and New Zealand, and the APR countries themselves, amounted to 3.0 percent of total world exports in 1963 and 5.8 percent in 1984. The share of total U.S. exports going to the APR has risen from 6.5 percent in 1968 to 13.1 percent in 1982. If Japan's share of U.S. exports is added to these figures, the share of U.S. exports taken by the devel-

Table 2.34   **Industry Distribution of a Country's Total Direct Investment from the United States, 1977 (percentage)**

Country	Mining	Petr.	Total Mfg.	Food	Chem.	Prim. Metal	Mach. exc. Elect. Eqpt.	Elect. Eqpt.
Indonesia	0.9	74.8	9.9	0.2	3.0	a	0.0	1.3
Malaysia	0.0	a	18.5	0.6	3.2	0.4	0.9	9.9
Philippines	0.0	32.6	37.9	11.9	10.5	1.7	0.1	4.1
Singapore	0.0	45.0	20.5	1.0	0.6	5.4	2.9	8.7
Thailand	2.5	a	21.5	3.8	3.8	1.7	0.0	4.6
Korea	0.0	a	41.5	2.0	22.8	0.3	a	4.3
Taiwan	0.0	6.2	68.7	3.5	19.7	0.4	1.2	34.0
Hong Kong	0.0	20.4	15.1	0.4	3.8	a	1.2	4.4

	Transp. Eqpt.	Other Mfg.	Trade	Bank-ing	Finance exc. Banking	Other Indus-tries
Indonesia	0.0	a	0.9	0.8	0.5	a
Malaysia	a	3.2	a	1.7	0.4	3.0
Philippines	a	a	9.1	11.1	3.1	6.2
Singapore	0.2	1.7	14.5	9.5	3.5	7.2
Thailand	0.0	7.6	a	11.4	2.5	3.4
Korea	a	1.3	a	4.3	2.8	2.3
Taiwan	2.7	6.9	8.5	13.9	1.9	0.8
Hong Kong	0.0	a	28.2	10.0	12.3	13.9

Source: U.S. Department of Commerce 1981.

aSuppressed to avoid disclosure of data on individual companies.

oped and developing countries of the APR increased from 15.0 percent in 1968 to 23.0 percent in 1982.

The United States has performed quite well in competing with the other major trading partners (defined as in the preceding paragraph) of the APR countries. The U.S. export share of this market rose from 21.6 percent in 1963 to 23.5 percent in 1980 and remained at 23.2 percent in 1984, despite the appreciation of the dollar relative to the currencies of Japan, the countries of the European Community, and other U.S. competitors in the region after 1980. Within the region, the U.S. gained slightly in market share in the markets of the ADCs (defined as Hong Kong, Korea, Taiwan, and Singapore), moving from 20 percent in 1963 to 21 percent in 1984, but lost in the RRCs (defined as the Philippines, Malaysia, Thailand, and Indonesia), falling from a 24 percent share in 1963 to a 16 percent share in 1984. In the Chinese market the United States had no market position in 1963, but by 1984 the U.S. share of China's imports from its major trading partners was 18 percent.

Table 2.35   **Industry Distribution of a Country's Total Direct Investment from the United States, 1984 (percentage)**

Country	Mining	Petr.	Total Mfg.	Food	Chem.	Prim. Metal Fab.	Mach. exc. Elec. Eqpt.	Elec. Eqpt.
Indonesia	[a]	88.3	3.4	0.3	0.9	[a]	0.0	0.6
Malaysia	0.2	62.4	32.1	[a]	2.5	0.8	[a]	23.2
Philippines	0.0	[a]	37.4	8.8	15.0	1.9	0.4	[a]
Singapore	0.0	24.0	45.4	[a]	4.3	3.4	[a]	20.4
Thailand	1.1	[a]	[a]	0.2	4.8	[a]	0.0	[a]
Korea	0.0	[a]	25.6	5.7	1.1	[a]	[a]	10.2
Taiwan	0.0	12.8	56.0	1.9	15.6	0.0	[a]	19.9
Hong Kong	0.0	9.2	16.6	0.5	3.8	1.4	[a]	4.7

Country	Transp. Eqpt.	Other Mfg.	Trade	Banking	Finance exc. Banking	Other Industries
Indonesia	0.0	[a]	1.2	0.7	0.2	[a]
Malaysia	[a]	3.6	8.3	1.6	[a]	[a]
Philippines	[a]	[a]	4.6	22.0	[a]	[a]
Singapore	[a]	[a]	13.7	9.4	3.2	4.3
Thailand	0.0	[a]	7.9	5.7	0.2	[a]
Korea	3.5	2.6	13.2	26.1	[a]	[a]
Taiwan	3.1	[a]	14.5	13.8	0.7	2.2
Hong Kong	0.0	[a]	30.0	13.5	15.7	15.1

Source: Survey of Current Business, August 1985, p. 36.
[a]Suppressed to avoid disclosure of data on individual companies.

The major competitor of the United States in the region is Japan. In 1984 Japan's share of the ADCs' market was 30 percent compared to the U.S. share of 21 percent, and the Japanese share of the RRCs' market was 26 percent compared to the U.S. share of 16 percent in that year. Japan supplied 43 percent of China's imports from its major trading partners in 1984, whereas the United States supplied only 18 percent.

Japan has also been the most successful competitor over the period in terms of gains in market shares. In 1963, for example, the U.S. and Japanese shares of imports into the ADCs and RRCs from their main trading partners were about the same, whereas, as noted above, the 1984 Japanese market shares exceeded the U.S. shares by about ten percentage points. The biggest loser in the competition for market shares has been the European Community. The EC's shares of the market for foreign goods in the ADCs and RRCs were only slightly below those of Japan and the United States in 1963, but they are now below the ADCs as supplier to the ADCs themselves and to the RRCs.

The rapid growth in the market shares achieved by the ADCs is one of the most important developments in the area. These countries are beginning to supply an increasing proportion of the market for manufactured goods in the APR. China, too, is now taking an appreciable part of this market.

The various methods used to reveal the comparative advantage position of the United States in the region indicate, as would be predicted from the factor-proportion theory of international trade, that the United States has a competitive advantage in commodities utilizing relatively large capital and skilled-labor factor shares. Furthermore, in the resource-scarce ADCs, the United States has a comparative advantage in land-intensive and other natural-resources-intensive commodities. The United States tends to be at a disadvantage in producing labor-intensive goods in the entire market and in providing land-intensive and natural-resource-intensive goods in the RRCs.

One observes the results of these basic factor conditions in the commodity composition of U.S. exports to the region. They tend to be concentrated in natural resource-intensive goods such as agricultural products and in technology-intensive goods, which, in turn, require a relatively high supply of professional and managerial skills to market successfully. Furthermore, the United States is competing most successfully against its export rivals in the APR market in high-technology products and, to some extent, natural-resource-intensive commodities. One would expect this pattern to continue, though it must be recognized that not only Japan but the ADCs and RRCs are shifting into the high-tech area. The United States must continually upgrade its level of high-tech products to maintain its market positions in the APR market as well as in other world markets.

Market opportunities for the United States depend on economic and political conditions in the countries of the region as well as on U.S. competitive abilities. It appears that the existing ADC governments will continue to pursue export-oriented economic policies. However, there is some political uncertainty stemming from outside pressures in Hong Kong and Taiwan, and from both outside and inside pressures in Korea. It is conceivable but unlikely that these pressures could bring governmental changes that reduce market opportunities in these countries. Even with the present governments in Korea and Taiwan, there is a need for the United States to apply pressures for the removal of various import barriers.

There is considerable political uncertainty in another important market for U.S. goods, the Philippines. One would expect economic policies to continue as they have, with alternate cycles of liberalization and control, resulting in a moderate rate of growth. But, there is also the possibility of a political shift resulting not only in more inward-looking economic policies but in the loss of U.S. military bases in the country. Indonesia is another country where there are strong political interests favoring import-substitution rather than export-promotion policies. Unlike the ADCs, resource-rich countries like Indonesia and the Philippines are not forced to promote exports of manufactures in order to produce a politically acceptable growth rate. Thailand and Malaysia are not only rich in resources but have adopted policies to utilize their abundant supplies of unskilled labor in producing manufactured goods for the export trade. They should continue to do well, but like the other countries must be pressured to open their own markets to a greater extent.

While this paper has been mainly concerned with the export opportunities of the United States and others in the APR market, data has also been collected on the performance of the APR countries in world export market. The picture that emerges is a familiar one. The developing countries of the APR have sent an increasing share of their exports to the United States, in many cases a significantly larger share. In 1984, U.S. trade with the RRCs was roughly in balance, but the United States bought $6 billion of goods from the ADCs than those countries purchased from the United States. The shares of exports sent to Japan by the APR countries have generally declined or, in a few cases, remained about the same. For the EC the share changes are mixed—some rising, some staying the same, and others declining.

Textiles and apparel are the most important category of imports from the ADCs and China, but products requiring higher skills, in particular, electrical machinery and electronic products, are becoming more significant. For the RRCs, oil and gas dominated their pattern of exports to the United States, but in recent years electrical and electronic products have challenged these products as the most important export category. Clearly, the APR countries are increasing the degree of complexity of their export product mix.

The 1980 volume of direct investment by the United States was greater in the ADCs than was Japan's, but Japanese direct investment in the entire region was greater than that by the United States. The United States is, however, increasingly enlarging its share of its total investment in the region, though this share is still quite small. It grew from 3.6 percent in 1977 to 6.7 percent in 1984. Oil and service activities, such as banking and trade, are the sectors in which direct investment in the APR countries takes the largest share of world investment in an industry. Services and manufacturing are the sectors in which investment in the developing countries of the Asian Pacific rim is growing most rapidly.

Notes

1. In this paper, APR will refer only to the developed countries of the Asian Pacific rim; Japan is not included.
2. The high proportion of primary product exports for Singapore reflects the large imports of crude petroleum and reexports of refined petroleum products.
3. Hong Kong's rate of population increase is relatively high because of immigration.
4. The account of Hong Kong's trade and development policies is based on Lin and Mok 1985; Chen 1984; Lin and Ho 1981; and Cooper 1986.
5. The account of Singapore's trade and development policies is based on Yue 1980 and 1986; Wong 1981; Roberts 1985; and Cooper 1986.
6. The account of Korea's trade and development policies is based on Frank 1975; Nam 1981; Hong 1977; Balassa 1986; and Cooper 1986.
7. The account of Taiwan's trade and development policies is based on Liang and Liang 1981; Kuo and Fei 1986; Ranis and Schive 1986; Balassa 1981; and Cooper 1986.
8. The account of the Philippines' trade and development policies is based on Bautista 1980; Baldwin 1975; Alburo and Shepherd 1986; and Niksch 1986.
9. Philippines export data for 1984 are not yet on the UNCTAD trade data tape.
10. The account of Malaysia's trade and development policies is based on Ariff 1980; Lim 1984; and Niksch 1986.
11. There are no export figures yet on the UNCTAD trade data tape for 1984.
12. The account of Thailand's trade and development policies is based on Akrasanee 1977 and 1980; World Bank 1980; Adjanant 1984; and Niksch 1986.
13. The account of Indonesia's trade and development policies is based on Rosendale 1977; Anwar 1980; World Bank 1981; and Pitt 1985.
14. The account of China's trade and development policies is based on Hardt and Boone 1986, and Ahearn 1986.
15. In interpreting the percentages in the table, note that the 1980 and 1984 figures do not include trade data on Taiwan.

References

Ahearn, Raymond J. 1986. Asian-Pacific economic development: The long-term historical perspective (1960–present). In *Economic changes in the Asian Pacific rim: Policy prospectus*. Washington, D.C.: Congressional Research Service.

Ahmad, Jaleel. 1985. South-south trade in manufactures: Implications for the north. Paper presented at the conference International Trade and Exchange Rates in the Late Eighties, Facultés Universitaires Notre-Dame de la Paix, Namur, Belgium. June.

Ajanant, Juanjai. 1984. Trade patterns and trends of Thailand. Paper presented at the conference Global Implications of the Trade Patterns of East and Southeast Asia, Kuala Lumpur. January.

Akrasanee, Narongchai. 1977. Industrialization and trade policies and employment effects in Thailand. In Narongchai Akrasanee, Seiji Naya, and Vinyr Vichit-Vadakan, eds., *Trade and Employment in Asia and the Pacific*. Manila: Council for Asian Manpower Studies.

———. 1980. Economic development of Thailand and ASEAN economic cooperation, with special reference to commodity problems. In Ross Garnaut, ed., *ASEAN in a changing Pacific and world economy*. Canberra: Australian National University Press.

Alburo, Florian, and Geoffrey Shepherd. 1986. Trade liberatlization: The Philippine Experience. Draft study prepared for a World Bank research project.

Anwar, M. Arsjad. 1980. Trade strategies and industrial development in Indonesia. In Ross Garnaut, ed., *ASEAN in a changing Pacific and world economy*. Canberra: Australian National University Press.

Ariff, Mohamed. 1980. Malaysia's trade and industrialization strategy: With special reference to ASEAN Industrial Cooperation. In Ross Garnaut, ed., *ASEAN in a changing Pacific and world economy*. Canberra: Australian National University Press.

Balassa, Bela. 1981. *The newly industrializing countries in the world economy*. New York: Pergamon Press.

———. 1986. The role of foreign trade in the economic development of Korea. In Walter Galenson, ed., *Foreign trade and investment: Economic development in the newly industralizing Asian countries*. Madison: University of Wisconsin Press.

Baldwin, Robert E. 1975. *Foreign trade regimes and economic development: The Philippines*. New York: National Bureau of Economic Research.

Bautista, Romero M. 1980. Trade strategies and industrial development in the Philippines: With special reference to Regional trade. In Ross Garnaut, ed., *ASEAN in a changing Pacific and world economy*. Canberra: Australian National University Press.

Beals, Ralph E. 1984. Trade patterns and trends of Indonesia. Paper presented at the conference Global Implications of the Trade Patterns of East and Southeast Asia, Kuala Lumpur. January.

Chen, Edward K. Y. 1984. Hong Kong's trade patterns and trends. Paper presented at the conference Global Implications of the Trade Patterns of East and Southeast Asia, Kuala Lumpur. January.

Cooper, William H. 1986. Export-led development: The East Asian NICs. In *Economic changes in the Asian Pacific rim: Policy prospectus*. Washington, D.C.: Congressional Research Service.

Frank, Charles R., Jr. 1975. Foreign trade regimes and economic development: Republic of Korea. In *Trade strategies for economic development: The Asian experience*. Manila: Asian Development Bank.

Hardt, John P., and Jean Boone. 1986. PRC modernization and openness: A new LDC and socialist model for the Pacific. In *Economic changes in the Asian Pacific rim: Policy prospectus*. Washington, D.C.: Congressional Research Service.

Hilton, R. Spence. 1983. Commodity trade and relative returns to factors of production. *Journal of International Economics* (16): 259–70.

Hong, Wontack. 1977. Trade and employment in Korea. In Narongchai Akrasanee, Seiji Naya, and Vinyr Vichit-Vadakan, eds., *Trade and employment in Asia and the Pacific*. Manila: Council for Asian Manpower Studies.

Hong, Wontack, and Lawrence B. Krause, eds. 1981. *Trade and growth of the advanced developing countries in the Pacific basin*. Seoul: Korean Development Institute.

Krause, Lawrence B. 1982. *U.S. economic policy toward the Association of Southeast Asian Nations: Meeting the Japanese challenge*. Washington, D.C.: Brookings Institution.

Kuo, Shirley W., and John C. H. Fei. 1986. Causes and roles of export expansion in the Republic of China. In Walter Galenson, ed., *Foreign trade* and investment: Economic development in the newly industrializing Asian countries. Madison: University of Wisconsin Press.

Liang, Kuo-shu, and Ching-ing H. Liang. 1981. Trade strategy and exchange-rate policies in Taiwan. In Wontack Hong and Lawrence B. Krause, eds., Trade and growth of the advanced developing countries in the Pacific basin. Seoul: Korean Development Institute.

Lim, Chee-peng. 1984. Changes in the Malaysian economy and trade trends and prospects. Paper presented at the conference Global Implications of the Trade Patterns of East and Southeast Asia, Kuala Lumpur. January.

Lin, Tzong-biau, and Victor Mok. 1985. Trade, foreign investment, and development in Hong Kong. In Walter Galenson, ed., Foreign trade and investment: Economic development in the newly industralizing Asian countries. Madison: University of Wisconsin Press.

Lin, Izong-biau, and Yin-ping Ho. 1981. Export-oriented growth and industrial diversification in Hong Kong. In Wontack Hong and Lawrence B. Krause, eds., Trade and growth of the advanced developing countries in the Pacific basin. Seoul: Korea Development Institute.

Nam, Chong-hyun. 1981. Trade, industrial policies, and the structure of protection in Korea. In Wonack Hong and Lawrence B. Krause, eds., Trade and growth of the advanced developing countries in the Pacific basin. Seoul: Korean Development Institute.

Naya, Seiji. 1986. Trade and investment opportunities in the NICs and ASEAN countries and the role of the United States. Presented at a Symposium on U.S. Pacific Relations, Joint Economic Committee of the U.S. Congress, Washington, D.C. December.

Niksch, Larry A. 1986. Indonesia, Malaysia, the Philippines, and Thailand. In Economic changes in the Asian Pacific rim: Policy prospectus. Washington, D.C.: Congressional Research Service.

Patrick, Hugh. 1983. The Asian developing market economies: How they have affected and been affected by the United States–Japan economic relationship. Paper presented at the conference United States, Japan, and Southeast Asia: Issues of Interdependence. December.

Pitt, Mark M. 1985. The timing and sequencing of a trade liberalization policy: Indonesia. Draft study prepared for World Bank research project.

Ranis, Gustav, and Chi Schive. 1986. Direct foreign investment in Taiwan's development. In Walter Galenson, ed., Foreign trade and investment: Economic development in the newly industrializing Asian countries. Madison: University of Wisconsin Press.

Roberts, Bee-yan. 1985. The timing and sequencing of a trade liberalization policy: The case of Singapore. Draft study prepared for World Bank research project.

Rosendale, Phillis. 1977. Trade and employment in Indonesia. In Narongchai Akrasanee, Seiji Naya, and Vinyr Vichit-Vadakan, eds., Trade and employment in Asia and the Pacific. Manila: Council for Asian Manpower Studies.

U.S. Department of Commerce. Office of Economic Research. 1976. Alternative measurements of technology-intensive trade. Staff Economics Report. OER/ER-17. September.

———. 1981. U.S. direct investment abroad, 1977. Washington, D.C. April.

Wong, Kum-poh. 1981. The financing of trade and development in the ADCs: The experience of Singapore. In Wontack Hong and Lawrence B. Krause, eds., Trade and growth of the advanced developing countries in the Pacific basin. Seoul: Korean Development Institute.

World Bank. 1980. *Thailand: Industrial Development Strategy in Thailand.* Washington, D.C.: World Bank.

————. 1981. *Indonesia: Selected issues of industrial development and trade strategy.* Washington, D.C.: World Bank.

Yue, Chia-siow. 1980. Singapore's trade and development strategy, and ASEAN economic co-operation, with special reference to the ASEAN common approach fo foreign economic relations. In Ross Garnaut, ed., *ASEAN in a changing Pacific and world economy.* Canberra: Australian National University Press.

————. 1986. The role of foreign trade and investment in the development of Singapore. In Walter Galenson, ed., *Foreign trade and investment: Economic development in the newly industrializing Asian countries.* Madison: University of Wisconsin Press.

2. Robert S. Ingersoll
East Asia and the U.S. Economy

In 1974 when I served as assistant secretary of state for East Asian and Pacific affairs, Henry Kissinger, recently installed as secretary of state, directed our bureau to draft a policy statement for our region. All of us realized immediately that this would be difficult because the countries we covered were so diverse. In our region there was no straightforward Communist/non-Communist rivalry, no cohesive structure like the EEC, no major isue that wove its way through all the nations of the region.

East Asia is still very diverse. Today, Japan is a world economic power and a power unto itself in the region. China, along with several other nations of the region, is still economically backward. The so-called newly industrializing countries—Hong Kong, Taiwan, Singapore, South Korea—have exhibited some of the fastest growth rates in the world. While China manages its economy through central planning, Japan employs market competition and government-business co-operation. Hong Kong's approach is almost laissez-faire.

Today, when I consider our economic relations with this diverse set of countries, I feel compelled to start not with a description of East Asia, but with a statement of the policy needs of the United States. First, year after year we have been suffering huge, utterly unacceptable trade deficits. Last year our overall deficit amounted to an unprecedented $170 billion, and 57 percent of that was with East Asia. This is a problem we have to solve, and the nations that are part of the problem are inevitably going to be affected. We want them to contribute to the solution.

Second, we are a major industrial power in an age of technological diffusion. Nations throughout the world are absorbing industrial know-how, and they are innovating. As a natural result, some of our industries are simply no longer competitive, and our economy is going through a wrenching adjustment. East Asia is a major cause for this adjustment. It is a source of products we love to buy, but at the same time it is a focus of resentment, especially among Americans whose jobs have moved to the region.

Deficits and resentment both lend themselves to protectionism, but this supposed remedy would only delay the inevitable for our uncompetitive industries and needlessly burden our competitive ones. Our economic policy in East Asia should be to support the multilateral framework of GATT and encourage the countries of the region to open their markets wide to foreign goods and foreign investment. We will not achieve our objectives without judicious pressure, and the United States—the chief market for these countries—will have to make clear that the alternative to GATT is a regime of ad hoc agreements on less than desirable terms.

Definition and Description of the Region

I view East Asia from a perspective acquired at the State Department, where East Asia and the Pacific are seen as one region. When I speak of East Asia or cite statistics for East Asia, I include, in addition to the nations already mentioned, Australia, Burma, Indonesia, Malaysia, New Zealand, the Philippines, Thailand, and the islands of the Pacific. I exclude the Soviet Union, Cambodia, Laos, North Korea, Outer Mongolia, and Vietnam—nations whose political and economic relations with the United States are severely circumscribed. Let me take a moment to describe the main features of the region.

Altogether, East Asia comprises about one-third of the world's population, compared to the 5 percent share of the United States. Total output of the region is around 13 percent to 15 percent of world GNP, compared to the roughly 23 percent to 25 percent share of the United States.

Japan has by far the largest economy in East Asia. With only one-thirteenth of the region's population, it produces an overwhelming 70 percent of the region's output. China, with two-thirds of East Asia's population, produces only 9 percent of the region's output. This nevertheless makes China the second largest economy in the region. Australia ranks third, South Korea Fourth, Indonesia fifth, and Taiwan sixth.

In terms of per capita income, Japan leads the major nations of the region at about $16,000 per year, according to data for 1986 (table 2.36). That figure was fairly close to U.S. per capita income of over $17,000

Table 2.36   **Population, Gross National Product, and Per Capita Income of East Asia, 1986**

	Population (000)	GNP/GDP (billion US$)	Per Capita GNP/GDP (US$)
Australia	15,900	164	10,275
Burma	39,300	9	220
China	1,056,000	252	239
Hong Kong	5,500	37	6,740
Indonesia	166,700	78	468
Japan	121,500	1,960	16,150
South Korea	41,600	94	2,371
Malaysia	16,000	26	1,620
New Zealand	3,300	31	9,300
Philippines	55,700	30	500
Singapore	2,590	18	7,025
Taiwan	19,400	73	3,748
Thailand	52,300	41	785
East Asia	1,595,790	2,813	1,762
Asian NICs	69,090	222	3,213
USA	241,900	4,207	17,390

Source: U.S. Department of State.

Note: Asia's newly industrializing countries (NICs) are Hong Kong, South Korea, Singapore, and Taiwan.

last year. Down the scale in East Asia is Australia, at about $10,000 per year. Thereafter comes New Zealand at about $9,000 and Singapore and Hong Kong, both around $7,000 per year. Far lower are Burma, with per capita income of about $220 per year, and China, at about $240 per year. Not surprisingly, many of the poorest countries are those in which the labor force is engaged primarily in agriculture.

East Asia has been the scene of some of the most remarkable stories in the history of economic development. Postwar Japan grew at breathtaking rates until the 1970s, and it has continued to grow impressively, despite oil shocks and its now advanced stage of development. Today Japan builds on a tremendous base. Its 4 percent average growth rate in the 1980s is more than the equivalent of adding a new Taiwan to the world's economy each year.

The newly industrializing countries, or NICs, began registering high rates of growth in the early 1970s, and generally they have continued to grow even in the difficult world economy of the 1980s. Recently, however, Singapore and Hong Kong have slowed considerably, although Taiwan and South Korea continue to move ahead.

The less developed countries of the region have grown fairly impressively since the early 1970s—6 percent to 7 percent annually in Indonesia, Malaysia, and Thailand, for example. But in the last two years, growth has slowed in most less developed countries, even registering zero or negative in Indonesia, Malaysia, and the troubled Philippines. GNP is still rising in China, however.

Exports have been a driving force behind much of the pace-setting growth in East Asia. As a consequence, the economies that have grown fastest are now highly dependent on exports, particularly exports to the United States (table 2.37). Taiwan, for example, exports over one-half of GNP, of which 53 percent goes to the United States. South Korea exports over one-third of GNP, of which 40 percent goes to the United States. Japan, having a more developed domestic economy, exports about one-tenth of GNP, of which 42 percent goes to the United States. Thus, the NICs and Japan depend heavily on exports, and they also depend heavily on the continued openness of the U.S. market. This means that we have considerable bargaining power in our relations with them.

Investment Issues

What problems does the United States face in its economic relations with this diverse and dynamic region? For the most part, frictions in our relations with East Asia can be divided into investment problems and trade problems. Where investment is concerned, Japan and the United States are by far the two dominant players in the region. U.S. direct investment in East Asia is $33 billion, which constitutes 14 percent of all U.S. investment abroad (table 2.38).

Of the $33 billion that the United States has invested in East Asia, only $9 billion is invested in Japan (table 2.39). This is a very low level,

Table 2.37   Export Dependence of East Asian Nations, 1986

	Exports as Percent of GNP	U.S. Share of Total Exports
Australia	13.6%	12.9%
Burma	5.4	3.3
China	11.1	18.6
Hong Kong	85.6	29.6
Indonesia	16.9	27.8
Japan	10.5	41.5
South Korea	36.0	39.8
Malaysia	55.1	17.8
New Zealand	19.0	18.9
Philippines	16.2	44.8
Singapore	122.5	21.9
Taiwan	54.9	53.4
Thailand	21.3	21.4

Source: Calculated from U.S. State Department data.

Table 2.38   **Composition of U.S. Direct Investment in East Asia, 1985**

	$ Millions	% Share
Petroleum	9,993[a]	30.6
Manufacturing	11,102	34.0
Wholesale trade	4,632	14.2
Banking	1,752[a]	5.4
Finance, insurance, real estate		
(excluding banking)	2,375	7.3
Services	565[a]	1.7
Other industries	1,824	5.6
Total	32,616	

Source: Calculated from *Survey of Current Business,* August 1986, table 15, p. 49.
[a]Figure is at least this amount. Disclosure limitations for individual countries prevent publication of exact amount.

given the size of the Japanese economy. In fact, the level of all foreign investment in Japan—U.S. and otherwise—is very low compared to the levels in other advanced nations of the world. This situation is a legacy of the strict laws against foreign investment that Japan maintained during much of the postwar period. These laws have been rescinded, but the government still retains broad administrative powers to reject investments that might endanger national security, damage existing Japanese businesses, or adversely affect the government's ability to guide the national economy.

Table 2.39   **Composition of U.S. Direct Investment in Japan, 1985**

	$ Millions	% Share
Petroleum	2,178	23.9
Manufacturing	4,621	49.7
Food and kindred products	127	1.4
Chemicals	1,244	13.7
Primary and fab. metals	50	0.5
Nonelectrical machinery	1,620	17.8
Electrical equipment	337	3.7
Transportation equipment	578	6.4
Other manufacturing	665	7.3
Wholesale trade	1,442	15.9
Banking	177	1.9
Finance, insurance, real		
estate (excluding banking)	519	5.7
Services	74	0.8
Other industries	83	0.9
Total	9,095	

Source: *Survey of Current Business,* August 1986, table 15, p. 49.

This means that many potential investors still face regulation. Usually this regulation follows the standard Japanese practice of private consultation between Japanese officials and Japanese companies in the potential investor's industry, often with the intention of maintaining "orderly markets" and preventing "excessive competition." While entrants to expanding markets may face few difficulties, entrants to mature or declining markets are likely to deal with Japanese officials who are under great pressure to obstruct the investment.

South Korea, perhaps following Japan's example, has maintained tight control over foreign investment. In recent years it has instituted new, more liberal guidelines, but the power of entrenched special interests is strong and the attitudes of many Koreans remain autarkic. The People's Republic of China partially opened to foreign investment in 1979, but procedures there are bureaucratic, foreign exchange is difficult to obtain, and control over local personnel is often limited. Potential investors face similar difficulties in many other countries of East Asia.

U.S. policymakers should recognize that fears of foreign economic domination on the part of the less developed nations of East Asia are legitimate, but at the same time they should strive to convince these nations to open their economies to the technology, jobs, and managerial skills that flow from foreign investment.

From Japan and the NICs, on the other hand, we should accept no excuses for restricting foreign investment. Japan is itself the world's greatest net holder of assets abroad. Apart from only the clearest reasons of national defense, Japan has no grounds for hindering foreign investment. And the NICs have advanced well beyond the point where they can justify restricting investment by claiming the vulnerability of a less developed economy.

Trade Issues

Greater freedom of investment is vital, but clearly the biggest issue in our relations with East Asia is trade. Last year we sold goods worth $59 billion to the region and purchased goods worth $155 billion from the region. We exported industrial machinery, high-technology goods such as aircraft and computers, and agricultural products and processed resource-based commodities such as aluminum and lumber. We imported a wide array of consumer goods and industrial products.

The United States' number one trading partner in the region is Japan. Last year the total value of United States–Japan trade—that is, the value of exports plus imports—was $112 billion. This constituted over half of total U.S. trade with the region. United States–Taiwan trade ranked second at $26 billion or 12 percent of total United States–East Asia trade. The volume of our Taiwan trade was over three times the volume of our trade with the People's Republic of China, despite the expansion of United States–China trade in recent years.

United States–East Asia trade is complementary—each party improves its welfare by importing goods that can be produced more cheaply abroad than at home. However, the net flow of goods has grown tremendously out of balance (fig. 2.1). In 1970 the U.S. deficit with the region was slightly less than $2 billion. In 1980 it was $18 billion. In 1985 it was $80 billion, and last year it reached $96 billion. With only two nations of the region—Australia and Brunei—did the United States run surpluses last year. Fifty-nine billion dollars of our trade deficit was with Japan, which sold over three times more goods to the United States than it bought from the United States. Sixteen billion dollars of our deficit was with Taiwan, which sold over four times more goods to the United States than it bought from the United States.

The United States' trade deficit with East Asia is clearly a problem of major proportions, and it should be acknowledged at the outset that U.S. economic policy is partly to blame. The need to fund staggering budget deficits has propped up dollar interest rates and consequently the dollar itself. An overvalued dollar has made imports attractive and has hampered the ability of U.S. industry to export. This has caused the United States to run record-high deficits with almost all of its trading partners, not just with East Asian countries (table 2.40).

Recently the value of the dollar has gone through a year-long fall, and the latest trade data suggest that the trade deficit may finally be declining. However, changing exchange rates will not eradicate the

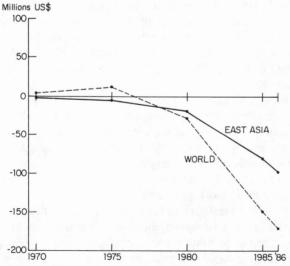

Fig. 2.1   U.S. Trade balance with East Asia and the world, 1970–86.

Table 2.40   U.S. Trade Balance with East Asia, 1986

	U.S. Surplus (deficit) (millions US$)	Percentage of Total U.S. Deficit
Australia	2,380	—
Brunei	137	—
Burma	(2)	0.0
China	(2,135)	1.3
Hong Kong	(6,444)	3.8
Indonesia	(2,757)	1.6
Japan	(58,837)	34.7
South Korea	(7,588)	4.5
Malaysia	(807)	0.5
New Zealand	(224)	0.1
Philippines	(805)	0.5
Singapore	(1,519)	0.9
Taiwan	(16,069)	9.5
Thailand	(1,018)	0.6
East Asia	(96,022)	56.6
Asian NICs	(31,619)	18.6
Western Europe	(33,583)	19.8
Latin America	(13,227)	7.8
World	(169,777)	—

Source: U.S. Department of State.

Note: Asia's newly industrializing countries (NICs) are Hong Kong, South Korea, Singapore, and Taiwan.

deficit—at least not soon. While the dollar has fallen about 40 percent against the Japanese yen over the past year, it has dropped less dramatically against the currencies of many other trading partners, particularly other East Asian trading partners (table 2.41). Even more important, a major component of the deficit problem is restrictions on the access of U.S. goods to many East Asian markets, and this situation is changing slowly.

Japan, for example, is a notoriously hard market for U.S. companies to crack. Although tariffs are low, domestic competition is keen, language is a nettlesome obstacle, and not least of all, many Japanese businessmen prefer the certainty of dealing with other Japanese to the uncertainty of dealing with foreigners. Japan should not be faulted for these barriers. They are facts of economic life in Japan, and our companies simply must work to overcome them.

However, there are barriers for which Japan should be faulted. For example, the Japanese government targets industries for growth. These industries receive, in addition to subsidies, a veil of official and unofficial protection against threatening foreign competition. This can

Table 2.41   **Japanese Yen/U.S. Dollar Exchange Rate Yearly Average, 1970-86**

Year	Rate
1970	358.15
1971	348.03
1972	303.11
1973	271.31
1974	291.90
1975	296.75
1976	296.48
1977	268.37
1978	210.40
1979	219.18
1980	226.53
1981	220.41
1982	249.05
1983	237.45
1984	237.58
1985	238.47
1986	168.50

lead to unending frustration for foreign companies that try to sell to Japan, even when they enjoy clear competitive advantages.

Barriers in Japan were once overt, legal, systematic, and pervasive. This is no longer the case. However, the protectionist orientation of the nation's early postwar period lives on in the minds of the business and governmental bureaucrats who administer, regulate, and purchase in Japan today. Certainly, Japan has carried out an extensive program of trade liberalization, and for this it deserves credit. In fact, Americans have probably been slow to grasp the changes. Clearly, our companies have not taken full advantage of the new access to Japanese markets. Nevertheless, Japan is still not as open as it ought to be, especially in view of the benefits it derives from the free trade policies of other nations.

What is most unfortunate about this situation, though, is that Japan is a model for other East Asian nations. Its constant reluctance to liberalize—indeed, almost never to concede except under pressure—is not going unobserved by other nations in the region. Perhaps with Japan in mind, perhaps not, these other nations are collaborating with local businesses to nurture infant industries until they are strong enough to compete on world markets. Sometimes this policy works. Sometimes it does not. When it does work, the result is trade friction. When it does not, the protectionist nation ends up, first, denying itself the benefits of foreign investment and second, creating hothouse industries that can survive only through protection and subsidy.

This is especially true for the smaller nations of the region. Their domestic markets are not big enough to do what Japan has done, that is, grow domestic industries to a scale sufficient to compete in international markets. When they try and fail, the result is misallocation of resources and harm to the national welfare.

Structural Adjustment

Trade is a tremendous problem in East Asia, but to properly understand it we should view it in the context of history. For a brief period after World War II, devastation in Europe and Asia gave the United States world superiority in industrial technology. So decided was this dominance that we produced more than 60 percent of the world's manufactures in the late 1940s. The revival of the industrial economies of Europe and Japan has eroded our share of world manufactures and exports.

Today we are witnessing the extension of industrial technology beyond Europe and Japan to regions of the world that were not industralized prior to World War II. In East Asia, the NICs are assimilating industrial technology at a ravenous pace. Eventually China will follow the same path, though it is still very far behind, building on a relatively small economic and educational base. As industrial technology continues to diffuse, East Asian economies will continue to shift the scales of comparative advantage in the world.

This will cause major changes in the United States. Heretofore, the United States has, both before and after its temporary postwar dominance, exported goods that are long on engineering and short on unskilled labor. We have imported goods that are short on eingineering and long on unskilled labor. The traditional sources of our comparative advantage have been our high level of technical education and our experience organizing for production. These are now being challenged by the nations of East Asia.

This need not harm us. Some of our industries will move offshore, but some will stay here and prosper. The real challenge to us is the challenge of adjustment. If we protect our industries, we will do no more than create uncompetitive subsidy-sustained cripples that will siphon resources from true job-creating enterprises. Instead we must retrain the workers in our uncompetitive industries. This is not a simple task, because education in the United States has fallen to the point where many of our workers today are not able to read, write, and calculate well enough to make retraining practical.

We must, of course, make every effort to increase our access to East Asian markets, whenever justified, so that our industries that are world competitive can achieve their full potential. Greater access to East Asian markets would also deflect U.S. domestic political pressure for protectionism. It is vital that we gain the access we deserve, and we should use our leverage with export-dependent NICs and Japan to ensure that we get it.

Conclusion: GATT or a Less Desirable Alternative

How do we translate this into policy? First, we should be careful not to throw our weight around until we have put our own house in order. We should cut our huge budget deficit and establish meaningful programs to retrain displaced workers. Also, we have to work harder to export to East Asia, rather than rely on our own domestic market as we have so much in the past. Once we have embarked on these tasks, however, we should carry out an active East Asian economic policy based on the premise that free trade under GATT is best for all nations of the region. This approach, with due safeguards for the economic independence of the less developed nations, clearly provides the best framework for balanced, equitable economic growth within the region.

However, not all nations will perceive their interests in this fashion. Some for reasons of ideology, others due to excessive nationalism, and still others because they misinterpret Japan's economic development will attempt to gain the benefits of GATT without meeting its obligations. For these nations a carrot and stick are called for. We should offer them a choice between GATT and tough bilateral agreements that restrict their exports to the United States, if necessary. The so-called voluntary restraint agreements are an example.

These are not tools we should want to use. They are protectionist measures, and they violate the multilateral spirit of GATT. When we use them we should recognize that we are courting the danger that they will cause world trade to degenerate into a melange of minor trading systems, each protectionist vis-à-vis the others. But this is a risk we must take when other nations follow policies that hinder the ability of our own industries to do what they do best.

This sounds threatening, perhaps, but it is based on the positive premise that free trade serves us better than protectionism. We know that tremendous structural adjustments are on the horizon for American industry. If we forget about protecting dying industries and instead devote ourselves to educating and retraining our people, we will continue to maintain our sources of comparative advantage. Then our own standard of living will increase along with the standard of living of the peoples of East Asia, as they and we increase our productivity.

3. Woo-choong Kim
The Era of Pacific Coprosperity

Many people think of Asia when the word *Pacific* is mentioned, but the Pacific is actually a huge area that includes North, Central, and South America, and Oceania, as well as the Far East and Southeast Asia.

This vast area includes nations highly divergent in history, culture, language, and stages of economic development, so it is easier to pinpoint differences rather than similarities among these many nations. Consequently, I focus on those nations where political, cultural, and economic considerations are closely interrelated, and where Western and Oriental civilizations come together, namely, the United States, Korea, Japan, and China.

Recent Changes in the Pacific Theater

The world has focused greater attention in recent years on the Pacific Theater. In recent decades, nations in the Pacific Theater have shown the largest and most consistent growth in trade volume and GNP in the world, accompanied by correspondingly rapid changes in their economic and social structures. These nations have quickly emerged as new markets and new competitors in the international economy.

This area of the world has most dramatically demonstrated the superiority of capitalism over communism, an ideology that had been dazzling many people in the region for a long time. In recent months, even the Soviet Union, the Eastern bloc nations, and China have been paying greater attention to the benefits of the capitalist system. In particular, the Asian NICs, by taking resolute steps for increased trade and the international division of labor, have aptly demonstrated the importance of free trade in promoting economic welfare and political stability.

For a variety of reasons, American interest in the Asian Pacific has developed rapidly in recent years. But we can look to World War II for the seeds of this interest. The role of the United States in the Pacific during the war was obvious, but it was in the postwar period that America had the opportunity to spread the development of democratic and capitalistic ideologies to highly different cultures and distant regions. Through national defense and foreign aid programs, the United States began to exert increased influence, while at the same time developing more interest in the Pacific at home.

As ties increased, so did trade. One result has been that the trade volume with the Pacific totaled $116.5 billion in 1985, some $20 billion larger than total American trade with the Atlantic for that year.

With the birth of a new international economic order influenced by the Asian Pacific, the United States has been required to make important changes in its trade and industrial structures. This has focused greater attention on the western Pacific as well. Competition by these nations with the United States on the global market has vastly increased.

Japan's targeting-industry strategy has been highly effective. And the NICs, mainly in the Asian Pacific, mass-produce and export low-cost, reasonable-quality products to world markets. This is made possible through their relatively low labor costs and use of newer equipment and improved medium-level technology. As a result, the American industrial structure is changing rapidly.

Also, we observe the gradual migration of population and industry from the northeastern United States to the South and West. As a result, the United States is looking increasingly more to neighbors to its west. Consequently, we see an increasing number of Americans with a more accurate understanding of Oriental society.

Rapid progress in shipping, transportation, and communications has led to tremendous increases in both material and human movement in the Pacific region. Also, the presence of American troops in many nations and the influx of large numbers of Asian students, military personnel, and civilians to the United States have resulted in adaptation of Western concepts and models of managerial strategies, the spread of Western production technology, and the promotion of cultural exchange.

One major result has been the rapid development of a production basis for multinational companies. This, in turn, has resulted in the proliferation of reasonably priced, quality industrial products for both domestic and world markets. But at the same time, a number of important questions have arisen concerning managerial strategies for such multinational companies.

For example, each of these big companies, competing with fewer domestic firms, has to develop strategies to become the lowest-cost producer in the international market. Or the companies are forced to induce flexible manufacturing systems which are, at this stage, rather unstable in the ever-changing international economic climate. And there is the important question of sharing profit margins between the home office and overseas operations. Furthermore, in addition to adapting to each host nation's policies and regulations, such firms must develop a total global strategy to encompass production, finance, personnel, and other facts of international operations. All of this becomes exceedingly complex.

Rapid technological development has also arisen as a major concern for all. Until recent decades, technological development has largely been centered in the United States and Europe. But Japan and the NICs have been rapidly expanding their technological development capabilities, and the technological gap with the United States continues to narrow. This means even greater and more diverse international competition in the years ahead. But the full impact of the importance of this issue is not yet clear.

With increased world and American attention on the Pacific, we are seeing greatly activated study on comparative culture. These efforts are aimed at defining the best that both East and West have to offer in terms of social and cultural development.

Considerable interest is now being shown in the merging of cultural differences. Western experts are showing marked interest in traditional Asian culture for the social and moral cohesion it provides. In the Pacific and particularly in East Asia we are seeing successful industrial development based on the gradual amalgamation and digestion of traditional Asian thought with Western concepts of practicality and individualism. Until now, much of Asia has been preoccupied with idealistic value and suppression of individualism for the common good through organizational control.

In contrast, Western industrialized society is based largely on contract, law, and the quest for individual profits. But with increased economic and cultural cooperation, the time has come for the West to realize the importance of restraint on short-term individual interest for the common good as found in Asian mentality. Acceptance of this notion should result in a strategic design that should affect not only short-term effectiveness in managing organizations, but also long-term motivations for improving interrelationships among different interest groups with different experiences or cultures.

The contrasts between East and West are interesting enough, but the merger of these two distinct approaches to life is proving to be even more so.

The Future of the Pacific Theater

It is safe to say that the Pacific region will continue with rapid economic growth, and we will see continued growth in terms of quality as well as quantity. Growth of the past, based mostly on extended trade, will become supplemented by increased technological improvements and advances. The nations mentioned should be increasing their role in becoming main suppliers of technology to the world in years to come. At the same time, their economic prosperity, good work ethics, and habitual frugality should bring continued increases in domestic savings, which in turn will make these nations future suppliers of capital to the rest of the world.

We can also expect a continued rise in the prominence of multinational conglomerates. They will become more realistic in adapting to ever-changing situations and more efficient in setting up global strategies, through increased experience and through harmonizing Eastern and Western cultures. This will, of course, result in expanded economic development as well.

Politically, through weakening support for the Communist system, we will see greatly reduced tensions between East and West, with the previous "ideological war" being replaced by détente and "ideological amalgamation." The Pacific region will also serve as evidence that democracy is possible even in Oriental countries, where no great respect for democracy has existed in their long history.

We can find many reasons to be optimistic about continued economic development for the Pacific Theater. One is the prospect for future markets. A full two-thirds of the world's population is in Asia, and much of this market is yet to be tapped.

Additionally, we can be optimistic about resources. China, ASEAN countries, the United States, and Australia have huge deposits of untapped natural resources which can be put to use over an extended period of time. They have human resources as well: There is plenty of manpower. People work hard, and there are relatively high levels of education in many nations in the region. And as China and India become more liberalized and open, we can expect increased practicalism and better utilization of both natural and human resources in the region.

Economic barriers to trade are also expected to lessen. This will be attributed to continued technological developments in shipping, transportation, and communications, wider use of information systems, and general trends toward international cooperation on all levels.

The current rigorous exchange of culture is developing a worldwide sympathy never experienced before. International understanding, as a result, should promote such a global consciousness even further and restrain unnecessary international frictions. However, a favorable environment cannot be the only factor in determining the future. A more important factor would be who will do what, and how.

We have seen history being made by people, especially by leaders of each era. Consequently, to see into and understand the future of the Pacific Theater, we should look to projected leading nations and ask about their approach to solving the problems before us.

Expected American Responses to the Pacific Era

Considering all regional aspects, we expect both the United States and Japan to maintain their positions as leaders in the region, sort of the locomotives pulling the train; the other nations will follow as manufacturers and suppliers to the world market. This is the reality. Therefore, it is useful for us to speculate on what would be the American response to the emerging Pacific era. Some of these responses and strategies may contribute considerably to further promotion of Pacific coprosperity, while others may be harmful even to America itself.

On the bright side, many Americans are proud that the United States is the international leader in all aspects and believe in her ability to accommodate to ever-changing situations and to compete with any nation in the world. I personally agree with this view. And I am happy to see that Americans have already started to heighten international competitiveness through greater fusion of economic and social issues. These movements of curing social incompetence include attempts to reduce the drug problem and to increase sociopsychological education for workers, to improve productivity at various levels, and to revitalize entrepreneurial culture and technical manpower—pursuing advanced technologies.

On the other hand, for political reasons, we may see increasing American protectionism, which had been the exclusive right of less developed countries. Current sectional or regional interests may easily become too influential on a national level. We may see American consumers begin to outspend themselves. And the extreme convergence of brains upon such careers as lawyer and investment banker may result in even lower productivity in the manufacturing industry in general.

America is now faced with some difficult economic situations. These situations may easily induce ordinary people to seek easy, short-term solutions rather than difficult, long-term, yet highly effective solutions for lasting prosperity. These situations are not unlike those that other nations are facing.

New Attitude for a New Era

Neither protectionism nor currency depreciation can be a valid recipe for this situation. No one will benefit from these measures. Only productivity increase itself can serve as a means of solving current and future problems intrinsically.

To promote this new era of coprosperity in the Pacific, all nations involved must develop new attitudes that will drive out the temptation for short-term and one-sided profits and that could bring long-term, mutual benefit for international society. In this sense, I ask you to reconfirm the belief in free trade. The new round of GATT talks is a necessary and urgent step in this direction.

Second, by restricting such movements as isolationism or new nationalism, we minimize the risk of making political issues of economic problems.

In the arena of international trade, some Americans have often asserted that the uncompetitiveness of American goods is due mainly to "unfair" trade practice by Japan and the NICs. We often hear about "manipulated" or "assaulting" industrial policies and "unfairly managed" exchange rate systems of other governments. But those people may not clearly perceive the total picture. In Japan and other NICs, people really work hard. They save as much as possible. They study foreign markets as much as their own domestic markets. Americans should be aware that the leaders and people of recently prospering countries have been ready to sacrifice their own short-term interest for their common good and better competitiveness. American pioneers did the same things, with the spirit of challenge, when they built this great society. The present situation may be different from the past in some ways, but the solution seems to be the same.

Also, fairness in all aspects of international cooperation must be stressed. For being fair in the long run, leader nations should bestow short-term favors to follower nations for their own, as well as for everyone's, long-term interests. History tells us that, in a solid society, leaders are willing to sacrifice their own interests for the long-term prosperity of the whole of society. Ultimately, followers are expected to accomplish their roles by learning from leaders.

Pacific Economic Community: An Example

I know this is not the time for vague ideas and soft rhetoric. It is the time to implement idealistic values with practical, concrete programs without further delay. Therefore, I propose a kind of "Pacific economic community" to create reliable and fruitful ways for the everlasting expansion of trade and coprosperity within the region.

Too many economic theories tell us the advantages of the free trade system, which we can never give up. But history tells us that no nation seeks a free trade policy without confidence in its ability to compete, without heartful needs for complementarity, and without deep trust in its trading partners. To satisfy these conditions we should have a synthetic agreement covering the forward directions each country should go into and the time schedule every government must keep in mind. Let me give an example.

Because we are aware that trade cannot be a zero-sum game, we need to prepare not ceaseless piecemeal negotiations but an omnibus plan that provides us with the steps to correct in a short time the ill-balanced balance of payment problems.

To resolve current problems with some nations' balance of payments, each government involved should draft a list of products that it would buy and that it could produce more economically than other nations. The products and related industrial policies should be adjusted gradually and with forward strategy by an intergovernmental committee considering balance of payment situations and industrial capabilities of each country. This would help make long-term planning by governments more reasonable and guide private companies to invest, produce, and market with higher confidence in the future international business environment.

At the same time, a new principle on a new international division of labor would have to be established; this would prevent any one nation from completely monopolizing any one industrial sector. In principle, the United States could concentrate on innovative technology, capital investment, and venture business, while Japan could make use of commercialization of technology development and capital investment. Korea and China would offer plenty of diligent manpower with acceptable levels of education and great willingness to learn from more advanced nations. Of course, formation of a research team backed up by every government would bring us more concrete programs.

In promoting further inter-Pacific cooperation, the leader nations could provide greater capital and technical support for the development of large deposits of natural resources in China and the ASEAN countries, while aiming at greater industrial development in these areas. The leader nations should keep in mind that an eternally poor nation can never be their market and that it is in their own interests to help bring nations out of poverty.

Essential to the success of the new system would be not only the willingness of all nations to establish valid systems for the efficient use of abundant resources, but also the determination to sacrifice short-term, sectional, and unilateral self-interest as well as the wisdom to develop more concrete programs to implement politically.

Since it is hard for any nation to sacrifice its own interests, even if they are sectional or regional, there is little chance of developing a common-benefit system without great efforts. So the development of a Pacific economic community requires decisive political action and determination to convince people that such a community would benefit all.

We are confronted with a difficult and historically important assignment which should be done without failure. The time has come for ideas and theories on such an economic community to be implemented for true coprosperity. Wishful thinking and vague ideas never build a better tomorrow. We all have a moral and historical responsibility to forge ahead into that better tomorrow through action and cooperation today.

Summary of Discussion

Woo-choong Kim noted that Hyundai had sold only about seven cars to Japan and remarked that it is difficult to market to Japan, suggesting that the Japanese should open their economy more. If they did so, he predicted, within five years Korea would have a favorable trade balance with Japan. Korea will produce parts and import the facilities from the United States and Europe. If the Japanese do not use Korean parts, they will not be able to compete.

Kim proposed that many people underestimate American competitiveness. Most American companies, he thought, have increased their competitiveness. He has some doubts, however, about whether American workers can work hard enough. Another concern is the brain drain in the United States into law and investment banking, both of which hurt industry. Furthermore, Americans overemphasize high technology to the detriment of medium technology. Americans must develop a consensus to support the country, not just themselves. Service industries are not sufficient in their own right. Financial markets, for example, follow the underlying industrial base; the Japanese are fast becoming financial powers because of their underlying strength.

Korea has succeeded because it has a new generation of leaders who graduated from school after independence. The country has a wonderful work force of educated, hardworking people. Koreans are ready to sacrifice, to work hard as a duty.

Korea's exchange rate is not necessarily undervalued. There remains $43 billion in debt. Furthermore the country faces the North and has to buy defense hardware, as well as satellites and other goods unavailable at home.

By 1990 or 1991, American trade will be in balance, Kim continued. In any case, Korea is not the problem since it is taking the Japanese or European share of the American market. The Japanese price six months to one year ahead, so they take time to adapt to the currency fall. They will soon start having problems.

The focus of the discussion shifted to the restrictive trade policies of Japan, Korea, and the other newly industralized countries. Robert Baldwin pointed out that we cannot attribute the U.S. trade deficit to the trade policy of Japan and the NICs because they were always closed while the trade deficit is only five years old; instead he emphasized macroeconomic factors and the budget deficit. He also argued that a nonmarket means of allocating production between countries would be politically unfeasible and economically inefficient.

Baldwin contended that reducing the large amount of protection in these countries should nonetheless be pursued. They will open up, he predicted, and when they do we will all benefit; recent economic history teaches that a liberal trade policy leads to rapid growth. The question is how to achieve this openness. Baldwin argued that bilateral pressure, a new phenomenon, is quite effective, partly since small countries get a free ride in GATT. For this approach to work, retaliation must be a possible recourse, and the voluntary export restraint is too much against GATT to be the weapon of choice. Rather, Baldwin prefers antidumping and countervailing duties as part of well-defined fair trade laws.

One participant said that in 1987 Korea was almost 94 percent free to imports, and he predicted close to 100 percent opening of the market by 1990. Koreans are willing to open to the United States in light of its growing trade deficit problems with Korea and other countries, but there is general apprehension that a broad opening up of the market might end up benefiting only countries like Japan, more so than the United States. So the problem is with countries that have no trade deficit problems; because they would attack a more open market aggressively, the Americans and Koreans should arrange for mutually profitable trade between themselves. The problem, he contended, is that U.S. companies think domestically, while exporting to Asia requires a more international perspective. Most Korean leaders, for example, have been educated in the United States.

Saburo Okita agreed with one aspect of the discussion, that inter-Asian trade is too small, amounting to something like 15 percent of Asian trade, while trade with the United States is 40 percent of the total. In Europe, by contrast, intraregional trade is 50 percent of the total while trade with the United States is 10 percent. Thus one way to reduce pressure on U.S. markets is to open markets to Asians.

Robert Ingersoll and Woo-choong Kim agreed, but both emphasized the need for mutual opening. Ingersoll suggested that the Japanese should take some responsibility in this area and should be the first Asian country to open up.

3

Our LDC Debts

1. Rudiger Dornbusch
2. Thomas S. Johnson
3. Anne O. Krueger

1. Rudiger Dornbusch

The United States has a major stake in the world debt problem because it affects the profitability and even the stability of our banking system. But it also matters because debt service requires trade surpluses for debtors. We are now experiencing the reverse side of the coin from collecting debt: debtor countries, having made their goods extra competitive, are selling in our market and are competing with our exports. The debt problem is therefore a part, though perhaps a small part, of the U.S. trade crisis. Finally, we have a major foreign policy stake in the debt crisis because debt collection brings about social and political instability.

This paper reviews these various aspects of the debt problem. Section 3.1 sets out debt facts, followed in section 3.2 with a brief look at the origins of the debt problem. That issue is important in laying the groundwork for solutions that involve sharing the adjustment. The "transfer problem" in section 3.3 is the general framework in which we discuss the problem of debt service for the debtor countries. Section 3.4 deals with bank exposure and the quality of less developed countries' (LDCs) debts. The U.S. trade implications of the debt crisis are briefly addressed in section 3.5. The paper concludes with an overview of alternative proposals for solving the debt problem.

3.1 Debt Facts

In this section I provide an overview of debt facts: in the aggregate and in country detail who owes whom how much, with what maturity, and in which currency.[1]

161

3.1.1   An Overview

Table 3.1 shows aggregate debt data for selected years both in current and constant dollars. There is a problem in finding a suitable deflator for the world economy. Possible candidates are the U.S. GNP deflator, or either import or export prices for LDCs. I select instead the price (export unit value) of industrial countries' exports as a broader price index of trends in the world economy. World trade prices since 1980 have declined and even in 1986 are below their 1980 level. Accordingly, this index behaves very differently from, for example, the U.S. deflator, which has been steadily increasing.

Since 1978, LDC debt has increased by 142 percent in nominal terms and 88 percent in real terms. In these aggregate data we observe the slowdown of debt growth since 1982 and the effect of changing trends in world prices with inflation in the early period and deflation since 1980.[2]

A second perspective is provided by looking at debt relative to some scale variables. The most common scale variables are exports of goods and services and GDP. Table 3.2 shows debt relative to GDP.

The most interesting point made by this data is that differences, at least at this aggregate level, are minor. Latin America is normally singled out as *the* problem case. But on a debt-income basis, non-oil Middle East countries stand out as carrying an even larger burden. The other point to note is the deterioration in debt ratios since 1982. This is surprising when one sees banks today rationing credit. The explanation lies primarily in the fact that GDP in U.S. dollars has declined for most debtor countries as a result of large real depreciation.[3]

There is another interesting presentation of debt-income ratios in singling out different groupings of countries. Interestingly small, low-income countries have a higher debt-GDP ratio (64.0 percent) than net oil imports (35.3 percent) or the group of problem debtors (46.6 per-

Table 3.1   **Capital-Importing LDC Debt (billions of U.S. dollars; billion 1980 dollars)**

	1978	1980	1982	1984	1986	1986 % Share
Total	399	570	763	849	967	100.0
Africa	72	94	117	128	144	14.9
Asia	93	135	180	212	265	27.4
Europe	48	68	77	82	101	10.4
Non-oil Middle East	30	43	56	68	75	7.8
Western Hemisphere	156	231	333	359	383	37.5
Total (1980 Prices)[a]	523	578	822	974	987	—

Sources: IMF *World Economic Outlook* and *IFS.*
[a]Deflated by industrial countries' unit export value.

Table 3.2   Debt GDP Ratios (percentage)

	Africa	Asia	Europe	Non-Oil Middle East	Western Hemisphere
1978	32.2	15.9	23.7	52.9	31.8
1982	36.3	21.5	30.8	66.6	43.5
1986	44.3	30.0	40.0	63.2	47.0
Cumulative Real GDP Growth, 1982–86	4.2	31.1	11.4	−0.3	5.5

Source: IMF *World Economic Outlook.*

cent). Thus countries in a group with Afghanistan and Bangladesh have higher debt ratios than the group including Brazil and Mexico. We shall see below that this does not translate into higher debt *burdens* since much of the poor countries' debt is concessional.

3.1.2   Short, Long, Official, and Private Debt

The maturity structure of the debt is primarily medium term. Throughout 1978–86, the share of short-term debt (less than one-year maturity) in total debt of all capital-importing LDCs never exceeded 20 percent. But, of course, there are significant differences between countries. The larger the borrowing from commercial banks, the shorter the maturity of debt. In the period to 1982 there was an increase in the share of short-term debt, reflecting the increasing recourse to commercial bank financing. But since then, with rescheduling and increased official lending, the share of short-term debt has declined from 20 percent to only 13 percent. Since most debtors are not in a position to amortize their debts, the distinction between short- and long-term debt is becoming increasingly irrelevant.

Table 3.3 shows the share of debt to official creditors in total debt. The table reports the data for various regions.

The differences among country groupings in their funding is quite striking. Latin America stands out as borrowing a very much larger

Table 3.3   Share of Long-Term Debt to Official Creditors in Total Debt
                         (percentage of total)

	Africa	Asia	Europe	Non-Oil Middle East	Western Hemisphere
1978	34.0	54.9	27.6	57.6	15.9
1982	38.9	42.5	30.7	58.5	12.4
1986	48.6	43.5	33.3	58.5	20.3

Source: IMF *World Economic Outlook.*

share from private sources than the remaining countries. But there is also an interesting difference in behavior over time. For Latin America and Africa, the absolute and relative increase in official credit since 1982 is much more substantial than for other regions. In 1985, for example, commercial bank exposure declined in absolute terms, while official exposure, especially of multilateral agencies, increased.

3.1.3   Debt Service Burdens

The burden of debt service is made up of interest payments and amortization. As such it is affected by three factors:

1. The maturity profile of debt, which dictates the amount of amortization in a given year. Any bunching of maturities would translate into large year-to-year fluctuations in debt service.

2. Interest rates on the debt. This factor depends on the private-official composition of the debt. Official debt may be concessional and long term while private debt typically involves floating-rate interest payments.

3. Debt service measured relative to some benchmark such as exports or GDP. The benchmark is affected by the country's real exchange rate. Real depreciation, as already noted, will reduce real GDP in dollars and hence raise the debt-income ratio. Measuring debt relative to exports implies that changes in the value of exports, say as a result of exchange rate policy or as a consequence of changes in world commodity prices, will affect the debt-export ratio.

The distinction between long- and short-term debt, in an environment of universal rescheduling, is becoming uninteresting. I thus focus only on interest payments. Table 3.4 shows debt service measured by interest payments as a fraction of debt, GDP, and exports. I again focus on the geographical distribution.

The first row makes apparent the difference in effective interest rates paid. Africa and Asia have a significantly larger share of concessional loans, and, accordingly, interest payments as a fraction of debt are in excess of two percentage points less than for Latin America. As a benchmark we can compare the effective interest rate with the LIBOR

Table 3.4   LDC Interest Payments, 1986

	Africa	Asia	Europe	Non-Oil Middle East	Western Hemisphere
Percent of Debt	6.8	5.8	8.0	7.3	8.4
Percent of GDP	3.0	1.7	3.2	4.6	3.9
Percent of Exports	14.4	6.1	10.8	17.0	27.7

Source: IMF *World Economic Outlook.*

(London Interbank Offered Rate), which in 1985–86 averaged 7.8 percent. Divergences of the effective rate from LIBOR reflect concessional loans and the spreads above LIBOR on commercial bank loans.

The interest burden as a fraction of GDP shows Africa and Europe in the middle range, a low figure for Asia, and a high indebtedness for Latin America and the non-oil Middle East. Differences between the GDP and export-based comparisons reflect economic structure. Europe is wide open while Latin America is much more closed. Latin America's export-to-GDP ratio is much lower than that for Asia, for example.

The difference between debtors with commercial as opposed to concessional debt becomes particularly apparent when comparing effective interest payments. While the effective interest rate for small, low-income countries in 1986 averaged 3.4 percent, for the remaining groups it was between 6.9 percent and 8.7 percent.

3.1.4   Currency Denomination

The currency composition of lending to LDCs is not well documented. There is litle doubt that the major part of loans, perhaps 60 percent to 70 percent, is in U.S. dollars. The denomination issue is very important since large fluctuations of real exchange rates between the United States, Europe, and Japan involve changing burdens of real debt and changing bank exposure.

Since February 1985 the dollar has declined in world markets by more than 50 percent relative to key currencies. Over the same period, prices of industrial countries' exports, which we might use as an index of prices in world trade, have fallen only 5 percent while prices of commodities exported by LDCs fell 7 percent over 1982–86. The movement of the dollar thus did not carry significant consequences for debtor countries if they were entirely denominated in dollars. If, however, a significant part was denominated in yen or in European currencies, the vast exchange rate movements would have meant an increase in real debt burdens.[4]

3.1.5   Major Problem Debtors

We conclude the review of facts with a listing of major *problem* debtors. This group of countries corresponds to the fifteen heavily indebted countries shown in Table 3.5, along with their total debts, interest payments, and debt per capita.

In this table, Chile, Peru, and Bolivia are shown as having the highest debt-GDP ratio, while Chile, Argentina, and Mexico show the highest per capita debt figures. Bolivia and Morocco are interesting in that their debts are predominantly to official creditors. Finally, Nigeria is of interest because of the relatively low per capita debt by comparison with the other countries.

Table 3.5   Fifteen Heavily Indebted Countries

Country	Debt[a]	Debt Per Capita[b]	Interest-GDP Ratio[c]	Share of Debt to Private Creditors
Argentina	50.8	1,662	7.9	86.8
Bolivia	4.0	622	10.0	39.3
Brazil	107.3	791	5.8	84.2
Chile	21.0	1,740	12.9	87.2
Colombia	11.3	395	3.3	57.5
Ecuador	8.5	906	6.0	73.8
Ivory Coast	8.0	846	8.7	64.1
Mexico	99.0	1,261	6.3	89.1
Morocco	14.0	842	8.2	39.1
Nigeria	19.3	210	1.9	88.2
Peru	13.4	680	10.8	60.7
Philippines	24.8	456	6.2	67.8
Uruguay	3.6	1,204	9.8	82.1
Venezuela	33.6	2,000	8.1	99.5
Yugoslavia	19.6	848	n.a.	64.0

Sources: *Fortune,* December 23, 1985; *Economist,* September 27, 1986; *International Financial Statistics;* and World Bank 1986.

[a]Billions of U.S. dollars.

[b]Thousands of U.S. dollars.

[c]Interest payments on the external debt as a percentage of GDP.

3.2   The Origins of the Debt Problem

In this section we review the origins of the debt problem. Three facts combined to produce the debt crisis of 1982. The proportions vary from one case to another, but in almost all instances there is a combination of the following factors: (1) poor macroeconomic policies of debtor countries, including overvaluation of their currencies; (2) the downturn in the world economy, involving sharply higher interest rates and lower growth; (3) initial overlending and subsequent credit denial by commercial banks.

3.2.1   Domestic Mismanagement

In the late 1970s, debtor countries worldwide, with rare exceptions, embarked on policies inducing currency overvaluation. The policies were motivated by a single purpose: to contain and reduce stubborn inflationary pressure. The popularity of the policy, in the short term, stems from the fact that real wages increase. The increase in real wages translates only gradually into lower employment. Hence there is a period of euphoria as standards of living are artificially inflated by the real appreciation while the resulting external imbalance is financed via reserve depletion and external borrowing.

Each of the countries in table 3.6 showed some real appreciation in 1979–82, indicated by an increase in the real exchange rate index. For

Table 3.6   **Real Exchange Rates (index 1980–82 = 100)**

	Argentina	Brazil	Chile	Mexico	Venezuela	Korea
1976–78	73	116	75	98	95	92
1979	101	96	79	98	94	95
1980	116	85	95	104	93	96
1981	107	103	108	114	100	101
1982	76	112	97	82	110	103
1983–85	74	85	86	86	98	96

Source: Morgan Guaranty *World Financial Markets.*

example, in Argentina the real exchange rate moves from a value of 73 in 1976–78 to 116 in 1980. Not all cases were as extreme, and the annual averages conceal some of the even higher peaks. But the basic point is that most debtor countries, sometime in 1979–82, experienced real appreciation of some degree.

The exact timing of real appreciation differs but the story is invariably the same. There are, however, significant differences in the magnitude of overvaluation. Argentina, Chile, Mexico, and Venezuela had much more extreme experiences than Brazil or Korea. Brazil is interesting because its policy of using (normally) a crawling peg geared to the United States–Brazil economywide inflation differentials assured that high-productivity growth in tradables translated into a steady real depreciation. Dollar depreciation reinforced the gain in competitiveness in the late 1970s, but when the dollar strengthened in the 1980–82 period, competitiveness was lost. In Korea's case the real appreciation was very short lived and in fact quite minor compared to, say, Argentina.

The particular details of mismanagement differ between countries. For example, we look at Argentina, Brazil, Chile, and Mexico.

Argentina

Under Finance Minister Martinez de Hoz in the post-Peronist military government, inflation was reduced from more than 600 percent in 1976 to less than 200 percent by 1978. But further inflation reduction was hard to achieve. A large budget deficit was an obvious reason, yet the government preferred to focus on the inflation-depreciation spiral and the role of expectations.

Appealing to the law of one price, and the critical role of expectations, the government implemented in December 1978 a policy of preannouncing the rate-of-exchange depreciation. The preannounced *tablita* showed a steady deceleration of the rate of depreciation, and this was actually implemented. But inflation reduction was very slow, hence the real exchange rate became steadily overvalued.[5] Even so the policy was continued until March 1981 when it ultimately broke down.

The consequences for debt of overvaluation came primarily from the side of the capital account. Argentina had liberalized international capital flows entirely. As a result, residents, aware of the growing over-valuation, could freely shift into foreign assets ranging from dollar bills to foreign deposits and securities or real estate. The extreme overvaluation, reaching more than 40 percent, led to large-scale capital flight. The government borrowed in New York, using the proceeds to sustain the exchange rate along its preannounced path. The public bought dollars and redeposited them in the very same banks from which the government had borrowed. And that process continued, in the fullest knowledge of all concerned, until a change in the military government led to a collapse of the policy.

My estimate of Argentine capital flight in 1978–82 is $23 billion, not counting unrepatriated interest earnings which would raise the figure to well above $30 billion.

Chile

The Pinochet government instituted free market reforms and fiscal orthodoxy in Chile. These included elimination of tariffs and quotas and a balancing of the budget.[6] But inflation, while sharply reduced from the near hyperinflation levels of 1972–74, would not disappear. By 1979, with inflation the only major economic problem, the government fixed the exchange rate. The rate was fixed at 39 pesos/$ even though inflation was still near 30 percent, way above world inflation, and wages were indexed in a backward-looking fashion.

Not surprisingly, the exchange rate became increasingly overvalued. Wage increases far outpaced world inflation and thus the real exchange rate appreciated steadily. In the short run the policy was popular since it raised living standards. But it became increasingly apparent that an unsustainable overvaluation was accumulating. By 1981 the system started to unravel. The public responded in their accustomed way. Taking advantage of what was perceived to be a very transitory "sale" of imports, the entire country participated in the flight into imports (in particular durables).

The real exchange rate appreciated by more than 25 percent between 1978 and 1981. The value of imports increased by 50 percent. Import volume indexes tell an extraordinary story: breeding stock +328 percent, automobiles +226 percent, electro domestic equipment +156 percent. The Chilean example highlights that, especially in the case of producer and consumer durables, a transitory exchange rate overvaluation has major effects on the timing of purchases. The government was not deterred by these developments. Steadfastly, the authorities maintained the exchange rate and asserted that the exchange rate policy was visibly successful as evidenced by the declining rate of inflation.

As in all other cases, the policy ultimately broke down. Tariffs are back today and so are quotas. Inflation is back to the point where the adventure started. The lasting difference is an extraordinary debt burden and extremely high unemployment. We return to these issues below.

Mexico

The large increase in oil prices during 1978–79 would lead one to expect that Mexico should have done well. But even with sharply increased revenues from oil, the current account deteriorated in 1979–81 from $5 billion to $13 billion. At the same time there was a major outflow of capital.[7]

An estimate by Morgan Guaranty places the amount of capital flight during 1976–82 at $36 billion while a World Bank estimate for 1979–82 gives $26.5 billion (*World Financial Markets,* March 1986; *World Development Report,* 1986). The extent of capital flight is associated with a peculiarly Mexican institution: the sixth and final year of the presidency. Such a year was 1982, and people expected, correctly, that overvaluation and an excess of spending would ultimately lead to a balance of payments crisis. Under these circumstances, capital flight became extreme.

Brazil

The Brazilian case is special in that the policy mistakes may well have been minor. Brazil certainly ran very large budget deficits. Oil price increases and increased world interest rates were absorbed by the public sector deficit, and the resulting external deficit was financed by increased borrowing abroad. But much of the earlier borrowing by state enterprises, especially in 1972–78, financed a massive national investment effort (Cardoso 1986).

In Brazil's case, tight restrictions on imports and the near absence of capital flight made for an experience very different from that of Argentina, Mexico, or Chile. The chief source of debt accumulation was the public sector, which meant that the damage was much more limited than was the case in the other countries. Indeed, by early 1985 it seemed that lower interest rates and a sharply reduced oil price helped solve Brazil's debt problems for the major part. Since then the current account has once again deteriorated, in part as a result of an overly expansionary policy. But even so, Brazil is among the debtor countries that are more likely to be able to sustain growth and debt service.

3.2.2   The World Macroeconomy

A major part in the origins of the debt crisis was played by the sharp downturn in the world economy during 1979–81. In the 1970s, partly as a result of the oil shocks, but also because of overexpansionary policies, the United States had experienced increasing inflation. In 1979–81, under the pressure of the collapsing dollar, U.S. policies changed sharply. The full-employment budget was cut by nearly 1.5 percentage points of GNP. Nominal interest rates were allowed to rise from 9 percent in 1978 to 17 percent in 1981, and real interest rates increased sharply.

The sharp change in the world economic environment is shown in table 3.7, which compares the early 1970s and the period preceding the debt crisis. The early 1970s favored debtors: strong growth, high inflation, and low interest rates. By comparison, in 1980–82 inflation was low, interest rates were extraordinarily high, and growth was stagnant.

It is particularly important in this context to see the *real* interest rate issue. For debtor LDCs the U.S. real interest rate is hardly appropriate. An alternative is provided by the inflation rate in world trade. Manufactures prices were declining by 2.4 percent while commodity prices fell by 13.3 percent per year. Any realistic estimate of real interest rates cannot fail to come up with extraordinarily high rates.

Commodity price developments have different effects depending on whether a particular debtor is a net exporter or a net importer of commodities. The point is important in a comparison of Korea and Latin America. Korea (like Japan, for example) is a net importer of commodities. As a result, the collapse of commodity prices in 1979–81 helped offset in part the oil price increase. Brazil, by contrast, is a net exporter of commodities and has a production structure that makes the country vulnerable to oil price increases and commodity price decreases. Table 3.8 shows terms of trade changes and highlights the very different experience of various debtor groups.

Table 3.7   **Key Macroeconomic Variables of the World Economy (annual percentage rates)**

		Inflation[a]		
	LIBOR	Manufactures	Commodities	OECD Growth
1970–73	7.6	12.4	14.4	5.9
1980–82	14.7	−2.4	−13.3	0.9

Sources: IMF *IFS* and World Bank *Commodity Trade and Price Trends.*
[a]Inflation rate in world trade

Table 3.8   **Terms of Trade Changes, 1978–82 (cumulative percentage change)**

Fuel Exporters	15 Heavy Debtors	Small Low-Income Countries	Non-Oil LDC Exporters	Net Oil Importers
54.5	7.9	−27.8	18.2	−20.1

Source: IMF *World Economic Outlook.*

These world economic developments meant that most LDCs experienced a sharp deterioration in their current account. Reduced export revenues, on account of the decline in commodity prices and world recession, were reinforced by sharply increased nominal debt service burdens. Thus debtors were made illiquid. To continue on the accustomed course, external financing needed to increase sharply. The lack of smooth financing in the case of Mexico then brought on generalized credit rationing.

3.2.3   Overlending and Credit Rationing

In the period to mid-1982, reckless lending was the rule. It is possible today to search the 1980–81 discussion of debt problems for warnings of the crisis to come. The Bank for International Settlements had expressed concern at least since 1978. A Group of Thirty inquiry in 1981 sought to uncover whether banks felt debt was a major issue and failed to find dominant concern (Group of Thirty 1981a, 1981b; Kraft 1984). In a survey of one hundred banks the question was posed, "Last time no serious debt defaults arose. This time do you think that a general debt problem affecting countries is likely to emerge?" In response, 72 percent of the banks questioned expressed the view that a debt crisis was not likely, 13 percent thought it might possibly happen, and only 15 percent replied in the affirmative (Group of Thirty, 1981b).

If there were some concerns, they were certainly not enough to stop a final lending boom. Table 3.9 shows Latin America's current account deficit and its financing. Between 1979 and 1981, private lending to Latin America exactly doubled. It is unclear how these credits were justified at the time. There were two arguments. One was the need for

Table 3.9   **Latin America: Current Account Imbalances and Financing (billions of U.S. dollars)**

		Borrowing	
	Current Account	Official Creditors[a]	Private Creditors
1978	19.4	2.2	25.8
1979	21.8	2.7	27.4
1980	30.2	6.1	35.9
1981	43.3	6.5	54.1
1982	42.0	14.6	28.8
1983	11.4	17.7	2.0
1984	4.9	10.7	7.0
1985	5.9	5.1	−0.6

Source: IMF *World Economic Outlook.*
[a]Including reserve-related liabilities. Private capital flows (flight) and errors and omissions make up the difference in the row sums.

recycling, which had worked well at the time of the first oil shock. The other was the lack of information on country exposure. Neither of course is a reasonable explanation.

Subsequent to overlending was credit rationing following the Mexican moratorium of August 1982. As shown in table 3.9, private lending fell off dramatically and in 1985 even turned negative. The credit rationing phenomenon is not surprising; faced with a country's inability to meet debt service, each individual lender is reluctant to put up money that would only serve to pay other banks' claims. Hence without a cartel there is no lending. But if there is no lending then, of course, debt service is impossible and hence debtors will default.

The problem in 1982 was therefore to develop a system that would organize creditors. They would have to provide the part of debt service that could not be extracted by improvements in debtor-country external balances. At the same time the cartel would serve, much as the occupation of customs houses in the old days, to extract a maximum of debt service by a lien on the debtor countries' macroeconomic policies. The IMF, having been ignored in the 1970s, eagerly (and skillfully) assumed the task of orchestrating debt collection, fiscal discipline, and forced lending.

3.3   The Transfer Problem and Debt Service Fatigue

We now ask why debt service appears to be such a major problem. In one sense the answer is quite straightforward: countries that used to spend, borrowing the resources from official and private creditors (with little thought of how to service or even less repay the loans), now no longer command these resources—they are limited to spending (this section draws on Dornbusch 1985b, 1986b, and 1986c). The adjustment in complicated by two facts. The first is the macroeconomics of earning foreign exchange; the second is the political economy problem of finding extra budget resources for debt service. These issues are familiar from the discussion of German reparation payments following World War I.[8] Exactly the same issues arise in the context of the involuntary debt service now underway.

3.3.1   The Reduction in Spending

The first issue is how a country adjusts to a reduction in its spendable resources. Before the debt crisis, foreign loans supplemented domestic income, enlarging the resources that could be spent. Interest payments on loans were automatically provided in the form of new money, and the principal on debts was automatically rolled over. With managing the debt so easy, and with ready access to resources beyond what was required to service the debt, spending ran high. After credit rationing began in 1982, spending had to be limited, and absorption fell below the level of output as interest now had to be paid out of current production. Interest payments now had to be earned by noninterest surpluses in the current account.

Table 3.10 shows the debt service process at work. In the post-1982 period of involuntary lending, debtor countries achieved a shift in their noninterest external balance of nearly 5 percent of GDP. This external balance improvement served to make net transfers of interest to the creditors. It was matched by a nearly equal reduction in investment in the debtor countries.

This perverse resource transfer, of course, came at the expense of living standards in the developing countries. But more important, the transfer had as a counterpart a sharp decline in investment. Interest payments thus were really financed by a mortgage on future standards of living and on the debtors' growth potential. In countries where population growth is high and income distribution is appalling, such a policy may turn out to be very shortsighted.

But there remained the issue of how to distribute the cut in spending between its various components: government, consumption, and investment. As we saw above, a large part of the cut took the form of reduced investment. There was, of course, also a decline in consumption. A fall in investment was not enough due to two special features of the adjustment process. First, cutting total demand has macroeconomic multiplier effects that translate into a reduction in output, income, and hence private spending. Second, at the same time that involuntary debt service started, there also occured a deterioration in the world economy that required an extra downward adjustment in spending.

3.3.2 The Foreign Exchange Problem

The second macroeconomic issue in adjusting to debt concerns the fact that the country needs to earn dollars, not pesos. In other words it needs to generate a trade surplus. The cut in spending will, of course, reduce import demand and also free exportables for sale abroad, but for two reasons that will not be enough. First, a sizable fraction of the

Table 3.10   **Latin America: Investment and the External Noninterest Surplus (percentage of GDP)**

	1977–82	1983–85	Change
Gross investment	24.3	18.5	−5.8
Noninterest external surplus	−0.6	4.7	5.3

Source: IMF *World Economic Outlook.*

expenditure cut will fall on domestic (nontraded) goods, not tradables. The spending cut thus creates directly unemployment rather than potential foreign exchange earnings. Even for those goods that are directly tradable it is not necessarily the case that increased supplies can be sold. Often there is the problem of obtaining market access, and, if the goods are not homogeneous commodities like cotton or copper, a cut in their price is required to realize increased sales. Even then, unless demand is sufficiently responsive, total earnings may not increase.

To translate the spending cut into foreign exchange earnings, a gain in competitiveness is required. The gain in competitiveness draws resources into the tradable goods sector and in the world market makes it possible to sell the increased production of tradable goods. Of course, the only way to gain competitiveness is by reducing the wage in dollars by a real depreciation. But the real wage cut also generates increased unemployment, at least in the short run, as the spendable income of workers is cut. The size of the required cut in real wages is larger, the larger the share of trade goods in income and the smaller the share of wages in GDP.

The overwhelming difficulty in the adjustment process is that external adjustment via a gain in competitiveness reduces employment. The dominant effect on employment is from the reduction in real wages and the resulting reduction in domestic demand. The positive employment response that would be expected in the tradable goods sector from the gain in competitiveness is often very weak and slow. One reason is that expectations of a *sustained* change in competitiveness do not take hold immediately. The traded goods sector thus adopts a wait-and-see attitude, which makes real depreciation a highly precarious policy tool. The Mexican experience in this respect is particularly instructive.

A second important difficulty arises from the worldwide adjustment to forced debt service. Since most debtor countries were overspending in the early 1980s and are now under a forced debt service regime, they all had to resort to real depreciation to enhance their competitiveness. But that means they are competitively cutting their wages relative to each other, and not only relative to those of the creditor countries. As a result, an isolated country, cutting its dollar wage, say, by 50 percent, will gain much less in terms of increased dollar revenues because all the competing LDCs are doing much the same.

3.3.3   The Budget Problem

The third macroeconomic problem in the adjustment process involves the budget. Much of the external debt is public or publicly guaranteed. Of the part that was not initially public, much has wound up in the public sector in the aftermath of the crises, as a result of bank failures. The government thus must service a debt that before was either in private hands or automatically serviced by new money. The problem, of course, is where to find the extra 3 percent or 4 percent of budget revenue that will pay these new interest costs.

There are basically four avenues: raising taxes and public sector prices, reducing government outlays, printing money, or issuing domestic debt. Raising taxes is notoriously difficult since most of the taxes are already levied in the form of social security taxes on workers. An easier solution is to raise public sector prices or to eliminate subsidies. The elimination of subsidies is particularly cheered by creditors and international agencies since it means moving closer to efficient resource allocation.[9] Of course, the imposition of extra taxes or the withdrawal of subsidies is inevitably inflationary from the price side unless the tax increase or subsidy cut is offset by a reduction in other prices or wages. Of course, via the revenue side reduces the growth in money and hence, in combination, it leads to a recession with inflationary pressure sustained by prevailing inflation.

Cutting government spending is another option. Attention here focuses on the often extreme inefficiency of the public sector. The public perceives that there must be a way to pay the bills out of increased efficiency, rather than reduced private absorption. The fact is, of course, that there is little room for public sector improvements in the short term. Large-scale firing of redundant workers would create an overwhelming political problem. Plant closings are of the same kind, and selling inefficient, overunionized firms runs into the obvious problem that the potential buyers might need to be paid to take over the liability. Perhaps the best advice may be that public sector firms should be simply given away. The problem is that the workers might oppose even that.

The most common adjustment is a cut in or freeze of public sector wages. This has happened in most of the debtor countries, and in some cases on a very large scale. It does help the budget, but it presents its own problems. The reduction in relative wages for the public sector promotes an exodus of the wrong kind. The efficient workers leave and only those with little alternative stay in the public sector.

In many of the debtor countries the answer to forced debt service has almost inevitably been to increase government budget deficits and to finance this by issuing debt or printing money. Money finance brings with it the problem of high and often extreme inflation. It is no accident that Argentina and Brazil experienced extraordinary inflation rates in the aftermath of the debt crisis. When deficits are financed by debt, while the imminent inflation problem may be absent, there is still the issue of excessive debt accumulation which ultimately poses the risk of an inflationary liquidation or a repudiation.

There is an interaction between the foreign exchange problem and the budget problem. The need to devalue to gain competitiveness implies that the value of debt service in home currency increases. A given payment of, say, $1 billion now amounts to more in pesos, produces a larger peso deficit, and hence gives rise to the need for increased inflationary finance. Thus devaluation is a source of inflation not just directly via the increased prices of traded goods and any accompanying indexation effects. It works also indirectly by raising the required inflation tax. In the classical hyperinflations, major movements in the exchange rate were the prelude to the outbreak of uncontrolled inflation; there is some evidence that exactly the same process is at work in the debtor countries today (see Dornbusch and Fischer 1986; Fischer 1986a, 1986b).

The budget is also adversely affected by the problem of capital flight. To stem capital flight, provoked by the inflationary consequences of debt service or perhaps by an impending tax reform, the country will have to raise real interest rates to very high levels. These high real interest rates in turn apply to the domestic debt, causing it to grow more rapidly, and thereby raising future budget deficits and hence the prospect of instability. That in turn feeds more capital flight and yet higher rates. There is thus an extraordinary vicious circle surrounding the sudden need to service debt and the inability to do so through ordinary taxation.

cess. To earn foreign exchange, the real wage must be cut in terms of tradable goods, thus enhancing competitiveness. But to balance the budget it is often necessary or at least recommended to cut subsidies for such items as food or transportation, and that also means a cut in real wages. There is thus competition between two targets—a cut in the dollar wage or a cut in the tortilla wage. A choice must be made because there is only so much one can cut. Because of the lags with which the trade sector adjusts, the competitiveness adjustment should take precedence and that budget balancing should follow once the economy's resources are reallocated. Since the real depreciation by itself is already bound to produce slack, there is no risk of overheating in this sequence of adjustment.

A final point is the link between budget cutting and the extraordinary fall in Latin American investment. In the category of government spending, the easiest cuts are in investment. Postponing investment and maintenance is much easier than firing workers. The resulting impact on aggregate investment is so large because the public sector, in the form of public sector enterprises, accounts for a large part of total investment and because the public sector was in the forefront of adjustment. This is a very ineffective means of adjustment because it fails to recognize the distinction between the public sector's current and capital accounts.

3.4.4   Case Study: Mexico

Mexico illustrates in a striking way many of these issues. The least noted fact, apparent in table 3.11, is the dramatic shift in the budget over the past three years. The *noninterest* or primary budget has improved by more than 7 percent of GDP. From a deficit of nearly 4 percent of GDP in 1982, the noninterest balance has shifted to an estimated surplus of 3.2 percent in 1986. The improvement is all the more impressive in view of the large decline in oil revenue in 1986. Note that the whole improvement in the noninterest budget went to finance increased interest payments on the domestic and foreign debt.

The total budget records a deficit of nearly 16 percent of GDP for 1986. The increase in interest payments is largely a reflection of inflation. Inflation and the accompanying exchange rate depreciation raise the nominal interest rates required to make Mexicans hold the depreciating asset. These interest rates in turn translate into a large interest bill in the budget. There is a budget deficit because there is inflation, not the other way around.

Table 3.12 shows further details on the Mexican macroeconomic situation. We already saw the cut in public sector investment. The table indicates that total investment shows a sharp decline, leaving little *net* investment.

Table 3.11   **Mexico's Budget (percentage of GDP)**

	1982	1983	1984	1985	1986[a]
Budget deficit	17.1	8.9	7.7	8.4	15.8
Primary deficit	3.7	− 5.2	− 5.4	− 4.2	− 3.2
Operational deficit	n.a.	− 0.2	− 0.7	− 0.9	− 2.1
Public investment	9.3	6.6	6.5	6.1	5.1

Source: Mexico, Presidencia de la Republica and Secretaria de Heacienda y Credito Publico.

[a]Estimate.

Table 3.12   **Mexico: Macroeconomic Indicators**

	1970–81	1982	1983	1984	1985	1986[a]
Per capita growth	3.5	− 2.8	− 7.5	1.4	0.4	− 6.3
Inflation	17	99	81	59	60	100
Investment/GDP	23.6	21.1	16.0	16.3	16.9	14.9
Real wage (1981 = 100)	n.a.	105	76	73	67	64
Current account/GDP	− 3.5	− 3.8	3.8	2.5	0.3	− 2.6
External interest/GDP	n.a.	7.5	7.1	7.0	6.0	6.4
Price of oil ($US/barrel)	12.4	28.6	26.4	26.8	25.4	11.2

Source: IMF and Secretaria de Hacienda y Credito Publico.

[a]Estimate.

Consider next the current account. There is a striking turnaround, from the deficits prior to the crisis to surpluses afterward. In 1983–84 the surpluses were enough to help finance capital flight and also meet the interest payments. In 1985, interest was paid out of these surpluses by attracting a reflow of private capital via very high interest rates. But with the oil price decline the external financing problem returned, forcing a choice between further real depreciation and an alteration in the terms of debt service.

The real exchange rate and the real wage both declined sharply in the past few years. Real wages today are 40 percent below their 1980 levels, and the external competitiveness has improved by 40 percent. These are extraordinary adjustments for any country to make. Finally there is the employment story. The labor force is growing at 3.5 percent per year, but employment after an initial decline has been entirely stagnant over the past four years. The informal sector and migration to the United States were the main shock absorbers in employment. Thus unemployment is growing and so too is social conflict. The lack of employment growth, even after so extreme a real depreciation, is an issue of major concern. It suggests that depreciation reduces employment for quite a while before the substitution takes over.

Early results for trade were disappointing. More recently Mexico has started to build up a strong non-oil export growth, but that has turned out to be a mixed blessing. U.S. trade concerns have spilled over to Mexico in the form of more than one hundred countervailing duty cases!

3.3.5 Case Study: Brazil

Brazil, just like Mexico, started off her adjustment with a large decline in per capita income and with a sharp acceleration of inflation. The inflation acceleration is largely due to the real depreciation required to generate a noninterest surplus. The presence of indexation translated exchange depreciation into an increase in inflation. The higher inflation in turn showed up in a sharply larger budget deficit (see table 3.13).

The noninterest external balance improved sharply. This is seen in table 3.13 in the shift of the noninterest current account from a deficit of 2 percent of GDP in 1982 to a 3.5–5 percent surplus in 1984–86. In contrast to Mexico, the Brazilian budget has not improved sharply, which has meant more stimulus to growth and to recovery.

The difference between the case studies of Mexico and Brazil, in 1986, is in both oil and macroeconomics. Lower oil prices in Brazil's case more than compensate for the adverse conditions of the boom on the external balance. But the external balance is certainly also improved by the import substitution and export capacity expansion made possible by the investments of the early 1970s, which came on line just in time to help service the debt.

Table 3.13   **Brazil: Macroeconomic Indicators**

	1982	1983	1984	1985	1986[a]
Inflation	99	142	197	227	65
Per capita growth	− 1.3	− 5.5	2.3	6.1	6.8
Budget deficit[b]					
Actual deficit	16.7	19.9	22.2	27.1	10.9
Operational deficit	6.5	3.0	1.6	3.5	5.1
Current account deficit[b]	8.5	3.5	—	0.1	− 0.1
External interest	6.5	5.3	5.4	4.7	3.7
Noninterest deficit	2.0	− 1.8	− 5.4	− 4.6	− 3.6

Source: Banco Central do Brasil.
[a]Estimate.
[b]Percentage of GDP.

3.4   Bank Exposure and the Quality of Debts

In this section we review the debt problem from the side of commercial bank creditors by looking at the extent of exposure and at the quality of debts.

3.4.1   Exposure

Table 3.14 gives a broad overview of loans by U.S. banks to regions other than the industrial countries or offshore banking centers. In these categories, Nigeria and Venezuela are included among the OPEC countries while Mexico is part of the non-OPEC countries.

Between 1977 and 1982, claims on non-OPEC countries more than doubled. By contrast, since then there has been a complete standstill in lending. The table shows that loans to Eastern Europe are small and relatively stable in size. Exposure to OPEC countries is more sizable and has declined since 1982.

Table 3.15 looks at lending to non-OPEC developing countries, this time disaggregating by size of bank. We also show how these claims have evolved relative to equity capital.

Three conclusions emerge from table 3.15. First, debt is a "big bank" problem. More than 60 percent of total debt is owed to the major money center banks, and nearly 85 percent to only twenty-five major banks.

Table 3.14   **U.S. Bank Claims on Nonindustrial Countries (billions of dollars)**

Year	OPEC	Non-OPEC	Eastern Europe
1977	14.3	45.0	7.0
1982	23.2	101.9	6.6
1985	20.4	100.9	5.1

Source: Federal Reserve.

Table 3.15   U.S. Bank Claims on Non-OPEC LDCs

	All Banks	9 Major	15 Major	All Other
Total claims (billion $)				
1978	52.5	33.4	9.9	8.9
1982	101.9	61.5	20.6	19.8
1985	100.9	63.5	19.8	16.9
Percentage of capital				
1978	110	163	107	57
1982	154	227	162	75
1985	99	156	99	41

Source: Federal Reserve.

Second, small banks have managed to reduce their claims over the past three years by 15 percent. Third, all banks and in particular the money center banks have been able to reduce their exposure measured as a percentage of capital. The exposure reduction has occurred primarily via a buildup of capital, in part by issuing equity commitment notes. But in part the exposure reduction is due to sell-off of loans, write-downs, and a slowdown or actual halt in new money commitments.

To judge the implications of LDC problem debts for the banking system, we look at table 3.16 at the group of most heavily indebted countries. For simplicity we take all of Latin America (including Venezuela) plus Nigeria, the Philippines, Morocco, and Yugoslavia. The total exposure in 1985 was close to $100 billion and approximately 90 percent of bank capital. Thus, in the extreme situation of all these debtors repudiating their debts completely, bank stockholders would be largely, though not altogether, wiped out, while depositors would be left fully intact. That picture is more favorable than much of the public discussion of the "LDC debt bomb" might lead one to believe. Of course, this point holds only in the aggregate and thus is not very

Table 3.16   U.S. Bank Exposure to Problem Debtors, 1985

	All Banks	9 Major	15 Major	All Other
Total exposure (billion $)				
Latin America	80.4	60.5	16.0	15.2
Other debtors	12.6	8.8	1.9	1.2
Percentage of capital				
Latin America	78.9	148.6	80.0	36.9
Other debtors	12.3	21.7	9.5	2.9

Source: Federal Reserve.

revealing. The more revealing comparison disaggregates by bank size. In this case it becomes apparent that their exposure is far in excess of their equity. Brazil, Argentina and the Philippines alone (to take the 1987 major confrontation cases) account already for more than half of the capital of major banks.

Even Latin America's debt is to a large extent held by non-U.S. banks. The Bank for International Settlements reports Latin American debt to banks in the reporting countries of $160 billion in 1985. Table 3.17 shows that only about one half of that debt is owed to U.S. banks. For the remaining problem debtors, the BIS total is $37 billion. In their case the U.S. loans are thus only one-third of the total of exposure to banks in the United States and elsewhere (Bank for International Settlements 1986).

There is an important difference, though, between European and U.S. banks. During the period of dollar appreciation, European banks were forced to increase their reserves against dollar loans. Furthermore these loan provisions were facilitated by tax advantages. Since 1985 the dollar has depreciated significantly, and this has worked to further increase European loan loss reserves relative to their claims. As a result, European banks are said to have been able, in some instances, to set aside loan loss reserves to fully cover problem debts. This, of course, is far from the case for U.S. banks.

Table 3.17   **Market Price of Problem Debt, December 1986 (billions of dollars)**

Country	Total Debt	Debt to U.S. Banks	Price[a]
Argentina	50.8	8.4	66.0
Bolivia	4.0	0.1	7.5
Brazil	107.3	22.2	75.5
Chile	21.0	6.5	68.0
Colombia	11.3	2.2	86.5
Ecuador	8.5	n.a.	65.5
Ivory Coast	8.0	0.4	77.0
Mexico	99.0	24.2	56.5
Morocco	14.0	0.8	69.5
Nigeria	19.3	0.9	39.0
Peru	13.4	1.5	19.0
Philippines	24.8	5.1	73.5
Uruguay	3.6	0.9	66.5
Venezuela	33.6	9.7	74.5
Yugoslavia	19.6	2.2	79.0
Weighted average			67.1

Source: Dealer information.

[a]Average of bid and offer price in cents per dollar debt.

3.4.2   The Quality of Debts

In the nineteenth century and until World War II, LDC debt mostly took the form of bonds traded on organized markets and widely held by the public. The postwar debt, by contrast, is owed to official institutions and commercial banks. Accordingly, there are no good price quotations that might be used as a measure of the quality of debts. Very little of claims on debtor LDCs takes the form of bonds.[10] But for some time, bank claims on various LDCs have been swapped between banks, sold outright between banks, and are now even being sold to nonbanks. The market has become central to discussions of debt-equity swaps. In these transactions, further discussed below, purchase of discounted debt is the starting point for a foreign investment in a debtor country.

Table 3.17 shows the average of the bid and offer price in the secondhand market. It would be a mistake to believe that all debts are actively traded, but even so the prices provide some indication of market valuation.

There are quite extraordinary divergences in prices. Bolivia, Peru, and Nigeria have low valuations, but perhaps more interesting is the difference between Mexico and Brazil. Why is Brazil thought to be so much better a credit risk than Mexico? The major difference would have to be between being an exporter and an importer of oil. The average price of problem debts is 67 cents per dollar. Discounts of 25 percent and more suggest that these are indeed problem debts and that the prospect of a return to voluntary lending might be very remote.

However, the story is not that simple. Consider the case of Uruquay. The country's debt stands at a discount of 23.5 percent, suggesting that the debt is poor. Yet in the fall of 1986, Uruquay issued a long-term public sector bond at the same rate as the U.S. Treasury. This suggests that the large discounts reflect above all a market that is too narrow, so it is illiquidity of banks that dominates in depressing the prices.

3.5   U.S. Trade Effects of the Debt Crisis

There is considerable difficulty in allocating the deterioration of the U.S. external balance between competing causes: the overly strong dollar, the rapid domestic growth relative to that abroad, the budget deficit, and the turn around forced on debtors' trade balances by the need to service external debts.

Table 3.18 gives some indication of the shift in our trade with Latin America. Not all of the shift can be attributed to the debt crisis since our loss in competitiveness must certainly account for some part of what happened. Also, the trade figures of the early 1980s are inflated by Latin America's overvaluation and spending spree. But even so,

Table 3.18 **U.S. Trade with South America (billions of U.S. dollars)**

	Exports	Imports	Trade Balance
1979	13.6	13.2	0.4
1980	17.4	14.4	3.0
1981	17.7	15.5	2.2
1982	15.3	14.4	0.9
1983	10.5	16.0	− 5.5
1984	11.0	21.0	− 10.0
1985	11.0	20.9	− 9.9

Source: Survey of Current Business.

there was a major shift in the bilateral balance amounting to $10–12 billion from 1979 to 1985.[11]

Table 3.19 compares the evolution of Latin American trade with different countries, showing a substantial shift toward bilateral surpluses with respect to each of these groups. While the surplus with the United States is far larger in absolute terms, this is not the case when the change is expressed relative to exports. This is a crude way of illustrating that the dollar appreciation may not be so dominant in this bilateral trade balance swing.

If $10 billion is taken as the change in the bilateral trade balance, even attributing it to the debt crisis, one does not come up with much damage to the United States. After all, this change is less than one-quarter of one percent of U.S. GNP! Of course, this does not exhaust the damage, and GNP is not the proper scale variable. Other damage to U.S. trade and investment interests occurs via the depression of demand and profitability in the debtor countries. U.S. multinationals that produce in those countries have sharply reduced sales and profits. Similarly, there are declines in U.S. exports of services (other than interest) to debtors. There are no ready estimates of losses in service exports.

In judging whether a $10 billion deterioration in the trade balance is large, one must bear in mind two points. The swing in the trade deficit helps facilitate a noninflationary absorption of our budget deficit.

Table 3.19 **Latin America's Bilateral Trade Balance with Various Groups (billions of dollars)**

	U.S.	Japan	EEC	Industrial Countries
1980	− 3.4	− 2.4	2.8	− 4.2
1985	10.8	0	7.7	18.7
Change as % of exports	42.9	54.8	20.8	35.1

Source: IMF Directions of Trade Statistics.

Switching lending from LDCs to the U.S. Treasury helps finance our own deficits under better (short-term) macroeconomic conditions. But there is clearly a cost for the affected industries. A large share of the trade deterioration, for example, is in the capital goods sector as Latin America's decline in investment reduced our exports. For this sector the trade deterioration with Latin America is, of course, far above the one-quarter of one percent of income. Even so, it would be difficult to make the debt crisis the main reason for our $150 billion trade problem.

3.6 Solutions to the Debt Problem

The ordinary aftermath of imprudent borrowing and adverse international conditions, as in the 1920s and 1930s most recently, is debt default.[12] Debts are normally written down or simply not serviced for many years. When servicing is ultimately resumed, it occurs without full payment of arrears and often at reduced interest rates.

The major differences in the present debt crisis are two. First, commercial banks and governments, rather than bondholders, are the main creditors. A more significant difference is that the governments of the major industrialized countries have insisted on debt service and have managed a system of debt collection, with the IMF as the chief coordinating agent. The system avoids illiquidity by making available essential "new money" at profitable spreads over the cost of funds to banks, and it enforces the debts by behind-the-scenes political pressure. The creditors are efficiently organized in this case-by-case approach, while debtors have been unable to put up a united front.[13]

The debtors' problem, especially in the case of Latin America, is how to gain debt relief or additional credit, so as to make available resources for investment and develop speculation in support of the government's ability to promote growth policies without risking financial instability. Tax reform and improved tax enforcement are certainly of overriding importance in this. Improved efficiency in the public sector is important, but measures to attract capital or secure relief on the external debt seem the most desirable or practicable alternatives. We review here five possible directions of change: an improved world macroeconomy, a facility, debt-equity swaps, a reversal of capital flight, and Bradley-style debt relief.

3.6.1 The World Macroeconomy

In 1982 the prospects of strong growth in the industrialized countries, lower interest rates, a weaker dollar, and stronger real commodity prices were the central scenario that encouraged the "muddling-through process." This favorable scenario implied that by the end of the decade, debt-export ratios would have declined significantly. Some of these developments have in fact occurred, and for some countries they have even been reinforced by an unexpectedly large decline in oil prices. But the expected benefits in terms of enhanced creditworthiness have not in general appeared. It is true that South Korea is at present not a problem debtor, but Brazil is and so are many other countries.

Looking ahead to the next few years, what macroeconomic developments can be expected and how will they affect the debt situation? The most important development for the world economy is U.S. budget balancing. There are basically three scenarios. In one case, rapid budget cutting is accommodated by monetary expansion in the United States and in the rest of the world. In this setting, interest rates decline sharply, growth is sustained, and the main exchange rates between industrial countries remain unaltered. This is a highly favorable scenario for LDCs in that much lower interest rates implicitly transfer to them resources in amounts far in excess of what can be expected from creditor-country taxpayers.

The second scenario envisages the same budget cutting, perhaps more spread out in time, but without monetary accommodation. In that case, interest rates decline somewhat, but there will be a world recession. Most debtors would not benefit, or at least very little, since the lower interest rates are offset by slack in their export markets.

A third scenario envisages a hard landing: budget cutting and a flight from the dollar that forces the Federal Reserve to *raise* interest rates to stem the inflationary impact of depreciation. Such a development would bring about systemwide illiquidity and likely default.

The world macroeconomy does hold out some promise. A Gramm-Rudman-Hollings budget cut, soon and with worldwide monetary accommodation, would make a major advance toward solving the debt problem. But for the time being there is not much of a sign of either the budget cutting or the monetary accommodation.

3.6.2 Debt-Equity Swaps

The debt problem has two aspects. The first is that debtors cannot service their debts as contracted. Moreover, the interest they pay comes largely at the expense of much needed investment in their economies. Thus debtors have a resource and investment shortage. On the lenders side, small banks are tired of the acrobatics involved in debt collection. They want to avoid yet another round of rescheduling. But there is no money in the debtor countries to pay them off, nor can the large banks do so, given their already extravagant exposure. These twin problems strain the skills of regulators, accountants, and policymakers worldwide.

The poor quality of LDC loans can be judged by the discount at which they trade in the emerging secondhand market. The large discounts suggest that an imminent return to voluntary lending is highly unlikely. Creditors' attention is therefore shifting to new ways of liquidating debts without taking outright and massive losses on the entire portfolio. But if banks are to get out, who will get in?

Debt-equity swaps have emerged as a seemingly attractive solution to the debt problem—clearly not *the* solution, but a sound contribution with all the rings of free enterprise.[14] Their apparent merit is in solving two problems at once: they allow banks to sell off loans without a massive decline in loan prices, and debtors can reduce their external debt and at the same time pull in foreign investment. All things considered, the swaps appear to be a good idea. But there are reasons for skepticism.

Before turning to these objections, a qualification is important. There should be no doubt that debt-equity swaps agreed to between private firms and their commercial bank creditors (without government intervention or subsidies) are entirely appropriate. Likewise, there can be no objection to direct foreign investment. On the contrary, there should have been more in the past, and the more there is in the future the better. The objections raised here concern exclusively the use of already strained debtor budgets to grease the wheels.

The basic difficulty is that debt-equity swaps amount to a budget subsidy by debtor countries that will allow banks to get out and foreign investors to get in. Here are the mechanics: First Regional Bank sells Brazilian government bonds at a discount to Dreams, Inc., a U.S. firm specializing in services. Dreams, Inc., presents the debt to the Banco Central do Brasil to be paid off in cruzados. The proceeds are used for the purchase of a Brazilian firm. It seems that everybody gains: the bank has found a way of selling some its illiquid portfolio without depressing the secondhand market; the investing firm gains the advantage of buying cruzados at a discount; and Brazil gains because she can pay the foreign debt in local currency rather than in dollars. Moreover, much needed investment takes place.

The debtor government will have to finance the repurchase of debt from the foreign investor. One cannot simply print local money to pay. In fact the government will issue domestic debt and use the proceeds to buy back its foreign debt as it is presented by the foreign investor. Hence, when everything is done, the government has a reduced external debt, but a matching increase in domestic debt. The country owns less of its capital stock, since the foreign investor will have bought some, and in return has redeemed some of its external debt.

Is there any advantage for the budget? In the budget there will now be reduced interest payments on external debt offset by increased domestic debt service. There is a net reduction in interest if the debtor country can appropriate most of the discount at which the external debt is traded and if the real domestic interest rate (in dollars) is not too high relative to the cost of servicing the external debt. The net result is likely to be an increase in debt service because real interest rates in debtor countries are exceptionally high.

On the balance of payments side, however, swaps might seem to be good news: foreign debt is reduced and as a result burdensome interest payments to abroad come down. But the reduced external interest payments are matched, at least potentially, by increased remittances of dividends or profits by the new foreign owners of the national capital stock. Hence, on the payments side the trick also does not do much good. In fact, the country becomes less liquid since it is much easier to control the service of bank debt than the remittances of multinationals. The massive outflow of remittances from Brazil in 1986 makes this point.

Debt-equity swaps are primarily a balance sheet operation, not a net resource transfer. One might argue that the government could target deals to make them less a transaction in existing assets and instead be directed toward new, extra investment. More likely, financial intermediaries will look for firms, domestic or foreign, that are already investing. They will approach the firms with a new kind of financing package involving debt-equity swap that, because of an implicit subsidy by the government, turns out to be less costly than alternative sources of finance. Thus debt-equity swaps will finance investment, but they finance at the budget cost of a subsidy investment that would have taken place anyway. This explains the reluctance of debtor countries to plunge into the scheme.

Debt-equity swaps bring together, with the glue of budget pesos, two entirely separate operations that would arise in a free, unregulated market. To solve the banks' problems, marking to market of LDC debts would occur and hence debts could be sold to the nonbank public. To cope with the resource problem, debtor countries would set up investment funds in which nonresidents can invest in the private economy with liberal facility for repatriation of dividends. The two separate steps assure that old, bad debts do not prevent new investment. The bad debts are distributed more widely, though at a possible loss to all the banks' stockholders. The debtor countries gain extra resources which they may use to expand investment or to buy back their debt, whichever appears more profitable. This is the market solution. Debt-equity swaps, by contrast, are a way of nationalizing the transaction, pushing budget subsidies to bank stockholders rather than to extra investment.

Balance sheet tricks are not a substitute for gaining extra real resources for investment. Improved government budgets in the debtor countries, increased private saving, increased efficiency in their public sector, and net resource transfers from abroad are the only way for investment and growth to return. Of course, debtor countries should open all doors to foreign direct investment—the sooner and wider, the better. But there is no justification for subsidizing such investment.

3.6.3   Reversal of Capital Flight

Wishful thinking turns to the $100 billion or more of Latin American assets that have fled from financial instability and taxation to the industrial countries, especially the United States. Reversing these capital flights, primarily in the case of Mexico or Argentina, would make it almost possible to pay off the external debt; much of the debt was incurred in the first place to finance the exodus of private capital.

Estimates of the amount of capital flight in the 1970s and early 1980s differ widely. But whatever the methods by which the magnitudes are estimated, the fact of at least a $100 billion capital flight from Latin America is not in question. Estimates are particularly large for Mexico, Argentina, and Venezuela and much smaller for Brazil and Chile. For both Argentina and Mexico, estimates of $25 billion to $35 billion are not uncommon, hence the suggestion that reversing the mammoth outflow could help pay off the debt without tears.

The idea that private capital could be the main solution, or at least provide an important contribution, is naïve. There is little historical precedent for a major reflow, and when it does happen it is the last wagon of the train. Einaudi once observed that savers "have the memory of an elephant, the heart of a lamb, and the legs of a hare." Capital will wait until the problems have been solved; it will not be part of the solution and is even less likely to provide a bridgehead.[15]

It is often argued that if only countries adopted policies guaranteeing savers a stable positive real rate of interest, there would be no capital flight problem. But that argument is not very realistic in three respects. First, in the context of adjustment programs, devaluation is often unavoidable. Compensating savers for the loss they would have avoided by holding dollar assets would place a fantastic burden on the budget, which in turn would breed financial instability. Second, maintaining high real interest rates poses a serious risk to public finance. The public debt that carries these high real rates snowballs, and that in turn is a source of instability. Third, raising the return on paper assets above the prospective return on real capital is terrible supply-side economics; it ultimately erodes the tax base and deteriorates the financial system by souring loans. A country in trouble simply cannot make its chief priority keeping the bondholders in place.

Capital controls, where feasible, are a better strategy for restoring order in public finance than papering over extreme difficulties for a while using extraordinarily high real interest rates. The latter strategy was, indeed, at the very source of the mess in Argentina under Martinez de Hoz and explains some of the difficulties in Mexico today.

The capital flight problem is encouraged by the fact that the U.S. administration no longer withholds taxes on nonresident assets. For with this tax-free U.S. return, anyone investing in Mexico (and actually paying taxes there) would need a yield differential, not counting exchange depreciation and other risks, of several extra percentage points.

There is much talk about the problems of banks putting in new money only to see it used by debtors such as Mexico to finance capital flight. Of an extra dollar of new money conceded by creditors, 70 cents are said to leave in extra capital flight. This indicates the need for a co-operative approach where debtor-country governments, the tax authorities in creditor countries, and the commercial banks cooperate in stopping capital flight and tax evasion. Of course, none of the three parties can succeed alone.

3.6.4   The Facility

A number of proposals have been made over the past four years by academics, business leaders, and politicians in an attempt to drive a wedge between old, bad debts and the recognized need for new investment in debtor countries. Old debts are seen in this context as oversized mortgages on the debtor countries that impede the free and voluntary flow of new funds. The means to achieve such a flow is a facility that buys up LDC debts from banks and reduces debt service costs for debtors.[16] Lightening the burden of old debts and using an international fund with its diversification possibilities and possible credit standing provides important opportunities for passing on benefits to the debtors, without destructive effects on the solvency of banks or the asset position of their stockholders.

The details of such facility schemes vary. Invariably they are administered by the World Bank and involve allusions to the Marshall Plan, recycling, and the sharing of international burdens by strong currency countries or countries with significant external surpluses. On the basis of a capital subscription to be made by an as yet undesignated donor, leveraged by significant borrowing in the world capital market, the facility would take LDC debts over from banks or buy these in the secondhand market. Benefits to the LDCs occur because the facility will have a lower cost of capital than the individual LDC, both because of diversification and guarantees. The benefit of the reduced cost of capital and of the facility's purchases at discount of debts from banks would be passed on to debtors in the form of more favorable interest rates or debt reduction.

The concept of a facility draws attention to an important practical problem in credit markets. The higher the interest rate charged on credit, the less likely that it can and will be paid. Hence a policy of risk premiums is exactly that—it makes loans risky. Thus the facility would avoid this problem by charging a common interest rate, but it would reward countries for performance by writing down outstanding debt.

Such a facility would introduce a new party into debt negotiations. Concerned with the solvency and productivity of the facility, the management could take positions on rescheduling agreements to assure that the value of the assets it carries is not impaired by extortionary settlements or unreasonable adjustment programs. One might imagine that the facility makes available a long-term reconstruction loan to a particular country, say Mexico, and in exchange secures from the banks extraordinary reductions in spreads or maturities. Of course, to perform this function aggressively would require that the manager of the facility have stature and independence beyond the immediate reach of the U.S. Treasury.

The main question about the facility, the issue of the donor aside, is Who should be the beneficiaries? The facility must, ultimately, involve taxpayers' money, although this may occur in a highly remote, off-budget, and leveraged fashion. The use of taxpayers' money makes it reasonable to ask whether the facility should benefit starving African debtors, middle-income Latin America, or winners such as Korea. Assigning the use of the fund primarily to Latin America rather than to Africa, whose debt is mainly to property authorities, is politically attractive.

3.6.5 Debt Relief

Debtor countries have failed to form an effective cartel that could impose debt relief in the form of a write-down, sharply reduced interest rates, generous grace periods, or the consolidation of debt into perpetuities. On the contrary, debtor countries have competed with each other and, as a result, have wound up with poor terms and a short leash.

So far, only two attempts have been made to turn debt service into a major political issue. One is the case of Peru, where the government unilaterally limited its debt service to a specified fraction of export revenue. The other is the Mexican case of 1986. In each instance the large domestic costs of debt service and the destructive effects on investment, inflation, and growth potential led the governments to try and limit the damage. It is hard to believe that Peru got very far, but it is certain that Mexico initiated an important change in policies and procedures. The Mexican success suggests to some observers that with enough determination (and a favorable geographic location), debtors can in fact secure reduced spreads, contingency funds, and even an underwriting of growth.

At the same time, the debt problem is starting to become a political issue. Henry Kissinger, Lord Lever, Sen. Bill Bradley, and an increasing number of policymakers and policy economists are advocating a more political approach to the debt problem. This is the case in part for reasons of foreign policy. But poor U.S. trade performance is also starting to be seen as a reflection of debtor countries' need to earn foreign exchange for debt service. This point has been emphasized especially by Senator Bradley (1986a, 1986b). The Bradley debt plan accordingly emphasizes the need to create a vehicle for trade-debt discussions. Focusing explicitly on the link between trade concessions by debtor countries and targeted, limited debt relief, this approach consciously makes debt a political issue. Besides adapting the regulatory system to facilitate write-downs agreed between debtors and creditors, the proposal also calls for reduced interest payments, extra money, and debt write-downs.

Several negative responses to the Bradley proposal have been voiced, suggesting that the plan is impractical or undesirable. One argument is that the particular details—for example, the annual debt summit—are implausible, complicated, or useless. The trade issue, viewed from the perspective of the U.S. external sector and growth, is small—there has been only a $12–15 billion swing in the bilateral balance with South America. Moreover, the write-downs are felt to be insufficiently conditioned on performance of the debtor countries and hence not worth making. Another criticism is more basic. It amounts to the assertion that any and all kinds of debt relief reduce or even destroy the beneficiaries ultimate chances of renewed access to the international capital market. Countries that accept debt relief, it is argued, will be tainted. Only those that service humbly will see the day of voluntary lending. Historical precedent for all of Latin America suggests the opposite.

Political solutions to the debt problem are likely to be close to the arrangement Mexico secured and far away from the ambitious Bradley Plan. Resistance to write-downs might soften, even if there is no indication of this at present, and terms might become more flexible. But even so the debt problem will remain an overwhelming burden on the growth prospects of Latin America. Taxpayers are unwilling to underwrite Latin American growth, and politicians are unwilling to underwrite the banks. Growth in Latin America will therefore depend in equal parts on a solution to the U.S. deficit problem with generous monetary accommodation and on the introduction of reasonable public finance in the debtor countries. With these two conditions met, and excepting extreme episodes such as the 1986 Mexican oil decline, growth can start again, although the losses of the 1980s will not be made up.

Debt relief can come from direct government intervention, but it can also come if governments withdraw from organizing the debt collection process. Meltzer (1984) has advocated this course and Milton Friedman (1984, p. 38) has observed: "So I think the way you solve the LDC 'debt bomb' problem is to require the people who make the loans to collect them. If they can, fine, and if they can't, that's their problem." There is little doubt that a withdrawal of governments (and the IMF) from the debt collection process would lead to a rapid disintegration of the creditors' cartel and a reduction of debts to levels more congenial to debtors.

3.6.6 Moral Hazard

Solutions to the debt crisis involving debt relief encounter one apparently overwhelming objection: Latin America's debt reflects to a large extent mismanagement and capital flight. Granting debt relief to Latin debtors, but not to countries where management was more careful, amounts to rewarding poor policy performance and thus invites repetition.

But the moral hazard argument can also be made in two other ways. First, not giving debt relief means that the governments of creditor countries enforce bad loans. They thus encourage poor lending policies on the part of commercial banks, which now expect their governments to help collect even the poorest sovereign loans. Second, in the context of capital flight it is frequently argued that amnesty for tax fraud and illegal capital transfers is an effective and desirable policy for encouraging a reflow. Of course, the same moral hazard argument applies, as future tax morality would be undermined.[17]

The major weakness of the moral hazard argument in cases such as Mexico and Argentina results from capital flight: those who pay are primarily workers whose real wages are cut. Owners of external assets are rewarded by capital gains and thus turn out to be net beneficiaries of the debt crisis. The moral hazard argument thus can be turned around to support the case for debt relief.

Notes

The author is indebted to Eliana Cardoso, Martin Feldstein, Stanley Fischer, and Simon Johnson for many helpful comments and suggestions.

1. There is a lot of flux in debt data. A good survey of the problems can be found in Mills 1986. We use here the IMF data, data reported by Morgan Guaranty *World Financial Markets,* and the U.S. country exposure survey, except where otherwise noted.

2. The classification of countries follows the IMF. See *World Economic Outlook* (October 1986): 31–34.

3. Note that real GDP and dollar GDP behave very differently. A real depreciation may raise real GDP but is certain to lower dollar GDP.

4. This increase in real debt burdens would have outpaced any advantages from cumulatively lower interest rates on nondollar debt. As is well known, exchange rate movements have far exceeded the depreciation implicit in international interest differentials.

5. See Dornbusch 1985 and 1986a on the Martinez de Hoz experiment.

6. On the Chilean experiment, see Edwards and Edwards 1987, and Ramos 1986.

7. On the Mexican case, see Cardoso and Levy 1986.

8. See especially Fraga 1986 for a comparison between Germany in the 1920s and Brazil in the 1980s. See, too, Dornbusch 1985b.

9. The fact that it is often food subsidies that are eliminated, without the proverbial neutral lumpsum tax to compensate the losers, does not seem to limit the case for the policy recommendation.

10. There are a few public sector bonds outstanding. Edwards 1986, and Dornbusch 1986b and 1986c look at the yields of Mexican, Argentine, Venezuelan, and Brazilian bonds.

11. The change in the bilateral trade balance in manufactures is more significant than the change in the total bilateral trade balance because declining oil and commodity prices reduce our import bill and hence are reflected in a smaller change of the total balance.

12. For an extensive discussion of solutions, see Lessard and Williamson 1985.

13. The Mexican settlement forced the commercial banks to put up an unexpectedly large contribution. The settlement has demonstrated that the debt problem is not dead, but also that government involvement might boomerang.

14. For a strong statement of support for debt-equity swaps, see the Morgan Guaranty *World Financial Markets* issue of September 1986.

15. The public opinion survey on Mexico reported in the *New York Times* on November 16, 1986, makes most apparent just how pessimistic nationals of debtor countries are about the chances of economic recovery.

16. The most recent proposals are the editorial by David Obey and Paul Sarbanes in the *New York Times,* November 9, 1986, and the suggestion for a Japan Fund made in various speeches by Jim Robinson of American Express.

17. There is an interesting difference in public finance ideology: government debt write-downs in the form of a capital levy are said to undermine the very foundations of government credit, but tax amnesty is viewed as a practical response.

References

Bell, Geoffrey L., and John G. Heimann. 1982. *Risks in international bank lending*. Group of Thirty.

Bergsten, Fred C., William R. Cline, and John Williamson. 1985. *Bank lending to developing countries: The policy alternatives*. Institute for International Economics. April.

Bradley, B. 1986a. Defusing the Latin debt bomb. *Washington Post,* October 5.

———. 1986b. A proposal for third world debt management. Paper presented in Zurich. June.

Cardoso, E. 1986. What policy makers can learn from Brazil and Mexico. *Challenge,* September/October.

Cardoso, E., and R. Dornbusch. 1987. Brazil's tropical plan. *American Economic Review* (papers and proceedings), May.

Cardoso, E., and S. Levy. 1986. Mexico. In R. Dornbusch and L. Helmers, eds., *The open economy: Tools for policy makers in developing countries.* World Bank.

Cline, W. 1983. International debt and stability of the world economy. Institute for International Economics, Washington, D.C., September.

Cohen, D., and J. Sachs. 1986. Growth and external debt under risk of repudiation. *European Economic Review,* June.

Cooper, R. N., and J. Sachs. 1985. Borrowing abroad: The debtors perspective. In G. Smith and J. Cuddington, eds., *International debt and the developing countries.* World Bank.

Dale, Richard, and Richard P. Mattione. 1983. *Managing global debt.* Washington, D.C.: Brookings Institution.

De Grauwe, P., and M. Fratianni. 1984. The political economy of international lending. *Cato Journal,* Spring/Summer.

Delamaide, D. 1985. *Debt shock.* New York: Anchor Press/Doubleday.

Dillon, Burke K., Maxwell C. Watson, Russell G. Kincaid, and Chanpen Puckahtikom. 1985. *Recent development in external debt restructuring.* International Monetary Fund. October.

Dornbusch, R. 1985a. External debt, budget deficits, and disequilibrium exchange rates. In G. Smith and J. Cuddington, eds., *International debt and the developing countries.* World Bank.

———. 1985b. Policy and performance links between LDC debtors and industrial countries. Brookings Papers on Economic Activity, no. 2.

———. 1986a. The Bradley Plan: A way out of the Latin debt mess. *Washington Post,* August 27.

———. 1986b. Impact on debtor countries of world economic conditions. In *External debt, investment and growth in Latin America.* International Monetary Fund.

———. 1986c. International debt and economic instability. In *Debt, financial stability and public policy.* Federal Reserve Bank of Kansas.

Dornbusch, R., and S. Fischer. 1986. Stopping hyperinflation. *Weltwirtschastliches Archiv,* April.

Eaton, J., M. Gersowitz, and J. Stiglitz. 1986. The pure theory of country risk. *European Economic Review,* June.

ECLA. 1985. *External debt in Latin America.* Denver, Colo.: Lynne Rienner Publishers; published in cooperation with the United Nations.

———. 1986. *Debt, adjustment, and renegotiation in Latin America.* Denver, Colo.: Lynne Rienner Publishers; published in cooperation with the United Nations.

Edwards, S. 1986. The pricing of bonds in and bank loans in international markets: An empirical analysis of developing countries' foreign borrowing. *European Economic Review,* June.

Edwards, S., and A. Cox Edwards. 1987. *Monetarism and liberalization.* Cambridge, Mass.: Balinger.

Eichengreen, B., and R. Portes. 1986. Debt and default in the 1930s: Causes and consequences. *European Economic Review,* June.

Feldstein, M. 1986. International debt service and economic growth: Some simple analytics. NBER Working Paper No. 2076.

Fischer, S. 1986a. The international debt problem and the Baler plan. Testimony before the Joint Economic Committee, January 23.

———. 1986b. Sharing the burden of the international debt crisis. *American Economic Review* (papers and proceedings), forthcoming.

Fishlow, A. 1985. Lessons from the past: Capital markets during the 19th century and the interwar period. *International Organization,* Summer.

Fraga, A. 1986. *German reparations and Brazilian debt: A comparative study.* Princeton Essays in International Finance, no. 163. September.

Friedman, M. 1984. *Politics and tyranny.* Pacific Institute for Public Policy Research.

Gersovitz, M. 1985. Banks' international lending decisions: What we know and implications for the future. In G. Smith and J. Cuddington, eds., *International debt and the developing countries.* World Bank.

Group of Thirty. 1981a. *The outlook for international bank lending.* New York.

———. 1981b. *Risks in international bank lending.* New York.

Guttentag, Jack, and Richard Herring. 1983. *The lender-of-last-resort function in an international context.* Princeton Essays in International Finance, no. 151. May.

———. 1986. *Disaster myopia in international banking.* Princeton Essays in International Finance, no. 164. September.

Hakim, P. 1986. The Baker Plan: Unfulfilled promises. *Challenge,* September/October.

Kaletsky, Anatole. 1985. *The costs of default.* 20th Century Fund.

Kenen, P. 1983. A bailout for the banks. *New York Times,* March 6.

Kindleberger, C. P. 1982. The cyclical pattern of longterm lending. In M. Gersovitz et al., *The theory and experience of economic development.* London: George Allen and Unwin.

Kraft, J. 1984. *The Mexican rescue.* Group of Thirty.

Krugman, P. 1985. International debt strategies in an uncertain world. In G. Smith and J. Cuddington, eds. *International debt and the developing countries.* World Bank.

Lessard, D., and J. Williamson. 1985. *Financial intermediation beyond the debt crisis.* Institute for International Economics, Washington, D.C. September.

Lever, H., and C. Huhne. 1986. *Debt and danger.* Boston: Atlantic Monthly Press.

Maddison, A. 1985. *Two crises: Latin America and Asia, 1929–38 and 1973–83.* Paris: OECD.

———, ed. 1986. *Latin America, the Caribbean and the OECD.* Paris: OECD.

Mehran, Hassanali. 1985. *External debt management.* International Monetary Fund.

Meltzer, A. 1984. The international debt problem. *Cato Journal,* Spring/Summer.

Mendelsohn, M. S., ed. 1981. *The outlook for international bank lending.* Group of Thirty.

Mills, R. H. 1986. Foreign lending by U.S. banks: A guide to international and U.S. statistics. *Federal Reserve Bulletin,* October.

Moreira-Marques, M. 1986. *The Brazilian quandary.* 20th Century Fund.

Niehans, J. 1985. International debt with unenforceable claims. Federal Reserve Bank of San Francisco. *Economic Review,* no. 1.

Nowzad, B., and R. C. Williams. 1981. *External indebtedness of developing countries.* International Monetary Fund. May.

Obey, D., and P. S. Sarbanes. 1986. Recycling surpluses to the third world. *New York Times,* November 9.

OECD. 1986. *Financing and external debt of developing countries: 1985 survey.*

Posner, M., ed. 1985. *Problems of international money, 1972–85.* International Monetary Fund.

Ramos, J. 1986. *Neoconservative economics in the Southern Cone of Latin America, 1973–83.* Baltimore: Johns Hopkins University Press.

Reiffel, A. 1985. *The role of the Paris Club in managing debt problems.* Princeton Essays in International Finance, no. 161. December.

Sachs, J. 1983. LDC debt in the 1980s: Risk and reforms. In Paul Wachtel, ed., *Crises in the economic and financial structure.*

———. 1984. *Theoretical issues in international borrowing.* Princeton Essays in International Finance, no. 54. July.

———. 1985. External debt and macroeconomic performance in Latin America and East Asia. Brookings Papers on Economic Activity, no. 2.

———. 1986. Conditionality and the debt crisis: Some thoughts for the World Bank. Harvard University. Typescript.

Simonsen, M. 1985. The developing country debt problem. In G. Smith and J. Cuddington, eds., *International debt and the developing countries.* World Bank.

Sjaastad, L. 1983. International debt quagmire: To whom do we owe it? *World Economy,* September.

U.S. Senate. Committee on Finance. 1932. *Sale of foreign bonds or securities in the United States.* January.

Watkins, Alfred J. 1986. *Till debt do us part.* Roosevelt Center for American Policy Studies. Washington, D.C.: University Press of America.

Watson, M., D. Mathieson, R. Kincaid, and E. Kalter. 1986. *International capital markets.* International Monetary Fund. February.

Weinert, R. 1983. Banks and bankruptcy. *Foreign Policy,* Spring.

Winkler, M. 1933. *Foreign bonds.* Philadelphia: Roland Swain Co.

World Bank. 1986. *A strategy for restoration of growth in middle-income countries that face debt-servicing difficulties.* Development Committee.

2. *Thomas S. Johnson*

U.S. External Debt and LDC Debt: Twin Problems

In 1982, when the international debt crisis burst into our collective consciousness, it was seen as a compartmentalized and "compartmentalizable" problem. Indeed, the strategy for dealing with it underscored that view. Emphasis was on the individual debtors, and debt restructurings were negotiated one at a time, each country with its group of creditor banks. Similarly, we handled the necessary macroeconomic adjustments on a case-by-case basis, each country working out its reforms and adjustment policies with the International Monetary Fund.

It will be up to economic historians to decide whether the compartmental approach was the correct one at the time—we think it was the right approach. Whatever the final answer to that historical question, however, today the international debt problem extends beyond the debtor countries and their creditor banks.

Considerable progress has been made—from both debtor and creditor perspectives—since the summer of 1982. The "Baker group" of fifteen countries—which together owe about $460 billion of the $1 trillion of LDC debt—have moved, in the aggregate, from deep current account deficit much closer to balance. Moreover, prices for their exports appear to have stabilized, interest rates on their debt have come down, and substantial debt restructuring has taken place.

We on the creditor side also have made progress. The five years since the problem became a crisis have allowed a substantial buildup of bank capital and reserves. As of late last year, lending exposure to the Baker-15 LDCs amounted to 125 percent of the capital of the nine largest U.S. banks, down from 200 percent in June 1982.

While acknowledging this progress, many believe that we may have come as far as we can using the compartmental approach alone and that systemic reform may now be needed. We will undoubtedly continue to succeed in restructuring and extending existing credits, but substantial impediments lie in the way of providing the flow of new funds that the LDCs need in order to grow:

- Unceasing negotiations with individual debtor countries are draining the analytical and managerial resources of official institutions, private creditors, and the developing nations themselves. For example, the energy toll among the top managers in our industry is very costly, and it clearly impairs, to some extent, our ability to do other things.
- The case-by-case approach had considerable merit in the early stages of the debt problem when adjustment was the priority. Now, when the emphasis has to shift to growth, reliance on the case-by-case approach alone may actually be inhibiting development of broader solutions.
- Multilateral programs for LDC financing that have been proposed thus far, such as the Baker Plan, continue almost exclusive reliance on commercial bank lending. Given the cloud that hangs over the commercial banks for the exposures they already have, continued emphasis on bank lending may be unrealistic at best and dangerous to the viability of the system at worst.

Beyond these institutional considerations, however, lie more fundamental reasons why further progress is problematic without going well beyond the case-by-case restructuring pattern. The United States, in acting as the world's largest consumer, has contributed to LDC progress in the short run, but, in becoming the world's largest debtor, in the longer run it has increased the vulnerability of the borrowing countries to shocks emanating from the industrialized world.

Between 1982 and 1985, the United States accounted for 75 percent of the rise in industrialized countries' total imports, and U.S. imports as a percentage of total world exports grew from 15 percent to more than 20 percent. Expansion of domestic demand in the United States has accounted disproportionately for expansion in worldwide demand and for growth of LDC exports. However, the unsustainability of U.S. consumer demand growth, complicated by our dangerously growing external imbalances, now exposes the LDCs to persistent and desta-bilizing concern over the potential for a sudden worsening of their situation.

How the industrialized world copes with its major imbalances will bear crucially on the ability of the LDCs to emerge from their debt crisis. A sudden loss of confidence in the United States as a debtor, or simply a portfolio preference shift away from U.S. financial instru-ments, would raise dollar interest rates and the LDC debt service burden and at the same time slow or shut down growth in the United States—the LDCs' major market.

However, a successful multilateral approach to the imbalances among industrialized nations would maintain demand for LDCs' products and reduce the risks of substantial increases in dollar interest rates. This is the challenge.

The accumulation of the U.S. debt in some ways is far more worrying and potentially disruptive than the accumulation of LDC debt. It is true that they differ in important ways. The U.S. debt is far smaller when measured against our income and resources. Moreover, we owe the debt in our own currency, rather than in the creditor's currency, so in that sense we can always repay.

In another sense, however, the debts are disturbingly similar. In each case, the borrowing has *postponed* an essential adjustment of real living standards. Borrowing in order to facilitate a more fundamental real adjustment is an appropriate use of credit for short periods of of time. But its use to avoid adjustment, as seen in the LDC experience, merely makes for a more wrenching adjustment eventually. Financial markets, of course, will ultimately cause the adjustments to occur, potentially in very destabilizing ways.

I am not reassured by the progress to date in attacking the imbalances present in the industrialized world. So far, there has been too much reliance on monetary policy in the coordination of G-5 policies, and too little movement toward correcting the saving-investment imbal-ances at the heart of the problem.

The massive lending to the developing nations in the late 1970s occurred in an environment of excessive worldwide liquidity growth. In retrospect, this occurred in the mistaken belief that the labor markets and physical plant of the developed world offered substantial margins of excess capacity.

Today, regulatory changes and sharp declines in nominal interest rates complicate interpretation of money growth rates. Nonetheless, there appears to be a similar complacency developing regarding the margins of unused capacity. There is no doubt in my mind that the strong growth of U.S. demand, which has in major part benefited the LDCs, has been encouraged by an accommodative U.S. monetary policy that may, with hindsight, prove to have been too easy.

Meanwhile, the call for foreign monetary authorities to finance faster growth ostensibly to stimulate U.S. and LDC export growth may amount, in effect, to a new way to monetize U.S. deficits. Similarly, efforts by foreign policymakers to stabilize nominal foreign exchange rates against the dollar will tend to create a potentially dangerous expansion of foreign money supplies. Such efforts already have entailed widespread acceleration of monetary aggregates and, in some cases, unwelcome overshooting of monetary targets. Time will tell whether the enormous lending to the United States is being facilitated by excess liquidity creation, as was the LDC lending. The danger, of course, is a new burst of inflationary pressures at some point.

There seems to be widespread agreement among policymakers that the fundamental imbalances are found in differential saving and investment patterns. It is a familiar theme, expressed at the Plaza, in Tokyo and most recently in Paris. The United States must reduce its budget deficit and thereby its excessive demands on the world's capital. The industrialized countries having external surpluses must find another outlet for their excess saving.

One way to effect these changes is identified in all of the G-5, G-6, and G-7 communiqués: stimulating domestic demand in the surplus countries through more aggressive use of fiscal and tax policies. This can be supplemented by exploring mechanisms to channel capital to LDCs, a subject to which I will return.

Before turning to some thoughts regarding an appropriate policy mix going forward, I must note that we are running out of time. While the LDC problem grew over a long period of time, the door to credit availability closed suddenly in 1982. Such a dramatic event is probably not likely to confront the United States as a debtor. Since our debts are in dollars, they will always be repaid, though at what real value is unknown. But developments over the last year suggest to me the door is beginning to close.

Through 1985, international investors appeared to view the United States as a good credit risk, given the size of its economy and its productive resources. More recently, there have been ominous signs of a shift away from preference for U.S. investments, perhaps because U.S. monetary policy has been so accommodative.

The middle two quarters of last year saw a sharp drop in spontaneous private inflows of capital to the United States. In 1985, net private capital inflows ran at $103 billion, exceeding the total recorded inflows, as official capital of $8 billion flowed out. In the second and third quarters of 1986, recorded private net capital inflows slowed to an annual rate of $65 billion—barely half the total capital inflows—as official flows into the United States accelerated to nearly $60 billion. Even that rate of official inflow was probably surpassed in the first quarter of 1987. Meanwhile, we have witnessed several worrisome episodes in the last twelve months in which the dollar's foreign exchange value has declined even as the U.S. interest rates have risen.

In this context, the Paris G-6 agreement is meaningless if it does not deliver substantial shifts in policies affecting fundamental saving-investment balances. The accord so far has apparently succeeded in relieving speculative pressures on the dollar, as currencies have traded in recent weeks over fairly narrow ranges. But the underlying market mood remains bearish, and a new speculative run—against which the central banks would have little leverage—could occur at any time. This makes it all the more important that policymakers move quickly to meet, or even exceed, the commitments they made to correct the saving-investment imbalances.

The litany of the required policy adjustment bears repeating: the U.S. administration and Congress must not let up on their efforts to reduce the federal budget deficit. Significant progress has been made, but I sense that a level of frustration is developing which threatens that progress.

The discipline inherent in Gramm-Rudman has put a significantly declining budget deficit within our reach. Regardless of whether we meet the arbitrary timetable set forth in the act, the main objective has to be creating credible expectations of declining budget deficits. The most important discipline has been resistance to any new programs. However, we now see our new programs—such as catastrophic health insurance and welform reform—being talked about, and it will require even greater efforts to hold the line. Budget deficit reduction in the United States will help maintain lower real U.S. interest rates and free up funds for productive private investment in the United States and abroad.

The surplus countries have taken some important steps and will have to continue their efforts to stimulate their domestic economies. My sense is that still more can be done through tax incentives for investment and local public works expenditures to replace export demand lost to the lower dollar. These initiatives, of course, must take place while making every effort to keep markets open to international trade.

We can add another dimension to these policies. A fundamental disequilibrium in the surplus industrialized countries is their excess of domestic savings. We also know that the LDCs require more diversified credit sources and markets for their products. A result of better economic policy balance among the developed countries should be a marginal, at least, improvement in the relative attractiveness of investments in the developing countries.

This challenge—providing a new flow of funds to promote growth—may require that we review the compartmental approach we have taken thus far on LDC debt. This debt is no longer a "bank" problem, and is too big for the banks to solve alone. The governments of the industrialized world, through excessive liquidity creation and mercantilist trade policies, helped create it, and governments must help solve it.

The ultimate answer may lie in some form of multilateral lending institution created to channel new capital to these countries and assist in diversifying the risks and the investor base. New cash for additional lending could be raised through some combination of equity contributions or credit guarantees from governments, together with more imaginative ways to deal with existing debt. The emphasis of the new approach, to which the creditor banks ought also to contribute, should be on new funds in response to longer-term economic reforms in the debtor nations.

The alternative—relying solely on case-by-case restructuring of existing debts—may not provide enough flexibility and time for the reforms to produce sustainably better performance in these countries. What we and they need now is breathing room.

Ideas of this sort require much more work. However, I am convinced that the problems confronting the LDCs and those of the industrialized world are really the same problems. They must be solved together, if they are to be solved at all.

3. Anne O. Krueger
The Problems of the LDCs' Debt

Debt-servicing difficulties are not a new phenomenon. American economic history contains episodes of default and servicing difficulties, and even in the "golden era" after the Second World War reschedulings often accompanied IMF stabilization programs. Until the 1980s, however, debt-servicing difficulties and reschedulings were seldom noted outside of the international institutions and country in which they happened.

In the 1980s, a number of large developing countries, with sufficiently sizable debt to arouse concern for the macroeconomic stability of the international financial system, encountered debt-servicing difficulties at almost the same time. Because these difficulties were simultaneous, it was natural that many observers took debt to be the problem, rather than a symptom. Indeed, there were perceived to be (at least) two problems: one, the financial institutions in credit countries, and the other the heavily indebted developing countries. While the two problems are not identical, it is clear that if the borrowers succeed in servicing their debt and restoring growth, both problems will be solved. I, therefore, concentrate on this issue in most of my remarks. In the conclusion, I briefly address the question of what might happen if there were an alternative outcome.

Almost any country confronted with debt-servicing difficulties has, by definition, a "balance of payments crisis." If it could service its debt, it could also obtain financing for its current obligations on international capital markets. This does not mean that debt-servicing obligations "caused" the balance of payments crisis; on the contrary, the usual story is one of chronic current account deficits that are financed by borrowing until creditors are unwilling to extend additional credit. It is not the existence of debt per se that triggers a crisis, but rather the inability to command yet more loans. However, in 1982–83 the world recognized the "crisis," but failed to appreciate the nature of the longer-term problems that had led to it.

For this reason, any assessment of the problems associated with the debt of individual developing countries must start with an understanding of the origins of the difficulties. I, therefore, address that question first. Thereafter, individual countries' prospects for resolution of their particular problems, given the current outlook for the global economy, are analyzed. On that basis, it is possible to evaluate potential changes in the international environment that might enhance economic prospects for some of the heavily indebted countries and for the world economy, which is the final topic.

What Led to the Debt Problem?

It is useful to recall the textbook explanation of capital flows, which for present purposes I shall equate with accumulation of debt. Capital-rich countries have relatively high savings rates (because of their high incomes) and relatively low rates of return on investment, contrasted with capital-poor, developing countries. Therefore, capital should flow from rich countries to poor countries because savers will receive higher returns and world economic growth will be enhanced.

During the 1970s, most observers viewed the expansion of private lending to developing countries as a sign of success with development: LDCs that had earlier been dependent on official capital flows (foreign aid and lending from government agencies and the multilateral development banks) were able to borrow from the private international capital market. That appeared to confirm the conventional wisdom and to signal that the private international capital market was functioning well in allocating the world's savings to high-return activities. Then came the "debt crisis" of the 1980s, which led some to question the textbook wisdom.

The conventional analysis is not wrong, but it is surely incomplete, at least as stated above. Borrowing to finance high rate-of-return investments can certainly yield a sufficient increment to income to permit the borrower to service the debt and simultaneously earn a higher income. But borrowing to finance an excess of consumption over income cannot be continued indefinitely. And, of course, investors' expectations may be wrong, either with regard to the stream of returns they will earn or with respect to the expected real interest rate they will pay over the life of their loan.

What happened in the 1970s was a combination of many things. Some countries' economic policies were conducive to high rates of return on investment, and they borrowed much as in the textbook story. Even those countries had to adjust in the early 1980s to worldwide recession and much higher real interest rates, but they were by and large able to do so, albeit not without difficulty.

Other countries, however, had macroeconomic policy stances in which domestic investment (some of which yielded low real returns) exceeded domestic saving, and foreign borrowing financed the difference. To some extent, the excess of domestic investment was the result of large public sector deficits (even when the authorities raised domestic interest rates to encourage the private sector to do the foreign borrowing); another contributing factor was the failure by some countries to have adjusted domestic incentives after the oil price increase in 1973. In a very permissive international environment, with negative real rates of interest and rising nominal export prices, these policy stances were not inconsistent with some growth of real per capita incomes and continued debt servicing, although alternative policies would have yielded even more rapid, and certainly more sustainable, growth. When the global environment changed in the early 1980s, however, these countries were confronted with major debt-servicing difficulties, and the economic policies that had earlier sustained satisfactory growth were no longer adequate to the task. To compound matters, there was a required adjustment to the almost-simultaneous sharp rise in real interest rates, deteriorating terms of trade, and decline in net capital flows.

Other countries fared even worse: their macroeconomic policies were so unrealistic that they were unable to sustain growth even in the 1970s. In some instances, there were debt crises and sharp shifts in policies even before the 1980s. Turkey is the most visible case. Many sub-Saharan African countries, of course, also experienced negative rates of growth of per capita income in the 1970s. However, a large portion of their debt was on concessional terms, and aid was sufficiently large so that many did not confront unmanageable debt-servicing difficulties until the 1980s. Then the impact of the altered global environment was magnified by the accumulated inefficiencies resulting from past policies.

To be sure, not all countries fell into any of these three categories. Some, most notably the South Asian countries, were sufficiently fiscally conservative that they did not borrow much from the private capital markets in the 1970s. Their situation is, therefore, not considered in what follows, although the fact that some low-income countries are not heavily indebted must be borne in the mind when considering policy options for improving the prospects of the heavily indebted countries.

The precise mix of internal and external factors that resulted in debt-servicing problems varied significantly from country to country. No one diagnosis pertains to all, or even the majority of countries. Nonetheless, all of the heavily indebted countries that encountered debt-servicing difficulties are confronted with a much harsher international economic environment in the 1980s: they cannot base their policies on the expectation that there will be a return to the conditions of the 1970s. This means that policies must be changed, not only or even primarily because of the need to service and perhaps reduce debt, but simply because the policies that were at least marginally sustainable throughout the 1970s are not feasible in the mid-1980s. New capital inflows, if and when they take place, will be economically warranted only in financing more efficient investment programs than was the case in the 1970s. Even without debt, therefore, policy shifts would have been necessary and economic prospects would have deteriorated for the heavily indebted developing countries under their policy regimes of the 1970s.

Prospects for Growth and Creditworthiness

Resumption/acceleration of economic growth is an important objective, not only for the well-being of people in developing countries, but also for American political and economic interests. It is difficult to imagine a continuation of debt servicing over the intermediate and longer-term with stagnant or falling living standards in the heavily in-debted countries. At any event, it is highly doubtful if exports could be increased enough to maintain debt service without growth in real output. Thus, while growth is desirable in itself, it is also a prerequisite for resolution of the debt problem.

The fundamental questions, in my judgment, are (1) What rates of economic growth would be attainable in the absence of any debt given a global environment not too different from that prevailing during the past several years? (2) To what extent do debt-servicing obligations reduce the attainable growth rate? and (3) What conflict is there, if any, between acceleration of growth and ability to maintain debt-servicing obligations and restore creditworthiness? Much public (and profes-sional) discussion of the debt problem has been muddled by confusion of these questions.

The attainable rate of economic growth of any country, given the global environment, is a function of its resource endowment, the rate at which it is accumulating resources, its policy stance (which is crucial in determining the efficiency with which resources are used and also the rate of saving and resource accumulation), and its willingness to alter its policies to improve growth prospects.

With a few exceptions, the policy reforms undertaken to date have been demonstrably inadequate to the task. In most heavily indebted developing countries, one would make similar policy prescriptions to enhance prospects for resuming/accelerating growth: adoption and maintenance of a realistic exchange rate; dismantling quantitative con-trols over imports and reducing the bias of the trade regime against exports by sharply reducing protection conferred to import-substituting industries and imposing a low ceiling on the height of any remaining tariffs; reduction in the size of the public sector deficit (but with ap-propriate attention to the investment/consumption composition of pub-lic expenditures and the incentive effects of the tax structure); removal of many domestic controls over private economic activity; reduction in the inefficiencies associated with parastatals; and movement toward more efficient mechanisms for channeling credit to its most productive uses.

If "ideal" or "near-ideal" reforms could be achieved, improved resource reallocation, increased inefficiency of resource utilization, and faster rates of growth of savings and investment would all conduce toward higher growth rates. Initially, one would anticipate a burst of exports and some degree of rationalization, if not reduction, in the size of the import-competing sector. Simply because incentives have been so distorted toward import-competing activities, the shift in incentives under this "ideal" reform would result in a period during which export growth would exceed GNP growth as the share of trade in GNP rose to a more appropriate level, and one would expect new private investment to be heavily oriented toward exportables and public investment to expansion of ports, communications, and other essential support services for expansion of international trade.

While the growth rate that might be achieved with such a shift in the policy environment would naturally vary from country to country, the historical evidence is that even during times of slow growth of the world economy, countries with reasonable policy environments have been able to achieve growth rates of 6–7 percent. If a country could somehow get to the 6–7 percent growth rate path, with an even more rapid rate of growth of export earnings for a half decade or so, debt-servicing problems would become manageable and diminish in importance with time.

There are, however, two reasons why things are not so easy as that even from the individual country's viewpoint (I later address the global issue of protectionism and what it does to export prospects). The first is that many countries' reform efforts have generally fallen far short of "ideal"; the second is that, in some countries, debt-servicing obligations may make the attainable rate of growth significantly lower than 6–7 percent without some capital inflow to supplement domestic savings.

Turning to the first issue, the needed "ideal" reforms are politically painful. Inevitably, the political process generates pressures to reduce the extent of reforms to the "necessary minimum." While economists can, to a considerable extent, identify larger and smaller deviations of policy from those most conducive to growth, it is not yet possible, given the state of the art, to quantify the essential minimum that will be effective in, for example, stopping a decline in per capita income or in permitting a growth rate of x percent per capita per annum, quite aside from the fact that any such quantification would necessarily be conditioned on the state of the international economy. Some "reform" programs, when whittled down by the political process, might succeed, if at all, only under highly favorable assumptions.

In these circumstances, many reform programs appear to be "too little, too late." And in some instances they are. Even in prospect, it was hard to understand how the international community gave its blessing to some of the programs; in many other instances, it could readily be judged that prospects were at best doubtful. To be sure, had global conditions returned to those prevailing in the mid-1970s, some of these programs would have been sufficient. But absent such conditions, it is almost certain that further policy reform programs will be essential in many of the heavily indebted countries.

Undertaking halfhearted and ill-fated reform programs has a number of costs. Political opposition (in other countries and in later efforts in the failing country) can point to the "failure" of these efforts as an argument against other attempts. And to the extent that international resources for supporting reform efforts are limited, the support of these programs diverts resources from more thoroughgoing efforts with far greater likelihood of success. Finally, there is some evidence that potential lenders cannot discriminate among reform programs: the failure of any makes them more reluctant to support all others without discrimination among them.

Thus, any attempt to evaluate prospects for growth and resolution of the debt problem must start with an assessment of the adequacy of the reforms undertaken thus far relative to the magnitude of those needed. I have already said enough to suggest that I am, in many instances, skeptical of the adequacy of the programs. But so far I have assumed there is no debt problem, only an international economic environment less permissive of policy mistakes than was that of the 1970s. The question next arises as to how the existence of debt and debt-servicing obligations complicates the analysis.

In most countries, the necessity for debt servicing creates a significant cost in that it diverts the attention of some of the most able policymakers from longer-term issues to the short-term problem of debt servicing and rescheduling. This "crisis management" mentality is not conducive to longer-term economic reforms, and it is all too easy to think of debt as the sole cause of difficulties. Ability to blame the debt also helps increase opposition to the necessary longer-term reforms.

Aside from that very real, but unmeasurable, cost, debt servicing poses two problems: (1) generating the foreign exchange for debt service, and (2) obtaining the necessary finance (since in most countries the debt is largely a government obligation).

For many countries, these problems would reduce the rate of growth attainable from "ideal," or even realistic, reforms. Nonetheless, the arithmetic is such that in most cases, attaining sufficient policy reform is the problem: export and GNP growth would and could be rapid enough to permit a fairly rapid reduction in debt-service ratios, with a consequent diminution of the debt problem.

There are some countries, however, whose debt obligations are so large, and whose incomes are so low, that it is difficult to imagine (on reasonable assumptions about the world environment) that even ideal reforms could deliver quick results without some additional external capital. New investment is usually needed to permit more than a short-term response out of excess capacity to newly realigned incentives. In countries where the domestic savings rate (public and private) is 12–14 percent of GNP, it is almost inconceivable that debt-servicing obligations (which usually have to be financed out of public revenues) of 6–7 percent of GNP can be met while simultaneously increasing net savings sufficiently to permit enough investment to achieve a reasonable rate of growth of exports and efficient import substitutes. If there were no "debt overhang," the high rates of return associated with realigned incentives would induce voluntary private capital flows. While an improved environment for direct private investment and other, non-debt, private capital flows can perhaps increase capital inflows (or reduce outflows) to some extent, it is highly unlikely that the order of magnitude can be sufficient to improve prospects significantly, given the reluctance of lenders to increase their exposure in countries encountering debt-servicing difficulties. And, until growth resumes, it is doubtful whether countries' prospects will appear sufficiently favorable to induce private lending from abroad. There thus may be a vicious circle in which the failure of capital inflows implies low growth which implies future debt-servicing difficulties.

This "debt overhang" problem is well known in the corporate finance literature: a burden of debt from past investments can act as a "tax" on future earnings so that even if companies have high prospective rates of return on new investments they may be unable to raise the finance for them (although it must be pointed out that holders of equity may have incentives to invest in some highly risky ventures even with negative expected returns since unfavorable outcomes cannot make their situations worse). Although a need to raise revenue for debt service equal to 5, 6, or 7 percent of GNP does not at first sight seem that high, it can be formidable when viewed in the context of economies where per capita incomes are very low and where there is an imperative to reduce the size and disincentive effects of the public sector.

The problem posed to policymakers by the debt (quite aside from whether the costs of reform may be high enough to be politically destabilizing) is to differentiate between cases of insufficient reforms, when prospects for growth and resumption of creditworthiness are in any event bleak (and where, therefore, additional debt will only make the problem worse when an adequate program is finally undertaken), and cases of "debt overhang" where reforms have been sufficiently far reaching but are unlikely to succeed because of the burden of debt service.

Based on these considerations, it is simple to answer the third question I posed. Except in cases of debt overhang, there is little, if any, conflict between resumption/acceleration of growth and resolution of the debt problem. To be sure, adequate reforms would yield even higher benefits in the absence of debt, but attainment of sufficient growth would surely permit the resumption of voluntary lending and thus reduce the drag. Indeed, it can be argued that the pressures created by debt-servicing obligations may, in some circumstances, induce more sizable reforms than would otherwise be undertaken and in that sense lead to more satisfactory long-term prospects.

That much said, however, the magnitude of policy reform required with debt service to achieve any "target" growth rate is certainly greater than it would be in the absence of debt. When there are political constraints on how much can be done, there may indeed be instances where the existence of debt-servicing obligations constitutes the critical margin of drain on resources. Nonetheless, in the longer term it remains true that the policy efforts that would accelerate growth are the same ones that would ease debt-servicing problems.

The Global Environment

Despite the feasibility of resuming satisfactory growth and of resolving the debt problem, the outlook that it will happen is not bright. Many countries' governments have undertaken what can at best be described as partial reform programs, and there are signs of political difficulties even then. Even in some of those countries where the policy package appears to be fairly far reaching, the "debt overhang" appears to be an issue.

At best, under present conditions, those few countries with the political strength to undertake sufficient reforms will accelerate growth and restore creditworthiness, or at least service their debt without major difficulties. Most of the heavily indebted countries, however, are more likely in the near term to suffer low growth and continuing debt service problems. In the longer term, of course, it is almost unthinkable that political stability could be maintained with stagnant or declining per capita incomes and continued voluntary debt servicing. But for the next three to five years, it is likely that there will be slow growth, with recurring suspensions of payments and protracted negotiations and reschedulings, with different countries taking center stage at different times. Of course, there will likely be a few lasting success stories, but they will be the exception unless something in the global environment changes.

The analysis thus far has been based on the assumption that world economic prospects are for a continuation of conditions much as they were in 1985–86: annual OECD growth of between 2.5 percent and 3 percent; growth of world trade about 5 percent; little new private lending to the heavily indebted countries except in support of reschedulings; and concessional flows to the very poor countries, especially sub-Saharan Africa, at approximately present levels.

Even this rather unsatisfactory outlook is premised on the continuation of existing growth rates of world trade. Existing protectionist pressures against developing countries' exports are worrisome not only for the long-run damage they could do to the economies of the protectionist countries but also because any significant effective increase in protection would spell macroeconomic doom for the prospects of the developing countries. Should the OECD, for example, limit the growth of exports from developing countries to the present share of OECD markets, that would imply expansion of LDC exports in the aggregate at a real average annual rate of 3 percent. Developing countries as a group could not then experience sufficiently satisfactory rates of export growth to finance both debt servicing and the growth of imports that would permit realization of satisfactory growth (and such protection would, in any event, provide further ammunition for the foes of policy reform in the developing countries).

Although the link between the Uruquay round of trade negotiations and the developing countries' prospects may seem remote, it is in fact very close: the restoration and maintenance of a liberalized trading regime is perhaps the single most important policy imperative from the developing countries' viewpoint. Recognizing that, more rapid growth of the OECD would also improve the odds. While maintenance of a liberalized trading regime would in any event be a necessary condition for sustained OECD growth, there is good reason to believe that something in the neighborhood of 3 percent OECD growth may be a watershed: historically, world trade had grown at about 1.5 times the rate of growth of the OECD GNP; developing countries have been able to increase their shares in trade, with growth rates about half as much again. On these norms (which presume no increase in protectionism), a 2.5 percent OECD growth rate would witness a 4 percent real rate of growth of world trade, which in turn could support about a 6 percent growth rate of developing countries' exports. That is barely above the real rate of interest; in these circumstances, the prospects for many developing countries would be poor indeed. By contrast, 3.5 percent OECD growth would probably permit about a 7.5 percent growth rate for developing countries' exports; this would provide a small margin for error and still permit some reduction in the overall debt service ratio for developing countries. To compound matters further, a lower rate of OECD growth would very likely be associated with a higher real rate of interest.

But while the world economy is important for the prospects of developing countries, the fate of issues that need to be addressed to assure more rapid growth will depend on political imperatives within the OECD countries and not on considerations of the debt problem or of developing countries' interests. The question, then, is whether other changes might improve prospects.

The obvious prescription is to increase capital flows, especially to those countries where policy reform appears to be reasonably far reaching and where debt overhang seems to be a significant issue. This would be doubly attractive. It would improve the long-term prospects for those countries where there are high real rates of return but insufficient savings to support a rate of investment that would allow a realistic change for growth. It would also increase the attractiveness of sufficiently bold policy changes in other countries to increase the likelihood that policy changes would in fact accomplish their intended goals.

To date, there has been insufficient differentiation between degrees of reform effort, and the developed countries and international institutions have fairly evenhandedly supported efforts in countries without as much regard to the adeququacy of reforms as might have been desirable. In part, this has been because assessment of what is adequate depends on one's forecast of future global conditions and other uncertainties. In part, however, political pressures have supported relatively uniform, and somewhat uncritical, reform efforts.

To be sure, augmented capital flows to the heavily indebted countries would reduce the needed degree of reform. But barring a large increase in capital flows, the case for greater targeting of available resources to those countries having undertaken adequate programs would appear very strong.

Some greater degree of concentration of limited resources would surely increase the rate of return on capital flows to developing countries. Assurances of support for a period of several years for, say, trade liberalization would provide needed credibility to reform efforts and often the critical margin between success and failure. Especially since more resources may otherwise result in less reform, the case for a highly selective targeting of available resources to the most thoroughgoing policy reform efforts seems very strong.

While it would require concerted action of the major OECD countries, such support could come through a special window of the IMF or World Bank, with eligibility limited to countries meeting reasonably stringent criteria. For example, countries might be eligible only if they undertook to maintain a policy regime with no quantitative restrictions on imports; no tariffs higher than, say, 10 percent; automatic adjustments in the exchange rate whenever the current account or trade balance deficit exceeded a certain figure (perhaps set as a percentage of GNP); no controls over domestic prices; a public sector deficit of less than 2 percent of GNP; and a real rate of return to domestic savers in excess of 3 percent. Whether additional requirements should be made judgmentally or not could be the subject for discussion, but my predeliction would be for reasonably tight automatic criteria so that political considerations not come into play. In saying this, I recognize that there are ways of "cooking the books" on the size of the public sector deficit, the tariff rate, and so on. Nonetheless, reasonably "clean" guidelines would provide support for those administering the window and simultaneously permit negotiation over the degree to which the numbers were a reasonable reflection of underlying reality.

What would induce countries to continue to adhere to the terms of the window and not reverse their reforms after a year or two? Obviously, there are no guarantees, but there could be a few inducements: (1) the assurance of support for the current account deficit up to the specified level; and (2) a negotiated debt repayment schedule that was annually effective contingent on satisfactory performance as agreed.

Such a facility, if it had adequate resources to underwrite thoroughgoing reform efforts of this nature, would do several things: (1) it would substantially increase the probability that reforms would be sustained and therefore would be effective, especially since a lack of credibility has often been a major reason for slow responses to altered incentives; and (2) it would probably increase the number of political leaderships willing to undertake policy reform packages of adequate proportions to induce results.

One fears, however, that the status quo—slow growth and recurring debt-servicing difficulties followed by new reschedulings—will continue to be the order of the day unless a major disaster focuses the attention of the international community on the problem or worldwide economic conditions revert to those prevailing in the mid-1970s. Given the enormous costs that would be associated with either of those outcomes, one can only hope that a buoyant international economy and a successful Uruquay round make a sufficient difference so that more countries can, more quickly, escape from their present difficulties.

Summary of Discussion

A major part of the discussion centered around the role of conditionality in solutions to the debt problem. Anne Krueger suggested that given the stop-and-go history of the policy reform apparatus in Latin America, the international community should assume the support of correct policy over the long horizon, laying down conditions in advance so that rollover can happen automatically. The problems should be handled in a more global and less case-by-case manner, and the political interests of the major bank/fund shareholders should be kept out of the process. The rules should be more clean.

Krueger contended that the Bradley plan did not recognize the scarcity of resources and the resulting fact that they should be carefully aimed. International competition for resources would increase the chances of successful policy reform. Currently the fund and bank resources are spread with insufficient selectivity to all countries that undertake any kind of reform. More resources are indeed needed, but in exchange for sufficient reforms.

Thomas Johnson agreed that any new institution to deal with the debt problem should get the rewards on the table ahead of the policy reform itself. From this perspective, he argued, an institution that buys debt from the banks, as in Bradley, could be counterproductive. Strict discipline with new credit over time could be quite effective.

Rudiger Dornbusch argued on the basis of a reading of Bradley's actual proposals that in the Bradley Plan a rolling revision of conditionality is matched to write-downs of debt and trade credit. Trade liberalization and other reforms are required. The problem with this plan for some is that the banks have to bear some of the burden. He warned that Congress is rampant with plans that would result in the reduction of stockholder equity.

Johnson agreed that the correct words about conditionality are there but asserted that the institutional setting is lacking.

The discussion shifted to the question of what might happen in the absence of a major new multilateral initiative. Johnson made a distinction between relief and write-down of debts. The marketplace is already doing the bookkeeping on the value of the loans, although there has been no forgiveness or write-downs by the banks. He raised the possibility of the banks walking away from the situation in 1989 or 1990, after they have increased reserves enough so that there will be no leverage over them, and argued that this scenario without a setting for new financing for the LDCs would be the worst possible outcome.

Martin Feldstein turned the issue around, asking why the big three debtors would not default, since they will not get as much in new loans as they have to pay in interest. He noted that the threat of exclusion from world trade might be credible. Krueger recalled the "dollar shortage," the Club of Rome predictions, and the "energy shortage." When the U.S. budget deficit shrinks, she contended, capital will flow to poor countries. The only hope for growth for debtor nations is integration into the world economy, and since trade credits will be the first to go, the debtor countries will hang on until they lose these credits. John Block wondered if the debtors could not improve their credit rating by walking out on their current obligations, which have such a depressing effect on prospects for growth. Krueger maintained that the fundamental determinants of growth would be the same.

Differences between the banks will not cause the situation to unravel, contended Johnson, who believes that the stakes are too big for the situation to fall apart.

The issue of book-market discounts was raised by several participants. Johnson pointed out that this market is highly illiquid. He explained that U.S. banks do not reflect market discounts but believes that there is room for growth to resume if imbalances in Western nations can be corrected. Gerald Corrigan agreed that the secondary market for LDC market is small, primarily used for debt-equity swaps, and should therefore not be considered a bellwether.

Thomas Enders pointed out that European banks have provisioned for much of their Latin American debtor portfolio, since their reserves are above the discounted value of the debt, and are moving it off their balance sheet. The Japanese may be doing the same thing, implying that U.S. banks would be the major holders as banks of LDC debt. U.S. banks have increased capital set-asides, but the recent drop in the LDC debt as percentage of equity from 90 percent to 45 percent masks an uneven distribution of debt, with the money center banks more exposed. Still, no U.S. banks are writing anything off.

Johnson agreed that the problem of the bank balance sheets is secondary to the question of how to deal with policy reform and growth, and how to maximize the likelihood that nations can play their financial and trading role in the world community.

4 Financial Innovations in International Financial Markets

1. Richard M. Levich
2. E. Gerald Corrigan
3. Charles S. Sanford, Jr., and George J. Votja

1. Richard M. Levich

4.1 Introduction

A wave of financial innovation begun in the early 1960s is now sweeping throughout the United States and other developed economies, producing major changes in the financial landscape. While the details of the process differ country by country, there are several common features, including (i) innovation—the development of new financial products and markets; (ii) securitization—a greater tendency toward market-determined interest rates and marketable financial instruments rather than bank loans; (iii) liberalization—of domestic financial market practices either through explicit deregulation or a breaking down of conventions; (iv) globalization—as national barriers erode and financial markets grow more integrated; and (v) increased competition among financial institutions, with many of the traditional distinctions between commercial banks, investment banks, and securities firms becoming blurred in the process.[1]

A major feature of this process has been the introduction of a wide variety of new products that trade in new market settings, thereby reducing the reliance upon banks for traditional credit instruments and credit evaluations. Many of these new products (e.g., currency and interest rate swaps, currency and interest rate options) are of obvious assistance for risk management purposes—to enable the individual or firm to tailor the various dimensions of risk (e.g., currency, maturity, credit, interest rate, default, and so forth) more precisely than before. Other products (e.g., note issuance facilities and Eurocurrency commercial paper) appear to directly reduce the cost of funding a desired financial position. The basic principles underlying today's new financial products are being extended and reapplied to yield still more products.[2]

It is not an exaggeration to claim that these developments are having a profound impact on all aspects of the financial services industry. For individual employees, innovation has affected the job description of the typical bank "lending" officer at major money center banks, the human capital needed to perform well, and even the definition of normal business hours. At the level of the financial services firm, innovation has affected the geographic location of activities, the financial product line, the risks that are being traded or carried, the identity of the major players, and the intensity of competition. Nonfinancial firms are faced with a vast array of financial choices—new financial markets and products, each with their own risk and return properties—that require increasingly sophisticated analysis. Naturally, all of these factors feed into macroeconomic performance. Policymakers and regulatory agencies are keen to understand the potential benefits (or costs) of these new products, new procedures, and new players and to incorporate these new factors into macroeconomic policies and regulatory decisions.

This paper provides a broad assessment of these recent developments surrounding financial innovation, including their impact on financial stability and national policy-making. This theme suggests several basic questions: (i) What financial product and process changes have occurred over the last twenty to twenty-five years in U.S. and international financial markets? (ii) What factors account for these changes? (iii) What are the implications of these changes for individuals and the aggregate macroeconomy from both a positive and policy perspective? This paper lays a foundation that will address these questions.

Section 4.2 outlines the dimensions of the international financial marketplace. Data presented on the volume of activity in the Eurocurrency and Eurobond markets offer a good reflection of the general phenomenon in financial markets—mushrooming volume, transforming markets once thought to be ancillary or for a specialized few into major centers of activity. Data on the extent of securitization and on trading in new risk management and funding vehicles (e.g., futures, options, and swaps) are also presented. Again the picture is one of securities or markets that were virtually nonexistent a decade ago, but now have grown to substantial importance.

Section 4.3 presents an overview of the types of new financial products that are available and their functions. Several financial market innovations are described to illustrate their workings and recent evolution and to demonstrate how the products add value for market participants. These examples also illustrate how new financial products might be engineered from existing products. This demonstrates that the new instruments need not add new price risk to the system, but by adding liquidity and new intermediaries they may contribute additional credit or liquidity risks.

The causes of financial market innovation are explored in section 4.4. I first consider the demand for financial market services in a "perfect capital market" setting and then argue that financial market innovations may be viewed as attempts to overcome real-world market imperfections. A distinction is made between imperfections that are man-made (e.g., taxes, regulatory barriers, and information disclosure) versus those that segment domestic markets and are naturally present (e.g., transaction costs, heterogeneous expectations, and heterogeneous consumption/investment/risk preferences). Innovations that overcome the former may directly thwart national economic policies, including useful prudential policies, while innovations that overcome the latter tend to increase economic (allocational) efficiency.

The implications of financial market innovation are discussed on two levels. First, in section 4.5, I examine the consequences of innovation on financial market prices, international price relationships, and financing opportunities. Then in section 4.6 I analyze the consequences of innovation for macroprudential policy and broader macroeconomic policy.

On the markets side, innovations act to reduce the impact of market imperfections, whether man-made or natural. As a result, we expect to observe greater capital mobility, greater similarity in the cost of funds in alternative capital markets, greater integration of international capital markets, and greater substitutability among assets as a result of improved hedging opportunities.

On the policy side, there are two major concerns. One is whether recent innovations have the capacity to impose negative externalities on society. As stated above, innovations act to reduce the impact of market imperfections, including those macroprudential policies designed to improve welfare by safeguarding the financial system. One specific concern is that the innovative process has led to a kind of "regulatory arbitrage," with financial institutions attempting to lower their costs and expand their activities by seeking out the least regulated environment. These shifts in activity have raised fears that innovation may increase the risk burden on financial institutions and adversely affect the safety and soundness of the financial system. These fears are compounded by the prospect of nations competing for financial services activity by further reductions in the regulatory burden.

Securitization poses another specific example of potential welfare losses associated with financial innovation. Securitization and the increased use of financial intermediaries place the burden of credit evaluation on a larger pool of participants; the increase in market linkages may itself be seen as a source of added risk. To some extent, this may be because the new instruments lack transparency (i.e., they are not well understood), and they have not stood the test of two or three business cycles. Increased reliance on the market system (i.e., adequate information disclosure of off-balance-sheet items, marking to market of financial positions, and so forth) may provide an adequate remedy for some of these fears.

The second major policy concern is the impact of financial innovation on macroeconomic policies in general and monetary policy in particular. At one level, these concerns are operational. The availability of variable-rate financing and hedging techniques makes the timing and incidence of monetary policy more uncertain. And related to this, the increasing ease of substitutability between assets and new techniques of obtaining credit may reduce the meaning and usefulness of traditional monetary and credit aggregates as indicators of monetary policy.

A more fundamental concern is that greater international mobility of capital and tighter integration of financial markets has altered the channels through which monetary policy works, ultimately threatening the welfare gains associated with international trade. Innovation appears to have reduced (to various degrees in different countries) the ability of authorities to adopt direct quantitative controls over credit or interest rate ceilings. With the effectiveness of the credit and controls channels reduced, it appears that monetary policy now has a greater impact on exchange rates, directly affecting the real competitiveness of domestic manufacturing. A country following a comparatively tight domestic monetary policy is therefore likely to lose international competitiveness, possibly setting off demands for trade protection. To the extent that countries seek to reduce the variability of exchange rate movements, the new financial environment limits the scope for effective and independent domestic monetary policies.

Viewed in isolation, the recent wave of financial innovations holds the potential to produce an international allocation of capital that is more consistent with economic risk-return considerations and allocational efficiency. An erosion of the gains from trade in manufactures and commodities would represent significant potential welfare losses. The major policy question, then, is whether free trade is antithetical to capital liberalization. Dealing with this added dimension of policy coordination will be the challenge for policy makers in the years to come.

4.2   Dimensions of International Financial Markets

The international financial marketplace has undergone a tremendous expansion in terms of the variety of products, the volume of trading, and the capitalized value of available securities. The data presented in this section suggest that a variety of financial markets, which were in their infancy or nonexistent two decades ago, have grown to become major centers of activity and influence. The growth of these markets demonstrates their significance and potential implications for investors, corporate managers, and national policymakers. We begin by reviewing the growth of three traditional international financial markets—the foreign exchange market, the Eurocurrency market, and the Eurobond market. Then data on the rise of securitization are presented, followed by measures of activity in the markets for futures, options, and swaps.

4.2.1   Foreign Exchange and the Euromarkets

The foreign exchange market, the interbank market for the exchange of bank deposits denominated in different currencies, has existed in one form or another for centuries and could hardly be called a modern innovation. In recent times, the foreign exchange market has been organized as a dispersed, broker-dealer market with high-speed telecommunications systems linking together the various participants in this worldwide, twenty-four-hour market. The volume and efficiency of the market is such that the spread between bid and offer prices in the spot market is often one-tenth of one percent, or less, for the major currencies.

The data in table 4.1 suggest the tremendous volume of activity handled in the foreign exchange market and its recent growth. Surveys carried out within the last year indicate that London is the most active

Table 4.1   **Average Daily Foreign Exchange Trading Volume by Location and Currency**

	Tokyo	London	New York	New York (1977)
Daily volume, March 1986 (billions of U.S. $)	$48	$90	$50	$ 5
Percentage share				
Sterling	—	30	19	17
DM	—	28	34	27
Yen	82	14	23	5
Swiss franc	—	9	10	14
French franc	—	4	4	6
Italian lire	—	2	—	1
Canadian dollar	—	2	6	19
Cross-currency and ECU	—	4	—	—
Dutch guilder	—	—	1	6
Other	18	7	3	5
Total	100	100	100	100

Sources: Press releases of the Bank of Tokyo, Bank of England, and the Federal Reserve Bank of New York.

foreign exchange trading location, with transactions totaling $90 billion per day. New York is the second most active center trading with $50 billion per day, and Tokyo is close behind with $48 billion per day. The total for these three centers is $188 billion per day. Adding the contributions from other centers (e.g., Frankfurt, Zurich, Hong Kong, and Singapore), worldwide foreign exchange could possibly exceed $250 billion per day or more than $60 trillion per year.[3] With an order flow of this size, many times in excess of world GNP and world trade, it becomes easy to understand the depth and speed of the foreign exchange market.

For comparison, daily trading volume in New York in 1977 was estimated to be only $5 billion, one-tenth of the estimated volume in 1986. The growth of trading in New York over this period was probably greater than that in London, and therefore overstates the worldwide growth in foreign exchange trading. Nevertheless, foreign exchange trading clearly grew at a faster pace than other nominal magnitudes over this ten-year period. The figures for New York also indicate changes in the composition of trading, away from the Canadian dollar and certain European currencies and toward the Japanese yen and the deutsche mark.

The Eurocurrency market has a much shorter tenure than the foreign exchange market. The Eurocurrency market, a market for deposits denominated in a currency different from the indigenous currency of the financial center, began to take shape in the early 1960s. The Russians played an important role in the early development of the market. They were reluctant in those cold war days to hold their U.S. dollars (needed for international trade transactions) in U.S. accounts. Instead, they deposited their dollars in Paris with an affiliate of a state-owned, Russian bank.[4] The true stimulus to the Eurocurrency market, however, was the differential regulation between offshore and onshore banking operations. Particular U.S. banking regulations (i.e., interest rate ceilings on time deposits, mandatory reserve requirements held at zero interest, and mandatory deposit insurance) became increasingly costly throughout the 1960s, resulting in a greater share of banking activity being pushed offshore. The innovation in the Eurocurrency market is an example of "unbundling"—in this case, taking the exchange risk of one currency (the U.S. dollar, for example) and combining it with the regulatory climate and political risk of another financial center.

The data in table 4.2 indicate the growth of the Eurocurrency deposit market, from roughly zero in 1960 to over $3.0 trillion on a gross basis and over $1.5 trillion on a net basis (netting out all interbank deposits) in 1986. The market, once exclusively dollar denominated, has now stabilized to become roughly 75–80 percent dollar based, with the

Table 4.2   **Dimensions of the Eurocurrency Deposit Market**
            (billions of U.S. dollars)

Year	Gross Size	Net Size	Eurodollars as % of Gross	U.S. Money Stock (M2)
1973	315	160	74%	861
1974	395	220	76	908
1975	485	255	78	1,023
1976	595	320	80	1,164
1977	740	390	76	1,287
1978	950	495	74	1,389
1979	1,235	590	72	1,498
1980	1,525	730	75	1,631
1981	1,954	1,018	79	1,794
1982	2,168	1,152	80	1,955
1983	2,278	1,237	81	2,189
1984	2,386	1,277	82	2,372
1985	2,846	1,480	75	2,564
1986 (June)	3,059	1,584	72	n.a.
Compound growth	19.9%	20.1%	—	9.5%

Sources: Morgan Guaranty Trust, *World Financial Markets*, various issues; *Economic Report of the President*, 1986, table B-64.

currencies of other industrialized countries making up the remainder of the market. The Eurocurrency market was once small enough to be ignored; today it rivals U.S. financial markets in terms of size and importance. The short-term lending rate in the Eurocurrency market (LIBOR, or London Interbank Offer Rate) as it has been determined largely by free market forces, has become the reference rate for many onshore loan agreements, floating rate notes, and other contracts as well as Euromarket loans.

Over the years, because of its rapid growth and apparent lack of regulation, the Euromarket has been feared by some as a source of macroeconomic instability or as a wobbly pyramid prone to crisis. Nearly all Eurocurrency banks are major players in their parents' domestic market and could be subject to regulation via this angle. In 1974, central bankers from the Group of Ten issued a general statement of responsibility (the Basle Concordant) indicating that countries would extend lender-of-last-resort facilities for the solvency of their Eurobanks (see Dam 1982, 322–26). The motivation here may have been to encourage national banking authorities to pay closer attention to their members' Eurobanking operations and to reduce the public's fear of an international banking panic. In 1980, the BIS announced another agreement requiring banks to produce consolidated statements of their worldwide activities, including offshore assets and liabilities. This consolidation would enable bank examiners to monitor the quality of off-shore lending on the same basis as domestic offices.

Eurocurrency markets and Eurobanking operations have become a commonplace feature in international finance. In 1981, the United States acknowledged the importance of these new offshore markets and authorized the establishment of international banking facilities within existing U.S. banking institutions. IBFs are not subject to the regulations that apply to domestic banking activity (reserve requirements and deposit insurance, in particular) and are free to engage in many offshore banking arrangements with *non*residents.[5]

The Eurobond market developed at approximately the same time as the market for Eurocurrency deposits. Again, differential regulation between offshore and onshore securities activities played a key role in stimulating the development of the market. In 1963, the United States adopted the so-called interest equalization tax, effectively an excise tax on American purchases of new or outstanding foreign stocks and bonds. To no one's surprise, the IET effectively closed foreigners' access to the U.S. bond market; to the surprise of some, the market simply migrated offshore to London and Luxembourg. Other costly U.S. regulations (further international capital controls and a 30 percent withholding tax on interest payments to foreigners) nurtured the environment for the Eurobond market.

The remarkable growth record of the Eurobond market is presented in table 4.3. From the first Eurobond floated in 1957, the volume of new offerings reached $6.3 billion in 1972. Two years later, the United States abolished the IET and its capital control program. Eurobond underwritings plunged to $2.1 billion in 1974 and the financial press was anticipating the death of the market. But Eurobonds and U.S. bonds continued to differ in several important ways—investors in Eurobonds paid no withholding tax and held bearer securities, and issuers of Eurobonds avoided costly and time-consuming SEC disclosure requirements. These differences proved substantial, and the Eurobond market expanded sixtyfold in the next eleven years.

New offerings in the U.S. dollar segment of the market now exceed the volume of new corporate bond issues in the United States. Treasurers of major corporations are now geared to conduct bond issues either offshore or onshore depending on market conditions. Even the U.S. Treasury has joined the parade to the Eurobond market with several so-called targeted treasury issues, in an attempt to lower the Treasury's funding costs.

4.2.2 Measures of Securitization

The increase in securitization, the tendency for an economy to have a greater proportion of its assets in the form of marketable securities

Table 4.3   **Dimensions of the Eurobond Market (billions of U.S. dollars)**

Year	Eurobonds		Foreign Bonds	Total International Bond Issues	U.S. Corporate Bond Issues
	Total	$-Denominated			
1970	3.0	—	1.6	4.6	29.0
1971	3.6	—	2.6	6.3	30.1
1972	6.3	3.9	3.4	9.7	25.6
1973	4.2	2.4	3.6	7.8	20.7
1974	2.1	1.0	4.7	6.9	31.5
1975	8.6	3.7	11.3	19.9	42.8
1976	14.3	9.1	18.2	32.5	42.2
1977	17.7	11.6	14.5	32.2	42.3
1978	14.1	7.3	20.2	34.3	20.5
1979	18.7	12.6	22.3	41.0	26.5
1980	24.0	16.4	17.9	41.9	44.6
1981	31.6	26.8	21.4	53.0	38.2
1982	51.6	44.0	26.4	78.0	45.4
1983	48.5	38.4	27.8	76.3	50.2
1984	79.5	63.6	28.0	107.4	59.6
1985	136.7	97.8	31.0	167.8	71.3[a]
1986 (Oct)[b]	163.4	102.7	30.7	194.1	n.a.
Compound growth[c]	29.0%	28.1%	21.9%	27.1%	

Sources: Morgan Guaranty Trust, *World Financial Markets*, various issues; *Economic Report of the President*, 1986, table B-90.

[a]First three quarters at annual rate.

[b]Through end of October, not annualized.

[c]Through end of 1985.

and bearing market-determined prices, can be seen from a variety of indicators. The par value of outstanding publicly traded bonds, as shown in table 4.4, totaled roughly $7.8 trillion at the end of 1986, reflecting a 25 percent increase over 1985. Salomon Brothers (1986) estimates that about half of this increase is the result of the dollar's depreciation. But the nearly fivefold increase in the market value of bonds relative to 1975 makes the long-term trend toward securitization apparent. The ratio of the market value of bonds to GDP has risen from 50 percent in 1980 to 71 percent in 1985, showing another measure of increasing securitization.

Another measure of securitization and its implications is presented in table 4.5. Net borrowings by U.S. nonfinancial corporations have traditionally relied heavily on bank loans, traditionally a nontraded asset. In 1981 and 1982, bank loans and securitized financing were roughly equal in magnitude; by 1986, more than three-quarters of net new financings were in a securitized form. One explanation for this phenomenon is that, for a variety of reasons (but primarily a deterio-

Table 4.4   **Par Value of Outstanding Publicly Issued Bonds (billions of U.S. dollars)**

| | Year-End | | | Annual Growth Rate | % of Total | | Ratio to |
	1975	1980	1985	1986[a]	1975–85	1975	1985	1985 GDP
U.S. dollar	$786	$1,473	$3,119	$3,660	14.8%	48.1%	50.4%	79%
Japanese yen	130	557	1,081	1,530	23.6	7.9	17.5	68
Deutsche mark	212	505	639	849	11.6	13.0	10.3	86
Italian lira	106	166	275	382	10.0	6.5	4.4	76
French franc	51	110	173	245	13.0	3.1	2.8	28
U.K. sterling	85	212	211	232	9.5	5.2	3.4	42
Dutch guilder	41	86	123	161	11.6	2.5	2.0	83
Belgian franc	46	105	111	150	9.2	2.8	1.8	117
Canadian dollar	57	91	131	146	8.6	3.5	2.1	39
Danish krone	32	71	102	135	12.2	2.0	1.6	151
Swedish krona	38	77	101	126	10.3	2.3	1.6	89
Swiss franc	25	54	77	106	12.0	1.5	1.2	70
Australian dollar	27	41	50	55	6.6	1.6	0.8	33
Total	$1,636	$3,566	$6,192	$7,776	14.2%			71%

Source: Salomon Brothers 1986.

[a]Estimate as of September 30, 1986.

Table 4.5   **Net Borrowing by U.S. Nonfinancial Corporations**
                 (billions of U.S. dollars)

	1981	1982	1983	1984	1985	1986
Securitized financing	45.0	37.7	27.2	78.4	90.5	98.6
Corporate bonds	28.1	44.2	24.6	55.3	77.0	90.5
Open market paper	16.9	−6.5	2.6	23.1	13.5	8.1
Bank loans	43.5	39.7	18.0	77.0	35.5	27.1
Ratio of securitized financing to bank loans	1.03	0.95	1.51	1.02	2.55	3.64

Source: Salomon Brothers 1986, 55.

ration in the quality of bank loan portfolios), the credit ratings of banks have fallen relative to their best customers. Corporations have observed that funding costs could be reduced by going directly to the market. As the most creditworthy customers are removed from a bank's portfolio, this trend is reinforced. The trend toward securitization is also reinforced to the extent that investors value liquidity and are willing to purchase marketable securities at lower yields than a bank might charge on loans.

The trend toward securitization in preference to traditional bank lending is also visible in the international markets. As shown in figure 4.1, syndicated bank loans captured nearly 60 percent of this market in 1982. In the years since, there has been a steady reduction in syndicated bank lending, along with a steady increase in international bond

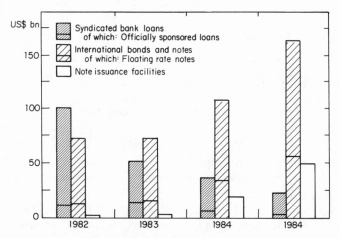

Fig. 4.1   International borrowing through syndicated bank loans versus tradable bonds and notes. *Source:* Bank for International Settlements, *Annual Report,* 1986.

issues and note issuance facilities. The preference for borrowing through marketable securities seems to be firmly established.

The market value of equity capital and its annual turnover provide further evidence on the securitization of international financial markets. The market value of equity shares reached $5.3 trillion at the end of 1986, up by 25 percent from 1985 and nearly fivefold from 1975, as reported in table 4.6. The U.S. share of the world market has fallen substantially since 1975, with Japan's share rising by a nearly offsetting amount. The extent of securitization, as measured by the ratio of market value of shares to GDP, shows considerable dispersion, from 13 percent in France to 77 percent in Switzerland. The recent trend toward privitization, the sale of state-owned assets to private investors, is helping to increase these measures of securitization. Plans to denationalize industries are in progress around the world. More than $19 billion was raised through equity sales of state-owned enterprises in 1986, roughly 25 percent of total new equity issues worldwide (Salomon Brothers 1986, 24).

The final innovative trend that enhances securitization is the transformation of formerly illiquid pools of assets into tradable securities, using pass-through certificates or collateralized obligations as a structure. GNMA (Government National Mortgage Association) pass-through certificates representing claims on a pool of GNMA-insured mortgages are perhaps the most well-known example, but other federal and private financial institutions began to issue similar certificates in the 1970s. New issues of asset-backed securities reached $269.0 billion in 1986, as reported in table 4.7. Residential mortgages remain the dominant component of this market. Securities representing commercial mortgages are now available, as well as securities backed by automobile and credit card receivables at the shorter end of the maturity spectrum.

4.2.3 New Risk Management and Funding Vehicles

The extent of financial innovation is perhaps best reflected in a set of new risk management and funding vehicles—futures, options, and swaps—that came into existence in the early 1970s and have experienced extraordinary growth and importance beyond what the numerical entities may suggest. The aggregate open interest in financial futures and options, a measure of the speculative capital at risk in the market, rose to $680 billion at the end of September 1986, an increase of nearly 75 percent over the year-end 1985 figure. Open interest, as reported in table 4.8, is split roughly two to one between futures contracts and option contracts. Futures and options written against contracts on interest-bearing securities account for by far the greatest open interest, 94 percent in the case of futures and 67 percent in the case of options.

Table 4.6 Stock Market Value of Exchange-Listed Domestic Companies (billions of U.S. dollars)

	Year-End				Annual Growth Rate 1975–85[a]	% of Total		Ratio to 1985 GDP
	1975	1980	1985	1986[a]		1975	1985	
U.S. dollar	$704	$1,237	$2,014	$2,202	11.1%	61.2%	49.5%	51%
Japanese yen	142	380	948	1,783	20.9	12.3	23.3	60
U.K. sterling	86	205	354	384	15.2	7.5	8.7	70
Deutsche mark	51	72	178	217	13.2	4.5	4.4	24
Canadian dollar	51	117	157	163	12.0	4.4	3.9	47
French franc	35	55	79	128	8.4	3.1	1.9	13
Italian lira	11	25	58	112	18.3	0.9	1.4	15
Swiss franc	17	43	84	97	17.7	1.4	2.1	77
Dutch guilder	18	29	59	77	12.5	1.6	1.5	40
Australian dollar	20	60	60	69	11.6	1.7	1.5	39
Swedish krona	2	13	37	57	32.7	0.2	0.9	33
Belgian franc	9	10	21	32	8.8	0.8	0.5	22
Danish krone	4	6	15	15	13.9	0.4	0.4	22
Total	$1,150	$2,251	$4,065	$5,335	13.5%	100.0	100.0	46%

Source: Salomon Brothers 1986.

[a]Estimate as of September 30, 1986.

Table 4.7   **Gross New Issues of Asset-Backed Securities (billions of U.S. dollars)**

	1980	1982	1984	1985	1986[a]	1987[b]
Residential mortgage	22.0	55.0	66.7	114.0	253.3	217.0
Commercial mortgage	—	—	1.3	6.0	5.6	7.0
Automobile receivables	—	—	—	—	10.0	15.0
Credit card receivables	—	—	—	—	.05	1.0
Total	22.0	55.0	67.0	120.0	269.0	240.0

Source: Salomon Brothers 1986.
[a]Estimate.
[b]Forecast.

Table 4.8   **Aggregate Open Interest in Major World Financial Futures and Options Contracts (billions of U.S. dollars)**

	1975	1980	1984	1985	1986:3
Futures	0.2	81.0	190.7	253.7	439.9
Interest rate contracts	0.0	78.8	182.1	236.0	412.4
Bonds	0.0	35.9	25.0	49.5	104.3
Money market	0.0	42.9	157.1	186.5	308.1
Stock index contracts	0.0	0.0	4.6	9.7	18.1
Currencies	0.2	2.2	4.0	8.0	9.4
Options	0.0	0.0	40.3	138.2	239.6
Interest rate contracts	0.0	0.0	21.5	88.8	161.9
Bonds	0.0	0.0	21.5	41.4	45.8
Money market	0.0	0.0	0.0	47.4	116.1
Stock index contracts	0.0	0.0	14.7	37.1	38.9
Currencies	0.0	0.0	4.1	12.3	38.8
Aggregate open interest[a]	0.2	81.0	231.0	391.9	679.5

Source: Salomon Brothers 1986, 23.
[a]Measured by dollar par or index value of outstanding positions on the last day of the period.

Daily trading volume for futures and options contracts, reported in table 4.9, mirrors the above findings. The dominate share of trading volume is in interest rate contracts, more so in the case of futures than in options. And among contracts on interest-bearing securities, the three-month Eurodollar futures contract is by far the most popular, accounting for about 75 percent of all activity. The three-month Eurodollar futures contract currently trades roughly fifty thousand to seventy-five thousand contracts per day, representing an aggregate face value of $50–75 billion. The Eurodollar contract is useful for hedging LIBOR interest rate exposure, which, as noted earlier, has become the major reference rate for pricing variable-rate bank lending and floating-rate note (FRN) securities.

Table 4.9   **Aggregate Daily Trading Volume in Major World Financial Futures and Options Contracts (billions of U.S. dollars)**

	1975	1980	1984	1985	1986:3
Futures	0.0	25.3	55.1	86.0	134.6
Interest rate contracts	0.0	24.2	46.7	73.4	115.9
Bonds	0.0	6.0	11.9	25.7	57.9
Money market	0.0	18.2	34.8	47.7	58.0
Stock index contracts	0.0	0.0	5.5	8.9	14.4
Currencies	0.0	1.1	2.9	3.7	4.3
Options	0.0	0.0	8.2	24.5	34.4
Interest rate contracts	0.0	0.0	1.9	11.5	16.3
Bonds	0.0	0.0	1.9	6.5	6.7
Money market	0.0	0.0	0.0	5.0	9.6
Stock index contracts	0.0	0.0	6.0	12.3	15.6
Currencies	0.0	0.0	0.3	0.7	2.5
Aggregate trading volume[a]	0.0	25.4	63.2	110.5	169.0

Source: Salomon Brothers 1986, 23.
[a]Daily average of the dollar par of index value of transactions.

Another indicator of the potential impact of financial futures markets on trading behavior is illustrated in figure 4.2, which graphs the daily volume of Treasury bond futures trading and the volume of trading in the underlying cash market. The data clearly show that the volume of trading in futures contracts now swamps the volume in the cash market by a factor of four. A similar ratio maintains between trading volume in stock index futures and underlying equity shares.

This development has raised fears that the heightened activity in financial futures markets may be contributing to volatility in underlying cash markets. In particular, "program trading" (transactions executed to remove arbitrage profits between futures and cash prices) and

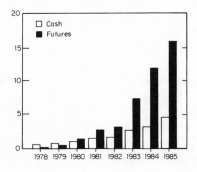

Fig. 4.2   Average daily trading volume in Treasury bond futures and underlying cash bonds (billions of U.S. dollars). *Source:* First Boston Corporation 1986, 225.

"witching-hour effects" (related to the convergence of futures and cash prices on the expiration day of the contracts) have been cited as examples of the disruptive power of the new financial futures and options markets. Careful studies need to examine these claims. Financial futures and options markets offer investors a combination of leverage and liquidity at exceedingly low transaction costs. When news occurs and expectations change, investors may feel that it is preferable to trade first in the futures market, leaving the cash market to adjust later in response.[6] Other evidence suggests that the addition of the futures markets has raised the pool of speculative capital in the market and that bid-offer spreads are lower in the cash market when the futures market is open (Miller 1986, 15).

Interest rate and currency swaps, the final products in this overview, may be thought of as either risk management or funding vehicles. As part of a financing plan, a swap enables the borrower to unbundle the terms (currency, fixed rate, variable rate, and so forth) under which he initially raises funds from the financing terms he is ultimately seeking. For example, it is not obvious that a corporation seeking variable-rate dollar financing ought to borrow in the variable-rate dollar market.[7] If the corporation has a comparative advantage or a window of opportunity in the fixed-rate DM bond market, it might obtain a lower cost of funds by borrowing in this segment and swapping the proceeds into variable-rate dollar funds. The new financing alternative might be presented to the corporation as a package, allowing a comparison between it and a straightforward issue of variable-rate dollar bonds. The alternatives could be identical in all respects, except that the package containing the swap carries the risk of default on the swap.

Swaps can also be used as risk management tools to alter the currency of denomination and interest rate structure of assets and liabilities. If the above corporation decides that variable-rate dollar financing is no longer in its best interest, and it prefers fixed-rate DM financing or fixed-rate Canadian dollar financing, the corporation can sell its swap or purchase other swaps to alter its position. This would likely be cheaper than redeeming its previous bond issue and incurring additional floatation costs.[8]

The limited information available on swap activity is reported in table 4.10. Information is incomplete because swaps are carried as off-balance-sheet entries and no formal reporting is now required. The volume of interest rate swaps outstanding is estimated to be $300 billion. Currency swaps associated with primary bond issues (so-called swap-driven bond issues) were estimated at $38 billion in 1986, or about 20 percent of new Eurobond issues. Other asset- or liability-based currency swaps were estimated to be as large as $76 billion in 1986.

Table 4.10   **Interest Rate and Currency Swap Activity**

Period	Interest Rate Swaps		Currency Swaps[a]	
	Amount[a]	No. of Contracts[b]	Primary Bond Related	Other
1982	—	—	2.3	—
1983	—	—	5.0	—
1984	—	—	11.0	—
1985:1	—	—	—	—
1985:2	109.9	—	—	—
1985:3	134.7	1,055	—	—
1985:4	170.2	1,621	18.0	—
1986:1	—	1,744	—	—
1986:2	—	2,209	—	—
1986:3	—	—	—	—
1986:4	300.0[c]	—	38.0	38–76[c]

Sources: Morgan Guaranty Trust, *World Financial Markets*, December 1986; Salomon Brothers 1986, 23.

[a]Total amount outstanding at end of period in billions of U.S. dollars.
[b]Number of contracts concluded during period.
[c]Estimated.

4.3   Characteristics of Recent Financial Innovations

4.3.1   Functions of International Financial Markets and Alternative Taxonomies

Innovation takes place when it becomes profitable to better fulfill any of the major functions of the international financial sector. These functions include (i) providing appropriate instruments for making payments, (ii) facilitating monetary exchange between currencies, (iii) facilitating the flow of savings toward investments across national boundaries, and (iv) providing mechanisms for allocating, diversifying, and compensating for risk. A partial list of new financial products, classified by their intermediation function, is presented in table 4.11. It may be useful to explore these innovations further using several alternative taxonomies.

Dufey and Giddy (1981) have argued that most financial innovations are either aimed at circumventing government regulations or taken in response to perceived relative price or relative risk changes. Government policies—in particular, regulations that are not applied uniformly across all parties or countries, and tax rates that are not uniform across different sources and uses of income—provide a fertile ground for the innovative process. Financial theory suggests that securities can be used to transform income from higher-taxed into lower-taxed forms, but the transformation is costly.[9] Individuals monitor the implied bur-

Table 4.11   A Classification of Innovations by Financial Intermediation Function

Innovation	Function				
	Price-Risk Transferring	Credit-Risk Transferring	Liquidity Enhancing	Credit Generating	Equity Generating
A. On-balance-sheet					
Adjustable-rate mortgages	X				
Floating-rate loans	X				
Back-to-back loans	X				
Asset sales without recourse		X			
Loan swaps		X			
Securitized assets		X	X		
Transferable loan contracts		X	X		
Sweep accounts and other cash management techniques			X		
Negotiable money-market instruments			X		
Money-market mutual funds			X		
Zero coupon bonds				X	
"Junk" bonds				X	
Equity participation financing				X	
Mandatory convertible debentures					X
B. Off-balance-sheet					
Futures	X				
Options and loan caps	X				
Swaps	X				
Forward rate arrangements	X				
Letters of credit		X			
Note issuance facilities	X	X	X		
Credit-enhancing guarantees on securities		X	X		

den of differential taxation and regulation, and shift their activities when the cost-benefit ratio is favorable. Dufey and Giddy argue that in the 1960s, the regulatory burden of the U.S. financial system became too costly, providing the incentive for the development of the Eurocurrency and Eurobond markets. In the 1970s, macroeconomic volatility increased the cost of carrying exposure, leading to a dramatic increase in the demand for risk management vehicles.

Another well-known taxonomy is the distinction between "product" and "process" innovations. The modern tradition of financial product innovation might begin with the negotiable time certificates of deposit introduced in the 1960s and include exchange-traded foreign currency futures contracts and equity option contracts introduced in 1972 and 1973 respectively. The innovative process has exploded since then. Exchange-traded financial futures and options contracts, which were virtually nonexistent in 1970, now cover dozens of securities and synthetic instruments (e.g., the S&P index) and are traded in at least nine countries on four continents. Active over-the-counter or interbank markets exist for other products. Some products are generic and fairly standardized (e.g., a spot DM contract or a fixed-rate currency swap). Other products have taken on proprietary names (e.g., CARS, certificates on automobile receivables, from Salomon Brothers) to afford some differentiated characteristics to products that can be imitated fairly easily. This kind of product differentiation may enable the innovating firm to appropriate a larger share of the returns from innovation, but it also may require the firm to invest heavily in a secondary market for its differentiated securities.

Modern examples of process innovations include the SWIFT (Society for Worldwide Interbank Financial Transfers) network for foreign exchange payments, the grey market (or premarket) in Eurobond trading, the Euro-clear and Cedel systems for clearing Eurobonds, the MESA network for clearing ECU transactions, and the establishment of formal linkages and dual listings between U.S. and foreign stock and commodity exchanges. The European Monetary System (EMS) might be viewed as a process innovation intended to stabilize European exchange rates and, in turn, facilitate the use of the ECU.

The Black-Scholes option-pricing model and other related models might also be thought of as process innovations. This line of theoretical research (i) provided a scientific underpinning for option pricing, (ii) indicated how option writers might manage their risks by "delta hedging," (iii) helped popularize a technique for pricing synthetic contracts (i.e., the replicating portfolio approach), and (iv) alerted analysts to the fact that many common financial contracts could be usefully viewed as embodying option-like features (that might be priced "scientifically")—all of which encouraged the development of new products and market-making activity. To take one example, Dufey and Giddy (1981) noted that despite articles describing the benefits of foreign exchange options, the market appeared to be failing because the contracts were too specialized and too difficult to hedge. Since banks will generally be selling call options to corporate customers, there is no obvious place for banks to buy options to mechanically square their books. The "delta hedging" procedure offered a reasonable alternative for risk management, which has enabled the interbank foreign exchange option market to develop.[10]

The theory of finance suggests another approach for understanding the recent wave of financial innovations. Investors and borrowers are typically characterized as risk-averse welfare maximizers. In this setting, we expect that individuals will desire the flexibility to hedge against any contingent risk. If the available set of financial assets does not "span" all possible contingencies, then individuals might be better off having access to additional securities whose payoffs depend on these contingencies. The introduction of interest rate futures, heating oil and crude oil futures, and mortgage-backed securities might be seen as products that help complete the menu of financial products, thus allowing individuals to reach their desired exposure to particular risks. Some of these innovations represent an "unbundling" of existing financial products.[11] Other new products, such as pass-through certificates, are simply tradable claims collateralized by previously existing financial positions, a process of financial disintermediation that closes the gap between ultimate borrowers and lenders.

Conditional on their exposure to risk, individuals also seek to maximize their expected investment returns, taking into account taxes and the transaction costs of managing their positions. Many new financial products (e.g., money market mutual funds, stock index options, and convertible bonds) represent a composition or "bundling" of more elementary financial instruments. Small investors have historically been attracted to mutual funds as a way to attain diversification and scale economies, which lower the cost of financial services, including professional management expertise. But now large, institutional investors have become attracted to composite products because they dramatically lower the cost of establishing and maintaining a leveraged position or acting upon fast-breaking news.[12]

A single innovation could draw on many of the characteristics just enumerated. The evolution of zero-coupon securities provides a good case in point.[13] Zero-coupon securities had existed for some time (e.g., Treasury bills and U.S. savings bonds). In the 1970s, aggressive reading of the federal tax code (regulatory channel) encouraged dealers and investors to separate (unbundle) the principal and coupon components of Treasury securities as distinct products. By selling the corpus at a deep discount, the dealer might recognize a capital loss; by purchasing this instrument, an investor might delay paying taxes until the security had matured or was sold. Taxable corporations also had an incentive to issue long-term zero-coupon bonds because of the Treasury's method of computing implicit interest expense. Even after the Treasury plugged these loopholes, demand for zero-coupon instruments persisted from foreign investors, who faced more favorable capital gains tax treatment on zeros, and from domestic investors, who used zeros to match future liabilities, eliminate reinvestment risk (hedging motives), and avoid bothering with coupons (convenience motive). The securities industry responded to this demand by stripping the coupons from existing securities, creating synthetic zeros (unbundling), some with exotic (and proprietary) names. In January 1985 the U.S. Treasury responded with its own innovation by announcing that all future issues with a maturity of greater than ten years would be transferable in their component pieces. The new product, STRIPS (separate trading of registered interest and principal securities), has been readily accepted with more than $90 billion of securities outstanding.

4.3.2   Engineering Innovative Financial Instruments

Swaps and Comparative Advantages

To set the stage for our later analysis, it is useful to point out the reciprocal nature of demand for swaps and other hedging instruments. This is clear from the typical diagrams used to illustrate the flows of funds in a swap transaction. For example,

(i) demand for five-year sterling ↔ supply of five-year dollars;
(ii) demand for fixed-rate funds ↔ supply of floating-rate funds; and
(iii) demand for LIBOR-basis funds ↔ supply of N.Y. Prime–basis funds.

The above situations are analogous to commodity trade in the sense that one country's demand for wheat is equivalent to its supply of cloth under the presumption that trade balances. A stylized result from classical trade theory is that countries are endowed with differential supplies of (immobile) capital and labor which gives rise to production cost differentials. To take advantage of the situation, countries tend to specialize in the production of their comparative advantage goods, which they then trade, capturing the gains from trade.

The principles underlying a financial swap bear a strong relationship to those of commodity trade and comparative advantage theory.[14] The feasibility of a swap (such as in cases i, ii, and iii) between parties A and B hinges on the possibility that they face different relative costs on the two pieces of the swap. The following example uses an interest rate swap, but the same principle would apply to a currency swap. Suppose that company A desires to borrow fixed-rate funds while company B desires floating-rate funds. Suppose further that the companies can borrow on the following terms:

	Company A	Company B	Differential
Fixed rate	11%	9.5%	1.5%
Floating rate	LIBOR + 0.5%	LIBOR + 0.25%	0.25%
			1.25%
Comparative advantage	Floating-rate funds	Fixed-rate funds	
Objective	Fixed-rate funds	Floating-rate funds	

Company B borrows at a lower rate in either case (it has an *absolute* advantage in both markets), but its *relative* or *comparative* advantage lies in the fixed-rate market. (A's comparative advantage is in the floating-rate market.) It can be easily shown that if A borrows at floating-rate terms and B borrows at fixed-rate terms and the companies then swap, there will be a 1.25 percent interest rate savings to divide between the two firms and any financial intermediaries who assist them.

What is the source of B's comparative advantage? A number of reasons might explain it: (1) Certain lenders (e.g., insurance companies) are constrained to lend to companies like B. Therefore, there is an excess supply of funds chasing firms like B. (2) Fixed-rate lenders are segmented from floating-rate lenders, and they have formed different expectations regarding A and B. (3) The assets and receivables of B are predominantly in fixed-rate terms. Consequently, lenders perceive lower risk associated with fixed-rate lending to B. If explanations (1) or (2) are behind B's comparative advantage, then for "small transactions," B may exploit its comparative advantage without losing it, much the same as commodity trade. In the aggregate, however, large-scale transacting would remove the segmentation barrier at the heart of this swap transaction. On the other hand, if explanation (3) is valid, the market may be signaling its preference to provide fixed-rate terms. If company B borrows at fixed-rate terms and swaps, the market may perceive that B is in a riskier position and turn its relative (fixed/floating) borrowing terms against it. In this case, B has traded away or reduced its comparative borrowing advantage. Explanation (3) clearly shows the need for disclosure of information on swap transactions so that the market can offer relative financing terms that are consistent with a firm's financial risks.

Several related issues can be raised by examining a currency swap. In the 1960s and 1970s, back-to-back loans and parallel loans (with cash flows essentially the same as a currency swap) were conducted to avoid the United Kingdom's investment sterling market or Latin American capital controls. Many observers point to the World Bank/

IBM swap in August 1981 as the beginning of the modern currency swap market. The funding and risk management strategy of the World Bank at that time called for borrowing in DM, Swiss francs, and other low-interest-rate currencies. In these smaller markets, repeated bond issues can cause lending terms to deteriorate as domestic buyers reach a saturation point (sometimes the result of prudential regulation) in their portfolios.

In the August 1981 deal, IBM borrowed DM and Swiss francs at preferential rates (because of IBM's credit rating and scarcity value), the World Bank borrowed dollars (without concern over market saturation), and the two parties then swapped the proceeds and the future obligations to make payments.[15] Each company exploited its comparative borrowing advantage and shared the gains from trade to produce a lower all-in cost of funds. The World Bank has continued to use currency swaps aggressively as an integral part of its funding strategy.

Building Synthetic Securities

Two further examples illustrate other aspects of the innovation process. Suppose that a market for short-term, unsecured borrowing similar to the U.S. commercial paper market, but denominated in DM, does not exist. Absent this market, companies can instead issue U.S. dollar commercial paper, sell the proceeds for DM, and cover by selling DM forward in exchange for dollars. The T-account in the first half of figure 4.3 demonstrates how these two transactions approximate a DM commercial paper instrument. The cost of funding in DM terms would be approximately the actual U.S. dollar commercial paper rate (for a

Euro-DM Commercial Paper	
Assets	Liabilities
{$ Cash} DM Cash	A/P: $Commercial Paper
A/R: $ forward purchase	A/P: DM forward sale

Euro-DM Bonds	
Assets	Liabilities
A/R: $ long-term forward purchase	A/P: Euro-$ Bond
	A/R: DM long-term forward sale

Fig. 4.3   Construction of synthetic securities: Euro-DM commercial paper and Euro-DM bonds

particular maturity and credit risk) plus the forward premium on foreign exchange.[16]

The gain from "constructing" DM commercial paper in this fashion might be measured by comparing the synthetic rate with the best alternative DM rate, perhaps a short-term Euro-DM loan. Synthetic DM commercial paper appears to offer a perfect substitute for "actual" DM commercial paper. Figure 4.4 shows that the savings from issuing constructed DM commercial paper were in the 30–90 basis pont rate during the early 1980s. An actual market for DM commercial paper will develop only if savings on transaction costs (including liquidity factors) warrant. If, in fact, a DM commercial paper market develops, actual prices must be set close to synthetic values so as to preclude arbitrage. Similarities between actual and synthetic commercial paper prices will not indicate that the gains from financial trade have vanished, only that the gains are now embodied directly in the interest rates themselves. Using synthetic commercial paper helps secure these gains from financial trade permanently.

A related example is the Eurobond market for DM, Swiss francs, and other currencies which at times in the recent past has been subject to queuing restrictions by national officials. Queuing imposes costs on a firm by restricting its ability to access the bond market at times when terms may be particularly favorable. The T-accounts in the bottom half of figure 4.3 demonstrate how the proceeds from a Eurodollar bond can be swapped for DM (or other currencies) to create a long-term DM obligation that approximates a Euro-DM bond. The cost of the constructed Euro-DM bond would be approximately the U.S. dollar Eurobond rate (for a particular maturity and risk class) plus the applicable forward premium on foreign exchange.[17]

The gain from constructing a Euro-DM bond in this fashion could be measured by comparing the constructed rate with the rate that might be obtained once the firm was allowed access to the actual Euro-DM

Fig. 4.4   Comparative spread relationship: Euro-DM rate minus constructed DM commercial paper rate (ninety-day term at percentage per annum). *Source:* Kreiner 1986.

bond market at sometime in the future. If the synthetic Euro-DM bond approach offers a liquid market, then queuing restrictions lose their force and countries would be inclined to drop these restrictions. Arbitrage would then insure that the current actual Euro-DM bond rate approximates the synthetic Euro-DM bond rate. By forcing these two rates toward equality, borrowers would enjoy permanent relief from queuing costs and other market access barriers.

Contract Innovation

A final area of financial innovation worth noting is in the design of futures contracts. Black (1986) has modeled the success and failure of futures contracts based on their commodity characteristics, their contract characteristics, and the interaction of these two variables. Commodity characteristics include the durability, storability, and homogeneity of the commodity as well as characteristics of the spot market. Contract characteristics refer to contract size, delivery dates, delivery locations, acceptable commodity grades for delivery, and so forth. Delivery conditions play a large role in contract specifications because even though most short contract positions are liquidated by offset, some physical delivery of the underlying commodity does take place.

The most important change in contract specification to affect futures trading has been to allow for cash settlement of futures contracts upon their expiration, rather than to require costly delivery of physicals. This innovation might have been adopted years ago except that a contract that could be settled only in cash was considered a wager and specifically outlawed in those states with major futures markets. In 1974, futures trading came under federal control (via the Commodity Futures Trading Commission), where no such rules regarding gambling were in effect. By 1981, all the regulatory channels had been cleared, and financial futures contracts specifying cash settlement began trading. The vast appeal of these new contracts is evident from the data on trading volume and open interest reviewed earlier.

4.3.3 Design and Evolution of Innovative Financial Instruments

Cooper (1986) has recently argued that in most new financial instruments, the underlying financial claims embodied in the contract are largely the same as in the past; what has changed is the packaging of the instruments as well as the speed, scope, and other aspects of the trading arrangements. As illustrated in the above examples, new financial contracts are often a transformation of existing financial instruments. This technique, the "replicating portfolio" approach, is central to the design of new financial instruments and to their pricing. Examination of many new instruments reveals that they reflect a bundling or unbundling of existing securities which allows them to replicate something that already exists at lower transaction costs.

Our examples demonstrate that new instruments may also replicate securities that *do not* exist but that the market may welcome (e.g., DM commercial paper or DM bonds without queuing restrictions). In principle, a security could be indexed to any contingent outcome in order to replicate any desired financial contract, although in practice it might have to be issued offshore to avoid prohibitive regulations.[18]

Once the general principle behind a financial innovation is well known (either its transaction costs savings or its risk-reducing properties), the possibility exists to move the product from a custom-design, small-volume market to a standardized product with high volume and lower transaction costs. This has been the evolution in several cases, as illustrated in table 4.12, for the currency and interest-rate swap market.

Product innovation is not a one-way street. There are numerous examples of failure among exchange-traded futures contracts which illustrates that these products, like consumer goods, must meet the market test.[19] Product innovation is costly, and because financial firms value their reputations and intend to be infinite-lived, we expect that new products will offer value-added, at least in the short run. But because financial innovations are likely to incorporate increasing complexity, it is essential for *nonfinancial firms* to gain the necessary expertise to evaluate the new products. And for these nonfinancial firms (as for regulatory authorities) it is essential that the evaluation be conducted on the basis of economic, risk-return criteria rather than accounting conventions.

4.4   Causes of Financial Market Innovation

4.4.1   Financial Services under Perfect Capital Markets

To better understand the role of swaps and other new financial instruments in the real world, it is useful to outline the nature of financial

Table 4.12   **Evolution of the Currency and Interest Rate Swap Market**

Date	Phase	Trading Arrangement	Volume
1970s	Arbitrage of regulation	Parallel loans	Small
1980–81	Arbitrage of market anomalies (1)	Intermediated agreements	Small
1982–83	Arbitrage of market anomalies (2)	Intermediated with bank inventories	$20 billion
1984	Standardized traded swaps	Market making on standard contracts	$100 billion
1985–	Derivative agreements on swaps (forward swaps, swap options)	Market making on standard contracts	$200–300 billion

Source: Adapted from Cooper 1986.

services that would exist in a "perfect" capital market. I will then argue that departures from "perfect" capital markets provide the necessary conditions for the development of new financial products such as swaps, options, and so forth.

For our purposes, the essential elements of a perfect capital market are (i) no transaction costs; (ii) no taxes; (iii) no regulatory barriers or restraints (but enforceable contracts); and (iv) a large number of small participants. Uncertainty regarding future economic outcomes is present, but investors view the future similarly.[20] The absence of transaction costs insures that all investors share the same information base and that they will agree on a fair valuation of securities. No transaction costs also implies that borrowers and lenders can act directly in the market without depending on agents or intermediaries. Finally, no transaction costs implies that securities are completely divisible and may be issued in arbitrarily small units.

To complete the story, we assume that investors are risk-averse and attempting to maximize their expected utility from lifetime consumption. Two questions are of interest: What financial instruments will be offered in the market and how will individuals and firms utilize these instruments?

In this stylized setting, investors will desire the flexibility to hedge against any contingent risk. It can be shown that if there are n independent sources of risk, then n financial instruments related to these sources of risk are sufficient for agents to form any portfolio of their choosing.[21] There could be more than n financial instruments in the · market, but these would represent combinations of the original n and would therefore be redundant. The financial market could be labeled "complete" in the sense that investors could hedge against any contingent risk and form a portfolio with any risk-return pattern.

In a perfect and complete market, any borrower or issuer could enter the market and directly sell financial instruments (i.e., a loan, option, or some other well-defined contract) for fair value. A lender or investor, on the other hand, could expect to find financial instruments capable of hedging any risk and enabling him to achieve any desired risk-return pattern. In a perfect and complete market, the menu of financial instruments allows everyone complete flexibility to meet their desired financial objectives.

4.4.2 Financial Services with Imperfect Capital Markets

The assumptions of perfect capital markets are substantially at odds with the real world. A variety of barriers exist that potentially might lead to departures from the various arbitrage and parity conditions applicable for international capital markets under perfect capital market assumptions. The most basic such parity condition is a variant of the law of one price applied to the financial market—similar securities (or combinations of securities) representing similar exposures to risk ought to sell for the same price regardless of the point of sale. This law predicts, for example, that an IBM seven-year straight U.S. dollar bond floated in London ought to command the same price as a similar security floated in New York or Tokyo. A financial market law of one price is, in essence, a statement about the integration of international capital markets and that capital flows (i.e., arbitrage) will take place to equalize currency-adjusted and risk-adjusted rates of return everywhere.

Real-world market imperfections can be divided into two groups: policy-related (or man-made) and behavioral (natural) barriers. Policy-related imperfections include taxes, rules regarding information disclosure or accounting conventions, and other regulatory barriers. The latter includes factors such as reserve requirements in banking, interest rate ceilings, market access rules (e.g., queuing), ownership restrictions on shares, legality of a monetary unit and other financial instruments (e.g., ECU-denominated debts and bearer securities), and rules regarding market entry and permissible activities (e.g., the Glass-Steagall Act). These national regulations are promulgated with diverse objectives in mind—domestic monetary control, the safety and soundness of the banking system, prudential management of pension and mutual funds, and desired competitive conditions in the financial services industry. The critical point here is that the incidence of the policy-related barriers is not similar across the world's capital markets, or even within a single capital market. Consequently these barriers lead to segmentation effects both between national capital markets and within individual markets.

Other capital market barriers are more a function of the natural economic environment or human behavioral patterns. Transaction costs—of bringing a new security to market, of discovering and verifying information regarding an issuer, of enforcing contracts—are an obvious natural barrier to complete integration of international capital markets. Perhaps as a result of different information sets, investors in different national markets may hold different expectations, resulting in different assessments of securities prices. And investors in different countries might have different age and income profiles, leading to different consumption/investment/risk preferences and, therefore, to different prices of similar securities across countries.

All of these barriers, whether policy related or natural, encourage the *segmentation* of international capital markets and the possibility that returns on similar securities (or portfolios of securities) may not equalize across countries. As a result, profit opportunities present themselves for borrowers and lenders who can circumvent barriers at low cost.[22] In addition, barriers also reduce the number and variety of securities below the level observed in perfect and complete markets. Profit opportunities also exist for agents who can create new instruments at low cost for hedging otherwise exposed risks.[23]

The above line of reasoning suggests that as long as investors are risk-averse utility maximizers, they will continue to search out arbitrage profit opportunities and to demand more complete financial markets. Demand for financial vehicles is always present, but with the existence of costly barriers, demand will be scaled by price and only a subset of financial vehicles will exist. What Ian Cooper (1986) called the proximate causes of financial innovation (i.e., the search for lower transaction costs, funding costs, new risk-transferring vehicles, and so forth) are always lurking. Why then has there been a surge in financial innovation over the last several years?

The simple answer to this question is that a set of factors (what Cooper labels the ultimate causes of innovation) has led to a substantial outward shift in both the demand and supply schedules for new financial products and processes. On the demand side, rising nominal and real funding costs in the late 1970s and early 1980s increased the willingness of borrowers to search out lower-cost funding. Volatility of asset prices, exchange rates, and inflation rates increased the price that investors and borrowers would pay for protection against these risks. Changing worldwide wealth patterns and the globalization of industrial markets increased the demand for global asset portfolios or funding strategies. Demand was also probably heightened by user education and advances such as option-pricing models.

On the supply side, advances in telecommunications and computer technology, increasing competition among financial intermediaries, and regulatory changes all combined to reduce the transaction costs of creating new financial instruments and offering market-making services. The impact of regulatory change cuts in two ways: permission to begin trading in financial futures and options clearly helped these instruments to develop, but persistence of other regulatory barriers most likely encouraged the search for close substitutes or parallel markets in order to overcome these barriers. Regulatory encouragement to increase the capital adequacy of banks and their return on assets is also credited as promoting the securitization of existing bank assets and the shift into new financial products that lead to off-balance-sheet exposures.

Distinguishing between demand and supply factors may be somewhat artificial because of the reciprocal nature of financial products—one side of the transaction cannot proceed without the other. The globalization of industrial activity suggests that it should be more common to find borrowers from around the world raising funds in diverse markets, units of account, and under diverse terms. The market for financial intermediary services has been responsive to link together the demand and supply for particular products. As noted earlier, the supply of intermediary services itself has followed an evolutionary process from specialty deals, to brokering, and finally to market-making in standardized products. The financial services industry appears particularly well suited to overcome some of the unique barriers (such as default risk, see n. 22) present in international capital markets.

4.5 Implications of Innovation on Financial Market Prices and Market Behavior

The process of financial market innovation that I have been describing leads directly to a number of important economic consequences. In this section, I outline the major effects on financial asset prices, international price relationships, and market behavior that we would expect to observe as a result of the innovative process. Then I review the empirical evidence on internationalization and integration of markets.

Given the steady financial innovation over the last two decades and the substantial amount of activity in these new markets, we should be able to observe and measure the following major economic differences:

1. Financial market behavior
   a. Lower transaction costs, greater liquidity, greater substitutability between domestic financial products
   b. Wider array of financial products giving improved opportunities for transfer of risks and risk optimization within investor portfolios
   c. Securitization of assets as investors value liquidity, financial disintermediation
   d. Improved opportunities for funding riskier credits
   e. Greater competition for financial services business
2. International financial market relationships
   a. Greater international capital mobility, existing barriers removed or more easily circumvented
   b. Greater integration of international capital markets, less segmentation
   c. Greater similarity between cost of funds (currency and risk adjusted) in alternative capital market locations
3. Macroeconomic effects
   a. Fewer opportunities for pursuing national monetary and policies using quantitative controls on credit availability or interest rate levels
   b. Greater impact of monetary policy on exchange rates and exchange rate variability

Central to the above hypotheses are the reduction in transaction costs because of supply-side factors (e.g., technological and regulatory change) and demand factors (e.g., scale economies and the development of secondary markets for new products). Arbitrage plays a key role in the process. As both borrowers and lenders monitor the risk-return properties of their portfolios in the face of a new menu of securities, expected rates of return on securities (adjusted for currency and risk factors) should be brought into closer conformity—that is, market integration. Arbitrage, as well as the creation of new synthetic securities, acts to reduce the burden of market imperfections. The greater similarity of capital market products across countries and their greater integration imply reduced scope for pursuing monetary and credit policies based on quantitative restrictions on credit or interest rate ceilings. They also suggest that as monetary policies differ across countries, exchange rate volatility will increase in response to capital mobility and portfolio rebalancing by borrowers and investors.

As these financial market transactions are completely voluntary, all those who directly participate should be better off as a result. These transactions enable borrowers and lenders to hold more desirable portfolios, given that they face lower transaction costs and an expanded opportunity set of financial instruments. For these players, capital allocations will be more in line with economic risk-return criteria. This should be a force tending to increase economic (allocational) efficiency, but other factors (discussed in the next section) may act in the opposite direction.

In his analysis of recent innovation in Japanese financial markets, Feldman (1986) suggests three approaches for measuring the degree of internationalization of a financial market. The *legal approach* focuses on the extent to which the law provides the right and opportunity for cross-border capital flows. The *quantity approach* posits that a larger volume of cross-border transactions is associated with greater internationalization. The *price approach* is the most exacting. It posits that the internationalization of a market is complete when its prices are brought into an international equilibrium. Feldman takes the interest rate parity relationship as his standard; when deviations from covered interest parity are small, markets are assumed to be integrated under the price approach.

What evidence is available to observe whether these financial market and macroeconomic effects listed earlier are actually taking place? The most obvious piece of evidence comes from the scope of new financial instruments and their trading activity outlined in section 4.2. The legal framework has been built to permit trading in a wide variety of financial futures and options contracts. The legal framework for swap transactionsis still developing, but substantial progress has been made to standardize various provisions and wordings of swap arrangements.[24] And many transactions have moved offshore, where the legal impediments to contract design and market entry are less severe. If we use quantity as a criteria, it is clear that these new securities play an important role in investors' portfolios.

On the international side, we also observe legal or institutional agreements that promote international linkages. Some companies have listed their securities on several exchanges around the world for years. Recent evidence suggests that this practice may be especially beneficial for firms from smaller countries which list their shares in the United States. Alexander and Eun (1985) conclude that the effect of dual listing on share price is greater for firms from smaller countries (e.g., Australia) that were more segmented from the U.S. capital market. As these dual-listed firms experience a price effect, arbitrage pricing suggests that other non-dual-listed firms may show a sympathetic price response, further integrating the international markets.

A variation on this theme is the recent agreement linking the Chicago Mercantile Exchange (CME), and the Singapore International Monetary Exchange (SIMEX). A futures position established on one exchange may be offset and closed with transactions on the other exchange. This linkage expands the number of hours of trading per day, which can be useful when prices are extremely volatile.[25]

Two kinds of evidence concern the integration of prices in international markets. The first addresses the law of one price for international securities. The dramatic growth of the Eurobond market suggests that many companies (as well as the United States Treasury) are "arbitraging" the funding differences between the offshore and onshore markets. The funding advantage of Eurobonds, which was estimated by Kidwell, Marr, and Trimble (1986) to be in the 70–140 basis point range in the 1977–81 period, declined to the 30–60 basis point range by 1983. A later study by Mahajan and Fraser (1986) examined ninety-two matched pairs of offerings in the Eurobond and U.S. bond markets between 1975 and 1983. Mahajan and Fraser concluded that once they had standardized for issuer, maturity, rating, and coupon, they could not reject the hypothesis that yields were similar in the two markets. This suggests an integration and harmonization of terms between the two markets.[26] The second source of evidence on the integration of international prices comes from tests of the interest rate parity condition and the existence of covered interest arbitrage profits. It has long been understood that covered interest arbitrage integrates the short-term Eurocurrency markets,[27] but it is now becoming more apparent that longer-term Eurocurrency markets, commercial paper markets (recall fig. 4.4), and onshore short-term financial markets are also being integrated by actual or potential arbitrage.[28] Feldman's (1986) analysis of the Japanese market is a good example. Figure 4.5 shows

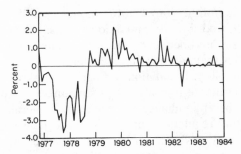

Fig. 4.5   Deviations from covered interest parity: Eurodollar versus Japanese gensakis, three-month rates. *Source:* Feldman 1986, 182.

the incentives for covered interest arbitrage between Eurodollar and gensaki instruments over the 1977–84 period.[29] Feldman argues that the deviation became insignificant in mid- to late 1981, suggesting a rise in internationalization. In addition, market professionals suggest that gains from interest rate and currency swaps are now relatively small, indicating that these markets provide for a high degree of integration in international capital markets (Morgan Guaranty Trust 1986, 3).

4.6 Policy Implications of Financial Market Innovation

The picture being painted sounds rosy, which should not be very surprising. If we begin with a market paradigm and open up more possibilities of choice and freedom for borrowers and lenders, in a potential sense, the world economy stands to be better off. Financial innovations act to overcome many of the natural barriers that divide and segment markets, and lead to allocational inefficiencies. But innovations also overcome many of the policy-related regulatory barriers that were put in place as safeguards or for particular policy objectives.

Concern about the recent wave of financial innovation centers around two themes: first, that increased reliance on the market mechanism— and the possibility of asset price overshooting, excessive competition among financial players, increased credit linkages between financial intermediaries, and anonymous market linkages between ultimate borrowers and lenders—may expose the financial system to additional risk in the aggregate; second, that the greater integration of international capital markets alters the channels through which traditional policy tools work—reducing the effectiveness of quantitative controls on credit availability and interest rates and increasing the impact of monetary policy on the external sector of the economy. At the theoretical extreme, a small, open economy subject to a high degree of capital mobility would find it difficult to follow a monetary policy independent of those being followed abroad. Innovation has made the financial markets of all countries more open and subject to greater capital mobility.

The first policy theme centers on the relationship between innovation and financial stability. Regulation of financial markets and institutions is intended to promote the safety and soundness of this sector of the economy and thereby enhance the economy's overall allocational efficiency. Existing regulations are designed to deal with a variety of problems that may adversely affect economic performance. The key objective is to protect the integrity of the payments system because this represents the lifeblood of business activity.

Financial institutions are known to be subject to *agency problems*, as shareholders and depositors may find it difficult to monitor the behavior of bank managers. Consequently, regulations to constrain or rule out certain kinds of activities may be warranted. Financial institutions may also be subject to so-called *insurance or moral hazard problems*, whereby managers feel the incentive to take excessive risks (given that the federal government is insuring them) or add to their off-balance-sheet positions. Financial institutions might also be subject to *conflict of interest problems* if they increased their activities to include lending and underwriting for nonfinancial firms, as well as brokerage sales and trust advisory services.

Financial innovation could clearly fuel additional fears over these kinds of problems. Requiring financial institutions to disclose their off-balance-sheet positions would be an obvious first step. Calculating insurance rates and capital adequacy requirements on the basis of risk-adjusted measures also makes sense but might present operational difficulties.

A related concern is whether financial innovation leads to an increase in aggregate financial risk. A review of the risk attribute of the new financial instruments is presented in table 4.13. These include market risk (the risk of moment-by-moment price fluctuations), credit risk (the risk of default by one counterparty in a transaction), settlement risk (the risk of default on the day of contract delivery or settlement), and liquidity risk (the risk of not being able to trade immediately). What is the overall impact of these new instruments on risk?

Financial instruments that transfer price risk do not create additional price risk. And to the extent that a more desirable distribution of risk is achieved (from the standpoint of each individual), the economy may be better able to withstand certain stressful periods. However, the transfer of risk through intermediaries creates additional linkages in the financial system and may raise its vulnerability to default, *particularly* in a period of financial stress. In addition, as more players are brought into the system, to carry individualized risks associated with

Table 4.13   Comparative Risks of New Financial Market Instruments

Instrument	Credit Risk	Market Risk	Settlement Risk	Market Liquidity Risk
Currency options	Writer for premium amount until paid, buyer for cost of replacement until exercised.	Limited for buyer, unlimited for writer.	Premium amount on payment date, principal amount for both parties if exercised. (One party pays currency A, one pays currency B.)	Exchange and OTC options new, liquidity of markets untested under stress. Liquidity of exchanges superior to OTC markets, also partially dependent on liquidity of market for underlying.
Interest rate options	Same as above.	Same as above.	Same as above except one party delivers cash, the other securities, if exercised. (Could be net amount if cash settled.)	Same as above.
Currency swaps	Default cancels future obligations. Risk limited to replacement cost. May be principal risk if agreed in original contract.	Equal to rate change on principal and interest amount.	Contractual amount on successive payment dates.	All OTC contracts: limited liquidity.
Interest rate swaps	Default cancels future obligations, risk limited to replacement cost. No principal risk.	Complex: equivalent to bond of equal maturity on fixed side. Risk to fixed payer in swap if rates have fallen, to fixed receiver if rates rise. Small on basis swap. No market risk on principal amount.	Interest payment amount only on successive payment dates.	All OTC contracts: limited liquidity.

Table 4.13 (continued)

Instrument	Credit Risk	Market Risk	Settlement Risk	Market Liquidity Risk
Note issuance facilities/ revolving underwriting facilities	Principal amount for holders of paper; same as other guarantees for writers of standbys.	Writers of standbys face risk they will be called on to lend at below-market spreads if market conditions change.	Principal amount on payment date for borrower.	Liquidity of paper largely untested.
Forward rate agreements	Mostly cash settled, credit risk limited to amount of market risk.	Equal to market risk on deposit.	Limited to amount of market risk if cash settled.	Small market, limited liquidity.
Eurobonds	Same as onshore bond.	Same as onshore fixed rate bond.	Largely same as onshore market.	Markets well developed, but secondary market less developed than major onshore markets.
Floating rate notes	Same as bond.	Same as on short-term paper.	Largely same as onshore market.	Relatively new market, liquidity untested, thin secondary market.
Securitized credits	Derivative from credit risk of underlying asset, sometimes with explicit insurance backup.	Same as conventional instrument of similar maturity.	Generally equal to similar conventional instruments, although some have payment date concentrations.	Markets well developed for long-standing instruments, less clear for new instruments. Thin secondary markets.
Asset sales (with recourse)	Equal to credit risk of selling institution.	Fixed by terms of sale.	Limited.	Limited liquidity.
Asset sales (without recourse)	Buyer takes credit risk of underlying debtor.	Set by terms of underlying credit.	Limited.	Limited liquidity.

Source: Bank for International Settlements, *Recent Innovations in International Banking*, 1986.

unbundled securities, more players need to make credit and pricing assessments. And there is no established track record to guide the market for making these assessments. Innovations may increase the availability of debt financing in the economy, raising the aggregate debt level and making it more vulnerable to shocks.

Another line of argument concerns the behavior of financial markets and unbridled competitive behavior. It is often argued that asset prices move quickly, and they may, in the short run, overshoot their long-run equilibrium value. If new financial instruments are subject to this sort of price behavior, a considerable risk could be added to the economy. Related to this concern is the possibility of excessive competition or excessive risk taking within financial institutions, perhaps related to the belief that behavior in these institutions may be guided by perverse incentives (e.g., compensation related to the volume of new business regardless of its risk). These concerns are enhanced because many of the new financial instruments lead to off-balance-sheet exposures that may or may not be adequately captured by existing accounting conventions and regulatory guidelines.

Dealing with the above concerns is possible, but obviously easier said than done. The general point is that a market system, to the extent that information is made available, has many built-in checks and balances that govern the behavior of market participants. To work in a stable and orderly manner, market participants need to make effective use of market information for decision making and performance evaluation. *Market information* implies accounting systems based on a continuous revaluation or "marking to market" of all financial positions (whether on the balance sheet or off) and assessment of risks on a portfolio basis. It may be that utilization of new financial instruments (interest rate swaps, for example) has actually lowered the exposure of their *portfolio positions* to interest rate risk, thereby reducing their capital needs.

Concern about mispricing of new financial instruments seems exaggerated, since it calls into question the ability of banks to make pricing and credit assessments of "traditional" instruments. The new instruments require an assessment of liquidity risks, traditionally represented by the bid-ask spread, and default risks, which until recently were the normal task of bank lending (credit) officers.

Excessive competition may be a concern associated with a new set of financial products, a scramble for an early dominant market position, and the inevitable shakeout. However, some observers have argued that regulatory ground rules (e.g., constant premium deposit insurance and historical cost accounting systems) build in incentives for managers to engage in excessive risk taking. A market-based regulatory system incorporating risk-adjusted insurance premiums and risk-adjusted capital adequacy requirements could put a natural brake on excessive behavior.

Given the mobility of capital, any regulatory response to financial innovation would need to be coordinated among national regulatory bodies. Otherwise, the markets will continue to engage in a kind of "regulatory arbitrage," seeking the lowest level of constraints in which to operate. National regulatory bodies may add to this problem if they compete with each other in terms of regulatory laxity in order to protect the market share of their domestic financial institutions. The recent accord between U.S. and British bank regulatory authorities announcing risk-based capital adequacy standards within a highly similar set of rules is a welcome first step toward international coordination (see Nash 1987, 1).

The second, and final, policy theme concerns the impact of financial innovation on domestic monetary policy. Financial innovation has lowered transaction costs, increased the menu of available assets, and increased the ease of substitution among assets. As a result, the ability of authorities to measure and control the money supply has been reduced. Individuals and firms also have increased their access to variable-rate financing and numerous risk-hedging instruments. The availability of variable-rate financing may reduce the sting of contractionary monetary policy because borrowers still have access to funds for which they may be willing temporarily to pay a higher rate. Lenders receive higher-interest income during these periods, which tends to increase aggregate spending.

The greater concern is that because of the increasing international mobility of capital, the dominant channel through which monetary policy is now felt may be the exchange rate. If countries are unable to coordinate their monetary policies effectively, then large exchange rate swings are more likely to develop. Countries then run the danger that protectionist pressures will mount, producing a contraction in international trade and reducing the gains from trade.

4.7 Summary and Conclusions

This paper has offered an overview of some of the financial market innovations we have seen over the last few years, the causes of innovation, and the implications of both in terms of economic effects and policy responses. The incentives for financial innovation are strong and at the foundation of a market system. Self-interest, profit maximization, risk optimization, and technological change are guiding the process. Benefits clearly accrue to those directly involved in the innovating and trading process. Natural barriers that segment world capital markets are under pressure, resulting in a tendency toward greater economic efficiency.

The transition from a segmented international capital market to one that is more integrated will also impose some costs. There will be greater demands for information and measures of the risk and return of the new financial instruments. Policy-related barriers (taxes, regulations, and so forth) will also lose some of their force, and to the extent that these were used for prudential control, other policies will have to take their place. The need to coordinate regulatory policies will increase. Monetary policy is more likely to effect the external sector of the economy via exchange rates, potentially raising the demand for trade protection. This prospect heightens the need for macroeconomic policy coordination.

In a potential sense, the world economy stands to benefit from the financial innovative process. But the process is not without its risks and not without increasing demands for policy coordination.

Notes

The author is grateful to participants in the conference Capital Market Developments and Financial Stability, organized by the Ditchley Foundation and the Graduate School of Business of the University of Chicago and held at Ditchley Park, England, for comments on a related paper, and to Michael Dooley and Martin Feldstein for helpful comments on an earlier draft of this paper. Julapa Rungkasiri provided efficient research assistance. The author retains responsibility for all errors.

1. Assessments of the recent experience have been prepared by Bank of England 1983; OECD 1984; and Germany and Morton 1985. By far the most comprehensive report describing recent innovations and their possible welfare and policy implications is that of the study group of the Group of Ten Countries (referred to in this paper as the G-10 report) published by the Bank for International Settlements in April 1986.

2. An interesting and potentially highly important area of financial innovation is that dealing,with the European currency unit (ECU). Since the introduction of the European Monetary System in March 1979, the ECU has been propelled to greater importance as a legal parallel currency for transactions throughout most of Europe. An array of innovative ECU products (e.g., ECU-denominated deposits, loans, swaps, bonds, futures, options, and numerous variations on these themes), applications (e.g., ECU invoicing), and institutions (e.g., the Mutual ECU Settlement Association for clearing transactions) have quickly developed. It is beyond the scope of this paper to discuss these developments in detail. The reader is referred to Levich 1987a and 1987b; Levich and Sommariva 1987; and the references cited therein for further discussion.

3. Informal estimates of the volume of foreign exchange trading in various centers are reported in Group of Thirty 1985, 11.

4. The bank, Banque Commerciale pour l'Europe du Nord, carried the cable address EUROBANK, which later became synonymous with the general activity of accepting deposits offshore. See Kvasnicka 1969.

5. For a further description of International Banking Facilities, see Chrystal 1984.

6. When asked whether the impact of Chicago's futures markets on the underlying asset markets was not an example of the tail wagging the dog, Richard Sandor replied that the questioner was mistaken—"the dog had moved to Chicago" (Proceedings of the Conference on Hedging with Financial Futures for Institutional Investors, Salomon Brothers Center, New York University).

7. More complex strategies are possible. For example, a corporation seeking five-year funds might borrow for ten years and sell the final five years' proceeds forward.

8. Gaz de France represents an interesting case study. Between 1983 and 1985 the company entered into 102 swap transactions totaling $7.4 billion to completely transform the currency profile of their financing away from U.S. dollars and toward European currencies, including the ECU. See Reboul 1987 for details.

9. See Miller 1977 for a discussion of the use of securities markets for tax shifting.

10. A thorough discussion of foreign exchange option pricing and market characteristics is presented in Grabbe 1986, chap. 6.

11. For example, a forward contract might be split into the combination of a put-and-call option. A U.S. Treasury security might be split into its principal and interest components.

12. Figlewski 1986 presents a thorough analysis of the use of financial futures for hedging portfolios of money market instruments.

13. For further details, see First Boston 1986, 218–22.

14. See Giddy and Hekman 1984 for a formal demonstration.

15. For further details, see Bock 1983.

16. The cost is approximate because we ignore (i) interest compounding, (ii) selling U.S. commercial paper for same-day delivery while foreign exchange quotations are sold for two-day delivery, and (iii) transactions costs in the commercial paper program and forward contracts. See Kreiner 1986 for a thorough analysis of these costs.

17. Alternative approaches for computing the cost of a long-term forward contract are reviewed in Antl 1983.

18. A good example are the so-called bull and bear bonds, which are Eurobonds with payoffs index-linked to the performance of the West German or Japanese stock markets. These instruments are a close substitute for actual stock index options on these markets that are currently outlawed. National regulators could attempt to impose sanctions on buyers or sellers of these offshore securities, but this form of control is untested.

19. Futures contracts were traded on over 128 products during the last century. Recently, only 45 commodities were actively traded on futures markets, including just 8 of the 23 commodities traded in 1929. See Black 1986 for a model of success and failure of futures contracts based on commodity and contract characteristics.

20. Classic definitions of perfect capital markets (for example, Fama and Miller 1972, 20–22) often begin with the case of certainty. In the certainty case, all individuals necessarily share the same information and expectations. Individuals still require financial markets under certainty to smooth their lifetime consumption to its desired path.

21. For a formal proof, see Cox and Rubinstein 1985, chap. 8, and the references cited therein.

22. A barrier that applies more in the case of international capital markets is the absence of a clear mechanism for enforcing legal contracts across borders.

The possibility of debt repudiation may be a significant factor leading to reduced international capital flows and the existence of apparent arbitrage profits. Dumas 1986 argues that financial service firms may be in a position to bridge this gap. Unlike the occasional borrower, the penalty for repudiation would be high; a major financial firm cannot afford to lose its reputation and so the chance of repudiation on their part is slim. In this way, financial services firms substitute for the nonexistence of a contract enforcement mechanism.

23. Black's (1986) model incorporates this result, predicting that futures contracts are more likely to be successful in the marketplace if they increase the ability of people to hedge their risks (i.e., if they increase the hedging effectiveness offered in the market). The presence of transaction costs might increase the number of useful hedging vehicles. For example, even if options contracts were traded on all five hundred securities of the Standard and Poor's 500 index, an S&P 500 index option would still be a cheaper way to take a position on all securities simultaneously.

24. The International Swap Dealers Associations (1986) has promulgated a code intended to standardize and simplify swap documentation. Parties to a swap agreement may adopt the code in its entirety or selectively. Express provisions in a swap contract always override anything to the contrary in the code.

25. Other formal linkages exist between the New York Commodities Exchange (COMEX) and the Sydney Futures Exchange (SFE), the Chicago Board of Trade (CBT) and the London International Financial Futures Exchange (LIFFE), and the SFE and LIFFE. The National Association of Security Dealers and the London Stock Exchange are conducting a pilot project for the exchange of stock price quotations, also aimed at expanding international trading opportunities.

26. Somewhat contrary evidence comes from the United States Treasury issues targeted to the Eurobond market. These data suggest that targeted Euro-U.S. Treasuries yield about thirty basis points less than comparable Treasury issues in the United States. By implication, the Treasury could increase the supply of offerings in the Eurobond market before interest rates would equalize with onshore Treasury issues.

27. See, for example, Aliber 1973, and Frenkel and Levich 1975.

28. See Dooley and Isard 1980, and Frenkel and Levich 1981.

29. Feldman's analysis on this point leaves some ambiguity. He discusses the interest rate parity relationship as the criterion for market integration, but then uses the expected rate of exchange rate change rather than the forward premium in his formulation.

References

Alexander, Gordon J., and Cheol S. Eun. 1985. International listings, stock prices and capital market integration. University of Maryland Working Paper.

Aliber, Robert Z. 1973. The interest rate parity theory: A reinterpretation. *Journal of Political Economy* (December): 1451–59.

Antl, Boris. 1983. Long-term forward contracts. In B. Antl, ed., *Swap financing techniques*. London: Euromoney Publications.

Bank for International Settlements. Various years *Annual report*.

Bank of England. 1983. The nature and implications of financial innovation. *Bank of England Quarterly Bulletin,* September.

Black, Deborah G. 1986. Success and failure of futures contracts: Theory and empirical evidence. Monograph Series in Finance and Economics, no. 1986–1. New York: New York University Salomon Brothers Center for the Study of Financial Institutions.

Bock, David. 1983. Exchanges of borrowings. In B. Antl, ed., *Swap financing techniques.* London: Euromoney Publications.

Chrystal, K. Alec. 1984. International banking facilities. Federal Reserve Bank of St. Louis. *Monthly Review* (April): 5–11.

Cooper, Ian. 1986. Innovations: New market instruments. *Oxford Review of Economic Policy* 2, no. 4 (Winter): 1–17.

Cox, John C., and Mark Rubinstein. 1985. *Options markets.* Englewood Cliffs, N.J.: Prentice-Hall.

Dam, Kenneth W. 1982. *The rules of the game.* Chicago: University of Chicago Press.

Dooley, Michael P., and Peter Isard. 1980. Capital controls, political risk, and deviations from interest rate parity. *Journal of Political Economy* (April): 370–84.

Dufey, Gunter, and Ian Giddy. 1981. Innovation in the international financial markets. *Journal of International Business Studies* (Fall): 33–51.

Dumas, Bernard. 1986. On the microeconomics of swaps and hedges: Comment. Paper presented at the conference on Swaps and Hedges, New York University Salomon Brothers Center. March.

Edwards, Franklin. 1986. Some regulatory implications of swaps: comment. Paper presented at the conference on Swaps and Hedges, New York University Salomon Brothers Center. March.

Fama, Eugene F., and Merton H. Miller. 1972. *The theory of finance.* New York: Holt, Rinehart and Winston.

Feldman, Robert Alan. 1986. *Japanese financial markets.* Cambridge, Mass.: MIT Press.

Figlewski, Stephen. 1986. *Hedging with financial futures for institutional investors.* Cambridge, Mass.: Ballinger Press.

First Boston Corporation. 1986. *Handbook of securities of the United States government and federal agencies.* New York.

Frenkel, Jacob A., and Richard M. Levich. 1975. Covered interest arbitrage: Unexploited profits? *Journal of Political Economy* (April): 325–38.

———. 1981. Covered interest arbitrage in the 1970s. *Economic Letters* (June): 267–74.

Germany, J. David, and John E. Morton. 1985. Financial innovation and deregulation in foreign industrial countries. *Federal Reserve Bulletin* (October): 743–53.

Giddy, Ian, and Christine Hekman. 1984. A theory of swaps. New York University. Typescript.

Grabbe, J. Orlin. 1986. *International financial markets.* New York: Elsevier Publishing.

Group of Thirty. 1985. The foreign exchange market in the 1980s. New York.

International Swap Dealers Association. 1986. Code of standard wording, assumptions and provisions for swaps. New York.

Kidwell, David S., M. Wayne Marr, and John L. Trimble. 1986. Domestic versus euromarket bond sale: A case of issuing arbitrage. Tulane University. Mimeo.

Kreiner, Irene J. 1986. Short-term multicurrency funding via the U.S. commercial paper market. NYU MBA Applied Business Project. January.

Kvasnicka, Joseph G. 1969. Eurodollars: An important source of funds for American banks. Federal Reserve Bank of Chicago. *Business Condition,* June.

Levich, Richard M. 1985. A view from the international capital markets. In I. Walter, ed., *Deregulating Wall Street.* New York: John Wiley.

————. 1986. On the microeconomics of swaps and hedges. Paper presented at the conference on Swaps and Hedges, New York University Salomon Brothers Center. March.

————. 1987a. Developing the ECU markets: Perspectives on financial innovation. In R. Levich and A. Sommariva, eds., *The ECU market: Current developments and future prospects.* Lexington, Mass.: D.C. Heath.

————, ed. 1987b. *The ECU market.* London: Euromoney Publications.

Levich, Richard M., and Andrea Sommariva, eds., 1987. *The ECU market: Current developments and future prospects.* Lexington, Mass.: D.C. Heath.

MacDougall, G. D. A. 1960. The benefits and costs of private investment abroad: A theoretical approach. *Economic Record* (March): 13–35.

Mahajan, Arvind, and Donald R. Fraser. 1986. Dollar Eurobond and U.S. bond pricing. *Journal of International Business Studies* (Summer): 21–36.

Miller, Merton H. 1977. Debt and taxes. *Journal of Finance* 32 (May): 261–75.

————. 1986. Financial innovation: The last twenty years and the next. University of Chicago Graduate School of Business, Selected Paper No. 63.

Morgan Guaranty Trust Co. Various issues. *World financial markets.*

Nash, Nathaniel C. 1987. Similar standards for banks are set by U.S. and Britain. *New York Times,* January 9.

Organization for Economic Cooperation and Development. 1984. The impact of new assets and intermediation techniques on the functioning of financial markets. *Financial Market Trends* (June): 12–24.

Reboul, Jean. 1987. Gaz de France and the ECU. In R. Levich, ed., *The ECU market.* London: Euromoney Publications.

Salomon Brothers, Inc. 1986. Prospects for financial markets in 1987. New York. December.

Study Group of the Group of Ten Countries. 1986. *Recent innovations in international banking.* Basle: Bank for International Settlements.

2. E. Gerald Corrigan
The Worldwide Implications of Financial Innovations

The subject of international financial innovation is obviously vast in scope, and it is only recently that we are seeing systematic efforts to categorize and analyze the many changes that are occurring in the character and operation of our international money and capital markets. Those efforts reached something of a watershed last spring with the publication by the Bank for International Settlements of the so-called Cross report, *Recent Innovations in International Banking.* But the cause of better analysis and understanding is now being advanced on many fronts.

Because so much of a descriptive nature on this subject is now available, I forgo the usually lengthy discussion of trends and developments in order to focus my remarks on some of the policy implications of the process of international financial innovation. However, as a starting point I want to briefly stress several aspects of the situation which seem to me essential to the evolution of our thinking.

First, the process of financial innovation has and will continue to provide important benefits to suppliers and users of financial services and to the larger goal of seeking to insure that the world's capital resources are allocated in the most efficient manner possible. However, even under the best of circumstances, there are bound to be some bumps along the road as new techniques, new instruments, and new systems are put to the test of the marketplace.

Second, while many of the new financial practices and instruments we are seeing gained popularity as devices to protect against unforeseen changes in credit, interest rate, or exchange rate conditions, they can, themselves, be the source of new and sometimes subtle elements of risk. At the very least, we know that none of these practices can eliminate risk; they can and do redistribute it, but even then it is unclear whether that process of redistribution works to heighten or to reduce risks to the system as a whole.

Third, many of today's financial transactions are very complex and may not always be fully understood by the principals to such transactions. Indeed, in some cases it is not so easy to distinguish principals from agents, a distinction that becomes vital in the face of adversity.

Fourth, looking at the financial system on a worldwide basis, there can be no doubt that innovation has increased the extent of operational, liquidity, and credit interdependencies among major markets and major institutions. In this sense, we should all be operating on the assumption that systemic risk probably has increased, even though some would debate that point of view.

Finally, we must be sensitive to the fact that much of what we call financial innovation has taken place in the post-1982 environment of expanding economies and declining interest rates. We all know that neither the business cycle nor the interest rate cycle is dead.

With these general observations in mind, all of us, I believe, can agree that the process of international financial innovation is raising a host of public policy questions ranging from the structure of our money and capital markets—including the structure and workings of the official "safety net" associated with those markets—to the workings of monetary policy in a much more financially integrated world. In addition, I believe we can also all agree that whatever else these forces may imply, they certainly imply that we must have a higher degree of international policy coordination, not just in regard to macroeconomic policy but also with regard to supervisory and related policies and practices bearing on activities of financial institutions and markets.

In some circles, the call for greater international policy coordination is greeted with sentiments ranging from doubt to outright skepticism as to whether the requisite degree of coordination is achievable. While the problems are formidable, international economic and financial policy coordination is working better than is often recognized. Several examples lead me to that conclusion.

First, the G-5, G-7 process has clearly led to a much higher degree of mutual understanding of problems and prospects while at the same time yielding important steps in policy coordination. That is not to say that all of the problems have been solved; clearly, they have not. However, progress has been made, and important building blocks for the future are in place. Having said that, I should also stress that the case for greater cooperation in the policy process does not mean that necessary policy initiatives of a unilateral nature can be ignored. To the contrary, policy coordination can only be fruitful to the extent that the individual countries are following broadly sensible policies in the first instance. Indeed, absent those fundamentals and the willingness to act unilaterally when needed, there is the obvious danger that policy coordination could become the coordination of bad policies.

Second, today's evident problems notwithstanding, I would also argue that the efforts to deal with the LDC debt problem over the past five years are a truly remarkable example of international cooperation among an incredibly large group of participants, public and private. Having said that, I am obviously sensitive to the fact that the process is under renewed strain as highlighted by Brazil's current difficulties and the greater difficulties in obtaining broad-based commercial bank support for and participation in restructuring and fresh money-lending programs. Clearly, these sources of strain must be overcome or we run the risk of reversing the hard-won gains of the past—a result that can only mean greater risks, greater instability, and greater tensions for all.

Third, in the area of bank supervision, there is also clear and important evidence of cooperation and coordination. The latest and perhaps most graphic example is the joint effort by authorities in the United States and the United Kingdom to promulgate comparable risk-based capital adequacy standards for internationally active banks in our respective countries. I regard that initiative as a genuine breakthrough in international cooperation, in part because we were able to agree on such a complex and technical subject, but also because the approach—as it applies to balance sheet and off-balance-sheet activities—is the first comprehensive effort, nationally or internationally, to substantially adapt basic supervisory standards to the wide range of the new activities and new instruments that have grown out of the process of financial innovation.

Finally, I cite another, more subtle, example of international cooperation: the monthly meeting of the central bank governors in Basle. The value of these meetings stems not merely from the fact that they provide a regular and recurring vehicle for discussion of timely issues of mutual concern but also because the central bank governors and their key staff personnel have come to know each other so well. The spirit of collegiality and trust growing out of the Basle meetings can be of considerable value in dealing with problems when they arise.

In citing these several examples of progress being made in the area of increased policy coordination, I do not want to leave the impression that any of us can be sanguine about the future. To the contrary, the agenda for the future is formidable. Therefore, I will touch on some of the areas that seem to me of particular importance, first in regard to the operation and supervision of financial institutions and markets and then in regard to monetary policy itself.

In banking and finance, the first order of business starts here at home and relates to our capacity as a nation to come up with a coherent point of view concerning what our banking and financial system should look like. That vision must take account not only of market and competitive realities here and around the world, but also of the public interest considerations associated with the stability, integrity, and public confidence in the operation of the system. Those public interest considerations, among other things, mean that the system must be strong enough to withstand the failure of those who abuse it, even when they are large in size. Indeed, the marketplace cannot live up to its promise of efficiency and order if even a few market participants believe that the public safety net will protect not just the system as a whole, but all participants, including those who have acted in an undisciplined or irresponsible fashion. We simply cannot have a system that combines the maximization of profits with the socialization of losses.

While the need to reshape the basic legislative and supervisory framework surrounding our banking and financial markets and institutions has been recognized for some time, today's international market realities make that case all the more compelling. As most of you know, I have recently suggested one longer-term view of what our banking and financial system ought to look like. In making that essay available, I hoped it would serve as a vehicle to help shape the debate—including its public policy elements—while at the same time providing, to use the comptroller of the currency's words, something of a script others can work from. Only others can judge whether it has been successful in that regard, but one thing is clear; namely, the case for fundamental reform is overwhelming and will not go away, nor will the need for some immediate legislative initiatives along the lines that have been persistently and aggressively espoused by the Federal Reserve and others.

Coming to grips with the structure of our own banking and financial system is, among other things, an indispensable prerequisite to coming to better grips with the structure of the supervisory system both domestically and internationally. Indeed, it strikes me as sheer folly to assume that we can better rationalize the structure of the banking and financial supervisory apparatus here in the United States while the system itself is in such a state of flux. However, and without prejudging what, if anything, should be done with it, it is clear that supervisory practices must, here and abroad, adjust to the new environment. For example, building on the U.S.-U.K. initiative, I hope that other major countries—especially those with large and active markets and institutions—will quickly begin the process of bringing capital standards for internationally active banking organizations into greater conformity with emerging international standards. To put it directly, the competitive and prudential implications of major banking organizations operating around the world with distinctly different capital requirements are simply not in the best long-run interests of strong, stable, and appropriately competitive international banking markets.

While internationally harmonious bank capital standards are important, they are only part of the task that lies ahead. Let me, therefore, briefly cite four other areas that I believe will require attention in the period ahead:

First, many of these issues that arise in the context of efforts to achieve a greater degree of harmony internationally in banking markets also arise in other areas. For example, a case can be made that greater convergence in securities market regulations among countries is a necessary corollary to greater harmony on the banking side. The case for greater convergence can also be made in regard to specific markets such as foreign exchange and swaps where banks and securities companies compete directly.

Second, the international payments system requires, in my judgment, continued attention with a view toward doing all we reasonably can to ensure its reliability and stability. This may be especially true for the vast flows of payments denominated in U.S. dollars, many of which are interbank in nature and almost all of which are associated with financial transactions. These dollar-denominated payments—many of which originate in London, Tokyo, and elsewhere and flash through New York as electronic blips—aggregate to more than $1 trillion per day. As such, they entail operational, liquidity, and credit interdependencies of very sizable proportions among virtually all the major banking organizations in the world.

Numerous efforts are underway within the Federal Reserve and within and among private banking organizations—foreign and domestic—aimed at strengthening credit and operational characteristics of these payments systems. However, these efforts take time, and as time passes the volume of transactions continues to grow very rapidly. In these circumstances, it important that parent organizations of foreign branches and affiliates with major operations in the United States, as well as their central banks, take steps to ensure they understand the risks that can be associated with international payments flows, including, but by no means limited to, dollar payments that are settled in New York.

Third, fresh questions are arising concerning the powers and privileges granted to financial institutions operating on foreign soil. We in the United States have for some years followed a policy of national treatment whereby foreign banks and securities firms operating in the United States have the same privileges and responsibilities as do our domestic institutions. Others follow that same policy, but in some countries reciprocity, or a blend of reciprocity and national treatment, is the rule. However, even where national treatment is the policy, questions arise as to whether practices are always consistent with that policy.

The policy of national treatment is coming under attack in the United States amid perceptions that U.S. firms are not always treated evenhandedly in some other countries. This situation requires our careful attention since protectionism in banking and finance is susceptible to those same insidious forces that we all fear on the trade side; in short, once unleashed, it is difficult to know where it will stop.

Fourth, there is a host of questions regarding the implications of efforts underway in a number of countries to reshape the basic legislative and regulatory framework within which banking and financial institutions operate, in the face of the changes that have been induced by market forces over the past decade or more. In addition to difficult issues of legal and regulatory philosophy, custom, and tradition, these efforts must also come to grips with differences in data reporting and consolidation requirements, tax policies, disclosure rules, and accounting standards.

As I said earlier, the agenda regarding the structure and supervision of banking and financial markets is formidable indeed, but there are also a number of important questions regarding monetary policy that grow out of the process of international financial innovation. For example, we know that at least for a transition period, financial innovation has played a role in undercutting relationships between monetary aggregates and key macroeconomic variables such as the GNP or the price level. We also know that the exchange rate is now more important than it once was insofar as its role in transmitting monetary policy changes to the economy. We also know that a variety of forces associated with the process of financial innovation implies that the role of credit-rationing devices in the monetary policy process has been reduced in importance, while price variables—interest rates and the exchange rate—have become more important. Finally, while we cannot be sure, many strongly suspect that the lags in the monetary policy process have become either longer or more unpredictable, or both.

In combination, these forces imply that the monetary policy process is subject to new sources of uncertainty and new tensions. This seems to me to imply that judgment and discretion will have to continue to play a large role in the process of monetary policy formulation and execution. I say this not just because there are the obvious questions surrounding the relevance of outdated empirical analysis and related "rules of thumb" concerning the workings of monetary policy, but also because the unbundling of the credit apparatus raises important questions as to the incidence of monetary restraint, not just its ultimate impact on the economy at large.

As I said earlier, it is clear that the international side of the monetary policy equation will be more important than it once was. That, in turn, implies the need for still greater communication and coordination, but the case for greater coordination internationally must not divert our attention from pressing matters here at home. Among the clear priorities in that regard are the need to better rationalize and strengthen our banking and financial system, and the need to reduce significantly and decisively the budget deficit, thereby narrowing and ultimately eliminating the domestic savings gap and thus providing the financial room to reduce our external deficits. Finally, financial institutions and financial market practitioners are going to have to gain a renewed sense of self-discipline and prior restraint if we are to avoid running the world's credit system too close to the soft shoulder of the high-speed expressway of international finance. None of these challenges will be easy to overcome, but if we are to reap the fullest benefits of financial innovation we must find the ways. I, for one, believe we can.

3. Charles S. Sanford, Jr., and George J. Votja

Deregulation, Technology, and the "Safety and Soundness" of the Financial System

Incomplete deregulation of the financial services industry and the dramatic advances in information technology are seriously damaging the safety and soundness of the commercial banking and thrift franchises in the United States, while at the same time creating a highly concentrated and protected securities industry.

The magnitude and pace of these powerful and irreversible changes are so great that the ability of adversely affected intermediaries and their responsible regulators to adapt is being severely tested. The result is progressive, increasing danger to the safety and soundness of the American financial system. The derivative consequence is that financial competition and innovation which improve service to the public are arrested because of accelerating systemic risk. Let us examine these issues one by one.

Incomplete Deregulation

During the Great Depression, interest rates on deposits were fixed by law or regulation at zero or relatively low levels, entry to banking was restricted, local banking markets were protected by limits to geographic expansion, federal insurance was provided for deposits, and banks gained exclusive access to the lender-of-last-resort window of the Federal Reserve system. At the same time, banks relinquished the right to underwrite securities. It was a package deal. The result was that commercial banks had the lowest cost of funds. Since they could charge less and yet maintain a decent profit, they had the pick of the most creditworthy and liquid assets. Banks became AAA "gilt-edged" credits, and few if any of them needed FDIC support to attract or hold deposits.

Today, the pact has been abrogated. The deregulation of the liability side of commercial banks' balance sheet, which occurred in the 1970s and 1980s, left the banks with a much higher relative cost of funds. Today the most creditworthy banks are unable to fund profitably, even on an acceptable mismatch basis, a loan to an A- or better-rated industrial company. As a result, the quality of the bank loan portfolios

Thanks to P. Daniel Borge for his assistance with this section.

has deteriorated and bank credit ratings have degraded significantly. Many banks now must have FDIC support to keep or attract funds. This process, far from being static, continues in a downward spiral.

Such an unpromising situation would not exist if, at the time of deposit deregulation, banks had been allowed to service the better credits in the open markets. The anomalies in the present situation are astonishing. A bank is not permitted to hold a liquid credit for five minutes, but is allowed to hold the same credit as an illiquid investment for fifty years. Banks cannot underwrite commercial paper, but they can underwrite the backup line of credit that comes into play when the credit behind commercial paper deteriorates.

One alternative is to return to the 1930s arrangement, which guaranteed banks the lowest cost of funds, an option that even the most politically naïve agree is impossible. Granting that premise, elimination of Glass-Steagall is the only rational cure for the decline of the safety and soundness of the banking business which has resulted from incomplete deregulation.

Foreign banks have been more fortunate. The advance of deregulation abroad seems inexorable. The British Big Bang and the changes taking place in Canada, to cite only recent events, are not isolated developments. At the same time, we see Swiss and German banks underwriting corporate bonds and stocks in the U.S. market. All of this is part of a global movement toward free competition in the financial markets. We hope that the completion of deregulation in the United States will follow soon.

Richard Levich's paper outlines clearly, with strong documentation, the broad picture. There is no need to refine his discussion of the process by which banks have lost ground to open market alternatives and seen their creditworthiness deteriorate. There is no escaping the conclusion that half of the Glass-Steagall arrangement has been repealed but the other half remains. U.S. banks are no longer protected from competition, but their powers to compete remain restricted.

Information Technology

The costs of gathering, storing, analyzing, and globally transmitting information have fallen dramatically. No end to this trend is in sight. The existence of financial intermediaries depends upon deficiencies in the information flow between borrowers and investors.

Information is not free and is not equally distributed across the population. It takes time and effort to find a counterparty to a bargain, and a suitable counterparty with complementary financial needs may be hard to find or may be nonexistent. Bargains cost money to structure and to enforce. Crafting a deal properly to reflect real-world legal, tax, and accounting considerations takes considerable skill. No one can be an expert on everything, so it pays to specialize—some of us build cars and some of us underwrite bonds. Some people are smarter than others; some people work harder than others; and some people are more willing to take risks than others.

Last, but certainly not least, governments may muddle up the works by supplanting the judgment of the market with the judgment of politicians. They do so sometimes in the name of high-minded goals like fairness, equality, and political stability, and sometimes in the service of special interests or entrenched mythologies, as in the case of the Glass-Steagall Act.

These shortcomings are what the economist likes to call "market imperfections," a term that may not do them justice. These imperfections cost society money by creating blockages and distortions in the flow of funds from investors to borrowers. Faulty investment decisions make society poorer than it would otherwise be.

The financial intermediary is a specialist whose job is to eliminate, circumvent, or reduce the cost of these financial market imperfections. The earnings of intermediaries depend upon the magnitude of the market imperfections that they face and their success in getting around them—whether by providing efficient information processing, by providing expert judgment, or by bearing unwanted risks. Improvements in information technology make it easier and cheaper to overcome those market imperfections that are caused by deficiencies in the flow of information between borrowers and investors. As these deficiencies are remedied by better and cheaper information technology, the demand for intermediation falls, increasing the competitive pressure on financial firms.

An important example of this phenomenon is the disappearance of the commercial banks' virtual monopoly on credit information. Years ago, banks gathered and evaluated information about the financial health of potential borrowers—a difficult and, in most cases, impossible if not prohibitively expensive task for individual investors. A bank pooled depositors' funds and lent to borrowers it determined were the best credit risks. Borrowers had few alternatives to the low-cost funds provided by banks.

Information technology has reduced the banks' comparative advantage in evaluating and taking credit risks. Computer and communication technology can quickly distribute financial news and data to the market in general. Rating agencies specialize in selling credit analysis on growing number of borrowers to a wider and wider audience. SEC disclosure requirements greatly improve the quantity and quality of available information. Banks have lost their relative monopoly in credit information; instead credit information is becoming a utility outside of the banking system.

Computer technology has also increased the efficiency of pooled investing via mutual funds, pension funds, and other institutional and individual investors. Investable funds are concentrated increasingly with these institutional and affluent individual investors, who are willing and able to do their own research and analysis. Investors now buy securities of the issuers directly, bypassing the bank loan and intermediation process. Since this disintermediation of banks begins with the better credits and works its way down, banks not only suffer a loss in business volume; they suffer a loss in the quality of the business that is left to them. As the competition for lesser credit increases, margins correspondingly decline. Thus, because of advances in information technology, and also because of incomplete deregulation, the bank loan and deposit business is under intense attack from more efficient, open markets and bank asset quality is deteriorating. But technology is transforming the nature of financial intermediaries as well.

It is hard to say whether intermediaries, as a group, will make more or less money as technology advances. What is clear is that successful financial firms will be structured and managed very differently from today. For example, as technology makes routine information cheaper and more widely available, financial professionals will have to find new ways to add value for their customers. More than a few of today's securities salespeople earn a handsome living by reciting current market prices, repeating conventional market chat, and helping customers evaluate simple trades. What happens when most of their customers have screens and expert systems to give the real-time prices and instant analysis of common trades?

As another example, artificial intelligence may make computer-to-computer trading a practical possibility. The more routine trades for the high-volume standardized instruments might be the first to be automated. Just as today's bond trader uses a programmed calculator, which is nothing more than an expert system, to do bond math and to evaluate simple trades, tomorrow's trading manager might use an automated trader to execute part of the firm's overall trading strategy. One early form of programmed trading is already achieving notoriety in the equities markets. The message is that the lower-order skills that are now the stock-in-trade of many traders, salespeople, loan officers, and other financial people are being taken over by technology and artificial intelligence of one form or another, leaving the higher-order skills to be performed by a new breed of financial professionals.

This new breed combines the talents of an artist with those of a technician and has enormous ability to craft creative solutions to customer-specific financial problems. This new person is comfortable with technology and demands "high-tech" research and analytical support to function. Information technology is no longer a black box in the back office but a critical front office tool. As firms employ greater and greater numbers of these new financial people, they will undergo significant organizational change, since these people will have to be managed differently. There will be fewer levels of management, weaker hierarchy, and less bureaucracy. A high-performance atmosphere will require greater autonomy and collegiality among professional members of the firm.

Also, the new technology will drive geographical expansion because the market is now global and requires a presence in all the major financial centers. Once the technology has become worldwide in scope and available to everyone who wishes access to the marketplace, then its specific location becomes irrelevant. Indeed, we can expect a certain geographical contraction to occur as firms focus their technology in the country where they are headquartered.

Information Technology and the New Global Market

Aside from the more obvious effects of technology on financial markets and institutions, another important structural change is occurring. Technology is allowing the creation of a globally integrated market for distinct, unbundled financial attributes.

Any financial instrument can be thought of as a bundle of financial attributes, such as amount, term, currency, repricing interval, base rate, credit risk, tax benefits, and so on. The new technologies, caps, floors, options, futures, and so forth are used to unbundle and repackage these attributes. Traditionally, a financial instrument was priced by comparing it to other instruments of the same name and the same structure trading in the same market. Today, it is common to price an instrument by comparing it to pieces or packages of other types of instruments in many different markets, that in combination produce the same financial result, that is, the same bundle of financial attributes.

For example, a U.S. dollar floating-rate loan from a U.S. bank is not simply compared to other floating-rate loans offered by other U.S. banks. It is also compared to a fixed-rate Eurodollar bond issue coupled with an interest rate swap and to a floating-rate sterling loan from a U.K. bank coupled with a currency swap. All produce the same bundle of attributes: funding in a given currency for a given term that floats off a given base rate at a given repricing interval.

Sophisticated borrowers and investors with ready access to the global markets approach financial needs by defining their underlying requirement for financial attributes—currency, term, repricing, and so on. They compare alternative packages of these attributes assembled from many markets around the world which meet optionally their requirements. Financial attributes are being priced and traded on world markets. As the volume of this activity expands, a single world price for each attribute will emerge. None of this would be possible without modern information technology to gather and analyze quickly data from all over the world.

In due course, every financial instrument will become a potential competitor to every other financial instrument. The ability to disassemble and repackage attributes into optional bundles means that anomalies in prices of different instruments will be arbitraged away more quickly. Artificial intelligence will accelerate this process by allowing the rapid comparison of many complex alternatives.

Similarly, segmentation and isolation of markets by political or institutional boundaries will be much harder to sustain because of competition from efficient synthetic substitutes available in the global market. Borrowers and investors will benefit greatly from this intense competition. The middleman's profit on basic intermediation will decline as a result of these developments. More important, it will be far easier to diversify away or hedge unwanted risks to achieve a customized financial position suited to the customer's situation. Successful financial professionals will be adept at using technology to help customers achieve their desired financial position.

Access to this new global market will be extremely valuable. Since the loss of market access will be costly, perhaps fatal, everyone will be subject to increased market discipline. It will be necessary to disclose all important information and, indeed, secrets will be much harder to keep. Failure to honor agreements may be suicidal.

The impact on financial intermediaries will be dramatic. Comfortable and profitable niches that are now protected by tradition, insulation, and regulation will be under relentless attack. The successful intermediary will not make its money from passive risk bearing or milking customers who have nowhere else to go. Instead, profit will be earned from (1) the creation and professional execution of effective solutions to unique financial problems; (2) the astute trading and positioning of financial attributes; and (3) the low-cost production and distribution of standard financial attributes in high volumes.

Relatively few firms will be capable of meeting the necessary standards of excellence over a wide range of customers and products. It will be vital to focus resources on a clearly defined and sustainable business franchise that is built upon a firm's unique strengths.

The advance of information technology will not be reversed unless some calamity returns the world to the Stone Age. Politicians may cause temporary setbacks, but technology will advance inexorably. Institutions and governments that ignore or resist the imperatives of technology will merely transfer their wealth to others who are more enlightened. Even the Kremlin cannot stop the PC from undermining its centralized monopoly on information.

How do regulators achieve safety and soundness in this new environment? They must create a financial system that responds to the challenges of technology and avoids stifling, harmful over-regulation. In these circumstances, over-regulation and restrictions on competition will create another perilous spiral. Suffocating regulation will breed evasive and desperate risk taking, which in turn will breed costly institutional failures, thus inviting further regulation, starting the cycle all over again. Reregulation in the United States runs the risk of generating such a process. We support three major changes in public policy with respect to the financial system: (1) reform of the "safety net"; (2) deposit insurance reform; and (3) removal of arbitrary restriction on product powers.

Reform of the "Safety Net"

When healthy market discipline and free competition are compromised by stifling regulation and an ambiguous "safety net," banks are denied the means and the incentives to build sound and sustainable businesses. There are many important roles for regulators to play, but it is unrealistic to pretend that they can be solely responsible for the health of individual banks *and* the system as a whole.

The erroneous assumption is that the safety of the financial system is synonymous with the safety of individual banking institutions. In this view, to protect the system, the government must restrain and protect each bank in hope of minimizing the number and severity of bank failures. A more promising approach is to return to the original purpose of the "safety net"—to protect small depositors and the system at large without protecting or guaranteeing the survival of individual institutions.

Protecting individual *institutions* is an expensive and self-defeating policy. Ultimately, it will be ineffective, for it

- breeds incompetent or reckless managers;
- places superhuman demands on regulators to prevent or salvage failures and forces them to say no to anything perceived to be "risky" or unfamiliar in terms of broadened competitive powers;
- creates excess capacity in the industry by preventing the exit of unfit and unneeded firms; and
- risks catastrophic losses to the insurance funds by encouraging insolvent firms to go for broke at the public's expense (the FSLIC has already been decimated by this process).

Gearing regulatory policy to try to prevent individual bank failures is at variance with providing a safe and sound financial system. We should focus instead on insulating the system from any serious consequences of bank failures rather than preventing individual failures themselves. It is possible to insure that the failure of one bank or group of banks will not spread to otherwise healthy banks in a contagion of failure that threatens the system as a whole.

In the absence of adequate safeguards, there is no denying that such an event could take place, given banks' illiquid assets, short liabilities, and interlocking transactions. There are safeguards in place now, however, and more could be added if necessary. Existing safeguards include banks' limits on credit extended to any one bank, daylight overdraft limits on Fedwire and CHIPS, and the ability of the Federal Reserve to lend to solvent but temporarily illiquid institutions. The deposit insurance system effectively precludes runs on retail deposits.

Technical changes in payment system procedures and policies might further reduce the risk of contagion. (Note that there is no risk of contagion on Fedwire now, since the Federal Reserve guarantees payments when made. The issue here is credit risk assumed by the Federal Reserve.) If even further safeguards are needed, and it is not obvious that they are, the payments mechanism could be transformed into a separately capitalized "exchange" that would absorb counterparty risks and establish rules for access and procedures for collateralizing transactions.

Deposit Insurance Reform

We must restore market discipline and reduce the ambiguity about which depositors are insured and under what circumstances. We offer the following program:

1. Regulators, stockholders, management, creditors, and depositors should know exactly what the rules are in advance. Ambiguity creates anxiety in the markets, undermining confidence in the banking system and increasing the potential for panic.

2. Only small depositors ($100,000 and under) should be insured. Everyone else should be at risk.

3. Insurance premiums should not be assessed on uninsured deposits, domestic or foreign.

4. Greater market discipline—the prospect of paying more for funds or not being able to raise enough funds at any price—is a powerful incentive for management to keep its house in order.

5. Effective market discipline depends upon disclosure of credible information about risks and performance of a bank.

6. If regulators intervene before a troubled bank has exhausted its capital cushion, the potential losses to insurance funds and the public are much smaller.

7. Mark-to-market accounting will inform both regulators and the market of the real value of a bank's assets so that their actions are informed and timely.

8. Risk-based capital requirements, if enforced, make it much less likely that a bank will ever approach insolvency.

9. An absolute requirement for the stability of our fractional reserve banking system is that the Federal Reserve must stand ready to act as the lender of last resort and to supply liquidity to solvent but temporarily illiquid banks.

10. Once it is determined that a bank is approaching insolvency, it must be allowed to fail. It does not follow that the bank is abruptly shut down. There can be an orderly process for reorganizing or liquidating a failed bank just as there is an orderly chapter 11 process for commercial firms.

It should be possible to construct a safety net for the *system* (but not for banks) without raising questions of subsidy or unfair advantage. If deposits are insured, fair premiums are paid and the fund is protected by risk-based capital and adequate collateral. There is no assumption that only banks (or thrifts) are entitled to insurance. If there are discount window borrowings, they are secured and at a fair market rate of interest. There is no assumption that only banks (or thrifts) are eligible to borrow.

Any other significant services provided by the government or the insurance funds are charged to their users at a fair price. Access to these services could be provided to any bank or nonbank if appropriate for system safety. Most important, the full consequences of risk taking fall on the risk takers and not on the public.

Functional Regulation

A direct route to competitive equity among suppliers of financial services is regulation according to function, rather than to types of institutions. This approach is especially important in view of the realities of the marketplace for financial attributes. The traditionally defined boundaries between different sorts of institutions and financial instruments are being obscured, even eliminated, as all institutions offer functional equivalents of one another's products.

Take, for instance, the case of transaction accounts. At one time, these were the exclusive preserve of banks. Eventually, investment banks established money funds that, because they were not in commercial banks, were free of reserve requirements, rate ceilings, and so forth. The regulators ultimately lifted interest rate ceilings and allowed banks to create money market accounts, although banks still face numerous competitive disadvantages.

Functional regulation not only promotes competitive equity because it deals with the world as it really is. Functional regulation also involves the most efficient use of regulatory resources, since it requires only primary regulatory for one generic activity or product.

Removal of Arbitrary Restrictions on Product Powers

The pressures created by advancing information technology—new products and new competitors—make it apparent that any system of regulation that is wedded to antique forms is dangerously obsolete. Yet that is exactly what we have: a major pillar of the regulatory framework, the Glass-Steagall Act, is based on the increasingly meaningless distinction between loans and securities.

Defenders of Glass-Steagall contend that allowing banks to underwrite domestic corporate securities would endanger the "safety and soundness" of the banking system. While there is no doubt that a stable, healthy system of banking and capital markets is vital to the nation's economy, there is considerable doubt that Glass-Steagall somehow protects the stability and health of banks. In fact, the notion that Glass-Steagall somehow protects banks is the truth stood on its head: Glass-Steagall *threatens* the "safety and soundness" of the financial system by limiting banks' ability to compete on an equal footing and to manage their business prudently.

Underwriting and Risk

The myth that bank underwriting activities caused the Great Depression has been debunked by careful economic analysis and examination of the historical record. There is no evidence that underwriting losses have caused any significant bank or securities firm to fail.

It is not difficult to see why the risks of securities underwriting are low and manageable. Underwriters hold securities for only a brief period—days or weeks at most. It is not unusual for an issue to be presold before it comes to market. Any securities that must be held by the underwriter can be substantially hedged against price changes by using options, futures, or short positions. The underwriting spread provides a further buffer against losses. A study by Ian Giddy of Columbia University showed that domestic equity underwritings between 1976 and 1983 rarely lost money for the syndicate involved and that those losses seldom exceeded $500,000—hardly a scary business.

The robust profits of the major securities firms are testimony to the relatively low risk (not to mention excessive concentration) of the domestic securities business. From 1979 to 1983, the after-tax rate of return on equity for the largest investment banks averaged over 26 percent, compared to less than 15 percent for the ten largest commercial banks.

Now consider lenders who originate and hold loans to maturity. Most of these are unmarketable medium- and long-term loans to borrowers who do not have good enough credit ratings to go to the open markets. Lenders also provide backup commitments to those borrowers who currently have access to the open markets but who will come to the banks if they are shut out of those markets because of deteriorating credit standing.

Can there be any doubt that securities underwriting is less risky than traditional lending? Skeptics should examine the case of Continental Illinois and Seattle First, whose risky and poorly diversified loan portfolios caused the bank to collapse. It is no accident that many banks are trying to liquify their loan portfolios to capture the value of loan origination and distribution skills without taking such large portfolio risks. This attempt to liquify loans will erase the few remaining financial distinctions between loans and securities—leaving only the artificial and archaic legal and emotional distinctions.

Diversification, Productivity, and Underwriting

If the arbitrary legal distinctions between loans and securities and between lenders and underwriters were eliminated, a bank could properly position itself within the generalized business of originating, distributing, trading, and investing in financial attributes, without regard to the form of the investment. The ability to compete freely in this wider arena would not only give banks a fair chance to regain some of the market share that has been lost to nonbank competitors; it would also dramatically expand banks' ability to diversify their portfolio risks, increase the liquidity of their balance sheets, and make more productive use of their capital and people. These benefits are potentially enormous and could dramatically increase the "safety and soundness" of banks both large and small.

Concentration of Power

Opponents of bank underwriting have waved the flag of bank domination. It is a curious concern in this day and age: the danger of concentrated market power of U.S. commercial banks seems remote, even absurd, in a time of global financial markets and the ascendancy of securitization over bank lending. Nevertheless, any excessive market power could and should be addressed by the antitrust laws. The real danger is the concentrated market power and inflated profits of domestic *investment* banks. The obvious cure for this malady is the entry of new competition from bank underwriters.

Implementation

Once we agree that banks need new powers, an interesting procedural question arises. Should these new powers be exercised in the bank itself or in a separately incorporated and capitalized subsidiary of the parent holding company?

It is difficult to see the point in granting banks expanded powers and then compromising their ability to employ them efficiently and effectively. Insisting that banks use their new powers through separately incorporated and capitalized subsidiaries is precisely such a compromise.

The separate subsidiary approach is inefficient as well as unnecessary. Again, competing in the new global markets will require a high degree of organizational flexibility, informal and temporary networks, coordination, and cooperation. Walls erected to provide an unnecessary insulation can only make it more difficult to achieve excellent competitive performance.

If it is a question of the deposit insurance fund inappropriately subsidizing securities activities, the answer is that the safety net should not subsidize or bail out any institution, bank or nonbank, big or small. Risk-based capital, fair insurance premiums, and market discipline—the abandonment of the "too big to fail" doctrine—and the prudent use of the lender-of last-resort powers of the Federal Reserve eliminate any question of subsidy without resorting to separate subsidiaries. Another approach would be for the banks to collateralize deposits under $100,000, thus obviating the need for the insurance fund entirely.

If it is a question of conflicts of interest, self-interest in preserving a good reputation and the penalties of the securities acts should be sufficient. It would be a shame to reach the sound conclusion that banks need new powers, only to dissipate some of the benefits by requiring an inefficient and unnecessary device for exercising those powers.

Proponents of the separate subsidiary approach usually cite a need for insulating the bank from the supposed dangers of the new activities. The argument is that this insulation is easier to accomplish and to monitor if new activities are in a separate legal entity.

It should be clear from everything that has gone before that insulation from the securities business is the last thing a bank needs. It is the *banking* activities that are dangerous, not the securities activities. Securities activities will strengthen the bank, not weaken it. Indeed, it is easy enough to imagine the employees of a securities firm wishing to be insulated from the *bank*.

The world of finance is changing irreversibly. In time, we suspect that public authorities will achieve consensus on five basic principles that must govern the world that is coming into being.

First, financial services firms must function as single, integrated institutions. These institutions will be confined to finance, however, and will not engage in commerce.

Second, regulators throughout the world will have to reach a meeting of the minds. Since the financial marketplace will be global, regulation will have to be consistent worldwide.

Third, financial institutions in this country will have to be able to compete equally in all markets, all exercising the same product powers.

Fourth, these institutions will have to be organized flexibly in order to respond to rapid change; institutions that are too large or too varied will have difficulty adapting to change.

Fifth, and finally, these jurisdictions will be accepted: the public responsibility is for the health of the financial system in general, and the system only; the private responsibility is for the health of individual institutions.

At this point, we shall truly have achieved safety and soundness in our financial system.

Summary of Discussion

The first theme of the discussion was the implications of financial innovation for macroeconomic policy. Geoffrey Carliner wondered if financial deregulation contributed to the unexpected decline in velocity during 1982, which in turn contributed to an unexpected change in the effect of Fed policy and to the depth of the 1982 recession. A 2 percent of GNP loss due to lack of Fed control associated with financial innovation would wipe out a lot of efficiency gain, he pointed out. Gerald Corrigan proposed that technical/measurement problems were not an overriding problem in the 1982 recession, and the ambiguity that did exist revolved around money market mutual funds prior to the availability of bank money markets. In any case, he noted, there is no choice involved in financial innovation, which is a technically driven process.

A question that is intellectually fascinating and policy relevant, according to Corrigan, is the issue of an inherent contradiction between the speed of capital and exchange rate movements and a monetary policy process compatible with a far more stable exchange rate environment. Another recent development is the disappearance of a stable private debt to GNP ratio since 1982. While some academics say not to worry, Corrigan does. Certainly innovation alters this relationship, and the question is how monetary restraint will work through a system with such a high degree of intermediation. Martin Feldstein pointed out that a high debt-to-GNP ratio implies a large degree of leverage, which in turn implies great interest sensitivity. Corrigan contended that the behavior of highly leveraged instruments is unknown and that the cumulative effect of financial innovation and leverage may be that a given degree of money restraint will require higher levels of interest rates.

Attention shifted to German and Japanese monetary aggregates when Jeffrey Frankel remarked that the Germans and Japanese resist American calls for more expansionary monetary policy by referring to high M1 growth in their countries. He wondered if the monetary authorities in these countries do not know about the breakdown in the M1-to-GNP relationship. Corrigan responded that little has changed in the monetary aggregates in these countries, except for a relatively minor change in the interest rate on Japanese postal savings accounts. He added that the situation in the United States is related not just to financial innovation but to the large drop in nominal interest rates over time.

Rudiger Dornbusch returned to the question of the benefits of financial innovation. He raised the possibility of an overproduction of varieties and pointed out that in manufacturing investment it would be preferable if financial analysis was done over horizons of longer than one quarter, suggesting that decisions become completely short term when financial instruments can be split up into attributes with little apparent connection to the real investment. Corrigan agreed that a series of questions existed about the costs of financial innovation, but he argued that the existence of an enormous flow of benefits is indisputable.

5 International Competition in the Products of U.S. Basic Industries

1. *Barry Eichengreen*
2. *Charles W. Parry*
3. *Philip Caldwell*

1. *Barry Eichengreen*

Capitalism, as Joseph Schumpeter defined it, is a process of creative destruction. In a market economy, one should expect new products, processes, and even producers to supplant their predecessors in the normal course of events. Yet Schumpeter's metaphor provides little comfort to employees and shareholders of basic industries in the United States, all of which are suffering the effects of foreign competition. The American steel industry is the most dramatic case in point: between 1979 and 1985, the number of wage employees there declined from 342,000 to 151,000, while the percentage rate of return on stockholders' equity fell from 5.8 to −18.5 (American Iron and Steel Institute 1986). Recent trends in the automobile, textile, and apparel industries, while somewhat less alarming, similarly convey an impression of U.S. basic industries in steady and perhaps irreversible decline.

In this paper, I first document the dramatic fall in the shares of U.S. basic industries in domestic employment and global production. I then consider explanations for these industries' relative—and, in some instances, absolute—decline. Those explanations fall into two categories: domestic and international. Domestic explanations focus on the decisions of three sets of actors: management, labor, and government. Management is blamed for ill-advised decisions (O'Boyle 1983), labor for high wage costs (Kreinin 1984), government for harmful tax, trade, and macroeconomic policies (Bluestone and Harrison 1982). International explanations focus on the tendency of the product cycle to continually shift the production of established products and standardized processes to newly industrializing countries (due to what Alexander Gerschenkron called, in now unfashionable parlance, the advantages of "economic backwardness").[1] Late industrializers, it is argued, while lacking the infrastructure to be in the forefront of innovation, have the advantage of low labor and material costs when it comes to the production of established goods using standardized technologies.

The problem that plagues this search for culprits should be familiar to fans of the board game Clue. As in Clue, the problem is one of too many suspects, and some method is required to eliminate candidates. One of the findings of section 5.1 is a striking contrast in the recent fortunes of the American steel industry on the one hand and the automotive and textile industries on the other—steel continuing to spiral downward, automobiles and textiles showing signs of greater stability. For an explanation of recent difficulties in the basic industries to be convincing, it must be capable of accounting for this contrast. Much of the analysis that follows is organized around the contrasting experiences of these industries.

After documenting recent trends in the U.S. basic industries, I decompose those trends into components associated with the rise of competing supplies, the growth of demand, and changes in competitiveness. First, I consider the rise of competing supplies, contrasting product cycle explanations that view shifts in the location of basic industries as a natural consequence of the international diffusion of standardized technologies with explanations that emphasize the influence of public policy. Evidence on the diffusion of established technologies, while confirming the importance of the product cycle, suggests also that continued innovation in the United States can preserve important segments of the U.S. basic industries. Next, I examine global trends in demand for the products of basic industries. Because there is a strong correlation between the intensity of demand-side pressures and the severity of the problems faced by the basic industries, I conclude that demand-side factors have played an important role in recent trends. Finally, I analyze factors influencing the competitiveness of basic industries in the United States and abroad, ranging from labor costs, work conditions, management strategies, and investment decisions to the macro, trade, and tax policies of governments.

A central message of this paper is that monocasual explanations for the recent difficulties of U.S. basic industries conceal more than they reveal. Those difficulties reflect both the efficient interplay of market forces (driven largely by economic development abroad) and inefficiencies resulting from labor, management, and government decisions that have proven ill advised in light of subsequent events. Insofar as product-cycle-based shifts in the international pattern of comparative advantage have contributed to recent difficulties, some decline in the

U.S. basic industries is both inevitable—barring measures to isolate the U.S. market from international competition—and justifiable on efficiency grounds. Insofar as labor, management, and government decisions share responsibility, the recent difficulties of U.S. basic industries may be at least partially reversible.

To the extent that these factors vary in importance across industries—indeed across segments of the same industry—it is misleading to offer an undifferentiated assessment of the prospects of the basic industries in the United States. Much depends on the facility with which different segments of those industries adopt new technologies emanating from the high-tech sector. The steel industry, for example, is increasingly bifurcated into a declining segment dominated by large-scale integrated works and a more profitable, technologically progressive segment dominated by minimills. Similarly, the application of new technologies holds out more promise for the survival and prosperity of some segments of the U.S. automobile and textile industries than for others. In consequence, it is increasingly difficult to analyze the basic industries as a monolithic bloc and even to distinguish them clearly from the high-tech sector.

5.1   Recent Trends in U.S. Basic Industries

It is not immediately clear which industries should be defined as basic. Basic industries are typically thought to be those that traditionally loomed large in U.S. industrial production and have fallen recently on hard times: iron and steel, textiles and apparel, and motor vehicles. These industries are lumped together more for their long-standing importance to the U.S. economy, their recent difficulties, and their regional concentration than for their innate economic characteristics. Technically, basic industries are those situated far upstream in the input-output table. Their products serve as inputs into production in a variety of other sectors. They are distinguished by the age of the industry and of the enterprise. Their technology is relatively standardized. Production is often capital-intensive, and there exist barriers to entry. Textiles, apparel, motor vehicles, and steel satisfy these criteria to differing extents. While the steel industry is relatively far upstream, aged, and capital-intensive, the speed with which its technology evolves resembles the high-tech industries. The textile and apparel industries, while relatively old and heavily dependent on standardized technologies, are not situated so far upstream (in the sense that they rely as much on consumer as producer goods markets), are labor- rather than capital-intensive, and until recently have exhibited few entry barriers. Despite the difficulties posed by the terminology, in this paper I adopt the popular definition of basic industries and focus on steel, motor vehicles, textiles, and apparel.

Figures 5.1–5.3 show trends and fluctuations in output, employment, and import penetration in these industries since the 1973 peak.[2] In figure 5.1, the cyclical volatility of steel and motor vehicle output contrasts with the relative stability of textile and apparel production. While textile and apparel production showed no trend through 1979, output in the two industries fell by 10 percent and 20 percent, respectively, between 1979 and 1985. In contrast, both steel and auto production fell sharply during the 1973–75 and 1979–81 recessions. While vehicle production tended to make up lost ground following each cyclical downturn, steel output appears to have ratcheted down to permanently lower levels. That ratchet effect was twice as severe in the 1979–82 recession as in 1973–75. Whereas automobile production had fully recovered by 1977, steel production remained 17 percent below 1973 levels. Similarly, whereas vehicle production had recovered to within 5 percent of 1979 levels by 1985, steel production remained 35 percent below these levels.

Trends in employment, in figure 5.2, mirror the trends in output in figure 5.1.[3] Textile and apparel employment declined gradually over the period (as it has since World War II), reflecting the loss of more than two hundred thousand jobs between 1973 and 1985 (amounting to nearly 10 percent of industry employment at the beginning of the period). Employment in steel moved in a similar manner until 1979, after which it declined sharply; by 1985, employment in the steel industry was barely 40 percent of 1973 levels. Employment in the motor vehicle and equipment industries, in contrast, has been dominated not by a sharp downward trend but by pronounced cyclical fluctuations, although, as foreign-based companies establish and increase production in the United States, the share of the four U.S.-based companies in U.S. vehicle employment continues to decline.

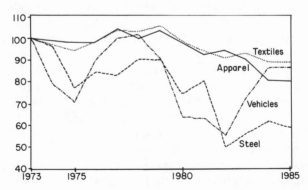

Fig. 5.1   Trends in U.S. basic industry output (1973 = 100).

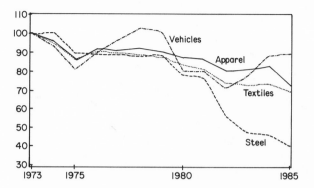

Fig. 5.2   Trends in U.S. basic industry employment (1973 = 100).

Together, changes in output and employment provide a perspective on industry adjustment. Comparing figures 5.1 and 5.2, one finds that only in motor vehicles did the percentage change in output significantly exceed the percentage change in employment between 1973 and 1985. In steel, employment has fallen considerably more than output, especially over the second half of the period when low-productivity plants were closed and a number of products with high labor requirements were abandoned. In textiles and apparel, employment has fallen slightly more than output, especially over the first half of the period. In both of these industries, the decline in labor-output ratios reflects substitution of capital for labor designed to increase productivity. In contrast, the maintenance of relatively high levels of employment in motor vehicles, especially between 1973 and 1979, reflects anticipations of producers that industry demand would soon recover.[4]

Figure 5.3 displays import penetration ratios (shares of domestic sales or apparent consumption accounted for by imports).[5] The reason for concern over imports is obvious. In all three industries, the share of the domestic market captured by imports has risen dramatically since the early 1970s—from approximately 15 percent to fully 25 percent in automobiles and steel and to nearly 35 percent in textiles. The timing of the import surge varies among industries, however, and there is no direct correspondence between movements in the import penetration ratio and trends in output and employment. In textiles and steel, the surge in import penetration began in 1980–81. In the case of textiles it proceeded steadily, while in the case of steel it was interrupted in 1983 and again in 1985, coincident with the implementation of two sets of voluntary export restraints. These two interruptions to the rise in steel imports fully account for the lower import penetration ratio in steel than in textiles in 1985. The case of automobiles is very different. The surge in import penetration began earlier, in 1978–79, but deceler-

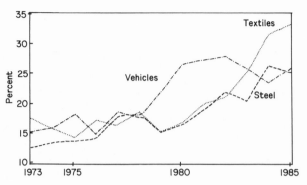

Fig. 5.3   U.S. basic industry import penetration ratios, 1973–85.

ated, leveled off, and ultimately declined in the early 1980s, again coinciding with the adoption of voluntary export restraints. Reinforcing the impression conveyed by their output and employment experiences, the import penetration performance of the automobile industry looks very different from that of textiles and steel.

Tables 5.1–5.7 provide an international perspective on trends in basic industry production. Three features stand out from tables 5.1–5.3 concerned with metals production. First, there has been a dramatic shift in the locus of production from developed to developing countries. The same pattern is evident in iron and steel, nonferrous metals and metal products alike, as if common market forces underlie recent trends. Second, trends in production in centrally planned economies (dominated in the 1980s by China and Romania) have tended to mirror trends in the developing world and hence to accentuate the international shift in the locus of production. Third, U.S. output has been sustained most successfully in the more technologically advanced stages of production.

As illustrated by the contrast between the 8.5 percent annual rate of growth of iron and steel production in developing countries and the 2.5 percent annual rate of decline in developed nations, the United States is not alone among developed countries in suffering a decline in iron and steel output (table 5.1). Even Japanese output fell between 1974 and 1983, a trend that has accelerated recently as Japanese finished steel production fell by 6.3 percent between the first half of 1985 and the first half of 1986, Japanese exports fell by 15.5 percent, and Japanese imports (notably from South Korea, Brazil, South Africa, and Taiwan) rose by 51.4 percent. But the rate of decline of the U.S. share of world output is exceptional: the U.S. share of total world raw steel production fell from 17 percent in 1976 to 11 percent in 1985 (calculated from American Iron and Steel Institute 1986).

Table 5.1   Changes in Global Iron and Steel Production, 1974–83 (percentage per annum)

	1974	1975	1976	1977	1978	1979	1980	1981	1982	1983	1974–81	1974–82	1974–83
Developed Countries	0.69	−16.79	7.22	−2.01	5.10	5.02	−7.24	−0.81	−16.40	−0.09	−1.10	−2.80	−2.53
U.S.	−2.50	−20.00	8.65	−0.88	8.93	0.00	−18.03	8.00	−37.96	14.93	−1.98	−5.98	−3.89
Canada	5.71	−10.00	−1.11	1.12	10.00	9.09	−7.41	0.00	−22.00	5.13	0.93	−1.62	−0.95
Japan	−2.31	−13.98	10.00	−2.27	3.49	10.11	2.04	−6.00	−3.19	−2.20	0.14	−0.23	−0.43
EEC	3.12	−17.83	6.98	−3.26	2.69	5.82	−5.33	−3.39	−9.75	−3.49	−1.40	−2.33	−2.44
Non-EEC	11.60	−8.26	−0.44	−1.98	4.92	8.59	−0.04	−2.26	0.11	3.64	1.52	1.36	1.59
Developing Countries	−6.63	31.93	15.12	7.74	7.63	16.11	6.63	7.13	−2.41	3.27	10.71	9.25	8.65
Centrally planned economies	6.73	6.35	3.83	5.67	5.55	0.62	0.57	−9.24	−2.50	4.17	2.56	2.00	2.21

Source: Constructed from United Nations, *Yearbook of Industrial Statistics*, various issues.

Notes: Year-to-year changes may be affected by the absence of data for some countries in some years and should therefore be treated cautiously. In "developed countries," 1983 excludes Australia. In "developing countries," (1) 1974 excludes Mexico and Hong Kong; (2) 1975 excludes Hong Kong; (3) 1978 excludes the Philippines; (4) 1982 excludes Colombia, Dominican Republic, Philippines, and Sri Lanka; and (5) 1983 excludes Colombia, El Salvador, Peru, Dominican Republic, Philippines, Sri Lanka, Ethiopia, Ivory Coast, and Kenya.

Table 5.2   Changes in Global Nonferrous Metals Production, 1974–83 (percentage per annum)

	1974	1975	1976	1977	1978	1979	1980	1981	1982	1983	1974–81	1974–82	1974–83
Developed countries	3.90	−19.74	15.83	2.82	4.26	2.64	−2.40	−2.44	−8.68	2.47	0.61	−0.42	−0.13
U.S.	−10.87	−19.00	27.16	0.97	5.77	2.73	−11.50	2.00	−18.63	10.84	0.76	−1.99	−1.05
Canada	12.50	−15.00	−3.53	15.85	0.00	−7.37	13.64	1.00	−16.83	15.48	2.14	0.03	1.57
Japan	9.30	−29.00	19.72	4.71	7.87	4.17	0.00	−4.00	−3.12	3.23	1.60	1.07	1.29
EEC	8.80	−17.76	12.29	2.37	1.75	1.89	1.61	−5.61	−3.09	0.81	0.67	0.25	0.30
Non-EEC	20.25	−14.30	5.81	2.39	1.05	5.26	1.26	−4.23	0.68	6.47	2.19	2.02	2.46
Developing countries	14.61	−0.87	25.50	30.39	22.78	45.28	44.61	27.72	18.10	−24.69	26.25	25.35	20.32
Centrally planned economies	12.34	9.89	5.88	4.97	5.12	0.20	−0.28	−5.31	1.75	4.04	4.10	3.84	3.85

Source: Constructed from United Nations, *Yearbook of Industrial Statistics*, various issues.

Notes: Year-to-year changes may be affected by the absence of data for some countries in some years and should therefore be treated cautiously. In "developed countries," 1983 excludes Australia. In "developing countries," (1) 1974 and 1975 exclude Hong Kong; (2) 1976 and 1978 exclude the Philippines; (3) 1982 excludes Bolivia, the Philippines, and Tunisia; (4) 1983 excludes all listed countries except Chile, India, Korea Republic, Singapore, and Mexico.

Trends in nonferrous metals (tin, copper, etc.), in table 5.2, display a similar pattern, with production by developing countries rising dramatically and that by developed nations stagnating. Of the country groups considered, only in the United States did production fall absolutely, however. Even that decline, at a rate of one percent per annum, is small compared to the experience of iron and steel.

Table 5.3 shows that the United States maintained its position relatively well in the more advanced stages of metal production and fabrication. Despite a decline in developed country output and a rise in developing country production not unlike those apparent in table 5.1, U.S. output remained steady over the 1974–83 period, in contrast to the less impressive performance of the Canadian and European industries. U.S. performance in metal fabrication in large part reflects the bouyant state of domestic demand, since it occurred despite a steady deterioration in the trade balance in steel-containing goods.

Trends in textiles, apparel, and footwear, in tables 5.4–5.6, are more heterogeneous. As in metals, production tended to shift from developed to developing and centrally planned economies over the course of the decade. In comparison to metals, however, these shifts were small, and in both textile and clothing the growth of output by centrally planned economies exceeded that by developing nations. Compared to steel there has also been more variation in output trends within the developed world. In textiles, for example, North American output rose slightly, while production elsewhere in the OECD fell. In clothing, in contrast, U.S. and Japanese output contracted, while production elsewhere in the OECD increased. Footwear production fell sharply in the United States and the EEC, while remaining stable in Japan and rising elsewhere in the OECD. The heterogeneity of response suggests that variations in trade and industrial policies (in nonmarket economies, planning) played an even larger role in textile trade and production than in iron and steel.

The experience of the global motor vehicle industry (table 5.7) contrasts with that of both textiles and steel. Production by developed countries grew respectably over the period, increasing most rapidly in Japan, of course, but expanding also in non-EEC Europe (notably Scandinavia), the United States and Canada. Only in the EEC did vehicle production actually decline. The astounding rates of growth of output in developing countries reflect the low levels from which production started in the early 1970s and the takeoff of automobile industries in Brazil, Mexico, South Korea, and Taiwan.

5.2 Growth of Competing Supplies

As the preceding analysis makes clear, a leading influence over the state of the U.S. basic industries has been the growth of competing

Table 5.3   Changes in Global Production of Metal Products, 1974–83 (percentage per annum)

	1974	1975	1976	1977	1978	1979	1980	1981	1982	1983	1974–81	1974–82	1974–83
Developed countries	-0.55	-10.76	11.60	5.75	5.95	5.74	-1.80	0.01	-20.57	-6.14	1.93	-0.51	-1.08
U.S.	-0.47	-11.38	12.20	6.52	8.16	4.72	-9.91	2.00	-15.69	4.65	1.42	-0.48	0.04
Canada	8.41	-9.28	6.82	-2.13	3.26	7.37	-1.96	0.00	-17.00	-3.61	1.56	-0.50	-0.81
Japan	-7.97	-18.89	17.81	6.98	8.70	2.00	-1.96	-4.00	-3.13	-5.05	0.33	0.64	0.07
EEC	2.31	-7.03	11.05	5.56	3.62	9.37	6.54	0.10	-38.00	-18.83	3.94	-0.72	-2.53
Non-EEC	7.49	-5.79	1.90	4.81	-0.26	1.80	5.35	-1.19	-2.99	1.27	1.76	1.24	1.24
Developing countries	0.40	11.44	29.96	13.13	32.49	22.43	26.68	25.84	15.07	-73.75	20.21	11.49	10.34
Centrally planned economies	9.34	9.50	7.27	7.75	4.16	4.13	2.56	-1.49	2.25	2.97	5.40	5.05	4.84

Source: Constructed from United Nations, *Yearbook of Industrial Statistics*, various issues.

Notes: Year-to-year changes may be affected by the absence of data for some countries in some years and should therefore be treated cautiously. In "developed countries, EEC and non-EEC," 1982 excludes Italy, Luxembourg, and Cyprus. In "developing countries," (1) 1974 excludes Hong Kong and Indonesia; (2) 1975 excludes Hong Kong and Malaysia; (3) 1977 excludes Malaysia; (4) 1980 excludes Bangladesh and Malaysia; (5) 1981 excludes Madagascar; (6) 1982 excludes Mexico, Dominican Republic, Sri Lanka, Bolivia, Fiji, Papua New Guinea, and Madagascar; and (7) 1983 excludes Mexico, Peru, Dominican Republic, Philippines, Sri Lanka, Malta, Papua New Guinea, Turkey, Ethiopia, Kenya, and Madagascar.

Table 5.4   Changes in Global Textile Production, 1974–83 (percentage per annum)

	1974	1975	1976	1977	1978	1979	1980	1981	1982	1983	1974–81	1974–82	1974–83
Developed countries	-4.85	-7.14	9.89	-2.00	-1.02	5.15	1.96	-3.00	-4.12	1.08	-0.13	-0.57	-0.41
U.S.	-7.62	-9.66	12.63	-1.64	1.83	6.05	-3.16	-2.07	-9.42	13.27	-0.46	-1.45	0.02
Canada	-2.00	-3.06	2.11	3.09	5.00	8.57	-3.51	3.64	19.30	9.78	1.73	-0.61	0.43
Japan	-10.00	-6.67	9.52	-2.17	2.22	1.09	-1.08	-2.17	-1.11	0.00	-1.16	-1.15	-1.04
EEC	-2.83	-7.77	10.52	-4.76	-2.00	5.10	-2.91	-4.00	-3.13	-3.23	-1.08	-0.47	-0.74
Non-EEC	0.81	-9.13	3.84	-3.53	-2.40	8.68	1.33	-6.68	-1.09	1.14	-0.89	-0.91[a]	-0.70[a]
Developing countries	2.38	1.16	6.90	0.00	3.23	2.08	2.04	0.00	-2.00	4.08	2.22	1.75	1.99
Centrally planned economies	5.26	6.25	4.71	4.49	4.30	1.03	2.04	1.00	-0.99	2.00	3.64	3.12	3.01

Source: Constructed from United Nations, *Yearbook of Industrial Statistics*, various issues.

Notes: Year-to-year changes may be affected by the absence of data for some countries in some years and should therefore be treated cautiously.

[a] Excluding Cyprus.

Table 5.5   Changes in Global Apparel Production, 1974–83 (percentage per annum)

	1974	1975	1976	1977	1978	1979	1980	1981	1982	1983	1974–81	1974–82	1974–83
Developed countries	-1.98	-2.02	7.22	0.00	-0.96	1.94	-4.76	-3.00	-3.09	0.00	-0.45	-0.74	-0.67
U.S.	-2.83	-5.21	14.11	4.59	0.11	-0.21	-4.84	-4.84	-10.98	7.60	0.11	-1.12	-0.25
Canada	0.34	1.74	7.19	-6.64	0.75	13.27	-7.40	1.20	-15.01	13.15	1.31	-0.51	0.86
Japan	-4.12	-5.65	6.44	-0.07	1.24	1.66	-3.82	1.49	-0.88	-1.52	-0.35	-0.14	-0.52
EEC	-0.93	2.80	3.85	-2.78	-1.90	2.91	-5.66	-3.00	0.00	-3.09	-0.59	-0.86	0.77
Non-EEC	0.60	12.68	4.55	-1.71	5.25	-1.29	-14.21	9.16	0.66	-0.02	1.88	1.74[a]	1.57[a]
Developing countries	7.89	2.44	8.33	-1.10	4.44	3.19	3.09	7.00	0.00	3.74	4.41	3.92	3.90
Centrally planned economies	7.14	6.67	6.25	3.53	4.55	3.26	5.26	2.00	0.98	1.94	4.83	4.40	4.16

Source: Constructed from United Nations, *Yearbook of Industrial Statistics*, various issues.

Notes: Year-to-year changes may be affected by the absence of data for some countries in some years and should therefore be treated cautiously.

[a] Excluding Cyprus.

Table 5.6   Changes in Global Production of Footwear, 1974–83 (percentage per annum)

	1974	1975	1976	1977	1978	1979	1980	1981	1982	1983	1974–81	1974–82	1974–83
Developed countries	-4.20	-3.98	0.74	-2.81	-0.63	1.50	-2.24	-2.80	-3.77	-4.58	-1.80	-2.02	-2.28
U.S.	-9.00	-2.65	-2.73	-8.41	1.02	-2.02	3.09	-6.00	-11.70	1.20	-3.34	-4.27	-3.72
Canada	2.39	-1.03	6.52	-8.16	11.11	8.00	-7.41	7.00	-15.89	11.11	2.30	0.28	1.36
Japan	-1.03	0.00	0.00	1.02	3.03	3.92	-5.66	2.00	-1.96	-4.00	0.41	0.15	-0.27
EEC	-1.48	-5.62	2.18	-0.55	-2.76	1.80	-5.46	-2.65	1.00	-4.38	-1.82	-1.50	-1.79
Non-EEC	-1.31	-4.19	7.10	2.45	-2.48	9.11	9.59	1.33	-3.12	-4.76	2.70	2.05	1.37
Developing countries	11.82	-0.19	36.19	12.50	21.68	16.24	23.13	53.32	1.17	-88.00	21.84	19.54	8.79
Centrally planned economies	7.80	6.95	3.53	4.12	5.17	3.49	2.62	-0.88	1.97	-0.33	4.01	3.79	3.37

Source: Constructed from United Nations, *Yearbook of Industrial Statistics*, various issues.

Notes: Year-to-year changes may be affected by the absence of data for some countries in some years and should therefore be treated cautiously. In "developed countries," 1983 excludes Australia. In "developing countries," (1) 1974 excludes Hong Kong and Madagascar; (2) 1975 excludes Hong Kong and Madagascar; (3) 1980 excludes Bangladesh and Malaysia; (4) 1981 excludes Madagascar; (5) 1982 excludes Dominican Republic, Fiji, India, and Madagascar; and (6) 1983 excludes all listed countries except Chile, Ecuador, Panama, and Korea Republic.

Table 5.7   **Changes in Global Production of Motor Vehicles, 1974–83 (percentage per annum)**

	1974	1975	1976	1977	1978	1979	1980	1981	1982	1983	1974–81	1974–82	1974–83
Developed countries	-3.87	-0.11	20.04	11.75	8.58	3.56	-9.81	3.49	-3.60	1.49	4.20	3.37	3.18
U.S.	-13.49	-2.27	26.74	13.76	8.06	0.00	-25.37	3.00	-10.68	25.00	1.30	-0.03	2.48
Canada	0.54	-12.20	18.52	7.81	0.00	0.00	-27.54	1.00	-3.96	26.80	-1.48	-1.76	1.10
Japan	18.35	10.85	17.85	16.35	12.90	12.62	16.19	11.35	1.73	5.11	14.56	13.13	12.33
EEC	-5.18	-7.61	13.12	5.41	2.05	1.28[a]	-3.80	-13.93[b]	-1.33	42.25[c]	-1.08	-1.11[b]	-5.22[c]
Non-EEC	16.12	10.97	11.90	13.97	9.47	16.87	1.69	-6.61[d]	12.80	-60.77[e]	10.90	11.11	3.92[e]
Developing countries	66.18	74.77	104.86	122.14	105.58	18.02	57.32	22.26	-46.52	n.a.	71.39	58.29	n.a.
Centrally planned economies	12.7	16.72	13.93	19.56	9.06	23.00	-0.03	-17.17	-0.77	103.83	9.72	8.56	18.08

Source: Constructed from United Nations, *Yearbook of Industrial Statistics*, various issues.

Notes: Year-to-year changes may be affected by the absence of data for some countries in some years and should therefore be treated cautiously. In "developed countries," (1) 1979 excludes Denmark; (2) 1980 excludes South Africa; (3) 1981 excludes Netherlands and Portugal; (4) 1982 excludes New Zealand; (5) 1983 excludes Denmark, Italy, Netherlands, United Kingdom, Austria, Portugal, Sweden, South Africa, New Zealand, and Australia. In "developing countries," (1) 1974 excludes Hong Kong and Indonesia; (2) 1975 excludes Hong Kong and Malaysia; (3) 1978 excludes Kuwait; (4) 1980 excludes Peru, Bangladesh, and Malaysia; (5) 1981 excludes Ecuador, El Salvador, Peru, and Kuwait; and (6) 1982 excludes Ecuador, El Salvador, Peru, Bangladesh, Fiji, India, Kuwait, and Tunisia. The abbreviation n.a. means not available.

[a] Excluding Denmark.

[b] Excluding Netherlands

[c] Excluding Denmark, Italy, Netherlands, United Kingdom.

[d] Excluding Portugal from 1981.

[e] Excluding Austria, Portugal, and Sweden.

supplies. Does this growth of foreign competition reflect inexorable shifts in the pattern of international comparative advantage, or should foreign government policies designed to promote the expansion of these industries be held responsible for recent trends?

5.2.1   The Product Cycle

According to models of the international product cycle, a pioneering producer of steel, automobiles, and textiles like the United States should expect its share of global output to erode as production processes are standardized and diffuse to newly industrializing countries. While an economy with a comparative advantage in the development of new products and processes will be the initial home of new industries, as products and processes are standardized and technological know-how spreads, the location of production will shift to other countries. The pioneering producer will retain a productivity advantage only if its rate of development of new processes exceeds their rate of international diffusion.

The first industry in which product cycle forces can be observed is cotton textiles. In the nineteenth century, the mechanism by which industrialization initially spread from Britain to the Continent, North America, and then other parts of the world was the diffusion of English-based spinning and weaving technologies. As early importers of British technologies, U.S. textile producers had begun to fear by the end of the nineteenth century that they were being placed at a competitive disadvantage by the continuing spread of textile technology to lower-wage parts of the world. Although innovation by the American industry helped stem this tide, other producers quickly began to emulate American example. Japanese firms, for example, after having turned for advice to English machinery manufacturers in the 1870s and 1880s and adopting the mule spinning technology favored in Britain, quickly shifted to the ring spinning technology developed in the United States. The Japanese industry expanded rapidly: by the interwar period, textile goods accounted for fully half of Japanese exports. But as the technology continued to diffuse, Japan's share of world textile exports fell. By the late 1950s Japan had begun to import textiles, and by 1978 imports reached 18 percent of domestic sales. In 1979, Japan's textile trade balance was in deficit for the first time in modern history.

The second phase in the textile industry product cycle, which took place between the late 1930s and early 1960s, was dominated by American technologies for the production of synthetics and blended fibers. Like their predecessors, these methods were labor-intensive and readily emulated. Hence the location of production continued to shift toward the NICs, for whom the textile industry is an important source of total manufacturing production and employment (see tables 5.4 and 5.5).

The diffusion of knowledge has been accelerated by the aggressive international sales activities of textile machinery companies, including those based in the United States. Today more than one hundred countries ship textile and apparel products to the United States.

The product cycle in the steel industry has been even more dramatic, since it has been compressed into such a short time span. In Japan, for example, where the steel industry was relatively small and inefficient prior to World War II, the transfer of advanced technologies was concentrated in the twenty-five years immediately following the war. In the 1960s, Japanese producers greatly expanded productive capacity, surpassing U.S. producers in their rate of adoption of new technologies such as the basic oxygen furnace and in construction of large greenfield plants offering economies of scale. A significant aspect of these programs was the Japanese industry's continued dependence on foreign technology. As late as 1961, over 60 percent of the Japanese industry's sales were dependent on technology imported from abroad, mainly from the United States. Over the course of that decade, foreign technologies were adapted and the pace of Japanese innovation accelerated. By 1967 the share of sales dependent on foreign technology had fallen to 8 percent, and by the 1970s Japan had begun to export technology to the United States (Oshima 1973, 313).

Production by third world countries, which remain heavily dependent on foreign technologies, increased dramatically (by nearly 150 percent) between 1970 and 1980.[6] While developing-country steel industries are only occasionally multinational, technology transfer still takes place through direct foreign involvement. China, for example, has relied successively on Soviet, Japanese, and, to a lesser extent, West German expertise, in 1978 signing an agreement with Nippon Steel for the construction of a greenfield, fully integrated plant at Shanghai and for the addition of a wide hot-strip mill to existing works at Wuhan. As part of this agreement, the Japanese offered to train Chinese technicians to operate the new works. In South Korea, advanced technology has been transferred whole with the assistance of foreign advisers. In Brazil, an exception to the rule that steel industries tend to be indigenous, two of the three largest private steel companies have significant European and Japanese participation. Brazil's new Tuberao plant is a joint venture with the Japanese and Italians. As a rule, however, government ownership predominates, and direct foreign financial involvement is rare.

As in steel, technology transfer in automobile production has been expedited by direct foreign involvement (often on the part of U.S. firms). But in contrast to steel, the multinational form dominates. This has been true even of Japan, GM and Ford having operated plants there from the mid-1920s to the end of the 1930s. The alternative—obtaining designs and tooling from abroad—is rendered difficult by foreign exchange shortages like those that hindered Japanese efforts in the 1950s and plague developing countries today. Compared to the other basic industries, product cycle forces operate slowly in the automobile industry since motor vehicles are exceedingly complex to produce and market. Major mechanical components such as engines and transmissions tend to be produced using automated, capital-intensive methods; because of high capital and low labor requirements, LDCs have no obvious comparative advantage. "Finish parts" such as exterior body stamping and moldings must fit precisely and be adapted to market demands. Again, there may be disadvantages associated with the use of relatively inexperienced labor and advantages from proximity to the consumer. LDCs' most obvious comparative advantage therefore lies in the production of minor mechanical components such as starters, springs, and wiring harnesses.

While for the immediate future foreign sourcing of minor mechanicals is likely to remain the principal form of LDC auto production affecting U.S. automakers, import competition from developing countries promises to have an increasingly powerful impact on the economy end of the U.S. market. The Hyundai, imported from Korea, in 1986 enjoyed the highest first-year sales ever recorded by an import and undoubtedly figured in GM's decision to halt production of its subcompact, the Chevrolet Chevette. This plus the introduction of the Yugo (manufactured in Yugoslavia) led to plans to import a similar economy car, the Proton Saga, from Malaysia. Meanwhile, established companies have developed plans to produce cars in LDCs for sale in the United States (Volkswagen in Brazil, Pontiac and Ford in Korea, Mercury in Mexico, Dodge in Thailand). For the time being, LDC competition is heavily concentrated at the bottom of the product line. The critical issue from the standpoint of U.S. companies is whether—or, more precisely, when and to what extent—these countries will begin to penetrate other segments of the American market.

5.2.2 Government Policy

Even while product cycle influences were shifting the locus of basic industry production from the United States to other parts of the world, foreign government policies could have been operating simultaneously to speed the process. The recent debate over the extent and effectiveness of foreign industrial targeting and export subsidization focuses on the latter set of influences. Following Krugman (1984), it is useful to distinguish three categories of policy: financial support (such as tax relief and privileged access to capital markets), control of product market access (through tariffs, quantitative restrictions, and administrative guidance), and government control of industry conduct (through the encouragement of mergers, joint ventures, and collusive pricing policies).

The efficacy of these policies might be judged according to several criteria. Did they raise foreign output, employment, and exports? Did they reduce foreign production costs? Did the returns on these policies exceed the costs from a national point of view? Finally, and this is the criterion relevant here, did foreign policies accentuate the shift in basic industry production from the United States and contribute to U.S. industry's competitive difficulties?

The extent to which governments have promoted the growth of their basic industries is notoriously difficult to quantify. How, for example, is one to measure the impact of moral suasion designed to encourage banks to lend money to enterprises in a particular sector? Despite these difficulties, some general conclusions about the impact of policy on the basic industries can be offered. It is clear, for example, that policy played an important role in the growth of the Japanese steel and au-tomobile industries in the 1950s; in the 1970s and 1980s, in comparison, its influence has been much diminished. In the 1950s, the Japanese steel market was protected by stringent import restrictions which in-creased the profitability of domestic production and permitted the in-dustry to produce at minimum efficient scale. Low-interest loans and tax concessions provided added incentive to invest. Although these policies remained in place into the 1970s, by the mid-1960s Japanese competitiveness had improved to a point where import restrictions were redundant. By the mid-1970s, policy shifted toward restraining the industry's growth to avoid exacerbating trade conflicts with other industrial countries.

As in steel, the growth of Japan's automobile industry was stimulated in the 1950s by prohibitive barriers to imports and by statutes requiring that companies be Japanese owned. Half the cost of a new automobile factory could be written off in the first year of operation. In the 1980s, in contrast, few such tax concessions have been available. Over the entire period 1966–81, Nissan paid an average effective corporate tax rate of 35 percent.[7]

Although various tax and financial incentives have been provided the Japanese textile industry, the government's basic strategy has been one of not interfering with the decline of employment. The share of textile manufacturing in Japanese employment fell from 23 percent in 1955 to 13.2 percent in 1979, with 18 percent of Japanese textile jobs lost in the 1970s alone. The late 1970s saw more than a thousand Japanese textile firm bankruptcies per annum. The implications of these developments for Japanese output are evident in tables 5.4 and 5.5. Some steps were taken to slow the industry's contraction, notably provision of concessional financing for development of new merchandise, modernization of equipment, and investment in R&D. But despite these examples to the contrary, Japanese textile-industry policy has generally emphasized adjustment rather than job retention.

Policy in Europe, in contrast, has focused more directly on stemming the decline of basic industry employment. In the early 1970s, government initiatives tended to be indirect, taking the form of measures to encourage private lending for rationalization and modernization, for example. Funds for the French steel industry were raised through government efforts to promote the formation of an industrywide syndicate to market bonds to the small investor. Banks were encouraged by the state to aid in the industry's modernization. As the financial condition of Europe's basic industries worsened, however, governments became increasingly involved directly in the provision of financial assistance. In 1978 the French government implemented a restructuring program that guaranteed the industry's debts.[8] In several other European countries, transfers from general revenues have been needed to permit publicly owned companies to service debt and continue operations. Subsidies and grants extended to the steel industry by members of the EC have been estimated at 70 billion DM between 1980 and 1985 (Gerken, Gross, and Lachler 1986, 775). Most of these measures have been taken in concert through the offices of the EC Commission.

As with its policy toward steel, the objective of European textile policy has been to prevent the erosion of employment. Starting in the 1970s, Belgium, Italy, and the United Kingdom offered textile firms substantial subsidies and in some cases experimented with nationalization. In Norway, the textile industry was provided relief from social security payments and financial support for investment in machinery. France provided transitional assistance to small- and medium-sized firms and subsidized technological research to increase productivity. The Netherlands initially permitted the market to operate freely but, once more than half of all textile jobs in Holland disappeared between 1970 and 1976, intervened with loans and with investment and current expenditure subsidies for cotton, rayon, linen, and clothing producers. If anything, the scope of such policies has expanded in recent years. France, for example, recently announced a program providing relief from social security contributions to textile firms that maintain or increase employment and investment. The Belgian government recently proposed extending loans and interest rate subsidies to firms promising to retain at least 90 percent of their labor forces (Toyne et al. 1984, 123–29).

Have these policies contributed in important ways to the competitive difficulties of U.S. basic industries? Krugman (1984) argues no. Taking steel as an example, he points out that Japanese policies served to subsidize industry expansion in the 1950s but not subsequently. One would have to document persistent links from the learning effects of the 1950s to costs of production in the 1970s in order to establish the relevance of Japanese subsidies to current trends in competitiveness. Krugman argues further that European policies have been "more a bailout for bondholders than a subsidy for production or for the creation of new capacity" (p. 117).

It is true that the direct effects of Japanese policies are small; one study estimates that between 1951 and 1975, loans by public institutions, export promotion schemes, and other assistance measures reduced the cost of a net ton of Japanese steel by no more than $0.45 US (out of an estimated Japanese cost of production in 1975 of roughly $150 US) (Mueller and Kawahito 1978, 25–26). Nearly every study of government assistance to the Japanese steel industry has arrived at similar conclusions. But European subsidies, in contrast with Japan's, have not been uniformly small; studies of European financial assistance to the steel industry in the mid-1970s yielded estimates of implicit subsidies in the range of $2 US per net product ton.

Even if European financial policies did not increase production or stimulate the creation of new capacity, as Krugman concludes, they surely prevented production and capacity from shrinking at the rates that would have been dictated by market forces alone. Even if European production subsidies and import restraints have primarily affected Japanese exporters, the U.S. industry is indirectly affected due to the integration of global commodity markets. Japanese steel exports that might be sold in Europe in the absence of governmental intervention there tend to be diverted to other countries, leading other producers, who might have concentrated on those markets in the absence of Japanese competition, to divert their own exports to still other markets, including that of the United States. Due to market integration, the mere fact that subsidies to the steel industry have been relatively generous in countries not among the leading exporters to the United States does not establish that they were without implications for the competitiveness of American producers. Policies increasing supply or restricting demand tend to have indirect repercussions on the United States wherever they occur.

Observers have argued further that Japanese firms have been favored by privileged access to borrowed funds, as a result of which their basic industries have enjoyed an artificially low cost of capital. The only systematic comparison of the corporate cost of capital in Japan and the United States, that of Ando and Auerbach (1985), suggests that, while this may have been true for the economy as a whole, the argument has not applied to the basic industries since the mid-1960s. Ando and Auerbach compare price-earnings ratios for samples of Japanese and U.S. companies as a measure of required rates of return. For their samples of roughly twenty U.S. and twenty Japanese companies for the period 1966–81, the median average return to (or cost of) capital is 10.3 percent for the United States and 9.5 percent for Japan. In other words, Japanese firms were able to pay their shareholders a rate of return 0.8 percent less than that required of their American counterparts. While the differences initially appear to be larger for steel and autos (in both industries, Japanese firms have substantially lower returns on, and costs of, capital than their U.S. counterparts), corrections for depreciation, inventories, and inflation change the picture.[9] While tending to further increase the cost-of-capital advantage for the Japanese economy as a whole, these corrections raise the returns to the U.S. steel and auto industries compared to their Japanese counterparts. For example, the before-tax cost of capital for U.S. Steel is estimated at 17.8 percent, compared with 22.0 percent for Kawasaki and 23.1 for Nippon Steel. Costs of capital for Ford and GM averaged 15.5 percent and 17.3 percent respectively, compared with 18.4 percent for Nissan. Adjustments for taxation only reinforce the conclusion, since Japanese industry in general and auto and steel firms in particular paid higher corporate taxes than their U.S. counterparts. Thus, if Japanese firms benefited from a lower cost of capital, the benefits did not extend to autos and steel. And, since the 1960s, direct government policy in the form of corporate tax policy has not worked in favor of Japan's basic industries.

5.3 Lagging Demand

The U.S. steel, textile, and automobile industries are all import-competing industries. Hence domestic market growth largely determines the state of industry demand.

The U.S. basic industries have all suffered from secular declines in demand, but to differing extents. The most dramatic decline, that experienced by the steel industry, is portrayed in figure 5.4, which shows U.S. apparent steel consumption relative to real GNP and its trend over a longer period starting in 1960. Although domestic steel use fell significantly over the period as a whole, domestic demand exhibited little trend in the 1960s but declined significantly after 1972 and again after 1978.[10]

The downward trend in U.S. steel consumption relative to GNP reflects the tendency of the steel intensity of production to decline as the economy matures.[11] Phases of rapid industrial expansion and reconstruction like those that followed World War II require inputs of steel for the construction of railroads, bridges, port facilities, power stations, and other infrastructure. Eventually, investment in infrastructure begins to slow and with it the demand for steel; the United States needs steel bridges for only one interstate highway network, for example. Figure 5.4 suggests that the United States had reached this stage of declining steel intensity by the early 1970s.[12]

Simultaneously, technological change created increasingly attractive substitutes for steel. Steel has been replaced by plastic and concrete tubing in many types of construction, by aluminum and plastic in the production of food and beverage containers, by plastics in various stages of automobile production. In several applications, notably automobiles, the shift toward lighter materials was accentuated by the energy price shocks of 1973 and 1979. In 1973, when 14.5 million vehicles were sold, Detroit consumed 23 million tons of steel; in 1985, 15.7 million vehicles accounted for only 13 million tons, a fall of 48 percent per unit.[13] The shift toward steel substitutes also can be seen as a corollary of economic maturity, as increasingly sophisticated technologies require the use of thinner and more formable materials. While there exist countervailing trends, such as the substitution of steel for timber, brick, and concrete in construction, overall these developments have tended to reduce the steel intensity of production (Keeling 1982, 15–17).

Figure 5.4 also reflects the cyclical sensitivity of steel consumption. During business cycle downturns, firms delay investment projects and consumers defer purchases of durables. The ratio of apparent steel consumption to real GNP therefore rises significantly during recoveries and falls during recessions.[14] Consequently, the absence of a notable decline of steel intensity in the 1960s is attributable in part to the relative buoyancy of the macroeconomy over the period. Analogously, slower growth over much of the period since 1973 and the exceptional severity of the post-1979 recession have exacerbated the industry's demand-side difficulties.

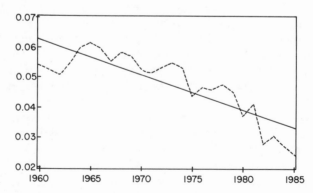

Fig. 5.4   Apparent steel consumption in ingots as a ratio of GNP at 1982 prices.

U.S. textile producers also have experienced stagnant domestic demand due to shifts in expenditure shares and a slowly growing macroeconomy. Global consumption of textiles has been rising less quickly than total manufacturing production since the early 1960s. The income elasticity of demand for clothing is less than unity and is thought to fall with rising incomes.[15] Consumers' expenditure on clothing and shoes as a percentage of total private consumption in the United States, calculated in current prices as in figure 5.5, has declined from nearly 9.5 percent in 1960 to less than 7 percent.[16] Measured in constant prices, that share has been more stable; while the constant-price share trends down over the period as a whole, most of its decline occurs in the decade of the sixties. Thus, it appears to be mainly falling prices rather than income inelastic demands or shifting expenditure patterns that account for the industry's demand-side difficulties. But the aggregate figures mask a shift toward casual wear at the expense of formal attire, stimulating the demand for the products of some segments of the industry while depressing the demand for others.

Motor vehicle apparent consumption as a share of GNP, shown in figure 5.6, while even more volatile than the share of steel, exhibits an almost imperceptible downward trend.[17] Trends in the share of spending on new motor vehicles in GNP can be decomposed into effects associated with changes in average vehicle life, "saturation" of the automobile market, and changes in the relative cost of purchasing and operating vehicles. The rising average age of passenger cars in use, from 5.7 years in 1973 to 7.5 years in 1984, reflects the combination of improving durability and relatively slow income growth over the period. Both the average price of a new car of constant quality and the real cost per mile of operating a passenger car actually declined between 1970 and 1983.[18] In 1984 the number of cars per thousand population

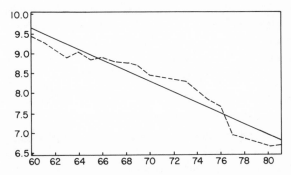

Fig. 5.5   Share of clothing in personal consumption (current prices), 1960–81.

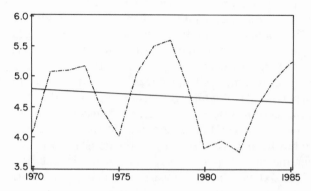

Fig. 5.6   Motor vehicle apparent consumption as percentage of GNP.

reached 549 in the United States, by far the world's highest (computed from *Motor Vehicle Facts and Figures '85*). OECD estimates put the saturation point at 700, however, suggesting that the industry is still far from wholly dependent on replacement demand (cited in Altshuler et al. 1984, 110). Thus, not only does the automobile industry differ from textiles and steel in that demand has remained relatively stable, but neither the saturation nor the operating cost argument provides much basis for pessimism about future demands. At the end of 1984 the Commerce Department forecast that the number of passenger cars sold in North America would rise by 11 percent between 1985 and 1990 (U.S. Department of Commerce 1984, 60). The principal factor likely to depress the quantity of new vehicles demanded is a rise in their relative price, perhaps due in part to the restrictive effect of voluntary export restraints on foreign producers. The effects of these restraints, which tend to raise the share of U.S. consumer expenditure on passenger cars even while depressing the quantity sold in the domestic market, are discussed in the section on trade policy below. But it is already clear that divergent trends in demand play an important role in explaining the differing fortunes of the automobile and textile industries on the one hand and iron and steel on the other.

5.4   Private Sector Determinants of Competitiveness

5.4.1   Labor Costs and Labor Productivity

No factor that figures in the debate over the competitiveness of U.S. basic industries has attracted more attention than labor costs (see, for example, Gomez-Ibanez and Harrison 1982). The importance of labor costs is incontrovertible: labor accounts for 46 percent of total costs in motor vehicles (Kreinin 1984, 41), roughly 28 percent of average

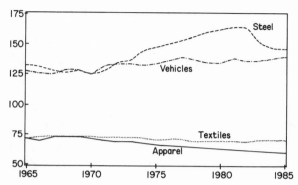

Fig. 5.7   Hourly earnings in U.S. basic industries (all manufacturing = 100).

total costs in steel (down from 39 percent in 1976; see Mueller and Kawahito 1978, 19), and for the great majority of manufacturing costs in apparel. The question is the extent to which high wages have contributed to competitive difficulties, particularly in automobiles and steel, and who bears the burden of responsibility.

Figure 5.7 shows trends over the last two decades in the average hourly earnings of employees in U.S. basic industries relative to all manufacturing employees. The need to distinguish among basic industries is again obvious. While earnings in textiles and apparel are only 75 percent of average manufacturing earnings and in the latter case have continued to decline, steel and vehicle earnings are at least 125 percent of the manufacturing average, with the differential favoring automotive workers rising slowly and that favoring steelworkers rising rapidly until 1982. The steelworkers' premium rose from 26 percent in 1970 to 64 percent in 1981–82, before falling to 43 percent in 1985.[19]

Productivity growth has not offset trends in labor costs, if anything exacerbating them instead. While hourly output in all manufacturing rose between 1977 and 1982, it changed only slightly in motor vehicles and declined markedly in iron and steel. Table 5.8 shows trends over time in U.S. unit labor costs (hourly labor costs adjusted for productivity). Nominal unit labor costs for all employees, which rose by 30 percent in all manufacturing between 1977 and 1982, rose by 56 percent in vehicles and 72 percent in steel. The impact on costs of the rise in steelworkers' hourly earnings, which was one and two-thirds as rapid as in all manufacturing, was reinforced by a 10 percent decline in output per hour. The rise in autoworkers' hourly earnings, which was one and a half times as rapid as in all manufacturing, was not offset by a relatively small increase in labor productivity.

Table 5.8 Percentage Increase of Average Hourly Earnings (current dollars) and in Output per Hour of Labor Input, Selected Periods

	Hourly Earnings		Output per Hour		Unit Labor Cost	
	All Workers[a]	Production Workers	All Workers[a]	Production Workers	All Workers[a]	Production Workers
All manufactures[b]						
1957–67	43	40	33	n.a.	10	n.a.
1967–72	35	35	16	n.a.	19	n.a.
1972–77	53	49	9	n.a.	44	n.a.
1977–82	37	48	7	n.a.	30	n.a.
Steel and steel products[c]						
1957–67	36	34	19	23	11	11
1967–72	42	43	13	14	29	29
1972–77	68	70	3	5	65	65
1977–82	62	82	−10	−4	72	86
Motor vehicles and parts[d]						
1957–67	51	46	45	48	6	2
1967–72	42	42	20	20	22	22
1972–77	55	55	19	18	36	37
1977–82	57	48	1	7	56	41

Source: Anderson and Kreinin 1981 and author's calculations. Calculations from data in *United States Census of Manufactures*, for 1957, 1967, 1972, 1977, and 1985, Bureau of the Census, U.S. Department of Commerce, Washington, D.C., for hourly earnings; *Handbook of Labor Statistics*, 1978 and 1985, Bureau of Labor Statistics, U.S. Department of Labor, Washington, D.C., for output per hour in aggregate manufacturing; and *Productivity Indexes for Selected Industries*, 1979, Bureau of Labor Statistics, U.S. Department of Labor, Washington, D.C., for SIC 331 and 371.

a. Nonproduction workers are assumed to work the same annual hours as production workers.

b. Output is gross domestic product (GDP) originating.

c. Standard Industrial Classification (SIC) 331; output is a physical production series constructed by the Bureau of Labor Statistics.

d. SIC 371.

Identifying the reasons for these earnings differentials is rendered difficult by the fact that they incorporate skill differentials, variations across industries in the use of cooperating factors (capital-labor ratios), differences in the organization of production, and differences in bargaining power. A significant portion of the differentials can be explained on the first three grounds without an appeal to market power or labor-market imperfections. A crude measure of skill differentials is educational attainment: in 1975, 30 percent and 35 percent of the workforce in textiles and apparel, respectively, had less than a ninth grade education, compared to 16 percent for U.S. industry as a whole (derived from U.S. Department of Labor 1975). This contrasts with 18 percent in primary metals, 15 percent in fabricated metals, and 12 percent in transport equipment. Since women comprise some 80 percent of apparel industry employees, in part because the industry provides a convenient port of entry for new labor force participants, the growth of female labor force participation may have depressed apparel industry wages by increasing the relevant labor supply. Yet Krueger and Summers (1986) find that controlling for age, education, and gender, among other variables, fails to eliminate most of the observed variation in interindustry wages. Even with controls, basic industry wages in 1984 differed from average wages by 19 percent in transport equipment, 18 percent in primary metals, -2 percent in textiles, and -16 percent in apparel. Krueger and Summers argue that the interdependence of tasks encourages the payment of efficiency wages in steel and autos which account for a portion of the differentials. In textiles and apparel, the diligence of workers is readily monitored through the inspection of output and the payment of piece rates, and the costs of employee turnover are relatively low because of the lesser importance of firm-specific skills. In steel and autos, in contrast, laborers work cooperatively, rendering their effort difficult to observe. In addition, turnover costs may be relatively high, making it efficient for firms to pay wage premia to attract and retain suitable employees.

None of these factors provides an obvious explanation for the growing differential between steel and automotive wages on the one hand and textile and apparel wages on the other, or for the surge in the premium enjoyed by steelworkers after 1970. This leaves the actions of unions and management. It appears that the two share responsibility for the surge in the steelworkers' premium after 1970 and that import competition played a critical role. When attempting to rationalize the rise in steel imports that occurred in the 1960s, management tended to focus on the threat of disruptions of domestic supply. A famous 116-day strike in 1959 forced U.S. steel users to search out alternative sources. As foreign supplies came to be seen as less volatile and uncertain than domestic sources, steel imports ratcheted upward every three years when contracts were negotiated and strike threats were renewed. Perceiving uncertainty about the availability of domestic supplies as the main factor contributing to the rise in import penetration and anticipating a strong domestic market for steel, management attempted to remove supply disruptions starting in 1974 by offering steelworkers real wage increases of not less than 3 percent per annum in return for foregoing the right to strike. It was easier for management to blame labor militancy than management decisions for the difficulty of competing with imports. While removing the cloud of uncertainty covering domestic supplies, this "experimental negotiating agreement" and its successors contributed greatly to the surge in steel industry labor costs. Thus, management and labor strategies led to the adoption of policies that in the long run exacerbated problems of cost competitiveness.

Only in 1983 did the accord break down. By that time the relationship of cost competitiveness to import penetration could no longer be denied. Management shifted its attention from supply disruptions to comparative labor costs, while labor, out of growing concern for employment, moderated its position on wages, negotiating a 9 percent reduction in total compensation in the first year of the new steel contract. In 1985, for the first time in twenty-five years, the United Steelworkers of America (USWA) struck a major steel company (Wheeling-Pittsburgh) after the company had filed for bankruptcy and unilaterally imposed court-approved reductions in wages and benefits.[20] Thus, both the rise and fall of the steelworkers' premium coincide with changes in management and labor strategy.

Alternative explanations for changes in labor costs are less satisfactory. Appealing to the presence of unions is insufficient; even in the low-wage apparel industry, more than half of employees were unionized in 1975.[21] Granting that unions in steel and autos were more cohesive than those in textiles and apparel, it remains unclear that their actions can account for the surge in the differential. Economic theory suggests that members of unions that effectively restrict entry will have higher wages than nonmembers, not that the differential will rise over time. Nor can the fact that union wage premiums tend to rise in recessions account for these trends in light of the almost uninterrupted rise in the steelworkers' premium over the decade of the 1970s. And while union workers, particularly members of the UAW and USWA, have had their positions protected by generous cost-of-living escalators, their earnings premiums rose uniformly in periods of low and high inflation alike.[22]

If the UAW or USWA were responsible for the widening differential, therefore, this must reflect changes in their bargaining power or strategy. In simple models (e.g., Oswald 1982), the level of wages for which unions bargain is a function of the elasticity of labor demand alone;

insofar as foreign competition has increased the price elasticity of final demand for the products of U.S. basic industries and, ceteris paribus, the elasticity of their derived demands for labor, this should have weakened the unions' bargaining power and reduced, not increased, the differential. Although voluntary restraint agreements have strengthened the bargaining position of U.S. auto- and steelworkers over what it would have been otherwise, the continued rise in the import share of the U.S. market suggests that foreign competition has weakened the bargaining position of the unions on balance. Moreover, the decline in the share of steel- and autoworkers unionized suggests that changes in labor market power have been working in the wrong direction.

This brings us to union strategy, the factor emphasized by Lawrence and Lawrence (1985). They suggest that the price elasticity of demand for labor is an increasing function of investment—that industries engaged in new investment are better able to substitute plant and equipment for labor when unions attempt to raise wages, thereby restraining wage demands. Declining industries in which investment is unprofitable are incapable of responding in this way, providing an incentive for unions to capture remaining profits by raising wages, a phenomenon known as "scooping."

The Lawrence and Lawrence interpretation has the virtue of consistency with recent trends in the automotive industry, where guarded optimism over medium-term prospects has sustained investment in recent years and declining automobile sales and plant closings starting in 1979 led to an immediate moderation in wage trends. After reporting record losses, Chrysler management entered national contract negotiations in 1979 and obtained a contract under which the UAW agreed to $203 million in wage concessions over three years. GM and Ford negotiated new contracts six months prior to the scheduled expiration of existing agreements; as at Chrysler, automatic wage increases both for inflation and other reasons were deferred. Only when industry conditions improved were traditional wage rules reinstated. This interpretation also provides a consistent explanation for the rise in steelworkers' wages relative to those of autoworkers, assuming that the steel industry's future was recognized as bleak from the early 1970s while the auto industry was expected to survive. This, however, imputes a remarkable degree of foresight to union leaders and fails to explain the falling steel industry premium after 1982. One might attempt to finesse this objection by positing that the U.S. steel industry is made up of two segments—an integrated sector facing terminal competitive difficulties, in which unions have been engaged in scooping, and another comprised of plants that can survive, in which unions have not engaged in this practice. The wave of plant closings since the early 1980s has shifted the mix toward the second segment and resulted in a decline in the steel earnings premium for the industry as a whole. Ultimately, however, the problem with this explanation is the implausibility of the notion that as long as fifteen years ago steelworkers recognized the future prospects of their industry as bleak, particularly in light of the optimism that pervaded the U.S. steel market in the mid-1970s.

How much labor cost differentials matter for international competitiveness depends on unit labor costs abroad. Comparing unit labor costs across countries is rendered difficult by differences in data, differences in product mix, and exchange rate fluctuations. The Department of Labor's estimates of hourly compensation, which attempt to adjust for these problems, are summarized in table 5.9.[23] Although these estimates should be regarded as approximations, it is clear, whether the comparison is for 1975 or 1985, that the ratio of U.S. to foreign labor costs is higher in automobiles and steel than in all manufacturing, whatever foreign country is considered. The U.S. steelworkers' and autoworkers' wage premiums that emerged in the 1970s were without counterpart in other countries. The only exceptions are Japanese steel- and autoworkers who, like their U.S. counterparts, are better paid than the average manufacturing worker. Still, at market exchange rates, U.S. steel and automotive wages were in 1975 and 1985 roughly double those of Japan.

Textiles and apparel exhibit a different pattern. In contrast to the United States, where textile and apparel workers earn less than the average manufacturing worker, in most developing countries they earn more. Nonetheless, there remains a dramatic labor cost differential between the Asian and Latin American industries on the one hand and those of industrial countries (including the United States) on the other. The United States is not alone; as early as 1975, textile and apparel wages in many European countries exceeded those in the United States. That they fell back below U.S. levels in 1985 illustrates the power of exchange rate movements to bring about dramatic shifts in relative labor costs (see section 5.5 and especially table 5.15 below).

To assess their implications for competitiveness, labor costs must be adjusted for productivity. Table 5.10 presents trends in unit labor costs in iron and steel in five countries since 1964.[24] It speaks to the question of whether unit labor costs in the United States have been rising relatively rapidly over time, thereby contributing the industry's competitive difficulties. Before 1977, steel-industry unit labor costs actually rose less rapidly in the United States. The U.S.-Japanese comparisons are of particular interest. Although Japanese labor productivity nearly tripled in a period when U.S. output per worker hour rose by only 16 percent, hourly earnings rose much more rapidly in Japan, reflecting the low level from which they started. Even though U.S. labor costs have been higher than Japan's, this shrinking disadvantage cannot ac-

Table 5.9   International Comparisons of Hourly Compensation, Production Workers, 1975–85, Relative to the United States (U.S. = 100)

	1975					1985[a]				
	Autos (SIC 371)	Steel (SIC 331)	Textiles[b] (SIC 22)	Apparel[b] (SIC 23)	All	Autos (SIC 371)	Steel (SIC 331)	Textiles[b] (SIC 22)	Apparel[b] (SIC 23)	All
Canada	77	74	104	102	92	65	70	100	87	84
Brazil	16	13	19	—	15	9	9	—	—	10
Mexico	—	23	46	—	15	—	—	19	—	—
Venezuela	—	19	—	—	31	—	—	—	—	—
Australia	—	—	—	—	85	—	—	—	—	—
Hong Kong	—	—	19	20	12	—	—	20	24	14
India	—	—	5	4	3	—	—	—	—	—
Israel	—	—	49	39	35	—	—	40	31	33
Japan[c]	37	51	52	42	48	40	52	57	48	50
Korea	5	—	8	6	6	9	10	13	13	11
New Zealand	—	—	—	—	51	—	—	—	—	34
Singapore	—	—	5	—	3	—	—	—	—	—
Sri Lanka	—	—	15	15	14	—	—	25	25	—
Taiwan	7	—	8	8	6	—	—	—	—	—

Table 5.9 (continued)

	1975					1985[a]				
	Autos (SIC 371)	Steel (SIC 331)	Textiles[b] (SIC 22)	Apparel[b] (SIC 23)	All	Autos (SIC 371)	Steel (SIC 331)	Textiles[b] (SIC 22)	Apparel[b] (SIC 23)	All
Austria	—	56	76	74	68	—	43	66	64	56
Belgium	75	79	129	118	101	50	56	85	93	71
Denmark	61	—	129	135	99	38	—	88	94	63
Finland	—	—	—	—	72	—	44	73	78	62
France	55	57	91	87	72	43	44	73	78	60
Germany	83	71	118	120	100	63	52	92	95	76
Greece	40	—	38	—	26	30	—	43	—	27
Ireland	—	—	63	50	47	40	—	58	49	45
Italy	54	58	94	88	73	—	42	—	—	60
Luxembourg	—	70	—	—	100	—	—	—	—	—
Netherlands	71	80	147	121	104	43	54	—	—	69
Norway	—	—	—	—	107	—	—	—	—	81
Portugal	—	—	33	30	25	—	—	—	—	—
Spain[c]	—	—	—	—	41	—	—	—	—	37
Sweden	78	—	153	151	113	51	—	99	109	74
Switzerland	—	—	118	106	94	—	—	98	89	73
Turkey	—	—	—	—	11	—	—	—	—	—
United Kingdom	42	38	65	54	51	35	35	54	52	48

Source: U.S. Department of Labor 1986a, 1986b, 1986c, 1986d, 1986e.

Note: Table includes nonwage earnings.

[a]Provisional estimates.

[b]1984.

[c]Japan: autos include motorcycles; Spain: autos include all transportation equipment.

Table 5.10   **Unit Labor Costs in Iron and Steel, Five Countries, 1964–81, All Employees (1964 = 100)**

	United States	Japan	France	Germany	United Kingdom
Output per hour					
1964	100.0	100.0	100.0	100.0	100.0
1972	116.1	219.8	157.1	157.7	130.0
1977	116.0	290.7	172.4	178.6	117.5
1982	107.0	315.7	222.2	212.0	156.9
Hourly labor cost[a]					
1964	100.0	100.0	100.0	100.0	100.0
1972	160.7	277.4	214.8	210.9	206.1
1977	277.0	645.1	529.1	362.3	507.6
1982	496.3	887.0	1,076.2	495.7	1,035.0
Unit labor cost (U.S. dollars)					
1964	100.0	100.0	100.0	100.0	100.0
1972	138.4	150.8	132.7	166.6	142.5
1977	238.7	300.3	305.8	347.2	271.0
1982	463.7	408.7	360.5	382.6	414.6

Source: U.S. Department of Labor, Bureau of Labor Statistics 1984.
[a]Includes nonwage earnings.

count for the American steel industry's continued loss of market share relative to Japan or for the industry's worsening (as opposed to persisting) competitive difficulties.

After 1977, conditions changed. The rise in hourly labor costs in the United States vastly exceeded the comparable rise in Japan. And while Japanese labor productivity rose, U.S. productivity fell. In part productivity trends reflect declining U.S. capacity utilization relative to capacity utilization in Japan, which may itself reflect the competitiveness effects with which we are concerned but in any case tends to exaggerate the underlying productivity differential. Nonetheless, the different trends are indicative of a rapidly worsening unit cost problem for the United States in the second half of the 1970s.

Fuss and Waverman (1985, 1986) find a similar situation in motor vehicles. They estimate that the trend rate of productivity growth in motor vehicles during the period 1970–80 was 4.3 percent per annum in Japan compared to only 1.6 percent per annum in the United States. By 1980, American producers, who possessed a considerable productivity advantage over their Japanese competitors at the beginning of the 1970s, had fallen behind. Combined with the labor cost differential apparent in Fuss and Waverman's table 4.2, U.S. producers were at a long-run competitive disadvantage of approximately 12 percent. As in steel, U.S. producers' competitive difficulties were reinforced by relatively low levels of capacity utilization.

5.4.2 Labor Relations and Work Organization

Labor productivity is not an exogenous variable to which labor costs must adapt. It depends prominently on four sets of factors: labor relations, the organization of work, physical investment, and technological change. Labor relations have attracted particular attention in the automotive industry, where Japanese work organization is sometimes viewed as a panacea for productivity ills. Reflection and experimentation have led to the realization that, while Japanese modes of organization provide useful lessons for American industry, it is neither feasible nor desirable simply to transplant Japanese approaches. Among the lessons is the inefficiency of an adversarial labor-management relationship which neither vests workers with responsibility for product quality nor taps their knowledge of the production process, and the ability of an implicit contract promising job security to reduce workers' fear that increased efficiency will lead to redundancy. How to apply these lessons in the U.S. context is the unanswered question.

In response to the Japanese example, automotive companies have adopted a variety of "employee involvement programs."[25] In the early 1970s, experiments were conducted replacing the assembly line with work teams. Initially, sharp separation was maintained between changes in work organization and bargaining over compensation, in contrast to Japan. With the expansion of quality- and productivity-related activities following the 1979 slump in auto sales, however, negotiations over work organization have become increasingly integrated with compensation issues, with union leaders trading changes in work rules and work conditions for changes in compensation and profit sharing.

To date, there exist no systematic comparisons of productivity in otherwise equivalent plants using assembly line and team production methods. Insofar as the main effect of the latter has been to increase the flow of information between labor and management, it is hard to see how it could fail to increase productivity. Whether the productivity increase is large is the open question.

5.4.3 Investment

The other central determinants of productivity growth are investment and technical progress. Insofar as technical progress in the steel, auto, and textile industries tends to be embodied in new plant and equipment, the importance of investment is heightened. Investment in the basic industries depends both on macroeconomic conditions and on sector-specific factors. To highlight the latter, figure 5.8 shows investment in U.S. basic industries as shares of total manufacturing investment.[26]

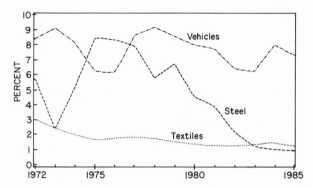

Fig. 5.8   Basic industry shares of total manufacturing investment, 1972–85.

After declining slightly in the early 1970s, investment in the textile industry has remained steady, even rising slightly as a share of manufacturing investment in the early 1980s. The share of automotive investment is more volatile but, like textiles and in contrast to steel, shows no decisive downward trend. The dramatic fall in steel industry investment over the past decade indicates that modernization has not proceeded at the same rate that it has in the textile and auto industries and provides additional evidence that future prospects for the U.S. steel industry are bleaker than those for textiles and autos.

Textile industry investment reflects attempts to cut costs rather than to expand capacity. Increasing the capital intensity of production enables firms to minimize the consequences of relatively high U.S. wages.[27] Open-ended spinning (which produces four to five times the output of ring spindles), the air-jet loom (which is three times as fast as the conventional shuttle), and computerized finishing are viewed as essential elements of the campaign to increase productivity. That investment has been maintained despite more than 250 plant closings since 1979 suggests that a leaner but more modern textile industry will survive into the foreseeable future. In these respects the situation in automobiles is similar to that in textiles, although there have been instances in recent years where capacity expansion has figured in investment decisions.

The behavior of steel industry investment—or disinvestment—differs markedly from the automotive and textile cases. Spokesmen assert that the American steel industry is vigorously "building for the future" by investing in new technologies.[28] However, calculations by Barnett and Schorsch (1983, chap. 6) suggest that industry investment has been inadequate to maintain the value of the capital stock since the early

1970s.[29] In the last five years, new expenditures have done little to offset depreciation of existing capital. Moreover, before 1980 much of this investment took the form of the development of new iron ore mines and iron pelletizing facilities, from which a shrunken integrated sector now derives little benefit. Since 1980, much of the investment that has been undertaken has gone into the construction of minimills rather than the updating of integrated works. Crandall (1985) calculates that Tobin's q (the market value of capacity in place relative to its replacement cost) is on the order of 0.1 for the integrated segment of the industry; it is not surprising that integrated firms, far from adding to capacity, are closing plants and disinvesting as quickly as possible. At the end of 1985, the most efficient minimill producers, in contrast to their integrated brethren, had a q of roughly 1.15, providing scope for continued investment.

This analysis of investment highlights two distinctions within the basic industries. First, investment trends imply bleaker prospects for American steel than for textiles and automobiles. Second, it is critically important to distinguish the prospects of the minimill subsector from those of integrated steel.

5.4.4   Choice of Technology

Choice of technology can exercise a decisive influence over production costs and international competitiveness. U.S. producers have been indicted for failing to adopt cost-minimizing technologies including continuous casting in steel and the air-jet loom in textiles. Since this debate has tended to center on the choice of technology by the steel industry, this section focuses on three recent developments in steel production: continuous casting, the basic oxygen furnace (BOF), and the complex of technologies comprising the minimill. (Section 5.7 below discusses subsequent innovations in steel and the other basic industries.)

Casting is the third of four main stages of primary steel making: smelting, melting, casting, and rolling. Continuous casting permits the elimination of costly and time-consuming discontinuities in the casting process. In ingot casting, liquid steel is transferred by ladle from the converter or furnace to ingot molds which are then trimmed, cooled, and solidified, after which the steel is withdrawn from the molds, reheated in soaking pits, and rolled into slabs, blooms, or billets. In continuous casting, liquid steel is transferred in an even stream first into a water-cooled mold and then to a cooling chamber, from which it is continuously withdrawn by a system of rollers and upon solidifying is cut into pieces of the required length. The advantages of continuous casting include yield, which exceeds 95 percent compared to approximately 80 percent for semifinished products made by rolling ingots in slabbing or blooming/billet mill facilities; improvements in metallurgical quality, including more consistent chemical composition and fewer surface defects; energy saving due to the elimination of the energy-intensive ingot processes; and increased productivity due to the elimination of several labor-intensive stages in the production process (see Association of American Iron and Steel Engineers 1986).

Following the development of experimental machines in the late 1940s, commercial introduction of continuous casting occurred between 1952 and the early 1960s. Continuous casting was first adopted on a large scale in the late 1960s. Figure 5.9 compares the course of adoption in the United States and abroad, illustrating the extent to which the United States has lagged other countries adopting this technology. Although the American industry began to close the gap by constructing or commissioning more than sixteen continuous casters between 1981 and 1983, a sizable shortfall remains (Cantor 1985, 2).

Why has the United States lagged in adopting this innovation? The answer has three components: differences in product mix, differences in related technologies, and differences in rates of growth and investment among national steel industries. Product mix matters because, until the 1970s, continuous casters as installed in the United States and Western Europe were suitable only for producing smaller sections (billets and blooms), which have a square cross section and are therefore relatively easy to cast. Slab continuous casting as developed in Japan is technologically more sophisticated than billet and bloom continuous casting and until the 1970s was not widely utilized. In the 1960s the share of U.S. crude steel production technically suited to billet and bloom continuous casting was lower than in a number of European countries.[30] These differences in product mix are attributable to the composition of end use. Flat-rolled products (sheets and plates, for

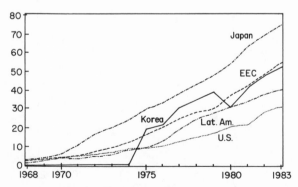

Fig. 5.9   Shares of continuously cast steel in total ingot-equivalent production.

example) are made from slabs, whereas beams and rails are made from blooms, wire rod and small structurals from billets. The U.S. industry's concentration on slabs partly reflects the importance of the U.S. automobile industry in final demand.

In addition, the cost savings derived from continuous casting depend on the type of furnace capacity in place. The diffusion of continuous casting was favored by the presence of oxygen converters and retarded by the presence of open hearth. As late as 1984, fully 9 percent of U.S. crude steel production used the open-hearth furnace, a technology that had disappeared in Japan and all but vanished in Europe (calculated from American Iron and Steel Institute 1985, table 27). But there must be more to the story: Figure 5.10 shows that, while the United States in 1984 had both a relatively low share of continuously cast steel and a relatively high share of open-hearth capacity, there exists no simple relationship between the two variables.[31] This is because the rate of adoption of continuous casting has also been influenced by the rate of expansion of steel industry capacity. Continuous casters are difficult to append to existing integrated works whose furnaces and rolling mills are not laid out in a manner that permits them to be easily connected by a casting machine. Countries that added capacity in the late sixties and early seventies, before the application of continuous casting to slabs was perfected, are likely to have a smaller share of current output continuously cast, while those that expanded their capacity subsequently tend to have a larger share.[32]

As our discussion of continuous casting makes clear, the basic oxygen furnace had advantages. In addition to its compatibility with con-

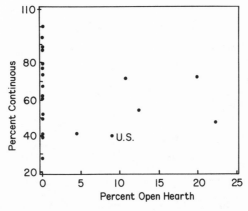

Fig. 5.10   Continuous casting and open-hearth production, 1984.

tinuous casting, the BOF, by replacing forced hot air with oxygen and relying solely on the heat generated by molten ore, eliminated the need for external fuel sources and reduced heat times by a factor of 12. Table 5.11 compares the adoption of basic oxygen furnaces by U.S. producers and their principal industrial competitors.[33] The United States lagged behind Japan in the adoption of the BOF from the late 1950s and behind Europe from the mid-1970s. As in the case of continuous casting, the lag reflects several factors. In the 1950s, when the new technology came on line, U.S. steel makers had a large amount of open-hearth capacity in place. The cost savings of replacing an open hearth with a BOF were less than the savings associated with installing a BOF rather than an open hearth for countries committed to capacity expansion. Rapidly growing national industries thus were better placed to install the new technology. In addition, BOFs could accept a maximum of 30 percent scrap rather than the 50 percent typical of open hearths; hence the relative abundance of scrap in the United States attenuated their advantages. Finally, entrepreneurial inertia cannot be dismissed; early BOFs were developed in Europe rather than the United States, and American producers were slow to appreciate the advantages of this foreign technology.[34]

As table 5.11 makes clear, some U.S. producers compensated for their failure to adopt the BOF by installing electric arc furnaces instead. In 1984, the share of electric furnaces in U.S. utilized capacity was 25

Table 5.11   **Adoption of New Furnace Technologies, 1960–84 (shares of total crude steel output)**

	U.S.	Japan	Nine EEC Countries	Canada
Basic oxygen furnace				
1960	3.1	11.9	1.6	28.1
1965	17.4	55.0	19.4	32.3
1970	48.1	79.1	42.9	31.1
1975	61.6	82.5	63.3	56.1
1981	60.6	75.2	75.1	58.6
1984	57.1	72.3	74.2	73.0
Basic oxygen or electric furnace				
1960	11.8	32.0	11.5	40.4
1965	27.9	75.3	31.5	45.1
1970	63.5	95.9	57.7	45.9
1975	81.0	98.9	82.6	76.4
1981	88.0	100.0	98.6	85.6
1984	91.0	100.0	100.0	100.0

Source: International Iron and Steel Institute 1985; *Steel Statistical Yearbook*, Brussels, IISI, various issues.

percent greater than in the other countries considered. Advantages of electric furnaces include small size and hence low capital requirements (minimum efficient scale of an electric furnace is 0.8 million tons of steel annually compared to 6 million tons for a BOF), ability to use 100 percent scrap (eliminating the need for coke ovens and blast furnaces and reducing the cost of raw material inputs by up to 50 percent), and compatibility with continuous casting. Karlson (1986) explains the growth of electric furnace capacity in the United States largely on the basis of these factors.

The electric furnace is a central component of the complex of technologies comprising the minimill. Minimills can be constructed for a fraction of the capital cost of a new integrated mill. Using electric furnaces in conjunction with continuous casters and a rolling mill, they initially tended to locate in scrap-abundant regions isolated from integrated producers by transport costs. Most minimill firms have not been organized by the USWA; they pay lower wages and operate under more flexible work rules than their integrated competitors. They have concentrated mainly on simple, low-value-added products such as wire rod and reinforcing bar that need not be produced to high metallurgical standards, leaving to integrated producers the flat-rolled sheet used in automobiles and appliances. Many minimill firms are increasingly adapting their methods to the production of high-quality bars and rods, however, and are expected to enter the market for sheet products by the end of the decade (Barnett and Schorsch 1983, 85). Since U.S. imports tend to be produced by foreign integrated firms (despite the growing importance of Japanese and Canadian minimills), the import penetration ratio in the market segment relevant to minimills is considerably lower than for the American steel industry as a whole. The same transport costs that provide minimills with natural protection from domestic integrated competitors provide protection from imports. This market segmentation has begun to break down, however, as minimill firms have expanded their capacity, moved into product lines traditionally dominated by integrated works, and penetrated the home turf of integrated firms.

The financial performance of the minimill firms has been consistently superior to that of their integrated competitors.[35] While a number of these firms have recently experienced financial difficulties, rendering overoptimistic the enthusiasm of some early analysts, as a group they continued to outperform their integrated competitors and now account for about 16 percent of the U.S. market and 22 percent of domestic shipments. Increasingly it appears that the U.S. industry is bifurcating into a relatively healthy minimill subsector and a declining integrated subsector.

As the example of minimills illustrates, U.S. steel producers remain active in adopting new technologies. At the same time, their record illustrates the disadvantages of an early start: having installed large amounts of capacity in the 1940s and 1950s before the new technologies were available, those established producers that dominated the integrated sector were ill placed to adopt subsequent alternatives.

5.4.5   Energy Prices

Higher energy prices have had two sets of countervailing effects on the competitive position of U.S. basic industries. Insofar as steel and vehicles are more energy-intensive than other sectors, higher energy costs raise prices and reduce industry employment both at home and abroad. At the same time, since the share of energy in total costs is greater in the EC and Japan than in the United States, higher energy prices tend to strengthen the competitive position of the U.S. industries vis-à-vis their foreign counterparts.[36] The share of energy in total costs has been relatively low in the United States due to abundant domestic energy supplies and minimal energy taxation. The importance of these effects varies greatly across industries, however. At one extreme, since textile and apparel manufacturing is far from energy-intensive, any comparative advantage accruing to the United States has been minimal.[37] At the other extreme, energy costs have a major impact on the demand for automobiles and are a major element in steel production. As of 1976, coal, fuel oil, natural gas, and electricity accounted for a quarter of major input costs in the U.S. steel industry. Although the impact of changes in energy costs on U.S. steel employment is theoretically ambiguous, Grossman (1986) estimates that U.S. steel industry employment would have been thirty-five hundred greater in 1976–78 had there been no change in the relative price of energy, and that higher energy prices led to the loss of an additional three thousand jobs between 1979 and 1983.[38] Insofar as the relative price of energy has fallen subsequently, these effects have been working in the other direction.

5.5   Government Policy and Competitiveness

Government policies affecting the basic industries are of two types: policies explicitly designed to influence output and employment in steel, autos, textiles, and apparel (trade policy, adjustment assistance) and policies targeted at the economy as a whole but with a special impact on those industries (macroeconomic policy, pollution abatement regulations).

5.5.1   Trade Policy

U.S. policies governing trade in steel, autos, textiles, and apparel differ from trade policy for other industries by virtue of their reliance on nontariff measures, notably voluntary export restraints. These forms of trade policy tend to be implemented on an incremental basis and to have a variety of unintended consequences which introduce unusual distortions into the pattern of basic industry trade.

Textiles illustrate those features that distinguish U.S. basic industry trade policy from trade policy for other sectors and show how a presumption of protection comes to be built into the policy debate with the passage of time. Voluntary export restraints by Japanese producers were first negotiated in 1937.[39] This agreement established the precedent of handling textile trade policy separate from the general trade program. In 1955, with Japan's admission to the GATT, tariffs on her exports were cut but replaced less than a year later by VERs (voluntary export restraints) and a five-year plan for controlling cotton textile and apparel exports to the United States. Thus, nontariff barriers have been a feature of U.S. textile market for fully half a century. Initially, U.S. textile trade policy was unique; subsequently, its distinguishing features—long-lived protection, reliance on voluntary export restraints, and industry-specific negotiations—spread to other basic industries, notably automobiles and steel.

Following an interlude during which textile imports were restricted by the Short-Term Arrangement on Cotton Textile Trade (1961–62) and the subsequent Long-Term Arrangement (1962–73), the Multifiber Agreement (MFA) was concluded as part of the 1973 GATT negotiations. The Long-Term Agreement had departed from GATT rules for manufactured goods by permitting import restrictions to be applied unilaterally, selectively, and without compensation to the exporter. Moreover, by restricting imports of cotton textiles without affecting imports of man-made fibers and apparel, these agreements induced developing countries to shift into the production of the latter. This provided impetus for the negotiation of a more comprehensive agreement, the MFA, which initially restricted the growth of textile imports from Japan to 5 percent per annum and from Taiwan, Hong Kong, South Korea, and Malaysia to 7–7.5 percent per annum. Imports from new entrants and small suppliers were treated more favorably. Governments were permitted to impose unilateral import controls in the event of market disruption (defined as serious damage to the domestic industry) and to negotiate lower rates of import growth for items upon which domestic producers were particularly dependent. Quotas were established through the negotiation of bilateral agreements covering more than 80 percent of U.S. textile and apparel imports in 1980. Since then, the quota system has been tightened further. In 1986, when Congress passed a textile quota bill and attempted to override the president's veto, the United States adopted new agreements with Korea, Taiwan, and Hong Kong. The first of these, for example, limits import growth to 0.8 percent per annum, compared to 8.6 percent from 1981 to 1984, and extends coverage to silk blends, ramie, and linen, fibers into which foreign producers have moved in response to previous restrictions.

Estimating the effects of textile trade policy is rendered difficult by the nontariff nature of the restrictions and the differentiated nature of the product (creating problems that arise in attempts to assess automotive and steel industry trade policy as well).[40] Fortunately, for at least some foreign products it is possible to estimate tariff equivalents indirectly. For the case of Hong Kong, where export quotas are freely traded, Hamilton (1986) used data on the unit values of U.S. textile imports and the market value of quotas to calculate the import tariff equivalent of U.S. quotas. These tariff equivalents, shown in figure 5.11, are both substantial and variable.

Nontariff barriers have significantly reduced U.S. imports of textile products. The value of U.S. textile and apparel imports (in equivalent square yards) grew by only 1.3 percent per annum between 1973 and 1981, while their composition shifted from textiles to apparel, reflecting differential treatment of the two categories under the MFA. Over the 1970s, the apparel share of U.S. textile and apparel imports rose from 35 percent to 58 percent. Insofar as the U.S. possesses a comparative advantage in the production of highly tailored, high-value-added merchandise rather than unfinished cloth, this side effect of quotas has functioned to the disadvantage of the domestic industry.

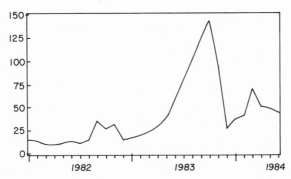

Fig. 5.11   Rate of import tariff equivalent on U.S. textile imports from Hong Kong.

Since 1981, import growth has accelerated to 15 percent per annum. How could this occur under the provisions of the MFA? First, a newly negotiated bilateral agreement with the Peoples Republic of China permitted quota growth of 10 percent per annum. Second, the NICs moved into those few remaining categories not under quota. Third, production shifted to countries such as Sri Lanka and Mauritius for which quotas did not exist. Fourth, merchandise may have been transshipped through third countries for which quotas were not binding. The incentive to respond in these ways was undoubtedly heightened by the dollar's sharp appreciation, which enhanced the profitability of exporting to the U.S. market. The American response was predictable. Firms lobbied for a tightening of import restrictions and, starting in December 1983, the administration moved to establish three hundred new textile quotas and to prevent their circumvention by transshipping. The rate of growth of textile imports fell to less than 7 percent in 1985. In effect, it appears that the rate of growth of U.S. imports is given exogenously by policy in the long run, despite various forms of slippage which offer scope for a positive price elasticity of supply over short periods of time.

Calculations by Hufbauer, Berliner, and Elliott (1986) imply that restraints depressed U.S. textile and apparel imports by approximately 28 percent in 1981. While offering widely differing estimates of the effect of imports on output and employment, studies of the textile industry uniformly conclude that output and employment effects are likely to be smaller than changes in import volumes. Quotas increase domestic production by less than they reduce imports because they raise domestic prices, reducing market demand. The percentage change in domestic textile industry employment should be roughly equal to the change in domestic production (Pelzman and Martin 1980, 16). Using assumptions such as these, Hufbauer, Berliner, and Elliott (1986) calculate that protection permitted the retention in 1981 of 150,000 jobs in textiles and 390,000 in apparel, increasing the total by 26 percent. Given the inelasticity of consumer demand for textiles and apparel, domestic consumers paid a high price per job, on the order of $37,000 1981 dollars.

The American steel industry is another long-time recipient of protection, the sector's early growth having been greatly stimulated by shelter from British competition. U.S. steel trade policy takes two forms—one traditional, one uniquely modern. The traditional form is antidumping law, which protects domestic producers against sales below cost and price discrimination by foreign competitors. Both practices are prevalent in the steel industry, since their capital intensity compels foreign firms to sell below average cost during cyclical downturns, and since cartelization and protection permit them to export at prices below those prevailing in their home markets. The United States has had statutes to deter predatory pricing in international trade for more than sixty years. Since 1974, antidumping investigations have focused on the "constructed value" criterion for dumping, according to which the United States estimates foreign material and fabrication costs and levies an antidumping duty if import prices fall short of those costs plus fixed margins for general expenses and profits. This constructed value criterion provided considerable incentive for U.S. producers to file antidumping suits, which soon exceeded the government's capacity to process them. This led in 1977 to the trigger price mechanism (TPM), under which the government monitored steel imports and, upon finding that steel was imported at a price below reference prices based on the constructed value of Japanese steel, automatically triggered a Treasury investigation. The TPM operated only so long as the industry refrained from filing antidumping suits. The advantages of this mechanism, from an administrative viewpoint, were that it not only eliminated the burden of antidumping suits but provided the authorities some insulation from industry pressure. But the TPM contained many special features and unintended effects, some of which worked to the U.S. industry's advantage, others which worked against it (for details, see Eichengreen and van der Ven 1984). Ultimately, the industry, concluding that the latter dominated, filed antidumping suits that led to the TPM's suspension and in 1982 to its demise.

The second, uniquely modern form that U.S. steel trade policy takes is VERs, like those in textile trade. VERs were negotiated with the Japanese and European steel industries in 1968, implemented in 1969, and renewed in 1972. Following the first oil shock and the steel market slump, the United States imposed a series of increasingly stringent trade restrictions, including new VERs and antidumping investigations culminating in the TPM. VERs on steel like VERs on textiles were a mixed blessing. As in textiles, foreign suppliers responded by trading up, shifting to higher-value products in which the United States might normally be thought to have a comparative advantage. As in textiles, sales by nonsignatory countries tended to replace restrained imports, and there were reports of shipments diverted through third countries. Once VERs were replaced by the TPM, a "somewhat porous price floor" (Barnett and Schorsch 1983, 240) for steel products was established, and the import share of the U.S. market stabilized in the neighborhood of 15 percent.[41] That the TPM's coverage was not limited to foreign producers that were party to explicit agreements was a major advantage from the U.S. industry's point of view.

Since the TPM's collapse in 1982, U.S. steel trade has again been governed by VERs. These differ from early agreements by defining permissible imports as shares of the U.S. market. The 1985 VERs were designed to limit import penetration to 20.5 percent of the steel market. European producers agreed to restrain their U.S. sales to shares of U.S. apparent consumption ranging from 2.2 percent for tin plate to 21.85 percent for sheet piling. Additional VERs were negotiated with Mexico, Brazil, and South Africa, and by the end of 1985 the number of VERs had increased to fifteen, covering 80 percent of the U.S. market. Quotas are administered by the exporting countries via licensing systems. As a quid pro quo for these agreements, the U.S. industry has refrained from filing antidumping suits against participating countries.

These VERs have not prevented imports from capturing a rising share of the U.S. market since 1981. Their coverage is incomplete (Canada as well as Argentina and Taiwan are excluded), and they can be circumvented by many of the devices utilized by textile producers. At the same time, their impact is reflected in the fact that the import penetration ratio fell from 26.2 percent to 20.5 percent the month following the conclusion of the mid-1985 VERs. One can get a sense of the stringency of these agreements by noting that the red cast-iron telephone booths sold off by British Telecom as souveniers have been counted against the European steel quota.

Since steel products are heterogeneous and import restrictions take nonprice forms, measuring their impact is not straightforward. The percentage premium of spot export prices over the U.S. user price is probably the best measure of the tariff equivalent of VERs and countervailing duties.[42] As shown in figure 5.12, except during the 1973–74 commodity boom, when imports subsided and U.S. exports rose, U.S. user prices have consistently remained above foreign export prices.

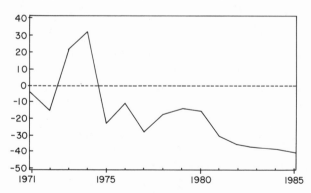

Fig. 5.12   Percentage premium of spot export prices over U.S. user price, 1971–85.

The differential hovered in the range of 15 percent to 30 percent over the second half of the 1970s and subsequently grew to nearly 40 percent, confirming the increasing stringency of U.S. import restraints. Measured as tariff equivalents, levels of protection received by the industry are substantial.

Tsao (1985) estimates for 1983–84 that VERs reduced U.S. imports from the EC by 17 percent and total U.S. imports by 15 percent. A Department of Commerce study estimates that net imports caused a loss of 148,000 jobs in steel in 1984; together with Tsao's estimate of the change in imports (and assuming no change in exports), this implies that U.S. import restrictions increased steel industry employment by 22,000 workers, or by 15 percent.[43] Grossman's (1986) estimates, in contrast, are predicated upon an elasticity of production employment with respect to import prices of approximately unity. Attributing the entire divergence of U.S. user prices from European spot export prices to the effects of VERs implies that U.S. trade restrictions, by raising effective import prices 30 percent, increased production employment by the same percentage.[44] This higher figure should be regarded as an upper bound, since other variables affecting employment, notably steelworkers' wages, would have adjusted to the change in import prices caused by the elimination of VERs; allowing wages to change by the same percentage as import prices halves the change in production employment, again resulting in an estimate of 15 percent. Still other estimates of the change in production employment are slightly lower (Hufbauer, Berliner, and Elliott 1986; Cantor 1984).

U.S. automotive trade policy takes the same form—voluntary restraints—as policy toward textiles and steel. Explicit VERs for automotive trade are a relatively recent innovation for which textile and steel policies provided inspiration. Until the mid-1970s, the growing U.S. market share of Japan was perceived as coming mostly at the expense of Germany and the United Kingdom. As late as 1970, Japan accounted for less than 20 percent of total U.S. imports (see table 5.12). But once the first oil price shock shifted demand toward smaller, more fuel efficient cars, Japanese producers were well situated to expand their exports. By 1979, Japan accounted for more than half of total U.S. imports and for 15 percent of the domestic market. In response to industry complaints, the United States then negotiated a voluntary restraint agreement under which the Japanese agreed to reduce car exports in the year beginning April 1, 1981, by 7.7 percent. Japanese exports were held to the same level for two subsequent years, after which the ceiling was raised by 10 percent. In 1985 MITI declined to renew the VERs in light of the record earnings of U.S. automakers, although the Japanese continue to restrain their exports to the United States using traditional forms of administrative guidance.

Table 5.12   U.S. Imports of Passenger Cars by Country of Origin, 1965–85 (as percentage of U.S. imports)

Year	Belgium	Canada	France	West Germany	Italy	Japan	Sweden	United Kingdom	Others	Total Imports[a]
1984	0.2	22.0	5.5	8.2	0.2	55.1	2.4	0.6	5.9.	4,879,560
1983	0.1	22.8	5.8	9.0	0.1	57.6	3.0	1.5	0.1	3,667,023
1982	0.1	22.9	2.9	11.0	0.3	59.4	2.5	0.4	0.1	3,066,992
1981	0.1	18.8	1.4	12.6	0.7	63.7	2.3	0.4	0.1	2,998,561
1980	0.1	18.3	1.5	14.5	1.4	61.3	1.9	1.0	0.1	3,248,266
1979	0.1	22.5	0.9	16.4	2.4	53.8	2.2	1.6	0.1	3,005,523
1975	1.8	35.4	0.8	17.8	4.9	33.5	2.5	3.2	0.1	2,074,653
1970	2.5	34.4	1.8	33.5	2.1	18.9	2.9	3.8	0.1	2,013,420
1965	0.1	5.2	4.5	67.3	1.7	4.6	4.6	11.9	0.1	559,430

Source: Calculated from Motor Vehicle Manufacturers Association, *MVMA Facts and Figures*, 1985.

Note: Percentages may not add to 100 due to rounding.

[a]Number of vehicles.

As in steel and textiles, auto industry VERs gave rise to a variety of distortions. They provided Japanese producers an incentive to shift into jeeps and light trucks not covered by the initial agreement (although this loophole was closed subsequently). They encouraged the export of components, leading Congress to consider domestic-content legislation. They provided nations not covered by the agreement, notably those of Europe, with an incentive to increase shipments to the United States and encouraged entry by other foreign producers, notably Korea and Yugoslavia. They led to direct investment by Japanese producers in the United States (see section 5.7 below). They provided an incentive for trading up, as Japanese producers shifted into the sale of more luxurious vehicles.

The effects of quota agreements are difficult to estimate because of the extent of trading up. Feenstra (1984) has estimated that two-thirds of the postagreement rise in Japanese car prices reflected quality change, yielding an estimate of the increase in quality-adjusted import prices in 1981–82 much smaller than those of other authors.[45] He estimates that the reduction in import volumes and rise in import prices increased domestic production by 8–9 percent in the first year of VERs and increased production employment by somewhat less (because of the existence of excess capacity). However, Feenstra's estimates for 1981–82, a period when U.S. auto demand remained relatively depressed, may understate the impact that fixed import quotas have had in subsequent years as the domestic market has expanded. Comparisons of the prices of a Toyota Corolla or a Nissan Sentra in Japan and the United States (e.g., Crandall 1986) show that American consumers, who had paid $500 more than Japanese consumers in 1979–80 before the imposition of VERs, paid $3,000 more in 1985. Assuming that the initial $500 reflects transportation and preparation, this suggests a tariff equivalent in excess of 25 percent (assuming an $8,000 U.S. sales price). As domestic demand has grown and quotas have become more binding, their domestic price and output effects appear to have increased. Auto import restraints are defined as absolute levels, in contrast to steel import restraints which are denominated as market shares. One would expect the former to grow more stringent over time. On the other hand, as new countries have entered the U.S. market—partly in response to Japanese VERs—the effects of these restraints may have been attenuated.

5.5.2   U.S. Industrial Policies

U.S. industrial policies fall into three categories: export promotion programs, investment subsidies for modernization, and import protection. The more internationally competitive a U.S. industry, the more policymakers tend to concentrate on export promotion schemes; the less competitive, the more they tend to concentrate on import protection. Not surprisingly, the predominant form of assistance for U.S. basic industries has been import protection. Policy toward the steel industry, for example, has been almost exclusively of this form.

Policy toward the textile industry has been more diverse. The Commerce Department has lobbied for the removal of foreign barriers to U.S. textile exports. For nearly two decades it has assisted U.S. textile and apparel producers wishing to develop export sales by helping them locate foreign sales agents, holding exhibitions, and organizing seminars on export marketing. While the U.S. industry has developed a few successful exports, notably blue jeans, it has essentially remained an import-competing rather than an exporting sector; in consequence, industrywide trends in output, employment, and profitability have been little affected by Commerce Department activities (Arpan et al. 1982, 263–64). In addition, the industry has received federal low-interest loans through the Public Works and Economic Development Act (EDA) of 1965, the Trade Acts of 1962 and 1974, and the Small Business Administration Program. Each of these schemes made funds available to firms unable to secure them through normal channels, so long as there was a reasonable expectation of repayment and the proceeds were used for expansion or modernization of capacity. In practice, the textile and apparel industries have not been major recipients of funds from these programs.

Although U.S. policy toward the automobile industry is dominated by import restraints, financial subsidies have also been important, notably in the case of Chrysler. Assistance to Chrysler starting in 1979 took the form of government loan guarantees, which subsidized borrowing by a firm for which the cost of credit would otherwise have been prohibitive due to bankruptcy risk. The availability of funds for modernization, in conjunction with the upturn in the U.S. auto market and the imposition of VERs upon Japan, permitted Chrysler to repay its government-guaranteed loans. That the loans were repaid does not change the fact that the government guarantee was a subsidy to the firm.

Besides protection, the most important form of U.S. policy toward the basic industries has been adjustment assistance. Adjustment assistance is designed to provide retraining, education, and transitional income for the newly unemployed. In practice, income transfers have been much more important than training schemes. According to Arpan et al. (1982), approximately 95 percent of adjustment assistance to former apparel-industry workers have gone into allowances to replace lost earnings rather than retraining or education. The number of workers that have been placed by the employment service remains negligible.

5.5.3   Macroeconomic Policy and Real Exchange Rates

Until recently, economists would have found it difficult to convince laymen that monetary and fiscal policies rather than sector-specific events had exercised a decisive impact on the basic industries. However, the dramatic post-1981 real appreciation of the dollar and its relationship to the monetary-fiscal mix have heightened awareness of the importance of macroeconomic factors (see the discussion in Branson 1986). In addition, the severity of the post-1979 recession has reminded observers of the sensitivity of the steel and automobile industries, as producers of durable goods and of inputs into their manufacture, to macroeconomic conditions (see section 5.3 above).

The budget deficits of the 1980s, combined with a tight anti-inflationary monetary policy, drove up the relative price of domestic goods by causing a rapid real appreciation of the dollar. The dollar's strength was a corollary of the capital inflow needed to absorb the debt issued to finance the deficit, and was reinforced by greater aggregate demand at home than abroad, which required for product market equilibrium that demand be shifted away from domestic goods (see Frankel, chap. 9, this volume). This real appreciation of the dollar impacted the basic industries because production costs in those industries are affected by economywide conditions and are imperfectly flexible in own-currency terms. For example, the 58 percent rise in the multilateral trade-weighted value of the dollar between 1980 and 1984 dramatically reduced the dollar value of the wages paid by foreign steel, textile, and automobile producers. Table 5.13 shows the dramatic decline in German hourly earnings in manufacturing expressed in U.S. dollars and the smaller but nonetheless significant decline in Japanese dollar-denominated labor costs over the period 1980:2–1985:1, when the value of the dollar rose by more than 80 percent against the deutsche mark and rose by nearly 20 percent against the yen. The rise in dollar-denominated foreign labor costs during the subsequent period of dollar depreciation is equally dramatic, although the relationship between the yen and the deutsche mark is reversed: whereas the fall in the nominal yen-dollar rate is nearly twice as fast the second period as its rise in the first, the fall in the deutsche mark–dollar rate is less than half as rapid in the second period as its rise in the first.

Nontariff barriers tend to reduce the price sensitivity of U.S. imports of basic industry products and hence to limit the impact of real exchange rates on employment in import-competing sectors. In addition, changes over time in the height of these nontariff barriers render the price elasticity of production employment extremely difficult to estimate. Estimates in the appendix (table 5.A.1) suggest that this elasticity ranges from roughly -0.2 in textiles and apparel to -0.5 in automobiles and

Table 5.13   Changes in Labor Costs in Manufacturing in Periods of Fluctuating Exchange Rates (in percentage points)

	1980:2–1985:1	1985:1–1986:2
U.S.[a]		
Total private	33.0	0.2
Textiles	34.5	4.6
Apparel	27.8	0.1
Primary metals	23.7	3.2
Transport equipment	41.9	1.8
Germany[b]		
Local currency	17.8	5.0
U.S. $	−67.4	36.0
Japan[c]		
Local currency	4.1	25.5
U.S. $	−14.3	59.5

Source: For U.S.: Department of Labor, Bureau of Labor Statistics, *Monthly Labor Review*, various issues. For Germany and Japan: OECD, *Main Economic Indicators*, various issues.

[a]Average hourly earnings of nonagricultural production or nonsupervisory workers, in current dollars.

[b]Hourly earnings in enterprises employing more than ten persons.

[c]Average monthly earnings.

steel. According to these estimates, the real appreciation of the dollar between the second half of the 1970s and the first half of the 1980s reduced employment in textiles and apparel by nearly 4 percent and employment in motor vehicles and steel by nearly 10 percent (table 5.A.2). The greater impact of exchange rate changes on autos and steel than on textiles and apparel makes sense when one observes that the dollar has fluctuated most dramatically (especially since the beginning of 1985) not against the currencies of developing countries, which are the principal suppliers of textile exports to the U.S. market, but against the currencies of industrial countries such as Germany and Japan, which are the main suppliers of autos and steel.

5.5.4 Pollution Abatement Expenditures

Unlike industry spokesmen, who attach great weight to the impact on international competitiveness of U.S. pollution abatement expenditures, academic analyses have generally concluded that the effects of these costs have been small. Table 5.14 shows pollution control expenditures as shares of GNP and investment for 1975, when concern over improving environmental quality was at its height. U.S. expenditure shares exceed those of its industrial competitors, with the notable exception of Japan. Table 5.15 presents three estimates of environ-

Table 5.14   **Private Sector Investment in Pollution Control, 1975**

	Percent of GDP	Percent of Total Private Investment
United States	0.44	3.4
Japan	1.00	4.6
Denmark	0.17	0.9
Finland	0.22	0.9
France	0.28	1.4
Germany	0.32	1.9
Netherlands	0.34	1.9
Norway	0.22	0.7
Sweden	0.19	1.1
United Kingdom	0.29	1.7

Source: Kalt 1985.

Table 5.15   **Direct and Indirect Regulatory Costs and Trade Performance**

	Direct Environmental Costs[a]	Direct and Indirect Environmental Costs[b]	All Regulatory Costs[b]	Net Exports[c]
Textiles	0.21	1.34	2.66	−0.68
Apparel	0.03	0.66	1.48	−12.39
Iron and steel	1.28	2.38	5.36	−8.70
Motor vehicles and equipment	0.14	0.99	6.75	−6.19
Average of 31 import-competing industries[d]	0.58	1.54	3.96	−7.64

Source: Kalt 1985 and author's calculations.

[a]Cents per dollar of industry output.

[b]Cents per dollar of final demand.

[c]Net exports as percent of value of shipments.

[d]Weighted by value of total industry output.

mental expenditure as shares of industry output or final demand for the U.S. basic industries and import-competing industry as a whole. Direct costs of environmental regulation include the capital, operating, and administrative costs of pollution abatement. Direct and indirect costs include in addition the expenditures of other sectors which produce inputs into the industries in question. Direct and indirect costs of all regulation add estimates of the costs of health, safety, and economic regulation (including price and entry restrictions).

The steel industry stands out for its disproportionate direct costs. The only other industries with comparable burdens are nonferrous metal mining, paper products, nonagricultural mechanicals, electric power generation, and the government sector (Kalt 1985, 9). In contrast, the direct environmental quality expenditures of the textile, apparel, and automotive industries are well below the U.S. average. When both direct and indirect costs are considered, costs to the steel industry remain above average, but to a lesser extent. Once other regulatory (notably mileage and carbon-dioxide-related) costs are added, vehicles join steel with regulatory burdens in excess of the U.S. average. Clearly, regulatory costs have affected steel and automobiles very differently than textiles and apparel.

Figure 5.13 takes a closer look at the direct pollution abatement expenditures of the U.S. and Japanese steel industries.[46] Japanese expenditures per ton of steel output peaked in 1976. (The year 1976 also marked the peak of Japanese environmental control expenditures as a share of total investment, at 21 percent.) Japanese expenditures fell thereafter, although they turned up in the early 1980s when more stringent water pollution, dust, and soot regulations were imposed. U.S. expenditures also rose in the early 1970s, but from a lower level, and remained stable at a higher plateau into the 1980s. Although the time profile of expenditure differed across countries, there is little evidence that the U.S. industry bore a heavier burden overall.

At the same time, expenditures by both the U.S. and Japanese steel industries have vastly exceeded those of semi-industrialized countries where the pressure to improve environmental quality generally is less intense, placing both industries at something of a disadvantage relative to competitors in lower-income countries.[47] Looking across industries,

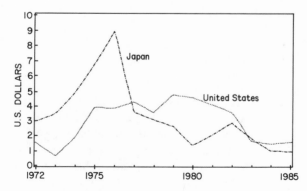

Fig. 5.13   Pollution control expenditures per thousand tons of crude steel output.

Kalt (1985) finds that higher environmental costs have led to a significant deterioration in U.S. trade performance. As incomes in developing countries continue to rise and their demands for environmental protection grow, any U.S. disadvantage due to environmental regulation can be expected to decline. But this is likely to be a source of little relief in the decades immediately ahead.

5.6   Wider Impact on the U.S. Economy

Import penetration and declining basic industry employment have wider implications for the American economy. Of the various effects that might be considered, this section focuses on three: implications for the current account of the balance of payments, implications for the income distribution, and implications for the regional location of industrial activity.

On the surface, the basic industries appear to have contributed significantly to the U.S. merchandise trade deficit. Steel imports are least important in the aggregate: in 1984, U.S. steel imports were only three percent of total merchandise imports, and the deficit on trade in steel was only 8 percent of the total merchandise deficit. The figures for textiles and apparel are larger: textile and apparel imports were 5.8 percent of total U.S. merchandise imports, while the textile and apparel deficit was 14.1 percent of the overall merchandise trade deficit. The most important basic industry deficit was that in motor vehicle trade: passenger cars accounted for 9.1 percent of U.S. imports and 22.4 percent of the deficit. Thus, together these four basic industries accounted for 44.5 percent of the merchandise trade deficit.

It does not follow that trends in the basic industries are a cause of the current account deficit in any meaningful economic sense. The current account is a macroeconomic variable determined by relationships among other macroeconomic variables, notably by any imbalance between savings and investment. Thus, the current account deficit results ultimately from those macroeconomic policies influencing aggregate savings and investment behavior. Developments affecting particular industries determine only the composition of the current account, not its level. Trends in the basic industries influence the current account only insofar as their prospects affect the economywide investment climate or their performance affects economywide levels of employment and profitability sufficiently to alter the aggregate level of savings.

Observers of the American economy have expressed concern that the real incomes of wage earners have failed to rise at historical rates or to keep pace with the cost of living. As figure 5.7 indicates, the declining shares of steel and motor vehicles in total manufacturing employment represent a shift from high-wage categories of manufacturing employment to lower-paid jobs. The elimination of "quality jobs," it is suggested, lowers blue-collar earnings and reduces labor's share of national income.

Were imports of steel and motor vehicles suddenly eliminated, employment in these industries could be considerably expanded even if the wage premiums enjoyed by steel- and autoworkers were maintained. But whether *average* blue-collar earnings and labor's share of the GNP rose or fell would depend on who financed the redistribution. The standard economic argument is that those factors of production used most intensively by the protected industries would benefit, while factors used intensively by other sectors would pay for the redistribution. That steel and motor vehicle production is highly capital-intensive compared to the economy as a whole suggests that protection for steel and automobiles would raise the demand for capital more than demand for labor. Shareholders would be the principal beneficiaries of protection for the steel and vehicle industries. While workers with industry-specific skills would benefit in the short run, in the long run artificial stimulus for these industries is likely to reduce—not increase—labor's share of national income.

The relative decline of the U.S. basic industries has major implications for the regional distribution of manufacturing employment. Tables 5.16–5.19 show how employment in apparel, textiles, steel, and vehicles has been concentrated regionally and how that concentration has shifted over time. Apparel industry employment, for example, already concentrated at the beginning of the 1970s in the Middle Atlantic

Table 5.16   **Apparel and Other Textile Products (SIC 23): Number of Employees and Number of Establishments (percentage of national totals)**

	U.S. Total					
	1970		1977		1984	
Region	Emp.	Est.	Emp.	Est.	Emp.	Est.
1. Pacific	5.6	6.5	9.0	17.9	10.7	20.6
2. Mountain	0.1	1.1	1.5	1.9	1.2	2.0
3. West N. Central	3.7	3.4	3.7	3.3	3.3	3.0
4. West S. Central	6.7	4.1	9.0	5.3	7.5	4.8
5. East S. Central	12.3	4.1	14.2	4.8	15.8	5.1
6. East N. Central	6.9	6.6	6.5	6.1	5.5	5.3
7. New England	5.6	6.6	4.9	5.1	5.0	4.7
8. Middle Atlantic	38.5	65.7	29.4	46.1	26.4	39.3
9. South Atlantic	19.8	2.1	21.8	9.7	24.7	15.2

Source: Calculated from *County Business Patterns*, various issues.

Note: Percentages may not sum to 100 due to rounding.

Table 5.17   **Textile Mill Products (SIC 22): Number of Employees and Number of Establishments (percentages in U.S. totals)**

| | U.S. Total | | | | | |
| | 1970 | | 1977 | | 1984 | |
Region	Emp.	Est.	Emp.	Est.	Emp.	Est.
1. Pacific	1.4	6.5	2.1	6.0	2.1	7.1
2. Mountain	0.1[a]	0.2	0.3	0.6	0.3	1.0
3. West N. Central	0.4	0.7	0.5	0.8	0.5	1.4
4. West S. Central	1.4	1.3	1.9	2.3	1.4	2.3
5. East S. Central	9.4	4.9	10.0	5.7	9.6	6.1
6. East N. Central	2.4	3.6	2.1	4.2	2.6	4.6
7. New England	8.9	12.2	7.6	10.3	7.9	9.9
8. Middle Atlantic	15.1	36.0	12.3	31.3	11.1	28.3
9. South Atlantic	61.0	34.5	63.3	38.8	64.4	39.4

Source: Calculated from *County Business Patterns*, various issues.

Note: Percentages may not sum to 100 due to rounding.

[a]Idaho and New Mexico not available.

region, has tended to shift south and westward (see table 5.16). In large part this reflects the attractions of low-wage labor in regions where unionization rates are low. Trends in textiles (table 5.17) resemble those in apparel. Textile industry employment is concentrated in six South Atlantic states, with North Carolina, South Carolina, and Georgia alone accounting for more than half of total industry employment. This geographical concentration has continued to increase over time.

Steel industry employment has been concentrated traditionally in western Pennsylvania, the vicinity of the Great Lakes, and to a lesser extent, California. Compared to the coasts, the Midwest retains a small margin of natural protection due to the transport costs of shipping steel from Europe or Japan.[48] Table 5.18 again reflects a tendency for industry to migrate toward the low-wage, nonunionized South, where the growth of minimills has been particularly rapid. The mid-Atlantic has been particularly hard hit by the decline in steel industry employment.

Motor vehicle industry employment is concentrated, of course, in the East North Central (table 5.19). But in this industry also, employment has tended to migrate toward the East South Central and South Atlantic regions.

A decline in basic industry employment need not imply either a persistent unemployment problem or the disappearance of manufacturing jobs. A dramatic counterexample is provided by Massachusetts, where a transition from dependence on the textile industry to sectors

Table 5.18 **Blast Furnace and Basic Steel Products (SIC 331): Number of Employees and Number of Establishments (percentages of U.S. totals)**

| Region | U.S. Total | | | | | |
| | 1970 | | 1977 | | 1984 | |
	Emp.	Est.	Emp.	Est.	Emp.	Est.
1. Pacific	4.1	10.2	4.1	11.3	3.0	9.8
2. Mountain	0.0[a]	0.5	2.1	1.5	2.5	1.8
3. West N. Central	1.7[b]	3.6	1.8	4.3	2.3	3.6
4. West S. Central	2.0[c]	5.4	3.1	8.0	4.6	8.2
5. East S. Central	6.0	6.8	5.5	6.3	4.8	15.7
6. East N. Central	42.4	32.7	41.6	30.7	45.0	27.9
7. New England	1.5[d]	6.6	1.7	6.9	1.7	6.9
8. Middle Atlantic	34.0[e]	27.1	31.4	21.5	25.9	17.5
9. South Atlantic	8.3[f]	7.2	8.8	9.5	10.2	8.5

Source: Calculated from *County Business Patterns*, various issues.

Note: Percentages may not sum to 100 due to rounding.

[a]Nevada, Utah, Colorado n.a.

[b]Iowa n.a.

[c]Oklahoma n.a.

[d]Rhode Island, New Hampshire n.a.

[e]New Jersey n.a.

[f]Delaware n.a.

Table 5.19 **Motor Vehicles and Equipment (SIC 371): Number of Employees and Number of Establishments (percentages of U.S. totals)**

| Region | U.S. Total | | | | | |
| | 1970 | | 1977 | | 1984 | |
	Emp.	Est.	Emp.	Est.	Emp.	Est.
1. Pacific	5.3	18.4	6.2	19.2	1.5	18.3
2. Mountain	0.2	1.9	0.5	3.9	1.3	3.9
3. West N. Central	6.9	9.4	7.2	8.3	10.7	7.9
4. West S. Central	2.0	8.3	2.6	9.6	7.1	9.7
5. East S. Central	2.6[a]	4.7	4.3	5.3	9.0	6.0
6. East N. Central	68.5	34.4	63.4	29.6	46.1	31.0
7. New England	1.7	3.7	1.4	3.1	2.3	3.0
8. Middle Atlantic	8.0[b]	10.2	8.2	11.5	11.4	10.2
9. South Atlantic	4.7[c]	8.9	6.2	9.4	10.6	10.1

Source: Calculated from *County Business Patterns*, various issues.

Note: Percentages may not sum to 100 due to rounding.

[a]Mississippi n.a.

[b]New Jersey n.a.

[c]Delaware n.a.

based on new technologies has been successfully completed (for details, see Ferguson and Ladd 1986). Yet this experience does not provide a case for untempered optimism. Massachusetts suffered from unemployment in excess of the national average for an extended period prior to its post-1975 recovery; thus, its experience does not suggest that adjustment will be either quick or painless. Second, the reduction in Massachusetts unemployment resulted not from exceptional rates of job creation but from below average population and labor force growth. Unemployment fell because Massachusetts was no less successful than the rest of the country in creating new jobs (a significant achievement itself) and because the commonwealth's depressed economy discouraged in-migration. Third, Massachusetts has singular advantages that enable it to exploit the opportunities offered by high-tech industries, notably a large educational complex. Whether other states can complete their transition with the same success remains to be determined. But by demonstrating the role of an educational infrastructure in facilitating the transfer of resources, the Massachusetts example may contain lessons for the design of public policy toward the regional problem.

5.7 Response of the Industries

Two avenues for enhancing competitiveness—reducing input costs and obtaining additional protection—have already been addressed. This section considers three additional means to this end: the development of new products and processes, investment in the U.S. by foreign companies, and diversification.

5.7.1 New Products and Processes

Criticism of U.S. basic industries for lagging their foreign competitors in the adoption of new technologies should not be allowed to obscure the technological dynamism of many firms. For the basic industries, advances in manufacturing methods offer more promise than the development of new products. The speed of process innovation will depend on the success with which basic industries apply new technologies developed in the high-tech sector. Much progress has already taken place. In the steel industry, automation and computer control of continuous caster operations enhance control of caster speed, liquid levels, and cooling rates while reducing labor requirements. Computers are increasingly used to regulate fuel consumption in rolling processes and to control the quality of feed input in blast furnaces.

Even in an industry whose output is apparently as homogenous as steel, there is scope for product innovation. Ladle-refining systems, which permit the production of higher-quality "clean" steel, have been widely adopted in recent years. Five electrolytic galvanizing lines, recently completed or currently under construction, promise to increase by 500 percent the industry's capacity to supply the automotive industry with corrosion resistant, uniformly formable electrogalvanized steel. Lasers are used to refine the magnetic domain structure of electrical steel for transformers, improving product quality and permitting a price premium to be charged (see Leonard and Collins 1986; Neiheisel 1986).

Process innovation in the automotive industry is proceeding apace.[49] Microprocessor-controlled flexible machining centers capable of fabricating parts for power-steering pumps and alternators have recently been introduced. These machines can change tools without operator assistance as needed for new jobs. Assembling the parts produced by such machines into completed components is a more delicate task; machines with these capabilities remain at the prototype stage, although robotics have been applied to stamping and to engine, body, and final assembly (Altshuler et al. 1984, 96–97). Computer numerical control has been introduced into engine and transmission machining. Computer-aided design has reduced design costs and lead times, while computer-aided engineering has reduced the cost of skilled tool-room labor. Computer modeling of production flows has reduced inventory costs, enhanced stock control, and helped automate product inspection.

As with steel, the scope for product innovation in the motor vehicle industry is less extensive than in many other sectors. Rather than fundamental changes in the nature of vehicles, it principally takes the form of incremental innovations that enhance their capabilities. For example, on-board computers are increasingly used to monitor engine performance. Electronic traction and skid control can be used to enhance operator control. While the cumulative impact of these improvements can be substantial, it remains unlikely, as Altshuler et al. (1984) conclude, that in the foreseeable future product innovation will radically transform the automobile.

In the textile and apparel industries, technological progress has been less rapid. Nonetheless, at the grading stage, new computer methods are available for selecting the best combination of fibers for a given end use and for eliminating the blend variations associated with hand feeding. At the spinning and weaving stages, technological progress has already led to refinements of existing technology. At the assembly stage, modest technological advances, such as the automated pocketmaker, have been adopted by many firms. The cost of these new technologies is prohibitive for all but the largest producers. This will be even more the case once research currently underway in Japan and New England leads to the development of flexible sewing systems based on robot technology like that already in place in the automobile industry.[50]

What relief from import competition does innovation offer the U.S. basic industries? Although process innovations will remain a critical determinant of comparative production costs, it is unlikely that their adoption will eliminate the gap between production costs in the United States and in its industrial competitors, notably Japan. New technologies applicable to the basic industries diffuse rapidly among industrial countries; there is no reason to anticipate that the United States will be able to appropriate such technologies and sustain a competitive advantage by adopting them to a greater extent than other industrial countries. Insofar as new manufacturing methods entail the substitution of capital for labor, new technologies that increase the scope for substitution may reduce the disadvantage of U.S. basic industries vis-à-vis their LDC competitors. But as the NICs continue to develop and their labor costs rise in the manner of Japan's, the importance of such savings will shrink.

Competitive advantages due to product innovation derive from producers' ability to tailor new products to the tastes and requirements of consumers. The proximity of U.S. producers to what remains a relatively large domestic market situates them favorably in this effort to adapt their products to the preferences of consumers and end users. The production of electrogalvanized steel for the U.S. automobile industry and designer clothing by the apparel industry, cited above, illustrates this potential. Yet the sobering example of the auto industry in the 1970s is a reminder that mere proximity to the market is no guarantee of success in tailoring products to final demand.

5.7.2 Joint Ventures and Onshore Production by Foreign Firms

The advent of Japanese automobile production in the United States is the most visible illustration of a general trend. Honda now operates a plant in Marysville, Ohio, and Nissan one in Smyrna, Tennessee, while Toyota and GM jointly produce a small car in what was formerly GM's Fremont, California, assembly plant. Together these three operations produced more than five hundred thousand vehicles in 1986. Mazda, Mitsubishi, and Isuzu/Fuji have plans for plants in Michigan, Illinois, and Indiana, respectively. In 1984, Nisshin Steel acquired a stake in Wheeling-Pittsburgh and Nippon Kokan obtained half of National Steel, while in 1986 Kawasaki Steel acquired half of California Steel. Moreover, there is an increasing foreign presence in the U.S. minimill sector.

To some extent these arrangements represent attempts to import Japanese technology, management, and labor relations techniques in efforts to boost productivity. For example, workers at the Nissan and Honda plants and at California Steel's plant in Fontana are organized into teams responsible not only for regular production duties but for inspection, materials handling, and housekeeping (Katz 1985, 144). Moreover, onshore production enhances the ability of Japanese steel makers to tailor output to their customers in the U.S. automobile industry, an important consideration for producers of coated-steel products. But the principal explanation for onshore production is as a response to U.S. protectionism and as a hedge against even more stringent measures. Not only can the Japanese protect against this risk by producing in the United States, but this strategy itself reduces the danger of tighter trade restrictions by diverting the sales of Japanese companies from goods manufactured abroad to those manufactured in the United States.

Japanese-owned automobile companies project that "immigrant plants" will produce 1.8 million vehicles for the U.S. market by 1990. Since domestic demand is projected to grow slowly, these sales are likely to come partly at the expense of Japanese exports and partly at that of the U.S. competition. While onshore production by foreign firms is likely to slow the decline of U.S. auto industry employment, it will only add to the difficulty domestic firms have had in maintaining market share.

5.7.3 Diversification

A final response on the part of U.S. basic industries is diversification, which can be understood as part of a long-standing strategy to make the basic industries "less basic." As early as 1969–71, 30 cents of every dollar invested by steel firms was invested outside of steel-producing activities; by the late 1970s the ratio had risen to 33 percent (Acs 1984, 136–37). USX (formerly the U.S. Steel Corporation) has found new outlets for its managerial and financial resources through acquisitions ranging from chemicals and engineering to real estate and railroads. The same strategy has been adopted by Japanese steel producers, who have branched into areas as diverse as industrial ceramics and silicon wafers. The principal thrust of USX's diversification has been into energy, notably through its acquisition of Marathon Oil in 1982 and Texas Oil and Gas in 1986. At present, only one-third of USX's revenues come from steel, with oil and gas now accounting for a majority of total sales. While this too represents an attempt to move into more promising sectors, it is also a continuance of the steel industry's traditional strategy of using diversification to reduce the cyclical risks of steel making. Since energy is an important component of the cost of producing steel, through the ownership of energy resources, steel companies can hedge against the effects of higher energy prices.

5.8 Future Prospects

What are the prospects for the basic industries in the United States? Clearly, the international product cycle will continue to operate. Competence in the production of the products of basic industries tends to be acquired in the early stages of industrialization. This international diffusion of standardized technologies is beyond the control of American producers and policymakers. Hence developing countries where the costs of labor and raw materials are low should have a continuing if not an increasing competitive advantage in the production of standardized basic industry goods. U.S. basic industries, particularly those segments using standardized processes to produce standardized products, will experience no relief from foreign competition.

The precise impact of this foreign competition will depend on the stance of U.S. trade policies. For the foreseeable future, trade in the products of these industries will continue to be regulated by "voluntary" restraints and bilateral quota agreements rather than tariff protection. There is no reason, if quotas are set at sufficiently restrictive levels, that production for the U.S. market could not take place domestically. Studies of U.S. trade policy unanimously conclude that the costs of such policies are high, however. Not only do the high prices charged domestic consumers of the products of basic industries translate into a very substantial cost per protected job, but they divert scarce U.S. resources into the basic industries and out of alternative uses where their productivity is higher. The competitive difficulties of the U.S. basic industries are the market's way of signaling that productivity there is relatively low. Permitting these industries to release resources and even facilitating their smooth transfer through adjustment assistance programs is a way of responding constructively to the productivity slowdown that has been the subject of so much recent attention.

None of this implies that the U.S. basic industries should or will vanish. U.S. producers will retain some comparative advantage vis-à-vis developing country competitors wherever product quality and marketing are important—that is, where skilled labor and proximity to the consumer confer comparative advantage. Those segments of the American automotive, steel, and apparel industries producing high-performance automobiles, electrogalvanized steel, and designer clothing, for example, have brighter prospects than the basic industries as a whole. The ability of the U.S. basic industries to exploit this advantage, which other industrial countries share, depends on their ability to maintain quality, to successfully tailor goods to market, and to moderate production costs, three areas where their record is not unblemished.

Most of all, the competitiveness of these segments of the U.S. basic industries will depend on their ability to apply the new technologies developed by the high-tech sector. Robots, computer-controlled machine tools, and other forms of automated technology continue to offer improvements in productivity and quality control. They are the domestic industries' hope of maintaining a competitive advantage as existing technologies continue to diffuse to newly industrializing countries. Located in a country rich in the human capital used to develop these new technologies, U.S. basic industries might be thought to possess a comparative advantage in their adoption. But much depends on the foresightedness of domestic producers and on public policy. If macroeconomic policies fail to keep domestic demand from declining and the real exchange rate from rising as wildly as in recent years, the investment required for the adoption of these technologies will not take place. If domestic producers are provided overly generous protection, they will have little incentive to develop and adopt these new technologies. Policies of protection that increase basic industry employment in the present may not be conducive to the prosperity of the U.S. basic industries in the future.

Appendix
Regression Results

This appendix presents regression results cited in the text. Using quarterly data for the period 1973:1–1986:1, employment is regressed on measures of the real exchange rate, the relative price of energy, the economywide unemployment rate, and the sectoral real wage. Data and specification follow Branson and Love (1986) with three modifications. First, the dependent variable is number of production employees instead of total employees. Second, a distributed lag on average hourly earnings is appended to their basic specification to permit the impact of labor costs on employment to be examined. Third, the sample period is altered, starting only in 1973:1 and extending through 1986:1. Data on both number of production employees and hourly earnings are drawn from U.S. Department of Labor, *Employment and Earnings* (various issues). Hourly earnings are deflated by the CPI to construct a measure of the real wage. Other data are as described by Branson and Love. The real exchange rate is the IMF index of relative unit labor costs; the real energy price index is the CPI-Urban energy price index divided by the CPI-Urban index for all consumer goods; the unemployment rate is for all workers, economywide.

Results appear in table 5.A.1. While the results for all manufacturing are quite satisfactory, the results for the four basic industries vary. In contrast to all manufacturing, employment in each shows a significant downward trend even after controlling for cyclical conditions, the real exchange rate, the real price of energy, and the sectoral real wage. Only the textile industry fails to exhibit strong sensitivity to the business cycle (as captured by the coefficients on the civilian unemployment rate). There is considerable variability in the impact of energy prices, which increases as one moves from textiles to apparel to steel and finally to motor vehicles. The large coefficients in the equations for vehicles and steel suggest that the energy price variable may also be picking up the impact of structural factors (shifts toward smaller cars or steel substitutes whose timing coincides with the energy price shocks). Similarly, changes in the real exchange rate had a more powerful impact on motor vehicles and steel than textiles and apparel, suggesting that the MFA limited the effects of import competition even more severely than automobile and steel VERs. Finally, the impact of real wages is generally negative but uniformly weak. (Before concluding from this that firms do not operate on their labor demand curves, it would be useful to adjust hourly earnings for productivity and to deflate them by a measure of sector-specific producer prices.)

Table 5.A.2 uses these regressions to decompose changes in U.S. competitiveness (as they are reflected in changes in production employment) into these four components and a residual. The first line shows that slack macroeconomic conditions, real exchange rate appreciation, and higher energy prices all tended to reduce U.S. manufacturing employment between the second half of the 1970s and the first half of the 1980s. Only some slight decline of real manufacturing wages moderated the trend. Of these factors, the dollar's real appreciation was the most important; by itself it would have caused production employment in manufacturing to fall by more than an eighth. But U.S. manufacturing employment declined considerably less than the movement of these variables would predict. Other sources of enhanced competitiveness ("other factors" in table 5.A.2) contributed significantly to the maintenance of manufacturing employment over the period.

The basic industries show many of the same patterns but important differences as well. Employment in steel and vehicles is more cyclically sensitive than employment in textiles and apparel, more strongly affected by movements in the real exchange rate, and more responsive to changes in the relative price of energy. Although the recent moderation of real manufacturing wages has stimulated employment in all

Table 5.A.1   Regression Results: Determinants of Production Employment, 1973:1–1986:1

Sector	Constant	Trend	Independent Variable (length of distributed lag)				p	R^2
			Unemployment (4)	Real Exchange Rate (6)	Real Energy Price (4)	Real Hourly Earnings (8)		
All manufacturing	10.916 (12.13)	-0.001 (0.19)	-0.300 (12.25)	-0.687 (3.45)	-0.097 (1.11)	-0.143 (1.40)	.057	.986
Textiles (SIC 22)	7.906 (2.02)	-0.006 (2.25)	-0.134 (1.01)	-0.246 (0.47)	0.060 (0.57)	-0.007 (0.26)	-.189	.863
Apparel (SIC 23)	7.655 (7.65)	-0.007 (6.20)	-0.147 (4.56)	-0.126 (0.70)	0.219 (1.30)	-0.513 (1.40)	.143	.984
Iron and steel (SIC 331)	11.104 (5.29)	-0.013 (5.55)	-0.256 (3.40)	-0.501 (1.79)	-1.057 (1.37)	-0.560 (0.68)	.546	.993
Motor vehicles (SIC 371)	14.491 (3.90)	-0.010 (2.97)	-0.238 (3.14)	-0.494 (1.55)	-1.142 (2.35)	0.404 (1.29)	.027	.947

Source: See text.

Note: Dependent variable is log of production employees. F-statistics for sum of coefficients are in parentheses below coefficient estimates. Numbers in parentheses below variable names denote number of lagged values of the explanatory variable included. The current values of all variables but real hourly earnings are also included. All equations are estimated on quarterly data using a Cohrane-Orcutt correction.

Table 5.A.2 **Decomposition of Trends in U.S. Basic Industry Employment from 1973:1–1980:1 to 1981:1–1986:1**

| | | Percentage Change in Production Employment | | | | |
| | | | Attributable to | | | |
	Total	Cyclical Factors	Real Exchange Rate	Energy Prices	Real Wages	Other Factors
All manufacturing	-8.4	-7.2	-13.3	-2.0	0.5	13.6
Textiles (SIC 22)	-20.2	-3.2	-4.7	1.4	0.1	-13.8
Apparel (SIC 23)	-13.9	-3.5	-2.4	5.0	5.4	-18.4
Iron and steel (SIC 331)	-47.9	-6.1	-9.7	-24.1	1.4	-9.4
Motor vehicles (SIC 371)	-16.5	-5.7	-9.6	-26.0	0.6	24.2

Source: Computed from regressions reported in table 5.A.1. "Other factors" incorporates the trend term and the regression residual.

four industries, the contribution of wage trends to the change in total industry employment has been relatively small. A striking feature of the table is the contrast in the impact of "other factors" between motor vehicles and the other basic industries. In textiles, apparel, and iron and steel, these other factors contributed to the decline in production employment over the period. The interpretation of this finding is that the further intensification of foreign competition tended to add to the three industries' competitive woes. In automobiles, in contrast, other factors account for a significant rise in production employment. Whether this has been due to increased barriers to foreign competition, notably the negotiation of Japanese export restraints in 1981, or to new investment, marketing, and product development strategies on the part of the U.S. automobile producers cannot be determined by regression alone.

Notes

Charles Butler, Carl Hamilton, Joseph Kalt, and James Love kindly provided data for this paper; Alan Auerbach, Robert Crandall, Kala Krishna, Peter Lindert, David Meerschwam, and Hans Mueller provided much-appreciated comments.

1. See Gerschenkron 1962. The basic reference on the international product cycle is Vernon 1966.

2. Raw steel production (in millions of net tons), average number of employees, and import penetration ratio in steel are taken from American Iron and Steel Institute 1986 and AISI Annual Statistical Bulletins. Motor vehicle production (cars, motor trucks, and buses), all employees in motor vehicle and equipment manufacturing, and import penetration ratio are constructed from Motor Vehicle Manufacturers Association, *Motor Vehicle Facts and Figures,* various issues. Employment in the textile mill products industry and in apparel and related products is from American Textile Manufacturers Institute, *Textile Hilights,* various issues. Output and import penetration ratios for textiles and apparel–apparel fabric are measured in square-yard equivalents and taken from American Textile Manufacturers Institute 1986.

3. Total employees is from U.S. Department of Commerce, *Employment and Earnings,* various issues.

4. Both Chrysler and Ford then reduced capacity and employment in the early 1980s. General Motors followed suit late in 1986, announcing that 11 facilities employing twenty-nine thousand workers would close permanently in 1987.

5. Figures for the steel industry, in millions of net tons, are taken from annual reports of the American Iron and Steel Institute, various issues. Figures for the automobile industry are percentage of domestic retail sales of passenger cars accounted for by imports, taken from *Motor Vehicle Facts and Figures.* Figures for textiles, imports as a share of domestic apparent consumption, are measured in square-yard equivalents and taken from American Textile Manufacturers Institute 1986.

6. This growth rate is for the nine leading third world producers, computed from Hogan 1983, 155.

7. The effective tax rate is from Ando and Auerbach 1985. For further discussion of these policies, see Saxonhouse 1983.

8. A significant share of these debts had been extended by the government itself, especially after 1970. The cost to the states of the restructuring program has been estimated variously at $2 billion to $6 billion (U.S. Congress, Joint Economic Committee 1981, 30–31).

9. As the authors are careful to note, their estimates must be interpreted cautiously, since relatively few steel companies (two Japanese, one American) and relatively few auto companies (one Japanese, three American) are included in their sample.

10. Apparent consumption is domestic production plus imports minus exports, taken from OECD 1985 and publications of the American Iron and Steel Institute, with figures from AISI publications converted to ingot equivalents by the OECD method. The trend line is the OLS regression:

$$\text{App. Cons./GNP} = 0.064 - 0.0012*\text{time}.$$
$$(26.82) \quad (7.66)$$

Here and in subsequent notes, figures in parentheses are t-statistics. Breaking the trend in 1973 and 1979:

$$\text{App. Cons./GNP} = 0.056 - 0.0001*\text{time} - 0.0015*\text{post72} - 0.0014*\text{post78}.$$
$$(28.13) \quad (0.32) \quad (2.54) \quad (1.76)$$

Equations such as these are not strictly interpretable as demand curves since they do not adjust the consumption ratio for relative price effects. In the case of steel, however, such adjustments are of little consequence. Adding the price of metals and metal products relative to the prices of all intermediate materials and supplies changes the coefficient on the time trend reported above only from 0.0012 to 0.0013.

11. See the discussion in Jones 1986, 56–58.

12. The data of Barnett and Schorsch (1983, 41) suggest that Germany reached this stage after 1970 and Japan after 1973. Cross-section data suggest that steel intensity declines once per capita GNP reaches $2,000 (1963 prices); see Jones 1986, 58.

13. For additional statistics, see Barnett and Schorsch 1983, 40.

14. An OLS regression of the apparent consumption/real GNP ratio on deviations of log real GNP from trend yields a coefficient significantly greater than zero at standard confidence levels:

$$\text{App. Cons./GNP} = 0.0479 + 0.132*(\text{deviation of log real GNP from trend}).$$
$$(25.47) \quad (2.69)$$

15. De la Torre 1984, 24. For evidence on Engel's law in the context of textile consumption, see OECD 1983, 29.

16. Data from OECD 1982 and previous issues. The trend is

$$\text{Expenditure share on clothing} = 9.760 - 0.134*\text{time}.$$
$$(82.94) \quad (15.00)$$

17. The slope of the OLS regression line, while negative, differs insignificantly from zero:

$$\text{App. Cons./GNP} = 4.960 - 0.015*\text{time}.$$
$$(7.57) \quad (0.43)$$

The regression for cyclical sensitivity of the apparent consumption ratio is

App. Cons./GNP = 4.674 + 8.979*(deviation of log real GNP from trend).
          (33.58)   (2.11)

18. Between 1973 and 1984, for example, real operating cost fell by nearly 19 percent. This calculation adjusts total cost per mile, from *Motor Vehicle Facts and Figures '85,* for changes in the cost of living index.

19. These figures from the U.S. Department of Labor omit nonpayroll items such as pensions, insurance, and supplemental unemployment benefits to facilitate the comparison with all manufacturing. Figures including estimates of nonwage compensation are used, however, in the international comparison of basic industries. Since nonwage earnings have been more important historically in steel and autos than elsewhere in the economy, fig. 5.7 presents a lower bound on the premium over all manufacturing received by workers in these two industries.

20. In 1986 there were short stoppages at LTV and Armco and a large-scale strike at USX (formerly U.S. Steel), the last of which left twenty-two thousand workers idle.

21. To be exact, 56.4 percent. See U.S. Department of Commerce 1978.

22. Their 1979 contract, for example, provided for a one percent hourly wage increase for every 0.26 point rise in the cost of living (Kreinin 1984, 46).

23. National currency compensation costs are converted to U.S. dollars using average market exchange rates. For well-known reasons, their dollar equivalents should not be taken as measures of living standards. Insofar as market exchange rates reflect the relative price of traded goods, however, this is the measure relevant to discussions of comparative costs in traded goods industries.

24. Note that estimates for steel in table 5.8 differ from those in table 5.10. Figures in the latter table have been adjusted by the Labor Department to enhance international comparability. See U.S. Department of Labor 1984.

25. Similarly, in steel the establishment of voluntary labor-management participation teams was encouraged by the 1980 basic steel agreement. By the end of 1985 there were approximately five hundred such teams functioning in the steel industry. The discussion of automotive labor relations that follows draws mainly Katz 1985, chap. 4, and National Academy of Engineering 1983, chap. 7.

26. Capital expenditures in millions of dollars are taken from American Iron and Steel Institute *Statistical Highlights,* various issues; American Textile Manufacturers Association *Textile Hilights,* various issues; and Motor Vehicle Manufacturers Association, *MVMA Facts and Figures,* various issues. Department of Commerce estimates of capital expenditures in U.S. manufacturing appear in the last two of these sources.

27. In a survey of textile industry executives, Toyne et al. (1984, 135–36) found this to be one of the principal motives for investment.

28. See, for example, AISI *Annual Report* for 1985, p. 9.

29. Although their methods, which assume a twenty-year life for plant and equipment, may exaggerate the rate of depreciation and thus overstate the extent of disinvestment, this is unlikely to affect the thrust of their conclusions. Acs (1984, 141), however, estimates that investment in new capacity exceeded depreciation in thirteen of twenty-one years from 1960 to 1980.

30. In the first half of the sixties the share of output technically suited to continuous casting was lower only in Austria; in the second half, it was lower only in Austria and Sweden (Schenk 1974, 245).

31. Continuously cast steel and crude steel production, in metric tons, and share of the total produced using open hearths are taken from International Iron and Steel Institute 1985, tables 2, 4, and 5. Linear regression yields

$$\% \text{ Continuously Cast} = 66.70 - 0.78 \% \text{ Open Hearth}; \quad R^2 = 0.05.$$
$$(13.60) \quad (1.14)$$

The sample is comprised of twenty-five developed and developing countries, all of those for which data could be obtained excluding Eastern Europe.

32. The regression is

$$\% \text{ Continuously Cast} = 12.18 - 0.621 \% \text{ Open Hearth}$$
$$(12.19)(-0.91)$$
$$- 1.10 \% \text{ Output Growth } 70\text{--}75 + 0.06 \% \text{ Output Growth } 75\text{--}84; \ R^2 = .12.$$
$$(1.10) \qquad\qquad\qquad (1.44)$$

Data are as above, with the addition of 1970 output from OECD 1985. One reason output growth does not have a stronger effect is that in some countries where there have been systematic programs of rationalization, the authorities, when shutting down excess capacity, have shut down those works without continuous casters. Hence in some countries where output has declined most rapidly, the share of steel continuously cast is highest.

33. Data are from International Iron and Steel Institute *Yearbooks,* various issues.

34. See for example Adams and Dirlam 1966. Oster (1982) found that large U.S. producers were slower to adopt the BOF than their smaller counterparts. However, in the subsequent study mentioned later, Karlson (1986) extended the analysis to encompass not only the choice between the BOF and the open hearth but the electric furnace as well, concluding that variations in adoption lag by plant size were trivial. It remains possible, however, as industry observers have argued, that all U.S. firms, irrespective of size, were slow to adopt the BOF.

35. For details, see Barnett and Crandall 1986.

36. Calculated from Mueller and Kawahito 1978, 19. Japanese energy intensity of production has fallen dramatically since the time of these calculations. Between 1973 and 1985, energy consumption per ton of crude steel production fell by 20 percent as the industry shifted toward coal-based energy in place of oil.

37. Arpan et al. 1982, 108–9. However, higher oil prices have improved the competitive position of U.S. national-gas-based synthetic fibre producers. The regressions in the appendix suggest that energy prices have had an insignificant impact on U.S. textile and apparel employment.

38. The estimates in the appendix suggest still larger employment effects.

39. Japan's 1937 exports of 124 million yards of cotton cloth were not matched until 1955 (Brandis 1982, 7).

40. There nonetheless exists a great number of studies of this question. Since they have recently been reviewed by Hufbauer, Berliner, and Elliott 1986, only a selection of the most recent estimates is discussed here.

41. Stabilizing the market share of imports may have been the underlying objective of the scheme, which was administered with varying severity so as to achieve it (Barnett and Schorsch 1983, 241).

42. Data are taken from Paine Webber, various issues. The export price is the Antwerp spot price.

43. The average number of production workers in 1983–84 was 170,000. Assuming it to have been 22,000 less in the absence of restraints, the share of employment accounted for by restraints is 22,000/(170,000−22,000) = 15 percent.

44. The point is not that domestic prices are 30 percent higher and domestic steel industry employment is correspondingly higher under VERs than they were in the preceding period of trigger prices. Rather it is that prices are approximately 30 percent higher than they would be under free trade.

45. See Hufbauer, Berliner, and Elliott 1986, 256, for other estimates.

46. U.S. capital expenditures for environmental control are the sum of air and water expenditures. Those for Japan are the sum of air and water and relatively small industrial waste, noise and vibration, and miscellaneous expenditures. U.S. total crude steel production is measured in net tons, while Japanese figures have been converted to net from metric tons. Sources are AISI Statistical Highlights, various issues, and unpublished MITI estimates supplied by the Japan Steel Information Center.

47. There are exceptions to this rule, such as substantial expenditures on pollution control by Brazilian steel companies.

48. Eichengreen and van der Ven 1984 reports estimates of these costs.

49. This is true of all industrial countries; see for example Marsden et al. 1985.

50. For details, see Toyne et al. 1984, chap. 4.

References

Acs, Zoltan J. 1984. *The changing structure of the U.S. economy: Lessons from the steel industry.* New York: Praeger.

Adams, Walter, and Joel Dirlam. 1966. Big steel, invention and innovation. *Quarterly Journal of Economics* 80:167–89.

Altshuler, Alan, et al. 1984. *The future of the automobile.* Cambridge, Mass.: MIT Press.

American Iron and Steel Institute. 1985. *Annual statistical report, 1984.* Washington, D.C.: AISI.

————. 1986. *Statistical highlights: U.S. iron and steel industry.* Washington, D.C.: AISI.

American Textile Manufacturers Institute. 1986. *The U.S. textile market measured in square yard equivalents, 1973–85.* Washington, D.C.: ATMI.

————. Various years. *Textile hilights.* Washington, D.C.: ATMI.

Anderson, Richard G., and Mordechai E. Kreinin. 1981. Labor costs in the American steel and auto industries. *The World Economy* 4 (June): 199–208.

Ando, Albert, and Alan Auerbach. 1985. The corporate cost of capital in Japan and the U.S.: A comparison. NBER Working Paper No. 1762. October.

Arpan, Jeffrey S., Jose de la Torre, and Brian Toyne. 1982. The *U.S. apparel industry: International challenge, domestic response.* Research monograph no. 88. College of Business Administration, Georgia State University, Atlanta.

Association of American Iron and Steel Engineers. 1986. *The making, shaping and treating of steel.* Pittsburgh, Pa.: AISE.

Barnett, Donald F., and Robert Crandall. 1986. *Up from the ashes.* Washington, D.C.: Brookings Institution.

Barnett, Donald F., and Louis Schorsch. 1983. *Steel: Upheaval in a basic industry.* Cambridge, Mass.: Ballinger.

Bluestone, Barry, and Bennett Harrison. 1982. *The deindustrialization of America.* New York: Basic Books.

Brandis, R. Buford. 1982. *The making of textile trade policy, 1935–1981*. Washington, D.C.: American Textile Manufacturers Institute.

Branson, William. 1986. Causes of appreciation and volatility of the dollar. In Federal Reserve Bank of Kansas City, *The U.S. dollar: Recent developments, outlook, and policy options*. Kansas City: Federal Reserve Bank of Kansas City.

Branson, William H., and James P. Love. 1986. The real exchange rate and employment and output in U.S. manufacturing, 1974–1985. Princeton University. Typescript.

Cantor, David J. 1984. Steel import limits: Estimated import reduction under three alternative proposals. Congressional Research Service, Report No. 84-759-E. September.

————. 1985. Steel industry continues long history of production process innovation. *Steel Comments*, August 29.

Crandall, Robert W. 1985. Trade protection and the "revitalization" of the steel industry. Brookings Institution. Typescript.

————. 1986. Detroit rode quotas to prosperity. *Wall Street Journal*, January 29.

Eichengreen, Barry, and Hans van der Ven. 1984. U.S. anti-dumping policies: The case of steel. In Robert Baldwin and Anne Krueger, eds., *The structure and conduct of recent U.S. trade policy*, 67–103. Chicago: University of Chicago Press.

Feenstra, Robert. 1984. Voluntary export restraint in U.S. autos, 1980–81: Quality, employment and welfare effects. In Robert Baldwin and Anne Krueger, eds., *The structure and conduct of recent U.S. trade policy*, 35–39. Chicago: University of Chicago Press.

Ferguson, Ronald, and Helen Ladd. 1986. Economic performance and economic development policy in Massachusetts. Kennedy School of Government, State, Local, and Intergovernmental Center, Harvard University, Discussion Paper D86-2. May.

Fuss, Melvyn, and Leonard Waverman. 1985. Productivity growth in the automobile industry, 1970–1980: A comparison of Canada, Japan and the United States. NBER Working Paper No. 1735. December.

————. 1986. The extent and sources of cost and efficiency differences between U.S. and Japanese automobile producers. NBER Working Paper No. 1849. March.

Gerken, Egbert, Martin Gross, and Ulrich Lachler. 1986. The causes and consequences of steel subsidization in Germany. *European Economic Review* 30: 773–804.

Gerschenkron, Alexander. 1962. *Economic backwardness in historical perspective*. Cambridge, Mass.: Harvard University Press.

Gomez-Ibanez, José, and David Harrison, Jr. 1982. Imports and the future of the U.S. automobile industry. *American Economic Review Papers and Proceedings*, 319–323.

Grossman, Gene M. 1986. Imports as a cause of injury: The case of the U.S. steel industry. *Journal of International Economics* 20: 201–24.

Hamilton, Carl. 1986. An assessment of voluntary restraints on Hong Kong exports to Europe and the USA. *Economica* 53: 339–50.

Hogan, William T. 1983. *World steel in the 1980s*. Lexington, Mass.: Lexington Books.

Hufbauer, Gary Clyde, Diane Berliner, and Kimberly Ann Elliott. 1986. *Trade protection in the United States: 31 case studies*. Washington, D.C.: Institute for International Economics.

International Iron and Steel Institute. 1985. *Steel statistical yearbook, 1985.* Brussels: IISI.

Jones, Kent. 1986. *Politics vs. economics in world steel trade.* London: Allen and Unwin.

Kalt, Joseph P. 1985. The impact of domestic regulatory policies on international competitiveness. Harvard Institute of Economic Research Discussion Paper No. 1141. March.

Karlson, Stephen H. 1986. Adoption of competing inventions by United States steel producers. *Review of Economics and Statistics* 68: 415–22.

Katz, Harry. 1985. *Shifting gears: Changing labor relations in the U.S. automobile industry.* Cambridge, Mass.: MIT Press.

Keeling, B. 1982. *The world steel industry: Structure and prospects in the 1980s.* Special Report No. 128. London: Economic Intelligence Unit.

Kreinin, Mordechai. 1984. Wage competitiveness in the U.S. auto and steel industries. *Contemporary Policy Issues* 4: 39–50.

Krueger, Alan, and Lawrence Summers. 1986. Reflections on the inter-industry wage structure. Harvard University. Typescript.

Krugman, Paul. 1984. The U.S. response to foreign industrial targeting. *Brookings Papers on Economic Activity* 1: 77–121.

Lawrence, Colin, and Robert Lawrence. 1985. Manufacturing wage dispersion: An end game interpretation. *Brookings Papers on Economic Activity,* 47–106.

Lawrence, Robert. 1985. Can America compete? Washington, D.C.: Brookings Institution.

Leonard, James H., and James F. Collins. 1986. Assuring steel's competitiveness for the automotive industry. *Steel Comments,* February 28.

Marsden, David, Timothy Morris, Paul Willman, and Stephen Wood. 1985. *The car industry.* London: Tavistock.

Meyer, J. R., and G. Herregat. 1974. The basic oxygen steel process. In L. Nabseth and G. F. Ray, eds, *The diffusion of new industrial processes,* 146–99. Cambridge: Cambridge University Press.

Motor Vehicle Manufacturers Association. Various years. *MVMA facts and figures.* MVMA: Detroit.

Mueller, Hans, and Kiyoshi Kawahito. 1978. *Steel industry economics.* New York: Japan Steel Information Center.

National Academy of Engineering. 1983. *The competitive status of the U.S. auto industry.* Washington, D.C.: National Academy Press.

Neiheisel, Gary L. 1986. High technology in the steel industry: Lasers, sensors, computers on the cutting edge. *Steel Comments,* March 31.

O'Boyle, Thomas F. 1983. Steel management has itself to blame. *Wall Street Journal,* May 17, 201, p. 34.

OECD. 1982. *Textile industry in OECD countries.* Paris: OECD.

———. 1983. *Textile and clothing industries: Structural problems and policies in OECD countries.* Paris: OECD.

———. 1985. *World steel trade developments, 1960–1983.* Paris: OECD.

Oshima, Keichi. 1973. Research and development and economic growth in Japan. In B. R. Williams, ed., *Science and technology in economic growth.* New York: Wiley.

Oster, Sharon. 1982. The diffusion of innovation among steel firms: The basic oxygen furnace. *Bell Journal of Economics* 13: 45–56.

Oswald, Andrew. 1982. The microeconomic theory of the trade union. *Economic Journal* 92: 576–95.

Paine Webber. Various issues. *World steel dynamics*.

Pelzman, Joseph, and Randolph Martin. 1980. Direct employment effect of imports on the U.S. steel industry. Economic Discussion Paper No. 6. U.S. Department of Labor. August.

Saxonhouse, Gary. 1983. What is all this about 'industrial targeting' in Japan? *World Economy* 6:253–74.

Schenk, W. 1974. Continuous casting of steel. In L. Nabseth and G. F. Ray, eds., *The diffusion of new industrial processes*, 232–50. Cambridge: Cambridge University Press.

Toyne, Brian, et al. 1984. *The global textile industry*. London: Allen and Unwin.

Tsao, James T. H. 1985. The economic effects of trade restrictions on U.S. steel mill products. Paper presented to the American Economic Association Annual Meetings, New York. December.

United Nations. Various issues. *Yearbook of industrial statistics*.

U.S. Congress. Joint Economic Committee. 1981. *Monetary policy, selective credit policy, and industrial policy in France, Britain, West Germany and Sweden*. 97th Cong., 1st sess. Washington, D.C.: GPO.

U.S. Department of Commerce. 1978. *Characteristics of the apparel industry*. Washington, D.C.: GPO.

———. 1984. *The U.S. automobile industry, 1983*. Washington, D.C.: GPO.

———. Various years. *Employment and earnings*. Washington, D.C.: GPO.

———. 1986. Trade ripples across U.S. industries. Office of Business Analysis. January.

U.S. Department of Labor. Bureau of Labor Statistics. 1975. *Educational attainment of workers, March 1975*. Special Labor Report No. 186. Washington, D.C.: GPO.

———. 1984. International comparisons of productivity and labor costs in the steel industry: United States, Japan, France, Germany, United Kingdom; 1964 and 1972–82. Unpublished data. January.

———. 1986a. Hourly compensation costs for production workers, textile mill products manufacturing (US SIC 22) 26 Countries, 1975–85. Typescript.

———. 1986b. Hourly compensation costs for production workers, apparel and other textile products manufacturing (US SIC 23), 24 Countries, 1975–85. Typescript.

———. 1986c. Hourly compensation costs for production workers, iron and steel manufacturing (US SIC 331), 21 Countries, 1975–85. Typescript.

———. 1986d. Hourly compensation costs for production workers, motor vehicles and equipment manufacturing (US SIC 371), 19 Countries, 1975–85. Typescript.

———. 1986e. Hourly compensation costs for production workers, all manufacturing, 34 Countries, 1975–85. Typescript.

U.S. International Trade Commission. 1985. *A review of recent developments in the U.S. automobile industry including an assessment of the Japanese voluntary restraint agreements*. Publication No. 1648. February.

Vernon, Raymond. 1966. International investment and international trade in the product cycle. *Quarterly Journal of Economics* 80: 190–207.

2. Charles W. Parry
Basic Materials in a Global Economy

In this comment I do not speak for all basic industry today, nor do I touch on those that were well covered in Barry Eichengreen's paper. Rather, I speak generally of factors affecting many basic industries and give some specific examples, using Alcoa as a proxy for other basic materials industries or producers.

Some underlying conditions affect almost all basic industries. They are (1) capacity exceeding demand; (2) low prices, a normal outcome of overcapacity; (3) inadequate financial returns; (4) high, if leveling, labor costs and an unproductive set of relationships between the three affected parties; (5) a broad and perhaps permanent reduction in the material intensity of the developed economies in general and the U.S. economy specifically; and (6) a permanent shift in comparative advantage and factor costs to LDCs and to government-owned operations where the reason for being is not necessarily return on investment.

I return to these characteristics in a moment. But some other, if less pervasive, problems also affect the basic industries, and I want to mention them briefly. All industries and all companies are not affected by them, but they prevail to a degree worth pointing out.

First, the macroeconomic environment in which U.S. industry operates is deteriorating. The combination of budget and trade deficits equals declining competitiveness. In fact, the so-called Tax Reform Act of 1986 will actually further reduce U.S. industrial competitiveness by stalling investment in productivity and by virtually eliminating the possibility of repatriating earnings from overseas operations.

Second, the strength of the dollar has created competitive pressures in recent years that have severely affected many basic industries. At its high, the strong dollar gave most European and Japanese aluminum producers a cost advantage of 20 percent or more vis-à-vis American producers. The result was a flood of imports of products that, all other things equal, would not have been competitive.

While the dollar has fallen against the yen, the deutsche mark, and some other currencies, the flood has not yet ebbed significantly. It seems to me that the dollar will have to fall another 15 percent to 20 percent before those imports retreat to a more typical level. Obviously, those basic industry companies that are multinational have not been as badly injured by the high dollar as those operating only within U.S. borders. But as the dollar falls, we must begin to worry about renewed inflation and the risking risk of disintermediation on the part of foreign investors.

Third, and perhaps more important, the production of basic goods today has changed dramatically and probably permanently. For many years, in some cases more than a century, the most economic production of basic materials came from vertically integrated systems. There were economies of scale that required the matching of various steps in the flow from raw material to finished product. Let me give you an example from the aluminum industry.

In our business the critical cost—and the technical fulcrum—was in smelting, where the refined ore was turned into metal. There was an optimum size for a smelter, depending on its power supply and its specific technology. To provide a feedstock, a refining plant had to be designed—not only to meet the needs of the smelter, but to take advantage of a particular body of bauxite. Assuring both a secure and profitable operation required some pretty deft planning and design work. In the early days, it was far more art than science.

Today, the need for an integrated system is at best questionable. The mines, the refining plants, and the smelters are all off the shelf, technically. Bauxite, alumina, and aluminum ingot are commodities, largely undifferentiated. What matters today lies downstream, in fabricated products and in parts and systems of parts made from those products. Recognizing this change, the U.S. aluminum industry is disintegrating. This change requires a wholly new mind-set, but it is driven by changes that are outside the control of the once-integrated companies.

Other basic industries have made similar responses where their production streams are complex. Steel, copper, tin, aluminum—all differ in their complexity, but all have the characteristics of a commodity. U.S. Steel today would be rolling British slabs at Fairless if the steelworkers had not objected. Aluminum was the last to go. If a definition of basic industry includes the automakers, an interesting parallel can be found in their complex assortment of outsourcing of parts, their joint ventures and international production systems.

My point is that the once familiar, self-contained, vertically integrated production systems are coming apart and that the trend will continue as basic industry continues to become globalized.

Now, let me return to my list of underlying conditions in basic industries.

In almost every basic industry, there is overcapacity. From customers' and consumers' points of view, this has been a good thing. Prices for basic materials have not contributed to inflation and, in the opinions of many, have actually been deflationary. But prices ultimately are a reflection of supply and demand, and shareholders are not known to be overly stupid for long.

In reaction, most basic industry companies in the United States have reduced excess capacity, cutting those facilities that are least competitive (which normally means those that are most technically out of date). In the case of my own company, we have written off uncompetitive capacity, even beyond the tonnage we typically carried for market development purposes. In the future, in periods of high demand we will buy what we are unable to produce. Reports in the media lead me to believe that we are not alone in this strategy.

There are, of course, real questions surrounding a strategy of limited capacity. Implicit in such a strategy is an assessment of limited market growth. There are also those who are uncomfortable with the long-term impact on national defense capabilities.

The reality of a world market in basic materials, however, effectively precludes any meaningful debate of those questions. Most, if not all, basic materials are not commodities. Commodities by definition are undifferentiated, so cost is the single determinant. In U.S. basic industry, critical costs are often determined by public policy, which has frequently been less than kind toward industry.

Again, an example. There are three major cost areas in producing primary aluminum: raw materials, labor, and electricity. In this example, raw materials are of lesser consideration, since economical ore sources do not exist in the United States; we must either import bauxite or its refined intermediates.

In the case of energy, to the extent that we have a national policy on electricity, it is a policy of populism. Power rates that once were based on cost of service have increasingly been based on the political expedient of keeping rates low for individual users. Since electricity is the largest single cost component in a pound of aluminum, it is critical. In the past decade, the United States has gone from being a low-cost aluminum producer to being a high-cost producer. That reality is reflected by the smelter shutdowns of recent years.

I mentioned the third factor of cost—labor. Basic industry in the United States has long been the country's most unionized sector. In recent years, however, declining demand in some industries and flattening growth rates in others have put great pressure on labor costs. The three components of labor cost—pay, benefits, and work rules—have all come under attack in varying degrees. But the real kicker here, and one that neither company nor union can control, is the development of the global economy. National unions, no matter how powerful, have precious little leverage in a global economy.

Union leaders have been in the forefront of those demanding protectionism. Yet union leaders—and past managements—share much of the blame for the noncompetitiveness of many U.S. basic materials. Those industries and companies whose operations lie entirely within the borders of the United States seem to have been hurt more by labor problems. Those of us with operations around the world are protected in varying degrees by our flexibility. While the steel industry, for example, joins with the United Steelworkers in demanding protection from imports, the aluminum industry concentrates instead on seeking fair trade and in opening markets in other developed economies. Other basic industries, such as tin and copper, have also been more global in their outlook.

I said at the start that high labor costs are a problem for basic industry. I also said that there is an unproductive set of relationships between the three affected parties. And there are *three* parties: management, employees, and the unions themselves.

My experience last year in dealing with the first simultaneous strike by both of Alcoa's major unions brings me to the conclusion that union leaders do not necessarily behave in the best interests of their members. Nor are union members necessarily hard-line, recalcitrant, or anti-management. In fact, the agenda of the union may be quite different from the agenda of the employee. This reality of separate agendas may serve the interests of both companies and employees in the future, providing common ground for experimentation and renewed trust. It remains to be seen whether the agenda of the international union becomes the odd man out.

So far, what I have discussed relates to some of the underlying causes of the general lack of competitiveness in basic industry. Those causes are fairly well known to anyone who has sought them out. I end my presentation by giving you my thoughts on the future for these enterprises.

First, basic industry has to make its case to the public for relief from those policies that affect it negatively. I refer specifically to such policies as a tax policy that penalizes investment, energy policies that pretty much rule out competitive costs, and trade policies that stifle rather than encourage competition. Changes in public policy are essential to create a supportive macroeconomic environment within which U.S. basic industry can become competitive.

Next, those of us in basic industry have got to get *our* act together and compete. This means coming to grips with new technologies, stepping up to the sometimes frightening prospect of reducing labor costs, and internationalizing mind-sets by internationalizing operations. We must rid ourselves of the false notion that the United States is a separate island in the sea of world trade.

In addition, U.S. basic industries need to get back to competing by going back into the marketplace. Products must compete on cost, but they also must compete differentially. The day of waiting for customers to call in an order is gone. This is especially true when basic materials are essentially undifferentiated. By adding value to a customer's product, a basic material is no longer the same as all others—a concept too many have either forgotten or never learned.

Finally, U.S. basic material producers must pursue quality. Quality must be redefined in terms of the user: quality products are those that add value because they eliminate rejects, cause no incidents in the customer's operations, and allow the customer to produce a quality product in turn.

Given a stable macroeconomic environment, U.S. basic industries *can* compete. The question then becomes one of whether it will *choose* to compete.

3. *Philip Caldwell*
U.S. Competitiveness in a Global Environment

While there are many differences among industries and companies, most of my more general observations on basic industries are intended to be applicable to manufacturing overall.

Success of a firm requires success in fundamentals in the way it plans, funds, and conducts its business. Product development, quality, cost, customer value—all achieved within the context that the incomings must exceed the outgoings over time—are the sine qua non; productivity, human resource management, and integrity are essential ingredients wherever the business is located. These qualities are not proprietary to the United States or to any nation, and the opportunities for competitive advantage for a firm or a country are not necessarily great or long lasting either.

Let me illustrate this fragility with an example from the automobile industry in the United States.

U.S. automakers have made *dramatic* gains in profitability, quality, productivity, supplier relations, and work force management. *But* in major market segments, foreign automakers *continue* to gain shares of markets. Foreign producers continue to make major innovations in product and manufacturing processes. If present economic relationships continue, *existing* U.S. *small car* and *sports car* manufacturing capacity will be largely redundant by 1990 in a free trade environment.

Analysts project that only two-thirds of domestic auto manufacturing capacity will be used. By 1990, auto-related employment at the *four domestic auto producers* will decline to 340,000 from 700,000 in 1978 and 400,000 in 1983. A similar situation also exists in Western Europe and may yet occur in Japan by the next decade.

Martin Feldstein (1986) gets to the heart of the problems and opportunities facing basic manufacturing industries in the United States:

> The principal problem with which the world economies must deal during the coming decade is the unsustainable imbalance of international trade. The United States cannot continue to have annual trade deficits of more than $100 billion financed by an ever increasing inflow of foreign capital. The U.S. trade deficit will therefore soon shrink and, as it does, the other countries of the world will experience a corresponding reduction in their trade surpluses. Indeed, within the next decade, the United States will shift from trade deficit to trade surplus. The challenge is to achieve this rebalancing of world demand in a way that avoids both a decline in real economic activity and an increase in the rate of inflation.

The United States has been in a competitive decline for the last two decades, losing out to countries like Japan, and more recently Taiwan and Korea. These countries have little natural wealth, but they have exploited technology—imported largely from the United States—while skillfully managing their human and financial resources and policies. As more countries successfully imitate this strategy, our ability to earn a rising standard of living becomes progressively more difficult.

Our basic industries began losing market shares in the last decade, but this was sometimes characterized as the failure of management, the stranglehold of unions, or unusual circumstances. Other segments were enjoying a boom as oil prices and exploration increased and high tech became the panacea, which some once thought would save us all in the United States.

Then in the 1980s Americans went on a credit binge—government, corporations, and individuals—consuming more than they produced—creating the twin deficits of budget and trade.

Feldstein (1986) describes the trade situation this way:

> The recentness of the U.S. shift from trade surplus to trade deficit deserves emphasis because it indicates that the cause of the trade deficit is not the character of the American workforce or of American management, as some have recently suggested. Such fundamental aspects of American industry cannot change in as short a time as the five years in which the United States has gone from a persistent trade surplus to a massive trade deficit. For the same reason it is wrong to attribute the massive trade deficit to a fundamental deterioration of U.S. productivity, of American product quality, or of other basic aspects of potential competitiveness. The primary reason for our deteriorating trade imbalance was the 70 percent rise of the

dollar that occurred between 1980 and the spring of 1985. This unprecedented increase in the dollar dramatically increased the price of American products relative to decline while merchandise imports have increased by nearly 50 percent.

Of course, there were other causes. Private sector managers and government politicians and administrators contributed their deficiencies. We all put some dirt in the carburetor, but the high value of the dollar was the common hurdle of discouragement across American industry and only a very few could jump it without injury.

Bruce Scott and others of the Harvard Business School have studied in depth the subject of national competitiveness. Since I find my own experiences in tune with their findings, in these remarks I quote liberally from their writings (Scott and Lodge 1984; Scott 1987).

National competitiveness is a national aspiration. In its most fundamental sense, it means the ability of a nation to earn a rising standard of living. As our trade deficit tells us, our present standard of living is only partially earned. More and more recently it has been borrowed.

Competitiveness in part is a question of goals. The United States is shouldering important international commitments for military security, economic aid, and various programs to insure a measure of economic security and to assist the least favored segments of other societies. Competitiveness for the United States means financing these various commitments without falling behind other industrial countries in standard of living. This sounds like perpetual motion to me, and I do not think we can do it. It is time this load be shared more broadly by Japan and others who enjoy the benefits and have the capacity to pay.

Reestablishment of a competitive economy will require changes in national priorities, policies, and institutional practices.

Public policy has promoted short-term consumer benefits on the one hand and added a growing array of consumer entitlements on the other. The role of Americans as producers has been taken for granted. The United States must adopt a more balanced view of Americans as producers as well as consumers. We really can kill the goose that laid the golden egg. The choice for the United States is either to increase the competitiveness of its economy or to revise downward its national goals and international commitments. Private firms do this or they do not survive.

In our quest for "free and fair competition," we say that true competitiveness can only be evaluated on a "level playing field." Such a definition overlooks the fact that countries have differing goals, differing economic strategies, and differing roles for their economic *actors*—notably for government. Countries have different ideas of what the game is all about and how to keep score as well as how to play.

Brazil, Japan, Korea, Mexico, and Taiwan do not necessarily share our view of the system. For them the goal is not so much to raise short-term living standards as to increase national wealth and economic power.

Government is an active participant in their economies; part player, part coach, perhaps part manager. As a player-coach, government is concerned with shaping the outcomes as well as establishing and enforcing the rules. We enact trade laws; our competitors complete trade programs.

The United States focuses on rules and procedures and complains that some other countries do not play according to the rules. This is an expression of an implicit U.S. economic strategy which assumes that free markets and interfirm competition give the best outcomes for the United States and presumably will for other countries as well. Government, in the U.S. view of the system, is a referee and not a player, coach, or manager. Government takes responsibility for the fairness of the game; the players, coaches, and their managers have responsibility for the outcome.

In part due to our munificence, some countries, which have been able to pursue strategies different from ours and whose governments play a role different from ours, have consistently had higher levels of performance and thus have been more competitive than us. These countries, notably Japan, have become models for other countries that are also trying to accelerate their economic growth. These countries, all of which have focused on manufactured exports as the leading economic sector, have had a remarkable impact on international competition.

True "leveling of the playing field" may require changes in our theory of international competition. It may mean that we as well as others must change.

Zysman and Cohen (1987) say that "we may have become a post industrial society, but we are not a post industrial economy" and "it is important that we not become one."

We need manufactured exports to pay for our imports. After deducting interest, dividends, and fees for "services" in our trade statistics, service income is only 15 percent of income from manufactures. At home we may make hamburgers for each other and take in the washing, but we cannot exchange those services overseas for automobiles and VCRs. Manufacturing is the core market for much of the services economy.

Technological innovation is frequently spawned in a manufacturing environment and engineering skills at home atrophy when production is located overseas. A healthy, vibrant manufacturing base is a must if our military security is to have real substance. Can we really forgo the capability to supply machine tools and semiconductors? I might risk leaving home without my American Express card, but it would be foolhardy and irresponsible to rely on a national security establishment supplied totally or primarily in its essentials by friend or foe overseas. Leadership of the free world requires strength and that includes economic strength.

I could spend considerable time enumerating the many steps we Americans need to take to keep America competitive. Since they have been well documented in a number of thoughtful studies, including most recently the report of the Young Commission on Competitiveness, I need not repeat them for this group.

I conclude these brief remarks, however, by posing two challenges, particularly relevant to this group and to the constituencies we represent.

1. In physical sciences, R&D programs are often directed toward finding solutions to problems standing in our way. Many times they are successful because we focus brainpower adequate to the task in quality and quantity. Could we do more of this in R&D in the social sciences? Most practitioners I know believe the international monetary system does not deal satisfactorily with establishing currency values. Is it possible that new technologies in communications and the impact of the rapid transfer of huge sums of money across national boundaries as compared to the transfer of physical goods have outmoded important facets of the present system? Could we concentrate our thoughts and launch a serious search for a more stable mechanism by which we can price our currencies?

2. Can there be a closer partnership between economists and the principles that guide economic thought and the practitioners of business in their pursuit of competitiveness in a global economy? A greater exposure to shared experiences could make both groups more effective for our country and for the world.

References

Cohen, Stephen S., and John Zysman. 1987. *Manufacturing matters.* New York: Basic Books.

Martin Feldstein. 1986. Correcting the world trade balance. Cambridge, Mass. Typescript.

Scott, Bruce R. 1987. U.S. competitiveness in the world economy: An update. Harvard University, Graduate School of Business Administration. February.

Scott, Bruce R., and George Lodge. 1984. *U.S. competitiveness in the world economy.* Boston: Harvard Business School Press.

Summary of Discussion

Saburo Okita asked whether the Japanese should move their parts manufacturing capacity to the United States as they have done with assembling, given the large surplus capacity that exists in the United States. Caldwell responded that surplus capacity is a problem in many industries and that what is needed is a solid dose of growth. The Japanese could have foreseen this excess capacity when they made their investment decisions.

In evaluating the global competitiveness of U.S. basic industries, Philip Caldwell identified exchange rates as the broadest and most troublesome factor for business management. Wide and rapid swings in currency values result primarily from macroeconomic factors. Individual companies and industries are incapable of dealing with these causes yet they bear the consequences from the frequent changes in relative value. Basic industries with heavy capital requirements needing long capital payback periods are particularly devastated. Such has been the effect in many parts of the U.S. economy during the 1980s.

He called for fresh thinking on this issue, arguing that exchange rates today are not predominantly established by the impact of the physical flow of goods, but by the overwhelming size of money flows across international boundaries. He suggested that many now feel that the floating regime is not a satisfactory long-term solution. He pointed out that the Japanese are just as upset as the Americans or any other nationality when there are major changes in exchange rate values.

Okita continued this line of thought by proposing a contradiction in liberalization of capital and commodity flows, in that liberalizing capital flows might lead to an excessively fluctuating exchange rate.

Robert Ingersoll contended that orderly marketing agreements and other government activity would not solve the problem. The Japanese circumvented the 1969 steel OMA by increasing the value of their products, and neither this OMA nor the current automobile restriction helps U.S. competitiveness. In the long run a managed economy is not as innovative or good for the general public as a more free economy. He proposed that Martin Feldstein's solution, involving a reduction in the trade deficit through a reduction in the value of the dollar, was attractive.

Caldwell suggested that the 1981 automobile voluntary import restraint program could have yielded much broader benefits for the United States if it had a three-dimensional characteristic. In exchange for a change in government policy that brought forth the voluntary restraint program, the industry could have been strongly encouraged to upgrade its product quality and productivity characteristics and organized labor could have been expected to modify the noncompetitive labor cost structure and work practices. He agreed that the exchange rate was very important and pointed out that even if the private sector fulfills its obligations in marketing, quality, cost structure, and labor management, the exchange rate can be a dominant factor. This, he argues, is part of government's responsibility.

He pointed out that the Chrysler situation had some elements of such a three-way deal. The critical parts of the solution to the Chrysler problem were a timely wage reduction and debt remission, both of which were largely engineered by people in government. The industrywide voluntary import restraint program could have been more fruitful if three-way cooperation had been brought to bear. This was suggested by some from the industry, but the government was not willing. As a result, in 1982 wages grew, albeit at a slower rate.

Unless the government, the unions, and management can work together on trade and wage restraint and new investment, automakers may have to look at the world from a more supranational point of view. There is no one in the auto industry who cannot produce anywhere in the world. In the case of a decision by automakers to move offshore, private sector judgments might not be in sync with public interest and there would be a change in the role of the United States in the world.

Anne Krueger emphasized the importance of macroeconomic factors and pointed out some dangers of protecting basic industries. She suggested that there might be a tension between competition and protection of basic industries. The United States has an interest in the global system, so U.S. interests are similar to global interests. A free trade regime must be maintained, she argued, since it is key to the debt problem.

What, Krueger asked rhetorically, is so special about basic industries? She pointed out that the service industry is no different; in fact, it is considered a service when a manufacturing firm contracts out work it would otherwise do in-house, whereas if the firm does the work itself it is manufacturing.

Macroeconomic solutions, Krueger suggested, are in the common interest. Furthermore, simply fixing or stabilizing exchange rates may be appealing, but without a reduction in the U.S. budget deficit there is no way to escape either high real interest rates or high inflation.

Caldwell recognized the importance of macroeconomic factors, but wondered whether we all are willing to accept the consequences of living only by macroeconomic objectives even when they will demolish fundamental national objectives. He reported a conversation with a key government economic official in 1979 who had been encouraging the free inflow of imports regardless of the adverse impact on the automobile, steel, machine tool, electronics, and many other basic industries. When it was suggested that if imports in overwhelming magnitude are good for our country, it would be even better for our country if all automobile producers moved all of their production overseas so that they could ship back to the United States products for the "consumer," he responded, "But you wouldn't do that, would you?" with a hopeful note in his voice.

Barry Eichengreen addressed the importance of the dollar in explaining the recent decline in basic industry employment, concluding that while the dollar has been key in predicting production in basic industries since 1981, its success was varied by industry. Cyclic factors, energy prices, wages, and productivity have also been very important, and the real exchange rate cannot explain the entire story.

Much of the discussion revolved around the globalization of the aluminum industry and its implications. Charles Parry explained that he was content with Alcoa's strategy of producing mostly secondary products in the United States. Venezuela, for example, has the bauxite and low energy costs to produce the primary product. There is also significant government support. National development and employment are the investment criteria.

This strategy is not available in steel, he noted, since steel does not have the variety of uses and opportunities that aluminum has. Steel production in the United States has fallen and will fall further, partly as a result of short-sighted management decisions and insufficient modernization. Copper production has been driven out of the United States by environmental regulations, which makes ironic the World Bank financing of a dirty copper smelter about twenty-five miles south of the Mexican border, with prevailing winds to the north. Aluminum production will be all right as long as the share of manufacturing in GNP is relatively stable. There will be increased dependence on foreign sources of primary products, and continued high levels of research and development are needed to maintain a position in finished aluminum products. Environmental regulations are not very onerous in the aluminum industry, he noted.

Parry explained that aluminum-finished imports are moderately sensitive to exchange rates. There has not been much decrease yet due to the fallen dollar, but Alcoa's calculations indicate that importers may be losing on each pound at the going exchange rate and prices.

George Vojta pointed out that the case of Alcoa illustrated the general themes of increasing deintegration and globalization of production. Parry agreed, noting that Alcoa has no worries about internationalizing the upstream end of production, which is simply a result of comparative advantage. Alcoa does not worry about the national defense issue.

James Schlesinger pursued this line of analysis, wondering if the United States can conceive of itself as providing military protection for the economy of the free world. For example, the producers of semiconductors on the Asian rim might need protecting. Compared to the consequences of the free Asian rim going to the Soviets, the risks associated with having aluminum production in Venezuela are not bad. He noted also that the United States was losing the edge in many militarily relevant areas, such as semiconductors and electronics, leading to a dilution of our abilities to formulate policies for the alliance.

Geoffrey Carliner mentioned a recent paper by Robert Lipsey which found that total exports of U.S. firms to third parties from onshore and offshore production have not fallen. This suggests that the problems with U.S. exports are not with management.

Parry addressed some questions associated with productivity-sharing arrangements. He acknowledged that the existence of industrywide unions creates problems. There is a big difference, he argued, between the individual worker and the union in attitudes toward work. Profit sharing of some sort is coming, however. Kaiser is doing what might be called pseudo–profit sharing now, and in 1989 Kaiser will start profit sharing. Alcoa neither can nor wants to decertify the union, and workers will not and should not give up collective bargaining. Profit sharing is the only way to equalize the base wage rate in healthy and unhealthy plants. Parry expressed hope for real productivity improvements, however, noting that during the recent strike Alcoa ran their operations with white-collar personnel and learned an enormous amount about productivity.

Parry acknowledged that assurances of continued employment will be a necessary accompaniment to profit sharing. Incentives and separation agreements will reduce the work force as productivity increases.

Robert Ingersoll pointed out that the Japanese use bonuses to achieve flexible labor costs. Parry agreed that this would be another implication of profit sharing. Profit sharing as a methodology of decreasing labor costs is one thing, but profit sharing could change the concept of the stakeholder and of the corporation.

Lionel Olmer wondered where the constituency for free trade lies, in an environment of wrenching structural adjustment in basic industries, cutthroat competition for market access, excess capacity, and fluctuating exchange rates. He has observed a trend to market sharing all over the world, in the aluminum industry as well as generally. Parry replied that the aluminum industry has always been for free trade. He expressed hope that bilateral negotiation with Japan, using the threat of a section 301 action, will lead to a bilateral agreement. European barriers too will come down by 1988. He suggested that enlightened management may explain this position. Olmer noted in this context that the apparent differences between GM and Ford on protectionism disappear on closer inspection, as GM wants it both ways behind the scenes, seeking special treatment for its own imports.

6 International Competition in Services

1. Rachel McCulloch
2. Maurice R. Greenberg
3. Lionel H. Olmer

1. Rachel McCulloch

6.1 Introduction

Production of services now dominates economic activity in the United States. Whether hailed as the dawn of a new "information economy" or deplored as the key symptom of American industrial decline, the trend in employment is itself beyond dispute. By the 1980s, only one U.S. worker in four was employed in the sectors of the economy producing tangible outputs—manufacturing plus mining, construction, and agriculture. But the increasing role of service-sector employment is by no means unique to the United States. Similar trends have been reshaping the economies of the other industrialized nations and even many less-developed countries.

Given this dramatic economic transformation at home and abroad, it may seem natural to find increasing attention on the part of U.S. policymakers to international competition in service activities. However, unlike domestic production, trade among nations is still dominated by exchange of tangible goods. Moreover, while the role of international service transactions is already significant and while some sectors show potential for rapid growth, the service transactions prominent in international commerce are quite different from the activities typical of the domestic "service economy."

In recent decades, national markets for tangible goods have become increasingly integrated, and virtually all U.S. goods-producing industries have experienced significant growth in both exports and competing imports. However, the rapid domestic expansion of service industries reflects the rising importance of health, education, housing, public administration, and other largely untraded service categories in final demand. The current U.S. interest in international service competition is focused on an entirely different group of industries, especially those supplying information-based business services. These industries are small relative to total domestic service-sector employment. And, although some part of their domestic output is "traded" internationally, that is, produced by residents of one nation for purchase by those of another, U.S. firms serve international markets primarily via local sales of foreign affiliates rather than exports.

6.1.1 Services on the Policy Agenda

Long ignored by trade officials as a generic issue, international competition in services has achieved high visibility on the global policy agenda just a few years after the subject was first raised by the United States. At the November 1982 ministerial meeting of the General Agreement on Tariffs and Trade (GATT), the United States trade representative called for inclusion of service transactions in forthcoming multilateral negotiations.[1] But the developing countries were strongly opposed, and the ministers merely recommended that members with an interest in service issues undertake their own national studies, exchange information, and report their results at the 1984 GATT session.[2]

Under continuing pressure from the United States, GATT members agreed in September 1986 to include services in the new Uruguay round of multilateral trade negotiations. Yet there remains widespread skepticism regarding progress on service issues. Abroad, the early and persistent enthusiasm of the United States for negotiations on services has caused U.S. trading partners to assume, perhaps incorrectly, that the United States will emerge as the major beneficiary of any liberalization achieved in this area.

The developing nations, led by Brazil and India, actively resisted inclusion of services on the GATT agenda. This resistance was overcome through a compromise that will keep services on a separate negotiating track from merchandise trade, but the developing nations are nonetheless suspicious of the outcome. While the other industrialized nations did eventually support the U.S. initiative on services, few trade officials abroad appear to view the prospects with any degree of enthusiasm. And even among the U.S. policymakers who pressed so vigorously for GATT negotiations on services, opinion remains divided on the best way to bring conflicting national policies toward services under the discipline of GATT rules.

Analysts in some U.S. government agencies worry that the GATT initiative on services may be premature. An extreme example is a recently issued report of the Office of Technology Assessment that openly suggests U.S. officials may have erred, perhaps because their decisions were based on inadequate data. The report's summary section gives this evaluation of the U.S. decision to promote negotiations on services:

> Consider, specifically, the decision by the United States prior to the 1982 GATT Ministerial to place a high priority on services in the next round—a decision taken in the midst of a period of deterioration in the ability of the world trading system to manage the impacts on trade in goods of nontariff barriers, bilateralism, and the national industrial policies that have become standard in many parts of the world. Would a better grasp of the prospects for U.S. exports of services have led to a different approach to the new round? Certainly the poor quality and coverage of the data impair the ability of policymakers to gauge the importance of services trade—as a whole, on a sector-by-sector basis, or bilaterally. (U.S. Congress, Office of Technology Assessment 1986, 7)

6.1.2   Analysis of Competition in Services

Although there is broad agreement on the poor quality of services data, progress in clarifying the nation's policy goals has been hampered also by lack of analytical guidance. Given the huge theoretical and empirical literature on international competition in goods, surprisingly little attention has been devoted until recently to international competition in services. In most empirical research on international trade, services are simply ignored or are treated as nontradable goods. Theorists, in contrast, often imply or state without elaboration that trade in services is conceptually no different from trade in goods, so that standard analyses in areas such as comparative advantage and gains from trade apply equally to international commerce in services.

Each approach has some economic justification. For the classic textbook example of haircuts and for many other types of services important in domestic production, foreign competition is indeed a negligible influence. Yet some important services, including shipping, transportation, and a variety of financial services, have been actively traded for centuries; for these, the determinants of trade and the gains from trade are fundamentally similar to those for merchandise trade.

But given the evident heterogeneity of the activities included in the category, does "services" even constitute a useful analytic classification, or is it merely a convenient label for a statistical residual?[3] The political and economic issues raised by international competition among producers of tangible goods have in practice proved far from simple to resolve, despite ample theoretical and empirical guidance; consideration of services introduces additional layers of complexity. These reflect the intangible nature of the outputs of many service activities, the locational and temporal constraints linking service providers to consumers, and the extensive role of domestic regulation in service activities. Analysts have only begun to grapple with the implications of these special features. In terms of both measurement and interpretation, analysis of service issues is still in its infancy.

All this raises obvious questions about the new GATT negotiations. Do policymakers have a sufficient knowledge base to shape international rules that will promote global efficiency? And do U.S. trade officials have a sufficient knowledge base to identify and pursue the nation's own economic interests in the area of service competition? If not, what can be gained by putting U.S. influence and prestige on the line to bring services into the GATT framework? Is the services item on the GATT agenda truly a generic issue, or is it fundamentally an attempt to improve the international position of a small set of U.S.-based multinational firms in a few industries?[4]

This paper surveys the main issues and evidence relating to U.S. international competition in services. The next section reviews the forces that have catapulted the services issue to the top of the U.S. agenda for forthcoming GATT negotiations.

Section 6.3 addresses what is meant by services and by trade in services, focusing on key ambiguities of definition. The discussion emphasizes similarities and differences within the service sector as conventionally defined and between "services" and tangible "goods."

Sections 6.4 and 6.5 interpret evidence on the growing importance of services in U.S. production and in international transactions. This evidence indicates the extent to which internationally traded services are unrepresentative of the services in domestic production.

Section 6.6 evaluates the influence of various types of national policies on international competition in services and compares barriers to services competition with nontariff distortions of merchandise trade.

Section 6.7 analyzes some of the choices facing U.S. officials and evaluates the advantages of alternative negotiating approaches in dealing with services issues.

The final section sums up principal conclusions emerging from the survey and emphasizes the links between international competition in services and other international issues on the policy agenda.

6.2 Services in the Policy Spotlight

For more than a generation, the majority of U.S. workers have been employed in service-producing sectors; for well over a century, employment in the service-producing sectors has been growing steadily as a share of the U.S. labor force (see tables 6.3–6.5 below). Thus, while the United States can accurately be described as a "service economy," this is hardly a recent development. Why then has the issue of services, barely mentioned in earlier GATT negotiations, emerged suddenly as a top U.S. priority for the Uruguay round? The burgeoning interest on the part of policymakers and the U.S. business community reflects several independent developments, each of which has generated some domestic support for market-opening measures in this area.

The first development is increasing concern in the United States about the nation's performance in international markets. Until the end of the 1960s, the technology gap between the United States and other industrialized nations appeared to provide a permanent advantage over foreign competitors, especially in the high-technology industries. Through massive research and development (R&D) expenditures, U.S. firms created a steady stream of new products and processes. These innovations allowed American manufacturing to remain internationally competitive, even given labor costs far higher than those abroad. But the technology gap narrowed with a speed that few anticipated. Through their global investments, American companies played a major role in the process.

In 1972, the United States recorded its first postwar deficit on merchandise trade. While the 1972 trade deficit of $2 billion seems insignificant relative to those of recent years, it stimulated questions about the course of the U.S. economy and its future position in world markets. The accompanying employment shift toward services, while not a new development, suggested the possibility that U.S. international comparative advantage was shifting from goods to services.

This impression was strengthened by U.S. balance of payments data that revealed a growing surplus in the "services" component of the current account. As U.S. merchandise trade performance deteriorated rapidly in the first half of the 1980s, services continued to make a significant positive contribution. As recently as 1982, the U.S. surplus on service transactions was large enough to reverse a sizable deficit on merchandise trade, so that the United States still showed a global surplus in the broader category of "goods and services" trade (see table 6.1). From this, some analysts inferred that increased market access abroad for U.S. service industries could further enhance their contribution to overall U.S. current account performance.[5]

Ironically, the healthy growth in the U.S. surplus on services was due mainly to increases in net earnings on foreign investments at a time of unusually high interest rates. Since then, interest rates worldwide have fallen dramatically. Moreover, the U.S. net investment position has reversed, with the United States emerging as the leading borrower in international capital markets. Accordingly, the contribution of investment income to U.S. current account performance is likely to become negative in the near future.

In contrast, as detailed in table 6.2, the types of service exports most likely to rise as a consequence of improved market access abroad

Table 6.1   U.S. Current Account by Major Component, 1977–85 (billions of dollars)

	1977	1980	1981	1982	1983	1984	1985
Merchandise trade							
Exports	120.8	224.3	237.1	211.2	201.7	219.9	214.0
Imports	151.9	249.7	265.1	247.6	268.9	334.0	338.3
Balance	31.1	−25.5	−28.0	−36.4	−67.2	−114.1	−124.3
Business services							
Exports	23.4	37.0	41.7	41.7	41.8	43.8	45.1
Imports	20.9	29.4	32.1	32.6	35.3	41.5	44.9
Balance	2.5	7.6	9.6	9.1	6.4	2.3	0.2
International investment income							
Exports (receipts)	32.2	72.5	86.4	84.8	78.0	87.6	90.5
Imports (payments)	14.2	42.1	52.3	55.3	52.6	68.5	65.8
Balance	18.0	30.4	34.1	29.5	25.4	19.1	24.7
Other goods and services							
Exports	7.9	8.7	10.5	12.4	13.0	10.7	10.2
Imports	7.2	12.2	13.1	14.5	14.7	14.0	13.6
Balance	0.7	−3.6	−2.5	−2.0	−1.7	−3.3	−3.4
Total goods and services							
Exports	184.3	342.5	375.8	350.1	334.5	362.0	359.7
Imports	194.2	333.5	362.6	350.0	371.5	458.0	462.6
Balance	−9.9	8.9	13.2	0.1	−37.0	−95.9	−102.9
Net unilateral transfers	−4.6	−7.1	−6.8	−8.1	−8.9	−11.4	−14.8
Current account balance	−14.5	1.9	6.3	−8.1	−46.0	−107.4	−117.7

Source: U.S. Department of Commerce 1986, table 40.

Table 6.2   **U.S. Business Services Trade by Component, 1977–85 (billions of dollars)**

	1977	1980	1981	1982	1983	1984	1985
Total business services							
Exports	23.4	37.0	41.7	41.7	41.8	43.8	45.1
Imports	20.9	29.4	32.1	32.6	35.3	41.5	44.9
Balance	2.5	7.6	9.6	9.1	6.4	2.3	0.2
Travel							
Exports	6.2	10.6	12.9	12.4	11.0	11.4	11.7
Imports	7.5	10.4	11.5	12.4	14.0	16.0	17.0
Balance	− 1.3	0.2	1.4	0.0	− 2.6	− 4.6	− 5.4
Passenger fares							
Exports	1.4	2.6	3.1	3.2	3.0	3.0	3.0
Imports	2.7	3.6	4.5	4.8	5.5	6.5	7.4
Balance	− 1.4	− 1.0	− 1.4	− 1.5	− 2.4	− 3.5	− 4.4
Shipping and other transportation							
Exports	7.1	11.6	12.6	12.3	12.6	13.8	14.3
Imports	8.0	11.8	12.5	11.7	12.3	14.7	16.3
Balance	− 0.9	− 0.2	0.1	0.6	0.3	− 0.9	− 2.0
Proprietary rights							
Exports	4.9	7.1	7.3	7.1	7.9	8.1	8.5
Imports	0.5	0.7	0.7	0.2	0.2	0.5	0.2
Balance	4.4	6.4	6.6	6.9	7.6	7.6	8.3
Other business services							
Exports	3.8	5.2	5.9	6.6	6.9	7.5	7.6
Imports	2.2	2.9	3.0	3.5	3.4	3.8	4.0
Balance	1.7	2.2	2.9	3.1	3.5	3.7	3.6

Source: U.S. Department of Commerce 1986, table 41.
Note: Details may not sum to totals due to rounding.

constitute a very minor portion of the relevant totals. Thus, even highly favorable conditions can be expected to have only a modest effect on the aggregate international position of the United States, although such conditions would provide substantial benefits to a number of U.S. firms.

While some proponents of GATT negotiations on services have stressed the expansion of service trade as a potential replacement for lost market share in manufactured products, others have emphasized complementarity with merchandise trade. In a variety of service activities that include distribution, training, repair, telecommunications, computer software, construction, and leasing, market access in services enhances market opportunities in related merchandise transactions.[6] This linkage implies that barriers to international competition in services may in effect constitute an important category of nontariff barrier to international competition in *goods,* especially manufactured goods.

An additional stimulus for attention to services arises from the national debate on "deindustrialization" of the American economy. At a time when U.S. manufacturing employment shows little promise of growth, expansion of the service industries represents an alternative means to improve the nation's economic prospects. Yet the forecast that newly created service jobs will replace jobs lost in manufacturing is itself controversial.

Optimists focus on a relatively narrow set of knowledge-based service activities, including ones closely linked to high-technology manufacturing. While some of these sectors have indeed enjoyed rapid growth in recent years, their size relative to the broad aggregate of services is quite small, both in the domestic market and in international transactions. Moreover, further decline in the size of the U.S. manufacturing sector is likely to slow or even reverse the growth of associated service activities as well. And U.S. labor unions, which are concentrated in manufacturing industries, point ominously to the low average earnings in many types of service employment and to the lower average rate of productivity increase in services relative to that in the goods-producing sectors.[7]

Support for including services in future GATT negotiations has also come from the U.S. public officials charged with forming and implementing the nation's policies toward trade. To many policymakers, services represent a promising area for continuing U.S. efforts to maintain open world markets. Negotiations on services could extend the discipline of GATT rules to a new and important category of transactions and might also help maintain the forward momentum of the liberalization process at a time when the prospect of further progress on merchandise trade issues appears dim. Anticipated trade and employment gains from increased service exports could help revitalize flagging political support at home for maintaining open markets (Feketekuty and Krause 1986, 89).

Finally, a major part of the impetus for the recent U.S. emphasis on service issues has come directly from the industries and specific firms with an important economic stake in serving international markets. Large international firms in insurance and other financial services activities and in business support services such as accounting, law, telecommunications, and data processing have actively promoted U.S. initiatives in the area of services. In many cases, U.S. firms expect their best customers abroad to be the foreign affiliates of major domestic clients. Thus, the global expansion of competition in services is in part a reflection of the earlier globalization of U.S. manufacturing industries.

In pressing their case for increased access to foreign markets, the interested firms and industry associations usually make no distinction between services exported from the United States and those provided locally to customers abroad by foreign affiliates of U.S. companies. Yet the two modes of serving foreign markets need to be separated for purposes of policy formation. Both types of transactions can provide substantial benefits to the U.S. economy. They will, however, generate quite different effects on domestic employment and income distribution.

Moreover, improved access for international sales via foreign subsidiaries is fundamentally not a trade issue at all, but rather a matter of national policy abroad toward direct foreign investments by U.S. firms. While consideration of trade in services already represents a significant extension of the GATT mandate beyond its current domain, the inclusion of service activities of foreign affiliates of U.S. firms would entail still a further expansion of GATT jurisdiction.[8] This initiative comes at a time when the GATT has been less than notably successful in its traditional work of maintaining open world markets for merchandise trade.

In sum, while a number of firms evidently anticipate substantial benefits from U.S. action on services, the national stake in the issue, whether in absolute terms or relative to other issues confronting members of the GATT, is less clear. Also, at least part of the broader enthusiasm for expanding U.S. market access in services reflects a superficial understanding of the role and importance of services in U.S. domestic production and in the nation's international transactions. Has liberalizing international competition in services been ranked too high on the nation's policy agenda? We return to this question at the end of the paper.

6.3 Analytical Issues

Despite continuing discussion of the nation's metamorphosis into a "service economy" and, more recently, of the growing importance of U.S. international competition in services, only meager attention has been paid to precisely what activities are entailed or exactly how these activities enter into international commerce. This section focuses on the fundamental issue of what is meant by services, emphasizing similarities and differences within the industries conventionally grouped together as "services" and between the categories of "services" and tangible "goods."

6.3.1 How Services Differ

Which are the industries included within the broad category of services? In terms of domestic employment, government (federal, state, and local) is by far the largest among U.S. service industries, obviously one for which international competition is not a pressing concern. Other major domestic service-producing sectors include transportation and public utilities, wholesale and retail trade, health, and financial and business services.[9] It is in the last category that the United States apparently hopes to make major gains via access to foreign markets. But in terms of international trade, travel and transportation currently account for the lion's share of total U.S. receipts from all "service" transactions (excluding income from direct foreign investment; see tables 6.1 and 6.2).

Although a number of scholars have attempted to identify the essential features that separate services from other economic activities, the inherent heterogeneity of the category implies that there will be important exceptions to any allegedly common feature. Heterogeneity may be on the rise, with the increasing importance of services that are "knowledge based" or "information based." These closely related categories include services that provide access to proprietary information (from mailing lists to industrial patents and trade secrets) and the services of individuals with specialized knowledge (from nursing to law). In practice, the two categories overlap; for example, an increasing range of services can be provided directly to the customer by skilled individuals or offered indirectly in the form of proprietary computer software packages.

Fundamentally, service activities may be distinguished either by the nature of their products or by the way in which those products are supplied.[10] Most service industries produce outputs that are intangible and nonstorable, although the rapidly growing category of information-based services offers important exceptions. For sectors such as telecommunications and computers, services and tangible goods are often provided together as part of a single transaction. Another characterizing feature of service products is high value-added relative to gross output. Again, however, there is a major exception, wholesale and retail trade, if the value of goods sold is included as an input.

Looking at the production process, services often require physical proximity of the producer and the consumer, a distinction that is particularly relevant for international competition in these sectors, although new communication technologies are changing the importance of this production constraint. For some knowledge-based services, a salient characteristic is strong economies of scale in production. Scale economies may reflect large fixed costs of physical equipment, as in telecommunications; large fixed costs of research and development, as for patented industrial knowledge; or large fixed costs of acquiring managerial or technical expertise which can then be extended inexpensively to additional customers, as in management consulting. Especially in financial service activities, scale offers the further cost advantage of internal risk diversification.

6.3.2   International Competition in Services

In general, international trade may be regarded as the *indirect* exchange of productive inputs embodied in the goods traded, that is, as a substitute for the direct movement of inputs across national boundaries.[11] Opportunities for and gains from international trade in services thus depend on the extent to which this indirect exchange is feasible. Since services are distinguished from tangible goods in part by greater constraints on the physical location of producer and consumer, it is helpful to classify services with respect to such constraints. There are four possible cases.[12]

1. No *required*[13] movement of providers or demanders. These have been called "separated" services (Sampson and Snape 1985) and "disembodied" or "long-distance" services (Bhagwati 1984). Such services are fundamentally similar to tangible goods with respect to opportunities for trade and gains from trade.

2. Required movement of providers (demander-located services). Where physical proximity to the market is essential, international competition necessarily entails movement of capital or labor to the production site, as in construction. However, the production process may also involve some inputs in another location (e.g., research and development or management). Deardorff (1985) calls these additional inputs "absent factors."

3. Required movement of demanders (provider-located services). The obvious example is tourism, but in practice, health and education are also important categories. Free "trade" in such services requires unrestricted international movement of potential demanders.

4. Required movement of either providers or demanders. In this case, production requires proximity, but the activity is "footloose" and can occur in the importing nation, the exporting nation, or even in a third location.

Another relevant classification of services is with respect to their relationship to merchandise trade. Some internationally provided services are complementary to trade in tangible goods (e.g., transportation, insurance, computer software), some offer alternatives to goods trade (e.g., licensing, computing services), while a third group is unrelated to goods trade (e.g., health and education).

Both classification schemes can be useful in sorting out issues of international competition (and barriers to international competition) in the broad range of activities usually lumped together in the category of services. However, any such taxonomy is necessarily arbitrary, and rapid changes in technology may in any case shift a particular activity from one niche into another.

U.S. firms may offer their services (and also tangible products) for sale abroad through direct exports or through local domestic transactions of a foreign affiliate.[14] In standard usage, a U.S. service "export" entails production by U.S. residents of a service purchased by a resident of another nation. It is thus the country of residence of the producer and buyer, rather than the site of production, that distinguishes trade in services. While the same definition applies for tangible goods, most trade in goods is accomplished by the movement of the goods themselves across national boundaries. But except for separated services (case 1 above), trade in services involves the movement of the producer and/or the buyer of the service.

As an alternative to exporting, a U.S. firm may establish a foreign subsidiary or enter into a joint venture with a foreign firm. In this case, the affiliate abroad can provide the service. Most of the affiliate's labor requirements will be met locally, although some skilled workers or managers may also move for a time period from the United States to the site of the foreign affiliate. In both trade and affiliate sales, there is a link to the U.S. firm, but sales abroad of U.S. affiliates do not necessarily entail a specific transaction between a U.S. resident and a resident of another nation and thus may not enter directly into the U.S. balance of payments accounts.

However, exporting and affiliate sales are not mutually exclusive modes of participation in foreign markets. In fact, they are often complementary activities of multinational corporations (see Bergsten, Horst, and Moran 1978, chap. 3). Likewise, trade and factor movements, or exports of goods and exports of services, have significant complementarity in actual transactions. The potential links among alternative modes of competition in foreign markets are highlighted in the following comparison, adapted from Feketekuty and Krause (1986), of the foreign sale of an automobile (tangible good) and of insurance (service). In both instances, movement abroad of U.S. factors, establishment of a foreign affiliate, and exporting are all potentially present.

To sell automobiles abroad, the U.S. producer usually establishes a dealer network in the foreign market. The U.S. firm need not own the dealerships, but in practice often does so. The firm also sends sales representatives to the foreign market to negotiate the terms under which the cars will be sold, government relations representatives to persuade foreign governments that safety and environmental standards have been met, and engineers to train and advise local mechanics. The automobiles themselves may be exported from the United States or produced by a local subsidiary. Often, market penetration begins with exporting and may be followed by establishment of a local subsidiary. Even then, the local operation may simply assemble automobiles from parts imported from the United States.

The U.S. insurance company wishing to sell policies abroad will likewise require a dealer network of local insurance brokers or agents to sell and service the policies. Again, the U.S. company need not own the brokerages but may do so. The U.S. insurance company will likewise need to send government relations managers to satisfy the foreign government that local regulatory requirements have been met, sales representatives to deal with local brokers, and perhaps management consultants to help train the local brokers.

For both automobiles and insurance, what is "exported" conceptually to the foreign market represents just a fraction of the value of the purchase made by the final consumer. Value added by local inputs, including sales and service personnel and transportation, makes up the difference. In the case of insurance, what is exported by the U.S. company is mainly risk bearing and related industry know-how, as well as other "headquarter services" of the parent corporation.

Attempting to classify any given transaction as either an export or an affiliate sale may thus produce a distorted overall picture of international competition. A more appropriate question concerns the relative importance of the two modes of foreign competition. The extent to which a given foreign transaction is carried out through affiliate sales rather than exporting obviously depends on technology but is also influenced by a variety of government policies toward transborder flows of products and data, movements of people, and direct foreign investment. Such policies at home and abroad may have a minor influence on the global market share of a given firm but a major influence on the firm's primary mode of participation in foreign markets.

6.3.3 Comparative Advantage in Services

Comparative advantage is the basic determinant of the direction of trade and of the gains from trade among nations: nations export the goods they can produce relatively cheaply and import goods that are relatively more costly to produce at home. Trade can thus be viewed as a superior indirect technology for producing certain goods. A given supply of primary inputs yields a greater total value of outputs when resources are concentrated in activities that are relatively more efficient.

Conceptually, comparative advantage may rest on differences in relative factor abundance, differences in technology, or the existence of scale economies. Most of the literature on merchandise trade has focused on the role of relative factor abundance. When countries have similar tastes and technologies, each will tend to export goods making relatively intensive use of its abundant factors and import goods requiring large amounts of its scarce factors.[15]

Accordingly, U.S. comparative advantage should lie in the high-technology areas, as these employ large amounts of skilled labor, the nation's abundant resource. Extending the same approach to services, there is a similar presumption that U.S. comparative advantage will lie in the high-technology end of the spectrum, and particularly in the production and export of knowledge itself.

However, recent theoretical research has emphasized the potential role of economies of scale in determining trade flows and the gains from trade. With restricted trade, large countries will tend to have lower prices for goods and services subject to important economies of scale.[16] But these lower prices do not necessarily predict the direction of trade when barriers are removed; with integrated markets, a firm located in a small nation no longer operates at a cost disadvantage.

Moreover, while scale economies increase the potential benefits from liberalization, they also complicate the issue of how these benefits are shared. In particular, the possibility that a given nation may lose by expanding trade even though global efficiency is improved is more difficult to rule out when scale economies are important. Mutual gains are assured only if each country is able, on average, to expand production in industries with scale economies.[17]

Information-based and knowledge-based services are the areas in which U.S. firms and U.S. policymakers seem most confident of expanding global sales. These services are likely to exhibit strong economies of scale. The theoretical analysis of comparative advantage and gains from trade suggests both that the apparent U.S. advantage in these industries (as measured by domestic prices) may be overstated under current conditions and that the cautious approach of other nations toward the liberalization of trade in services may have a firm economic basis.

6.4   Services in the Domestic Economy

This section reviews evidence on the growing importance of services in U.S. employment and production, and compares U.S. trends with experience of other nations. Tables 6.3–6.8 indicate the division of U.S. economic activity into service and nonservice components according to two alternative criteria. As discussed below, the most important categories of internationally traded services (see tables 6.1 and 6.2) are not the same ones that are most important in terms of recent growth of domestic employment.

6.4.1   Services in U.S. Employment

Sectoral employment is the yardstick that demonstrates most clearly the extent to which the United States has become a "postindustrial" or service economy. Tables 6.3 and 6.4 show recent nonagricultural employment of U.S. workers by type of industry. The service-producing

Table 6.3   U.S. Employment on Nonagricultural Payrolls by Industry, 1984–86 (thousands)

Industry	1984	1985	1986
Total	94,496	97,614	99,918
Private sector	78,472	81.199	83,198
Goods producing	24,727	24,930	24,965
Mining	966	930	790
Construction	4,383	4,687	4,974
Manufacturing	19,378	19,314	19,201
Service producing	69,769	72,684	74,953
Transportation and public utilities	5,159	5,242	5,265
Transportation	2,917	3,006	3,037
Communications and public utilities	2,242	2,236	2,228
Wholesale trade	5,555	5,740	5,872
Retail trade	16,545	17,360	17,464
General merchandise stores	2,267	2,320	2,344
Food stores	2,637	2,779	2,917
Auto dealers and service stations	1,799	1,892	1,944
Eating and drinking places	5,388	5,715	5,889
Financial, insurance, and real estate	5,689	5,953	6,261
Finance	2,854	2,979	3,137
Insurance	1,757	1,830	1,918
Real estate	1,078	1,144	1,206
Services	20,797	21,974	22,924
Business services	4,057	4,452	4,755
Health services	6,122	6,310	6,543
Government	16,024	16,415	16,720
Federal	2,807	2,875	2,889
State	3,734	3,848	3,936
Local	9,482	9,692	9,885

Source: Monthly Labor Review, October 1986, table 13.
Note: Data for 1984 and 1985 are annual averages; 1986 data are for May.

sectors are distinguished here by the intangible nature of their output and include both final-demand and intermediate-input categories.

As table 6.3 shows, U.S. employment is now heavily concentrated in the industries broadly described as service producing: transportation, public utilities, wholesale and retail trade, finance, insurance, real estate, miscellaneous business services, health, and government. This broad range of activities comprises all industries that are *not* included in the goods-producing sector, that is, manufacturing, construction, mining, and agriculture. The employment classification in table 6.3 is made on the basis of the industry's main output, which may be sold to final consumers (health, education), used as an intermediate input (business services), or both (restaurants).

Table 6.4   **U.S. Employment on Nonagricultural Payrolls by Industry, 1919–83 (millions of workers)**

Industry	1919	1930	1940	1950	1960	1970	1980	1983
Total	27.1	29.4	32.4	45.2	54.1	70.9	90.4	90.1
Private sector	24.4	26.3	28.2	39.2	45.8	58.3	74.2	74.3
Goods producing	12.8	12.0	13.2	18.5	20.4	23.6	25.7	23.4
Mining	1.1	1.0	0.9	0.9	0.7	0.6	1.0	1.0
Construction	1.0	1.4	1.4	2.4	3.0	3.6	4.3	3.9
Manufacturing	10.7	9.6	11.0	15.2	16.8	19.4	20.3	18.5
Service producing	14.3	17.5	19.1	26.7	33.8	47.3	64.7	66.7
Transportation and public utilities	3.7	3.7	3.0	4.0	4.0	4.5	5.1	4.9
Wholesale trade	n.a.	n.a.	1.8	2.6	3.1	4.0	5.3	5.3
Retail trade	n.a.	n.a.	4.9	6.8	8.2	11.0	15.0	15.5
Financial, insurance, and real estate	1.1	1.5	1.5	1.9	2.6	3.6	5.2	5.5
Services	2.3	3.4	3.7	5.4	7.4	11.5	17.9	19.7
Government	2.7	3.1	4.2	6.0	8.4	12.6	16.2	15.9
Federal	n.a.	0.5	1.0	1.9	2.3	2.7	2.9	2.8
State	n.a.	n.a.	n.a.	n.a.	1.5	2.7	3.6	3.7
Local	n.a.	n.a.	n.a.	n.a.	4.5	7.2	9.8	9.4

Source: U.S. Department of Labor 1985, table 63.

Note: Data include Alaska and Hawaii beginning in 1960. Details may not sum to totals due to rounding.

Tables 6.4 and 6.5 indicate the nation's labor force allocation in longer-term perspective. Table 6.5 shows the division of U.S. employment among three major sectors: agriculture, goods, and services. Here agriculture includes forestry and fisheries; goods-producing employment includes mining and construction. Government employment is allocated according to industry, with only public administration listed as a separate service category.

Table 6.5 reveals that the growth of service-sector employment as a share of the U.S. labor force is a trend going back to 1850, the earliest year for which data are available. However, until recent years that growth was accommodated mainly through the secular contraction of agriculture's share. Agriculture accounted for about two-thirds of U.S. employment in 1850 but less than 4 percent by the 1980s.

In contrast, the share of goods-producing employment increased steadily until the turn of the century and moved cyclically around the one-third mark for many years thereafter. Only in the past twenty years has growth of employment in service-producing industries come mainly at the expense of manufacturing and the other nonagricultural goods-producing sectors.

Even so, it is primarily the *share* of the goods-producing sectors in total employment, rather than the *level* of such employment, that has

Table 6.5   U.S. Employment by Major Sector, 1850–1982 (percentage
                   of total)

Year	Agriculture	Goods Producing	Service Producing
1850	64.5	17.7	17.8
1860	59.9	20.1	20.0
1870	50.8	25.0	24.2
1890	43.1	28.3	28.6
1900	38.0	30.5	31.4
1910	32.1	32.1	35.9
1920	27.6	34.6	37.7
1930	21.8	31.7	46.6
1940	18.3	33.1	48.6
1952	11.3	35.5	53.3
1957	9.8	34.3	56.0
1962	7.8	33.1	59.1
1967	5.3	34.7	60.1
1972	4.4	31.4	64.2
1977	3.7	29.7	66.6
1979	3.6	30.2	66.3
1982	3.6	27.2	69.2

Source: Urquhart 1984, table 1.

fallen in recent years. As table 6.6 indicates, the number of workers in goods-producing employment actually rose between 1967 and 1979, even though the share of these sectors fell from 34.7 percent to 30.2 percent of the U.S. labor force. But a sharp recession in 1980–82 produced a substantial fall in goods-producing employment. Although employment growth resumed in 1983, by 1986 the total number of workers in the goods-producing industries was still well below previous peaks. Of course, employment in manufacturing and other goods-producing sectors fell even more relative to the levels that would have been attained had the distribution of the larger labor force among the major sectors remained unchanged from the 1967 pattern.

6.4.2 Services in Gross National Product

A similar pattern emerges from an examination of U.S. gross national product (GNP) by industry, as shown in table 6.7. In current dollars, the service-producing sectors now account for over two-thirds of U.S. GNP, up from about 55 percent immediately after World War II. The industrial classifications used in tables 6.3–6.7 include both intermediate and final products, and both government and private activities.

An alternative measure of the economic importance of services is their share in final demand as measured by consumer spending. As shown in table 6.8, expenditure for services now accounts for about

Table 6.6   **Estimated Employment Shifts by Sector and Industry, 1967–79 (millions)**

Sector and Industry	1967 Actual	1979 Actual	1979 with 1967 Distribution	Relative Gain or Loss
Total	74.4	98.8	—	—
Agriculture	3.9	3.5	5.2	−1.7
Goods producing	25.8	29.8	34.3	−4.5
Manufacturing	20.7	22.5	27.5	−5.0
Service producing	44.7	65.5	59.4	+6.2
Transp., communication, and public util.	4.9	6.5	6.5	+0.0
Trade	13.9	20.1	18.5	+1.6
Wholesale	2.6	3.9	3.4	+0.5
Retail	11.3	16.2	15.1	+1.2
Eating and drinking establishments	2.3	4.2	3.0	+1.2
Finance, insurance, and real estate	3.5	5.9	4.7	+1.2
Services	18.2	27.8	24.1	+3.7
Business and repair	2.1	3.7	2.7	+1.0
Personal	4.4	3.9	5.9	+2.0
Entertainment and recreation	0.7	1.1	0.9	+0.2
Professional	11.0	19.2	14.6	+4.6
Health	3.8	7.0	5.1	+1.9
Education	5.2	8.0	6.9	+1.1
Legal	0.3	0.7	0.5	+0.2
Welfare and religious	0.7	1.6	1.0	+0.6
Public administration	4.2	5.2	5.6	−0.4
Postal	0.7	0.7	1.0	−0.3
Other federal	1.5	1.6	2.0	−0.4
State	0.6	0.9	0.8	+0.1
Local	1.1	1.9	1.8	+0.1

Source: Urquhart 1984, table 2.

Note: Details may not add to totals due to rounding.

one-half of total personal consumption expenditures, up from about 40 percent in 1929 and as little as one-third in 1950. The main categories of service expenditures in final demand are housing, utilities and other services used in household operation, transportation, and medical care.[18] However, these data tend to understate the relative importance of services in final consumption, since they do not include important government-financed consumption services such as education and recreation.

Table 6.7   U.S. Gross National Product by Industry, 1947–85 (billions of dollars)

	1947	1950	1960	1965	1970	1975	1980	1985
Total GNP	235.2	288.3	515.3	705.1	1015.5	1598.4	2732.0	3998.1
Goods producing	102.9	127.3	203.2	271.3	352.3	531.4	903.2	1192.3
Agriculture, forestry, and fisheries	20.8	20.8	21.7	24.2	29.9	56.3	77.2	91.5
Mining	6.8	9.3	12.8	14.0	18.7	41.3	107.3	122.8
Construction	9.1	13.2	24.3	34.7	51.4	76.5	137.7	182.2
Manufacturing	66.2	84.0	144.4	198.4	252.3	357.3	581.0	795.8
Service producing	129.4	158.7	311.4	429.3	657.1	1047.0	1776.3	2770.3
Transp. and public utilities	21.0	26.6	47.3	62.6	88.4	141.7	240.8	374.4
Wholesale and retail trade	44.2	51.5	85.7	115.0	168.7	273.7	438.8	652.5
Financial, insurance, and real estate	23.8	32.2	72.8	98.9	145.8	221.7	400.6	626.6
Services	20.2	24.2	51.4	74.6	120.2	199.8	374.0	639.4
Government and government enterprises	20.2	24.2	54.2	78.2	134.0	210.1	322.1	477.4
Statistical discrepancy	1.8	0.8	-2.8	-1.2	-1.1	2.5	4.9	-5.5
Rest of the world	1.2	1.5	3.5	5.8	7.3	17.5	47.6	41.2

Source: Economic Report of the President, 1987, table B-10.

Notes: Industry classification is on an establishment basis and is based on the 1972 Standard Industry Classification. Details may not add to totals due to rounding.

Table 6.8   U.S. Personal Consumption Expenditures, 1929–86 (billions of dollars)

	1929	1940	1950	1960	1970	1975	1980	1986
Total	77.3	71.0	192.1	330.7	640.0	1012.8	1732.6	2762.4
Durable goods	9.2	7.8	30.8	43.5	85.7	135.4	219.3	388.3
Nondurable goods	37.7	37.0	98.2	153.2	270.3	416.2	681.4	932.7
Services	30.4	26.2	63.2	134.0	284.0	461.2	831.9	1441.3
Housing	11.7	9.7	21.7	48.2	94.0	148.4	261.5	438.5
Household operation	4.0	4.0	9.5	20.3	37.7	63.5	113.9	178.4
Transportation	2.6	2.1	6.2	11.2	23.7	35.7	64.5	95.9
Medical care	2.2	2.2	6.9	16.4	46.1	84.2	164.2	315.9
Other	9.9	8.2	18.8	38.0	82.5	129.3	227.9	412.6

Source: Economic Report of the President, 1987, table B-14.

Notes: Housing includes imputed value of owner-occupied housing. Data for 1986 are preliminary.

6.4.3 Why and How Services Grew

The summary tables presented in the previous sections document the evolution of today's "service economy" but give little insight into the causes of these dramatic changes. In brief, the employment and output shifts reflect the combined impact of three basic forces: changes in the sectoral allocation of final demand (in turn reflecting rising per capita income and systematic changes in relative prices as well as demographic shifts), relative rates of productivity improvement, and changes in the organization of economic activity.

Looking first at the long-term shift of employment out of agriculture offers some perspective on the more recent movements from goods-producing to service-producing employment. In the case of agriculture, low income and price elasticities of demand, changing dietary preferences, and sustained high rates of productivity improvement have all contributed to agriculture's declining share of total employment, even over the periods when the United States was increasing its penetration of foreign markets.

Changes in the organization of economic activity reinforced the effects of demand and productivity changes, with specialized processing, transportation, distribution, and business-services units gradually taking over many functions once handled by workers classified as agricultural employees. But the nation is by no means losing its "agricultural base" in terms of production. On the contrary, agricultural outputs have continued to grow with dismaying rapidity despite the steady decline in the number of workers employed in the sector.

While the shift from goods-producing to service-producing employment is more complex, some of the same forces were important. Changes in the age composition of the population and in the labor force participation of women have fueled increases in the demand for some services that have experienced high rates of growth. These include health and education among professional services, and eating and drinking establishments, a major component of retail trade. Moreover, the goods-producing sectors have maintained relatively high rates of productivity increase, so that outputs of most sectors have continued to rise even when employment has stabilized or dipped. Finally, changes in the degree of vertical integration of goods-producing firms have led to a reclassification of many workers from other industrial categories as service employees, although the work performed by these employees is basically unchanged.

In recent years, "business services" has been the most rapidly growing sector of the U.S. economy in terms of employment. The business services sector comprises seven major industries:[19] advertising; consumer credit reporting and collection; mailing, reproduction, and stenographic services; services to buildings, including cleaning, maintenance, and exterminating services; personnel supply services, including both temporary-help suppliers and employment agencies; computer and data processing services; and miscellaneous business services, which include research and development, management and consulting, and protective services.

Firms in this industry provide a variety of business services on an ongoing contractual basis (e.g., janitorial services, data processing, advertising) or to accommodate temporary or cyclical requirements (e.g., office personnel, unskilled labor). While some of the included activities are new (computer services), the growth of others reflects changes in the way U.S. firms are doing business and particularly in employer-employee relationships in the goods-producing sectors of the economy.[20]

6.4.4   Services, Labor Supply, and Productivity

Changes in the composition of the labor force may affect growth of service employment through changes in productivity as well as through changes in the pattern of final demand. The recent bulge of new entrants into the labor force was absorbed in large part through expansion of employment in the services sector, with slow or negative increases in compensation. One recent study found that women hired in the service sector were much more likely not to have worked at all in the previous year than to have worked previously in the goods sector.[21] The rapidly growing retail trade sector (which includes the infamous fast-food outlets) experienced the largest relative decline in average hourly earnings between 1977 and 1983 of any major employment sector (U.S. Department of Labor 1985, table 78).

With fewer new entrants to the labor force, or with greater downward rigidity of wages and employee benefits (as in the European community), a smaller number of new jobs would have been created in services, while the higher cost of employing additional workers would have induced employers to adopt more capital-intensive (i.e., more "productive") technologies.[22]

The relatively strong productivity performance and accordingly low employment growth of the goods-producing sectors may have a similar explanation. With more extensive unionization and less flexibility in compensation and work rules, faster adaptation of new labor-saving technologies would typically mean slower employment growth but higher measured increases in labor productivity for any given growth rate of output. Thus, for both tangible goods and for services, sectoral patterns of labor productivity growth are appropriately viewed as endogenous, reflecting the interaction of such forces as technological advance, labor market developments, and tax policy.

6.4.5   International Comparisons

The relative importance of the U.S. service sector in total employment has increased over time with the nation's rising per capita income. Cross-country evidence also points to a strong positive correlation between service employment and per capita GNP. As table 6.9 shows, in 1980 service employment absorbed just 15 percent of the labor force of the world's poorest countries, while agriculture occupied nearly three workers of every four—a pattern not too different from the United States in the mid-1800s.[23]

Among the industrialized nations, the average share of service employment was 58 percent, with the United States eight percentage points higher. Moreover, between 1965 and 1980, every industrialized country showed an increase in the share of services in total employment. The same was true also for the nonmarket economies of Eastern Europe and for almost all other nations, whether rich or poor. In most cases, the increase in the share of services has come at the expense of agricultural employment, presumably reflecting the dissemination worldwide of modern agricultural technologies as well as the industrialization goals of many nations.[24]

A similar pattern emerges for the percentage share of services in gross domestic product (GDP). As table 6.10 indicates, the percentage share of services in GDP averaged 62 percent in 1984 for the industrialized nations but only 29 percent for the world's poorest nations. The table also shows that the share of services has been increasing over time for every industrialized nation, while that of industry broadly and of manufacturing specifically has been declining.

These shares are calculated on the basis of local domestic prices. However, prices of services tend to be higher relative to those of tangible goods in countries with higher per capita GNP. When a common set of international prices is used to value outputs, the percentage shares of services in GDP differ less markedly over time for a given country or between rich and poor nations in a given year. Using real-quantity indexes in place of value shares, Kravis, Heston, and Summers (1983) show that in real terms, low-income countries may actually consume services in higher proportions than wealthier nations. This finding presumably reflects the very low relative prices of services in poor countries.

6.5 International Service Transactions

The high priority placed by the United States on negotiations on trade in services is frequently justified by assertions that this trade is currently or potentially very important to the nation's overall international position. Yet the data on U.S. trade in services provide only weak support for such a claim. Globally and also for the United States, the aggregate size of services trade as reflected in balance of payments data is roughly one-fourth that of merchandise trade. Moreover, that

Table 6.9   **Distribution of Labor Force by Industry, 1965 and 1980 (percentage of total labor force)**

	Agriculture		Industry		Services	
Country Group	1965	1980	1965	1980	1965	1980
Low-income economies	77	73	9	13	14	15
Middle-income economies	57	44	17	22	26	34
Oil exporters	61	49	14	19	24	32
Oil importers	53	40	19	23	28	36
High-income oil exporters	56	36	15	21	28	44
Industrialized market economies	14	7	38	35	48	58
Canada	10	5	33	29	57	65
France	17	9	39	35	43	56
Germany	10	6	48	44	42	50
Italy	24	12	42	41	34	48
Japan	26	11	32	34	42	55
United Kingdom	3	3	47	38	50	59
United States	5	4	35	31	60	66
Eastern European nonmarket economies	35	21	34	40	31	39

Source: World Development Report, 1986, table 30.

Notes: Country groups are as defined by the World Bank. Group averages are weighted by population.

Table 6.10   **Structure of Production by Major Sector, 1965 and 1984 (percentage of total gross domestic product)**

Country Group	Agriculture 1965	Agriculture 1984	Industry 1965	Industry 1984	Manufacturing 1965	Manufacturing 1984	Services 1965	Services 1984
Low-income economies	43	37	29	34	14	14	28	29
Middle-income economies	21	15	31	36	20	21	47	49
Oil exporters	22	16	28	39	16	18	50	46
Oil importers	21	13	33	35	22	25	46	52
High-income oil exporters	5	2	65	61	5	7	30	37
Industrialized market economies	5	3	39	35	29	25	56	62
Canada	5	3	34	24	23	—	71	72
France	—	4	—	34	—	25	—	62
Germany	—	2	—	46	—	36	—	52
Italy	11	5	41	40	32	30	48	55
Japan	9	3	43	41	32	30	48	56
United Kingdom	3	2	41	36	30	22	56	62
United States	3	2	38	32	29	21	59	66

Source: World Development Report, 1986, table 3.

Notes: Country groups are as defined by the World Bank. Group averages are weighted by population. Japanese data are for 1965 and 1983.

proportion has been relatively stable in recent years. Thus, neither the absolute size nor the rate of growth of trade transactions in services by themselves makes a compelling case for its recent promotion to a top position on the trade policy agenda of the United States.

Although there is ample reason to believe that official trade data seriously underestimate the true value of both U.S. service exports and imports, even improved and expanded services data do not provide credible support for a major push on services trade. If there is a strong argument for broad-based negotiations on services, it appears to apply less to trade than to the alternative mode of international competition, sales abroad of U.S. affiliates.

Tables 6.11 and 6.12 show the value and composition of international service exports in 1980 for the twenty-five leading service-exporting nations. The United States is indeed largest in terms of services exports, as well as merchandise exports and income from foreign investment. However, the relative importance of services, as measured by the ratio of service exports to GDP, is *less* for the United States than for most of the other nations. This should perhaps not be surprising, given the very large absolute size of the U.S. market. But the ratio of service exports to merchandise exports is also far below that of other major service exporters.

Still, these data provide only a partial indication of the importance of international competition in services to the U.S. economy. As described in section 6.3, a U.S. firm may compete in markets abroad through direct exports or through a foreign affiliate. A service export entails production by U.S. residents of a service purchased by the resident of another nation. At least in principle, the total value of service export sales appears in the services section of the U.S. balance of payments accounts.[25] As shown in table 6.12, the most important service export categories by value for the United States and most other nations are travel and transportation.

Unlike export sales, sales abroad of U.S. affiliates do not enter directly into the U.S. international accounts, as such sales do not necessarily entail a specific transaction between a U.S. resident and a resident of another nation. Affiliate sales probably have important indirect effects on two items in the services section of balance of payments accounts—earnings of U.S. investments abroad and intrafirm payments of royalties and licensing fees. But neither item provides a reliable measure of the U.S. stake in the foreign market, because payments between the parent and foreign affiliates are shaped by tax considerations and other dimensions of national regulation.

For the firms and industries that have shown the greatest interest in a U.S. initiative on services trade, sales abroad by foreign affiliates are substantially larger than exports from U.S. operations, although the

Table 6.11   Twenty-five Largest Services Exporters in 1980 (billions of U.S. dollars)

Country	Value of Services Exports	Value of Foreign Investment Income	Value of Merchandise Exports	Services Exports to GDP Ratio (%)	Services Exports to Merchandise Exports Ratio (%)
U.S.	34.9	70.2	224.3	1.4	15.6
U.K.	34.2	17.1	110.9	6.5	30.9
France	33.0	18.4	107.6	5.1	30.7
Germany	22.4	8.5	185.5	3.9	17.2
Italy	22.4	5.3	76.8	5.7	30.2
Japan	18.9	7.2	126.8	1.8	14.9
Netherlands	17.7	10.0	67.5	10.5	26.2
Belgium	14.5	17.6	55.2	12.1	26.3
Spain	11.7	0.2	20.5	5.6	56.9
Austria	10.8	2.5	17.2	14.0	62.6
Switzerland	8.4	n.a.	29.3	8.3	28.9
Sweden	7.5	0.8	30.7	6.0	24.3
Mexico	7.4	1.0	16.2	4.0	45.8
Norway	7.3	0.5	18.7	12.7	39.2
Canada	7.0	2.9	67.6	2.7	10.3
Singapore	5.9	n.a.	18.2	54.1	32.7
Korea	4.5	0.3	17.2	7.7	26.1
Yugoslavia	4.5	0.2	9.0	7.1	49.9
Greece	4.0	0.0	4.1	9.9	97.6
Saudi Arabia	3.7	n.a.	100.7	3.2	3.7
Australia	3.5	0.7	21.7	2.5	16.2
Israel	3.2	0.7	5.8	15.9	55.8
South Africa	3.0	0.4	25.5	3.8	11.8
Finland	2.8	0.2	14.1	5.6	19.6
Egypt	2.3	0.3	3.9	9.8	60.2

Source: U.S. Trade Representative 1983, table 2.

Notes: Values converted to U.S. dollars at current exchange rates. Services exports exclude official transactions and investment earnings. Foreign investment earnings include private direct investment income and portfolio income but exclude foreign official income.

industries' own discussions typically do not distinguish these two types of foreign operations or divide revenues from foreign markets into exports and affiliate transactions.

The importance of subsidiary sales in total foreign sales of U.S. service firms is qualitatively similar to the situation of international competition in tangible goods. In the manufacturing industries, U.S. firms have maintained a roughly constant share of world exports in recent decades. But exports from the United States have constituted a declining share of total U.S. sales in international markets, with exports from U.S. affiliates abroad increasing to maintain overall constancy of the total market share (Lipsey and Kravis 1985).

Table 6.12   **Major Categories of Service Exports, 1980 (billions of U.S. dollars)**

	Total	Shipment	Other Transp. and Passenger Fares	Travel and Tourism	Other Private Services
U.S.	37.5	4.0	12.9	10.0	10.8
U.K.	37.1	5.8	11.2	6.9	13.3
France	33.0	1.3	10.7	8.2	12.8
Germany	33.8	5.3	6.5	6.6	15.5
Italy	23.5	3.3	3.4	8.9	7.8
Japan	19.4	7.4	6.1	0.6	5.3
Netherlands	18.6	3.7	7.2	1.7	6.1
Belgium	14.9	2.4	2.3	1.8	8.4
Spain	12.2	1.2	2.4	6.9	1.7
Austria	10.8	0.7	0.1	6.5	3.6
Switzerland	8.4	0.4	n.a.	4.1	3.9
Sweden	8.0	1.8	1.9	1.0	3.4
Mexico	7.7	n.a.	0.7	5.2	1.8
Norway	9.2	5.0	2.1	0.8	1.4
Canada	7.0	0.8	0.7	2.9	2.6
Singapore	5.9	0.6	2.0	1.4	1.9
Korea	4.8	1.0	1.0	0.4	2.5
Yugoslavia	4.6	0.4	1.0	1.6	1.5
Greece	4.0	0.1	0.9	1.7	1.2
Saudi Arabia	4.3	n.a.	2.2	1.3	0.7
Australia	3.5	0.5	1.8	1.0	0.3
Israel	3.1	0.6	0.7	0.9	0.9
South Africa	3.2	0.3	1.2	0.6	1.1
Finland	3.0	0.5	0.8	0.7	1.0
Egypt	2.5	n.a.	1.4	0.6	0.5

Source: U.S. Trade Representative 1983, table 3.

Notes: Values converted to U.S. dollars at current exchange rates. Other private services include IMF balance of payments categories "other goods, services and income," "labor income, n.i.e.," and "property income, n.i.e." Totals on this table may not match data in table 6.11 because of intervening revisions in the IMF data tapes used.

In the case of services, available data are sketchy for both exports and foreign sales. One estimate suggests that revenues from sales abroad of U.S. affiliates exceed those from U.S. exports on average by about 50 percent (U.S. Congress, Office of Technology Assessment, 1986). Since profit rates of foreign subsidiaries are usually higher than those of domestic operations, this would mean that, in terms of profits to U.S. firms competing internationally, affiliate sales probably account for well over half of all profits generated by operations abroad. However, affiliate sales translate into a smaller demand for domestic labor input than the same dollar volume of export sales.

The importance of affiliate sales relative to direct exporting varies substantially across those industries with important international transactions. For some major service industries, including travel, educational and legal services, and technology licensing, direct exports account for nearly all revenues from international transactions. In a second group, including insurance, advertising, and accounting, affiliate sales provide the bulk of foreign revenues. For a third group, including transportation, construction, consulting, and computer software, both direct exports and affiliate sales are significant. Table 6.13 shows Office of Technology Assessment estimates of 1983 revenues in both categories for U.S. service firms. Banking, an important service industry both domestically and in international transactions, was treated separately because of the special problem of distinguishing investment income from the service component of foreign revenues.

Given that affiliate sales greatly exceed exports for many service providers, a broader measure of the importance of international transactions to U.S. service industries is the size of total foreign revenues

Table 6.13   **OTA Estimates of Foreign Revenues of U.S. Service Firms, 1983 (billions of dollars)**

Activity	Direct Exports	Affiliate Sales	Total Foreign Revenues
Accounting	0.2–0.5	3.7–4.0	3.9–4.5
Advertising	0.1–0.5	1.7	1.8–2.2
Construction	4.8	2.9–3.3	7.7–8.1
Data processing	0.1–1.2	2.5–3.7	2.6–4.9
Education	1.6–2.3	0.0–0.1	1.6–2.4
Engineering	1.1–1.6	4.0	5.1–5.6
Franchising	0.2–1.1	0.0	0.2–1.1
Health	1.0–2.5	1.1	2.1–3.6
Information	0.0–2.9	0.0–2.9	2.9
Insurance	2.7–3.6	10.1–12.1	12.8–15.7
Investment banking/brokerage	1.0–2.0	7.7	8.9–9.7
Leasing	0.2–1.2	3.7–5.4	4.5–5.6
Legal	0.0–2.0	0.1	0.1–2.1
Licensing	5.2	0.0	5.2
Management/consulting	0.6–1.4	1.2	1.8–2.6
Motion pictures	1.9	2.0	3.9
Retailing	0.0	25.4	25.4
Software	2.5–2.6	3.2–4.4	5.7–7.0
Telecommunications	1.3	1.3	2.6
Transportation	17.1	10.9	28.0
Travel	14.1	0.0	14.1
Miscellaneous	5.3	6.0	11.3
Subtotal (excluding banking)	61.0–75.1	87.5–97.3	152–169
Banking	n.a.	n.a.	9.4
Total	n.a.	n.a.	161–178

Source: U.S. Congress, Office of Technology Assessment 1986, table 5.

from both sources relative to overall sales. For the major U.S. service industries as ranked on the basis of domestic employment, including health services and education, foreign revenues from exporting plus affiliate sales are small relative to the value of total output. Moreover, as with merchandise trade, a few large firms account for the lion's share of all U.S. international service transactions in a given industry.

While there is no "typical" service sector, the insurance industry can provide an illustration of the relative magnitudes. According to Stalson (1985, 94), there are about ten thousand insurance companies worldwide, with half of those in the United States alone. But only a few hundred have significant foreign sales. Of this group, about fifty are U.S. firms; among the U.S. firms, five are very large and operate in many countries. Revenues from foreign sales constitute about one-tenth of total revenues for the U.S. industry, with most of that going to five firms.

Although the data for many service industries are seriously deficient, a more significant problem is in interpretation. None of the available measures can give an accurate indication of the contribution of foreign sales to profits. For information-based service industries, including telecommunications and most business services, fixed costs may account for a very large portion of total costs. Expansion into foreign markets (whether through exports or sales of affiliates abroad) may thus make a contribution to profits far in excess of the proportion of foreign sales to total revenues.[26] Of course, the actual or potential contribution to profits of U.S. firms is still far from a measure of the *national* stake in pursuing multilateral liberalization of barriers to international competition in the service sector. This is particularly relevant at a time when attaining U.S. goals will surely require trade concessions affecting the prospects of other domestic industries.

6.6 Barriers to International Competition

The U.S. move to promote inclusion of services in the new round of GATT negotiations reflects the belief not only that international service transactions are important to the American economy but also that significant barriers hamper the access of U.S. firms to foreign markets. This section considers the types of barriers that might be included in efforts to maintain open markets for services transactions, and prospects for success based on experience in negotiating limits on barriers to merchandise trade.

6.6.1 Barriers to Merchandise Transactions

Even for the relatively straightforward case of tangible goods, barriers to trade are anything but straightforward. Tariffs, the classic trade barrier, have not entirely disappeared, and high tariffs are still present for some products. However, in recent decades focus has shifted to nontariff barriers (NTBs) to trade, meaning all other national policies that potentially affect the volume of and gains from international trade. The Kennedy round of GATT negotiations succeeded in slicing most tariff rates to postwar lows. The subsequent Tokyo round was the first to tackle the much broader issue of nontariff barriers, but with only modest results.

At least four major reasons account for the slow progress. First, NTBs are not one problem but fifty or three hundred separate problems, ranging from relatively straightforward quantitative trade restrictions to such complex mechanisms as product standards, government procurement procedures, and labor market policies. In most cases, the impact on foreign competition is not the primary motivation of the policy, although in practice such policies are nonetheless administered in a way that puts foreign firms at a disadvantage in serving the local market.

A second reason for slow progress in limiting the proliferation of nontariff barriers is that their use arises partly from basic deficiencies of the GATT structure in handling problems of adjustment to changing international conditions. For example, the widespread use of "voluntary" export restraints (VERs) reflects general dissatisfaction with the provisions of article 19, which in principle governs members' response to unanticipated changes in international competition.

Third, the GATT was designed under the assumption that national policies can be viewed as having both "domestic" and "international" components. The GATT rules focus primarily on the latter—that is, policies applied at the national border. But the increased integration of national markets has made this dichotomy almost obsolete.

Finally and perhaps most important, both the GATT negotiation process and the GATT rules are predicated on a mercantilistic view of the gains from international trade, that is, that the "gains" from open markets are expanded exports and that any increased imports represent the price paid for the opportunity to expand exports. By failing to emphasize the real mutual gains from integrated global markets, GATT member nations have shifted negotiating efforts in inappropriate directions, even to the point of forcing GATT to become a party to global cartelization of the markets for textiles and apparel.[27]

Unfortunately, the factors that apply to merchandise trade are at least equally relevant for international competition in services, where movement of "traded" products across national borders is the exception rather than the rule. This does not necessarily imply that inclusion of services in forthcoming negotiations is unprofitable. It does, however, mean that the very basic problems now confronting the GATT are likely to be exacerbated rather than eased by broadening its mandate to include services.

6.6.2 Barriers to Competition in Services

Diverse in many respects, the service industries do not share common objectives with respect to expansion abroad. Indeed, some industries with well-established foreign operations are hesitant to participate in a generic sectoral push to expand market access abroad lest their own firm-specific and industry-specific needs receive less favorable attention from foreign governments. Even information on the relative importance of particular types of barriers is not easily collected. Some U.S. firms are reluctant to divulge information that might indicate their competitive position to foreign or domestic rivals, and the service firms as a group are less accustomed than those in the goods-producing sectors to providing detailed information about their business operations to government agencies on a regular basis (U.S. International Trade Commission 1982, 1).

To provide better support for U.S. efforts, the International Trade Commission conducted a voluntary survey of 479 international service firms in fourteen service industries. Only about one-fourth of the firms responded to the survey, and the response rate was much lower in some industries. In communication services, only one firm out of eight responded to the questionnaire.

Respondents identified the degree to which specific nontariff barriers were encountered in foreign markets. Most important were restrictions affecting the basic "right of establishment" in the foreign market (63 percent of all respondents), specific barriers to provision of a service by foreign firms (62 percent), and foreign exchange controls (54 percent). Other barriers in order of frequency included government procurement (30 percent), technical issues (27 percent), restrictions on related trade in goods (21 percent), subsidies and countervailing duties (21 percent), licensing requirements (18 percent), standards and certification (17 percent), inadequate protection of intellectual property (12 percent), and professional qualification restrictions (10 percent).

Despite the ubiquitous nature of these barriers, one-fourth of the firms did not anticipate any increase in foreign revenues from their removal. Presumably profits would rise, however. Half of the firms surveyed did expect revenues to increase, but the anticipated increase was surprisingly small—$1 billion in total, plus another $2 billion in associated merchandise trade exports.[28]

6.6.3 Why Liberalization Is Opposed

Looking at specific barriers and speculating on the prospects for limiting their future use ignore the more basic question of why most countries have responded coolly to U.S. proposals for liberalization of trade in services. If the experience with merchandise trade is indicative, agreeing to eliminate specific barriers without regard to their domestic objectives usually means that other policies, possibly less desirable from an efficiency perspective, will be substituted in short order.

Obviously, all the same kinds of economic and political considerations—employment, adjustment, regional effects, and so forth—that arise with liberalization of merchandise trade are equally relevant for trade in services. But some additional domestic considerations appear to be more important for services as a group than for goods.

First, many types of services, from banking and telecommunications to haircuts and restaurants, are subject to extensive local regulation, either because they are considered essential to national welfare and security or because they have important potential effects on consumer health and safety. Whatever their motive, regulatory barriers typically ensure above-normal profits for successful entrants, making current domestic providers particularly reluctant to share the market and potential foreign providers particularly keen to enter.

Moreover, local regulation is likely to act as a barrier to international competition even when the regulation is applied evenhandedly to both domestic and foreign firms; the same requirement is often more difficult and costly for a foreign firm to meet because of language barriers or general unfamiliarity with local legal and administrative procedures. But regulation often discriminates explicitly between domestic firms and foreign-controlled suppliers.

For some particular sectors deemed "essential," a foreign presence is considered undesirable or even unacceptable. For example, the United States prohibits foreign ownership of radio and television stations, while Brazil and Japan exclude foreign firms in some telecommunications sectors. Many countries provide essential services via a public monopoly. Even the United States maintains a government monopoly in postal service.

For such sectors there are really two different cases for excluding foreign firms. In some instances a nation may desire to maintain permanent local control over a particular sector, even if this control comes at a cost in terms of efficiency. Presumably a national security motive is present in most such cases. For a second group, the need of "temporary" protection is justified by a variant of the usual infant industry argument.

The perceived need to protect infant service industries is an important factor underlying the strong resistance of some developing nations to GATT negotiations on services. Financial services as well as telecommunications and associated information-based services are frequently protected, with the goal of nurturing a domestic provider not yet able to confront international competition. However, because these services are important intermediate inputs, protection raises costs and lowers efficiency for all the using industries, thus lowering the odds of survival for other, perhaps more promising, infants.

As noted in section 6.3, however, it is theoretically possible for liberalization to reduce national welfare unless a country is able on average to expand its outputs in activities with scale economies. This condition is unlikely to be met for most developing nations, so the theoretical case for developing-country liberalization of service sectors is not airtight.

Finally, some countries generally concerned about foreign influence within their borders see liberalization of "trade" in services as the start of a general assault on national policies restricting direct foreign investment. Their alarm has some justification, since U.S. firms pressing for expanded markets abroad rarely distinguish between opportunities for trade and opportunities for affiliate sales.

Overall, as in the case of merchandise trade, a variety of arguments may be used to justify barriers against foreign competition in service sectors. But, as in the case of merchandise trade, the "national interest" arguments for continued protection are put forward mainly by those whose own commercial interests would be threatened by liberalization.

6.7   Where and How to Negotiate on Services

Although the United States has succeeded in putting the services issue on the agenda for the new GATT round, many questions concerning future U.S. negotiations in this area remain to be answered. This section considers two. First, what are the merits of pursuing the services issue in other bilateral or multilateral forums, in addition to or instead of the GATT? Second, what are the alternative strategies that might be used to make progress on this admittedly difficult issue?

6.7.1   Where to Negotiate on Services

As a practical matter, it is too late to wonder whether the United States is prepared to lead international negotiations on service issues in the GATT.[29] For better or worse, the decision has been made and cannot be reversed without substantial loss of credibility for the United States. Gaps in knowledge, both analytical and empirical, remain significant but are beginning to be filled. However, the Uruguay round of GATT negotiations is expected to extend over a number of years. In the meantime, what might be accomplished by pursuing some of the same issues with selected trading partners in other forums?

Since progress on service issues will require countries to grapple with a whole new set of nontariff distortions of international commerce, bilateral negotiations offer an opportunity to explore these issues with just one partner. In the case of Canada, where broader bilateral negotiations on a free trade area are already in progress, there is a natural opportunity to test out possible negotiating strategies. One special complication in this case is Canada's provincial regulatory structure. However, given the generally cordial relationship between the United States and Canada and the high degree of integration of the two economies, any approach that fails in this test case can probably be scrapped without trying it out in the GATT.

A second possibility is to work initially within a group of countries with a particular interest in pursuing liberalization in the services area. This has been termed a "minilateral" approach or a "GATT of the like-minded." Since the developing nations have expressed the greatest reservations about services, such a group would presumably be drawn from the OECD, or the OECD might become the formal sponsor of a parallel negotiation.[30] Agreements reached within the group would have a conditional most-favored-nation (MFN) status, applying only to the nations agreeing to abide by the terms.[31] However, others could join the group later by agreeing to the same terms.

While the benefits of learning by doing in a smaller negotiation are real, there are some risks as well. Bilateral or minilateral negotiations create preferential trading arrangements that become vested interests. This may reduce the motivation of some GATT members to press for broader and more inclusive agreements later on (Aho and Aronson 1985). Another danger is that the terms of a bilateral agreement with, say, Canada, may be difficult to extend to other trading partners with stronger comparative advantage in certain sectors (e.g., transport, construction).

6.7.2 How to Negotiate on Services

Here the basic choice is whether to organize the discussions along sectoral lines (e.g., insurance, telecommunications) or to attempt as in the Tokyo round to develop codes that cover particular types of policies (e.g., subsidies, government procurement policies) for all or most types of traded services.[32] Given the vast universe of policies that impinge on international services competition, it is not possible to handle all relevant issues through the second approach, so the question is really about the degree of emphasis accorded to each.

One strategy to prevent the task from becoming unmanageable is to begin by extending as far as possible the current GATT framework on merchandise trade to services transactions. This approach would identify any "easy" liberalization gains from moving negotiating efforts into virgin territory. At the same time, information would be gained about the important specific issues that do not fall easily into a framework paralleling that for goods.

Another important issue is the extent to which liberalization in service trade is linked to issues on goods. The two-track compromise agreed on at Punta del Este suggests that linkage will be minimal, at least at the start. Unfortunately, complete separation places limits on the efficiency gains attainable through multilateral negotiations, and especially potential north-south agreements to make liberalization in labor-intensive manufactured goods in the north the quid pro quo for high-technology and services liberalization in the south.

One final strategic issue concerns timing. The conventional wisdom is that the pressure of deadlines and media attention can help negotiators to reach mutually beneficial compromises that might otherwise prove elusive. With perhaps a decade of slogging through difficult issues ahead, there is need for some short-term goals where progress can be made, and announced, sooner.

6.8   Summing Up

The United States has indeed become a "service economy"—and so have most U.S. trading partners, both industrialized and developing. But although domestic employment at home and abroad is now heavily concentrated in the service industries, tangible goods still dominate international trade. Moreover, the services that absorb most of the labor force at home are not the same services that account for most international service transactions or even the ones ripe for global expansion in the near future.

Thus, the need to press forward on liberalization of services must be justified along other lines—for example, to maintain the forward momentum in multilateral negotiations or to restore domestic support in the United States for open international markets. Yet these arguments seem shaky if services are allowed to displace important unfinished business in the traditional areas of GATT efforts, especially safeguards. Also, if U.S. service firms are interested mainly in expanding sales abroad of their foreign affiliates rather than exports, as the greater importance of the former in total revenues suggests, then the resulting base for domestic support may be rather narrow.

There are important positive aspects to bringing services into the GATT, however. Despite its sometimes disappointing record, the GATT remains the only international organization where rules are taken seriously.[33] Because services would be a new issue in the GATT, there could be some easy gains to be made initially; in merchandise trade, only the hard things are left to tackle. Consideration of services would necessitate greater attention to the links between trade and direct investment and between trade and international movements of labor—further complicating the task of GATT, but in a way likely to serve its ultimate objective of pushing the world economy toward greater efficiency. And, finally, because goods and services are inextricably (and increasingly) intertwined in real transactions, progress on merchandise trade will surely be slowed unless trade negotiators begin to think seriously about services too.

Notes

The author is indebted to Robert E. Baldwin and J. David Richardson for helpful suggestions, to Robert E. Lipsey and Irving B. Kravis for detailed comments on an earlier version of the paper, and to the Ford Foundation for research support.

1. With a few minor exceptions, the rules of the GATT currently apply only to merchandise trade. Outside the GATT framework, long-established regimes govern international competition in some specific service activities, such as ocean shipping and air transport. However, cartelization rather than liberalization has been the dominant theme. In a few other cases, such as telecommunications, there are sector-specific bodies dealing primarily with regulatory and technical issues and only incidentally with barriers to trade. Also see Stalson 1985, 30–36.

2. See U.S. Trade Representative 1983. This is the national study submitted to the GATT by the United States in December 1983.

3. In U.S. statistics for the domestic economy, "services" are usually defined to include all sectors except manufacturing, construction, mining, and agriculture. Balance of payments accounting conventionally divides current account transactions into merchandise trade and "invisibles." The "services" added to merchandise trade to form the broader "goods and services" balance in the U.S. international accounts are income from foreign investments, military transactions, travel and transportation, and "other services." (The remaining category of "invisible" transaction is unilateral transfers.) The U.S. Department of Commerce uses the term *business services* to refer to travel, transportation, and "other services" as recorded in the U.S. international accounts.

4. In a footnote to a statement by the Committee on Changing International Realities of the National Planning Association endorsing Stalson's generally favorable assessment of the prospects for U.S. negotiations on service issues, John C. Carroll of the Communications Workers of America writes, "I sometimes feel that it is a disservice to the public interest to use the code words of 'barriers to trade in services' to fight for the foreign interests of a handful of large construction, banking, and insurance firms" (Stalson 1985, 7).

5. Optimism about the outcome of trade negotiations almost always reflects a belief that the nation's exports will increase more than its imports. Progress toward liberalization thus typically rests on the shaky foundation of mercantilistic goals and inconsistent expectations, rather than an accurate perception of mutual gains to be achieved through expansion of both exports and imports along lines of comparative advantage.

6. See, for example, U.S. International Trade Commission 1982. The Office of Technology Assessment regards prospective direct benefits from expanded service exports as modest but acknowledges the possibility that exports of

goods may follow from sales of services such as engineering and construction contracts (U.S. Congress, Office of Technology Assessment 1986, 5).

7. Based on an analysis of recent job creation in the United States, the Industrial Union Department of the AFL-CIO concluded that service occupations "experiencing the largest net growth in the number of jobs demand little skill, are only weakly organized into unions, and usually offer little pay— ranging from building custodians to fast food workers. . . . prospects for upward mobility out of these lower rung jobs . . . are slight" (AFL-CIO 1984, 11–12). However, other researchers view growing service-sector employment in a more favorable light. For example, see Lawrence 1984 and Urquhart 1984.

8. However, trade-related investment policies have also been ranked high on the agenda for the new GATT round by U.S. trade negotiators, along with a third "new" issue, protection of intellectual property.

9. See table 6.3. Construction, considered a service activity in the international accounts of the United States, is included in the goods-producing sectors in the tabulation of domestic employment by industry.

10. For more extensive discussion of the distinguishing properties of services as economic activities, see Bhagwati 1984; Deardorff 1985; Gray 1983; Kravis 1983; Sampson and Snape 1985; and Stern and Hoekman 1986.

11. A large part of the theoretical literature on international trade deals with the extent to which indirect exchange of factors via trade can achieve the same efficiency benefits in production and consumption as free international movements of the factors themselves.

12. The following discussion is based on Stern and Hoekman 1986.

13. What is technologically required needs to be distinguished from what is cost efficient or profitable. This distinction is elaborated in the examples below.

14. Most analyses of international competition in services exclude factor services, that is, the employment abroad of a country's labor or capital by a foreign firm.

15. The theory of comparative advantage explains the source of mutual gains to nations from international trade and, in particular, shows that a nation can gain from trade even if it is at an absolute disadvantage in all productive activities. The theory of comparative advantage does not suggest that every resident of a given nation will be made better off by trade. Actual trade flows are determined by international competitiveness, of which comparative advantage is just one element, along with exchange rates and national policies. Comparative advantage is a reliable predictor of a nation's trade flows only when exchange rates are consistent with globally balanced trade and the influence of trade-distorting policies is minor.

16. "Large" refers here to the size of the market for a given product. This tendency has been termed "false comparative advantage" by Lancaster 1979. Also see Helpman and Krugman 1985, 152.

17. This problem was discussed by Frank Graham more than half a century ago. For a modern treatment, see Helpman and Krugman 1985.

18. Housing services in table 6.8 include the imputed rental value of owner-occupied housing, but transportation services does not include a similar imputed value for motor vehicles.

19. This definition is the one used in the employment data published by the Bureau of Labor Statistics. Business services is sometimes defined more broadly to include all services purchased mainly by businesses rather than households, adding in particular business-oriented financial and communication services. Also, the U.S. Department of Commerce uses the term *business services* in its balance of payments reporting to refer to all nonfactor services traded internationally.

20. Like the broader services category, employment in business services includes workers at every level of skill. See Howe 1986 for a detailed assessment of employment growth in the business services industry.

21. Urquhart 1984. Men hired in the service sector were more likely to have worked in the goods-producing sector rather than not to have worked at all during the previous year.

22. A related issue is the extent to which firms in service industries earn rents, which are shared with workers through higher wages. Using microdata, Krueger and Summers (1986) show that most service industries are low paying even when the usual adjustments are made for worker characteristics. The exceptions include banking and insurance, industries that are characterized by substantial barriers to entry.

23. Final demands are typically met by a combination of goods and services selected on the basis of both income and relative prices. Intermediate-input service needs are met by direct employment or by purchases from specialized service-providers. Again, the choice depends on relative prices. The observed long-term correlation between per capita income growth and the importance of service employment necessarily reflects changes in relative prices as well as systematic effects of rising income (Kravis 1983; Kravis, Heston, and Summers 1983). The same is of course true for cross-country comparisons in a given year.

24. Some developing nations are belatedly recognizing their strong comparative advantage in agricultural production as well as the concentration of poverty in rural areas. A few are attempting to alter domestic policies that have favored industrial production at the expense of agriculture.

25. In practice, many service exports are misreported or unreported. Some service exports are bundled together with merchandise exports (e.g., computer equipment and software). For these, the total value of the bundle is reported as a merchandise export. In others including tourism, reported amounts are based on voluntary surveys with low response rates. Some categories of service exports are estimated from conceptually flawed or incomplete data, while still others are simply omitted. For further details on measurement issues, see U.S. Congress, Office of Technology Assessment 1986 and references cited there.

26. The existence of scale economies is, of course, not unique to for-profit activities. Both health and education, largely organized on a not-for-profit basis, offer similar examples of potential benefits from "exporting" services in excess of the share in total revenues.

27. The small GATT secretariat has remained an important voice for liberal policies, but these efforts have had scant influence on the actions of major nations.

28. U.S. International Trade Commission 1982, 4–7. This document also provides information by industry for each of the fourteen service industries.

29. Krommenacker 1984 provides an insider's evaluation of the potential role of the GATT in liberalizing trade in services.

30. The OECD has already sponsored considerable consultative work on services. See Schott 1983 for an evaluation of OECD initiatives and the relative merits of proceeding within the OECD rather than the GATT.

31. Such conditionality represents a departure from the central GATT principle of MFN treatment (nondiscrimination), under which tariff concessions made by any member apply to all other members. However, a similar approach was used in the Tokyo round for the codes of conduct on specific types of nontariff barriers.

32. Strategies for negotiating on services are discussed in greater detail by Aronson and Cowhey 1984; Brock 1982; Gray 1983; Malmgren 1985; Stalson 1985; and Sapir 1985.

33. Not necessarily followed, but at least taken seriously. A good example is the prolonged effort by the United States to find a "GATT-able" variant on its domestic international sales corporation (DISC) device for subsidizing exports.

References

AFL-CIO. Industrial Union Department. 1984. *Deindustrialization and the two tier society: Challenges for an industrial policy.* Washington, D.C.: Industrial Union Department, AFL-CIO.

Aho, C. Michael, and Jonathan David Aronson. 1985. *Trade talks.* New York: Council on Foreign Relations.

Aronson, Jonathan, and Peter Cowhey. 1984. *Trade in services: A case for open markets.* Washington, D.C.: American Enterprise Institute.

Bergsten, C. Fred, Thomas Horst, and Theodore H. Moran. 1978. *American multinationals and American interests.* Washington, D.C.: Brookings Institution.

Bhagwati, Jagdish. 1984. Splintering and disembodiment of services and developing nations. *World Economy.* 7:133–44.

Brock, William A. 1982. A simple plan for negotiating on trade in services. *World Economy* 5:229–40.

Deardorff, Alan V. 1985. Comparative advantage and international trade and investment in services. In *Trade and investment in services: Canada/U.S. perspectives,* ed. Robert M. Stern. Toronto: Ontario Economic Council.

Feketekuty, Geza, and Lawrence B. Krause. 1986. Services and high technology goods in the new GATT round. In *Pacific trade policy cooperation: Goals and Initiatives,* 87–99. Korea Development Institute.

Feldman, Robert A., and Allen J. Proctor. 1983. U.S. international trade in services. *Federal Reserve Bank of New York Quarterly Review* 8 (1):30–36.

Gray, H. Peter. 1983. A negotiating strategy for trade in services. *Journal of World Trade Law* 17:377–87.

Helpman, Elhanan, and Paul R. Krugman. 1985. *Market structure and foreign trade.* Cambridge, Mass.: MIT Press.

Howe, Wayne J. 1986. The business services industry sets pace in employment growth. *Monthly Labor Review* 109 (April) 29–36.

Kravis, Irving B. 1983. Services in the domestic economy and in world transactions. National Bureau of Economic Research Working Paper No. 1124. May.

Kravis, Irving B., Alan W. Heston, and Robert Summers. 1983. The share of services in economic growth. In *Global Econometrics: Essays in honor of Lawrence R. Klein,* ed. F. G. Adams and B. Hickman, 188–218. Cambridge, Mass.: MIT Press.

Krommenacker, Raymond J. 1984. *World-traded services: The challenge for the eighties.* Dedham, Mass.: Artech House.

Krueger, Alan B., and Lawrence H. Summers. 1986. Reflections on the inter-industry wage structure. Harvard Institute of Economic Research Discussion Paper No. 1252. July.

Kutscher, Ronald E., and Valerie A. Personick. 1986. Deindustrialization and the shift to services. *Monthly Labor Review* 109 (June):3–13.

Lancaster, Kelvin. 1979. *Variety, equity, and efficiency.* New York: Columbia University Press.

Lawrence, Robert Z. 1984. *Can America compete?* Washington, D.C.: Brookings Institution.

Lipsey, Robert E., and Irving B. Kravis. 1985. The competitive position of U.S. manufacturing firms. *Banca Nazionale del Lavoro Quarterly Review* 153:127–54.

Malmgren, Harald B. 1985. Negotiating international rules for trade in services. *World Economy* 8:11–26.

Price Waterhouse. 1985. Exporting services: A Fortune 500 view. *Export Today* 1:53–57.

Sampson, Gary P., and Richard H. Snape. 1985. Identifying the issues in trade in services. *World Economy* 8:171–82.

Sapir, André. 1985. North-south issues in trade in services. *World Economy* 8:27–42.

Schott, Jeffrey J. 1983. Protectionist threat to trade and investment in services. *World Economy* 6:195–214.

Stalson, Helena. 1985. *U.S. service exports and foreign barriers: An agenda for negotiations.* Washington, D.C.: National Planning Association.

Stern, Robert M. 1985. Global dimensions of international trade and investment in services. In *Trade and investment in Services: Canada/U.S. Perspectives,* ed. Robert M. Stern. Toronto: Ontario Economic Council.

Stern, Robert M., and Bernard M. Hoekman. 1986. GATT negotiations on services: Analytical issues and data needs. Research Seminar in International Economics, University of Michigan. Seminar Discussion Paper No. 189.

Urquhart, Michael. 1984. The employment shift to services: Where did it come from? *Monthly Labor Review* 107 (April):15–22.

U.S. Congress. Office of Technology Assessment. 1986. *Trade in services: Exports and foreign revenues—Special report.* Washington, D.C.: GPO.

U.S. Department of Commerce. 1986. *United States trade: Performance in 1985 and outlook.* Washington, D.C.: GPO.

U.S. Department of Labor. 1985. *Handbook of labor statistics.* Washington, D.C.: GPO.

U.S. International Trade Commission. 1982. *The relationship of exports in selected U.S. service industries to U.S. merchandise exports.* USITC Publication 1290. Washington, D.C.: U.S. International Trade Commission.

U.S. Trade Representative. 1983. *U.S. national study on trade in services: A submission by the United States government to the General Agreement on Tariffs and Trade.* Washington, D.C.: Office of the U.S. Trade Representative.

Whalley, John. 1986. Some reflections on the current trade in services debate. University of Western Ontario.

2. *Maurice R. Greenberg*
The United States and World Services Trade

My company, AIG, is the largest international insurance organization in the world—with thirty thousand employees and $20 billion in assets. We do business in 140 countries and jurisdictions. In every one of them, insurance is a highly regulated activity; when governments even *think* about policies that affect trade in services, we feel the heat.

Direct economic interest is one reason I care about services, but there is also another, bigger reason for my concern over trade in services. It is such an important area of U.S. economic activity, yet has gotten so little attention. We, as a nation, have a tremendous economic stake in the health of our service sector—a stake that is only now starting to be understood and appreciated.

Unfortunately, we are well past the point at which understanding and appreciation are enough. As in other trade areas, the growth of intense worldwide competition and the spread of nontariff barriers have hurt U.S. economic interests in services trade—and will continue to hurt us in the absence of firm, direct, and immediate action on our part and on the part of our principal trading partners.

My feelings of alarm are not eased when a labor leader describes the service economy as fast food and video games; when the head of one of the world's biggest banks describes the service economy as one where we take in each other's laundry; when a former presidential candidate describes the service economy as one where Americans serve hamburgers and sweep floors.

One of the reasons services have gotten such short shrift is that they are hard to understand. What is a "service" anyway? You cannot see it, touch it, store it, or measure it in any meaningful way that is also easily understood. We are dealing here with a "product"—in quotes—that is really a process; something that was once integral to the production and distribution of goods—organizing inputs, throughputs, and outputs—that has been broken away into any number of separate, distinct, profit-producing activities.

A lot of service industries have been around for a long time. In my own business, even Lloyd's was a latecomer: insurers were writing covers on caravan goods when Hammurabi ruled Babylonia four thousand years ago. What makes today different is the rapid growth of the telecommunications infrastructure, the integration of the world's capital markets, and the shifting basis of comparative advantage from natural endowments to human resources.

Today, we talk routinely of world cars, outsourcing, and focused manufacturing as if they had been around forever. In fact, they are recent developments, made possible by the vast, technology-driven expansion of the service sector. Microchips and microwaves have given us the ability to allocate and manage resources globally, on a scale and to an extent that none of us could have imagined when John Kennedy was president.

That ability to deliver services globally has, in turn, fueled economic transformation and division of labor on a global scale—a degree of economic integration that boggles the mind, occurring at a pace that leaves us breathless. In turn, this quantum leap in economic development has both multiplied demand for services and dramatically increased supply of the necessary ingredients for a modern service economy—technology, expertise, and capital.

World trade figures reflect this fundamental change. In 1976, service transactions represented just over one-quarter of total world trade; in 1985, they accounted for 30 percent.

At the same time, the U.S. position in worldwide services trade has slipped significantly in a number of ways. For one thing, the dramatic growth in service exports—over 400 percent between 1970 and 1980—has come to a grinding halt. Since 1980, our exports, measured in current dollars, have grown only 26 percent—that is actually a net loss of almost 8 percent when corrected for inflation.

We have also seen significant erosion of our market share. Up through the early 1970s, U.S. service exports accounted for a dependable 25 percent of the worldwide total. In recent years, they have averaged 20 percent or less.

To our credit, services—including investment income—have been our best trade performer. In every year since 1972, services have shown a surplus. In five of those years, the surplus was even big enough to offset deficits in the merchandise account. That, of course, was when our merchandise deficits were a small fraction of their present size.

A lot of the glimmer fades, however, when we take a closer look. For one thing, our overall trade performance is deteriorating significantly. Since 1981, when we hit a high of $41 billion, our overall surplus has steadily fallen to its current level of around $24 billion.

Most of the decline comes not from eroding exports, but from explosive growth in service imports—growth that is likely to continue. Our transformation to net debtor status is going to increase that pressure, since every penny of the interest we pay to our foreign creditors—and every penny of profit on U.S. operations they repatriate—counts as a service import.

But most disturbing of all is the deterioration of our trade in business services—finance, brokerage, insurance, professional services and so on—the growth industries of the service sector. In 1981, our peak year, business services generated a surplus of $10 billion. In 1985, that figure was down to less than half a billion. Last year's numbers could well show deficit. Stated in other terms, our share of that market has fallen from almost 15 percent in 1973 to just under 8 percent in 1984. However you look at it, we are not in good shape.

Before we all get terminally depressed, however, let me hasten to point out that these numbers are, at best, imprecise. Despite the best efforts of that huge statistical machine in Washington, we know very little about our true performance.

Nobody ever paid very much attention to giving services their due. We were a manufacturing economy at the end of World War II—or at least we thought we were—and statistically speaking we were going to stay a manufacturing economy. Last September, the congressional Office of Technology Assessment suggested that our service exports between 1982 and 1984 may have been underestimated by as much as $128 billion, but nobody really knows, because nobody keeps close track of the numbers.

How can we make policy if we do not know what we are dealing with?

One thing I do know, and which we all know without a doubt, is that the United States is very much a service economy—with all due respect to the labor leader, banker, and presidential candidate I quoted earlier. Well over two-thirds of our GNP comes out of services. Three-quarters of our work force is directly employed in service industries: the actual proportion probably exceeds 90 percent when we include service employees in the goods-producing sector—managers, planners, accountants, R&D personnel, and so on. Forty percent of our exports are services; a quarter of our imports are services.

America's overwhelming national interest in the strength of the service sector is self-evident. Service industries have a critical role to play not only in contributing to the vitality of our international economic performance but also—and perhaps especially—in enhancing the efficiency and global competitiveness of our goods-producing industries as well.

One way we can work toward strengthening our service sector is by improving our ability to compete in the global marketplace for services.

There is nothing fundamentally wrong with the U.S. service sector. Our technological base, our human resource base, and our access to capital are second to none. Indeed, if anything, the vastness and complexity of our domestic marketplace have given us a substantial lead in the learning curve of resource allocation and infrastructure management that lie at the core of service activities.

So why haven't we been able to translate that head start into sustained leadership in the world marketplace? In a word, the reason is protectionism. By their very nature, services are among the world's most closely regulated economic activities. Traditionally, governments have granted themselves tight control over access to their financial, communications, and internal transport markets.

That is all well and good, so long as a national government is willing and able to live in isolation from the rest of the world community. Maybe Albania can do that, but I cannot think of many others. The fact is that the integration of world markets, deregulation, and the wholesale privatization of former public and quasi-public monopolies have effectively demolished whatever rationale may have existed for constraints on market access in most, if not all, nonmilitary economic activities.

Yet such constraints not only exist, but have grown perniciously over the last several years. As in merchandise trade, trade in services has become a viper's nest of governmentally inspired economic distortion and obstruction at every turn. Not that this is surprising: increased competition is a natural and predictable consequence of the substantial and continued growth in both the demand for services and capacity I noted earlier.

The problem is that this license to obstruct with impunity is a direct result of the exclusion of services from the multilateral trading regime. And it is hurting the United States and others committed to open markets.

Without negotiated rules, we are left with an ad hoc system of expedient means based on the narrowest of national interests. Now, I am certainly not arguing against self-interest: if anything, self-interest is the only thing that lets agreements work. What I am arguing against is short-term, unilateral action that inevitably leads to long-term, multilateral conflict.

Obviously, we have made some progress. The Reagan administration's successful effort to get services onto the GATT agenda has built a strong multilateral consensus on the need for negotiated rules and set a major precedent as well. At the same time, however, we cannot forget that last September's success at Punta del Este came only after six years of incessant jawboning and arm-twisting on the part of William Brock, Clayton Yeutter, and dozens of others in every forum imaginable.

One voice that made a great deal of difference is the Coalition of Service Industries, a group formed in 1982, which I served as chairman until last year. The purpose of the coalition is to build public awareness of the role of service industries in the U.S. economy and to speak out on public policy issues affecting the U.S. service sector.

So far, we have done well. Among other things, the coalition supported passage of the Omnibus Trade Act of 1984, made a strong commitment to reducing barriers to trade in services at the 1984 London

Economic Summit and to completing the U.S. National Study on Services, and experienced success at Punta del Este.

However, let me also emphasize that our initiative, precedent-setting though it was, is still only an agenda victory. If the Kennedy and Tokyo rounds are any indication, we are not going to see Draft Codes, let alone signed agreements, for a long time—perhaps, if things go well, by the turn of the century.

This is not to dismiss GATT. It is an organization that has contributed a great deal to our trading system and still has an important contribution to make. But its potential for contribution may not be strongest in the services area. I would much rather see a series of linked bilateral or multilateral agreements that could eventually be integrated into a broader multilateral code subject to further negotiation in the GATT forum.

Certainly the constituencies exist. As a key player in services, Japan was the first to support our initiative. The United Kingdom has also understood its stake in services—what they call "invisible trade"—for a long time. As a result of the national studies on services mandated by the GATT ministerial conference in 1982, we have discovered that France is an even bigger exporter of services than the United Kingdom: as a whole, EEC service exports are more than three times the size of ours. And speaking of blocs, the ASEAN countries are also starting to recognize their stake in services. I think most of those governments would be willing to negotiate under the right conditions.

The executive power exists: The Omnibus Trade Act of 1984 not only opened the way for bilateral sectoral trade agreements in services and investment; it also strengthened the president's power to impose sanctions for unfair trade practices in services.

And there are precedents as well: a few years ago, for example, Canada offered to open negotiations around a sectoral free trade agreement on traded computer services, and services are included in the U.S.-Israel free trade agreement of 1985.

If we can build a framework of bilateral agreements on a services regime, we will be more than halfway—much more than halfway—toward full GATT sanction. But before we can enter into any kind of international negotiations, we have to get our own act together and that is not going to be easy.

The first thing we must do is decide that we are going to speak with one voice and then execute the decision. Right now, there are at least five executive branch departments that have some say over trade policy—Commerce, Agriculture, State, Defense, and the trade representative's office. A few years ago, Donald Regan and Malcolm Baldridge floated the idea of a Department of Trade, but it died. Recently, Dan Rostenkowski raised the idea again as part of his trade bill. I think we need to do it, regardless of the turf battles these things invariably create.

Another necessary step is beefing up our collection and analysis of service-sector economic data. The Omnibus Trade Act of 1984 mandated such changes, but the various departments have been slow to respond. Three years after the act's passage, for example, it is still impossible to get more than the sketchiest annual figures on trade in business services. We will not be able to make realistic, workable policy.

The last thing we have to do before we sit down at the negotiating table is to make some fundamental decisions about the kind of agreements we want and then adopt appropriate strategy and tactics. If we want a single broad agreement, we have to decide that. If we want a "constitution" for services trade that sets out some general rules, plus a series of sectoral codes that can be signed, we have to decide that too. The one thing we cannot do is go in unprepared and negotiate ad hoc.

There are a number of pressing issues on the services agenda. From my perspective, the most pressing of these is national treatment—the right of foreign service businesses to receive fair and equal treatment under the laws of the host country. At present, governments can, and do, discriminate against service businesses in ways that are clearly prohibited in the agreements that govern trade in goods. Those practices seriously impair our ability to compete on a level playing field.

Discrimination can take place in many forms: the most common are in fiscal policy, taxation, and government procurement practices. Discriminatory fiscal policy generally works by setting up unequal and onerous requirements for foreign businesses. In some countries, for example, foreign insurers are obliged to make deposits of assets that are not required of domestic insurers—in situations that the government specifies.

Taxation is also an easy way to discriminate. In several European countries, foreign insurers are required to pay taxes on premium income, while domestic companies pay taxes on profits. In another European country, premium taxes can be 400 percent greater for foreign insurers than for their domestic competitors.

One of the great successes of the Tokyo round was the agreement on rules for opening up government procurement of merchandise. We need the same thing in services. Today, foreign insurers are still methodically shut out of the bidding on government-sponsored projects, both at home and in third countries. They are systematically excluded from subsidized or guaranteed government export credits—even when those credits can benefit domestic industries.

Nor is the insurance industry alone. Any number of industry and government surveys show that other service industries face the same kinds of discriminatory and unequal treatment in foreign markets. To counteract this, we have to insist that any agreement guarantees, to the largest extent possible, the right of market access and the principles of transparency and national treatment.

In conclusion, I want to reemphasize the need for negotiated rules on trade in services. Such an agreement would benefit not just the service sector but every sector of the U.S. economy—manufacturing, mining, and agriculture—by improving efficiency and enhancing competitiveness. It would strengthen our trade position immeasurably by establishing a level playing field on which we can compete. And it would make a positive contribution to the further integration of the world economy.

Our success or failure at the negotiation table will depend on how we trade access to our markets for access to other markets. Most of our trading partners appreciate the size and wealth of our economy and understand the implicit power of the leverage we possess. It is time we understand and appreciate them as well.

3. Lionel H. Olmer
The Role of Services

A couple of hundred years ago Adam Smith, the eighteenth-century father of classical economics (or so I am told by ideologues among Reagan administration policy officials past and present) is said to have criticized the role of services in the economy. He wrote that services are "unproductive of any value because they do not fix or realize themselves in any permanent subject or vendible commodity which endures after labor is passed." A service, he remarked, "perishes in the very instant of its production."

I believe, to the contrary, that services are important and increasingly so. The U.S. economy seems to be driven more and more by the services sector rather than by manufacturing or agriculture, both in terms of economic output and employment. Indeed, the crown jewel in the Reagan administration's display of accomplishments, the "great American job machine," which has produced 13 million new jobs over the last six years, is a record of truly glittering proportions compared with other industrial nations, particularly those in Western Europe where no new jobs have been added over a ten-year period. None of this additional employment has been in the manufacturing sector; virtually all of it has been created in the services: since 1980, retailing, which now represents 16 percent of the U.S. work force, has experienced a 20 percent increase, and finance and real estate have each experienced roughly a 25 percent rise in employment during the six-year period. These three categories alone, retailing, finance, and real estate, now account for more than one out of every five jobs in America, while all services comprise three of every four jobs in our economy. Because there has been no increase in jobs in manufacturing, as the economy grows, manufacturing employment will make up a smaller and smaller percentage of the total.

The role and significance of services in our economy are neither well understood nor accurately measured and evaluated. Part of this problem stems from an archaic statistical system which has not kept pace with changes in our economy and does not provide adequate data. For example, an emerging pattern in recent years has been for manufacturing companies to remove from their direct-hire payrolls workers needed for custodial, security, and cafeteria services and instead to contract out to specialty firms for the performance of those functions. There might not be any net change in the number of employees, but U.S. labor statistics would reflect a reduction in manufacturing employment and an increase in services jobs. The extent of this trend has not been determined. On another level, and notwithstanding Adam Smith's peroration, some services may exert a strong "pull" on manufacturing sales; that is, the performance of a service, such as engineering consulting, may result in sales contracts for equipment specified as a consequence of the engineering service. This phenomenon has been experienced often in connection with large construction contracts, in the developing world especially.

In the field of informatics, that is, the integration of telecommunications, computers, and related services, the relative value of software continues to escalate in comparison with hardware. Among some leading manufacturers of digital telephone switching equipment—machines that receive, store, relay, and forward hundreds of thousands of telephone calls, computer linkups, and video signals simultaneously—fully 80 percent of the cost is in the software that permits the equipment to operate, and only 20 percent of the total cost of production lies in the machinery. One switch manufacturer has told me his company's objective is to "drive down the cost of the hardware to close to zero, and we have a good chance of reaching this goal within five years." The production of the switching software for computers and telecommunications equipment and the design of microchips and related tasks are classified as services.

Finally, it can be said with some justification that the world of finance has overshadowed the manufacturing sector in terms of overall importance to national economies. Financial flows exceed the value of trade in goods by more than twenty to one. Finance is clearly the lubricant that makes possible the smooth flow of international commerce. In the absence of credit, trade grinds to a virtual halt: over a three-year period in the early 1980s, U.S. exports to six countries in Latin America suffered a $17 billion decline mostly because financing was simply not available as lending institutions panicked in the face of the enormous buildup of foreign debt by these countries. The impact on the U.S. trading community generally, and in particular among export-related industry in south Florida, was staggering. And so it is fair to state that financial services to a great degree underpin manufacturing jobs and the performance of U.S. companies in international trade.

Having declared that I believe services are increasingly significant yet not well understood and that their contribution to the manufacturing sector may be underestimated, let me now put a different perspective on the role of services in the U.S. economy. I shall make four points:

1. The export potential of services in relation to international trade in goods has been exaggerated, and thus the importance of services in the context of America's staggering trade and current account deficits is being vastly overstated.

2. The prospects are dim for achieving a more open and liberal regime of rules to guide world trade in services, as for example through the new round of multinational negotiations initiated in September 1986 under the auspices of the General Agreement on Tariffs and Trade (GATT).

3. Yet even if a GATT agreement on services is not possible to achieve, say, over the next five years, and even though the value of services exports is relatively small, the effort to liberalize markets and regulations is still worthwhile.

4. The United States, however, would be better advised to place greater emphasis on bilateral and sector-specific negotiations rather than on those that are multilateral and generic in character.

The size and pervasiveness of the U.S. trade deficit (we are now experiencing a deficit even in high-technology trade, a field in which we had long thought ourselves preeminent) has finally aroused the body politic and convinced virtually everyone in and out of government that the United States has a severe problem. The problem will not be corrected by market forces but through negotiation on an "even playing field" on which U.S. businessmen are allowed to compete on terms equivalent to those permitted to foreigners in the U.S. marketplace. Nor will it be solved merely by encouraging faster economic growth in major industrialized countries or by some magic stroke that would eliminate the debt and interest payment obligations of less developed countries so that they could, presumably, buy more U.S. goods and services. No, the realization has taken hold that the United States cannot export its way back to a balance of accounts.

Some argue that, in the end, accounts will balance "because they must," that when foreigners cease loaning money to the United States, the U.S. foreign debt will increase even faster (it is already larger than any other single country's external debt and arguably within a few years will be larger than the combined debt of all other nations in the world) and the value of our currency will plummet, making U.S. goods price competitive in both world markets and our own market. I am not so sanguine about this unhappy forecast! Price competitiveness is only one factor in the sale of manufactures: market presence, technological superiority, quality, and service weigh heavily in the decision-making calculus of most purchasers. In some sectors, once a presence has been established, it is extremely difficult to dislodge even with an offer of significant cost savings.

Although statistics on trade in services are inadequate, and even to a degree misleading, an examination of our economic accounts is nonetheless revealing of the relative unimportance and lack of potential contribution by services to the resolution of the overwhelming deficits we confront. The most comprehensive yardstick of international economic activity is the *current account,* which includes the total of U.S. trade and other transactions in goods and services. The current account is comprised of five component parts: the *merchandise trade* account which measures the exchange of goods but not services; the *business services* account which is the aggregation of all services; the *international investment income* account; the *other goods and services* account which measures mostly government transactions; and the *unilateral transfers* account which is comprised almost entirely of payments to U.S. citizens living abroad. Table 6.14 shows how the Department of Commerce reports the performance of these various accounts for 1986.

A closer focus on the 1986 *business services* account accomplishes two purposes (see table 6.15): it demonstrates that little comfort should be drawn from believing that success in trade in services will do more than contribute at the margin to a turnaround of our deficits; more important, it underscores the critical primacy of trade in goods and the burden on the manufacturing sector[1] for any serious reduction in the current account imbalance.

The point is that the largest categories in the business services account have nothing whatever to do with the substance or rhetoric associated with the popular discourse on services trade as the wave of the future.[2] And the part of the account that does deal with insurance, engineering consulting, financial management, and the like amounts to a very small fraction of the U.S. trade picture, hardly enough to make a difference in the context of present and foreseeable economic realities. Indeed, it is reasonable to expect that U.S. service companies will not have an easy time holding on to existing surpluses as, for

Table 6.14   **Current Account (billions of dollars)**

	Imports	Exports	Balance (−$140)
Merchandise trade	398 (CIF)	228	−170
			(−148 FOB)
International investment income	68	91	+23
Unilateral transfers	−15.1	—	−15.1
Business services	45.1	48	+2.9
Other goods and services	13.7	10.2	−3.5

Table 6.15   **Business Services (billions of dollars)**

	Imports (45.3)	Exports (48.2)	Balance (+2.9)
Travel	17.8	12.9	−4.9
Passenger fares	6.8	3.3	−3.5
Shipping	16.4	14.7	−1.7
Proprietary rights	—	9.6	+9.6
Other: (communications services, contractor/ consulting fees, financial management, insurance, film rentals, etc.)	4.3	7.7	+3.4

example, Japan becomes a more experienced international center of finance, as Korea increases its participation in international construction projects, and as the U.S. share of world patents continues to decline as it has for a decade.

The government and industry should make substantial efforts to improve the performance and opportunity for U.S. companies to compete in these areas, but we must bear in mind the fact that services cannot come close to bailing us out of our international economic morass.

GATT negotiation on services will produce results that are disappointing at best and possibly harmful if the United States grants concessions and assumes obligation in anticipation of equivalent commitments from its trading partners. This is not farfetched if one looks at the historical record of GATT agreements outside the realm of mutual and balanced tariff reductions. The Tokyo round of GATT negotiations concluded in 1979, and one would be hard pressed to find many (if any!) in the private sector who would testify to the utility or value of the variety of nontariff agreements that those negotiations produced amid much-heralded and highly publicized fanfare (e.g., agreements on government procurement and civil aviation have neither produced significant sales opportunities for U.S. exporters nor dissuaded foreign governments from subsidizing national aerospace companies).

Services trade is by its nature less amenable to multinational negotiations and agreement. Not only are the problems harder to define, but they are often unique to particular regions and countries. The "problems" as we might see them may, from the foreigners point of view, not represent a problem or a barrier to the entry of nondomestic suppliers; rather they exist as a reflection of the history, culture, and custom of the local society.[3] Moreover, the two fundamental principles of GATT are *national treatment,* that is, the proposition that outside competitors will be treated the same as domestic citizens, and *most favored nation* (MFN) *treatment,* which makes available to all GATT members concessions granted to any. Often, national treatment is not enough to provide U.S. suppliers with an opportunity to compete. For example, in countries where government policy that supports monopoly services and paternalistic regulations represents the primary barriers to U.S. services trade, reciprocal market access would require those countries either to adopt the regulatory philosophy for the United States or to otherwise accommodate U.S. concerns in ways that far exceed national treatment. "Reciprocity" is simply unacceptable to most countries as a comprehensive international standard.

Telecommunications are much in the news. The United States has concluded formal negotiations with Japan on terms pronounced "90 percent satisfactory" by segments of the U.S. industry. Talks with Germany, Italy, and France, however, continue with little progress being reported and with high potential for major confrontation looming. Thus, the U.S. Congress, feeling increasingly pressured to do "something" about the U.S. trade deficit lest members be characterized as ineffective, threatens to pass telecommunications reciprocity legislation. Supporters of such legislation, which would force the president to retaliate if bilateral negotiations fail, assert that the breakup of AT&T and the consequent opening up of the U.S. telecommunications markets constitute a unilateral trade concession by the United States. Because most of the rest of the world chooses not to follow the U.S. lead in deregulation, the only way to obtain foreign concessions is to negotiate accommodations of U.S. grievances on a bilateral, sectoral basis. This is not compatible within the framework of MFN, and it is highly unlikely that any nation would open its borders to all members without assurances that each subscribed to and would seriously implement a world agreement. From the point of view of U.S. national interests, we should become more comfortable with the policy of negotiating market access on a bilateral basis even in the face of criticism that it appears to lessen U.S. commitments to a multilateral trade regime.

Private sector companies with major interests that would be advanced through open markets and liberal regulations governing trade in services have done a superb job of maintaining pressure on the U.S. government. The administration has secured an agreement from GATT members to put services on the agenda when serious negotiations begin in Geneva, Switzerland, later this year. Had it not been for U.S. insistence starting at the ministerial level in 1981 and continuing through the start of the Uruguay round in September 1986, more delay would certainly have been the result of intransigence on the part of the leading advanced developed nations, most especially Brazil and India. (It was not long ago, 1982 to be exact, that the EC resisted U.S. blandishments on services and agreed only to "study" the various issues. After four years of desultory "study," the EC seems willing to accept services on the agenda, although this should not be seen as tantamount to embracing the subject enthusiastically.) That in the final hours at Punta del Este a concession was forged and the United States achieved "victory" in the sense of incorporating services as part of the Uruguay declaration on the new GATT round should not obscure the long, torturous road ahead or raise unrealistic expectations for what might be achieved in the course of the next several years of negotiations. Plow ahead we should, but with eyes wide open as to what the costs and benefits might be for *all* American interests and without encouraging the belief that mere grudging acceptance to discuss services in the GATT is close to a great leap forward in U.S. export trade.

The United States needs to press hard for greater market access throughout the many difference service areas and to insist on improved protections for intellectual property rights lest we slowly lose the present advantages and permit by abdication or ineffective negotiations the steady erosion of the existing trade surpluses in these fields. In the case of patents, copyrights, and semiconductor chip design (which was created as a sui generis right by the U.S. Congress in 1984 and which, by dint of strict reciprocal standards embodied in the statute, is slowly being emulated by certain of our leading trade partners to the great advantage of the U.S. high-technology community), tough negotiations, strict enforcement, effective oversight, and dispute settlement are more likely to be productive if pursued bilaterally among like-minded nations perceiving a shared interest in reaching a conclusion.

In summary, there is every reason to push ahead vigorously for expanding services trade through the mechanism of the GATT, but to achieve faster results more meaningful to most U.S. companies, we would probably be better off pressing hardest on a sector-by-sector basis with those countries most likely to perceive a benefit from reaching agreement with the United States. But we must recognize that success in liberalizing services trade will be difficult to achieve and long in coming; above all else we should know that such success would not approach the magnitude of manufactures trade which must remain dominant in the U.S. economy.

Notes

1. This burden on the manufacturing sector will become even heavier as the current account deficit continues to rise in the face of increasing interest payments on U.S. foreign debt and as remittances increase on foreign investment in the United States. Historically in surplus, or at least less in arrears than the merchandise trade balance, the current account deficit will grow to exceed the trade deficit this year or next. It represents roughly 3.3 percent of U.S. GNP in 1986, and if U.S. foreign debt reaches $600–800 billion in the early 1990s, the current account deficit will approach 15 percent of our entire growth national product. Merchandise trade is the only area of our trading economy large enough to make a difference in reducing the deficit.

2. Articles in newspapers, congressional testimony by "experts," and administration witnesses speaking on behalf of services, perhaps in part to reduce pressures on other areas, frequently cite the entire business services account, which lumps together all manner of transactions into what appears to be a respectably large accumulation of trade—$93 billion in 1986. For example, in an op-ed piece in the September 14, 1986, *New York Times,* Leslie Wayne writes of services exports as "the new symbol of America's grandeur abroad. They are the bright spot in an otherwise bleak trade picture [and] represent about one-third of the nation's $800 billion-plus flow of exports and imports." In fact, this "new wave" totaled $12 billion in 1986 with a $3.4 billion surplus, statistics that remain roughly unchanged.

3. This is not to suggest that the United States should accept the status quo, but to make clearer that what we often see as a barrier is something of deep fundamental significance to the foreign country and that its elimination is likely to be several orders of magnitude more difficult (impossible?) than reducing tariffs.

Summary of Discussion

Several issues in the negotiations for freer trade in services were discussed. On the question of whether the forthcoming U.S. trade bill would demand reciprocity or national treatment for services, Lionel Olmer explained that the administration report "Quest for Excellence" is a grab bag of ideas that does not make a clear statement on this point. According to section 301, the absence of reciprocity can be grounds for the initiation of a trade complaint, but there is no definition of reciprocal treatment in the legislation, and in any case, Olmer contended, the presence of such a basis in law would be unreliable.

The aluminum industry deals bilaterally with trade problems whenever possible, reported Charles Parry. GATT promises to be a tidy solution, but in practice it fails. Services in particular will be a farce in GATT. Olmer defended the emphasis on services in the current GATT round as a justifiable strategy for bleeding off congressional protectionist pressures. He noted, however, that Congress has become extremely cynical about GATT. Furthermore, the current GATT negotiations will not be over for several years, and any agreement on services will be very nonspecific in any case. Services should not be neglected, but should be placed in perspective with a realization that manufacturing is by far the dominant traded sector in terms of jobs and the future health of the economy. Thomas Enders supported a pessimistic outlook for service trade negotiations, citing as an example the bilateral negotiations between the United States and Canada, where despite great commitment and similar policies, skilled negotiators, minimal cultural problems, and a systematic attack on the issues, a major step forward cannot be expected.

Maurice Greenberg rejected any analysis of service trade based on available statistics, which he claimed are faulty. His personal experience suggests that the value of service trade is much greater than evoked by the data. No one suggests, according to Greenberg, that service-sector income will balance merchandise trade; both issues are important. He pointed out that there is international support for expanded service trade, particularly from the United Kingdom, France, and Japan and that India and Brazil form the principal resistance. He downplayed the doubts expressed about GATT, suggesting that it is a worthwhile forum for this type of negotiation.

The discussion shifted to questions of the merits of bilateral versus multilateral and codified versus case-by-case approaches. Robert Baldwin suggested that even in the case of trade in manufactured goods, the codes of the Tokyo round were ineffective and the panel dispute resolution not satisfactorily uniform in outcome. In his view, bilateral approaches are a waste of time; a more promising approach would be to attack nontariff barriers in a multilateral forum on an item-by-item basis, with countervailing duties available as the proverbial stick. Greenberg agreed that nontariff barriers cannot be codified and expressed some hope in the application of the section 301 stick as a threat in bilateral negotiations.

Thomas Johnson brought up the case of the regulation of financial transactions, where the problem is not with London or New York but Tokyo. There is a complex set of institutional questions, due to the existence in Japan of a Glass-Steagall-type law. Licensing of U.S. banking institutions to operate directly in securities markets is not prohibited by Japanese law, but the resistance has so far been insurmountable. U.S. regulators are helping, although the admittance by the Fed of three Japanese participants as primary dealers of U.S. government securities might not help because it removes the stick. The U.S. banks need reciprocal, not national, treatment in Japan.

On the question of the importance of the exchange rate in service trade, Maurice Greenberg said that it matters only a little, since in the books the earnings or losses in foreign exchange are balanced out.

Sebastian Edwards raised the issue of what is to be considered fair game in service trade, wondering why LDCs should not claim that housekeeping, for example, is a service. Rudiger Dornbusch suggested that Mexican dentists might want to fly to Texas for the day to export their particular service.

7 International Competition in Agriculture and U.S. Farm Policy

1. *Bruce L. Gardner*
2. *H. B. Atwater, Jr.*
3. *John R. Block*

1. *Bruce L. Gardner*

7.1 Introduction

The United States has been the world leader in agricultural technology and the dominant factor in world grain markets. Between 1970 and 1980 the value of U.S. agricultural exports more than doubled in real terms, with the real value of grain exports more than tripling. Yet by 1986 the export and net trade positions had returned almost to the 1970 levels (table 7.1). What happened?

During the 1980s the following additional and interrelated events have caused concern about the U.S. farm economy: market prices of the grains have fallen about 30 percent (nominal) between 1980 and 1986; the average price of farmland has fallen 21 percent during the period; perhaps 150,000 commercial-scale farms, 20 percent of the total, are under severe financial stress; U.S. farm commodity programs in the 1980s were larger and more costly than ever before in real terms, even than in the 1930s and 1950s.

This paper assesses the available explanations of the decline in agricultural exports, the possible policy responses to the situation, and prospects for the near future.

Some leading hypotheses explaining weakness in the foreign market for U.S. farm products are (1) expansion of world agricultural output abroad; (2) declining (rate of increase of) demand in the developing countries; (3) macroeconomic or financial factors, notably a rise in the foreign exchange value of the dollar and weakened import demand due to events associated with the "debt crisis" in many countries; (4)

Table 7.1   U.S. Agricultural Trade (billions of dollars)

	Exports					Net
Year	Grains[a]	Other Crops[b]	Livestock Products	Total[c]	Imports	Net Trade
1940	1.5	1.5	.7	3.8	9.9	-6.1
1945	2.5	3.2	5.7	14.6	10.8	3.2
1950	3.3	6.3	1.2	12.1	16.7	-4.6
1955	3.3	4.8	3.7	11.8	14.7	-2.9
1960	5.5	6.5	1.9	15.5	12.3	3.2
1965	7.4	6.2	2.4	18.3	12.1	6.2
1970	6.2	6.2	2.2	18.2	14.5	3.7
1971	5.2	7.4	2.2	17.3	13.1	4.3
1972	7.1	7.7	2.4	20.2	13.9	6.2
1973	2.7	11.9	3.2	35.7	16.9	18.8
1974	18.5	13.9	3.3	40.5	18.9	21.7
1975	19.1	10.8	2.9	36.9	15.7	21.1
1976	17.0	11.1	3.8	36.4	17.4	19.0
1977	12.6	13.4	4.0	35.0	19.9	15.1
1978	15.8	15.6	4.1	40.7	20.5	20.2
1979	17.8	15.6	4.8	44.1	21.2	22.9
1980	20.6	15.9	4.4	48.1	20.4	27.9
1981	20.2	13.8	4.5	46.0	17.9	28.3
1982	14.3	12.6	3.9	36.6	15.3	21.3
1983	14.1	11.6	3.7	34.8	15.9	18.9
1984	14.4	11.4	3.9	34.9	17.8	17.1
1985	10.2	8.5	3.7	26.5	17.4	9.1
1986[d]				22.9	18.2	4.7

Source: Council of Economic Advisers.
Note: Dollars are deflated by implicit GNP deflator; 1982 = 100.
[a]Wheat, rice, and feed grains.
[b]Cotton, tobacco, oilseed products.
[c]Includes commodities not itemized.
[d]Author's estimate based on data through November 1986.

protectionist policies among industrial-country food importers; and (5) U.S. agricultural policies that overprice exported commodities.

Each hypothesis embodies several more specific causes of reduced demand for U.S. commodities. For example, expansion of world output occurs because of improvements in technology in developing countries, as in the Green Revolution, or because countries change their policies, as in Indonesia's promoting of self-sufficiency in rice. Also, some issues cut across several of these hypotheses, notably the issue of whether the U.S. grain export decline reflects mainly a deterioration in U.S. competitiveness as compared to other countries or a worldwide shrinkage in commodity demand compared to supplies. To present the evidence in an orderly fashion, the discussion is organized as it bears on the five hypotheses listed.

7.2 World Agricultural Output

In response to pessimistic appraisals of the prospects for food production in the developing countries (e.g., U.S. Council on Environmental Quality 1980; Brandt Commission 1980), several authors have pointed to evidence that technical progress in farming is accelerating in many countries (Avery 1984; Sanderson 1984; Johnson 1983). Impressive recent technical advances have occurred in milk production, control of livestock disease (e.g., new vaccine for foot-and-mouth disease), improved varieties of traditional crops, and development of nontraditional crops that are drought resistant or insensitive to water salinity. In addition, changes in the agricultural policies of some countries have been cited as causing increased output. India's freer pricing and regional trade and Argentina's cutting of grain export taxes are examples. The most important case, however, is China, whose agricultural output is estimated to have increased 31 percent between 1980 and 1984.[1]

While these and other such episodes provide concrete evidence about emerging events, an aggregate account—the account that really matters—requires combining the well-documented instances of growth with less successful commodities and countries. While the accuracy of measured year-to-year output changes is questionable, we have no better choice than to base our overall judgment of world output trends on collections of national data, particularly as published by the Food and Agricultural Organization (FAO) of the U.N.

To see how the pre- and post-1980 data fit in with longer-term trends, figures 7.1–7.3 summarize statistics of the recent history of world agricultural production. The data are given in the appendix in table 7.A.1. Figures 7.1–7.3 are plotted on a semilogarithmic scale so that the slope indicates the rate of growth.

Figure 7.1 shows an index of worldwide aggregate agricultural production, constructed by the U.S. Department of Agriculture. The index grows at a trend rate of 2.3 percent over the 1955–85 period. This rate exceeds the world population growth rate, so we should not expect to see price rises owing to population-food pressure. Perhaps less well known, in view of the emphasis on droughts and famines in popular discussion of agriculture, is the stability of the growth of output. The index never departs from a band ± 4 percent of the trend value, and the lowest point relative to trend in recent years, in 1983, is largely attributable to the United States idling about 20 percent of its cropland under its payment-in-kind (PIK) acreage idling program.

The most significant point for U.S. exports in the 1980s is lack of evidence that the rate of growth of output in the 1980s is different from that of the preceding twenty-five years. There have been subperiods in which the growth of output accelerated, most notably between 1961

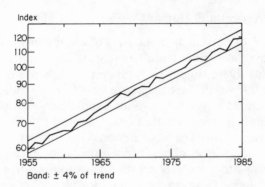

Fig. 7.1   World agricultural production.

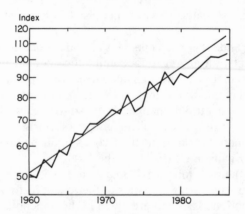

Fig. 7.2   Grain production outside the United States.

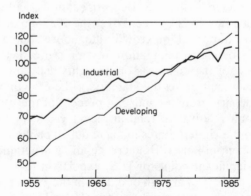

Fig. 7.3   Agricultural production in developing and industrial countries.

and 1968, and this could help explain the general agricultural price weakness of the 1960s. But nothing here explains the price weakness of the 1980s.

To focus more directly on the most discussed source of U.S. farm export problems, figure 7.2 shows the production of grains (wheat and coarse grains aggregated) outside the United States. The trend rate of growth, 3.1 percent annually in 1960–80, is higher than for all food, and grain output is less stable. A band of about 7 percent around trend is necessary to encompass all the observations, with output on several occasions rising or falling 8 percent to 10 percent within a year. The salient fact about the 1980s is that even more clearly than for all agricultural output, the production of grain outside the United States provides no explanation for the weak export market of the 1980s. Indeed, if non-U.S. production were the dominant market force, U.S. exports would be greater in the 1980s than in the 1970s. Every observation in the 1980s lies below the 1960–80 trend line drawn in these figures.

Figure 7.3 disaggregates to show developing and industrial countries separately. Aggregate agricultural output in the developing countries is growing more rapidly than in the industrial countries, at a trend rate of 2.7 percent annually in 1955–85 in the former compared to 1.6 percent in the industrial countries. The rate does not seem to have changed appreciably during this period. Although there is an apparent acceleration in the late 1960s, the Green Revolution and recent technical advances and policy changes have not shifted agricultural output in these countries either to a higher output growth rate or to a higher base level from which future growth may proceed (i.e., no apparent one-time permanent output increases shifting the trend line). The relatively slow growth of output in the industrial countries has to temper (but it does not negate) the notion that output-promoting policies of the industrial countries are a prime cause of world price weakness (as argued, for example, in World Bank 1986).

The lack of fluctuation of annual output around trend in developing countries as compared to the industrial countries—all observations of developing countries in 1955–85 being within 3 percent of the trend output—could reflect data problems. Statistics on annual changes in farm output for some countries are unreliable, and even ex post a year's stated output may be partly a trend extrapolation of the previous year's value. In this sense the observed stability may be a statistical artifact. Nonetheless, the maintenance of a steady trend for thirty years must surely reflect a real underlying stability in output growth.

The centrally planned economies also have a substantial 2.5 percent annual growth rate of agricultural output over the thirty-year period (not shown in figure 7.1–7.3—data in appendix). This may be surprising in view of the recurrent stories of problems in the agricultural economies of these countries. The data for China dominate the aggregate. Output in the Soviet Union grew less than 1 percent annually in 1970–85. Perhaps more striking than output trends in the centrally planned economies, given that we call them "planned," is the variability of output around trend. While the world as a whole and the developing countries as a group are always within a 4 percent bank around trend output in 1955–85, the centrally planned economies in aggregate are more often than not outside this band. Even for this group, however, production in the 1980s is not above the thirty-year trend line.

7.2.1 Trends in Competitive Advantage

The United States is thought to be an efficient, some say the world's most efficient, agricultural producer, but the evidence for this proposition is thin. Total factor productivity as an index of aggregate output, divided by an index of land, labor, and other inputs, can be revealing, but data appropriate for international comparisons are not available. Partial productivity measures, such as yields per acre or output per worker, are available, but must be used with care. For example, in 1982 Indonesia harvested 2.5 tons of rice per hectare while the U.S. yield was 3.9 tons. But we cannot draw conclusions about productivity without information about nonland inputs per hectare in the two countries. And even if we could obtain total cost-of-rice comparisons for the two countries, we need information about the cost of producing rice relative to other goods.

These difficulties notwithstanding, the most pertinent productivity indicators are as follows. The index of total factor productivity in U.S. agriculture published by the USDA has a trend rate of growth of 2.0 percent annually between 1950 and 1985. During the 1980s the index has been unusually volatile. It ranged from a low in 1983 of 98 (compared to a base level of 100 in 1977) to a high of 127 in 1985. The index's average in 1981–85 was 114, compared to 101 in the previous five-year period, 1976–80, implying a 2.5 percent annual productivity growth rate. This is above the thirty-five-year trend rate of productivity growth, but the volatility of measured productivity in the 1980s is too large to infer that the increase is significant. Still, there is no evidence that U.S. agricultural productivity growth is slackening, and so no reason to suspect declining international competitiveness on this score.

Cross-country partial productivity comparisons can be made using data on grain output per hectare. For the 1960–85 period my estimate of the trend rate of growth of wheat and coarse grain yield is 2.4 percent annually in the United States. For the countries outside the United States, as an aggregate the rate of increase in grain yield is 2.6 percent for the same period. So U.S. yields are growing slightly less rapidly. But the non-U.S. countries started at a much lower yield level, and in

1986 U.S. grain yields at 4.7 tons per hectare are still more than double the 2.1 tons yield in the non-U.S. aggregate. Looking at more recent trends, the rate of growth in grain yields seems to have slowed slightly in the non-U.S. countries in the 1970s, and then accelerated in the 1980s to about a 3.0 percent annual rate of growth. The United States has remained more nearly at a steady 2.4 percent growth rate. The year-to-year volatility in yields is such that one cannot be confident that the differences between growth rates in different time periods are significant. And as the earlier caveats indicate, cross-country comparisons of yields are dubious indicators of productivity because they omit nonland inputs from the accounting. But such as they are, the grain yield data provide no cause for worry about a loss of U.S. competitiveness in agriculture.

Another approach to competitiveness is to compare the export price of competing commodities from different countries, as in the indexes of price competitiveness of Kravis and Lipsey (1971, 44). The U.S. Department of Agriculture estimates that in June 1986, when the U.S. Gulf Coast price of no. 2 hard red winter wheat averaged $2.94 per bushel, the most nearly comparable Argentine wheat price was $2.32, while Canadian and Australian wheat was selling from $2.40 to $2.70 per bushel. Moreover, since 1981 the price of Argentinian wheat declined from a 7 percent premium over the U.S. Gulf price to the 21 percent discount as of June 1986. The USDA attributes lagging U.S. wheat sales to these differences, which in their calculations persist after accounting for transportation cost and quality differences (U.S. Department of Agriculture 1986a, 2).

The significance of such price differentials is unclear; in particular, it is unclear whether they say anything about competitiveness. Neither of the two plausible views about the nature of the world wheat market permits a straightforward measure of competitiveness using the price differences. One view is that (quality-adjusted) wheat is essentially a homogeneous good. In exporting grain, international grain-trading companies such as Cargill, Continental, and others compete for sales to importers by acquiring grain interchangeably from that available at various exporting locations, according to which is cheapest at the moment. Their joint bidding and action establishes something close to competitive pricing structure in which export prices from different countries differ only because of locational or quality advantages. The price ratios then are uninformative about countries' relative production costs or competitiveness.

Still, price ratios of grain from different countries change over time in ways that cannot readily be explained by changes in marketing costs, as in the Argentina wheat case cited above, and these changes are associated with shifts in market shares (U.S. Department of Agriculture

1986c). A view that explains such observations is that wheat from different countries is a different commodity, not just quality-adjusted versions of the same commodity, so, for example, demand shifts can change what counts as "high-quality" wheat. For example, some wheats are good for spaghetti, others for bread; which kind sells at a premium to the other depends on relative supply of and demand for the two types. Since exporting countries produce different proportions of different types, they are selling different or at least differentiated products. Grennes, Johnson, and Thursby (1978) develop the argument that the world wheat market is like this. In this situation, we can speak of U.S. wheat becoming more or less competitive with imperfectly substitutable wheat from other countries and look at changing relative prices of wheat from different countries to measure competitiveness.

The most conclusive evidence that the United States is efficient or competitive in agriculture has been its dominance of the export markets. But now that dominance is slipping. U.S. farm output grew 1.9 percent annually in 1955–85 and 1.8 percent in 1970–85. Since the agricultural output of the developing countries—indeed that of the non–United States generally—grew at a faster rate while all countries faced the same world market prices, can we conclude that the United States is becoming less competitive in agriculture? No. Most countries insulate their domestic producer prices from world prices, and differential trends have occurred in the degree of protection. Some developing countries have moved from taxing their agricultures (paying producers less than world prices) to subsidizing them by paying more.

Such changes in policy could explain the decline in the U.S. share of world agricultural production that is implied by the slower U.S. output growth rate. But our knowledge of the effects of these policies is not sufficient to determine if this hypothesis explains the facts. Alternative hypotheses involve changes in factor supplies—changing trade patterns as some countries increase their ratio of farmland to labor, or farmland to other resources, by clearing jungles, constructing irrigation projects, and the like. But again our knowledge is too sketchy to draw conclusions.

A problem with any numerical indicator of efficiency or competitiveness is that the indicator may change as supply and demand conditions change. For example, the U.S. corn belt could well be the most efficient supplier of corn to the world market—the supply activity including both producing the crop and getting it shipped to importing locations—in the sense that as world prices fall low enough to squeeze out corn suppliers, the corn belt would stay in business at the lowest world prices. But at the current level of production, the U.S. marginal cost is at the higher levels that prevail in other regions. An indicator based on this cost level might show the United States as declining in competitiveness. As this example suggests, however, the real issue is not any overall indicator of competitiveness, but rather changes in the demand for and supply of the exported commodities in the United States and elsewhere.

7.3 World Food Demand

One of the principal recurring reasons for optimism about increasing demand for U.S. agricultural commodities has been pessimism about world population growth confronting limited food production capacity. Increasing scarcity of food would in this scenario result in an increasing real price of agricultural commodities, and of land as a specific factor in agriculture, and thus real gains to food-exporting countries. In fact, real prices of agricultural commodities for which long-time series are available, such as wheat or sugar from colonial times to the present, show a persistent downward trend. For grains in the twentieth century the trend rate of price decline is about one percent annually, so real prices have declined by little more than one-half since 1900. The main reasons seem to be technical change in food production and marketing, together with a failure of demand to grow fast enough to pressure specific factors in agriculture.

Notwithstanding the long-term trend, the sharp price rises of agricultural commodities in the 1970s rekindled worries about global food scarcity. Evidence of this worry is contained not only in alarming articles, but also in speculative commodity price rises and increases in agricultural land prices. Between 1970 and 1980, U.S. crop prices received by farmers increased by 17 percent in real terms. During this same period the USDA's farm real estate price index rose 52 percent in real terms. The land price increases were large enough that they must have embodied expectations that high rental returns would persist or continue to increase for many years.[2]

The preceding section indicates that the failure of these expectations to be realized in 1982–86 is not attributable to a detectable surge in world food output. The natural alternative cause to look for is a decline (relative to other commodities) in world food demand. The two main possibilities for a decline from earlier expectations in demand involve the rate of population growth and the rate of consumer income growth.

Population has not grown as fast in the 1980s as forecast in some earlier projections, but it is still positive enough to add significantly to food demand each year. The U.S. Department of Agriculture publishes an index of food output per capita (fig. 7.4) that indicates world food demand pressure on available supplies. The rate of growth of agricultural output per capita over the 1955–85 period is one-half of one percent annually for the world as a whole; the same rate (to the nearest

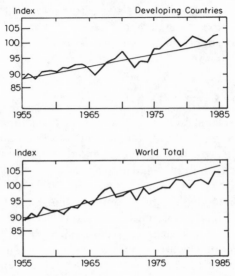

Fig. 7.4   Indexes of agricultural output per capita.

tenth of one percent) is found for the developing countries. Both time series look as if a constant-rate-of-growth trend line would fit well, but there are statistically significant departures from a constant trend. The least-squares trend lines for both the developing and whole world are drawn in figure 7.4 as estimated, using 1955–70 as the sample period. The post-1975 data depart significantly from this trend line. For the world as a whole, every observation after 1975 lies below the trend line—agricultural output is increasing faster than population, but not at as fast a rate in 1975–85 as in 1955–70. On the other hand, in the developing countries no observation after 1975 lies below the trend line. Thus, comparing figure 7.4 with figure 7.1–7.3 shows that the period of the Green Revolution and after experienced a lessening of food-population pressure in these countries because population grew slower, rather than because output grew faster.

Although the data show no trend toward an expanding *necessity* for agricultural imports prior to 1980, or a reduction in such necessity since, there is evidence that the demand for food imports rose through the 1970s and declined in the 1980s. Table 7.2 shows relevant data for some important regions. Africa, Asia, and Latin America all have been increasing their net imports of grains, at least up to 1980, in quantities that are unlikely to be caused by movements along a demand curve as real prices fell. Indeed, in 1973 and 1980, prices were high and yet imports were highest in these years. Therefore, the demand for imports must be increasing. Why? Having cast doubt on population–food supply pressure, the likely candidate is real income.

Table 7.2   **Annual Net Imports of Grain (million metric tons)**

Date	Africa	Asia	Latin America	East Europe and USSR	Western Europe
1948–52	0	6	−1	no data	22
1960	−2	17	0	0	25
1966	7	34	−5	4	27
1973–74	6	45	2	18	20
1980	18	64	16	43	11
1985	46	14	1	32	−16

Sources: 1948–80: *Development,* 1982:4, p. 5; 1985: U.S. Department of Agriculture 1986b.

Although the demand for food products in the industrial countries does not increase as much as income increases, perhaps 1 percent to 3 percent for each 10 percent increase in real income, the demand for food is more responsive to income in the developing countries, typically, 6 percent to 7 percent for each 10 percent income increase (see Ritson 1982, 34, for summary of estimates). Nonfood commodities as an aggregate must have an even higher income elasticity if that for food commodities is less than one, so the income growth scenario is consistent with a declining relative price of food. Still, the empirical evidence is that income growth is associated with increased food imports. The key factor in grain import demand for some rapidly growing economies is the switch from food to feed use of these commodities as the demand for meat increases. Mellor and Johnston (1984) cite the case of Taiwan, where feed use of cereals rose from 1 percent to 60 percent of total use between 1961 and 1981.

Thus, the most plausible reason for increases in cereal imports by developing countries despite rising output per capita is increasing real income in these countries. Projecting increased per capita income into the future leads to quite substantial increases in projected imports by developing countries. For example, a report by Winrock International (1983, 42) projects cereal imports of 152 million metric tons by Africa, Asia, and Latin America in 1993. A recent study by the U.S. Department of Agriculture's Economic Research Service projects an increase of 40 million metric tons in grain imports by the developing countries during the 1980s (White, Mathia, and Overton 1986, 143). However, the 1985 data of table 7.2 are not on the paths to these outcomes. Except in Africa, imports have decreased substantially in the 1980s.

What happened? Since real income growth is credited with causing agricultural imports to rise until 1980, perhaps real income per capita has stopped growing in the developing countries. The World Bank estimates that real GDP per capita in the developing countries as a group increased at an annual rate of 3.2 percent in 1973–80 and 1.3 percent in 1980–85 (World Bank 1986, 45). This decline seems small, but it could have had a significant effect because the market for traded grains is thin. The developing countries produce about four-fifths of the grains and over 95 percent of the rice they consume. If the rate of growth of demand fell by 1 percent, while the rate of growth of output continued to rise at almost 3 percent per year, it is not hard to accumulate a 20 percent to 30 percent reduction in excess demand over five years. Suppose the decline in the rate of GNP growth of 1.9 percent (from 3.2 to 1.3) caused a decline in the rate of food demand growth of 1 percent (income elasticity of .5), from 2.5 percent to 1.5 percent per year. With output growing at 2.7 percent per year, excess demand decreases by 1.2 percent of consumption each year. This 1.2 percent is about 5 percent of quantities imported. If this occurs every year between 1981 and 1986, we accumulate a 25 percent reduction in aggregate food import demand.

The slow-income-growth explanation does not, at first glance, fit well with less aggregated data for the developing countries. Low-income countries in Asia had faster-growing real GNP in 1980–85 than in 1973–80, yet their agricultural imports declined most, as seen in table 7.2. Low-income countries in Africa had a 2 percent annual decline in per capita real GNP in 1980–85, yet their cereal imports increased. These apparent anomalies are explained by concurrent changes in other determinants of demand growth. In Asia, because of technical change, increased price incentives for producers, and decreasing rates of population growth, increases in supply outpaced the growth of demand; some Asian countries achieved self-sufficiency in cereals, particularly rice. In Africa, the income decline was accompanied by, and indeed was in part caused by, slumping growth in agricultural output. And the population growth rate remained high. Between 1974–76 and 1982–84, food production per capita declined by more than 10 percent in Somalia, Ghana, Kenya, Mozambique, Zambia, Lesotho, Zimbabwe, South Africa, Cameroon, and Botswanna (World Bank 1986, 190). The potential for increased import demand was realized without the income growth normally required, in part because of increased food aid shipments, which count as imports.

Several recent papers have argued that an important cause of developing-country import increases in the 1970s was cheap (negative real interest rate) credit plentifully supplied by the industrial countries. Then the "debt crisis" of the 1980s turned this situation on its head and caused import demand to weaken (see White, Mathia, and Overton 1986, 128; Insel 1986; Watkins and Galston 1986). A helpful review of arguments and evidence on this hypothesis is provided in Dutton, Grennes, and Johnson (1986).

There seems to be no clear a priori reason for debt to be strongly associated with food imports. Nonetheless, there is an empirical linkage between decline in growth of debt and declining agricultural imports in the 1980s. Dutton, Grennes, and Johnson estimate that for a set of debtor countries that bought U.S. farm products in 1972–84, each $1 billion in annual net financial inflow induced $400 million in agricultural imports.

7.4 Macroeconomic and International Financial Policies

Monetary and fiscal policies in both the United States and abroad have been linked to the export performance of U.S. agrculture. To the extent that these policies influence real income growth or debt, they affect the demand for imports as discussed in the preceding section. The macroeconomic effects that have received most attention, however, are the consequences of changes in exchange rates. A recent assessment by the World Bank (1986, chap. 4) finds exchange rate overvaluation to be one of the principal sources of a bias against agriculture that is widespread among developing countries. The bias works against agriculture mainly because many of the overvaluing countries are traditional agricultural exporters; by overpricing their currencies they overprice their commodities from the viewpoint of foreign buyers. While movements in real exchange rates track agricultural exports quite well—the World Bank summarizes studies of Nigeria, Ghana, Argentina, and Brazil—the direction of the changes has been mixed. The African countries have been losing export markets and the Latin American countries gaining.

With respect to U.S. exchange rates, three events concerning the value of the dollar have received much emphasis: the fall in the dollar in the early 1970s, the rise in 1980–85, and the decline since the first quarter of 1985.

The importance of the depreciation of the dollar for encouraging U.S. agricultural exports during the period when the flexible exchange rate regime was introduced has been emphasized by Schuh (1975). Subsequent empirical work, notably by Chambers and Just (1981), confirmed the importance of exchange rate movements. They estimated that in 1969–77, each 1 percent decline in the value of the dollar, measured as the exchange rate of dollars for SDRs, caused exports of wheat, corn, and soybeans to rise 0.7 percent to 4.1 percent (depending on the commodity and whether a short-run or long-run adjustment). Orden (1984) attempts to distinguish the effects of exchange rates on U.S. corn exports from effects of standard supply and demand variables such as yields and foreign income, using 1970–80 data. He finds that exchange rate movements explain more of the observed variations in export quantities in the early 1970s, during the shift in exchange rate regimes, but less in the late 1970s as compared to the standard supply-demand variables.

Assessment of the relative importance of these causal factors requires an econometric model incorporating them. Three approaches to such modeling are (1) estimation of particular structural relationships between putative causal variables and trade flows, for example, Chambers and Just's (1981) examination of the effect of the exchange rate on grain exports; (2) reduced form equations in which trade flows are explained by a list of variables assumed to be exogenous, without attempting to model the structural mechanisms that relate subsets of endogenous or exogenous variables to one another, for example, Dutton, Grennes, and Johnson (1986); (3) multivariate time series analyses of trade and related variables, attempting to deduce by leads and lags which variables cause which, for example, Chambers (1981), and Orden (1984).

The third approach can be viewed as a preliminary exploration that should be undertaken before trying either of the other two. Chambers (1981) found that the money supply influenced agricultural trade, but that a null hypothesis that interest rates influenced trade could not be rejected. Batten and Belongia (1986) found that while the real exchange rate influenced agricultural exports, they could not find any influence of monetary policy on the real exchange rate in the 1980s (through 1984:3), the particular period we are most interested in. No investigators have reported significant effects of agricultural sector variables on macroeconomic variables such as interest rates or GNP growth in recent years, although such effects were found in 1970s. While large price shocks emanating from commodity markets or policies can undoubtedly influence the overall economy—and even more so the measurement of GNP-account effects, as discussed by Tatom (1986)—persistent effects do not show up in time series data. Consequently there is some warrant for proceeding, as most investigators have proceeded, by taking macroeconomic variables as exogenous to agriculture and estimating reduced-form or structural relationships in approach (2) or (1).

The particular relationships of interest involve effects of exchange rates, foreign income and debt, non-U.S. production, and other countries' policies on the demand for U.S. agricultural commodities. The empirical work indicates great difficulty pinning down the effects. Results are sensitive to ways variables are measured (which exchange rate, which money supply), specification of estimating equation (variables excluded and econometric technique), and data period covered. The last is particularly important in limiting the usefulness of earlier studies because evidence shows that the 1980s are not like the 1970s

(Orden 1984). This situation is disappointing but not surprising, given the large range of estimated parameters for even the much-investigated domestic commodity supply and demand elasticities, not to mention the elasticity of demand for U.S. farm exports (see Gardiner and Dixit 1986).

Although econometric studies of exchange rates and agricultural exports concentrating on data of the 1980s are lacking, the results of work on earlier periods reinforce the presumption that the rise of the dollar in 1980–84 must have been an important factor in the weakening market for U.S. exports (see Schuh 1985). Relevant data for the grain markets are shown in table 7.3. Between 1980 and 1984 the real trade-weighted dollar index of the Federal Reserve Board rose by 41 percent (from 84.8 to 128.5), while grain export quantities fell by 15 percent from 111 million to 95 million tons. However, the big drop in exports did not occur until 1985, when the real trade-weighted dollar rose only 3 percent.

Short-term relationships are difficult to isolate in the annual data because of lags between price changes as perceived by importers and the induced shipments of U.S. grain. Also, the annual data show the exchange rate on a calendar-year basis but exports on a marketing-year basis, for example, 1985–86 wheat exports as shipments of the crop harvested in 1985, and shipped between June 1, 1985, and May

Table 7.3   **U.S. Grain Exports and the Value of the Dollar**

Marketing Year	Exports (million metric tons)	Trade-Weighted Dollar, Real (FRB)
1970–71	38.5	
1971–72	40.5	
1972–73	69.1	
1973–74	73.8	98.8
1974–75	63.6	99.2
1975–76	82.0	93.9
1976–77	76.5	97.3
1977–78	86.9	93.1
1978–79	92.7	84.2
1979–80	108.8	83.2
1980–81	110.7	84.8
1981–82	108.0	100.8
1982–83	116.4	111.7
1983–84	95.5	117.3
1984–85	95.4	128.5
1985–86	61.0	132.0
1986–87[a]	74.6	

Sources: U.S. Department of Agriculture; Council of Economic Advisers.
[a]Forecast by U.S. Department of Agriculture, December 1986.

31, 1986. Thus, the value of 132.0 for the value of the dollar corresponding to exports in 1985–86 is the calendar-year 1985 value. This seems roughly appropriate since even though much grain harvested in 1985 is shipped in 1986, the contracting for these shipments is done largely in 1985. Still, because the extent and length of time in advance that is typical of forward sales vary, and because on average there appear to be one- or two-quarter lags between price changes and exports, it is possible that the export decline in 1985–86 reflects in part earlier rises in the value of the dollar.

Dunmore and Longmire (1984) attempt a synthesis of existing evidence to explain the relative importance of the following factors as causes of declining U.S. exports of grains and oilseeds in 1980–83: the change in production of these commodities outside the United States, the change in population and real per capita income abroad, the exchange rate between the importing countries' currencies and the dollar, purchase decisions by the Soviet Union, the EC's policy-determined exports, changes in freight rates, and the debt situation in importing countries. Dunmore and Longmire find foreign production and exchange rate movements to be the most important short-term contributors to the weakening export market in 1980–82. From the earlier discussion, the picture looks somewhat different for the longer-term comparison of the mid-1970s with the mid-1980s. Foreign production is less important, real income growth more important.

Haley and Krissoff (1986) estimate the effect of the value of the dollar on U.S. wheat exports during 1973–85. They improve on the work cited earlier by using multicountry real exchange rate indexes weighted by each county's share of the world wheat market. Their inflation-adjusted index of the dollar's value compared to currencies of wheat importers rose 46 percent between 1979 and 1985, and their index for competing wheat exports rose 43 percent.[3] This is somewhat less than the increase of 59 percent in the real FRB index of table 7.3, but all the indexes track fairly closely in the 1980s. They estimate that a 1 percent permanent increase in the exchange rate reduces wheat export quantity by 2.5 percent over a period of eleven quarters, with essentially no effect until the fifth quarter after an exchange rate change.

Given the evidence for 1980–84, it is disappointing that there appears to have been no appreciable response of quantities exported to the decline in the value of the nominal FRB trade-weighted dollar index from a peak of 156 in the first quarter of 1985 to 124 in the second quarter of 1986, a fall of 23 percent. This could be a matter of lagged effects, but even a six-quarter lag should be showing more results than so far observed in the grains. The lack of effect is more surprising in that a principal difference between U.S. grain markets of the 1980s and the 1970s is the determination of domestic nominal commodity prices by stock accumulation at support prices in the 1980s. There should be more pronounced export quantity response to exchange rates under 1980s conditions. A shift in foreign demand for U.S. commodities has a bigger quantity effect and a smaller price effect when the supply of marketed quantities out of stocks is very elastic at the support level.

The best explanation for the apparent lack of effect of the dollar's fall to date is that while the trade-weighted dollar has fallen, the dollar has not fallen against our principal market-oriented export competitors—Canada, Australia, and Argentina (Dutton and Grennes 1985)— or against developing country importers; the countries in Europe and Japan against which the dollar has fallen have effective quantity limits on imports and insulate their domestic producer and consumer prices. So all the falling dollar does is to increase the border protection necessary to maintain the internal price and the size of export subsidies required to meet U.S. competition for EC exports in third-country markets. The demand for imports is essentially unresponsive to lower prices offered on world markets. To consider carefully the policy options for dealing with this situation requires prior discussion of farm policies, both abroad and in the United States.

7.5   Agricultural Policies Abroad

The U.S. position in agricultural trade has undoubtedly been harmed by the agricultural policies of importers and competing exporters. Not all countries have increased their protection of agriculture in the 1980s, however; in these instances they cannot be blamed for the problems of recent years. Japan has achieved self-sufficiency in rice by paying producers and charging consumers three to five times the world price, and has set severe limitations on imports of other agricultural products. This policy has been unchanged in the 1980s, but maintaining internal prices has caused border protection to increase as world prices fell.

The more damaging change among industrialized-country importers has been that of the European community. The EC has converted itself from a net importer of 10 million (metric) tons of grain in 1975 to an exporter of 16 million tons in 1985. The internal price has been kept at about the same level relative to the world level over time, via variable levies on imports, but production at the supported price has increased so much that a substantial surplus over EC consumption occurs. This is disposed of on world markets via export subsidies. Thus, the mid-1980s world prices of grains are lower than they would be without EC agricultural protection. The policy-induced net export volume of about 20 million tons amounts to about 1.5 percent of annual world wheat and feed grain production (10–15 percent of world grain trade), which could itself drive down the world price by 10 percent to 20 percent, given the inelastic aggregate world non-EC demand and supply functions typically estimated for grains.

Developing-country importers and exporters of grains have also changed their policies in the 1970s and 1980s in such a way as to encourage production and thus reduce the market for U.S. grain. In some cases, notably for rice in China, Indonesia, and Thailand, policies that formerly held farm prices down were replaced by policies that increased farm prices, in some cases providing effective net protection by subsidizing inputs, particularly fertilizer. This probably explains part of the reduction in Asian grain imports between 1980 and 1985. Nonetheless, as discussed with reference to figure 7.1–7.3, there has been no evident acceleration in agricultural output growth in the developing countries as a whole. Therefore, unlike the case of the EC, there is no good reason to blame developing-country farm or trade policies for the decline in the market for U.S. grains in the 1980s as compared to the 1970s.

Among competing exporters, Brazil in soybeans and Argentina in grains made substantial inroads in world markets in the 1970s. The industrial-country grain exporters, Canada and Australia, have maintained fairly low levels of intervention in the form of maintaining slightly higher domestic prices than export prices, but have not made significant changes in the 1980s.

The overall picture consists of two parts: the effects of policies on world agricultural commodity trade; and the effects of policies that reduce the U.S. share of the export market. On the first aspect, Tyers and Anderson (1986) provide simulations of the consequences for all OECD countries, all developing countries, and both groups together when they abandon their border distortions in seven commodity markets: wheat, rice, feed grains, beef, pork and chicken, dairy products, and sugar. Tyers and Anderson use supply and demand equations for each commodity, including cross-price effects, for thirty countries and regions. They assume removal of policy-created differences between world prices and internal prices for each country or region as of 1980–82. Some of their results are given in table 7.4. Liberalization by industrial countries, developing countries, or both groups jointly increases trade substantially for all commodities and raises the world price for all but rice and poultry. Exporting countries like the United States would be gainers, although the price effects as simulated are small for grains and sugar. There is a net gain worldwide of $40 billion annually.

With respect to recent changes in the U.S. share of world commodity trade, table 7.5 summarizes recent data. The U.S. share has fallen off since 1975, mostly because of shifts to the EC. The gains of traditional exporters, Canada and Australia, for example, have been smaller. This

Table 7.4 **Simulated Effects of Liberalization of Commodity Markets (percentage changes)**

	OECD Liberalization	Developing Country Liberalization	Liberalization in All Market Economies
World Prices			
Wheat	2	7	9
Coarse grain	1	3	4
Rice	5	− 12	− 8
Beef	16	0	16
Pork and poultry	2	− 4	− 2
Dairy products	27	36	67
Sugar	5	3	8
Trade Volume			
Wheat	− 1	7	6
Coarse grain	19	12	30
Rice	32	75	97
Beef	195	68	235
Pork and poultry	18	260	295
Dairy products	95	330	196
Sugar	2	60	60

Source: Tyers and Anderson 1986.

Table 7.5 **Shares of World Grain Exports (percentage)**

Year[a]	United States	EC − 10	Other Exporters[b]
1960	57	− 42[c]	45
1965	58	− 26	43
1970	50	− 28	51
1975	66	− 9	35
1980	64	2	34
1981	61	4	35
1982	58	6	38
1983	56	6	40
1984	52	10	39
1985	49	10	41

Source: U.S. Department of Agriculture, Foreign Agriculture Service.

[a]Year refers to crop year, e.g., 1960 is the period of time, July 1960 through June 1961, when the 1960 crops were sold.

[b]Canada, Australia, Argentina, South Africa, and Thailand.

[c]Minus sign indicates share of world imports.

suggests a greater weight for export subsidies and a lesser weight for the value of the dollar in explaining the decline in the U.S. export share in the 1980s.

7.6 U.S. Agricultural Policies

Wide agreement exists that U.S. farm commodity programs are important in determining the U.S. position in world trade, but there is much disagreement about what particular policies have done. There is even more disagreement about what policies are appropriate in 1987. Because of the range of policies for different commodities, the complexity of some of them, and disagreements about their effects, it is difficult to provide a discussion that is complete and comprehensive in a small space. This section concentrates on some of the main events and programs for key commodities.

7.6.1 Price Supports

In trade discussions, European countries argue that U.S. farm policies are equivalent to export subsidies in that these policies pay U.S. producers more than the world price and increase supplies on world markets. The opposite concern was important in U.S. farm policy discussions in 1985—that U.S. farm programs were supporting the world market price and hindering U.S. exports. An extraordinary document (U.S. Department of Agriculture 1985), authored jointly by four former secretaries of agriculture of both political parties, Freeman (Kennedy administration), Hardin (Nixon), Butz (Nixon-Ford), and Bergland (Carter), stated that cuts in market price support levels were essential to help the United States regain its former competitiveness in world markets. An assessment of which view is correct is not as straightforward as might be expected because U.S. policies have some elements that encourage exports but at the same time have other features that discourage exports.

Corn Price Support Program

Consider the price support program for corn. It has three main elements: (1) a "loan rate," or market support price, (2) a "target" price, and (3) an acreage reduction program. These are explained in turn, with examples drawn from the program for corn up to 1985.

Loan rate. The loan rate is not an interest rate but the price at which the Commodity Credit Corporation (CCC) values corn as collateral for nonrecourse loans under provisions established by law. *Nonrecourse* means that the CCC must accept corn valued at the loan rate as payment in full, including interest. The corn loan rate for the 1985 crop was $2.55 per bushel; thus a farmer could place 1,000 bushels under loan (meaning having the corn in commercial storage or approved on-farm bins) and receive a loan of $2,550. If the market price rises above the loan rate plus interest charges, the farmer repays the loan and reclaims the corn. If not, the farmer turns over the corn to the CCC. Since this program guarantees the loan rate (less storage costs), it places a floor under the market price at roughly the loan-rate level. Whatever excess supply exists at the loan rate ends up in CCC stocks.

The implication for international trade is that no one is going to sell corn for export at less than the market support level. When the United States sets its loan rate at above the U.S. border price that would prevail in the absence of intervention, corn goes under loan instead of being exported. The only reason exports are not choked off completely is that as U.S. corn is withdrawn from the world market, world prices rise. The United States is not a small country in the sense of being able to sell any quantity at the prevailing world price. Between 1972 and 1980 the market price of corn was generally above the loan rate. But in 1981, market prices fell and CCC stocks began to accumulate rapidly. By the time the 1982 crops were harvested, it was clear that CCC stocks of corn were going to approach the levels that had characterized the 1960s. This situation led to the Payment-in-Kind (PIK) Program of 1983, which reduced harvested area by about one-fourth of 1982 acreage, drove up prices in the world market, and placed U.S. prices well above the loan levels. Higher prices permitted carryover stocks to be reduced from 3.5 billion to 1.0 billion bushels. However, support prices were not reduced, and with no PIK in 1984, stocks began building up again. By the fall of 1985, CCC corn stocks were projected at 4.0 billion bushels, larger than ever. This realization led to the view that loan rates should be cut in the new farm legislation being debated in 1985.

Complications in the loan program are that Congress establishes a national loan level or range within which the secretary of agriculture can establish it, but variations from state to state occur, presumably reflecting the price surface justified by regional differences in normal prices. Also, loan rates are defined for particular grades of the commodity, with discounts or disqualification for lower quality. Moreover, to receive the CCC loan, grain must be in approved on-farm storage facilities or in commercial storage which the farmer must pay for. Therefore, particularly in the immediate postharvest period, the U.S. average farm price can fall well below the loan rate. For example, in November 1985 the average price received by farmers was estimated by the USDA to be $2.20 per bushel, even though the loan rate was $2.55 and there was no lack of corn eligible for the loan program. Thus the price floor is somewhat spongy. The average price for the 1985–86 crop year (September 1–August 31) was $2.35, 20 cents below the loan rate.

Bruce L. Gardner/H. B. Atwater, Jr./John R. Block

Target price. The target price is a support level for producer receipts but not for the market price. Producers receive deficiency payments equal to the difference between the target price and higher of the loan rate or the average farm price for the first five months of the marketing year. In 1984 and 1985 the corn target price was $3.03 per bushel, 48 cents above the $2.55 loan rate. Farmers cannot realize $3.03 on all they wish to produce. The net benefits to farmers are reduced by the requirement that acreage be idled in order to qualify for payments.

Acreage reduction. In 1985, program participants had to idle 10 percent of their corn base acreage, a percentage established by the U.S. Department of Agriculture. To obtain a notion of the cost to farmers, suppose land yields 140 bushels per acre and has an annual rental value of $100 per acre, or $.71 per bushel. For each bushel that would normally have been produced, the participating farmer receives the deficiency payment of $.48 on 0.9 bushel, but has to give up the rental value of $.71 on idled land that could have produced 0.1 bushel. Therefore, the net gain is ($.48 × .9) − ($.71 × .10) = $.36 per bushel. The alternative action, not participating, provides the farmer $2.55, assuming the market price is supported at that level. The effective price guarantee for a participating farmer is thus $2.55 + .36 = $2.91.

Complications change the program benefits further. There are complications that make things better for producers: (1) a farmer may have low-quality land to idle, with rent foregone of less than $100 per acre; (2) in a special provision for 1985, hay could be harvested from certain nominally idled land; (3) a portion of deficiency payments is paid in advance, at planting time, so the farmer gets about six-months interest on part of the $.48; (4) although the regulations proscribe this, if the farmer only idles 9 percent rather than 10 percent of the corn base, the government will probably not discover the fact, and it is probably also safe to grow potatoes or melons, or run cattle on some idled land for a short time, even though these activities are not permitted. There are also complications that make things worse for producers: (1) the regulations require that land be idled, but weeds must be controlled and conservation practices followed; (2) the farmer may have fixed resources, equipment, and perhaps the farmer's own labor which will be idled along with the land; (3) when the market price on a U.S. average annual farm-level basis falls 20 cents below the loan level, the guaranteed price is correspondingly 20 cents below the target price.

The acreage reduction program's complications mean that a 10 percent set-aside does not simply reduce output by 10 percent from the no-program output. Although participation generates a net gain in the example given above, and does so also for plausible parameter values using U.S.- or state-average yield and rental values, there are evidently farmers for whom participation does not pay since only 69 percent of corn production was enrolled in the 1985 program. This means actual output is reduced by less than 10 percent. Moreover, since we expect lower-quality land to be idled, and perhaps even some cheating, output will be reduced by less than the 6.9 (10 × 69) percent of the acreage base enrolled. Finally, since the payment increases the net incentive to produce corn, we expect farmers to try to produce more corn on their reduced acreage by using more fertilizer, pesticides, or other measures. So output falls by an even smaller percentage than quality-adjusted, truly idled land does. These complications all work in the same direction and taken together constitute "slippage." Slippage has proven difficult to measure beyond the nonparticipation aspect, but the aggregate evidence indicates that in recent years, for both corn and wheat, it has been about 30 percent for a given output price (Norton 1985). That is, the 10 percent corn ARP of 1985, which reduced base acreage by 6.9 percent, probably reduced output by (6.9 × .7) about 5 percent from what would have been produced on the base acreage.

What is the effect of all three program elements together? The target price protection causes farmers to produce more than they would with no price supports, and their excess production drives down world and U.S. prices, providing justification for the European complaints. But the acreage reductions work in the other direction, tending to hold world prices up. Which effect dominates? The acreage reductions have already been estimated to have reduced corn output by 5 percent from what otherwise would have been produced given the price incentive that existed. But how much extra production potential was caused by target-price protection?

To estimate the output effect, two facts are needed: the producer price under the 1985 guarantee compared to the market price that would have existed in the absence of the program, and the response of production to higher prices, that is, the elasticity of supply of corn.

To estimate the market price in the absence of the program, we need a judgment about how low prices would have to go to make annual U.S. corn production equal domestic consumption plus exports. In the 1985 crop year, 6.5 billion bushels of corn were marketed, giving an indicator of demand. On the supply side, to estimate no-program output at trend yields (to abstract from random yield fluctuations) we add 5 percent additional acreage to reflect the absence of acreage controls, giving output of 9.1 billion bushels. Thus the excess supply is 2.6 billion bushels. The 6.5 billion bushels were marketed at an average farm level price of $2.35 per bushel. The 9.1 billion bushels correspond to output at a producer price of $2.91, from earlier calculations. How much would prices have to fall to achieve a common producer and consumer price that would clear the market? To answer this question requires an estimate of elasticity of demand as well as supply. Neither elasticity is known with precision, but a demand elasticity in the range $-.35$ to $-.70$ and a supply elasticity of .15 to .40 seem defensible (see Gardner 1986 or Lin 1986 for further discussion). The most price-responsive elasticities, .4 and $-.7$, imply that price would have to fall to \$1.87 per bushel to clear the market. The least price-responsive elasticities imply that price would have to fall to \$1.28.[4] The corresponding quantities at which production equals use are 8.0 billion bushels and 7.6 billion bushels. The largest no-program quantity would occur with the more elastic demand and less elastic supply combination, in which case no-program output would be 8.4 billion bushels.

For the whole range of assumptions, the quantity of corn produced in the absence of the corn program is less than the 8.6 billion bushels, given the 1985 program. Therefore, the Europeans seem to be correct in asserting that U.S. policy increases supplies and is expected to be world-price depressing. However, the CCC loan program must still be considered. The 6.5 billion bushels that go onto the markets at the \$2.35 supported price are less than the lowest simulated output with no program. Therefore, because of the CCC loan program the European view cannot be sustained—the three elements of U.S. price support policy taken together result in world prices higher than they would be if the U.S. abandoned its programs.

The preceding simulations pertain to the corn program of 1985. The story would be essentially the same for all the crops marketed under the Agriculture and Food Act of 1981, that is, the 1982–85 crops. The biggest departure from the calculations would have occurred in 1983. Then the acreage reductions were larger, and U.S. policy was world-price supporting even without the CCC loan program.

The situation is different in detail but qualitatively the same for the other exported feed grains—barley and sorghum—as well as for wheat, rice, and cotton. In each case the U.S. loan program tended throughout 1982–85 to support the world price by diverting commodities that would otherwise have been exported or consumed domestically into CCC stocks. So there is no case for the programs through 1985 being world-price depressing. It is more nearly correct to argue, as many did, that U.S. price supports were providing an umbrella under which other exporters could expand output at prices higher than would prevail in the absence of U.S. programs. Thus the commodity programs of the 1980s must have caused a decline in the share of world grain trade accounted for by U.S. exports. In cotton, the United States was essentially priced out of the market in 1985, as exports declined from 6 million to 2 million bales between the 1984–85 and 1985–86 marketing years.

The Food Security Act of 1985

The 1985 Food Security Act, in effect since January 1986, is in some respects a response to the situation of export depression and stock accumulation. The act reduces the loan rates and, moreover, introduces provisions that completely divorce the loan rate from market prices for rice and cotton, and provide options for doing so in wheat and corn. The corn loan rate, for example, fell from $2.55 in 1985 to $1.92 per bushel for the 1986 crop (28 percent); the Gramm-Rudman budget reduction legislation resulted in a further 4.3 percent cut. For changes in other commodities, see table 7.6. In the fall of 1986 and early 1987, the cash price of corn at Chicago was in the $1.50–1.60 range, about $1.00 lower than a year earlier. In real terms these prices are about one-fifth the corn prices of 1974–75 and are about half the levels of 1969–71, before the commodity boom began. In cotton the percentage declines in market price were about the same, and in rice even larger, with 1986 prices about one-half the 1985 level.

While the 1986 programs cut market support levels, this was much less a move toward market orientation than one might at first suppose. The target prices were left unchanged. Acreage controls were tightened. And export subsidy activities were intensified.

Table 7.6   **U.S. Support Prices in 1985 and 1986**

Commodity	Type of Support	1985	1986[a]
Wheat	target	$ 4.38/bu	$ 4.38
	loan	3.30	2.40
Corn	target	3.03	3.03
	loan	2.55	1.92
Soybean	loan	5.02	4.77
Cotton	target	81.0¢/lb	81.0
	loan	57.3	ineffective
Rice	target	$11.90/cwt	11.90
	loan	8.00	3.60 minimum
Milk	support	11.60 (after July 1)	11.20[b]
Sugar	support (attained via quotas)	18.0¢/lb	18.0

[a]Gramm-Rudman-Hollings budget reduction act results in 4.3 percent cut in effective target prices and loan rates.

[b]CCC support remains at $11.60, but a 40 cent per hundredweight producer assessment was introduced in April 1986.

Freezing the target prices while loan rates were cut meant big increases in deficiency payments. The payment in corn goes from $.48 in 1985 to $1.11 per bushel in 1986. Moreover, farmers' participation jumped from 69 percent to 83 percent of the acreage base. After Gramm-Rudman adjustment we still end up with about $6 billion to be paid on corn. In the case of rice, the target price is at $11.90 per hundredweight, and the 1986 program let the market price fall from $8.00 to about $4.00. Thus, government payments to rice producers will be about twice the market value of the rice crop.

Keeping target prices up while cutting market prices makes the commodity programs more like production subsidies, so the Europeans' complaints seem more appropriate in 1986 than 1985. And one can sympathize with the other rice exporters, notably Thailand, who, with a halving of the U.S. export price along with the depreciating dollar, face a much tougher marketplace. However, a complicating factor is that acreage controls were tightened in 1986. Plantings of corn in 1986 were down 8 percent from 1985, with wheat down 5 percent, rice 4 percent, and cotton 10 percent. However, these cuts are probably not large enough to reduce production to no-program levels.

Moreover, further steps were taken in 1986 that, coupled with loan rate cuts, place U.S. policy indubitably in the world-price-depressing category. These steps involve the disposal of CCC stocks accumulated from past (1982–85) surpluses and the export subsidies that accompany this action. Carryover stocks of corn and rice are currently about one-half of a year's production, and carryover stocks of wheat three-fourths of annual output. Cutting loan rates can prevent further accumulation, but existing stocks have to be pared down to economically appropriate levels. Since current production is not randomly large, nor is export demand high because of transitorily low production abroad, carryover stock levels that can be justified for stabilization purposes are probably quite low—no more than 10 percent of normal production. Therefore it makes sense in terms of financial management by the government to dispose of some of existing stocks, even at a loss. The U.S. government has been disposing of stocks by using them in food aid, in payments in kind to producers to compensate program participants for some acreage diversion, and to exporters as an in-kind subsidy.

The Export Enhancement Program (EEP) is intended to be targeted specifically at markets into which the EC has sent subsidized commodities. Under this program, exporting companies can bid for sales to markets designated by the secretary of agriculture, undercutting competitors' prices by amounts negotiated between the importer and the company. If the negotiated price is approved by the U.S. Department of Agriculture, the company receives sufficient CCC grain to compensate the company for the difference between the negotiated sale price and the prevailing U.S. domestic price taken as the company's cost of grain exported. An example is shown in table 7.7 for wheat sales to Morocco. The availability of subsidies for 1.5 million tons of wheat sales to Morocco was announced in September 1985. In December 1985 and December 1986, deals were consumated as shown in table 7.7. Given the negotiated sale price and terms, the Department of Agriculture payment ("bonus") varies according to judgments about the loss the exporting company would incur if not compensated. The bonus is then paid in bushels of wheat from CCC stocks, valued at the U.S. price deemed appropriate. The subsidy varies from sale to sale, averaging $22.56, or 20 percent of the average f.o.b. price.

Overall, between June 1985 and December 1986, sales under the EEP amounted to 7.3 million tons of wheat and flour, 1.5 million tons of barley, 17,750 head of dairy cattle, and small amounts of rice, semolina, and frozen poultry. The aggregate value of the commodities is $921 million, with CCC book value (an overstatement of the market value) of bonuses equal to $534 million.

The effects of the EEP are difficult to estimate. Because the quantities subsidized are limited, and less than the total imports of the buying countries, it is doubtful that the program has added to consumption in these countries. Instead, the main consequence is an income transfer from U.S. taxpayers to whoever gets the right to buy at the subsidized U.S. price and sell in favored importing-country markets. Since the subsidy does not add to consumption, to a first approximation, it does not change world prices even if it causes shuffling of export and import customers. But the release of CCC stocks to pay the subsidies, stocks that would otherwise be held off the market, must place some down-

Table 7.7   **Export Enhancement Program, Wheat Sales to Morocco**

Date of Sale	Type of Wheat[a]	Quantity (tons)	Sale Price ($/ton)	Terms of Sale[b]	Bonus ($/ton)
12-20-85	SRW	180,000	131.00	c&f	20.55
12-30-85	HRW	120,000	131.50	c&f	20.60
1-17-86	HRW	200,000	113.50	fob	22.81
1-17-86	HRW	60,000	113.50	fob	22.81
1-21-86	HRW	120,000	106.00	fob	25.38
1-21-86	SRW	80,000	106.50	fob	24.95

Source: U.S. Department of Agriculture.

[a]SRW is a soft red winter wheat; HRW is hard red winter wheat. (SRW has less than 12 percent protein and is used in unleavened bakery products such as crackers; HRW has 8–15 percent protein and is used in bread making.)

[b]C&f means priced at Moroccan port; fob means priced at U.S. port. The roughly $18 per ton difference is transportation cost.

ward pressure on world market prices. These quantities are not re-cycled into CCC stocks via new loans because the loan rates for the 1986 crops have been cut while the release prices for previously ac-quired CCC stocks have not.

Prospects for 1987

The constellation of 1986 programs—cutting loan rates, unloading stocks, and subsidizing exports—will continue in 1987 and has real promise of causing exports to rebound. The effects to date are most apparent in cotton, where exports from the 1986 crop are projected by USDA at triple the very depressed exports from the 1985 crop. USDA projects 1986 crop exports, as compared to 1985, to be up 30 percent for rice and 25 percent for wheat and corn (U.S. Department of Agriculture 1986a). These estimates are quite uncertain, in that export projections have had considerable error in recent years. The grain export markets have remained weak and suggest that USDA may have been too optimistic. The sluggishness of exports, given that loan rate cuts and the dollar's decline have reduced the price of U.S. grain as seen by industrial-country importers by about half in the past two years, has led to criticism of the 1985 act and calls for changes in farm leg-islation. Congress is expected to consider several reforms in 1987.

The main recent change in farm policy discussion bearing on inter-national trade is renewed interest in production controls. The 1985 act required that a nonbinding poll of wheat producers be conducted on their preference for a production control program. To the question; "Do you favor imposition of mandatory limits on the production of wheat that will result in wheat prices that are not lower than 125 percent of the cost of production (excluding land and residual returns to man-agement)?", 54 percent of 319,000 valid ballots said yes. Nonetheless it appears unlikely that such mandatory controls will be imposed. The 1987 programs already announced use 1985-act authorities of the sec-retary of agriculture to idle an additional 15 percent of corn acreage and maintain acreage reduction at 1986 levels for wheat, rice, and cotton. Hopes for farm price increases from production cutbacks that persisted for more than a year or two seem doomed because the demand for U.S. commodities abroad is too price-responsive.

Attempts to move further toward market pricing by additional cuts in CCC price supports for corn or wheat have the great drawback of increasing budgetary costs, which are already seen as too high. With full participation by farmers, each 13 cent cut in the CCC loan rate adds $1 billion to government outlays through deficiency payments.

Intensification of export subsidy efforts is another possibility that runs afoul of budgetary costs. The dubious cost-effectiveness of the targeted subsidies of 1985 and 1986 in expanding export quantities has also tarnished this approach (see U.S. Department of Agriculture 1986b).

The Reagan administration has proposed cutting target prices 10 percent in 1988 from the 2 percent reductions scheduled in the 1985 act. This would reduce budgetary costs and begin the phaseout of supporting U.S. producer prices 50 percent to 100 percent above world market prices, a phaseout that economic efficiency will sooner or later require. But this step will be difficult for Congress.

7.6.2 Policies Other Than Price Support Programs

Although the commodity programs are the most important current determinant of U.S. exports, other policies have also played a role. The export embargoes of 1973–80 continue to be controversial, as do food aid programs. More important than either for the future, however, may be multilateral agreement on agricultural policy and trade issues resulting from GATT negotiations.

The Legacy of Embargoes

The U.S. embargoed exports of soybeans in 1973, and in 1974, 1975, and 1980 suspended grain sales to the Soviet Union. Congress in 1985 enacted legislation requiring the Department of Agriculture to conduct a study to determine the losses to U.S. farmers caused by past export embargoes. Since the last such embargo occurred five years previously, in a year during which U.S. grain export quantities nonetheless reached their all-time high, this legislation shows the remarkable political strength of what would appear to be an economically minor event. The resulting study, listing as principal contributors more than twenty economists from universities across the country in addition to USDA staff, concluded that the embargoes were not a significant cause of the economic problems of U.S. agriculture in the 1980s (U.S. Department of Agriculture 1986b). Nonetheless, farm commodity groups expressed amazement and the secretary of agriculture disavowed the study.

Could the study have been so badly mistaken? The notion that there must have been significant effects has been well expressed by a spokesman for the American Soybean Association: "four embargoes in eight years set up a trend. . . . We know our reputation as a reliable supplier has been injured" (*Washington Post,* November 28, 1986). The best observable indicator of this phenomenon is that the U.S. share of Soviet grain imports dropped throughout the 1980s, until in the 1986–87 marketing year the Soviets have bought no U.S. grain. This plausibly reflects a Soviet desire to reduce its dependence on the United States, encouraged by the embargoes. However, it is far less clear that the decline in the U.S. share of worldwide aggregate grain imports has been caused by aversion to buying from the United States as opposed to other sources. Such aversion should show up as unwillingness to pay as much for U.S. grain as for that from other sources; but as indicated earlier, U.S. prices in the mid-1980s have if anything tended to be premium rather than discounted compared to grain from other sources. Thus, the most accessible but inconclusive evidence suggests no significant lasting impact of the embargoes. More detailed investigations intended to sort out embargo effects from other events have reached the same finding.

Export Subsidies via Surplus Disposal

Going back to the P.L. 480 program initiated in the mid-1950s, the idea of disposing of surplus commodities by shipping them abroad at below-market prices has been a key element in farm commodity support efforts, especially for rice and wheat.

Some information on concessional sales is presented in table 7.8. P.L. 480 exports have remained quite constant over thirty years in dollar terms, meaning they have declined in real terms. Despite recent increased interest in these programs, they still account for a much smaller percentage of U.S. exports than they did in 1956–70.

As is the case for the targeted export subsidies of 1985 and 1986, the effectiveness of these programs is questionable. The USDA (1986b, I-20) estimates that the subsidies necessary to cause an additional ton of U.S. wheat exports would be larger than the cost of simply destroying the wheat. Surplus disposal also has been criticized for reducing production incentives in other countries, which would tend to increase

Table 7.8   **Government-Assisted Agricultural Exports (billions of dollars)**

Fiscal Year	P.L. 480	CCC Subsidized Sales	Subsidized Credit	Total	Percent of All Agricultural Exports
1956–60 (ave.)	1.4	1.0	0.1	2.5	61
1961–65	1.5	1.2	0.1	2.8	51
1966–70	1.2	1.4	0.3	2.9	45
1971–75	1.1	1.9	0.5	3.5	23
1976–80	1.4	0.0	1.3	2.7	9
1981	1.5	0.0	1.9	3.4	8
1982	1.2	0.0	1.5	2.7	7
1983	1.3	0.1	4.2	5.6	16
1984	1.5	0.0	3.9	5.4	14
1985	1.7	0.0[a]	2.9	4.6	15

Source: U.S. Department of Agriculture.
[a]Excludes EEP sales, which were neglible until FY 1986.

demand for imports in these countries. But we do not have good evidence on these effects.

In addition to their direct effects, these programs and the Export Enhancement Program discussed earlier have strategic aims. They are intended to increase the cost of other countries' agricultural support prices. The particular aim is to increase the cost of the EEC's export subsidies. The EEC pays the difference between its internal price and the world market price on the grain it exports. If U.S. policy cuts the world price by $30 per ton—and the wholesale price of U.S. corn has fallen by more than this in the past year—the cost to the EEC is about $500 million based on their 1985 exports of 16 million tons. The EEP is intended strategically to force the EEC on a country-by-country basis to either match the U.S. sale price or abandon the market. Matching the EEP subsidies to date has not been nearly as problematical as the threat posed by the lower loan rates on grains. The biggest strategic success to date may well have been the EEC's response to seeing the U.S. price of rice fall from $8.00 to $4.00 per ton in the spring of 1986; the contemplation of what would result from similar policies in wheat and feed grains is likely behind the increased willingness of EEC countries to place agriculture on the GATT agenda, as discussed below.

At the same time, the strategic risk exists of escalating retaliation. The lower feed grain prices resulting from 1986 programs pushed the Canadians to a finding that deficiency payments constituted an implicit export subsidy and a consequent retaliatory Canadian duty on imports of U.S. corn. The effects of this duty are quantitatively negligible, but illustrative of the risks in strategic action in trade policy. Another side of the EEP subsidies is that the USSR, in reneging on its long-term agreement to buy U.S. wheat and corn, gave as a reason for not buying in 1986–87 that the USSR could not get the subsidized prices while other countries could.

Of course, strategic action typically involves differences between stated and really intended plans, and between stated reasons and real reasons for what is actually done. The Canadian corn tariff issue must be considered jointly with U.S. hog producers complaints against imports of Canadian pork and the U.S. International Trade Commission's 1986 finding (reversing an earlier decision) that Canadian timber sales policy amounted to an export subsidy on lumber. The possible additional motives for the USSR's decision are too tangled even to attempt to list.

The highest-profile agricultural trade dispute in early 1987—the threatened U.S. tariffs on certain European wine, cheese, and related products—does seem independent of the 1986 U.S. policy initiatives, however. The issue here is proper U.S. compensation under GATT rules for the U.S. loss of feed grain markets in Spain and Portugal as they come under the EEC's agricultural protection umbrella. This brings us to the general topic of agriculture and the GATT.

Trade Negotiations in Agriculture

The demand for U.S. commodities has been reduced by other countries' protection of agriculture. Much of the protection is consistent with the outcome of trade negotiations under the General Agreement on Tariffs and Trade, and ironically it was at the insistence of the United States that agricultural exemptions to free trade principles were introduced. The United States to the present day relies on tight import quotas to maintain its sugar and dairy price supports, in the former case achieving U.S. prices three to five times higher than world prices. In January 1987 the New York offshore price of raw sugar was 6.5 cents per pound while the New York domestic price was 21 cents. In the 1950s the United States was concerned more generally with defending its grain and cotton price supports from imports at the support levels and so achieved a GATT waiver for import restrictions necessary to maintain domestic farm programs.

Now that other countries make more use of import restrictions in maintaining domestic producer price protection, the picture is different from the U.S. viewpoint. The United States sought and achieved inclusion of agriculture in the agenda for the upcoming round of GATT negotiations. Equally important, at the Tokyo Summit in May 1986 the leaders of the United States, Japan, France, Germany, and the United Kingdom agreed that liberalization of agricultural trade was desirable and that current trade problems were inseparable from the domestic farm policies of the countries involved.

With respect to the developing countries, there is a risk that they may emulate the industrial countries and subsidize farmers in pursuit of food self-sufficiency. Dorosh and Pearson (1985) provide an interesting case study of Indonesia, and the World Bank's *World Development Report* (1986) outlines others. It is evident that such policies can make comparative advantage irrelevant. If Saudi Arabia can become a surplus grain producer, and it has, any country can. The argument for trade is that self-sufficiency can be quite costly. Saudi Arabia pays producers about $25.00 per bushel for wheat, while the U.S. target price at $4.38 is too high (in the sense that U.S. producers would be willing to produce more than they do now at a lower price).

The policy implication is that both the United States and other countries could make themselves significantly better off by joint agreement to reduce their protection of agricultural commodities. The deadweight losses are not the small triangles that one finds for excise taxes because instead of 5 percent or 10 percent price distortions we have ones that are 100 percent or 200 percent for some commodities, notably sugar and dairy products. Tyers and Anderson (1986) estimate the net world-wide gains from liberalization of their seven agricultural commodities to be $40 billion. I have estimated that unilateral liberalization of the U.S. farm programs would cost U.S. farmers about $10 billion per year and benefit consumers and taxpayers by $15 billion (Gardner 1986). Most of the $5 billion deadweight loss is the opportunity cost of idled land and losses on stored commodities (not the usual triangles). If other countries liberalized jointly with the United States, the costs to U.S. farmers would be less because world prices would be raised.

While this could make U.S. liberalization more palatable politically, it is not in the cards at present despite the attention given to this year's $25 billion budgetary cost of farm programs. Candidates of both major parties campaigned in 1986 with promises to do more for farmers; no candidate in any state promised to work to cut back farm supports; Congress, in its pre-election positioning, acted to increase, not to reduce, farm program costs; and in the election itself the Democrats, who had promised farmers most, gained in both houses. In this climate the preliminary agreement to place agriculture on the agenda in the upcoming GATT negotiations is the only bright spot on either the domestic or international agricultural policy scene. Belated discussions between the United States and Canada and the United States and the EC have succeeded only in the limited sense of having prevented recent increases in agricultural protection from accelerating as rapidly as they have threatened to do.

7.7 Conclusion

Several hypotheses concerning the decline of U.S. agricultural exports in the 1980s have been discussed, along with some evidence bearing on them. The hypotheses that seem most important are (1) the slowdown in population and real income growth among importers and accompanying debt problems, (2) EC agricultural policies, (3) the rise in real foreign exchange value of the dollar, and (4) the U.S. CCC loan program. Recent events point to an improved export situation as far as (3) and (4) are concerned, but for (1) and (2) the prospects are less clear. Hypotheses that do not appear to be as important are expansion of agricultural output in developing countries and the legacy of past embargoes. However, there are reasons to believe that agricultural protection and the rate of growth of developing-country output might accelerate (see Avery 1984 and references cited therein). And there is a real risk that more of these countries may choose to pursue food self-sufficiency.

The outlook for world agricultural commodity markets and for the U.S. position in them is highly uncertain. Most consistent with events observed to date, using world trading prices as a measure of market conditions, is that these prices will continue a random walk with downward drift in real terms of about one percent annually, punctuated by periodic "commodity booms." Characteristic of the three booms observed in this century, roughly corresponding to World War I, World War II, and 1973–76, is the lack of a convincing explanation of why prices rose as much as they did in any of them. In all three episodes, none of the supply and demand shift variables discussed in this paper contributes as much as dummy variables for the years in question to the explanation of why prices rose above trend in those years. The economic picture for producers is a period averaging about twenty five years of subsistence returns, irregularly interrupted by a few years of extraordinary profits. The position of U.S. agriculture in the future depends on trends in productivity and demand variables in the U.S. compared to the rest of the world, and on policies in the various countries. It is difficult to be at all confident about any projection for either the economic or political events. The volume of agricultural trade will probably resume an increasing trend, as continuing economic development fosters specialization on a worldwide basis; but the U.S. share of world agricultural production and trade could as well increase or decrease. It does seem unlikely that the U.S. share will decrease enough that its agricultural export volume will fall over time.

The problem is that even if U.S. export volume increases, but at a low rate, this will require a continuing shrinkage of not only the agricultural labor force—which is almost certain in any event—but also of capital and land in agriculture. Suppose that total factor productivity in U.S. agriculture continues to increase at about 2 percent annually, and domestic demand at 1 percent of U.S. production. This means that 1 percent of annual production must be added to agricultural exports each year to keep the current level of resources employed in agriculture. With one-fourth of output exported, this means that U.S. export volume must grow at 4 percent annually to fill the gap (and exports must continue to increase as a fraction of farm production). This rate of increase in real export value has been achieved by the United States over the past thirty years. Although there are many plausible scenarios under which the rate of U.S. export expansion could be faster or slower in the next thirty years, the theory and evidence discussed in this paper are insufficient to provide a forecast.

The implications of this uncertain situation for U.S. agricultural policy are that flexibility is required and that policies that would isolate the United States from the world market are a nonstarter for either U.S. farmers or the overall national interest. Whatever the objectives of U.S. agricultural policy, the appropriate steps in pursuit of them will change as currently unpredictable events unfold. And for any policy that seeks to maintain a healthy farm sector over the long term, isolation is untenable because productivity trends imply that farm exports cannot simply be maintained but must grow unless the sector as a whole is to decline; yet if steps are taken to reduce U.S. productivity growth, such as a cutback in biotechnical research, the United States will lose the export markets it still retains to countries in which agricultural productivity continues to grow.

Appendix

Table 7.A.1   **Indexes of Agricultural Production, 1955–85 (1976–78 = 100)**

Year	United States	All Industrial Countries	Centrally Planned Countries	Developing Countries	World Total
1955	65	69	54	53	59
1956	66	70	59	55	62
1957	65	69	60	56	62
1958	69	72	63	59	65
1959	70	74	62	61	66
1960	72	78	60	62	67
1961	73	77	60	64	67
1962	73	80	61	66	70
1963	76	82	62	68	71
1964	76	82	70	69	74
1965	78	83	71	71	76
1966	77	84	78	71	78
1967	81	89	80	74	81
1968	83	91	82	77	84
1969	84	89	80	80	83
1970	62	89	85	82	86
1971	89	92	87	84	88
1972	90	92	86	84	88
1973	92	95	97	86	93
1974	87	94	95	89	93
1975	94	97	93	94	95
1976	96	96	98	96	97
1977	102	100	97	100	99
1978	102	103	104	104	104
1979	109	107	104	104	105
1980	102	105	102	107	104
1981	113	108	103	112	108
1982	113	110	110	113	111
1983	92	102	115	116	110
1984	109	112	120	120	117
1985	115	113	119	125	119

Source: U.S. Department of Agriculture 1986a.

Notes

1. Percentage changes in this paper are calculated as changes in natural logarithms. The source of production data used in this section is primarily from the U.S. Department of Agriculture 1986a, 1986b, and 1986c.

2. The land price rises were consistent with the expectations that land rental rates of the mid-1970s would continue forever, but these expectations are not possible to distinguish, in these data, from high rents existing for ten to fifteen years and then falling back. For evidence on U.S. land prices and land rents, see Alston 1986 and Burt 1986, which follow up on Melichar 1979 and Feldstein 1980.

3. Construction of these indexes is tricky because of the existence of several exchanges rates, some in parallel markets, in some of the importing countries, and because of high inflation rates that may not be measured accurately. For example, the value of the dollar against the countries that import U.S. wheat, weighted by each country's share of U.S. sales, rose from an index value of 85 in 1982 to 105 in 1985. But the nominal value of the dollar, before adjusting for inflation rates, rose from 488 in 1982 to 11,841 in 1985 (U.S. Department of Agriculture 1986a).

4. The calculations are as follows. To fit the with-program price-quantity points, the constant elasticity supply curve at the elasticity extremes must be $Q_s = 7.75\, P_s^{.15}$ or $Q_s = 5.94\, P_s^{.40}$, where Q_s is quantity produced and P_s is the producer price. The demand curves must be $Q_d = 8.77\, P_d = 8.77\, P_d^{-.35}$ or $Q_d = 11.8\, P_d^{-.70}$. Finding equilibrium by equating $Q^s = Q^d$ and $P^s = P^d$, the implied prices and quantities are as stated for the elasticity extremes.

References

Alston, Julian M. 1986. An analysis of the growth of U.S. land prices. *American Journal of Agricultural Economics* 68:1–9.

Avery, Dennis. 1984. World food productivity: Rising fast. Bureau of Intelligence and Research, U.S. Department of State. Report 969-AR.

Batten, D. S., and M. T. Belongia. 1986. Monetary policy, real exchange rates, and U.S. agricultural exports. *American Journal of Agricultural Economics* 68:422–27.

Brandt Commission. 1980. *North-South: The report of the Independent Commission on International Development Issues*. London: Pan Books.

Burt, Oscar R. 1986. Econometric modeling of the capitalization formula for farmland prices. *American Journal of Agricultural Economics* 63:934–41.

Chambers, Robert G. 1981. Interrelationships between monetary instruments and agricultural commodity trade. *American Journal of Agricultural Economics* 63:934–41.

Chambers, Robert G., and R. E. Just. 1981. Effects of exchange rate changes on U.S. agriculture. *American Journal of Agricultural Economics* 63:32–46.

Dorosh, Paul A., and S. R. Pearson. 1985. Macroeconomic policy and agricultural development in Indonesia. Food Research Institute, Stanford University Mimeo.

Dutton, John, and Thomas Grennes. 1985. Measurement of effective exchange rates appropriate for agricultural trade. North Carolina State University. Economic Research Report, no. 51.

Dutton, John, Thomas Grennes, and P. R. Johnson. 1986. International capital flows and agricultural exports. *American Journal of Agricultural Economics* 68 (forthcoming).

Dunmore, John, and James Longmire. 1984. Sources of recent changes in U.S. agricultural exports. Economic Research Service, USDA. ERS Staff Report no. AGES 831219.

Feldstein, Martin. 1980. Inflation, portfolio choice, and the prices of land and corporate stock. *American Journal of Agricultural Economics* 62:910–16.

Gardiner, W. H., and P. V. Dixit. 1986. Price elasticity of export demand. USDA. ERS Staff Report no. AGES 860 408.

Gardner, Bruce. 1986. Economic consequences of U.S. agricultural policies. World Development Report background paper. World Bank, Washington, D.C.

Grennes, T. J., P. R. Johnson, and M. Thursby. 1978. *The economics of world grain trade*. New York: Praeger.

Haley, S. L., and B. Krissoff. 1981. The value of the dollar and competitiveness of U.S. wheat exports. U.S. Department of Agriculture. ERS Staff Report no. AGES 860611.

Insel, Barbara. 1986. Comment. In R. Paarlberg, ed., *U.S. agricultural exports and third world development*. Curry Foundation, Washington, D.C.

Johnson, D. Gale. 1983. The world food situation. In D. G. Johnson and G. E. Schuh, eds., *The role of markets in the world food economy*. Boulder, Colo.: Westview Press.

Kravis, Irving B., and Robert E. Lipsey. 1971. *Price competitiveness in world trade*. Studies in International Relations, no. 6. National Bureau of Economic Research, New York.

Lamm, R. 1980. The role of agriculture in the macroeconomy. *Applied Economics* 12:19–35.

Lin, William. 1986. Effects of farm commodity programs: The cases of corn and rice. Paper presented at the American Agricultural Economic Association meetings, Reno, Nevada.

Longmire, Jim, and Art Morey. 1982. Exchange rates, U.S. agricultural export prices, and U.S. farm program stocks. USDA, International Economics Division.

Melichar, E. 1979. Capital gains versus current income in the farming sector. *American Journal of Agricultural Economics* 61:1058–92.

Mellor, J. W., and B. F. Johnston. 1984. The world food equation. *Journal of Economic Literature* 22:531–74.

Norton, Nancy. 1985. *The effect of acreage reduction programs on the production of corn, wheat, and cotton*. M.S. thesis, University of Maryland.

Orden, David. 1984. The exchange rate and international corn market. Virginia Polytechnic and State University. Mimeo.

Ritson, Christopher. 1982. *Agricultural economics*. Boulder, Colo.: Westview Press.

Sanderson, Fred H. 1984. World food prospects to the year 2000. *Food Policy*.

Schuh, G. Edward. 1975. The exchange rate and U.S. agriculture. *American Journal of Agricultural Economics*.

———. 1985. International agricultural and trade policies. In B. Gardner, ed., *U.S. agricultural policy*, 56–78. American Enterprise Institute, Washington, D.C.

Tatom, J. A. 1986. How federal farm spending distorts measures of economic activity. Federal Reserve Bank of St. Louis. *Review* 68:16–22.

Thompson, Robert L. 1981. A survey of recent developments in international agricultural trade models. USDA-ERS, Washington, D.C.

Tyers, Rod, and Kym Anderson. 1986. Distortions in world food markets: A quantitative analysis. World Bank. Mimeo.

U.S. Council on Environmental Quality. 1980. *The global 2000 report*. Washington, D.C.: GPO.

U.S. Department of Agriculture. 1985. Joint statement on agricultural policy by former secretaries of agriculture, Freeman, Hardin, Butz, and Bergland. Press release.

———. 1986a. *Agricultural outlook*. August and October issues.

———. 1986b. Embargoes, surplus disposal, and U.S. agriculture. Economic Research Service. Staff Report no. AGES 860910.

———. 1986c. World indices of agricultural and food production. Economic Research Service. Statistical Bulletin no. 744.

Watkins, A. J., and W. A. Galston. 1986. International debt, domestic credit, and the rural economy. Mimeo.

White, T. K., G. Mathia, and E. Overton. 1986. Global trends in agricultural production and trade. In *U.S. agricultural exports and third world development*. Curry Foundation, Washington, D.C.

Winrock International. 1983. World agriculture: Review and prospects for the 1990s. Morrilton, Ark.

World Bank. 1986. *World development report 1986*. New York: Oxford University Press.

2. H. B. Atwater, Jr.

From the Club of Rome to Agricultural Surplus: The Dramatic Reversal in World Agricultural Trade

The dramatic reversal in world agricultural trade in the last ten years has confounded the predictions of grain traders and economic pundits alike. In the 1970s, world agricultural markets were booming. There was even a high level of hysteria that widespread starvation was inevitable because production could never keep up with growing demand. By 1987 there had been a complete reversal of these trends, with heavy worldwide stocks of grain and a slackening in world demand for agricultural imports. In particular, the position of the United States as the dominant supplier has deteriorated rapidly and dramatically.

I explore the factors responsible for the export boom of the 1970s and the export bust of the 1980s. With that background, and bearing in mind the hazards of forecasting, I then talk very gingerly about the future direction of world agricultural trade and our political choices in the United States.

The thesis I develop is that world agricultural markets have changed dramatically and will not return to their previous condition. The United States has gone from being the world's largest net exporter of agricultural commodities to the point where we were a net importer for two months last year. I do not expect the United States will regain the position we enjoyed in world agricultural trade during the 1970s. Furthermore, we can no longer expect a large U.S. agricultural trade surplus to offset trade deficits in manufacturing and services.

All the evidence in the 1970s would have sharply contradicted this thesis. International agricultural trade was growing rapidly, and most experts predicted continuing growth. For example, total world wheat imports grew by 71 percent from 1970 to 1980. Some other grains and commodities more than doubled their world imports from 1970 to 1980.

The lesser developed countries of Asia, Africa, and Latin America were major players in this import growth. Four factors stimulated LDC imports: first, rapid population growth; second, a deemphasis of agricultural development relative to urban industrial development; third, a belief that their mineral, oil, and industrial exports would be able to pay for a greater dependence on agricultural imports; and fourth, readily available debt in international financial markets, which they used, in part, to pay for agricultural imports.

In addition to the LDC pressures for imports, the farm economy of Eastern Europe and Asia was in disarray, as poor weather, particularly in the Soviet Union, exacerbated the problems of command economies with few incentives for agriculture.

Frightening projections of future supply and demand for food became the conventional wisdom. The Club of Rome issued a siren call noting the rapidly increasing growth in world population and predicting drastic shortages of all raw materials and commodities, including food, by 1985. In 1974 the environmental fund issued a declaration on population and food, stating, "we have reached, or nearly reached, the limit of the world's ability to feed even our present numbers adequately." To offset the terrible consequences of this anticipated world food shortage, books such as Frances Moore Lappé's *Diet for a Small Planet* urged us to eat grains and other complex carbohydrates rather than meats and heavily processed foods. Since it takes roughly seven pounds of grain to produce one pound of beef, a switch from beef to grain consumption in the richer countries of the world would free up food supplies which could be shifted to the starving and malnourished in the lesser developed countries.

These concerns were not the mere doomsday prophecies of well-meaning Cassandras: the prices of agricultural commodities and of the factors of production in agriculture were increasing substantially. Food prices were escalating dramatically in the United States, and, as a food marketer, I can well remember the consumer boycotts of supermarkets in cities across the United States during the mid-1970s. Grain prices were skyrocketing, and the price of farmland was escalating. Companies in the grain-trading business dramatically expanded their investment in barges, ships, and grain terminal facilities, as it appeared that continued increases in worldwide demand were inevitable.

The United States was uniquely positioned to take advantage of the opportunity provided by expanding international markets in agriculture. We had the world's best technological infrastructure, including superb internal transportation, a system of land grant colleges and agricultural extension services, and plenty of capital for agricultural investment. U.S. farmland was planted from fence row to fence row, and we moved aggressively, building our share of the world grain trade in the late 1970s to a position of such dominance that it enabled some to talk of the possibility of the United States exercising "green power" in a fashion analogous to OPEC's exercise of oil power.

All of this kind had a very positive effect on U.S. trade statistics. The U.S. agricultural trade balance grew from a $1 billion surplus in 1960 to a $26.6 billion surplus in 1980. Our very success in building our agricultural export business masked the fact that we were running an increasingly large trade deficit in manufacturing. Without the agricultural surplus, the U.S. trade account would have been in deficit for sixteen of the last eighteen years, instead of only ten of those last eighteen. Our 1981 agricultural trade surplus of over $25 billion enabled the United States to report a current account surplus of $6.3 billion.

The 1980s have witnessed a virtually complete reversal. The boom markets of the 1970s have stagnated worldwide as import demand for agricultural commodities slackened. World wheat imports, for example, increased by less than 7 percent over the first four years of the 1980s after growing by 71 percent over the previous ten years. Indeed, from 1981 through 1983 there was *no* increase in the world volume of wheat imports. And this pattern is characteristic of many agricultural commodities in the 1980s.

The conventional wisdom of the impending global catastrophe of world food shortages has been changed in the 1980s: now we live in an era of tremendous agricultural surplus. In mid-1986, for example, the stored grain surplus of the United States and EEC alone amounted to approximately one-sixth of total world consumption, an amount considerably larger than the total volume of grain traded in international markets that year.

As agricultural trade slowed and world stocks expanded, prices fell. Falling prices and incomes are measured in the agony of our farm economy, with numerous personal bankruptcies, failing agricultural banks, and the great distress of agricultural implement manufacturers and other agribusiness segments.

This agony is compounded by the sharp deterioration of the position of the United States as principal world supplier. Whereas in 1981 a trade surplus of over $25 billion contributed to a current account surplus of $6.3 billion, by 1986 the United States had a current account deficit of more than $100 billion and an agricultural trade surplus of only $5.4 billion. Furthermore, our share of world grain trade, which was over 50 percent in 1980, had dropped to 34 percent by 1986. For every year from 1980 through 1986, the U.S. share of world grain exports declined, without exception. In the space of seven years we have gone from dominating world trade in agriculture to having a net deficit in agricultural trade for two months last summer.

These are dramatic changes that mark an unprecedented reversal. The question is What caused this dramatic reversal and what does it tell us about the future? And why has the U.S. position of market dominance deteriorated so sharply in this stagnant, oversupplied international market?

The most basic and important long-term cause has been the change in agricultural policies by the governments of countries that were traditionally major agricultural importers. These policies have transformed former importers into self-sufficient and, in some cases, exporting countries. As a result, world import markets have been reduced.

The most important changes are in the lesser developed countries. Today, the conventional wisdom in many of these countries is that the key to economic development lies first in strengthening the agricultural sector of the economy. This is almost a complete reversal of the situation in the 1960s, when most development programs ignored the agricultural sector entirely. The political leaders of LDCs are now recognizing that the agricultural sector offers a number of important opportunities not available in other parts of the economy. Agriculture tends to be much more labor-intensive than manufacturing. Therefore, an investment in the agriculture sector tends to create more jobs. More jobs in rural areas means less urban crowding. Most lesser developed countries have found that the rush to the cities is a socially destabilizing process. Increases in the price of food in a highly urban economy can topple a government. Also, the necessary capital investments required for successful agricultural development tend to be smaller than the capital requirements for manufacturing development projects. Furthermore, many of the roads and other infrastructure improvements required for agriculture also serve other segments of the economy.

The recent *World Development Report* for 1986 issued by the World Bank noted the dramatic effect that third world agricultural policy changes could have. For instance, the introduction of market incentives for the production of agricultural goods has had stunning results in a number of countries. Chinese wheat production more than doubled over the last ten years, due to the introduction of market incentives.

Technological changes in the agricultural sectors of the LDCs is another important policy-induced factor in increasing their self-sufficiency and reducing import demand. India has gone from being a country plagued by food shortages and starvation to the point where it is now a significant exporter of grains, particularly wheat. While the introduction of new strains of wheat and similar "high technology" efforts have been central to the success of India's Green Revolution, the use of very simple technology has played an important role as well. Improvements in the transportation system and storage infrastructure have cut waste to 20 percent of production from its previous level of 80 percent in the 1950s.

The LDCs are no longer dependent upon the developed countries for agricultural technology. During the 1970s, LDC spending on agricultural research and development tripled. Further, the Office of Technology Assessment, in a recent study, listed twenty-nine different technical areas with at least a medium potential for significant productivity increases in agriculture. In nine of those areas, developing countries are playing a leading role. The OTA also noted that the diffusion of existing agricultural technology was occurring much more rapidly than in the past.

In a few countries, most notably Brazil and Mexico, the government has designed policies expressly to foster the development of agricultural export sectors. This effort has been spurred by the massive foreign debt accumulated during the 1970s, which contributed to the expansion of the international agricultural market in that decade. Mexican production now accounts for more than 50 percent of the consumption of fresh fruits and vegetables in the United States during the winter months. Brazil, with the largest debt of all the third world countries, has expanded soybean exports so that they account for 12 percent of Brazil's total foreign exchange earnings.

Africa is the one part of the world that is a significant food problem area. There is great potential for the expansion of agricultural production in Africa, but the biggest stumbling block is the role of the African governments. With few exceptions, they have managed to effectively thwart any significant increase in agricultural production. Should they adopt constructive agricultural policies in their countries, as some are now beginning to do, they could easily become self-sufficient. This is made clear by the fact that "for the first time in more than a decade and a half, agricultural output in Africa in 1986 grew by more than 3 percent—a figure which is more than the population growth rate," according to the executive secretary of the U.N. Economic Commission for Africa.

Developed countries can also create major changes in agricultural trade. The EEC in 1970 was a substantial net importer of grains, with 28 percent of net world imports. In 1985, by contrast, the EEC acounted for 10 percent of net total world exports of grains, in large part due to the production incentives built into the common agricultural policy.

The special political position of the farm community in the United States has also worked to our disadvantage in agricultural trade. That special relationship has been manifested for the past fifty years in a set of agricultural support policies that induce a degree of productive inefficiency: price supports, surplus storage programs, and acreage reduction policies. While these pograms were largely irrelevant to U.S. export performance during the boom markets of the 1970s, their inefficiency-inducing effects may be quite significant for American competitiveness in a relatively sluggish and highly competitive world market in the 1980s.

There are at least two reasons beyond the policy considerations discussed above for the current stagnation in agricultural trade. First, the effects of the global recession in the early 1980s have not been overcome in many parts of the world, and personal income growth rates have been sluggish. This is especially relevant because of the strong relationship between rising income and increased food consumption in lesser developed countries. Current statistics show that in developing countries with annual per capita income above $1,250, food consumption is ten times greater than in those countries with incomes below $250 per capita.

As per capita incomes increase, diets tend to be upgraded, switching from vegetable protein first to rudimentary baked goods and sugars, and then to meats and poultry. Obviously these kinds of consumption changes would create increased markets for feed grains and processed agricultural goods.

A second factor has been the third world debt crisis. The heavily indebted countries have curtailed agricultural imports and have added aggressive export promotion policies in agriculture. For example, effective January 1, 1987, Nigeria, which was the second largest purchaser of American wheat, has banned all imports of wheat. In the past year and a half, Nigeria has banned imports of rice, corn, vegetable oil, and day-old chicks. The reason is simple—Nigeria cannot afford to import food, given its huge debt service requirements. At independence in 1960, Nigeria was largely self-sufficient in agriculture, and agricultural exports, such as cocoa, peanuts and palm oil, accounted for 70 percent of Nigeria's total export earnings. In 1985, food exports accounted for only 3 percent of total exports and Nigeria had to import both peanuts and cooking oil. In response to these trends, Nigeria has set an extremely ambitious goal. It intends to make this nation of 100 million people totally self-sufficient in food by the end of 1987. Once there, they intend to stay self-sufficient.

Another example of the impact of the debt crisis in the 1980s is provided by Argentina, whose total foreign debt equals 46 percent of its GNP. Argentina has expanded its agricultural exports by 43 percent in volume in an effort to meet its debt service requirements. Costa Rica, while admittedly not one of the major players in international markets, nevertheless also illustrates in interesting ways the impact of the debt crisis. Reprocessed coffee wastes, which are abundant in that country, are now being used to replace imported corn in the diets of cattle. Such innovations, born of the fear of additional international debt, can have a significant effect in reducing world demand for agricultural imports, when aggregated across many similar countries.

An additional factor that put pressure on U.S. agricultural trade was the strengthening of the dollar between 1980 and 1985, which dramatically raised the price of our exports. Because this increase in the value of the dollar was substantial relative to almost all of the world's currencies, it gave a significant boost to the agricultural export promotion policies of all of our principal competitors. As a result, the United States lost some market share to many other exporters. The post-1985 decline in the value of the dollar has been great relative only to our major industrial trading partners; the value of the currencies of some of our primary competitors in international agricultural markets, such as Argentina, Australia, Brazil, and Canada, has remained relatively low.

The United States has also been hurt by the perception that we are an unreliable supplier. This was an outgrowth of the U.S. grain embargoes, which not only opened the door to new suppliers, as in the case of Brazil and soybeans, but also destabilized established customer relationships as with the Soviet Union. These agreements are only now beginning to be reestablished.

Finally, the increasingly intense, subsidized agricultural trade war being waged with the EEC is hurting our exports. Last August the European community offered butter on international markets at a price that was 3 percent of the EEC's cost to purchase it. The Common Agricultural Program is inducing budget crises in the EEC, but for a number of domestic reasons—particularly the special political position of farmers, notably in France—it is not clear that they will abandon this subsidized trade policy.

While U.S. agricultural trade will not return to the booming situation of the 1970s, conditions *can* be made better than they are now. There is not a single and simple solution, but a package of reforms on several fronts should serve to improve the current picture.

First, the long-term special political position of the farm community in the United States must be transformed. The agricultural support policies that have been in place for the past fifty years are not working now, except as a restraint on our international competitiveness.

The United States needs to replace governmental incentives for production with market incentives. The return on investment for farmers varies dramatically with the size of their farm, the level of sophistication of the farmer, the kind of job the farm represents—full time or part time—and the cost of the major capital factors of land and equipment. In other words, farmers with reasonably priced capital inputs are making money at farming even with today's prices. Small farms, hobby farms, and farms with high-priced assets and heavy interest burdens are in terrible financial shape. Rather than spending $26 billion to support farm prices for an existing farm, farmers who cannot compete in the new environment must be helped to move to new employment.

We must avoid the temptation to take large quantities of agricultural land out of production by paying farmers for acreage set-asides. This delivers money to the wrong hands and slows down the necessary process of having inefficient farmers leave agriculture. Furthermore, it has the potential of dramatically raising prices for American consumers and absolutely pricing us out of export markets without heavy export subsidies. Congress will not easily give up its special relationship with agriculture, but long-term prospects for America's role in international agricultural trade are rather dim if it does not.

Second, as a step toward reinvigorating the international agricultural markets, the United States should do its part to spur world economic growth, especially in the third world. As much as anything, this probably means avoiding the increasingly strong temptation in Congress to impose import restrictions on manufactured goods from the newly industrialized countries of the third world and more vigorously attempting to reduce our government budget deficit, which annually drains some $200 billion of potential investment finances out of the world economy. Healthy world economic growth will not resume without a resolution of the debt problems of the lesser developed countries.

Lastly, the United States needs urgently to resolve its growing agricultural trade war with the EEC. International agricultural markets have been more subject to governmental intervention than virtually any other international economic sector. The consequence is a very expensive and market-distorting burden for the world's consumers and taxpayers. We must move now to the bargaining table to negotiate joint reductions in the level of subsidization of agricultural exports.

While the seemingly endless "good times" of the 1970s will not return to agriculture, both the United States as well as individual American farmers must be able to profit from participation in international agricultural markets. We must have the political will to craft our agricultural programs so that they reflect the realities of international markets. U.S. policies must help move the domestic agricultural sector to become an effective competitor in the new world agriculture scenario.

3. John R. Block
Food Policy in an Evolving World Marketplace

I speak from personal experience because I have spent a lifetime in agriculture. I was born and raised on a farm and have lived the agriculture industry from a tractor seat to the cabinet room, and seen a lot of things happen—some of them good and some of them not particularly good.

If you look back to the year 1700, one farmer was feeding three people, only three. By the year 2000, one farmer in the United States will be feeding more than a hundred people. When I was a boy, we had two old horses called Bert and Bill, and my sisters and I milked ten cows with my father, by hand, morning and night. And those old horses pulled a two-row corn planter. It took a long time to plant the corn under those conditions.

Today we have a farming operation of seven people. Those seven people are producing ten thousand head of hogs a year, and three thousand acres of corn and soy beans. Not only is the operation vastly different today, but it is a capital-intensive business. Then it was much more labor-intensive. But also the things you talked about and look toward were entirely different.

As a boy we would bale the hay in the afternoon and, with the hay put away, would sit around visiting with the neighbors. The men were always talking about the weather and a host of things, but they never talked about the international market place. They did not talk about the strength of the dollar; they did not talk about penetrating the Soviet market and sending another million metric tons of wheat into the Soviet Union; they did not talk about any of those things because we had an industry that was labor-intensive. It was national, and in some cases even regional and local, in scope.

We bottled our own milk in the basement and took it and sold it in my grandfather's store. We gathered the eggs and took them to town and sold them in his store. It is certainly not like that today.

Agriculture is a global industry. And for the most part, this has happened in my lifetime and yours. If you look back to the 1930s, 25 percent of the people in this country lived on farms. Today 2 percent live on farms. Even more important, of that small percentage who live on farms and farm, 14 percent of the farmers produce 75 percent of the farm production.

As Bruce Gardner pointed out, when we went into the 1970s, the world market exploded. Earl Butz was out selling grain everywhere, all around the world, and the expectations were just unbelievable. Those expectations carried forward to the day I went to the office of secretary of agriculture. Just two months before I stepped into that chair, the *Wall Street Journal,* on November 28, 1980, was telling the world: "Big increases in food prices loom as world demands more U.S. grain. U.S. can no longer be a bread basket to the world. Food will be in the 80s what oil became in the 70s. Scarce and expensive." It goes on and on, and the situation we know does not resemble anything in that article. It just shows how the whole country and the whole industry and the whole world was caught up in these expectations; it is no different from people who thought we would see $100 a barrel of oil. The high-price incentive brings on more production, regardless of what it is, and the whole thing collapsed as we went into the 1980s.

In the agricultural industry, prices plunged, and land values declined. Frankly they were in a free-fall in the early part of the 1980s, but they have started to change a little bit now. You sit in the Cabinet Council of Economic Affairs and the cabinet room and you wish you could get your hand on the handle to straighten it out. But there is no handle to pull. Because the handle is all wrapped up in international macroeconomic policies. And no one really understands what those policies are.

So you have got all these problems to deal with, with a strong dollar. Bruce Gardner pointed out that the ability of our customers to buy products from us collapsed, the European economic community turned into a big exporter, and they are subsidizing exports all over the world because they have to get rid of them too—they don't know what to do with the stuff. We have a farm program in place that was put in place in 1981; it, unfortunately, is designed in a way to encourage production. It provides for an escalating support price, escalating target prices, targets and supports that everyone in the world shot for because they knew they were guaranteed. One of the things we have to fix is a farm program that is not related to the conditions of the day. That means lowering supports, and you know how many people want to lower supports under those conditions. That is the kind of situation we wrote the 1985 farm bill under, I might add.

Of course not all farm commodities are given these direct supports. In fact, in dollar terms, more than half of our commodities are not supported this way. They may have some indirect support, however. Wheat, feed grains, rice, cotton and dairy, peanuts, and tobacco are supported, but all the meats and all the special crops are unsupported. Meats of course get an indirect support because they rely on the grain that must be fed to the animals.

The 1985 farm bill did some good things. We lowered the loan rate dramatically so that we did not have that guarantee to our farmers and the rest of the world that the price was always going to be high. In Bruce Gardner's paper, table 7.6 really shows how the loan rate came down. In some cases it needs to come down still more. Prices in some cases are about half what they once were.

Where are we today? I will talk a little about our domestic farm programs, because you cannot divorce domestic policy from trade policy.

Our domestic policies impact Europe. European domestic policies impact the Caribbean because they are dumping sugar all over the world, depressing the price of sugar. Frankly, they would not be able to compete if they had to do it on an open market. But farm programs in different countries are impacting everyone else in the world.

American agriculture is starting to stabilize somewhat, after being in a free-fall since about 1981 or 1982. Land values, although declining, are not declining as fast today. Exports, in terms of dollar sales and especially in terms of volume, look like they may be starting to turn back up again.

The United States is using a host of subsidy programs to penetrate markets and to pressure the European community into abandoning their farm policies that have been disastrous for us and a lot of other countries.

And we are using our surpluses to push product into the market. We'll sell something, and then we'll give them a little extra wheat so they'll have a good deal, and we'll be able to sell more product that way. We are zapping countries all over the world. We are taking markets away from Argentina by selling beef to Brazil. We took sugar markets from Australia by selling sugar to China. We have everyone in the world angry at us for what we are doing. So we are successful in getting the world's attention that agricultural subsidies are a world problem.

When you look at the rest of the world, a very important point is the battle cry for food self-sufficiency. I think it is going to have a big impact. It is already starting to.

I saw the sands of Saudi Arabia green with wheat. They should not have been raising any wheat there at all, but Saudi Arabia is now a net wheat exporter. They are an exporter of wheat which is absolutely insane. They are paying their farmers a thousand dollars a ton to produce, raise, and sell wheat. I could raise wheat on this floor for a thousand dollars a ton and make money.

But it is a fact of life—there is a battle cry for food self-sufficiency. But wanting it is one thing; knowing how to achieve it is another. Many of them have figured this out because they realize that price incentive is the way to get it done. Let the prices rise and then technology will flow, and they will produce more food as time goes on.

Technology is flowing now. You get farm people complaining that we are transferring our technology to other countries so they can compete against us. I don't buy that. We do some of that, but technology just plain flows. Technology is for sale. It is for sale because we are a country of private companies.

I went to Hungary a year and a half ago to visit their agriculture experiment station—the most beautiful corn you have ever seen outside of corn in Illinois. What do you think those experiment station people were wearing. They were wearing Pioneer caps, all of them. And that is in Hungary. You can find similar examples everywhere. Technology transfer is occurring.

Finally, the other agricultural exporting countries in the world are feeling a pinch like the United States. In Europe, in many cases, the price of product in real terms has gone down. Their budgets are being taxed to the limit; they are trying to find more revenue to keep their supports in place; and land values have declined, in France in particular.

I have read reports that in Australia, with these lower prices, which is a disincentive to produce wheat in Australia, that by year 1991 their acres in wheat production will be about half what they were at their peak in 1981 or 1982, unless they turn around the policies. And in Canada, they are cutting their acres for corn because the prices are not as attractive as they once were. This tells us that these lower prices are working. But it takes a while for them to work, to put this disincentive through the whole system.

I suggest that the 1985 farm bill will not be changed very much. There is a lot of talk of wild-eyed ideas, like Senator Harkins' supply management, but the closer the proponents of that idea get to it, the more they are going to run away from it like the plague. It would raise the cost of food dramatically, and politically it is an untenable position. I am amazed at Gephardt. I am not amazed at Harkins. That is his populist mentality, but I can not imagine why Gephardt signed on to that kind of approach. I say it is not going to happen.

The administration's dramatic cuts are not going to happen either, this year, because politics will not allow it.

The longer-range solution to the farm problem should involve what they popularly talk about as decoupling, as promoted by Senators Boschwitz and Boren. This solution really says, let's see which farmers receive subsidies, let's figure out about how much they were getting, and let's just give them those subsidies. We'll give them a little less each year, but we won't ask them to do anything. You don't have to cut production; you can go down to the breakers and enjoy the weather; you can do anything you want with those subsidies.

That is a good solution because it buys farmers off of this kick of being on the dole of the farm program. And in the final analysis the farmer will start responding to market signals. The key to it is not to have any production requirements placed on the farmer. Let him raise what he wants, whatever he wants.

The time for that approach has finally arrived. Farmers argue that it is a welfare-type program. Well, call it what you like—I call it a transition program to get out from under the heavy hand of government. I think something like that will be written into the next farm bill, but it is not due to be written until 1990. Maybe they will write it before then, but Congress never does anything until it has to. It won't write a new farm bill until the old one expires.

The rules for trade in agricultural products are going to be written or not written with these GATT talks that we talked about before. It is important that agriculture have a priority there. Writing new rules is going to be enormously difficult because countries are still providing a great many special privileges to agriculture. All over the world, there is no industry that has been given this kind of special consideration. In my judgment, agriculture should not be given special treatment in the world, especially in the developed countries. It should take its place alongside other businesses and industry in the world economy since it is a global industry today. But to break away from these old ties of special support will not be easy. I am optimistic that, given the kind of change we have seen in our lifetimes in trade and agricultural, in the next twenty years we will see more dramatic changes, where many of these national borders will melt away or diminish. And hopefully the tension in the world will diminish as trade tends to increase, and we will have a little safer place in the world.

I will close my remarks by quoting a few words that have to do with food diplomacy, agriculture, and the food industry as the foremost diplomatic tool in world affairs. In fact this quote shows beyond a shadow of a doubt that food and agriculture are the foremost diplomatic tool. This is a letter written to a newspaper in my state of Illinois. Peoria, Illinois, How does it play in Peoria? Well, this was written to a Peoria newspaper. "I saw a newspaper picture of the Soviet Minister of Agriculture holding a pig while standing next to U.S. Secretary John Block who was also holding a pig. A year ago I saw another picture of the President of France and Block, holding pigs, during a visit to Block's Illinois farm. Obviously I'm missing something because I don't understand this. Can you help me."

The newspaper writes back: "Not really. For reasons that not even the State Department understands, whenever foreign dignitaries arrive in the United States, they immediately ask if they can hold a pig with John Block. It's simply one of those international mysteries. It's pig diplomacy."

Summary of Discussion

John Block explained the apparent contradiction between the huge increase in federal farm payments and the desperate shape of so many farmers: most of the money passes through the hands of the farmers on to their bankers. The real question, he said, is how we got to where we are. He proposed that under the scenario given in a 1980 *Wall Street Journal* article that predicted food shortages in the 1980s, the programs as designed would not have been so expensive. In the seventies the same types of programs worked reasonably well, since the farm economy stayed ahead of the support prices. The 1985 farm bill represents some improvement, since the lowering of the loan rate makes agriculture more competitive in world markets, although the outlay is still enormous since the difference was made up with direct payments to farmers. Obviously, farmers have enormous clout in Congress.

Bruce Atwater attributed the special treatment of farm debtors to the strength of the farm block. When small farms approach bankruptcy, there is significant political reaction; when small industrial companies borrow too much, prices fall, and they approach bankruptcy, there is not a similar political reaction. Government lending agencies were encouraging farmers to borrow in the late seventies, since the petrodollars had to be recycled and agriculture was considered to be a sector of comparative advantage. James Schlesinger added that Iowa has an early presidential primary.

Block saw little cause to predict rapid change in the strength of farm interests, pointing out that it is especially difficult to change a program that is already in place. He added that while there are relatively few farmers, rural America, which is closely related to farm America, is very important, since 25 percent of Americans are rural, as are 75 percent of governmental units and 90 percent of natural resources. He predicted nonetheless that we have seen the high water mark for agricultural outlays both in the United States and Europe. The fall in the dollar helps, as does the effect of the 1985 farm bill on export prices, and while Japan says it will be self-sufficient in rice at any cost, it will be importing in ten years. Block noted that it is a myth that the family farm will disappear. Almost all farms are and will be family farms.

Several discussants speculated on the fate of the EEC farm policy. Schlesinger suggested that the EEC situation will fall apart when the Left takes over in the United Kingdom and Germany, as the support for the current conservative governments is very rural, and the high domestic food prices will not be tolerated, particularly at an exchange rate of one DM to the dollar. Atwater disagreed, citing the support of the French government for the current agriculture policy and the proagricultural implications of the addition of Spain to the community and the growing strength of Italy. Anne Krueger expressed the belief that the European common agricultural policy (CAP) would encounter trouble due to budgetary issues within the community, and remarked that the French generated only token flack about the 1986 World Bank *World Development Report,* which was critical of aspects of the EEC farm policy.

The prospects for a large contribution of U.S. agriculture exports to the resolution of the trade imbalance were discussed by several people. Block reported the forecasts of the National Association of Food Producers, which projected an increase of food exports in volume (64 percent) and value (42 percent) by 1991. He expressed less bullishness but agreed that exports would recover, and predicted that imports would increase at a slower pace. He noted that the prospects for serious discussion of agriculture at GATT are good since current U.S. policy of stealing markets from the EEC and LDCs has created a desire in these countries for some rules on trade in agriculture.

Bruce Gardner tempered this optimism with the remark that the striking aspect of the trend in per capita food production since the mid-1970s is not so much that the rate of increase in food production has gone up but that the rate of population growth has slowed. The relationship of this trend to income growth is the key to an increase in food exports; since little can be done to change it, at least in the remainder of the 1980s, this is gloomy news for agricultural exports.

Krueger saw hope for U.S. agricultural exports in the immanent changes in EEC policy, in the prospective takeoff of Japan and Korea as food importers, and in the importance of the dollar exchange rate in agricultural trade. She noted that while macro forecasts often turn out to be self-fulfilling, micro forecasts are generally the reverse of the truth.

Jack Sawyer suggested that economists not ignore questions of political economy. For example, on the issue of competitiveness, much of the current discussion is couched in overly general language. He wondered if some politically useful ideas about entitlement programs could not be framed in terms of consumption subsidies and savings incentives. Peter Peterson predicted an eventual revolution against the entitlement constituencies, but pointed out that currently there is no sign of this. A modest proposal to reduce the COLA frequency from twice to once per year generated armfuls of negative mail, for example.

8 Changing Patterns of International Investment in and by the United States

1. *Robert E. Lipsey*
2. *Mario Schimberni*
3. *Robert V. Lindsay*

1. *Robert E. Lipsey*

8.1 Introduction

After World War II, the United States became the major supplier of capital in world markets, and for many years that role appeared to be a permanent one. The United States' recent swing to being the world's largest borrower is a reminder that in this respect our history has been cyclical since the late nineteenth century, alternating between periods of capital exporting and capital importing. These swings were mainly based on economic circumstances, but at times wars and threats of wars, revolutions, and other types of government instability made investment flow uphill, against the pull of purely economic forces.

A more constant feature than the direction of the capital flow has been the association of U.S. capital exports with the export of technology and management. Americans were the innovators in exporting the package of management, technology, and capital, sometimes even without the capital, that is known as foreign direct investment: the ownership of production facilities in one country by firms based in another country.

The development of this type of multinational enterprise and the changes that have taken place within it reflect the evolution of the competitiveness and comparative advantage of American firms and their responses to changes in political and economic circumstances. The innovation represented by these U.S. enterprises has been increasingly copied by firms based in other countries, with the result that many foreign firms have entered the U.S. market, and multinational activity has become a feature of firms even from developing countries.

Against the relatively steady growth of direct investment, first out of the United States and then into it, there have been large swings in other forms of investment. Most foreign investment in the United States has been portfolio rather than direct investment; that is, it has not included foreign control of U.S. enterprises. The United States too has engaged in brief, but very large, spurts in portfolio investing in foreign countries. These are important, despite their infrequency, because they have been so large, at times outrunning the steadier trends in direct investment.

8.2   Historical Background

8.2.1   Foreign Investment in the United States before World War I

The recent metamorphosis of the United States into a large international borrower has been unsettling. It has been an unfamiliar role for many decades, but it is not a totally new one. It is a return to the pattern of the United States' first century of existence. Most of the time, from George Washington's inauguration until an abrupt turn to capital exporting at the end of the nineteenth century, the United States had been a net borrower in foreign financial markets (see table 8.1).

The cumulation of borrowing year after year until the end of the nineteenth century meant that the United States was a net debtor throughout these years; it was still a net debtor at the beginning of World War I, despite fifteen or twenty years in which the United States was a net foreign lender most of the time (see table 8.2).

Table 8.1   **Net Inflow of Capital to the United States (millions of dollars, current prices)**

Years	Inflow
1790–99	21
1800–1809	11
1810–19	97
1820–29	−6
1830–39	209
1840–49	−80
1850–59	196
1860–69	768
1870–79	402
1880–89	1,146
1890–99	97
1900–1909	−600
1910–14	341

Source: U.S. Bureau of the Census 1975, Series U 18–U 23.

Table 8.2   **Net Liabilities (−) of the United States, 1789–1914 (millions of dollars, current prices)**

	From Cumulation of Net Capital Flows	From Compilation of Assets and Liabilities	
		Net	Gross
1789	−60		
1800	−83		
1815	−80		
1820	−88[a]		
1830	−75		
1840	−261		
1850	−217[b]		
1860	−377		
1870	−1,252		
1880	−1,584		
1890	−2,894		
1900	−2,501		
1897	−3,305	−2,710	−3,395
1908		−3,875	−6,400
1914		−3,686	−7,200

Sources: Cumulation of net capital flows from U.S. Bureau of the Census 1975, Series U 40. Compilation of assets and liabilities from Lewis 1938, 445.

[a]After defaults of $50 million in 1816–19.

[b]After defaults of $12 million in 1841 and 1842.

An indication of the size of the debt relative to the U.S. economy is that the net indebtedness was about 3 percent of U.S. national wealth or tangible assets (land, structures, equipment, and inventories) in 1900; the indebtedness of 1914 was a little over 2 percent of national wealth in 1912. U.S. gross indebtedness in 1914, including foreign holdings of direct investment, was about 2.5 percent of total tangible and financial assets in the United States in 1912 (U.S. Bureau of the Census 1975, Series F 377 and F 378).

There are several ways to view the role of these flows of financial capital in American development. One is as a source of financing for aggregate capital formation, permitting faster accumulation of capital than would have taken place if only domestic financing had been available. On this basis, it is hard to suppose that imports of capital had a great influence on the rate of development, at least during most of the nineteenth century. The capital inflows never reached more than 1.5 percent of total output in any decade from the 1830s through the first ten years of the twentieth century and were probably never more than 6 percent or possible 7 percent of gross capital formation (see table 8.3).

Table 8.3   Net Inflow of Capital in 1860 Prices

	As Percent of Gross National Product	As Percent of Gross Domestic Capital Formation
1834–43	0.6	6.2
1839–48	−0.3	−2.8
1844–53	0.4	3.1
1849–58	0.5	3.4
1854–63	0.5	n.a.
1859–68	0.9	n.a.
1864–73	1.5	n.a.
1869–78	1.1	4.9
1874–83	−0.1	−0.5
1879–88	0.8	3.5
1884–93	1.5	5.6
1889–98	0.5	1.8
1894–1903	−0.8	−3.1
1899–1908	−0.5	−1.8

Source: Edelstein 1982, 234, table 10.1, cols. 1 and 3.

In general, U.S. borrowing from foreign countries rose when U.S. capital formation surged; borrowing tapered off as U.S. saving, rising more gradually and steadily, caught up with capital formation. Thus, investment from abroad accommodated the large spurts in the demand for capital that characterized the rapidly growing economy.

There may have been other roles for borrowing from abroad. One might have been to supply funds for particularly risky forms of capital formation at a lower interest rate than would have been required by domestic lenders. Another might have been to supply funds when, in the face of heavy demands by rapidly growing sectors, U.S. domestic lenders' needs for diversification of risks made them reluctant to offer sufficient financing to these sectors. Another interpretation is that U.S. railway and government securities, relatively safe and requiring less local knowledge than investment in smaller-scale enterprises in agriculture, mining, and manufacturing, tended to be sold overseas, while domestic suppliers of capital invested in the riskier, but more profitable, sectors (Edelstein 1982, 237–38).

The bulk of foreign investment in the United States was portfolio investment rather than direct investment (table 8.4). That is, it consisted of purchases of bonds or, to a small extent, equities that did not involve control over the enterprise receiving the capital. Just before World War I, about 80 percent of the stock of long-term foreign investment in the United States was portfolio investment; the same had been true for the flow over a long period (Edelstein 1982, 36 and 37). Governments and railways were the chief borrowers, and most of the financing was

Table 8.4   **Composition of U.S. Liabilities, 1869–1914 (millions of dollars, current prices)**

	1869	1897	1908	1914
Direct investment ⎱				⎧ 1,310
Securities ⎰	1,390	3,145	6,000	⎩ 5,440
Short-term credits	150	250	400	450
Total	1,540	3,395	6,400	7,200

Source: Lewis 1938, 442 and 445.

in the form of bonds rather than equities. Most of the foreign investment, whether for governments or private companies, went to large,
lumpy, social overhead capital projects, such as canals, railways, electrical utilities, and telephone and telegraph systems (Edelstein 1982,
39–41). Manufacturing enterprises were probably almost all too small
to seek foreign financing or even, in most cases, public financing from
domestic sources.

There were instances of manufacturing enterprises set up by foreign
craftsmen or entrepreneurs with special knowledge or skill. However,
in an era in which transportation and communication were slow by
modern standards, these often involved the migration of the owners
and eventual conversion of their enterprises into domestic entitites.
Thus, these enterprises involved mainly a flow of human capital to the
United States.

We do not deal with the flow of human capital here, but it may have
been more important to U.S. development than the flows of financial
capital. In terms of numbers, immigration into the United States in
each decade from the 1830s through the beginning of World War I
ranged from about 5 percent to 10 percent of the number already in
the country (U.S. Bureau of the Census 1975, Series A 6 and C 89).
Furthermore, most of the immigrants (a 50 percent larger proportion
than in the population as a whole) were between fifteen and forty-four
years of age (U.S. Bureau of the Census 1975, Series C 119, C 122-27,
C 138, and C 141). They came to the United States with most of their
rearing costs already incurred and with a large part of their working
lives still ahead of them.

8.2.2   The Beginnings of U.S. Direct Investment Abroad

The United States has been unique among the major investing countries in that the principal form of its investment has been, from the
earliest times recorded, direct rather than portfolio investment (table
8.5). That is, it has typically involved control of foreign operations
rather than simply the lending of capital to foreign-controlled firms or

Table 8.5   Stock of U.S. Investment Abroad, by Type (millions of dollars, current prices)

	Direct	Portfolio[a]
1897	634.5	50.0
1908	1,638.5	886.3
1914	2,652.3	861.5

Source: Lewis 1938, 605.
[a]Net of repatriations and repudiations.

to governments. The earliest estimates, for 1897, show over 90 percent of U.S. investment to have been of this type.

The earliest examples of U.S. direct investment took place while the United States was still, on net balance, an importer of capital. They illustrate the key role of the export of technology, or other firm-specific assets, as contrasted to the pure export of capital, as is the case with portfolio investment.

U.S. direct investment abroad, in the sense of production abroad by subsidiaries or branches of U.S. companies, began soon after the Civil War and involved companies "with national sales plans and unique products" (Wilkins 1970, 35). Wilkins describes Singer, the manufacturer of sewing machines, as "the first American international business" (p. 37), with salaried sales representatives abroad in the early 1860s and its first foreign factory by the late 1860s (p. 42). Other early American production abroad during the period when the United States was still a capital importer was done by Hoe (printing presses), Babcock and Wilcox (boilers), International Bell Telephone and Western Electric, Edison Electric, Thomson-Houston Electric, a component of General Electric when it was formed later, Westinghouse Air Brake, Kodak, McCormick, Worthington Pump, Chicago Pneumatic Tool, Otis Elevator, National Cash Register, and Libbey-Owens (Southard 1931; Wilkins 1970, chap. 3). These companies were typically early technological leaders in their fields. Another indication of the importance of technology rather than capital is the number of instances in which the parent's investment consisted entirely or largely of patent rights, as in the case of Ford in Canada, Libbey-Owens Glass in various European countries, and Westinghouse Electric in the United Kingdom (Lewis 1938, 300–301).

8.2.3   The Transformation of the U.S. International Balance Sheet, 1914–19

The beginning of World War I found the United States still a substantial international net debtor, but the events of the next few years transformed the country's international balance sheet. As a result of wartime lending by the United States, and especially the liquidation of foreign claims against the United States in the form of holdings of U.S. securities, this country ended the period as a net creditor in international markets (table 8.6). The United States became a net creditor even on private account, aside from the intergovernment debt of almost $10 billion that was to bedevil international negotiations on reparations and other topics through the interwar years.

8.2.4   The United States as an International Investor, 1919–29

The period of the 1920s, and particularly the late 1920s, was exceptional in the history of U.S. investing abroad in two respects. One was that the growth of portfolio investment was far greater than that of direct investment, to the extent that the stock of portfolio investment exceeded that of direct investment for the first and only time at the end of that period (table 8.7). The other was that, in the late 1920s, direct investment in foreign public utilities, which represented only 4 percent of the stock of direct investment in 1924, accounted for over a third of the increase during the next five years (table 8.8).

Almost the whole history of U.S. direct investment in foreign public utilities is concentrated in the few years between 1924 and 1929. The increase in the stock of public utility investment in these years was almost 80 percent of the 1929 total as compared with less than 30 percent for all industries combined (table 8.9). The direct investment in foreign public utilities was very concentrated, both geographically and by company. The most detailed geographical breakdown, available only for 1940, probably reflects the distribution in 1929 (table 8.10). Over 60 percent of the public utility investment was in Latin America,

Table 8.6   **The International Balance Sheet of the United States (millions of dollars, current prices)**

	July 1, 1914	Dec. 31, 1919
Assets (private account)		
Securities	862	2,576
Direct investments	2,652	3,880
Short-term credits	—	500
Total	3,514	6,956
Liabilities		
Securities	5,400	1,623
Direct investments	1,310	900
Sequestrated property and securities	—	662
Short-term credits	450	800
Total	7,200	3,985
Net privately held	−3,686	2,971
Net government	—	9,591
Private and government	−3,686	12,562

Source: Lewis 1938, 447.

Table 8.7 Value of Stock of Private Foreign Assets of the United States (millions of dollars, current prices)

Type of Investment	1919	1924	1929	1924 minus 1919	1929 minus 1924
Direct	3,880	5,389	7,553	1,509	2,164
Portfolio, incl. short term	3,076	5,365	9,456	2,289	4,091
Total	6,957	10,754	17,010	3,797	6,256

Source: Lewis 1938, 450 and 605.

Table 8.8 Percentage Distribution by Industry of the Value and the Growth in Value of the Stock of U.S. Direct Investment

	1924	1929	1929 minus 1924
Primary production[a]	45.6	40.6	28.2
Manufacturing	23.2	24.1	26.3
Public utilities	4.2	13.6	37.0
Distribution, incl. petroleum[b]	13.1	11.5	7.2
Other	13.9	10.3	1.3
Total	100.0	100.0	100.0

Source: Lewis 1938, 450 and 605.
[a]Agriculture, mining, and petroleum production.
[b]Sales and purchasing, including petroleum distribution.

Table 8.9 Growth in Value of the Stock of U.S. Direct Investment, 1924–29, as Percentage of the 1929 Stock, by Industry

	1929 minus 1924 as Percent of 1929
Primary production, excl. petroleum distribution	19.9
Manufacturing	31.2
Public utilities	78.2
Distribution incl. petroleum distribution	18.1
Other	3.5
Total	28.7

Source: Lewis 1938, 450 and 605.

Table 8.10   **Percentage Distribution (%) of U.S. Direct Investment in Public Utilities**

	1940
Canada and Newfoundland	26.9
Latin America	63.6
Other	9.5
Total	100.0

Source: Sammons and Abelson 1942, 21.

mainly South America, far above that area's share in total direct investment.

Portfolio investment, as well as direct investment, was concentrated in South America during the 1920s (table 8.11). More than a third of the growth in direct investment between 1924 and 1929 was in South America, the location of less than a fifth of such investment in 1924, and over a quarter of the growth in portfolio investment was directed there in these years, although the initial share was only 10 percent. Another way of describing the temporal concentration of investment in South America is that almost half of the stock of direct investment and almost two-thirds of the stock of portfolio investment in South America in 1929 were accounted for by the growth between 1924 and 1929 (table 8.12).

Table 8.11   **Percentage Distribution by Geographical Area of the Value and the Growth in Value of U.S. Direct Investment**

	1924	1929	1929 minus 1924
Direct investment			
Europe	17.5	18.0	19.4
Canada and Newfoundland	20.5	22.3	26.7
Cuba and other West Indies	18.9	13.8	1.5
Mexico and Central America	16.7	12.9	3.8
South America	18.0	23.2	35.7
Africa, Asia, and Oceania	8.4	9.8	13.1
Total excl. banking	100.0	100.0	100.0
Portfolio investment			
Europe	37.9	41.7	46.9
Canada and Newfoundland	34.0	25.6	13.9
Cuba and other West Indies	2.4	1.6	.6
Mexico and Central America	6.2	3.9	.6
South America	10.2	16.5	25.5
Africa, Asia, and Oceania	9.4	10.7	12.5
Total excl. international	100.0	100.0	100.0

Source: Lewis 1938, 606.

Table 8.12   Growth in Value of the Stock of U.S. Direct and Portfolio
                    Investment, 1924–29, as Percentage of the 1929 Stock, by Area

	Percentage of 1929 Stock
Direct investment	
Europe	31.3
Canada and Newfoundland	34.8
Cuba and other West Indies	3.1
Mexico and Central America	8.5
South America	44.9
Africa, Asia, and Oceania	39.0
Total excl. banking	29.1
Portfolio investment	
Europe	46.9
Canada and Newfoundland	22.5
Cuba and other West Indies	15.8
Mexico and Central America	6.6
South America	64.1
Africa, Asia, and Oceania	48.8
Total excl. international	41.7

Source: Lewis 1938, 606.

The changes in value, especially for portfolio investment, reflect some price changes as well as new investment. However, these data do not reflect the price changes on individual issues but only changes in exchange rates. In any case, very little of the investment was in common stock (about 5 percent), and almost all the loans were dollar loans (about 95 percent), so neither possible source of price change, stock prices or exchange rates, could have been of much importance. Thus, the changes in portfolio investment must represent a tremendous flurry of new financing during this period.

The reasons for this concentrated burst of portfolio investment were probably different from those behind the direct investment in utilities. The two U.S. companies that were the ultimate parents of most of the utility affiliates were major manufacturers of the capital goods purchased by the utilities. Neither one was a domestic company in the industries in which these affiliates operated. The ownership of foreign utilities was, in effect, a way of exploiting the parents' advantages in technology and marketing in the telephone and electric power equipment manufacturing industries. The concentration of these investments in Latin America and their decline were at least partly the result of government monopolization and regulation, earlier in Europe and later in Latin America and Asia as well.

The burst of portfolio investment in the late 1920s was fueled by some of the same speculative spirit that propelled the U.S. stock

market in those years. The concentration in South American investment represented, according to one very thorough study (Mintz 1951)
and many contemporary accounts, a large decline in the quality of
credit extended, as the boom of the late 1920s progressed. The fall
in quality is summarized by the fact that of the loans extended in
the first half of the 1920s, only 18 percent went into default later,
while the share of defaults was 50 percent for loans extended in 1925–
29 (Mintz 1951, 6).

8.2.5 Defaults and Liquidations, 1929–35

After the large build-up of portfolio assets and liabilities in the last
few years of the 1920s, the depression of the 1930s led to a wave of
liquidations of security holdings and of defaults on foreign bonds among
U.S. investments abroad as well. In addition, asset and liability values
decreased as a result of declines in prices, but much of this decline is
concealed by the use of book values for bonds. We do have a rough
estimate of U.S. international assets with defaulted bonds valued at
market, but we do not have a similar estimate for market values of
other securities or direct investment.

Even without any allowance for default or price depreciation on
bonds, we observe a decline of more than a quarter in securities assets,
a reduction of short-term assets by almost half, and a decline of about
20 percent in securities liabilities (table 8.13). The market value of U.S.
security holdings, taking account of depreciation on defaulted bonds
but not on other securities, declined almost 50 percent.

Table 8.13   **The International Balance Sheet of the United States, 1929 and
1935 (millions of dollars, current prices)**

	1929	1935	
		All Bonds at Par	Defaulted Bonds at Market
U.S. private investments abroad			
Direct investment	7,553	7,219	7,219
Securities	7,839	5,622	4,222
Short-term credits	1,617	853	853
Total private	17,009	13,694	12,294
U.S. liabilities			
Direct investment	1,400	1,580	
Securities	4,304	3,529	
Sequestrated properties	150	—	
Short-term credits	3,077	1,220	
Total private liabilities	8,931	6,329	

Source: Lewis 1938, 454.

By 1935, the primacy of direct investment among U.S. assets had reappeared. Some of the direct investment values may be inflated by the use of book values. Still, mismeasurement of capital stock is not responsible for the main story, as can be seen from the capital flow data (table 8.14). The United States continued to invest in controlled companies abroad, at least for the first couple of years, and the decline in value of these investments must therefore have stemmed largely from exchange rate changes, and from declines before sale in the value of assets sold during the period.

The data for long-term portfolio and short-term investment reveal a repatriation to the United States of about $2 billion. The rest of the $3 billion decline in the U.S. portfolio assets may reflect some losses from declines in the value of foreign currencies relative to the U.S. dollar. On the other side, the decline in foreign portfolio and short-term assets in the United States of almost $3 billion was less than half accounted for by capital flows during the period.

The United States ran a surplus on goods and services during this period of more than $3 billion. The deficits of the U.S. partner countries were financed not by private capital flows but by an absorption of gold by the United States of about $3 billion in the last two years of the period.

8.2.6   The United States as a Destination of Flight Capital, 1935–40

Despite the low level of economic activity in the United States in the second half of the 1930s, foreign private investment in the United States more than doubled. The fastest growth was in short-term investment, which more than quadrupled, but every category of foreign investment grew.

In contrast, both U.S. direct and U.S. portfolio investment abroad declined, especially the latter. The $7 billion increase in foreign in-

Table 8.14   Capital Flows, 1930–35 (millions of dollars, current prices)

	Capital ($-$ = outflow) Flow
U.S. private investment	
Direct investment	-483
Other long term	751
Short term	1,237
Total private	1,505
Government	106
Total U.S.	1,611
Foreign investment in U.S.	
Long term	566
Short term	$-1,906$
Total	$-1,340$

Source: U.S. Bureau of the Census 1975, Series U 18–U 23.

vestment in the United States, combined with a cumulative U.S. surplus on goods and services of almost $5 billion, was financed largely by a $12 billion flow of reserve assets into the U.S. government's account (table 8.15).

An indication of the size of this capital flow is that over the five years it was almost 20 percent of gross capital formation and greater than net capital formation. In effect, the capital inflow was financing all net capital formation in the United States during this period. With this large inflow of capital, the United States, after twenty or so years as a net creditor on private account, slipped back into the position of a net debtor, aside from U.S. government holdings of official reserve assets.

8.2.7 Effects of World War II and the Reconstruction Period on the U.S. International Capital Position

In contrast to World War I, when foreigners liquidated well over half their long-term investments in the United States, foreign holdings of private U.S. assets were unchanged between the beginning and end of World War II (table 8.16). Foreign holdings of U.S. government securities grew substantially, while the U.S. private sector raised its foreign assets by about 20 percent. The United States remained a net debtor outside of its official reserve assets.

After 1945, the United States resumed its acquisition of private foreign assets, mainly direct investments, and by 1950 the United States was once again a net creditor even outside its official reserve assets. A $35 billion cumulative surplus in net exports of goods and services in the late 1940s was financed partly by the growth of U.S. assets and

Table 8.15   **The International Balance Sheet of the United States, 1935 and 1940 (billions of dollars, current prices)**

	1935	1940
U.S. private investment abroad		
Direct	7.8	7.3
Other private long term	4.8	4.0
Total private long term	12.6	11.3
Private short term	.9	.9
Total private	13.5	12.2
Foreign investment in the U.S.		
Direct	1.6	2.9
Other private long term	3.5	5.2
Total private long term	5.1	8.1
Private short term	1.2	5.1
Total private	6.3	13.2
U.S. government	—	.3
Total	6.4	13.5

Source: U.S. Bureau of the Census 1975, Series U 26–U 39.

Table 8.16   **International Balance Sheet of the United States before and after World War II (billions of dollars, current prices)**

	1940	1945	1950
U.S. investment abroad			
Direct	7.3	8.4	11.8
Other private long term	4.0	5.3	5.7
Total private long term	11.3	13.7	17.5
Private short term	.9	1.0	1.5
Total private	12.2	14.7	19.0
Foreign investment in the U.S.			
Direct	2.9	2.5	3.4
Other private long term	5.2	5.5	4.6
Total private long term	8.1	8.0	8.0
Private short term	5.1	5.3	6.6
Total private	13.2	13.3	14.6
U.S. government	.3	3.7	3.1
Total	13.5	17.0	17.6
U.S. government	22.1	22.2	35.4

Source: U.S. Bureau of the Census 1975, Series U 26–U 39.

by transfers, but a large fraction—more than a third—was financed by an accumulation of official reserve in the hands of the United States.

8.3   The Internationalization of U.S. Companies

8.3.1   The Growth of U.S. Direct Investment Abroad after World War II

After 1950, the growth of U.S. direct investment abroad, slowed by the Great Depression and World War II, resumed its rise. One measure of the spread of U.S. firms, the number of new affiliates established, rose rapidly to a peak until the late 1960s, and then slowed down (table 8.17).

These data are confined to a fixed group of corporations that had become multinational by the time the sample was selected, and the decline in the rate of establishment may have represented only the exhaustion of profitable locations for new affiliates by this particular group of parents. Furthermore, the data take no account of the size of the newly established affiliates or of their growth after establishment.

Another measure of foreign direct investment is the value of such investment, measured as the book value of parent investment in affiliates as reported on the books of affiliates. Since these values are affected by inflation and by the growth of the economy in general, we compare the value of direct investment in foreign countries with the total assets of U.S. corporations (table 8.18). These ratios suggest that

Table 8.17   **New Foreign Affiliates Established per Year by 180 Parent Firms**

	Number of Affiliates
1946–52[a]	55
1951–55	84
1956–60	192
1961–65	322
1966–67	390
1968–69	508
1970–71	431
1972–73	378
1974–75	236

Source: Hood and Young 1979, 22.
[a]For 187 parent firms.

the peak importance of foreign investment relative to all U.S. corporate assets was in the early or mid-1970s, although the year-to-year fluctuations make it difficult to identify a precise peak.

Foreign investment was always less important in finance than in other industries, and the ratio for all industries is greatly affected by the inclusion of financial corporations. Overseas investment was a much

Table 8.18   **Value of U.S. Direct Investment Abroad as Percentage of Assets of U.S. Corporations**

	All Corporations	Nonfinancial Corporations
1950	2.08	4.21
1957	2.76	5.59
1966	3.06	6.72
1967	3.05	n.a.
1968	3.03	n.a.
1969	3.11	n.a.
1970	3.19	n.a.
1971	3.13	n.a.
1972	3.02	n.a.
1973	3.08	n.a.
1974	3.06	n.a.
1975	3.11	n.a.
1976	3.10	n.a.
1977	2.97	5.82
1982	2.45	5.07
1983	2.24	4.83
1984	2.10	4.67
1985	2.07	4.74

Sources: Value of U.S. direct investment abroad from appendix, table 8.A.1, and U.S. Department of Commerce 1982; assets of U.S. corporations from Federal Reserve Board 1979 and 1986, and Musgrave 1986a and 1986b.

higher proportion of the assets of nonfinancial corporations than of those of financial corporations or all corporations, but the time pattern appears to have been similar: a peak at some point between 1966 and 1977 (comparable data for intervening years are not available) and then a decline to the levels of the 1950s.

The amount of investment relative to assets is only one of several possible measures of the international activities of U.S. firms. It is the one that can be carried back the furthest, but it has several drawbacks. At best it measures the financial stake in overseas affilitates, but it does not reflect the level of activity carried on there. U.S. firms could be increasing the share of production they carry on abroad or the share of their employment abroad while reducing their investment in foreign affiliates and still retaining control of them. More serious problems of measurement arise from the fact that the investment in foreign affiliates is measured in book values rather than current values and that these are subject to the vagaries of currency translation. The tangible assets of all U.S. firms, in the denominator of the ratio, are estimated current values. The high inflation rates of the late 1970s and early 1980s must have raised the totals for U.S. firms' assets relative to the values on the books of affiliates, and the rise in the value of the dollar from 1982 to 1985 must have had a similar effect. We must therefore be somewhat skeptical about this evidence for a decline in the importance of overseas activities.

A measure free of problems of valuation is provided by data on employment, although this measure is also subject to question (table 8.19). Relative to private nonagricultural employment in the United States (U.S. Department of Commerce, 1985a), employment in majority-owned affiliates (the only figures available for 1966) rose between 1966

Table 8.19   **Employment in Foreign Affiliates as Percentage of U.S. Private Sector Nonagricultural Employment**

	All Affiliates		Majority-Owned Affiliates	
	Total	Nonbank	Total	Nonbank
1966			7.3	7.2
1977	10.9	10.7	8.2[a]	8.0
1982	9.2	9.0	7.0[a]	6.8
1983		8.6		6.5
1984		8.1		6.2

Sources: U.S. private nonagricultural employment from U.S. Department of Commerce 1985a; employment in affiliates from Brereton 1986 and U.S. Department of Commerce 1975, 1981, and 1985f.

[a]Including minority-owned bank affiliates.

and 1977 (U.S. Department of Commerce 1975 and 1981). Between that date and 1982, all measures of employment declined relative to U.S. employment, and nonbank affiliate employment continued to decline relatively through 1984 (U.S. Department of Commerce 1985f; Brereton 1986).

The main question about this measure is whether employment is a good measure for comparing domestic and overseas labor input. For one thing, there was a shift toward female and part-time employment in the United States that may not have been matched overseas. Aside from the measurement problem, it is hard to know whether the relative drop in affiliate employment from 1977 to 1982 reflects mainly the effect of the 1982 recession or is part of a declining trend.

One indication in the opposite direction, discussed later, is that exports from overseas affiliates have, within manufacturing, increased relative to exports from the United States by the affiliates' parents and

Table 8.20   **Distribution, by Type of Industry, of U.S. Direct Investment Abroad**

	1985	1982	1977	1966	1957
TOTAL	100.0	100.0	100.0	100.0	100.0
Primary production[a]	17.8	18.4	14.4	27.2	33.9
Manufacturing, incl. petroleum refining	44.0	43.4	49.6	44.7	35.7
GOODS PRODUCTION, INCL. CONSTRUCTION	62.3	62.4	64.6	72.6	70.0
Public utilities and transportation, incl. petroleum transportation	1.6	1.9	3.4[b]	6.8	13.2
GOODS, PUBLIC UTILITIES, & TRANSPORTATION INCL. CONSTRUCTION	63.9	64.3	68.1	79.4	83.2
Trade, incl. petroleum	15.6	17.1	16.4[c]	12.4	11.4
Finance	15.6	13.8	11.3	4.8	3.8
Other services, incl. oil field services	4.9	4.8	4.3	3.4[d]	1.6
TRADE, FINANCE & OTHER SERVICES	36.1	35.7	31.9[c]	20.6[d]	16.8

Source: Appendix, table 8.A.1.

Note: Table excludes holding companies and finance affiliates in the Netherlands Antilles.

[a]Including petroleum extraction and integrated extraction and refining but not separate refining, transportation, or distribution of petroleum or oil field services.

[b]Including gasoline service stations.

[c]Excludes gasoline service stations.

[d]Includes all other industries and inactive.

by the United States as a whole. This measure also has defects. It has the advantage that all measures are in current values, but it also reflects the changing degree of export orientation of affiliates, parents, and U.S. firms in general.

The main changes in the composition of U.S. investment abroad are described in table 8.20. The major shifts over the thirty years have been the declines in importance of investment in the production of goods, especially primary products, and in public utilities and transportation, and the rise in importance of investment in trade and services. The fall in investment in primary production took place before 1977, prior to the oil crises. Investment in public utilities and transportation, accounting for 13 percent of investment in 1957, had been reduced to under 2 percent by 1982. Within the trade and services group, finance was responsible for the great increase in importance of the sector. There was some growth in the importance of trade, but other services, especially outside of oil field services, remained of small importance throughout, although they probably did grow.

8.3.2   The Competitiveness and Comparative Advantage of U.S. Multinational Firms

It is customary to discuss the competitiveness of countries and of industries in them in terms of their shares in world markets or of particular markets. A country's competitiveness depends in the short run on the effects of its monetary and fiscal policies on prices and exchange rates and over longer periods on the rate and direction of its advances in productivity.

To some extent, companies that become multinational in their operations loosen their dependence on these home-country determinants of competitiveness. If home-country production becomes more expensive relative to foreign production because of rapid inflation at home or because the exchange value of the home country's currency has risen, or because labor has risen in price or decreased in efficiency, the multinational firm has some opportunity to shift its production to locations in other countries.

The competitiveness of the multinational firm depends on the firm's characteristics rather than on those of its home country. It may rest on the possession of patents or other technological assets based on the firm's R&D. It may rest on the ability to manage or control certain types of production or distribution operations. It may originate in access to raw materials on favorable terms or in access to home-country markets. All these factors have in common that they can be exploited wherever the firm operates. That is, they are mobile geographically within the firm but relatively immobile between firms (Lipsey and Kravis 1985).

We can imagine a number of possible indicators of the competitiveness of a firm or a group of firms. One would be its shares in world production or world consumption of some set of products. Another would be the share in world trade or in world exports of products or groups of products. Still others would be shares in value-added, employment, or capital. All the indicators have drawbacks. The use of employment or capital shares relies on a single factor of production when others may be equally important or may behave differently. Value-added may be affected by the shifting of profits to minimize taxes or for other reasons. Production or consumption is difficult to use because world and area aggregates are difficult to assemble. They may also be subject to manipulation by host-country governments controlling access to their home markets.

Shares in export trade, used here as a competitiveness measure, have drawbacks also—for one, they slight firms and industries making products that, because of weight or bulk, or for other reasons, tend to be supplied from within the countries where they are consumed. Despite the drawbacks, export shares have a number of advantages as measures of competitiveness. One is that there are reasonably comprehensive world and regional aggregates against which to measure a firm's share. The main advantage of using exports rather than production for this purpose is that exports are more footloose. A country has more power to determine which producers supply its home market than which supply export markets. Shares in export markets may, therefore, represent the underlying economic advantages of firms and countries to a greater degree than do shares in production.

That is not to say that export markets are unaffected by government interventions or other noneconomic factors. The imposition of export requirements on U.S. affiliates by some governments as the price for acquisition of a local firm in the host country or even for continued operation in the country has been a source of much friction between the United States and these countries. However, these export-promoting policies are circumscribed by the ability of companies to leave markets where the costs imposed on them are too high. They are also limited by the watchfulness of other countries over their own home and export markets.

The competitiveness of U.S. multinationals, measured by their export shares, can be described and compared to that of the United States as a country by the figures in table 8.21. The shares of the United States and its multinationals were about equal in 1966, but the multinationals kept their share remarkably constant while that of the United States declined, particularly in the earlier years. The parent firms of the U.S. multinationals did not escape the forces that led to the fall in the U.S. export share, but the fall in the parents' share was a little smaller than that of the United States.

Table 8.21   **Share of World Exports of Manufactures (percentage)**

	U.S. Multinationals	U.S.	U.S. Parent Firms
1966	17.7	17.5	11.0
1977	17.6	13.3	9.2
1982	17.7	14.3	9.5
1983	17.7	13.9	9.1

Source: Lipsey and Kravis 1986.

The multinationals were more successful than nonmultinational U.S. firms in world markets for manufactured goods. What kept the multinationals' share in world exports up was the success of their exports from their foreign affiliates, a record that can be traced back twenty-five years (table 8.22). In the first twenty years, the shares of U.S. multinationals' affiliates in both developed countries and LDCs grew rapidly, but after that, only the shares of the LDC affiliates grew, while affiliates in the developed countries more or less held their shares steady.

This growth in exports from foreign affiliates implies that larger and larger portions of world market shares outside the United States held by U.S. multinationals and by all U.S. firms were being supplied from production outside the United States, as can be seen from table 8.23. By 1983, almost half of all manufactured exports by U.S. multinationals and over 40 percent of manufactured exports by all U.S. firms were supplied by foreign affiliates of the multinationals.

We can identify the comparative advantage of U.S. multinationals by the industry distribution of their exports relative to that of the United States as a country or of the world. Another way of putting this measure is saying that we take the multinationals' share of exports in each industry relative to their share in all industries combined. This measure

Table 8.22   **Share in World Exports of Manufactures of U.S. Majority-Owned Foreign Affiliates (percentage)**

	In All Countries	In Developed Countries	In LDCs
1957	4.5	4.1	0.5
1966	6.8 (6.6)[a]	6.3 (6.2)[a]	0.5
1977	8.4	7.6	0.8
1982	8.3	7.3	1.0
1983	8.6	7.6	1.1

Source: Lipsey and Kravis 1986, appendix, table U–1a.
[a]Comparable to 1957.

Table 8.23   **Share of U.S. Majority-Owned Affiliates in Exports of Manufactures (percentage)**

	Share by U.S. Multinationals	Share by All U.S. Firms
1957	n.a.	17.6
1966	38.1	27.8 (28.9)[a]
1977	47.7	40.0
1982	46.7	38.7
1983	48.7	40.2

Source: Lipsey and Kravis 1986.
[a]Comparable to 1957.

is sometimes referred to as "revealed comparative advantage" and has the drawbacks of such measures. For example, it is not based on the presumed determinants of comparative advantage and incorporates the effects of trade barriers, subsidies, and many other factors that can affect trade flows.

If we take these distributions for 1966, the first year for which we have the data, we find that the United States as a country enjoyed comparative advantages relative to the world as a whole in chemicals, machinery, and transport equipment, and comparative disadvantages in food products, metals, and miscellaneous manufacturing industries.

The comparative advantages of U.S. multinationals were in the same industries, but to a larger degree, and the same was true for the comparative disadvantages of the multinationals. Thus, if we compare U.S. multinationals with the United States as a country, the multinationals had comparative advantages over other U.S. firms in chemicals, machinery, and especially transport equipment, and disadvantages relative to the United States in foods, metals, and miscellaneous manufacturing industries (see table 8.24). In other words, where the United States was strong, U.S. multinationals, taken as a group, were stronger. And where the United States was weak, U.S. multinationals as a group were

Table 8.24   **Industry Share in Manufactured Exports Relative to Share in World Exports, 1966**

	U.S.	U.S. Multinationals
Foods	66.7	44.1
Chemicals	123.8	128.6
Metals	76.6	47.1
Machinery	138.3	142.2
Transport equipment	142.4	202.0
Other manufacturing	68.8	61.4

Source: Lipsey and Kravis 1986, appendix, table U–9.

weaker. That is not to say that there were no individual U.S. multinationals with comparative advantages in foods or metals that permitted them to operate in many countries. The data show that such firms were less common in these industries than in chemicals or machinery.

Sixteen years later, the main outlines of the story were similar (table 8.25). There was a slight weakening of the U.S. position in chemicals and transport equipment, as well as in the already weak metals area, and a stronger comparative advantage in machinery. Within machinery, the U.S. comparative advantage in nonelectrical machinery increased and that in electrical machinery declined.

U.S. multinationals increased their comparative advantage in chemicals relative to the world and to the United States as a country, but their previously very large comparative advantage relative to the world in transport equipment was substantially reduced. Their comparative disadvantages in foods and metals were also reduced, but remained large. In 1982, U.S. multinationals still showed a large comparative advantage relative to the world in chemicals, nonelectrical and electrical machinery, and transport equipment, but there was one exception to the rule that their comparative advantages were an accentuated version of U.S. comparative advantage. That exception was in nonelectrical machinery, in which the comparative advantage of the United States as a country exceeded that of the U.S. multinationals.

For 1977 and 1982 it is possible to examine the comparative advantage of U.S. multinationals for a much finer breakdown of industry groups into thirty or more industries. The industries in which U.S. multinationals exhibited the largest comparative advantage relative to the world were, in order: (1) tobacco products, (2) office and computing machinery, (3) electronic components, (4) soaps, cleansers, and so forth, (5) drugs, and (6) construction machinery (see the appendix, table 8.A.3). Of the six, four were also among the industries of greatest comparative

Table 8.25   Industry Share in Exports by the United States and by U.S. Multinationals Relative to Share in World Exports, 1982

	U.S.	U.S. Multinationals
Foods	67.3	45.8
Chemicals	112.9	143.1
Metals	64.0	44.6
Machinery	142.3	131.9
Nonelectrical	163.8	127.7
Electrical	110.8	138.0
Transport equipment	116.8	158.8
Other manufacturing	73.0	58.3

Source: Lipsey and Kravis 1986, appendix, table U–9.

advantage for the United States as a country, exceptions being the two chemical groups. These industries are characterized by high expenditures on R&D (office and computing machinery, drugs, and electronic components) and on advertising (tobacco products, drugs, soaps, cleansers, etc.).

The 1977–82 period was one in which the shift by multinationals from the United States to their overseas affiliates as their export base, which was strong in the previous decade, was interrupted and even reversed to a small extent. As might be expected, there was wide variation among industries in this respect. Most of the industries in which U.S. multinationals' exports rose rapidly saw a continuation of the shift to overseas production for export. That category included drugs, industrial chemicals, other chemicals, other transport equipment, plastic products, and instruments. Two major exceptions were office and computing machinery and electronic components. There was not a major shift back to the United States (in percentage terms) in these two industries, but there was clearly no move away from U.S. operations.

By comparing the distributions of exports of U.S. multinationals for 1977 and 1982 with those of the United States for the same year, we can get some notion of the distinctive comparative advantages of these firms, as compared with the United States as a geographical entity (appendix, table 8.A.5). Among the major groups, the multinationals showed comparative advantages in chemicals, electrical machinery, and transport equipment, but not in foods, metals, nonelectrical machinery, and "other manufacturing."

The ratios for more detailed industries are suggestive. Within foods, the multinationals held a large advantage over other U.S. firms in beverages, probably an advertising-intensive industry. In chemicals, the largest advantage was in soaps, cleaners, and the like, also an advertising-intensive field, followed by drugs and, by a small margin, industrial chemicals, the former extremely R&D-intensive, the latter a little above average. In nonelectrical machinery, the largest advantage of multinationals over other U.S. firms was in office and computing machinery, by far the most R&D-intensive group. In the electrical machinery group, the multinationals' advantages were large relative to the United States in electronic components and, in 1982, also in communications equipment, both R&D-intensive industries, but not in "other electrical machinery," the most R&D-intensive. However, in electrical machinery, the lines are quite blurry among the detailed industries. Many parents seem to cross these detailed industry lines.

There are a number of indications here that both R&D intensity and advertising intensity are major factors in the comparative advantage of U.S. multinationals, and both have been associated with U.S. firms' shares in foreign markets (for example, in Caves 1974). R&D intensity is a variable that has been associated in many studies with the comparative advantage of the United States as a country (for example, Baldwin 1979; Stern and Maskus 1981). Our data confirm that association. If we relate the share of an industry in U.S. exports relative to its share in world exports (*US/W*) to the R&D intensity of industries, as measured by the ratio of R&D expenditures to sales (*RD/S*), we find we can explain a substantial part (40 percent) of the interindustry differences in U.S. export shares in 1977 with that factor alone (t-statistics in parentheses).

(1) $$US/W = .089 + .022\ RD/S; \qquad \bar{R}^2 = .40.$$
$$(5.96)\quad (4.40)$$

However, the same R&D intensities are even more strongly related to the comparative advantage of U.S. multinationals in the same year, measured in the same way (share of industry in multinationals' exports relative to its share in world exports, (or *USMNC/W*).

(2) $$USMNC/W = 0.98 + .052\ RD/S; \qquad \bar{R}^2 = .49.$$
$$(3.39)\quad (5.26)$$

The foreign investment survey does not include data on advertising intensity, the other characteristic associated with U.S. multinationals' comparative advantage, but R&D intensity at least is one attribute explaining the comparative advantages of the United States and of U.S. multinationals, especially that of the multinationals.

8.3.3   Changing Characteristics of U.S.-Owned Foreign Operations

U.S. affiliates in foreign countries exist mainly to serve local markets. About two-thirds of their sales have been in their host countries in the last few years. Exporting is most important for affiliates in primary production—agriculture, mining, and the extraction of petroleum—in all of which a majority of sales were outside the host country (table 8.26). The reason for the export orientation of affiliates in these industries is that they were drawn to their locations not by the prospect of breaking into or enlarging their shares of the host country's market but by the presence of relatively cheap resources.

At the other end of the scale, affiliates in some noncommodity industries—public utilities, retail trade, and business and personal services—concentrated heavily in their host-country markets.

Over the last quarter century, the trend has been for affiliates to become more export oriented. The share of exports in total sales more than doubled for manufacturing affiliates. That is a substantial shift in orientation, but not as large as the rise in the share of exports in GNP or in output of goods in the United States and in other countries.

Table 8.26   **Affiliate Exports as Percentage of Sales, Majority-Owned Affiliates, by Industry**

	1957	1966	1977	1982	1983	1984
All industries	27.4	24.9	38.2	34.5	35.2	36.5
Agriculture, forestry, and fishing	63.0	n.a.	58.2	72.6	73.5	74.6
Mining	84.0	75.2	77.5	82.4	79.5	80.7
Petroleum	34.3	29.9	49.5	35.4	37.0	36.4
Extraction	n.a.	n.a.	54.1	61.4	61.0	61.0
Other, incl. oil field services	n.a.	n.a.	48.8	30.1	31.7	29.6
Manufacturing	15.9	18.6	30.8	33.9	35.1	37.5
Construction	n.a.	n.a.	13.5	9.5	10.6	11.1
Public utilities and transport	24.4	11.1	1.7	9.2	6.3	8.3
Trade	n.a.	29.1	34.6	36.9	34.6	35.2
Wholesale	n.a.	n.a.	41.1	41.7	39.8	40.3
Retail	n.a.	n.a.	2.0	2.2	2.1	1.5
Finance (excl. banking), insurance, real estate	n.a.	n.a.	12.0	37.8	41.2	46.2
Services	n.a.	14.8	22.0	19.8	20.3	20.3

Source: Appendix, table 8.A.7.

The export orientation of affiliates varies by location as well as by industry (table 8.27). Affiliates in all industries combined were more export oriented in developing than in developed countries, partly because those in natural resource industries were large exporters and partly because of the high ratios for the Asia and Pacific countries. In manufacturing, the affiliates in Asia and Pacific countries exported over 40 percent of their sales. Affiliates in Japan and in Oceania were very

Table 8.27   **Exports as Percentage of Sales, Majority-Owned Affiliates, by Location, 1982**

	All Industries	Mfg. Industries
All countries	34.5	33.9
Developed	31.2	36.6
Canada	23.3	34.5
Europe	37.3	41.2
Japan	8.7	11.0[a]
Australia, New Zealand, S. Africa	10.9	12.7[a]
Developing	45.8	22.0
Latin America	40.4	11.9
Middle East	25.0	31.9
Asia and Pacific	58.7	41.1[b]

Source: U.S. Department of Commerce 1985f, tables III.D3, III.E1, and III.E3.
[a]Suppressed observations estimated by the author.
[b]Including sub-Saharan Africa.

inward-looking, perhaps because these countries had comparatively protected markets.

For the most part, overseas affiliates have relied little on the United States as a market, with slightly more than 10 percent of their sales in the two most recent years for which we have data and a similar proportion for twenty-five years earlier (table 8.28). The unusually low share in 1966 and the exceptionally high U.S. share in 1977 both reflected mainly the fluctuations of the petroleum industry.

Affiliates in primary production—agriculture, mining, and petroleum extraction—have, in general, been the most dependent on the U.S. market, although the finance (except banking), insurance, and real estate group entered that category in 1982. In the other broad industry groups—manufacturing, construction, public utilities and transportation, wholesale and retail trade, and services—sales to the United States have ranged from less than one percent of affiliate sales to a little over 10 percent.

If there has been any trend in some of the groups, it seems to be toward an increasing dependence on the U.S. market. The largest jump was in the finance group, as mentioned above, but there have been persistent increases in manufacturing (more than a doubling of the share of sales to the United States) and, over the last few years, a substantial one in wholesale trade. The rise of almost 50 percent in the dependence of manufacturing affiliates on the U.S. market suggests the influence

Table 8.28   **Exports to the United States as Percentage of Sales, Majority-Owned Affiliates, by Industry**

	1957	1966	1977	1982	1983	1984
All industries	9.9[a]	6.4	18.5	10.5	10.9	12.4
Agriculture, forestry, fishing	38.2	n.a.	30.1	40.7	39.7	39.1
Mining	44.2	37.9	28.1	28.5	30.9	32.3
Petroleum	9.9	5.4	35.7	13.7	12.4	13.5
Extraction	n.a.	n.a.	36.0	40.1	35.7	31.4
Other, incl. oil field services	n.a.	n.a.	35.7	8.3	7.3	8.5
Manufacturing	6.0	5.6	9.1	9.7	11.6	14.0
Construction	n.a.	n.a.	.7	.3	.3	.4
Public utilities and transportation	n.a.	7.4	.6	6.4	3.2	4.2
Trade	n.a.	3.6	2.9	4.3	5.0	5.3
Wholesale	n.a.	n.a.	3.4	4.8	5.7	6.1
Retail	n.a.	n.a.	.2	.2	.5	.2
Finance, insurance, and real estate (excl. banking)	n.a.	n.a.	5.9	23.0	25.3	25.5
Services	n.a.	n.a.	4.2	5.4	5.3	6.0

Source: Appendix, table 8.A.7.

[a]Excluding trade and finance.

of the increasing exchange value of the dollar in those years. It remains to be seen whether the reversal in exchange rates will undo this shift in orientation.

A widely discussed trend in the character of direct investment by the United States and by other countries has been the move toward shared ownership, and particularly toward minority ownership, with majority shares in the hands of citizens of the host country. The less developed countries, particularly in Latin America, have promoted this trend. Restrictions on majority ownership were written into the Andean Pact and into Mexican law.

Despite the pressure from host-country governments, U.S. parent companies have been more reluctant to share ownership in affiliates than companies from other countries. Of the multinationals' affiliates surveyed in the Harvard program that were established before 1951, 58 percent of the U.S.-owned affiliates, 39 percent of European affiliates, and 27 percent of affiliates of firms in other countries were wholly owned. All these proportions had decreased by the late 1960s to 46 percent, 19 percent, and 6 percent, but the preference of U.S. firms for 100 percent ownership remains clear (OECD 1981, 50).

There has been some move by U.S. multinationals toward sharing ownership. The proportion of total affiliate sales made by majority-owned affiliates fell from 88 percent in 1966 to 77 percent in 1982. The decline took place in the first ten years of that period, however, and there was actually a small rise between 1977 and 1982.

There are large differences among industries in the shares of majority-owned affiliates, and the reduced share in the aggregate could represent shifts among, as well as within, industries. It is clear, however (see appendix, table 8.A.8) that in all the major industry groups, the proportion of sales by affiliates less than majority owned grew between 1966 and 1982 in both developed countries and LDCs. The rise of these affiliates was important in mining, retail trade, and public utilities and transportation, and in LDCs they accounted for half or more of affiliate sales in these industries by 1982. Thus, if the growth of these firms has been a response to host countries' efforts to gain substantial shares in the equity of foreign-owned affiliates, the efforts have met with some success.

Given that technological or proprietary information is the basis for the competitive advantage of multinational firms, one might expect that the more important these factors were in an industry, the greater would be the reluctance of parent companies to share these advantages and the stronger the insistence on control or, preferably, total ownership of affiliates. It is indeed the case that among manufacturing industries, those that rank high with respect to spending on R&D are also among those with the highest shares of majority ownership (table 8.29). The

Table 8.29   Sales of Majority-Owned Affiliates as Percentage of Affiliate Sales

	1977		1982	
	Developed Countries	LDCs	Developed Countries	LDCs
All manufacturing	80.5	71.0	76.5	71.1
Drugs	93.8	86.0	96.2	93.8
Office and computer machines	94.7	97.5	94.0	99.5
Electronic comp. and access.	80.5	95.3	78.9	96.0

Source: Appendix, table 8.A.8.

only exception was electronic components and accessories in developed countries, largely in Japan (a country in which less than 20 percent of manufacturing affiliate sales are from majority-owned affiliates). In fact, in these industries, the share of majority-owned affiliates actually increased between 1977 and 1982, despite the decline in the majority-owned share in manufacturing as a whole.

It is clear, then, that the policy of forcing shared ownership has not been very successful for the LDCs in R&D-intensive industries. The cost of enforcing the policy may have been too great: a reduction in foreign investment in these industries and in the consequent transfer of technology.

8.4   The United States as a Recipient of Foreign Direct Investment

8.4.1   The Recent Growth of Foreign Direct Investment in the United States

During the 1960s, as U.S. direct investment in foreign countries was reaching its peak rate of growth, hardly any of the world's flow of new direct investment was coming to the United States (table 8.30). From 1961 through 1967, less than 3 percent of the flow to developed countries came to the United States, and in 1967 the United States was the location of less than 10 percent of the world stock of direct investment (Hood and Young 1979, 18; U.S. Bureau of the Census 1975, Series U-35). The U.S. share of inflows of direct investment to developed countries rose to over 10 percent in 1968–73, and since then has been over 20 percent in every year through 1983. It has stayed over one-third since 1978 and reached as high as two-thirds in 1981. The U.S. share of inflows to all countries has been over a quarter since the late 1970s and reached a peak close to 50 percent in 1981. The United States has absorbed more than all developing countries together since 1978 and usually more than all the European countries combined.

With this large inflow of direct investment, the stock of foreign direct investment in the United States has been growing very rapidly. One

Table 8.30   **Direct Investment Inflows to the United States as Percentage of Inflows to the World and Developed Countries**

	World	Developed Countries
1961–67		2.6
1968–73		11.4
1970	15.0	18.5
1971	3.4	4.6
1972	7.4	9.3
1973	17.5	23.2
1974	25.8	26.6
1975	13.4	22.1
1976	30.9	38.6
1977	14.6	23.6
1978	26.4	35.2
1979	30.0	40.5
1980	35.6	46.0
1981	47.5	66.0
1982	36.9	55.0
1983	29.0	39.0

Sources: United Nations 1983, annex table II.2, and 1985, table II.1; OECD 1981.

indication of the growth is the comparison with assets of all U.S. corporations (table 8.31). After staying around one-half of one percent from 1950 through 1966, the ratio tripled in the next twenty years, and more than doubled in the eight years from 1977 to 1985.

Another way of describing the growth of foreign direct investment in the United States is by comparing it with U.S. investment abroad (table 8.32). The greatest leap in foreign investment in the United States relative to U.S. investment abroad took place in the five years from 1977 to 1982, when foreign direct investment grew from less than a quarter of U.S. direct investment abroad to 60 percent of it, and the ratio has continued to increase rapidly since 1982.

Table 8.31   **Stock (Book Value) of Foreign Direct Investment in the United States as Percentage of Assets of All U.S. Corporations**

Year	Percentage
1950	.6
1960	.6
1966	.5
1974	.7
1977	.7
1980	1.2
1982	1.5
1985	1.6

Sources: Appendix, table 8.A.9; Federal Reserve Board 1979 and 1986; and Musgrave 1986a and 1986b.

Table 8.32   **Stock (Book Value) of Foreign Direct Investment in the United States as Percentage of U.S. Direct Investment Abroad.**

1950	28.8
1966	17.5
1977	23.7
1982	60.0
1983	66.1
1984	77.3
1985	78.6

Sources: Appendix, tables 8.A.1 and 8.A.9.

Since these are book values, they are subject to the familiar doubts about their meaning and comparability. The U.S. direct investments abroad are much older, on average, than the foreign direct investments in the United States and were made in periods of much lower asset prices. It is therefore likely that the use of book values understates the value of U.S. investments relative to market values much more than it does the foreign investments. Thus, the extent and growth of foreign investment in the United States relative to U.S. investment abroad is probably considerably exaggerated in these figures.

Another fact that points to such a bias is the difference in income. Despite the relatively small ostensible difference in the value of the stocks, income on U.S. direct investment abroad was more than four times as large as income on foreign direct investment in the United States in 1985 (U.S. Department of Commerce 1986a and 1986b).

For the most recent decade or so, data on employment provide a measure of foreign firms' participation in the U.S. economy that is free of the effects of exchange rate changes and conversion methods. This measure too demonstrates the rapid growth of foreign-owned operations, but also indicates that their role in the U.S. economy as a whole remains small (table 8.33).

A point to keep in mind in comparing inward and outward direct investment is that U.S. firms became multinational earlier than did

Table 8.33   **Employment in Nonbank U.S. Affiliates of Foreign Companies as Percentage of U.S. Private Sector Nonagricultural Employment**

1974	1.6
1977	1.8
1980	2.7
1982	3.3
1984	3.4

Sources: Appendix, table 8.A.10; U.S. Department of Commerce 1985a, 46–48.

most foreign firms and probably reached something like an equilibrium stock of foreign assets by the end of the 1960s. After that, there was not a large net movement of U.S. firms into multinational status. Foreign firms, in contrast, have, for the most part, become multinational fairly recently and are adding to their overseas operations rapidly because they have not reached the goals they have set. One indication of the relative maturity in this sense of U.S. direct investment is that all (and more) of its growth came from reinvested earnings in 1984 and 1985, while most of the growth of other countries' direct investment in the United States is from flows of new equity and debt (table 8.34). U.S. parents were bringing some of their foreign assets back to the United States by reducing equity and intercompany debt, while foreign companies were increasing their holdings of U.S. assets far beyond their accumulation of reinvested earnings.

8.4.2 Characteristics of Foreign-Owned Affiliates in the United States

The fact that the share of foreign-owned firms in U.S. employment was still only about 3.5 percent in 1985 might appear to deflate the anxieties that have been aroused by the inflow of direct investment. However, the explanation for that concern lies in the concentration of the investment; half of the employment in foreign-owned firms is in manufacturing, which accounted for only about 15 percent of total nonagricultural employment in the United States in 1984 (appendix, table 8.A.10).

Aside from mining, the ratios for which are affected seriously by incomparabilities between numerator and denominator, the greatest foreign share in U.S. employment—7 percent—is in manufacturing. That share almost tripled in ten years (table 8.35).

Employment in foreign-owned manufacturing operations more than doubled, while total U.S. employment in manufacturing stayed about constant or even declined a little. Employment in foreign service af-

Table 8.34 **Shares in Changes in the Value of Direct Investment, 1984 and 1985 (percentage)**

	U.S. in Foreign Countries	Foreign Countries In U.S.
Equity and intercompany debt	−28.2	85.4
Reinvested earnings	117.0	8.7
Valuation adjustment	11.2	5.8
Total	100.0	100.0

Sources: U.S. Department of Commerce 1986a and 1986b.

Table 8.35   Employment in U.S. Affiliates of Foreign Corporations as Percentage of Total U.S. Private Sector Employment, by Broad Industry Groups

	1974	1977	1980	1982	1984
Mining[a]	16.8	13.0	12.4	14.5	16.1
Manufacturing	2.7	3.5	5.4	6.6	7.1
Construction	.2	.3	1.0	1.3	1.0
GOODS PRODUCTION	2.8	3.3	5.0	6.2	6.4
Transportation and public utilities	1.0	.5	.7	1.1	1.2
GOODS, TRANSP., & PUB. UTIL.	2.5	2.9	4.3	5.3	5.5
Wholesale trade	2.8	3.2	4.1	5.3	5.3
Retail trade	1.0	1.0	2.0	2.6	2.7
Finance, insurance and real estate[b]	1.1[c]	1.1	2.1	2.3	2.2
Services	.3	.2	.5	.6	.9
TRADE & SERVICES	1.0	1.0	1.6	2.1	2.2

Sources: Appendix, table 8.A.10; U.S. Department of Commerce 1985a, 46–48.
[a]Including petroleum.
[b]Banking included in denominator but not in numerator.
[c]Including banking would be 1.8 percent.

filiates rose at an even faster rate than in goods production. However, in these industries U.S. total employment was also rising, by about 50 percent over ten years. As a result, although the foreign share increased, it did not grow as rapidly as in manufacturing.

At the end of the period, among trade, finance, and services, it was only in wholesale trade, probably closely tied to the distribution of imported goods, that the share of employment in foreign-owned firms reached 5 percent. In other groups the foreign share was under 3 percent. However, the ratios for finance, insurance, and real estate are understated because the data for foreign-owned firms omit banks. It seems clear, however, that foreign penetration of the service sectors was relatively small.

Within manufacturing, also, there were wide differences among industries in the degree of foreign penetration. In 1984, almost 40 percent of manufacturing employment in the chemical industry was in foreign-owned firms, while the proportions in other industries were all under 10 percent (table 8.36).

The foreign share increased substantially in every group, at least doubling within each industry. However, the ranking of the industries hardly changed at all. The greatest degree of foreign penetration was in chemicals at the beginning and end of the period, followed by food manufacturing industries, and there was a relatively small foreign employment share in nonelectrical machinery in both periods. Thus the comparative advantages of foreign firms relative to U.S. firms seemed to remain in the same industries.

Table 8.36   **Employment in U.S. Affiliates of Foreign Corporations as Percentage of Employment in All U.S. Firms, by Industry within Manufacturing**

	1974	1984
All manufacturing	2.7	7.1
Food and kindred products	4.4	9.0
Chemicals	10.8	38.7
Metals	3.0	7.1
Machinery, excl. electrical	1.9	5.8
Electrical machinery and equipment	2.8	8.2
Transportation equipment	} 1.7	3.2
Other manufactures		3.6

Sources: Appendix, table 8.A.10; U.S. Department of Commerce 1985a, 46–48.

The industry distribution of employment in foreign firms in 1984 was much more concentrated in manufacturing and petroleum, and in goods-producing industries as a group, than was U.S. employment in general, as can be seen in table 8.37. The shares in trade and finance did not diverge as much from those of the United States as a whole, especially if one takes account of the omission of banks from the total of foreign holdings. However, the share of employment in foreign-owned companies that was in service industries was less than a third of that for U.S. firms.

The differences in the distributions reflect two influences. Foreign firms may have had a comparative advantage in goods production and U.S. firms in service production. However, the results may also reflect differences in the difficulty of carrying across national boundaries the comparative advantages of firms. Whatever gives firms a comparative advantage or competitiveness in manufacturing industries, whether ownership of patents or knowledge of production techniques or management abilities, may be easier to move across national boundaries than the characteristics that distinguish firms in trade and service industries. That might be because of inherent characteristics of the two groups of industries or because there are many more regulatory and similar obstacles placed in the path of service industry producers than in the path of goods-producing companies. Since entry into the U.S. market is relatively unrestricted and the share of foreign firms in services is small, the suspicion that there are inherent obstacles to service industry direct investment is reinforced.

The main trends in the industry distribution of foreign firms' employment appear to move it toward the U.S. pattern. That is, the share of mining and petroleum was declining, as was that of manufacturing, after 1977. The main increase in importance within foreign-owned companies was in the service industries.

Table 8.37   Distribution by Industry of Employment in Foreign-Owned Firms in the United States

	Employment in Foreign-Owned Firms					Empl. in All Private Sector U.S. Firms
	1974	1977	1980	1982	1984	1984
All nonagricultural	100.0	100.0	100.0	100.0	100.0	100.0
Mining	2.2	1.3	1.2	1.7	1.2	} 1.2
Petroleum	9.0	7.4	5.0	5.0	4.6	
Manufacturing	52.5	56.7	54.6	51.0	50.9	24.7
Construction	.8	1.1	2.1	2.1	1.6	5.5
GOODS PRODUCTION	64.4	66.5	63.0	59.8	58.3	31.5
Transportation and public utilities	4.3	1.9	1.8	2.3	2.3	6.6
GOODS, TRANSP., & PUBL UTIL.	68.7	68.4	64.8	62.1	60.6	38.1
Wholesale trade	11.6	12.6	10.7	11.5	10.8	7.1
Retail trade	11.5	11.7	15.0	16.3	16.8	21.1
Finance, Insurance, and real estate	4.5[a]	4.2	5.3	5.0	4.7	7.2[b]
Services	3.9	3.1	4.2	5.0	7.1	26.5
TRADE & SERVICES	31.6	31.7	35.2	37.9	39.4	61.9[b]

Sources: Appendix, table 8.A.10; U.S. Department of Commerce 1985a, 46–48.
Note: Foreign-owned firms means U.S. nonbank affiliates of foreign corporations.
[a]Including banking, 6.6 percent.
[b]Including banking.

8.4.3   Sources of Foreign Direct Investment in the United States

As foreign direct investment has flowed into the United States in the last few years there have been periodic alarms about increasing control of U.S. industry by companies from the Middle East or Japan. Despite the publicized incidents of investments from these countries, the great bulk—two-thirds of the total—of foreign direct investment in the United States continues to be controlled by European firms. Over 40 percent of the foreign investment is concentrated in two countries, the Netherlands and the United Kingdom (table 8.38).

The identification of firms by nationality is often uncertain. These ratios may well understate the ultimate Japanese and middle eastern stake that is partly held through firms incorporated in Europe. Data on U.S. direct investment abroad include investments by U.S. firms controlled by foreigners, and data on foreign direct investment in the United States include investment by foreign firms controlled by U.S. parents. In the latter case, however, the surveys include a classification by ultimate beneficial ownership.

The shares of the different countries and areas vary from industry to industry. Invesment in the petroleum industry, for example, is over-

Table 8.38   **Share in Foreign Direct Investment Position in the United States, 1985**

	Percentage
Canada	9
Europe	66
France	3
Germany	8
Netherlands	20
U.K.	24
Switzerland	6
Japan	10
Latin America	9
Neth. Antilles	6
Middle East	3
Kuwait	2

Source: Appendix, table 8.A.11.

whelmingly from Europe, over 80 percent of the total from the Netherlands and the United Kingdom (appendix, table 8.A.11). Investment in manufacturing, the area that receives most public attention, is also largely from Europe—about three-quarters—but several countries participate: 9 percent from France, 10 percent from Germany, and 12 percent from Switzerland, aside from the usual high proportion, over 40 percent, from the Netherlands and the United Kingdom. Japan accounts for less than 5 percent of this investment.

Japan's investment is concentrated in wholesale trade. That investment is more than half of Japan's total investment position in the United States and is more than 40 percent of total foreign direct investment in the industry. Japan also plays a larger role in investment in U.S. banking—almost a fifth—than in the other industries.

Investment from Latin America, largely from the Netherlands Antilles, is more concentrated in the U.S. real estate industry than that from any other source. More than a quarter of Latin America direct investment and that from the Netherlands Antilles is in real estate, and over a quarter of total foreign direct investment in real estate is from Latin America, most from the Netherlands Antilles.

The sources of the most recent growth in the foreign investment position in the United States do not suggest revolutionary changes in the pattern (table 8.39). Europe accounted for two-thirds of the additions over the last five years, as it did for the stock. The major change was that Japan was the source of 14 percent of the additions, as compared to only 6 percent of the 1980 stock, and the Netherlands and the United Kingdom less than 50 percent of additions as compared with a share in the 1980 stock of almost 60 percent. Within manufacturing,

Table 8.39   Share in Changes in Foreign Direct Investment Position in the
              United States, 1980–85

	Percentage
Canada	4
Europe	66
France	3
Germany	7
Netherlands	17
U.K.	30
Switzerland	6
Japan	14
Latin America	7
Middle East	4

Source: Appendix, table 8.A.11.

increases in investment from France were small relative to the initial
stock and those from Switzerland and Japan were relatively large, the
latter from a very small base of only 3 percent of total foreign investment in manufacturing.

8.5 Portfolio Investment and Aggregate Investment Flows
       and Stocks

The capital account of the United States has gone through wide
swings, representing what appears to be an underlying evolution of the
United States from steady capital exporter in the 1960s to the world's
major capital importer in the mid-1980s. The major element of the U.S.
capital outflow in the first decade was the steadily growing direct investment flow to foreign countries, averaging about $4.5 billion per
year (table 8.40). That trend of direct investment was not interrupted
in the next few years, but it was outweighed in 1971 and 1972 by the
monetary troubles of the United States, reflected in the additions to
foreign official holdings in the United States of over $18.5 billion a year

Table 8.40   Net U.S. Capital Outflow (−) or Inflow (+) Annual Averages
              (billions of dollars, current prices)

	U.S. Capital Outflow/Inflow
1960–70	−2.8
1971–72	+8.7
1973–82	−13.3
1983–85	+69.8

Source: Appendix, table 8.A.12.

and, until the devaluation of the dollar, by the running down of foreign deposits in U.S. banks.

The next ten years were turbulent, including the two oil price shocks and two U.S. recessions that were severe by post–World War II standards. U.S. direct investment abroad continued to grow and accounted for capital export averaging about $12.5 billion a year, but it was reduced severely by the 1982 recession and did not recover to earlier levels until 1985. However, a new element entered the picture in this decade: foreign lending by U.S. banks at the rate of over $37 billion a year, dwarfing the direct investment that had been dominant in the 1960s. As U.S. banks lent abroad, they also absorbed deposits from abroad that were far larger than in earlier years, averaging over $20 billion a year. While the two series were not perfectly synchronized, the bank lending and bank borrowing did move more or less in step, as U.S. banks acted as intermediaries between the countries accumulating assets and those absorbing them. The inflow of capital to the United States also included large additions to foreign holdings of U.S. Treasury securities and, beginning in the late 1970s, large direct investment flows to the United States.

The next few years were to see a spectacular reversal of the U.S. position. U.S. bank lending, which had averaged over $37 billion a year in the 1973–82 decade and over $80 billion a year in 1980–82, dropped to under a billion dollars in 1985. At the same time, U.S. bank borrowing from abroad, which had averaged a little over $20 billion a year during 1973–82 and almost $40 billion in 1980–82, continued to average over $40 billion in 1983–85. Thus, the United States was absorbing foreign capital through U.S. banks, through foreign purchases of Treasury securities, and through foreign purchases of other U.S. securities (table 8.41). Most of the foreign purchases of U.S. securities other than Treasury securities in the last couple of years have been of bonds rather than stocks, although stocks predominated earlier (tables 8.42 and 8.43). The main sources of these funds were Western European countries, especially the United Kingdom.

The sources of other U.S. borrowing, including purchases of U.S. Treasury securities and additions to U.S. bank liabilities other than foreign official assets, were more widely dispersed (table 8.44). In this case, too, the industrial countries have been the main sources of funds, but among them, Japan, included in the other industrial countries, played a larger role than in purchases of corporate bonds. The Caribbean centers are intermediaries, the origins of whose funds are not reported. The rest of the U.S. borrowing, about a fifth, came mainly from the developing countries of Latin America and Asia.

Changes in foreign official assets in the United States were relatively small on net balance in 1983–85, but there were significant shifts among countries (table 8.45).

Table 8.41   **Additions to Foreign Holdings of U.S. Assets, Annual Averages (billions of dollars, current prices)**

	1973–82	1983–85
U.S. Treasury securities	+2.6	+17.4
Other U.S. securities	+3.3	+24.1

Source: Appendix, table 8.A.12.

Table 8.42   **Additions to Foreign Holdings of U.S. Corporate Stocks and Bonds Other than Treasury Securities (millions of dollars, current prices)**

	1981–83	1984–85
Stocks	15,017	3,949
Bonds	7,182	59,670

Source: Appendix, table 8.A.13.

Table 8.43   **Foreign Purchases of U.S. Bonds Other than Treasury Securities, 1983–85 Annual Average, by Country (billions of dollars, current prices)**

	Purchases
Total	20.6
Germany	1.4
Switzerland	1.7
U.K.	13.8
Japan	2.5

Source: Appendix, table 8.A.13.

Table 8.44   **Purchases of U.S. Treasury Securities and Additions to Foreign Liabilities of U.S. Banks, 1983–85 Annual Averages, by Country (billions of dollars, current prices)**

	Purchases and Additions
Total	59.0
Industrial countries	32.8
Western Europe	17.9
Canada	2.7
Other	12.3
Caribbean banking centers	13.3
Other countries	12.8
Of which OPEC	1.7
By area, incl. OPEC	
Latin America	5.6
Asia	4.5
Other	2.7

Source: Appendix, table 8.A.14.

Table 8.45   **Changes in Foreign Official Assets in the United States, Annual Averages (billions of dollars, current prices)**

	1974–78	1979–82	1983–85
Total	21.1	2.5	2.5
Industrial countries	13.0	−9.6	4.0
OPEC members	6.5	9.8	−6.4
Other countries	1.5	2.4	4.9

Source: Appendix, table 8.A.14.

Since the collapse of oil prices, OPEC countries have been drawing down reserves in the United States while the industrial countries and the developing countries have been increasing them. In contrast, in the four years before, OPEC countries had been increasing their official reserve holdings in the United States by almost $10 billion a year and the industrial countries had been reducing theirs just about as fast. In the years after the first oil shock, all three groups of countries were adding to the official reserves held in the United States.

The collapse of U.S. bank lending during the last three years includes very different behavior toward industrial and developing countries (table 8.46). Lending to developed countries changed little, but with respect to the developing countries of Latin America and Asia the United States turned from net lending to net repayment of debt.

Over longer periods, the concentration of the growth of debt in a very few years becomes evident: almost two-thirds of the total since the first oil shock was extended during 1981 and 1982, and that pattern was repeated in almost all the borrowing countries (table 8.47). Then the next period, 1983–85, saw reductions of 80–85 percent in the rate at which U.S. banks were extending credit, and that pattern too was repeated in each of the individual countries.

Table 8.46   **Changes in Claims on Foreigners Reported by U.S. Banks, by Area (billions of dollars, current prices)**

	1983	1984	1985
Total	−29.9	−11.1	−.7
Industrial countries	−8.8	−8.4	−7.3
Caribbean banking centers	−6.7	−.7	−.2
Other areas	−14.4	−2.0	+6.8
Latin America	−9.3	−1.1	+4.7
Asia	−4.6	−.8	+1.7

Source: Appendix, table 8.A.15.

Note: (−) = increase in U.S. assets.

514   Robert E. Lipsey/Mario Schimberni/Robert V. Lindsay

Table 8.47   Changes in Claims on Foreigners Reported by U.S. Banks, by Areas, Annual Averages (billions of dollars, current prices)

	1976–80	1981–82	1983–85
Total	−27.9	−97.6	−13.9
Industrial countries	−10.8	−41.3	−8.2
Western Europe	n.a.	−33.6	−4.9
U.K.	−4.2	−21.6	−3.3
Other	n.a.	−12.0	−1.6
Canada	n.a.	−3.8	−1.0
Japan	n.a.	−2.8	−1.7
Caribbean banking centers	−6.8	−23.5	−2.5
Other Areas	−10.4	−32.8	−3.2
OPEC	−1.5	−4.0	−.6
Latin America	−6.2	−24.6[a]	−1.9[a]
Asia	−2.3	−7.4[a]	−1.2[a]
Other	−.4	−.9	−.1

Source: Appendix, table 8.A.15.
Note: (−) = increase in U.S. Assets.
[a]Including OPEC.

8.6 Conclusion

The United States has gone through several cycles in the state of its foreign investment account. It was a borrower and international debtor before World War I, first a lender and then a refuge for foreign capital between the wars, the world's major lender and creditor after World War II, and, in the last few years, a borrower again and, according to the official accounts, even a net debtor. Most foreign investment in the United States has always been portfolio investment, although direct investment has been growing rapidly in recent years, while most U.S. investment abroad has typically been direct investment. The major episodes of foreign portfolio investment by the United States have not been happy ones. One was the intergovernment lending during World War I, eventually written off. A second was the burst of lending to Latin America in the late 1920s, a good part of which ended in default. And the third was the large international lending of the period after the first oil crisis, much of which is of questionable standing now.

The long period of U.S. borrowing before 1900 does not seem to have brought enough foreign capital into the United States for the transfer of resources involved to have made a great difference in the long-run growth of the country. The role of foreign capital appears to have been that of accommodating capital needs for sharp bursts in U.S. growth or in the growth of particular sectors, especially capital-intensive ones, until domestic saving caught up with capital formation. If the irregularity of capital requirements was an intrinsic feature of rapid growth, the inflow of foreign capital was more important than its size would indicate.

U.S. direct investment abroad began while the United States was still an overall borrower and debtor, as the technological leaders among U.S. manufacturing firms pioneered in the technique of exploiting their firm advantages by producing in other countries. The major expansion in U.S. direct investment took place in the 1950s and 1960s, as U.S. firms took advantage of the great advances in communication and transportation to spread their production activities around the world. The peak in the stock of foreign assets relative to domestic assets was probably reached during the early 1970s, although the share of their exports that multinational U.S. manufacturing firms produced abroad continued to increase after that.

The bulk of U.S. direct investment abroad has always been in goods production. However, there was a brief period in the 1920s in which almost all of U.S. investment in public utilities was concentrated, presumably a reflection of the U.S. lead in telephone systems and electric power production and distribution. Within the production of goods there has been a shift away from primary production, between a third and a half of the total in the 1950s, to manufacturing, which reached its peak share in the late 1960s or early 1970s. Since then there has been growth in the trade and services sector, the share of which roughly doubled between the mid-1950s and the mid-1980s and reached almost a third of total direct investment. Most of this growth is in wholesale trade and finance, with other services, even including oil field services, still less than 5 percent of U.S. direct investment abroad in 1985.

Using foreign production to retain their competitiveness in world markets, U.S. multinational manufacturing firms have been able to retain a constant share of world exports of manufactures over the last fifteen or twenty years, while the share of the United States as a country has fallen sharply. What sustained the share of U.S. multinationals was the growth in their exports from locations outside the United States to the point that almost half of their exports now originate from their foreign production.

The comparative advantage of both the United States and its multinational firms is concentrated in chemicals, machinery, and transport equipment, to judge by export performance. The multinationals' share is large relative to that of the United States in chemicals, electrical machinery, and transport equipment, but the share of the United States as a country is greater in nonelectrical machinery. Among more narrowly defined industries, the multinationals' comparative advantage is strongest in industries with heavy investments in advertising and R&D. R&D intensity, a major explanation of the comparative advantage of the United States as a country, explains the comparative advantage of U.S. multinationals to an even greater degree.

Over the last quarter century, U.S. affiliates in foreign countries have changed their operations in several respects. One is that they have become more dependent on the U.S. market. However, they still sell mainly in their host-country markets, and what they do export goes mainly to countries other than the United States. Exports to the U.S. market are only 14 percent of their total sales.

There has been an increase in the proportion of affiliates in which parents own less than a majority share, although that trend has at least slowed. Affiliates in the most technologically advanced industries continue to be majority owned in most cases, presumably because sharing of ownership would erode the very advantages that make direct investment profitable.

While the flow of direct investment from the United States has slowed, there has recently been a large inflow of foreign direct investment into the United States, roughly tripling the share of foreign-owned companies in the United States since 1950, doubling it in the last decade, and reaching to about three-quarters of the value of U.S. investment abroad if those book value figures are taken literally. They probably exaggerate the size of inward direct investment relative to outward investment because so much of the inward investment has occurred in recent years.

While foreign-owned firms accounted for only about 3.5 percent of total U.S. employment after all the recent growth in foreign investment, the shares in manufacturing and wholesale trade were considerably higher. Within manufacturing there was also considerable variation, with foreign firms accounting for almost 40 percent of chemical industry employment, but in all the other industries for less than 10 percent. The foreign shares in service industries, aside from wholesale trade, increased, but remained below 3 percent. To some extent, these figures reflect U.S. comparative advantage in service industry production, but the fact that U.S. companies' direct investment in foreign service industries is not itself very large suggests that it may be difficult to carry firm advantages in these industries across national borders.

The sources of these foreign investment flows into the United States continue to be mainly European countries, particularly the United Kingdom and the Netherlands. However, there has been some increase in the flow from Japan, mainly into wholesale trade. Most of that is probably connected with exporting from and importing to Japan rather than with wholesale trading among U.S. companies.

Aside from the increased flow of direct investment into the United States in recent years, there have been major shifts in the U.S. international capital position, stemming largely from changes in portfolio investment. The United States became a very large capital importer in 1983–85 as U.S. banks reduced their net lending to insignificant amounts overall and foreign countries added greatly to their holdings not only of direct investment but also of U.S. Treasury securities, other U.S. securities, and deposits in U.S. banks. Most of the flows have been from Europe, as in the case of direct investment, but Japan has also become an important investor, particularly in U.S. Treasury securities.

The growth of U.S. bank claims on foreigners was concentrated in a very short period after the second rise in oil prices, with most being accumulated in 1981 and 1982. That concentration is unpleasantly reminiscent of the concentration of portfolio investment in the late 1920s, but there has already been a substantial reduction in those claims in 1985 alone.

Appendix

Tables 8.A.1–8.A.15 are on pages 518–42.

Table 8.A.1   U.S. Direct Investment Abroad, by Industry of Affiliate (millions of dollars, current prices)

	1985	1984	1983	1982	1977	1966	1957	1950	1943	1936	1929
Agriculture	679	739	528	504	528	322	680	589	503	482	880
Mining	4,797	5,230	5,514	5,210	5,998	3,983	2,361	1,129	973	1,032	1,185
Petroleum, total	*58,347*	*59,089*	*57,574*	*57,817*	*28,030*	*13,893*	*9,055*	*3,390*	*1,393*	*1,074*	*1,117*
Extract. & integ. ref. & ext.	35,967	36,501	33,003	32,693	12,987	9,136	5,518	n.a.	n.a.	n.a.	n.a.
Petrol. ref. & petrol. & coal prod.	6,508	6,091	7,085	7,028	5,259	1,366	1,009	n.a.	n.a.	n.a.	n.a.
Tankers, pipelines, storage	1,338	1,465	1,740	1,648	2,490[a]	1,104	1,198	n.a.	n.a.	n.a.	n.a.
Distribution & marketing	8,377	8,895	9,692	11,057	5,380	1,804	1,212	n.a.	n.a.	n.a.	n.a.
Wholesale	n.a.	n.a.	n.a.	10,835		n.a.	n.a.	n.a.	n.a.	n.a.	n.a.
Oil & gas field service	6,157	6,137	6,053	5,392	1,914	482	117	n.a.	n.a.	n.a.	n.a.
PRIMARY, incl. all petrol.	63,823	65,058	63,616	63,531	34,556	18,198	12,096	5,108	2,869	2,588	3,182
PRIMARY, excl. petrol. ref., dist. & serv.	41,443	42,470	39,045	38,407	19,513	13,442	8,560	n.a.	n.a.	n.a.	n.a.
Manufacturing	95,586	85,253	82,907	83,452	62,019	20,740	8,009	3,831	2,276	1,710	1,813
Mfg., incl. petrol. ref.	102,094	91,344	89,992	90,480	67,278	22,106	9,018	n.a.	n.a.	n.a.	n.a.
Construction	1,159	1,014	937	1,061	905	362	118	—[d]	—[d]	—[d]	—[d]
TOTAL GOODS, incl. all petrol.	160,568	151,325	147,460	148,044	97,480	39,300	20,223	8,939	5,145	4,298	4,995

Goods, excl. petrol. transp., trade & serv.	144,696	134,828	129,975	129,947	87,696	35,910	17,696	n.a.	n.a.	n.a.	n.a.
Public utilities & transp., excl. petrol.	2,333	2,322	2,427	2,273	2,186	2,260	2,145	1,425	1,390	1,640	1,610
Public utilities & transp., incl. petrol. transp.	3,671	3,757	4,167	3,921	4,676[a]	3,364	3,343	n.a.	n.a.	n.a.	n.a.
Goods & Publ. Util., incl. all petrol.	162,901	153,647	149,887	150,317	99,666	41,560	22,368	10,364	6,535	5,938	6,605
Goods & Publ. Util., excl. petrol. trade, & service	148,367	138,585	134,142	133,868	92,372	39,274	21,039	n.a.	n.a.	n.a.	n.a.
Trade, excl. petrol.	*27,863*	*25,650*	*25,184*	*24,485*	*16,836*	*4,331*	*1,668*	*762*	*654*	*391*	*368*
Wholesale, excl. petrol.	23,822	21,790	21,278	20,788	14,011	3,427	1,156	542			
Wholesale, incl. petrol.	31,921	30,408	30,712	31,623	19,391	n.a.	n.a.	n.a.	n.a.	n.a.	n.a.
Retail, excl. petrol.	4,041	3,860	3,906	3,697	2,825	905	513	221			
Retail, incl. petrol.	4,319	4,137	4,164	3,919	n.a.	n.a.	n.a.	n.a.			
Trade, incl. petrol.	36,240	34,545	34,876	35,542	22,216[b]	6,135	2,880	n.a.			
Finance & other serv., excl. petrol.											
Banking	14,728	13,246	12,387	10,317	4,370	280	131	—[g]			
Finance (exc. bank), ins., & RE	21,914	15,828	15,075	18,018	21,248	4,423	934	463[h]			

Table 8.A.1 (continued)

	1985	1984	1983	1982	1977	1966	1957	1950	1943	1936	1929
Of which Neth Antilles	−21,994	−25,040	−23,300	−20,089	−1,215	—	—	—	674	362	555
Of which holding comp.	22,398	20,584	19,666	19,597	11,477	2,311	111	56			
Insur., RE, & other finance	21,510	20,284	18,709	18,510	10,986	2,112	823	407[h]			
Insur. & RE						769	400	237			
Other Services, excl. petrol.	5,260	4,625	4,670	4,615	3,870	1,199[c]	293	199			
TRADE & SERV., excl. petrol.	69,765	59,349	57,316	57,435	46,324	10,233	3,026	1,424	1,328	753	923
TRADE & SERV., excl. petrol., Neth., Antilles, & Holding cos.	69,361	63,805	60,950	57,927	36,062	7,922	2,915	1,368	n.a.	n.a.	n.a.
TRADE & SERV., incl. petrol., excl. Neth. Ant. & hold. cos.	83,895	78,837	76,695	74,376	43,336[b]	10,208	4,244	n.a.	n.a.	n.a.	n.a.
Total	*232,667*	*212,994*	*207,203*	*207,752*	*145,990*	*51,792[e]*	*25,394[f]*	*11,788*	*7,862*	*6,691*	*7,528*
Total, excluding Neth. Antilles	254,661	238,034	230,503	227,841	147,205						
TOTAL, Excl. Neth. Antilles and holding companies	232,263	217,450	210,837	208,244	135,728	49,481	25,283	11,732			

Sources: 1982–85: U.S. Department of Commerce 1986a, table 37; 1977: U.S. Dept. of Commerce 1981; 1966: U.S. Dept. of Commerce 1975, table A-15; 1929–57: U.S. Dept. of Commerce 1960, tables 5 and 6, pp. 93, 94.

[a]Includes gasoline service stations.
[b]Excludes gasoline service stations.
[c]Hotels, advertising & other business services, motion pictures, and all other, including inactive.
[d]Included with other services.
[e]Figure comparable to 1957 is 54,799.
[f]Figure comparable to 1950 is 26,278.
[g]Included with other finance.
[h]Includes banking.

Table 8.A.2   Distribution of Exports of Manufactures by the United States and the World, by Detailed Industry, 1966, 1977, and 1982

	1966		1977		1982	
	World	U.S.	World	U.S.	World	U.S.
All manufacturing industries	100.00	100.00	100.00	100.00	100.00	100.00
Foods and kindred products	*13.03*	*8.69*	*11.09*	*7.58*	*9.92*	*6.68*
Grain-mill. & bakery prod.	1.27	2.23	.87	1.42	.91	1.41
Beverages	1.13	.08	.86	.13	.88	.12
Other food products	10.63	6.38	9.36	6.03	8.13	5.14
Chemicals & allied products	*10.30*	*12.75*	*10.73*	*12.04*	*11.82*	*13.35*
Drugs	1.16	1.18	1.12	1.14	1.24	1.47
Soaps, cleansers, etc.	.41	.41	.43	.35	.50	.40
Agricultural chemicals	.95	1.16	.74	1.06	.81	1.49
Industrial chemicals	6.44	8.33	7.17	7.95	7.88	8.34
Other chemicals	1.35	1.67	1.27	1.53	1.38	1.65
Metals	*15.53*	*11.90*	*13.08*	*7.50*	*12.41*	*7.94*
Primary iron and steel	5.82	2.08	5.57	1.49	5.27	1.08
Primary nonferrous	6.12	3.01	3.76	1.72	3.29	1.96
Fabricated metal prod.	3.58	6.81	3.75	4.29	3.84	4.90
Nonelectrical machinery	*13.96*	*20.85*	*13.81*	*20.93*	*14.17*	*23.21*
Farm and garden mach.	1.43	2.75	1.10	2.01	.89	1.49
Construction mach.	2.09	4.34	2.44	4.81	2.56	5.52
Office and comp. mach.	1.43	2.44	1.63	3.93	2.44	6.09
Other nonelect. mach.	9.01	11.32	8.63	10.17	8.28	10.11
Electrical machinery	*6.82*	*7.88*	*8.90*	*9.94*	*9.70*	*10.75*
Household appliances	1.02	.80	1.01	.71	.94	.56
Communications equip.	2.18	2.05	3.14	2.51	3.29	2.42
Electronic components	.58	1.09	1.09	2.14	1.64	3.08
Other electrical mach.	3.04	3.94	3.66	4.58	3.82	4.70
Transport equipment	*13.78*	*19.62*	*17.14*	*23.68*	*16.93*	*19.78*
Motor vehicles & equip.	9.16	12.70	12.06	15.75	11.81	10.63
Other transport equip.	4.62	6.93	5.07	7.92	5.13	9.15
Other manufacturing	*26.58*	*18.30*	*25.25*	*18.34*	*25.06*	*18.30*
Tobacco products	.28	.57	.28	.67	.34	.81
Textiles & clothing	8.54	3.17	7.26	2.70	7.00	2.33
Paper & pulp	3.53	2.58	2.39	2.19	2.37	2.10
Paper products	.37	.37	.41	.50	.46	.60
Printing & publishing	.84	1.17	.71	.72	.71	.86
Rubber products	.84	.78	.97	.64	.95	.63
Plastic products	.35	.36	.57	.48	.58	.41
Lumber & wood furn.	3.02	1.74	3.04	2.48	2.67	2.14
Glass products	.62	.63	.56	.54	.57	.50
Nonmetallic minerals	1.12	.65	1.23	.47	1.24	.48
Instruments	2.98	4.34	3.30	4.77	3.77	5.66
Other manufacturing	4.09	1.94	4.53	2.18	4.40	1.77

Source: U.N. Tapes.

Table 8.A.3 **Industry Distribution of Exports of Manufactures by U.S. Multinationals, by Detailed Industry, 1977 and 1982**

	1977	1982	1982/1977
All manufacturing industries	100.00	100.00	1.00
Foods and kindred products	4.71	4.54	.96
Grain-mill. & bakery prod.	1.37	1.12	.82
Beverages	.495[b]	.505	1.02
Other food products	2.84	2.92	1.03
Chemicals & allied products	13.99	16.92	1.21
Drugs	2.39	2.89	1.21
Soaps, cleansers, etc.	1.09	1.26	1.16
Agricultural chemicals	.698	.794	1.14
Industrial chemicals	8.63	10.34	1.20
Other chemicals	1.18	1.63	1.38
Metals	5.86	5.54	.95
Primary iron and steel	1.37	1.03	.75
Primary nonferrous	1.88	1.96	1.04
Fabricated metal prod.	2.61	2.55	.98
Nonelectrical Machinery	18.23	18.10	.99
Farm and garden mach.	a	1.27	a
Construction mach.	5.32	4.69	.88
Office and comp. mach.	5.91	7.92	1.34
Other nonelect. mach.	7.00[b]	4.22	.78[b]
Electrical machinery	11.14	13.39	1.20
Household appliances	1.04	.552	.53
Communications equip.	2.98	3.75	1.26
Electronic components	3.33	4.67	1.40
Other electrical mach.	3.78	4.42	1.17
Transport equipment	30.65	26.89	.88
Motor vehicles & equip.	24.22	19.52	.81
Other transport equip.	6.43	7.37	1.15
Other manufacturing	15.43	14.61	.95
Tobacco products	c	1.58	c
Textiles & clothing	1.37	1.05	.77
Pulp & paper Paper products	2.65	2.09	.79
Printing & publishing	.418	.406	.97
Rubber products	1.59	1.09	.69
Plastic products	.305	.527	1.73
Lumber & wood furn.	1.39	.95	.68
Glass products	.582	.530	.91
Nonmetallic minerals	.837	.637	.76
Instruments	4.03	5.09	1.26
Other manufacturing	2.25[d]	.65	.99[d]

Sources: U.S. Department of Commerce 1981, tables III.H2 and II.T1, and 1985f, tables III.E2 and II.P1.

Note: *Multinationals* refers to manufacturing industry parents and majority-owned affiliates in manufacturing industries.

[a]Included in other nonelectrical machinery.

[b]Includes farm and garden machinery.

[c]Included in other manufacturing.

[d]Includes tobacco products.

Table 8.A.4   **Industry Share in Exports of Manufactures, United States and U.S. Multinationals Relative to the World, by Detailed Industry, 1966, 1977, and 1982**

	Industry Share of Exports				
	U.S. Relative to the World			U.S. Multinationals Relative to the World	
	1966	1977	1982	1977	1982
Foods and kindred products	*.67*	*.68*	*.67*	*.42*	*.46*
Grain-mill. & bakery prod.	1.76	1.63	1.55	1.57	1.23
Beverages	.07	.16	.14	.58	.58
Other food products	.60	.64	.63	.30	.36
Chemicals & allied products	*1.24*	*1.12*	*1.13*	*1.30*	*1.44*
Drugs	1.02	1.02	1.19	2.13	2.33
Soaps, cleansers, etc.	1.00	.81	.80	2.53	2.52
Agricultural chemicals	1.22	1.43	1.84	.94	.98
Industrial chemicals	1.29	1.11	1.06	1.20	1.31
Other chemicals	1.24	1.20	1.20	.93	1.19
Metals	*.77*	*.57*	*.64*	*.45*	*.45*
Primary iron and steel	.36	.27	.20	.25	.20
Primary nonferrous	.49	.46	.60	.50	.60
Fabricated metal prod.	1.90	1.14	1.28	.70	.66
Nonelectrical machinery	*1.49*	*1.52*	*1.64*	*1.32*	*1.28*
Farm and garden mach.	1.92	1.83	1.67	a	1.43
Construction mach.	2.08	1.97	2.16	2.18	1.83
Office and comp. mach.	1.71	2.41	2.50	3.63	3.25
Other nonelect. mach.	1.26	1.18	1.22	.72[b]	.51
Electrical Machinery	*1.16*	*1.12*	*1.11*	*1.25*	*1.38*
Household appliances	.78	.70	.60	1.03	.59
Communications equip.	.94	.80	.74	.95	1.14
Electronic components	1.88	1.96	1.88	3.06	2.85
Other electrical mach.	1.30	1.25	1.23	1.03	1.16
Transport equipment	*1.42*	*1.38*	*1.17*	*1.79*	*1.59*
Motor vehicles & equip.	1.39	1.31	.90	2.01	1.66
Other transport equip.	1.50	1.56	1.78	1.27	1.43
Other Manufacturing	*.69*	*.73*	*.73*	*.61*	*.58*
Tobacco products	2.04	2.39	2.38	c	4.65
Textiles & clothing	.37	.37	.33	.19	.15
Pulp & paper	.73	.92	.89	.95	.74
Paper products	1.00	1.22	1.30	.95	.74
Printing & publishing	1.39	1.01	1.21	.59	.58
Rubber products	.93	.66	.66	1.64	1.15
Plastic products	1.03	.84	.71	.54	.91
Lumber & wood furn.	.58	.82	.80	.46	.36
Glass products	1.02	.96	.88	1.07	.93
Nonmetallic minerals	.58	.38	.39	.68	.51
Instruments	1.46	1.45	1.50	1.22	1.35
Other manufacturing	.47	.48	.40	.47[d]	.15

Sources: Tables 8.A.2 and 8.A.3.

[a]Included in other nonelectrical machinery.

[b]Includes farm and garden machinery.

[c]Included in other manufacturing.

[d]Includes tobacco products.

Table 8.A.5   **Industry Shares in Exports by U.S. Multinationals Relative to Shares in U.S. Exports of Manufactures, by Detailed Industry, 1977 and 1982**

	1977	1982
Foods and kindred products	.62	.68
Grain-mill. & bakery prod.	.96	.79
Beverages	3.81	4.22
Other food products	.47	.57
Chemicals & allied products	1.16	1.27
Drugs	2.10	1.97
Soaps, cleansers, etc.	3.11	3.15
Agricultural chemicals	.66	.53
Industrial chemicals	1.09	1.24
Other chemicals	.77	.99
Metals	.78	.70
Primary iron and steel	.92	.95
Primary nonferrous	1.09	1.00
Fabricated metal prod.	.61	.52
Nonelectrical machinery	.87	.78
Farm and garden mach.	a	.85
Construction mach.	1.11	.85
Office and comp. mach.	1.50	1.30
Other nonelect. mach.	.57[b]	.42
Electrical machinery	1.12	1.25
Household appliances	1.46	.99
Communications equip.	1.19	1.55
Electronic components	1.56	1.52
Other electrical mach.	.83	.94
Transport equipment	1.30	1.36
Motor vehicles & equip.	1.54	1.84
Other transport equip.	.81	.81
Other manufacturing	.84	.80
Tobacco products	c	1.95
Textiles & clothing	.51	.45
Pulp & paper Paper products	.99	.77
Printing & publishing	.58	.47
Rubber products	2.48	1.73
Plastic products	.64	1.29
Lumber & wood furn.	.56	.45
Glass products	1.08	1.06
Nonmetallic minerals	1.78	1.33
Instruments	.84	.90
Other manufacturing	.79[d]	.37

Sources: Tables 8.A.2 and 8.A.3.

Note: *Multinationals* refers to manufacturing industry parents and affiliates in manufacturing industries.

[a]Included in other nonelectrical machinery.

[b]Includes farm and garden machinery; comparable 1982 ratio was .47.

[c]Included in other manufacturing.

[d]Includes tobacco products; comparable 1982 ratio was .86.

Table 8.A.6   **R&D Expenditures by Manufacturing Parents and Relation to Parent Sales, 1977 (millions of dollars)**

	R&D Expend.	Sales	R&D Expend. as % of Sales
Total Manufacturing	17,039	739,460	2.30
Foods and kindred products	395	83,422	.47
Grain-mill. & bakery prod.	94	14,497	.65
Beverages	29	9,679	.30
Other food products	273	59,245	.46
Chemicals & allied products	2,892	96,474	3.00
Drugs	950	16,423	5.78
Soaps, cleansers, etc.	277	14,790	1.87
Agricultural chemicals	a	3,303	a
Industrial chemicals	1,481	53,985	2.74
Other chemicals	184[b]	7,974	.74[b]
Metals	751	94,563	.79
Primary iron and steel	314	46,902	.67
Primary nonferrous	183	19,250	.95
Fabricated metal prod.	255	28,411	.90
Nonelectrical machinery	3,395	80,174	4.23
Farm and garden mach.	203	6,559	3.09
Construction mach.	356	18,211	1.95
Office and comp. mach.	2,191	23,950	9.15
Other nonelect. mach.	645	31,455	2.05
Electrical machinery	2,284	62,631	3.65
Household appliances	102	8,436	1.21
Communications equip.	446	16,723	2.67
Electronic components	238	6,247	3.81
Other electrical mach.	1,498	31,225	4.80
Transport equipment	5,046	165,681	3.05
Motor vehicles & equip.	3,242	115,877	2.80
Other transport equip.	1,804	49,804	3.62
Other manufacturing	2,275	156,516	1.45
Tobacco products	52	10,845	.48
Textiles & clothing	74	25,342	.29
Pulp & paper / Paper products	315	22,570	1.40
Printing & publishing	14	13,734	.10
Rubber products	312	16,401	1.90
Plastic products	30	3,251	.92
Lumber & wood furn.	84	18,218	.46
Glass products	94	6,053	1.55
Nonmetallic minerals	115	10,409	1.10
Instruments	1,058	19,087	5.54
Other manufacturing	127	10,607	1.20

Source: U.S. Department of Commerce 1981.

[a]Included in "other chemicals."

[b]Includes "agricultural chemicals."

Table 8.A.7   **Sales and Exports by U.S. Majority-Owned Affiliates (millions of dollars)**

	Total Sales					
	1957	1966	1977	1982	1983	1984
All Industries	38,154[a]	97,783	507,019	730,235	705,811	716,410
Agriculture, forestry, fishing	856	[b]	1,195	1,286	1,353	1,490
Mining	2,032	3,321	5,086	4,336	3,220	3,260
Petroleum	14,501	27,457	198,624	266,304	245,340	235,267
Extraction	n.a.	n.a.	24,753	45,143	44,462	51,174
Other	n.a.	n.a.	173,871	221,161	200,878	184,093
Manufacturing	18,331	47,375	194,200	271,099	270,363	284,581
Construction	[b]	[b]	7,871	12,208	10,544	7,094
Public utilities and trans.	1,216	1,366	3,629	4,233	4,460	4,276
Trade	n.a.	14,066	77,362	129,333	128,584	134,545
Wholesale	n.a.	n.a.	64,463	113,622	110,929	116,796
Retail	n.a.	n.a.	12,899	15,711	17,655	17,749
Finance, ins., & real estate (excl. banking)	n.a.	n.a.[e]	10,002	23,526	23,690	28,517
Services	1,217[c]	4,181[d]	9,051	17,911	18,256	17,380

	Total Exports					
	1957	1966	1977	1982	1983	1984
All Industries	10,459[a]	24,393	193,712	252,274	248,763	261,328
Agriculture, forestry, fishing	539	[b]	695	934	994	1,111
Mining	1,707	2,496	3,940	3,572	2,560	2,632
Petroleum	4,980	8,206	98,254	94,205	90,882	85,748
Extraction	n.a.	n.a.	13,392	27,736	27,125	31,211
Other	n.a.	n.a.	84,862	66,469	63,757	54,537
Manufacturing	2,912	8,817	59,773	91,832	94,973	106,587
Construction	[b]	[b]	1,060	1,155	1,118	787
Public utilities and transp.	297	151	60	388	281	356
Trade	n.a.	4,100	26,737	47,754	44,482	47,395
Wholesale	n.a.	n.a.	26,483	47,410	44,118	47,125
Retail	n.a.	n.a.	254	344	364	270
Finance, ins., & real estate (excl. banking)	n.a.	n.a.[e]	1,198	8,897	9,771	13,181
Services	n.a.	623	1,994	3,539	3,700	3,529

Table 8.A.7 (continued)

	Exports to the U.S.					
	1957	1966	1977	1982	1983	1984
All Industries	3,770[a]	6,300	93,573	76,780	76,814	88,956
Agriculture, forestry, fishing	327	[b]	360	524	537	583
Mining	898	1,260	1,429	1,234	995	1,052
Petroleum	1,441	1,491	70,916	36,567	30,514	31,780
Extraction	n.a.	n.a.	8,909	18,113	15,854	16,048
Other	n.a.	n.a.	62,007	18,454	14,660	15,732
Manufacturing	1,093	2,679	17,601	26,244	31,258	39,858
Construction	[b]	[b]	56	33	30	29
Public utilities and transp.	n.a.	101	20	273	144	179
Trade	n.a.	504	2,225	5,538	6,387	7,157
Wholesale	n.a.	n.a.	2,195	5,501	6,297	7,122
Retail	n.a.	n.a.	30	37	90	35
Finance, ins., & real estate (excl. banking)	n.a.	n.a.	591	5,401	5,984	7,277
Services	n.a.	n.a.	377	966	966	1,040

Sources: U.S. Department of Commerce 1960, tables 22 and 23; 1975, table L-1; 1981, table III.H2; 1985f, table III.E2; 1986d, table 35; 1986c, table 35.

[a]Excluding trade and finance.

[b]Included with services.

[c]Including construction.

[d]Including agriculture, forestry, fishing, and construction.

[e]The division of sales between local sales and exports was not reported by companies in "finance, insurance, and real estate."

Table 8.A.8   Sales of Majority-Owned Affiliates as Percentage of Sales of All Affiliates

	1966		1977		1982	
	Developed Countries	LDCs	Developed Countries	LDCs	Developed Countries	LDCs
All Industries	88.0	88.7	75.4	84.2	77.3	80.3
Agriculture	a	a	58.8	87.5	68.2	86.2
Mining	92.7	74.8	54.6	48.3	61.9	42.6
Petroleum	90.2	100.0	72.8	93.4	78.2	86.4
Manufacturing	88.8	80.2	80.5	71.0	76.5	71.1
Chemicals	91.1	83.3			82.1	68.2
Drugs	n.a.	n.a.	93.8	86.0	96.2	93.8
Soaps, cleansers, etc.	n.a.	n.a.	96.6	88.6	99.3	88.8
Machinery	90.2	87.2	86.3	77.8	86.1	79.1
Office & computing mach.	n.a.	n.a.	94.7	97.5	94.0	99.5
Radio, TV, & commun. eq.	n.a.	n.a.	94.1	77.6	83.3	71.1
Electronic comp. & access.	n.a.	n.a.	80.5	95.3	78.9	96.0
Instruments & related prod.	n.a.	n.a.	89.2	76.8	88.5	78.7
Transportation, comm., & public util.	88.5	68.3[c]	19.5	29.4	6.3	50.3
Construction	a	a	80.8	75.3	96.5	82.7
Wholesale trade	94.8	91.8	75.6	79.5	93.4	87.3
Retail trade	95.4[b]	91.5[c]	71.6	60.5	58.9	46.4
Finance, insur., & real estate	a	a	75.6[d]	53.9[d]	76.3[d]	92.6[d]
Services	a	a			90.3	
Other industries	94.4	93.3[c]	73.1	76.0	81.0	

Sources: U.S. Department of Commerce 1975, tables J-3, J-4, J-18 and L-3; 1981, tables II.F6 and III.F6; and 1985f, tables II.D4 and III.D4.

[a] Included with "other industries."

[b] Based on income in place of sales. The sales figures for majority-owned affiliates in the source appear to be incorrect.

[c] Suppressed observations estimated by the author.

[d] Excluding banks.

Table 8.A.9   Foreign Direct Investment in the United States, by Industry of Affiliate (millions of dollars)

	1985	1984	1983	1982	1981	1980	1977	1974	1966	1960	1950
Total	182,951	164,583	137,061	124,677	108,714	83,046	34,595	26,512	9,054	6,910	3,391
Agriculture, forestry, & fishing	1,110	1,150	1,148	1,049	948	773	n.a.	31c			
Mining	4,070	3,920	1,928	1,876	2,152	1,320	n.a.	427			
Petroleum, total	28,123	25,400	18,209	17,660	15,246	12,200	6,573	6,354	1,740	1,238	405
Extraction & integ. ref. & ext.	24,256	21,913	15,385	14,199	12,452	10,229	n.a.	6,174			
Petrol. refin. & petrol. & coal prod.	29	28	31	44	48	39	n.a.				
Tankers, pipelines & storage[a]	520	538	587	457	393	368	n.a.				
Distribution & marketing[b]	2,398	1,930	1,202	1,909	1,365	962	n.a.	180			
Oil & gas field service	919	990	1,005	1,051	988	601	n.a.				
PRIMARY, incl. all petrol.	33,303	30,470	21,285	20,585	18,346	14,293	n.a.	6,812			
PRIMARY, excl. petrol., transp., dist., & service	29,466	27,012	18,491	17,168	15,600	12,362	n.a.	6,632			
Manufacturing	60,798	51,802	47,665	44,065	40,533	33,011	14,030	8,242	3,789	2,611	1,138
Chemicals	19,502	16,631	15,766	14,377	13,701	10,439	n.a.	2,672			
Machinery	9,447	9,682	8,608	8,595	8,297	6,995	n.a.	1,093			
Transp. equip.	2,134	1,880	1,656	1,507	994	955	n.a.				
Other	29,715	23,609	21,635	19,586	17,541	14,622	n.a.	4,477			
Construction	4,024	4,337	3,676	3,692	3,152	522	n.a.	36c			
TOTAL GOODS, incl. all petrol.	98,125	86,609	72,626	68,342	62,031	47,826	n.a.	15,090			
GOODS, excl. petrol., transp., dist., & service	94,288	83,151	69,832	64,925	59,285	45,895	n.a.	14,910			
Public util. & transp., excl. petrol.	1,885	1,633	1,572	1,379	1,103	774	n.a.	347			
Public util. & transp., incl. petrol.	2,405	2,171	2,159	1,836	1,496	1,142	n.a.	n.a.			
GOODS & PUB. UTIL., incl. all petrol.	100,010	88,242	74,198	69,721	63,134	48,600	n.a.	15,437			
GOODS & PUB. UTIL., excl. petrol. trade & service	96,693	85,322	71,991	66,761	60,781	47,037	n.a.	15,257			

Trade, excl. petrol.	34,212	31,219	26,513	23,604	20,537	15,210	n.a.	4,578			
Wholesale, excl. petrol.	27,514	24,455	21,031	18,397	16,012	11,560	7,237	4,153	739		
Wholesale, incl. petrol.	29,912	26,385	22,233	20,306	17,377	12,522	n.a.	425			
Retail	6,698	6,764	5,482	5,207	4,525	3,650	n.a.				
Trade, incl. petrol.	36,610	33,149	27,715	25,513	21,902	16,172	n.a.				
Finance & other serv., excl. petrol.											
Banking	11,503	10,326	8,697	7,846	6,553	4,617		510			
Finance (exc. bank), insur., & real estate	34,334	32,316	25,570	21,607	17,159	13,530	5,398	5,686	2,072	1,810	1,065
Holding companies	3,783	3,687	2,213	1,772	1,044	857		3,807			
Other finance	30,551	28,629	23,357	19,835	16,115	12,673		1,879			
Other services, excl. petrol.	2,893	2,479	2,082	1,899	1,330	1,089		302			
Other industries							1,357[d]	714[d]	1,251[e]		784[e]
TRADE & SERV., excl. petrol.	82,942	76,340	62,862	54,956	45,579	34,446		11,076			
TRADE & SERV., excl. petrol. & hold cos.	79,159	72,653	60,649	53,184	44,535	33,589		7,269			
TRADE & SERV., incl. petrol. excl. hold. cos.	81,557	74,583	61,851	55,093	45,900	34,551		n.a.			

Sources: 1981–85: U.S. Department of Commerce 1986a, table 23; 1980: U.S. Department of Commerce 1985b, table 34; 1974: U.S. Department of Commerce 1976, table A-4. These data have been revised in the source listed for 1977 and earlier years, but we used this source for its superior detail. 1950, 1960, 1966, 1977: U.S. Department of Commerce 1984b, tables 1 and 17.

[a] Includes gasoline service stations.

[b] Wholesale only.

[c] Investment in unincorporated affiliates in agriculture and construction is combined in the source. We assumed that half was in agriculture and half was in construction.

[d] Including agriculture, mining, construction, public utilities and transportation, retail trade, and other services.

[e] Same coverage as note d, plus wholesale trade.

Table 8.A.10 Employment of Nonbank U.S. Affiliates of Foreign Corporations, by Industry of Affiliate (thousands)

	1984	1983	1982	1981	1980	1979	1978	1977	1974
All Industries	2,715	2,547	2,448	2,417	2,034	1,753	1,430	1,219	1,057
Agriculture, forestry, & fishing	9	11	11	11	10	10	10	9	8
Mining	32	29	41	40	25	18	16	16	23
Petroleum	125	121	122	128	102	86	98	90	94
PRIMARY PRODUCTION	166	161	174	179	137	114	124	115	125
Manufacturing	1,378	1,321	1,242	1,300	1,105	1,006	804	686	551
Food & kindred prod.	145	139	126	128	120	111	84	72	75
Chemicals	406	398	390	414	284	261	224	198	115
Primary & fabric. metals	164	146	103	111	113	107	84	85	88
Machinery, excl. elect.	128	125	132	138	117	112	86	65	43
Elect. mach. & equip.	181	168	153	164	173	149	110	95	56
Transport. equip.	61	65	71	73	65	50	21	3	} 174
Other manuf.	294	281	266	273	233	217	195	167	
Construction	42	45	52	58	43	28	23	13	8
GOODS PRODUCTION	1,586	1,527	1,468	1,537	1,285	1,148	951	814	684
Public utilities & transportation	63	56	57	43	36	27	25	23	45
GOODS, PUBLIC UTIL. & TRANSP.	1,649	1,583	1,525	1,580	1,321	1,175	976	837	729
Wholesale trade	293	269	280	254	217	196	172	153	122
Retail trade	454	420	398	344	304	236	172	142	121
Finance, exc. bank. & insur.	38	37	25	18	25	13	11	10	9[a]
Insurance	62	68	71	68	62	45	38	33	33
Real estate	27	27	26	29	20	22	11	8	5
Services	192	143	123	124	85	66	51	37	41
TRADE AND SERVICES	1,066	964	923	837	713	578	455	383	331

Sources: Shea 1986; Howenstine 1985; U.S. Department of Commerce 1984a, table F-1; U.S. Department of Commerce 1985c, table F-1; U.S. Department of Commerce 1976, table L-1.

[a]Banking: 26 thousand.

Table 8.A.11   **Foreign Direct Investment Position in the United States by Industry and Country (billions of dollars, current prices)**

	1985	1984	1983	1982	1981	1980
All Industries	*183.0*	*164.6*	*137.1*	*124.7*	*108.7*	*83.0*
Canada	16.7	15.3	11.4	11.7	12.1	12.2
Europe	*120.9*	*108.2*	*92.9*	*83.2*	*72.4*	*54.7*
Germany	14.4	12.3	10.8	9.8	9.5	7.6
Netherlands	36.1	33.7	29.2	26.2	26.8	19.1
U.K.	43.8	38.4	32.2	28.4	18.6	14.1
Switzerland	11.0	8.1	7.5	6.4	5.5	5.1
Japan	19.1	16.0	11.3	9.7	7.7	4.7
Latin America	*17.0*	*16.2*	*15.0*	*14.2*	*11.7*	*9.7*
Neth. Antilles	10.6	10.9	9.9	9.2	8.2	6.7
Middle East	5.0	5.3	4.4	4.4	3.6	.9
Petroleum	*28.1*	*25.4*	*18.2*	*17.7*	*15.2*	*12.2*
Europe	25.4	23.1	16.3	15.1	12.9	n.a.
Netherlands & U.K.	23.6	21.0	14.6	13.5	11.4	n.a.
Manufacturing	*60.8*	*51.8*	*47.7*	*44.1*	*40.5*	*33.0*
Canada	5.1	4.1	3.3	3.5	3.4	n.a.
Europe	*46.5*	*39.1*	*36.9*	*33.0*	*30.9*	n.a.
France	5.5	5.4	5.5	5.0	4.9	n.a.
Germany	6.2	4.4	4.5	4.2	4.2	n.a.
Netherlands	13.0	12.5	11.2	9.9	9.0	n.a.
U.K.	11.9	9.7	9.2	8.5	7.6	n.a.
Switzerland	7.4	4.8	4.2	3.6	3.3	n.a.
Japan	2.6	2.5	1.6	1.6	1.3	n.a.
Latin America	5.6	5.5	5.2	5.4	4.5	n.a.
Neth. Antilles	3.7	4.1	3.8	3.7	4.0	n.a.
Wholesale trade	*27.5*	*24.5*	*21.0*	*18.4*	*16.0*	*11.6*
Europe	12.5	11.7	10.1	9.0	8.0	n.a.
Japan	11.6	9.7	7.8	6.1	5.0	n.a.
Retail trade	*6.7*	*6.8*	*5.5*	*5.2*	*4.5*	*3.6*
Europe	5.1	5.2	4.4	4.3	3.8	n.a.
Banking	11.5	10.3	8.7	7.8	6.6	4.6
Europe	6.0	5.7	5.6	4.9	4.0	n.a.
Finance, excl. bank.	*4.7*	*5.6*	*2.3*	*2.2*	*1.1*	*1.3*
Europe	2.4	3.5	1.2	1.4	.6	n.a.
Insurance	*11.1*	*8.9*	*8.7*	*7.9*	*7.1*	*6.1*
Europe	*8.9*	*6.7*	*7.2*	*6.3*	*5.5*	n.a.
Netherlands & U.K.	5.7	3.9	4.2	3.9	3.5	n.a.
Real estate	*18.6*	*17.8*	*14.6*	*11.5*	*9.0*	*6.1*
Europe	8.8	8.3	6.8	5.1	3.7	n.a.
Latin America	4.8	4.7	4.1	3.3	2.6	n.a.
Neth. Antilles	3.9	3.7	3.2	2.6	1.9	n.a.
Other	9.9	9.5	8.5	8.0	6.5	3.2

Sources: U.S. Department of Commerce 1986a and earlier articles in the same series.

Table 8.A.12 U.S. International Capital Transactions, 1960–85 (millions of dollars, current prices)

	1960	1961	1962	1963	1964	1965	1966	1967	1968	1969	1970	1971	1972
U.S. AND FOREIGN ASSETS, NET	−1,805	−2,833	−2,263	−4,053	−5,917	−4,974	−3,660	−2,378	−1,049	+1,117	−2,978	+10,495	+6,964
U.S. ASSETS ABROAD, NET (increase/capital outflow (−))	−4,099	−5,538	−4,174	−7,270	−9,560	−5,716	−7,321	−9,757	−10,977	−11,585	−9,337	−12,475	−14,497
U.S. official reserve assets, net	2,145	607	1,535	378	171	1,225	570	53	−870	−1,179	2,481	2,349	−4
U.S. government assets, other than official reserve assets, net	−1,100	−910	−1,085	−1,662	−1,680	−1,605	−1,543	−2,423	−2,274	−2,200	−1,589	−1,884	−1,568
U.S. private assets, net	−5,144	−5,235	−4,623	−5,986	−8,050	−5,336	−6,347	−7,386	−7,833	−8,206	−10,229	−12,940	−12,925
Direct investment	−2,940	−2,653	−2,851	−3,483	−3,760	−5,011	−5,418	−4,805	−5,295	−5,960	−7,590	−7,618	−7,747
Foreign securities	−663	−762	−969	−1,105	−677	−759	−720	−1,308	−1,569	−1,549	−1,076	−1,113	−618
U.S. claims on unaffiliated foreigners reported by nonbanking concerns	−394	−558	−354	157	−1,108	341	−442	−779	−1,203	−126	−596	−1,229	−1,054
U.S. claims reported by U.S. banks, not included elsewhere	−1,148	−1,261	−450	−1,556	−2,505	93	233	−495	233	−570	−967	−2,980	−3,506

Foreign Assets in the United States, net (increase/capital inflow (+))	2,294	2,705	1,911	3,217	3,643	742	3,661	7,379	9,928	12,702	6,359	22,970	21,461
Foreign official assets in the U.S., net	1,473	765	1,270	1,986	1,660	134	-672	3,451	-774	-1,301	6,908	26,879	10,475
U.S. government securities	655	233	1,409	816	432	-141	-1,527	2,261	-769	-2,343	9,439	26,570	8,470
U.S. Treasury securities	655	233	1,410	803	434	-134	-1,548	2,222	-798	-2,269	9,411	26,578	8,213
Other	—	—	-1	12	-2	-7	21	39	29	-74	28	-8	257
Other U.S. government liabilities	215	25	152	429	298	65	113	83	-15	251	-456	-510	182
U.S. liabilities reported by U.S. banks, not included elsewhere	603	508	-291	742	930	210	742	1,106	10	792	-2,075	819	1,638
Other foreign official assets	—	—	—	—	—	—	—	—	—	—	—	—	185
Other foreign assets in the United States, net	821	1,939	641	1,231	1,983	607	4,333	3,928	10,703	14,002	-550	-3,909	10,986
Direct investment	315	311	346	231	322	415	425	698	807	1,263	1,464	367	949
U.S. Treasury securities	-364	151	-66	-149	-146	-131	-356	-135	136	-68	81	-24	-39
U.S. Securities other than U.S. Treasury securities	282	324	134	287	-85	-358	906	1,016	4,414	3,130	2,189	2,289	4,507

Table 8.A.12 (continued)

	1960	1961	1962	1963	1964	1965	1966	1967	1968	1969	1970	1971	1972
U.S. liabilities to unaffiliated foreigners reported by U.S. nonbanking concerns	-90	226	-110	-37	75	178	476	584	1,475	792	2,014	369	815
U.S. liabilities reported by U.S. banks, not included elsewhere	678	928	336	898	1,818	503	2,882	1,765	3,871	8,886	-6,298	-6,911	4,754
Allocations of special drawing rights	—	—	—	—	—	—	—	—	—	—	867	717	710
Statistical discrepancy	-1,019	-989	-1,124	-360	-907	-457	629	-205	438	-1,516	-219	-9,779	-1,879

	1973	1974	1975	1976	1977	1978	1979	1980	1981	1982	1983	1984	1985
U.S. AND FOREIGN ASSETS, NET	-4,486	-504	-24,033	-14,751	+16,534	+2,906	-25,579	-28,006	-27,709	-27,195	+35,474	+79,128	+94,670
U.S. ASSETS ABROAD, NET (increase/capital outflow (−))	-22,874	-34,745	-39,703	-51,269	-34,785	-61,130	-64,331	-86,118	-111,031	-121,273	-50,022	-23,639	-32,436
U.S. official reserve assets, net	158	-1,467	-849	-2,558	-375	732	-1,133	-8,155	-5,175	-4,965	-1,196	-3,131	-3,858
U.S. government assets, other than official reserve assets, net	-2,644	366	-3,474	-4,214	-3,693	-4,660	-3,746	-5,162	-5,097	-6,131	-5,005	-5,523	-2,824

U.S. private assets, net	−20,388	−33,643	−35,380	−44,498	−30,717	−57,202	−59,453	−72,802	−100,758	−110,177	−43,821	−14,986	−25,754
Direct investment	−11,353	−9,052	−14,244	−11,949	−11,890	−16,056	−25,222	−19,222	−9,624	2,369	−373	−3,858	−18,752
Foreign securities	−671	−1,854	−6,247	−8,885	−5,460	−3,626	−4,726	−3,568	−5,778	−8,102	−7,007	−5,082	−7,977
U.S. claims on unaffiliated foreigners reported by nonbanking concerns	−2,383	−3,221	−1,357	−2,296	−1,940	−3,853	−3,291	−3,174	−1,181	6,626	−6,513	5,081	1,665
U.S. claims reported by U.S. banks, not included elsewhere	−5,980	−19,516	−13,532	−21,368	−11,427	−33,667	−26,213	−46,838	−84,175	−111,070	−29,928	−11,127	−691
FOREIGN ASSETS IN THE UNITED STATES, NET (increase/capital inflow (+))	18,388	34,241	15,670	36,518	51,319	64,036	38,752	58,112	83,322	94,078	85,496	102,767	127,106
Foreign official assets in the U.S., net	6,026	10,546	7,027	17,693	36,816	33,678	−13,665	15,497	4,960	3,593	5,968	3,037	−1,324
U.S. government securities	641	4,172	5,563	9,892	32,538	24,221	−21,972	11,895	6,322	5,085	6,496	4,703	−841
U.S. Treasury securities	59	3,270	4,658	9,319	30,230	23,555	−22,435	9,708	5,019	5,779	6,972	4,690	−546
Other	582	902	905	573	2,308	p −666	463	2,187	1,303	−694	−476	13	−295
Other U.S. government liabilities	936	301	1,517	4,627	1,400	2,476	−40	615	−338	605	725	436	438
U.S. liabilities reported by U.S. banks, not included elsewhere	4,126	5,818	−2,158	969	773	5,551	7,213	−159	−3,670	−1,747	545	555	522

Table 8.A.12 (continued)

	1973	1974	1975	1976	1977	1978	1979	1980	1981	1982	1983	1984	1985
Other foreign official assets	323	254	2,104	2,205	2,105	1,430	1,135	3,145	2,646	−350	−1,798	−2,657	−1,488
Other foreign assets in the U.S., net	12,362	23,696	8,643	18,826	14,503	30,358	52,416	42,615	78,362	90,486	79,527	99,730	128,430
Direct investment	2,800	4,760	2,603	4,347	3,728	7,897	11,877	16,918	25,195	13,792	11,946	25,359	17,856
U.S. Treasury securities	−216	697	2,590	2,783	534	2,178	4,960	2,645	2,946	7,052	8,721	23,059	20,500
U.S. securities other than U.S. Treasury securities	4,041	378	2,503	1,284	2,437	2,254	1,351	5,457	7,176	6,392	8,636	12,759	50,859
U.S. liabilities to unaffiliated foreigners reported by U.S. nonbanking concerns	1,035	1,844	319	−578	1,086	1,889	1,621	6,852	917	−2,383	−118	4,704	−1,172
U.S. liabilities reported by U.S. banks, not included elsewhere	4,702	16,017	628	10,990	6,719	16,141	32,607	10,743	42,128	65,633	50,342	33,849	40,387
Allocations of special drawing rights	—	—	—	—	—	—	1,139	1,152	1,093	—	—	—	—
Statistical discrepancy	−2,654	−1,458	5,917	10,544	−2,023	12,521	25,431	24,982	20,276	36,325	11,130	27,338	23,006

Source: Krueger 1986, table 1.

Table 8.A.13   **Foreign Purchases of U.S. Corporate Stocks and Corporate and Other Bonds, excluding Treasury Securities and Transactions of Foreign Official Agencies (millions of dollars, current prices)**

	1985	1984	1983	1982	1981
Stocks, net foreign purchases	4,855	−906	6,395	3,566	5,056
Western Europe	2,079	−3,061	3,947	2,518	3,655
Germany	730	−48	1,046	334	−22
Switzerland	−75	−1,542	1,325	−579	288
U.K.	1,686	−676	1,771	3,096	2,216
Other	−262	−794	−195	−333	1,173
Canada	355	1,691	1,151	223	1,046
Japan	298	−148	274	—	118
Other	2,123	612	1,023	826	237
Corporate & other bonds, net foreign purchases	46,004	13,666	2,241	2,826	2,115
Western Europe	39,424	11,192	1,204	2,678	1,713
Germany	2,001	1,727	345	2,011	848
Switzerland	3,987	639	583	158	108
U.K.	32,488	8,436	406	189	661
Other	948	390	−130	320	96
Canada	188	−62	123	24	−12
Japan	5,420	1,455	682	29	175
Other countries	1,086	787	223	123	198
Intl. financial inst.	−114	294	9	−28	41

Sources: 1983–85: Krueger 1986, table 6; others from earlier articles in the same series
Notes: (+) = net foreign purchases; (−) = net foreign sales

Table 8.A.14 Foreign Purchases of U.S. Treasury Securities and Additions to Liabilities Reported by U.S. Banks (millions of dollars, current prices)

	1985	1984	1983	1982	1981	1980	1979	1978	1977	1976	1975	1974
Changes in foreign official assets in the U.S., net	-1,324	3,037	5,795	3,318	5,430	15,442	-13,757	33,293	36,656	18,073	6,336	10,981
Industrial countries	1,178	463	10,284	-6,506	-11,544	914	-21,151	34,293	28,766	3,887	-1,040	-713
Members of OPEC	-6,599	-4,304	-8,283	7,291	13,581	12,769	5,543	-1,137	6,351	9,581	6,881	10,841
Other countries	4,097	6,878	3,794	2,533	3,393	1,759	1,851	137	1,539	4,605	495	853
Other purchases of U.S. Treasury Securities and additions to liabilities Reported by U.S. banks, not												

incl. elsewhere	60,887	56,908	59,063	72,974	45,074	13,388	37,567	18,456	7,253	13,773
Industrial c'ntries	35,988	36,255	26,299	38,585	13,209	6,062	18,150	10,931	1,183	6,312
Western Eur.	10,964	23,343	19,296	33,975	11,029					
Canada	777	3,392	3,989	2,027	−23					
Other	24,247	9,520	3,014	2,583	2,193					
Caribbean banking centers	11,287	6,972	21,770	18,894	24,817	2,980	14,006	3,911	3,128	1,618
Other areas	13,612	13,681	10,994	15,495	7,048					
Of which members of										
OPEC[a]	2,464	2,023	573	4,736	90	861	1,808	1,070	989	1,161
By area[b]						4,311	3,565	2,473	2,674	1,968
Latin America	5,361	6,350	4,989	11,533	4,681					
Asia	5,538	3,651	4,358	2,915	1,009					
Africa	1,079	243	−57	−36	−45					
Other	1,634[A]	3,437	1,704	1,083	1,403					
Intl. fin. inst.				776	1,472	−826	38	71	−721	2,714

Sources: 1983–85: Krueger 1985 and 1986, tables B and 9; others from earlier articles in the same series.

Notes: (+) = credits, increase in foreign assets; (−) = debits, decrease in foreign assets.

[a] Previous to 1981, oil-exporting countries.

[b] OPEC members included in area totals from 1981 through 1985; oil-exporting countries excluded from area totals before 1981.

Table 8.A.15   Changes in Claims on Foreigners Reported by U.S. Banks, by Area (millions of dollars, current prices)

	1985	1984	1983	1982	1981	1980	1979	1978	1977	1976
Total	-691	-11,127	-29,928	-111,070	-84,175	-46,838	-26,213	-33,631	-11,427	-21,368
Industrial countries	-7,291	-8,384	-8,846	-49,183	-33,464	-14,255	-13,906	-18,107	-3,125	-4,507
Western Europe	-6,445	-6,411	-1,868	-43,053	-24,092					
U.K.	-4,450	-7,994	2,527	-26,076	-17,094	-2,812	-10,009	-4,610	-1,942	-1,799
Other	-1,995	1,583	-4,395	-16,977	-6,998					
Canada	1,319	-349	-3,905	-3,241	-4,352					
Japan	-2,659	-663	-1,752	-1,591	-4,019					
Other	494	-961	-1,321	-1,298	-1,001					
Caribbean banking centers	200	-717	-6,696	-25,462	-21,475	-16,845	2,335	-1,930	-5,825	-11,518
Other Areas	6,800	-2,026	-14,386	-36,425	-29,236	-15,738	-14,642	-13,594	-2,477	-5,343
Of which OPEC members[a]	1,321	124	-3,105	-5,698	-2,302	-1,684	241	-3,472	-906	-1,712
By area[b]						-14,054	-14,883	-10,122	-1,571	-3,631
Latin America	4,702	-1,122	-9,269	-26,344	-22,763	-8,870	-11,436	-7,045	-609	-3,095
Asia	1,713	-761	-4,567	-9,499	-5,341	-4,407	-2,795	-2,879	-928	-366
Africa	385	280	-570	-867	-511	-303	-99	-109	-111	59
Other	—	-423	20	285	-621	-474	-553	-89	77	-229

Notes: (+) = credits, decrease in U.S. assets; (−) = debits, increase in U.S. assets.

[a] Previous to 1981, oil-exporting countries.

[b] OPEC members included in area totals from 1981 through 1985; oil-exporting countries excluded from area totals before 1981.

Note

This paper draws on research carried on under grants from the National Science Foundation and the Ford Foundation and a PSC-CUNY research award. The author is indebted to J. David Richardson and Richard Levich for very helpful comments on an earlier draft and to James Hayes, Linda Molinari, Marinella Moscheni, and Rosa Schupbach for help in checking his work and in preparing the manuscript. The views expressed are the author's own and do not necessarily represent those of the National Bureau or of any of the sponsors of the research cited.

References

Baldwin, Robert E. 1979. Determinants of trade and foreign investment: Further evidence, *Review of Economics and Statistics* 61 (1).
Brereton, Barbara F. 1986. U.S. multinational companies: Operations in 1984. *Survey of Current Business* (9).
Caves, Richard E. 1974. The causes of direct investment: Foreign firms' share in Canadian and U.K. manufacturing industries. *Review of Economics and Statistics* 56: 279–93.
Edelstein, Michael. 1982. *Overseas investment in the age of high imperialism: The United Kingdom, 1850–1914*. New York: Columbia University Press.
Federal Reserve Board. 1979. *Flow of funds accounts, 1949–1978: Annual total flows and year-end assets and liabilities*. Board of Governors of the Federal Reserve System. December.
———. 1986. *Flow of funds accounts: Financial assets and liabililties, year-end, 1962–85*. Board of Governors of the Federal Reserve System. September.
Hood, Neil, and Stephen Young. 1979. *The economics of multinational enterprise*. London and New York: Longman.
Howenstine, Ned G. 1985. U.S. affiliates of foreign companies: Operations in 1983. *Survey of Current Business* (11): 36–50.
Krueger, Russell C. 1985. U.S. international transactions, first quarter 1985. *Survey of Current Business* 65 (6): 34–71.
———. 1986. U.S. international transactions, first quarter 1986. *Survey of Current Business* (6): 36–73.
Lewis, Cleona. 1938. *America's stake in international investments*. Washington, D.C.: Brookings Institution.
Lipsey, Robert E., and Irving B. Kravis. 1985. The competitive position of U.S. manufacturing firms. *Banca Nazionale del Lavoro Quarterly Review* 153: 127–54.
———. 1986. The competitiveness and comparative advantage of U.S. multinationals, 1957–1983. NBER Working Paper 2051. October.
Mintz, Ilse. 1951. *Deterioration in the quality of foreign bonds issued in the United States, 1920–1930*. New York: National Bureau of Economic Research.
Musgrave, John C. 1986a. Fixed reproducible tangible wealth in the United States, 1982–85. *Survey of Current Business* 66 (8): 36–39.
———. 1986b. Fixed reproducible tangible wealth in the United States: Revised estimates. *Survey of Current Business* 66 (1): 51–75.
OECD. 1981. *International investment and multinational enterprises: Recent international direct investment trends*. Paris: OECD.
Sammons, Robert L., and Milton Abelson. 1942. *American direct investments in Foreign Countries, 1940*. U.S. Department of Commerce. Washington, D.C.

Shea, Michael A. 1986. U.S. affiliates of foreign companies: Operations in 1984. *Survey of Current Business* 66 (10): 31–45.

Southard, Frank A. 1931. *American industry in Europe.* Boston and New York: Houghton-Mifflin.

Stern, Robert M., and Keith E. Maskus. 1981. Determinants of the structure of U.S. foreign trade, 1958–76. *Journal of International Economics* 11 (2).

United Nations. 1983. *Transnational corporations in world development, third survey.* U.N. Centre on Transnational Corporations.

———. 1985. *Trends and issues in foreign direct investment and related forms.* U.N. Centre on Transnational Corporations.

U.S. Bureau of the Census. 1975. *Historical statistics of the United States, colonial times to 1970.* Washington, D.C.

U.S. Department of Commerce. 1953. *Foreign investments of the United States, census of 1950.* Office of Business Economics. Washington, D.C.: GPO.

———. 1960. *U.S. business investments in foreign countries.* Office of Business Economics. Washington, D.C.: GPO.

———. 1975. *U.S. direct investment abroad, 1966.* Bureau of Economic Analysis. Washington, D.C.: GPO.

———. 1976. *Foreign direct investment in the United States.* Report to the Congress, vol. 2. Report of the Secretary of Commerce, Benchmark Survey, 1974. Washington, D.C.

———. 1981. *U.S. direct investment abroad, 1977.* Bureau of Economic Analysis. Washington, D.C.: GPO.

———. 1982. *Selected data on U.S. direct investment abroad, 1950–76.* Bureau of Economic Analysis. February. Washington, D.C.

———. 1983. *Foreign direct investment in the United States, 1980.* October. Washington, D.C.

———. 1984a. *Foreign direct investment in the United States: Annual survey results, revised 1981 estimates.* Bureau of Economic Analysis. December. Washington, D.C.

———. 1984b. *Selected data on foreign direct investment in the United States, 1950–79.* Bureau of Economic Analysis. December. Washington, D.C.

———. 1985a. *Business statistics, 1984.* Supplement to the *Survey of Current Business.*

———. 1985b. Foreign direct investment in the United States: Country and industry detail for position and balance of payment flows, 1984. *Survey of Current Business* 65 (8): 47–66.

———. 1985c. *Foreign direct investment in the U.S.: Operations of U.S. affiliates, 1977–80.* Bureau of Economic Analysis. Washington, D.C.

———. 1985d. *Foreign direct investment in the U.S.: Operations of U.S. affiliates of foreign companies, preliminary 1983 estimates.* Bureau of Economic Analysis. December. Washington, D.C.

———. 1985e. *Foreign direct investment in the U.S.: Operations of U.S. affiliates of foreign companies, revised 1982 Estimates.* Bureau of Economic Analysis. December. Washington, D.C.

———. 1985f. *U.S. direct investment abroad: 1982 benchmark survey data.* Bureau of Economic Analysis. December. Washington, D.C.

———. 1985g. *U.S. direct investment abroad: Operations of U.S. parents and their foreign affiliates, preliminary 1983 estimates.* Bureau of Economic Analysis. December. Washington, D.C.

———. 1986a. Foreign direct investment in the U.S.: Detail for position and balance of payments flows, 1985. *Survey of Current Business* 66 (8): 74–88.

_____. 1986b. U.S. direct investment abroad: Detail for position and balance of payments flows, 1985. *Survey of Current Business* 66 (8): 40–73.

_____. 1986c. *U.S. direct investment abroad: Operations of U.S. parents and their foreign affiliates, preliminary 1984 estimates.* Bureau of Economic Analysis. October. Washington, D.C.

_____. 1986d. *U.S. direct investment abroad: Operations of U.S. parents and their foreign affiliates, revised 1983 estimates.* Bureau of Economic Analysis. October. Washington, D.C.

Wilkins, Mira. 1970. *The emergence of multinational enterprise.* Cambridge, Mass.: Harvard University Press.

2. *Mario Schimberni*
Investing to and from the United States

I have been asked to explain why European businessmen are interested in entering, operating, and investing in the U.S. market. The explanation is complex and associated with all the components of a global strategy. Briefly, for a European company a presence in the United States is an important step toward competing successfully with American firms in the world market.

We live in a low- or no-growth economy, where markets are more competitive, partly due to the presence of new competitors, sometimes from new geographical areas or from industries outside the ranks of traditional rivals. Being present in the United States may enable us to acquire useful competitive factors and be successful in this context.

The 1980s have been characterized by increasing interrelations among the various economies. If we measure the degree of openness of an economy by the incidence of imports and exports on GNP, we observe that it rose from 8 percent to 30 percent in the OECD countries between 1970 and 1985.

This indicator is not sufficient, however, to fully describe the internationalization process in economies and business strategies, which today is characterized by qualitative elements difficult to measure in monetary terms. Traditionally, it was the industrial and commercial aspects of economic activity that were affected by the process of foreign openness, through the flows of imports and exports and direct investments. Now the elements upstream from the market competition phase also take part in the internationalization process. For this reason it is more correct to speak of "globalization."

In a global market, business can find market outlets perhaps with differentiated classes of users for its products, but also it can find (1) new financial opportunities in terms of markets, instruments, and currencies of denomination; and (2) new occasions for innovation, through forms of collaboration and interaction with other companies and with advanced research centers. This change in the objectives of internationalization is also reflected in the greater diversification of available instruments. In contrast to the past, companies are going beyond the alternative between exports and direct investments and utilizing a "continual" range of instruments that lend themselves to flexible use and rapid termination.

Joint ventures, nonequity collaboration agreements between companies, minority shareholdings in firms that are strategic from the standpoint of innovation and research, acquisitions, mergers: these are the instruments and opportunities available to global companies today. European businessmen have a growing interest in the American economy precisely because of the complex, diversified nature of the *motivations* and *methods* of the internationalization process.

In addition to its continental "commercial" dimension, the American market is strategic because it offers a series of industrial, technological, scientific, distributional, financial, and managerial resources. The *existence* and *accessibility* of these resources have attracted European economic operators even during strong dollar periods, demonstrating that their interest is strategic and long range, not speculative or linked to short-term profits.

We may attempt to "quantify" interest in the American economy by analyzing collaboration agreements, which have been a highly important flexible instrument at the service of corporate "global requirements."

Out of a broad sample of 1,883 agreements concluded during the 1982–85 period, almost 50 percent included an American partner. In the electronic and pharmaceutical industries, the percentages were even higher: 55 percent and 68 percent, respectively.

I describe, based on the experience of the Montedison Group, the significant reasons for this interest. We begin with the scientific-technological reason.

Of the 1,883 agreements signed during the 1982–85 period, 41 percent were sought for reasons of R&D or technology transfer. The important role of the United States in this field of know-how diffusion is shown by the fact that out of 204 agreements in which there was a unilateral transfer of technology, 132 had the United States as a source, with Europe and Japan as the principal recipients. The American balance is strongly positive, Japan's slightly positive, Europe's negative.

At the basis of these tendencies is the existence of a "system effect" that increases the efficiency with which each company, large or small, American or not, participates in the innovation process. At the foundation there is a high level of scientific research, particularly that conducted in university laboratories, but European universities (and especially Italian) are far away from these standards.

The results of scientific and technological research are "transferred" from the university world to industry: the United States offers great possibilities and capacity for applying scientific progress. This is particularly important in a phase like the present when innovation has a high concentration of scientific knowledge, and the competitive position of a company depends to a great extent on the quantity and quality of scientific knowledge incorporated into its productive processes.

The facility and rapidity with which ideas, information, and research results circulate, and the mobility of scientists from the university to industry, enable most production organizations, even those of small dimensions, to be involved in the innovation process at a high level. In other words, even small and midsize companies enter the innovation system and enrich it. This permits the association between high-quality research and the entrepreneurial flexibility and creativity of small business.

The "system effect" lies precisely in the *pervasiveness* of scientific and technological progress, also boosted by (1) efficient mechanisms for financing innovation (like venture capital); and (2) the existence, in some cases, of physical facilities that institutionalize this intermingling of the relationships and communication channels which multiply innovation (the case of science parks).

A "system effect" of this type is lacking in Italy and, I would say, in all of Europe. As a consequence, this limits innovation in the fabric of small and midsize firms characteristic of our economy. This limited capacity to generate product innovations has negative effects on competitiveness throughout the system. In Montedison we have sought to overcome these structural deficiencies in two ways. On the one hand, we have consolidated our presence and our network of contacts here in the United States. For example, we have concluded two research agreements, the first with the creation of Keramont (joint venture with MER) in the field of advanced ceramics, the second with the acquisition of Plant Cell Research Institute of Palo Alto in the field of biotechnology. On the other hand, we are working on two projects: the first creates together with other European firms a scientific research center on the American model of MIT; the second founds a liasion agency to organize joint ventures between small Italian firms and U.S. high-tech companies.

A second reason for European interest in the United States is of a financial nature. The American capital market has some important characteristics that in Europe are present only to a limited degree (or totally nonexistent).

1. *Magnitude*. The New York Stock Exchange has a ratio of capitalization to GNP of 50 percent, while the Milan Stock Exchange has

a ratio of 18 percent. This great magnitude also concerns the secondary market, where it is possible to make large unit transactions without upsetting the market. An important consequence of these characteristics is stability. The European capital market is still segmented by the various national regulations, and we cannot speak of integrated European financial structures.

2. *The number and type of intermediaries*. The U.S. market is endowed with a diversified system of financial intermediation: the activity of collecting deposits and granting loans is accompanied by forms and channels of intermediation sufficient to finance investments through risk capital and debt capital. In Italy, for example, the government regulations constituting investment banks were approved only a month ago.

3. *Broad presence of institutional investors*. In the United States there is a type of institutional investor, the complementary pension funds, that because of its method of collecting savings is able to invest significant amounts on the stock market. This circumstance, absent in the Italian system, gives the American market great stability and offers business a large source of risk capital to finance its investments. An important consequence is that it reduces the entire structure of long-term interest rates.

The need to overcome the structural limitations of the Italian capital market has induced the Montedison group; on the one hand, to strengthen the presence of foreign investors in its ownership. Almost one-third of shares outstanding are owned by foreign operators, including U.S. investors. On the other, the group has listed the shares of some group companies on foreign stock exchanges. Erbamont, a subholding in the health care field, and Ausimont, a subholding in specialty chemicals, are quoted on the New York Stock Exchange. In addition, the shares of the holding company (Montedison S.p.A.) will be listed on some European exchanges (Frankfurt, London, Paris, Zurich) within a few months. This global financial strategy is also one way for diversifying our sources of financing and making our financial structure consistent with our production and commercial structures.

A third reason for the interest of European businessmen in the U.S. market comes from its *dimension* and *homogeneity*. The European market as a whole is quite large, but it is segmented and not homogeneous due to national barriers of a regulatory and institutional nature.

The chemical market in Europe, for example, in terms of apparent dimensions (the subtotal of internal production plus imports less imports), is 22 percent larger than that of the United States and over twice that of Japan. What is lacking is homogeneity in the market. The physiological need to consider Europe as a single domestic market is contrasted by national economic and monetary policies which are often divergent—a fact that has a negative impact on the exchange agreement linking European currencies—and by the differences and complexities of national legislation. Let us not forget that completion of the EEC internal market is scheduled only for 1992.

Based in part on these considerations of dimension and homogeneity, the Montedison group has taken several initiatives, such as the creation of a 50-50 joint venture with Hercules in the polypropylene field, in which Montedison provided the technology and Hercules its strong penetration capacity in a broad market area. Today Himont, as this joint venture is called, controls 22 percent of the world polypropylene market.

The U.S. market, besides being large and homogeneous, has a high quality of demand. For a company like Montedison, which is increasing the proportion of its high-value-added and high-tech products, it is important to be able to count on an advanced level of consumers. For this reason, our production of Fomblin, a high-performance lubricant employed in electronics and aerospace, is sold predominantly in the United States.

Perhaps having to live with situations of instability, a lack of homogeneity, and greater difficulties than in the U.S. system has developed in European businessmen an aptitude for internationalization, for looking beyond their own borders, for managing situations of uncertainty with flexible instruments and methods. This "adaptable mentality" may be useful in the future low- or no-growth economy. It will be an important asset when the implementation of global strategies leads European companies to rapidly exploit opportunities for investments and growth in economic systems other than America's, such as in Japan, for example. The future of the global European company may include a wider spread of investments among geographic areas.

It is here that we perhaps find an element of relative weakness in the American strategic approach: Compared to the capacity, especially Japanese, to compete on the U.S. market, and the keen activity, especially European, of monitoring U.S. technology, we find that U.S. firms, with the exception of the multinationals, have difficulty going beyond national borders and confronting other realities. With regard to the global economy, the American mentality today appears "domestic oriented."

I would like to recall one fact concerning the chemical industry. Several European firms have increased their sales on the American market at a *faster rate* than their overall sales. On the other hand, most of the American companies have registered a *lower* rate of growth in European sales than in overall sales. Some U.S. chemical companies have greatly reduced their European sales. Keeping in mind that most of the agreements and joint ventures between European and American chemical companies have taken place on U.S. soil, we could deduce that the enterprises of the Old Continent have been more skillful than their American competitors at grasping opportunities, at increasing technological level, at penetrating strategic markets. These considerations seem confirmed by the superior performance of Europe's chemical companies with respect to their American counterparts.

---

3. Robert V. Lindsay
Direct Investment into the United States

My observations on direct investment in the United States are those of an individual banker—drawing on market developments rather than depth of research. Given those limitations, I hope I can contribute a few points.

In contemplating a theme for this chapter, I thought one might paraphrase *res ipsa loquitur,* modifying "actions speak for themselves" to "markets speak for themselves." For the flow of direct investments is based on many specific corporate decisions dictated by specific market opportunities and by a supportive market climate. Broader political and economic forces can encourage or deter, but individual corporate strategies are paramount. I believe that current market opportunities and market conditions are such that direct investments will grow in number, in overall dollar value, and in diversity of origin.

To support that conclusion, I review briefly the earlier pattern of U.S. business expansion abroad; the nature and sources of recent foreign direct investments into this country; the forces at work in the U.S. and international business scenarios that are highly encouraging to foreign direct investors; and the financial market environment which is equally encouraging. I make a few comments specifically related to Japanese direct investment and finally highlight some overall positives and negatives from the U.S. point of view.

When I arrived in London in the early 1970s, U.S. corporate expansion abroad was at a peak. From the first establishment or reestablishment of foreign sales offices and subsidiaries after the Second World War, there developed a broader outreach through acquisitions, green field manufacturing entities, and marketing organizations. This growth was well documented in Robert Lipsey's paper published in this volume.

Our bank and its counterparts devoted significant people and financial resources to the service of our U.S. corporate clients as they pursued a goal of greater market share in a rebuilding Europe. We worked with them on local financing and on such problems as exchange and other controls in the various European centers. Our clients for the most part identified their offshore expansion as a discrete and separate part of their organizations, and we dealt with a combination of expatriate corporate officers and international specialists in the corporate treasury staffs.

Fifteen years late, the U.S. direct investment totals continue to grow, but from high levels. Mistakes made in the push for overseas market share have in many cases been rectified and overseas operations rationalized. In effect the U.S. overseas investment process has matured.

At the same time, the U.S. multinational has integrated its overseas investments into the structure and strategy of the corporate whole. Outsourcing, interborder component sales, cross-border financings— all are part of an overall strategic thrust. As Lipsey points out, a growing portion of offshore market share for these companies is supplied by their offshore subsidiaries. Their bankers, to compete successfully, must serve the corporate clients on an integrated basis in all markets rather than dealing separately with the parts. And the integrated corporation works to serve its shareholders rather than any specific national interest.

To some extent there may be a parallel though more recent pattern involved in the development of foreign direct investment into the United States. From the 1960s on, a growing number of foreign companies with sufficient capital and management talent to expand beyond their national or regional areas directed their attention to building market share in the United States. This was done primarily by acquisition or joint venture rather than through start-ups. As in the case of their U.S. counterparts, mistakes were made, particularly but not exclusively in the earlier years. *Forbes* noted in an issue last July that of the 101 foreign-owned U.S. companies for which a separate profit and loss statement can be broken out, 23 operations lost $1.3 billion in the previous fiscal year. However, there have been enough successes of sufficient size so that the Morgan Bank, for example, now has a fully staffed department of banking officers specifically assigned to servicing the U.S. subsidiaries of the bank's offshore corporate clients. That department did not exist a decade ago.

What distinguishes the foreign corporate invasion from the U.S. expansion abroad is that the process has by no means peaked; if anything it is gathering momentum. One also has the impression that most foreign corporate entities have from the outset devoted their most senior time and attention to their U.S. strategic moves, reflecting perhaps the enormous potential of the U.S. market and their own inherently multinational backgrounds. Here again, understandably, corporate self-interest tends to transcend specific national interests.

Who has been coming in from abroad, what have they been buying, and at what cost? The figures show that total foreign direct investments increased 11 percent in 1985, the last year for which there are complete figures, to a total of $183 billion. Of the $17.9 billion net additional investment, nearly $12 billion represented equity capital inflows. The figures from the first nine months of 1986 indicate a dropoff of nearly 50 percent in net additional investment, but these figures were importantly affected by several repayments of capital and debts by U.S. affiliates to their European parents.

As to who is doing the buying, Jeffrey Frankel points out in his paper that 66 percent of foreign direct investments at the end of 1985 were owned by Europeans. The British and Dutch were by far the largest holders within the European totals. Other countries are also important—the United Kingdom, Switzerland, Germany, and Canada together accounted for 74 percent of the increase in investment in 1985—but the United Kingdom itself doubled its net additional investments from $4.3 billion in 1984 to $8.7 billion in 1985. The Japanese presence has been much smaller but may grow apace in future years. Total Japanese investment in the United States nearly tripled from 1980 to 1985; *Business Week* reports that MITI expects a 14 percent growth annually until the year 2000. As I mention later, the direct investment percentage of the Japanese total should itself increase.

What is being bought? The list runs the gamut from manufacturing to natural resources to trade and service industries of all kinds. Food, chemicals, and machinery were important in 1985, and several major investments in petroleum and oil services were made. Retail trade, banking, other finance and insurance have all been well represented in recent years. Real estate is significant in its own right, with representation in several categories as direct investments, portfolio investments, and joint venture start-ups. Clearly whatever is not prohibited by statute is fair game, and the fact that an industry is at least temporarily depressed is no bar to the acquisition or joint venture process.

What are the forces at work that give impetus to the flow of direct investment into the United States? Some result from the changing world economic environment and some relate to U.S. domestic market developments within the global environment.

In the first category we begin with currency relationships. One could argue that a falling dollar is discouraging in that existing dollar investments fall in value and the foreign currency value of earnings from existing or new investments will be lower. However, those negatives are more than offset by the lower capital cost of new investments for offshore buyers. America can be bought on the cheap, as the press points out, all the more so when compared to the cost of alternative investments in other developed countries with relatively flat growth rates. Another point worth making, even though it cannot be supported by hard evidence, is that offshore investors, as we will see, have increasing means of partial exchange rate protection at their disposal; however, they are not as concerned with the risks of currency gains and losses as their American counterparts. Europeans in particular tend to take the longer view, having lived with currency fluctuations over centuries; the effects of currency gains and losses in the income statement are reported as a fact of doing business rather than a management sin. If the underlying market strategy is seen to make sense, a currency risk will not outweigh it, unless political risk is also a factor.

Clearly economic growth in the countries of ultimate ownership have helped build the capital and earning power of acquiring companies. The process of both growth and rationalization in postwar Europe has resulted in the emergence of strong multinational entities and investment pools fully capable of financing and managing sizable U.S. acquisitions. Some companies in smaller domestic markets like Scandinavia *must* go offshore to grow, but all are impressed with the necessity of a U.S. base for diversification, on both economic and political grounds.

Differences in labor practices, particularly between the United States and Europe, are well known and do not need amplification here. However, despite a trend toward a slightly less restrictive labor environment in Europe, most notably in England, the gap is seen to be widening in favor of the United States as a more flexible place to do business.

Another characteristic in the world environment which is unfortunate but must be recognized is the lack of alternatives in the world investment climate. Businesses measure success by growth; successful businesses are not static by their nature. In a different world, Eastern Europe, Africa, Latin America, and the Asian land mass would provide outlets for that growth; as it is, the realistic options have *narrowed* in recent years, making a U.S. investment even more of an imperative.

The U.S. environment is itself supportive of direct investment in several ways. Our wrenching readjustments in the face of world competition have resulted in low valuation of some corporate assets, making those assets more likely targets for offshore acquisition. Corporate restructuring has thrown up divisions or subsidiaries that are unprofitable or outside the strategic thrust of the original owner, but that represent a market fit or point of entry for the foreign buyer. Obviously interstate competition for new investment has gone well beyond southern lures to northern manufacturers; the trade mission from Nashville is as likely to be in Tokyo as in Detroit. Threats of protectionism, either through tariffs or quotas, are a more recent spur to a manufacturing presence in the U.S. domestic market, outweighing the negatives of higher labor costs. In sum the economic trends in the world and in the United States not only support further direct investment; they create an environment in which *not* to have a presence in the United States can be seen to represent an undue risk.

What about financial market developments that are supportive of investment from the outside? They are may, and in my view they are crucial to the decision process, since they provide at least initial comfort to the decision makers. They make managements and their boards of directors *feel* better.

Let's look at the decision process and how it relates to the market. First, it is fair to say that most decisions are taken against a five-year time frame. Ten-year forecasts can be drawn as part of strategic planning, but only the super confident or super gutsy will pay much attention beyond the fifth year. In the process, strategic options are examined and the broader environmental factors previously mentioned are taken into consideration. If as I concluded earlier those point to a presence in the United States, one or more of several steps will be taken by a potential acquirer. Its existing line organization will be advised to locate appropriate U.S. acquisitions through its own sources of information. Investment and commercial bankers will be apprised of acquisition interests. Consultants may be called upon to abet or confuse the process. A chain of events will be set in motion designed to seek out an opportunity or react quickly when an opportunity arises. The intermediaries not only will arrive in force with screens at the ready; they will also include representatives of home-grown financial institutions as well as those of the United States, the United Kingdom, and other key money centers. Everybody is either in or getting in the M&A game these days, and advice and ideas, some good, some bad, will flow in. Morgan Guaranty as a case in point not only is represented in all the major money centers; it also has 120 research professionals around the world maintaining data bases and analytical papers on every important industry, jurisdiction by jurisdiction. Clearly, such talents are in place to develop business with and stimulate the process of investment by potential acquirers.

Along the line, management will concern itself with financial support of the strategic decision. Here is where those innovations discussed in Richard Levich's paper came into play, but frst let me underscore two points: (1) the world is awash in money; and (2), it is a near certainty that our acquirer's banks and investment banks have branches or home bases in the United States competing strenuously to finance this piece of business. Management will be comforted by multilingual liquidity and multilingual competition. It will also be comforted, as well perhaps as irritated, by transnational documentation—the lawyers have not been slow to follow their clients from and into the United States, and even law firms from as far off as Australia now have American resident offices and partners.

As to the innovations so ably documented by Levich, let me simply highlight two and mention a third that deserves attention. I pointed out that management primarily plans within a five-year horizon. What a comfort therefore that long-dated forward exchange contracts have become a commonplace, going in some cases well beyond five years. As I said earlier, foreign exchange risks may not drive the decision, but partial protection over the medium term puts smiles in the board room. If one adds interest rate swaps, commercial paper bridges, and other means of minimizing the cost of financing the acquisition, the board's comfort will be limited only by its capacity to understand what its financial team is talking about! Finally, the international equity markets are developing an underpinning to the acquisition process. In 1980 Morgan had 270 American depositary receipt (ADR) accounts representing 244 million shares. As of this January we had 450 accounts representing 1.4 billion shares. Out of such statistics flow potential liquidity for the American seller and greatly enhanced flexibility for the buyer. Reuters, for example, set up their ADR facility in 1984 and used its mechanism in 1985 to acquire Rich Inc. by the issuance of new depositary shares. One would assume that British Telecom or British Gas will expand via the same process, having incorporated ADRs in their initial privatization.

These are just a few examples to make the point: the markets are developing techniques that support the globalization process to the same extent that the market makers themselves have become globalized, and as long as the United States is a strategic business target, the support systems will push the decision makers in that direction.

As noted earlier, Japanese investments in the United States are expected to grow at a remarkable rate. Within that growth, however, direct investment will increase proportionately, a point most recently made by Michiya Matsukawa of Nikko Securities in the latest paper published by the Group of Thirty, and a point reflecting also the experience of Morgan's M&A group in Tokyo. A deterrent has been Japanese skepticism about acquisitions—joint ventures and green field start-ups have been preferred. However, protectionist concerns and the high cost of doing business in Japan are forcing a reexamination of policy on acquisitions and a drive toward better execution, in which they have been weak heretofore. Among other things, for example, acquisition strategy requires fast decisions as all those last-minute hurdles appear, a real problem for the Japanese, but one they are addressing.

The problem for U.S. manufacturing employment going forward may be that the Japanese are tending to outsource their manufacturing in lower- cost locations elsewhere in Asia and looking to the United States for technology and services, notably finance. And with a year-end 1986 market capitalization of $34 billion for Nomura Securities alone, as against $8 billion for J. P. Morgan, $3.6 billion for Merrill Lynch, and $2.7 billion for Chase Manhattan, the prospect of Japanese direct investment concentrated in finance is a bit scary, to say the least! There is also the potential problem of imbalances in U.S. real estate ownership and valuations, as Japanese annual purchases of our real estate have moved to a $6 billion level in 1986.

Over and above specific questions relating to the Japanese, there is the broader subject of the impact for better or worse of a growing inflow of direct investment in this country. Let me mention a few of the positives and negatives, both for U.S. businesses and for the nation as a whole.

For the American businessman, an important factor in acquisition by a foreign buyer may be the perception of greater continuing job stability for the selling management and staff, since there is less likelihood of duplication of experience and local knowledge. The ability to move ahead without fear of being swallowed by domestic competitors is a corollary plus, an example being the acquisition by Allied Irish Banks of a major interest in the First National Bank of Maryland, leaving the latter intact and with a substantial infusion of capital. There are similarities in the Sumitomo investment in Goldman Sachs. Also, a foreign acquirer can offer its U.S. target a built-in expansion into foreign markets—a quick widening of business horizons. Negatives include the obvious problem of differing business cultures and the flip side of the management picture, that is, the good younger American executive may see promotion to the upper ranks of the parent as unlikely, if not impossible. This is a real problem for the Japanese, but also for more compatible cultures such as Scandinavia, where high personal taxation is a major deterrent to influx of otherwise mobile American managers. There is no one answer to these questions. As a general rule, if the underlying transaction made sense, the positives will outweigh the negatives in the glow of subsequent success.

The nation as a whole should benefit from infusions of capital and business brainpower, capital that by its nature will be more stable than the massive offshore holdings of liquid assets (although parenthetically, when concerns are expressed about foreign investors pulling out of their U.S. holdings, I am more inclined to think, as Martin Feldstein does, of satiation rather than outright withdrawal). A negative, apart from the political concerns of loss of control of our economic destiny—somewhat farfetched at this point—is pointed out in Jeffrey Frankel's paper: earnings on direct investment tend to be greater than interest earned on bonds, and to that extent the underlying current account problem is worsened. Also, as pointed out earlier, multinational self-interests will prevail and may run a political collision course with perceived interests of U.S. voting constituencies.

I conclude by repeating the original theme—the markets speak for themselves, and at the moment they tell us that most signals are go for direct investment, including accumulations of offshore capital, attraction to the United States as a market, and a highly accommodative acquisition environment for corporate decision takers. I see little on the horizon likely to change that market consensus.

Summary of Discussion

Several participants commented on the consequences of direct investment for trade. Thomas Enders recalled that when U.S. multinationals went abroad, exports, through sales to subsidiaries, for example, followed. Later, there may have been a reverse flow, he suggested. Robert Lindsay argued that direct investment is not a substitute for firm or country exports but is rather an effort to hold onto or expand foreign markets. The Swedish investments here, for example, expanded Swedish exports to the United States.

On a different topic, Lionel Olmer expressed some doubt that the EEC internal market would be complete by 1992, and Mario Schimberni conceded that there was some doubt that this target was achievable; he noted that he was doing everything he could to help, but suggested that unification will require great political leadership.

There was some discussion of the reasonableness of the scenario in which foreign investors in the United States lose confidence in their U.S. securities and shift their portfolios quickly overseas, precipitating a crisis. Schimberni accepted the possibility that foreign investors might desire eventually to stop the huge inflow of foreign flows, but he wondered if there were markets anywhere else with the depth and breadth of U.S. markets. Olmer agreed that a sudden collapse was unlikely because the only possibility is the gradual acceptance of the mark and the yen as reerve currencies. Schimberni contended that the macroeconomic climate of low inflation and uncertain growth in Germany and Italy is not conducive to their absorption of capital that had rejected the United States.

Rachel McCulloch opened a discussion on strategies for direct investment by noting that U.S. companies abroad tend to like wholly owned subsidiaries, while foreigners in the United States avail themselves of a range of options. She wondered whether this could be explained by differences between the types of firms. Lindsay considered that the desire of U.S. firms to hold onto their technological advantage and of foreign firms to acquire technology could explain the different behaviors.

Schimberni predicted two basic changes in direct investment. First, the slow rate of overall growth implies that businesses should avoid overcapacity and the resulting competition. Second, the acceleration of the timing of technical change means that a new discovery does not last long and the product cycle is short. The reduction in the number of actors and the bigger critical mass required for the larger amounts of research and development necessary imply that Americans will have to consider partnerships and joint ventures too. In fact some American firms, such as Dupont, already are, which was unheard of five years ago.

Peter Peterson proposed that the trend was toward the global rationalization of the business, not as a U.S. firm with several subsidiaries, for example, but as one global profit center. This makes partial ownership awkward. Robert Ingersoll agreed that partnership and globalization of production and marketing are not compatible. Charles Parry said that Alcoa has not seen this coordination problem, although he remarked that IBM has had difficulties with cross-border transport of components. He observed a problem for the national interest in the possibly conflicting desires to preserve national technological leads and to optimize the location of manufacturing.

The issue goes beyond ownership integration to management itegration, pointed out Bruce Atwater. In the 1950s and 1960s the European subsidiaries of U.S. companies primarily were run by American managers. Now most European subsidiaries are run by national managers, and the issue has moved to internationalizing parent-company management. George Voita suggested that the early stages of direct investment involve the acquisition of technology or markets and hence imply subsidiary arrangements, while the more mature stage, where foreign direct investment in the United States may be in ten or fifteen years, involves a more global structure and management.

Schimberni argued that the joint venture may have some advantages from a cultural point of view, The difference in organizations might reflect a difference in management styles, not a more primitive stage of investment. The flexibility of European firms comes from the necessity to be international in orientation. The management must fit the community. IBM, for example, suffers in Japan because it is wholly owned and has partly American managers. To successfully penetrate Japanese markets will require joint ventures and a long-term point of view. His firm's joint venture with Hercules, a fifty-fifty proposition, would not have been more successful as a wholly owned subsidiary.

9 International Capital Flows and Domestic Economic Policies

1. Jeffrey A. Frankel
2. Saburo Okita
3. Peter G. Peterson
4. James R. Schlesinger

1. Jeffrey A. Frankel

9.1 Introduction

When consumer electronics roll off the assembly line in Singapore, when there is a bumper wheat crop in China, or when shoe production expands in Italy, the relevance to U.S. producers and consumers is tangible. The large U.S. trade deficit has become a source of concern familiar to Americans. When Japan liberalizes portfolio guidelines for life insurance companies, when there is a collapse of investment opportunities in Latin America, or when fixed brokerage commissions are abolished in the City of London, the relevance for Americans is much less tangible. But the international flow of capital is no less important than the flow of goods. Indeed, there is an important sense in which capital flows have been the cause of the U.S. trade deficit in the 1980s, with U.S. government macroeconomic policies the driving force behind it all.

International capital movements affect the U.S. economy in a number of ways. Banks, securities companies, and other providers of financial services constitute the sector of the American economy that is most directly affected. They now compete with financial institutions in Tokyo, London, and Frankfurt, and around the world. Exports of financial and other services are a growing credit item in the U.S. balance of payments, and the current U.S. administration has placed a high priority on more favorable treatment of U.S. financial institutions in bilateral trade negotiations, and on liberalization of trade in services generally in the Uruguay round of negotiations under GATT (General Agreement on Tariffs and Trade).

The impact of international capital flows reaches far beyond a single sector of the American economy, however. Every U.S. firm feels the effect, which comes through two main channels. First is the availability of capital, as reflected in interest rates. Large corporations increasingly often borrow from foreign residents, and portfolio managers increasingly invest abroad. But even the many firms that borrow only at home, or the many individuals who hold only domestic assets, are affected, because U.S. interest rates are increasingly determined on world capital markets jointly with other countries' interest rates. The second channel through which U.S. producers are affected is the exchange rate, which by the 1980s has become overwhelmingly determined by flows of capital rather than flows of goods. Again, even those firms that do not export are affected, to the extent that they compete with imports or buy imported inputs.

This paper is organized in five sections. Section 9.2 reviews briefly the postwar history of the U.S. capital account up to the 1970s, a period throughout which Americans were steadily building up a positive net foreign investment position. Section 9.3 considers those factors, other than expected rates of return, that discourage or encourage international capital flow: transactions costs, government controls, taxes, default and other political risk, and exchange risk. The record is generally one of gradually diminishing barriers. Section 9.4 describes the historic swing of the U.S. capital account in the 1980s toward massive borrowing from abroad. Section 9.5 examines international differences in rates of return on various assets and shows how the increase in interest rates in the United States in the early 1980s attracted the large net capital inflows. Section 9.6 concludes the paper with an analysis of U.S. government policies—monetary, tax, and spending—in determining U.S. saving, investment, and the net capital inflow. The lesson that emerges is that the primary source of the large U.S. borrowing from abroad, and therefore of its counterpart the large U.S. trade deficit, is the federal budget deficit.

9.2   Net U.S. Capital Outflows in the Period 1946–80

Table 9.1 presents the figures for the U.S. balance of payments from 1946 to 1985. The first half of the table breaks down the current account into its components: merchandise trade, investment income, travel and transportation, other services, and so forth. The second half of the table shows the components of the reverse side of the balance of payments coin, the capital account. Until the last few years of this period, private capital was on net steadily flowing out of the country. But the story nevertheless features a number of twists and turns over the years.

9.2.1   The Period of "Dollar Shortage"

In the immediate aftermath of World War II, the United States ran large trade surpluses, as measured either by the merchandise balance (goods alone) or the balance on goods and services. These surpluses were the counterpart to large trade deficits in Europe and elsewhere in the world. The war-ravaged countries had lost much of their industrial and agricultural capacity, and needed to import basic necessities of consumption, as well as capital goods to rebuild their economies. They had a shortage of dollars with which to buy such goods. The flow of goods from the United States to Europe was financed partly by foreign aid and other transfers, partly by lending, and partly by an increase in U.S. official holdings of international reserves. This last means that the United States was running a surplus in its overall balance of payments: the surplus in the current account—defined as goods, services, and transfers—was greater than the net private capital outflows.

In the 1950s, as the European and other economies recovered, their trade balances improved and, as a natural consequence, the U.S. trade surplus returned to more normal levels. By the end of the decade, the surplus in goods and services had fallen below the deficit in transfers and private capital flows, so the United States was running substantial overall balance of payments deficits.

9.2.2   The Balance of Payments Problem in the 1960s

One could view the emerging U.S. deficit of this period, and the rest of the world's surplus, as the natural outcome of steady worldwide growth under the "dollar standard." Although the 1944 conference at Bretton Woods, New Hampshire, that established the postwar international monetary system did not give the U.S. dollar this role officially, the dollar soon became the de facto reserve currency of the system, because it was convertible into gold and because of the economic wealth and political prestige of the United States. As world trade grew, countries needed to hold growing levels of reserves, and running balance of payments surpluses was the only way other countries had of acquiring dollar reserves. This is the sense in which the U.S. balance of payments deficits could be viewed as a natural consequence of worldwide economic growth under the monetary system. Nevertheless, the increasing ratio of dollars held abroad to gold held by the U.S. government began to cause concern. It seemed that the system could only become more and more vulnerable over time to a crisis in which the holders of dollars around the world would try to cash in their claims for gold and the United States would be unable to pay.

In the early 1960s, the balance of payments deficit was entirely a deficit of the capital account. The merchandise trade balance, goods and services balances, and current account were all in substantial sur-

Table 9.1   International Statistics of U.S. International Transactions, 1946–85 (millions of dollars)

Year or Quarter	Merchandise[a,b]			Investment Income[c]			Net Military Transactions	Net Travel and Transportation	Other Services Net[c]	Balance on Goods and Services[a,d]	Remittances, Pensions, and Other Unilateral Transfers[a]	Current Account[a,d]
	Exports	Imports	Net	Receipts	Payments	Net						
1946	11,764	−5,067	6,697	772	−212	20,565	−493	733	310	7,807	−2,922	4,885
1947	16,097	−5,973	10,124	1,102	−245	857	−455	946	145	11,617	−2,625	8,992
1948	13,265	−7,557	5,708	1,921	−437	1,484	−799	374	175	6,942	−4,525	2,417
1949	12,213	−6,874	5,339	1,831	−476	1,355	−621	230	208	6,511	−5,638	873
1950	10,203	−9,081	1,122	2,068	−559	1,509	−576	−120	242	2,177	−4,017	−1,840
1951	14,243	−11,176	3,067	2,633	−583	2,050	−1,270	298	254	4,399	−3,515	884
1952	13,449	−10,838	2,611	2,751	−555	2,196	−2,054	83	309	3,145	−2,531	614
1953	12,412	−10,975	1,437	2,736	−624	2,112	−2,423	−238	307	1,195	−2,481	−1,286
1954	12,929	−10,353	2,576	2,929	−582	2,347	−2,460	−269	305	2,499	−2,280	219
1955	14,424	−11,527	2,897	3,406	−676	2,730	−2,701	−297	299	2,928	−2,498	430
1956	17,556	−12,803	4,753	3,837	−735	3,102	−2,788	−361	447	5,153	−2,423	2,730
1957	19,562	−13,291	6,271	4,180	−796	3,384	−2,841	−189	482	7,107	−2,345	4,762
1958	16,414	−12,952	3,462	3,790	−825	2,965	−3,135	−633	486	3,145	−2,361	784
1959	16,548	−15,310	1,148	4,132	−1,061	3,071	−2,805	−821	573	1,166	−2,448	−1,282
1960	19,650	−14,758	4,892	4,616	−1,237	3,379	−2,752	−964	579	5,132	−2,308	2,824
1961	20,108	−14,537	5,571	4,999	−1,245	3,754	−2,596	−978	594	6,346	−2,524	3,822

Year												
1962	20,781	−16,620	4,521	5,618	−1,324	4,294	−2,449	−1,152	809	6,025	−2,638	3,387
1963	22,272	−17,048	5,224	6,157	−1,561	4,596	−2,304	−1,309	960	7,167	−2,754	4,414
1964	25,501	−18,700	6,801	6,824	−1,784	5,040	−2,133	−1,146	1,041	9,604	−2,781	6,823
1965	26,461	−21,510	4,951	7,437	−2,088	5,349	−2,122	−1,280	1,387	8,285	−2,854	5,432
1966	29,310	−25,493	3,817	7,528	−2,481	5,047	−2,935	−1,331	1,365	5,963	−2,932	3,031
1967	30,666	−26,866	3,800	8,020	−2,747	5,273	−3,226	−1,750	1,612	5,708	−3,125	2,583
1968	33,626	−32,991	635	9,368	−3,378	5,990	−3,143	−1,548	1,630	3,563	−2,952	611
1969	36,414	−35,807	607	10,912	−4,869	6,043	−3,328	−1,763	1,833	3,393	−2,994	399
1970	42,469	−39,866	2,603	11,747	−5,516	6,231	−3,354	−2,038	2,180	5,625	−3,294	2,331
1971	43,319	−45,579	−2,260	12,707	−5,436	7,271	−2,893	−2,345	2,495	2,269	−3,701	−1,433
1972	49,381	−55,797	−6,416	14,764	−6,572	8,192	−3,420	−3,063	2,766	−1,941	−3,854	−5,795
1973	71,410	−70,499	911	21,808	−9,655	12,153	−2,070	−3,158	3,184	11,021	−3,881	7,140
1974	98,306	−103,811	−5,505	27,587	−12,084	15,503	−1,653	−3,184	3,986	9,147	−7,186^c	1,962
1975	107,088	−99,185	8,903	25,351	−12,564	12,787	−746	−2,182	4,598	22,729	−4,613	18,116
1976	114,745	−124,228	−9,453	29,286	−13,311	15,975	559	−2,558	4,711	9,205	−4,998	4,207
1977	120,816	−151,907	−31,091	32,179	−14,217	17,962	1,528	−3,565	5,272	−9,894	−4,167	−14,511
1978	142,054	−176,001	−33,947	42,245	−21,680	20,565	621	−3,573	6,013	−10,321	−5,106	−15,427
1979	184,473	−212,009	−27,536	64,132	−32,960	31,172	−1,778	−2,995	6,214	5,138	−6,128	−991
1980	224,269	−249,749	−25,480	72,506	−42,120	30,386	−2,237	−997	7,793	9,466	−7,593	1,873
1981	237,085	−265,063	−27,978	86,411	−52,329	34,082	−1,183	144	8,699	13,764	−7,425	6,339
1982	211,198	−247,642	−36,444	85,549	−54,883	28,666	−274	−992	8,829	−214	−8,917	−9,131
1983	201,820	−268,900	−67,080	77,251	−52,410	24,841	−369	−4,227	9,711	−37,123	−9,481	−46,604
1984	219,900	−322,422	−112,522	86,221	−67,469	18,752	−1,827	−8,593	9,881	−94,308	−12,157	−106,466
1985	214,424	−338,863	−124,439	89,991	−64,803	25,188	−2,917	−11,128	10,603	−102,694	−14,983	−117,677

Table 9.1 (continued)

| Year or Quarter | U.S. Assets Abroad, Net (increase/capital outflow [−]) | | | | Foreign Assets in the U.S., Net (increase/capital outflow [−]) | | | Allocations of Special Drawing Rights (SDRs) | Statistical Discrepancy | |
	Total	U.S. Official Reserve Assets[f]	Other U.S. Government Assets	U.S. Private Assets	Total	Foreign Official Assets	Other Foreign Assets		Total (Sum of the Items with Sign Reversed)	Overall
1946	—	−623	—	—	—	—	—	—	—	—
1947	—	−3,315	—	—	—	—	—	—	—	—
1948	—	−1,736	—	—	—	—	—	—	—	—
1949	—	−266	—	—	—	—	—	—	—	—
1950	—	1,758	—	—	—	—	—	—	—	—
1951	—	−33	—	—	—	—	—	—	—	—
1952	—	−415	—	—	—	—	—	—	—	—
1953	—	1,256	—	—	—	—	—	—	—	—
1954	—	480	—	—	—	—	—	—	—	—
1955	—	182	—	—	—	—	—	—	—	—
1956	—	−869	—	—	—	—	—	—	—	—
1957	—	−1,165	—	—	—	—	—	—	—	—
1958	—	2,292	—	—	—	—	—	—	—	—
1959	—	1,035	—	—	—	—	—	—	—	—
1960	−4,099	2,145	−1,100	−5,144	2,294	1,473	821	—	−1,019	−3,618
1961	−5,538	607	−910	−5,235	2,705	765	1,939	—	−989	−1,372
1962	−4,174	1,535	−1,085	−4,623	1,911	1,270	641	—	−1,124	−2,805
1963	−7,270	378	−1,662	−5,986	3,217	1,986	1,231	—	−360	−2,354
1964	−9,560	171	−1,680	−8,050	3,643	1,660	1,983	—	−907	−1,831
1965	−5,716	1,225	−1,605	−5,336	742	134	607	—	−458	−1,359

Year									
1966	−7,321	570	−1,543	−6,347	3,661	−672	4,333	—	629	102
1967	−9,757	53	−2,423	−7,386	7,379	3,451	3,928	—	−205	−3,604
1968	−10,977	−870	−2,274	−7,833	9,928	−774	10,703	—	438	1,644
1968	−11,585	−1,179	−2,200	−8,206	12,702	−1,301	14,002	—	−1,516	2,470
1970	−9,337	2,481	−1,589	−10,229	6,359	6,908	−550	867	−219	−10,258
1971	−12,475	2,349	−1,884	−12,940	22,970	26,879	−3,909	717	−9,779	−29,945
1972	−14,497	−4	−1,568	−12,925	21,461	10,475	10,986	710	−1,879	−11,181
1973	−22,874	158	−2,644	−20,388	18,388	6,026	12,362	—	−2,654	−6,184
1974	−34,745	−1,467	366e	−33,643	34,241	10,546	23,696	—	−1,458	−9,077
1975	−39,703	−849	−3,474	−35,380	15,670	7,027	8,643	—	5,917	−6,173
1976	−51,269	−2,558	−4,214	−44,498	36,518	17,693	18,826	—	10,544	−15,135
1977	−34,785	−375	−3,693	−30,717	51,319	36,816	14,503	—	−2,023	−36,441
1978	−61,130	732	−4,660	−57,202	64,036	33,678	30,358	—	12,521	−34,410
1979	−64,331	−1,133	−3,746	−59,453	38,752	−13,665	52,416	1,139	25,431	13,654
1980	−86,118	−8,155	−5,162	−72,802	58,112	15,497	42,615	1,152	24,982	8,494
1981	−111,031	−5,175	−5,097	−100,758	83,322	4,960	78,362	1,093	20,276	878
1982	−121,273	−4,965	−6,131	−110,177	94,078	3,593	90,486	—	36,325	1,372
1983	−50,022	−1,196	−5,005	−43,821	85,496	5,968	79,527	—	11,130	−4,772
1984	−23,639	−3,131	−5,523	−14,986	102,767	3,037	99,730	—	27,338	54
1985	−32,436	−3,858	−2,824	−25,754	127,106	−1,324	128,430	—	22,006	5,182

Source: Department of Commerce, Bureau of Economic Analysis.

Notes: The data are seasonally adjusted, except as noted; (+) = credits; (−) = debits.

aExcludes military.

bAdjusted from census data for differences in valuation, coverage, and timing.

cFees and royalties from U.S. direct investments abroad or from foreign direct investments in the United States are excluded from investment income and included in other services net.

dIn concept, balance on goods and services is equal to net exports and imports in the national income and product accounts (and the sum of balance on current account and allocations of special drawing rights is equal to net foreign investment in the accounts), although the series differ because of different handling of certain items (gold, capital gains and losses, etc.), revisions, etc.

eIncludes extraordinary U.S. government transactions with India.

fConsists of gold, special drawing rights, convertible currencies, and U.S. reserve position in the International Monetary Fund (IMF).

plus. But, beginning under the Kennedy administration, capital outflows became the subject of increasing concern. Under Operation Twist, monetary policy sought to raise short-term interest rates to attract short-term capital from abroad, at the same time as long-term interest rates were kept low with the aim of stimulating investment. A series of increasingly strong direct controls on the outflow of capital were also put into place, though they were not very effective: the rise of the Euromarket, outside the grasp of U.S. regulators, dates from this period.

Much of the capital outflow took the form of U.S. direct investment in Europe and elsewhere. Outward direct investment increased from $2.9 billion in 1960 to $10.2 billion in 1970, explaining most of the increase in measured private capital outflow.[1] One view was that the United States was playing a useful role as the world's banker: borrowing short term and lending long term. A bank does it by taking deposits and lending to businesses and homeowners; the world's banker would do it by creating liquid dollar reserves for others to hold and investing in plant and equipment abroad. But some, the French in particular, resented the idea that Americans were buying out their factories and land, offering in return only paper that was less and less adequately backed by gold.

9.2.3   The Breakup of the Bretton Woods System

In the late 1960s, the U.S. balance of payments problem became more of a trade balance problem. The reason was expansionary macroeconomic policies. After 1965, military spending increased rapidly because of the escalation of the Vietnam War. At the same time, domestic spending was increasing under Lyndon Johnson's Great Society program. Furthermore, monetary policy accommodated the expansion, with the exception of a couple of brief attempts at braking. Rapid growth in income resulted directly in rapid growth in imports. The economy also became overheated, giving rise to inflation. U.S. inflation, in a system under which the dollar was supposedly not allowed to devalue, resulted in a gradual loss of competitiveness by American firms on world markets. In 1971, the U.S. trade balance went into deficit for the first time in the postwar period. In response to the trade deficit and to a corresponding loss in reserves, Richard Nixon unilaterally devalued the dollar in terms of both gold and foreign currencies, placed a tariff surcharge on imports, and ended the U.S. government's commitment to sell gold for dollars to foreign central banks. This marked the end of the Bretton Woods system. Most foreign central banks continued to cooperate in the effort to prop up the system of fixed exchange rates, buying up unwanted dollars. But by now, private speculators knew that selling dollars was a good bet. As a result, capital outflows were very high throughout the early 1970s. In the accounts in table

9.1, they show up as an increase in the rate at which U.S. residents acquired claims abroad (and in the statistical discrepancy). In the first few months of 1973, several of the major central banks had to absorb unprecedented quantities of dollars, with no end in sight. In March 1973, they ceased their commitments to buy and sell dollars at fixed exchange rates. In other words, the world moved from the fixed exchange rate system to the current system of floating exchange rates.

With the exchange rate now free to move, the desire of investors to allocate a higher proportion of their portfolios to foreign assets suddenly took the form of an increase in the price of foreign assets in terms of dollars, that is, a depreciation of the dollar. The depreciation meant that American manufacturers and farmers could once again compete in world markets on favorable terms. The current account returned to surplus in the years 1973–76.

9.2.4   Capital Outflow in the Mid-1970s

The rate of net private capital outflow reached a stable plateau in the mid-1970s. This outflow was not primarily a sign of lack of confidence in the U.S. economy, as it had been in 1970–73. Indeed, there were times, for example, in the immediate aftermath of the late-1973 oil crisis, when investors increased their demand for dollar assets.[2] Rather, the United States was behaving as a mature industrialized country generally is expected to behave: running a current account surplus ($18.1 billion in 1975) and investing the proceeds in other countries where they can earn a higher rate of return.

The financial situation began to deteriorate, however, in the latter half of the decade. Following the oil crisis and the 1975 world recession, there was concern, particularly in the United States and in developing countries, that worldwide saving was too high and expenditure too low to sustain growth. There had been a massive transfer of wealth to the members of OPEC, many of whom had a high tendency to save the wealth rather than spend it. The United States undertook steady fiscal and monetary expansion, with the Europeans following only reluctantly and with a delay. The result was rapid growth in U.S. imports and a fall in the trade balance; in 1977 and 1978, the current account registered substantial $15 billion deficits. The Carter administration could have argued that the trade deficits were not cause for concern, but to the contrary, were precisely what was needed: The expansion in demand was sustaining recovery in the United States, and at the same time was allowing those developing countries that were faced with sharply increased oil import bills to earn the foreign exchange to pay them by exporting to the United States. But the record deficits did generate concern. In 1977–78, as it was to again in 1985–87, the U.S. Treasury pressured foreign governments to expand their own economies in order to increase purchases from the United States. In both episodes, reluctant foreign governments had to face the alternative that the same goal, reducing the U.S. trade deficit, would instead be accomplished by an accelerated depreciation of the dollar.

I will discuss in later sections the declines in real interest rates and in the value of the dollar during this period. Here we note that the swing from surplus to deficit on the current account in 1977–78 was not associated with an offsetting swing from deficit to surplus on the private capital account. Private capital on net continued to flow out at a steady rate of about $20 billion a year.[3] The U.S. current account deficit was financed by increased holdings of U.S. assets on the part of foreign central banks ("official foreign assets" in table 9.1), rather than on the part of foreign private citizens. Much as at the beginning of the decade, foreign central banks were buying dollars in an unsuccessful attempt to prevent the dollar from depreciating and their own currencies from appreciating.

The depreciation of the dollar stimulated exports enough to return the country to a surplus in goods and services in 1979 and 1980. At the same time, the nature of capital flows began to change. This was the end of a long period of steady U.S. net investment abroad.[4] In the 1980s, capital on net began to flow in to finance U.S. trade deficits, reversing the pattern of the preceding ninety years. We will be picking up the story of the capital inflows in section 9.4.

9.3   Risk, Government Controls, and Other Barriers or Incentives to International Capital Movements

Many factors influence investors' decisions to move capital internationally. The most obvious factor is the expected rate of return that can be earned in one country or another. In section 9.5, we will be looking at various measures of rates of return in the United States and other major countries, with special reference to the increased attractiveness of U.S. assets in the early 1980s. But other factors are important as well. Indeed, if investors cared only about expected returns and nothing else, then one would not observe *any* differentials in rates of return. Investors would refuse to buy the assets with the lower return and would have an unlimited demand for the assets with the higher return. In other words, arbitrage would quickly insure that expected returns were equalized.[5] We will see in section 9.5 that this does not quite seem to be the case. In this section we consider factors other than expected rates of return: transactions costs, capital controls, taxes, default risk, and exchange risk.

9.3.1 Transactions Costs

An unavoidable barrier to international capital movements is transactions costs, as represented in the case of securities by a brokerage fee or a bid-ask spread. But this barrier is extremely small for countries with developed financial markets. Several factors have worked to reduce transactions costs steadily over the years. Deregulation, innovation, and economies of scale in international dealings, particularly in the Euromarket, have made the world banking and securities industry more efficient. Some of the many recent innovations in international markets to make the issuance of securities, or the management of the accompanying risk, more convenient for borrowers or lenders include currency and interest rate swaps, dual currency issues, mismatched floating rate notes, zero coupon bonds, equity-related issues, note issuance facilities, and Eurocommercial paper.[6] Reduced telecommunications costs and other technological advances have also been important. The real cost of sending a telegraphic message from New York to London or Paris in 1985 was only 8–9 percent of what it was in 1900, and the real cost of a three-minute off-peak phone call between Washington and Frankfurt was only 5 percent of what it was in 1950 (Cooper 1986, 10).

Another factor, exchange rate variability, has worked to *raise* foreign exchange transactions costs since curencies began to float. To make a market in foreign exchange, banks have to take open positions in foreign currency, even if only briefly, and the riskiness of doing so has gone up with the variability of exchange rates. As a result, bid-ask spreads have generally been higher since 1973 than in the past (Levich 1985, 997–99). Nevertheless, they are still on average small—not high enough to create much of a deterrent to investors' shifting their portfolios in response to a change in the attractiveness of a country's assets.

The result of these reduced costs is a very high volume of financial transactions internationally. For example, a survey by the Federal Reserve Bank of New York in March 1986 documented a very high level of turnover in the New York foreign exchange market: $50 billion a day among banks, 92 percent above the previous survey in April 1983, and $26 billion a day among nonbank financial institutions, up 84 percent over three years earlier.[7] The volume of foreign exchange trading was even greater in London at $90 billion a day.[8]

Due to economies of scale, transactions costs tend to be lower in currencies that are widely used in trade and financial transactions. The U.S. dollar has been the world's vehicle currency ever since it inherited the role from the pound sterling early in the century. A non-U.S. resident wishing to buy assets of a third country generally must buy dollars

Table 9.2   **International Bond Markets, 1982–First Half 1986**
(billions of U.S. dollars)

	1982	1983	1984	1985	1986[a]
Eurodollar issues	42.2	39.2	65.3	96.5	108.2
Foreign dollar issues	6.0	4.7	4.3	4.7	5.8
Total international dollar issues	48.2	43.9	69.6	101.2	114.0
Borrowers (percent of total)					
Australia	1.9	3.2	2.2	2.3	5.9
Canada	17.2	9.8	4.5	5.3	7.8
France	11.6	10.5	8.8	7.3	4.9
Japan	8.3	14.3	14.4	11.9	15.3
United States	25.5	12.9	28.0	28.9	29.3
Euroyen issues	0.6	0.2	1.2	6.5	16.1
Foreign yen issues	3.3	3.9	4.9	6.4	6.7
Total international yen issues	3.9	4.1	6.1	12.9	22.8
Borrowers (percent of total)					
China	—	—	—	3.0	7.8
France	8.8	10.8	8.6	7.6	5.6
Japan	5.3	—	1.3	5.8	8.2
United States	0.1	—	10.7	26.5	30.4
International development organizations	17.1	27.3	25.2	18.4	6.4
Eurodeutsche mark issues	3.3	4.0	4.3	9.5	18.2
Foreign deutsche mark issues	2.1	2.6	2.4	1.7	—
Total international deutsche mark issues	5.4	6.6	6.7	11.2	18.2
Borrowers (percent of total)					
Austria	—	—	—	—	9.1
Germany	1.5	6.0	5.7	13.8	24.6
United States	11.5	4.2	9.3	9.7	7.4
EEC institutions	16.2	15.5	15.5	5.3	8.0
International development organizations	13.8	37.0	21.2	15.0	12.0
Euro–Swiss franc issues	0.1	—	—	—	—
Foreign Swiss franc issues	11.3	13.5	13.1	15.0	23.5
Total international Swiss franc issues	11.4	13.5	13.1	15.0	23.5
Borrowers (percent of total)					
Australia	3.0	1.7	5.3	7.9	4.7
Canada	11.3	9.2	7.6	7.3	3.6
Japan	32.9	49.3	44.4	45.1	30.5
United States	13.0	8.9	9.5	19.0	26.3
International development organizations	10.8	9.9	11.2	11.7	4.7
Other Eurobond issues	4.1	6.7	10.9	22.9	37.7
Other foreign bond issues	2.4	2.3	3.1	3.2	3.1
Total other international bond issues	6.5	9.0	14.0	26.1	40.8
International bond issues	75.4	77.1	109.5	166.4	219.3

Source: Organization for Economic Cooperation and Development, *Financial Statistics Monthly.*

Note: Total international bond issues for 1986 was $225 billion.

[a]First half 1986 annualized.

first, before converting them into the third currency. Banks and large corporations around the world hold dollar transactions balances. In 1985 over 60 percent of international bond issues were denominated in dollars, as can be seen from table 9.2. A disproportionately high share of world trade is also invoiced in dollars.

Other currencies also play a role in international transactions. In ascending order of transactions costs in the ninety-day forward markets, as measured by the percentage bid-offer spread in the period September 1982–December 1985, are the mark, yen, Canadian dollar, Dutch guilder, pound, and Swiss franc.[9] This ranking of the currencies corresponds roughly to their ranking in volume of foreign exchange trading in New York: mark, yen, pound, Swiss franc, Canadian dollar, French franc, and Dutch guilder.[10] In the 1980s, there has been talk of the yen beginning to play a more central role. The use of the yen as a currency in which to invoice trade, issue bonds, and hold reserves is indeed increasing relative to the low levels of the past. The share of yen-denominated issues in international bond markets has gone from 5.2 percent in 1982 to 10.4 percent in 1986, including many U.S. borrowers. This is now a greater share than that of the deutsche mark, as can be seen in table 9.2.[11] However, there is little prospect of the dollar being seriously challenged as the world's vehicle currency.

One might also include the cost of obtaining information in the category of transactions costs as another barrier discouraging residents of one country from holding assets in another. Information costs are relevant, for example, for mortgage holdings because of the difficulty of evaluating the creditworthiness of the borrower. Foreigners hold essentially no mortgages in the United States, while Americans in the aggregate hold about 25 percent of their portfolio in that form. Information costs are not a problem for U.S. Treasury securities on the other hand; indeed the safety and liquidity of U.S. government securities are so attractive to foreigners that they hold about 43 percent of their U.S. portfolio in that form, as compared to about 21 percent for Americans (see table 9.3). Eurobonds issued by well-known U.S. corporations have also been very popular with foreigners in recent years for the same reason.

9.3.2 Capital Controls

In many countries, government controls have been serious barriers to the international flow of capital. The postwar international economic system established at Bretton Woods did not incorporate a presumption, analogous to the one incorporated regarding international trade, about the undesirability of government intervention in international capital markets.

Table 9.3   **Foreign versus Domestic Holdings of Financial Assets, 1984 (billions of dollars)**

	Foreign Holders		Domestic Holders	
	Amount	% of Total	Amount	% of Total
Checkable deposits and currency	$ 19.7	4.4%	$ 582.2	7.1%
Large time deposits	39.4	8.8	392.3	4.8
Short-term U.S. government securities	72.0	16.0		
Long-term U.S. government securities	120.8	26.9	1,709.5	20.8
Other short-term paper	40.9	9.1	266.4	3.2
Corporate bonds	61.8	13.8	588.1	7.2
State-local government securities	0.0	0.0	543.6	6.6
Mortgages	0.0	0.0	2,028.9	24.7
Corporate equities	94.5	21.0	2,090.3	25.5
Total	449.1	100.0	8,201.3	100.0

Sources: Board of Governors of the Federal Reserve System, *Flow of Funds*, various issues; table from Friedman 1986.

Notes: Amount and percentage of total are year-end figures. Short-term U.S. government securities include marketable securities only. Other short-term paper includes commercial paper and bankers acceptances. Foreign holdings of corporate equities exclude foreign direct investment. Totals exclude small time and saving deposits, money market mutual funds, interbank claims, and other miscellaneous assets.

The more common use of controls is to discourage the outflow of capital from a weak-currency country, as in many developing countries, or as in the United States in the 1960s and early 1970s. But they are also sometimes used to discourage capital from flowing into a country, when it wishes to avoid a real appreciation of its currency or is worried about a potential loss in monetary control. For example, Germany and Switzerland had special taxes on interest payments to nonresidents, and maintained other measures to discourage foreigners from holding assets in their countries, until 1975.[12] Though the controls on capital inflow into Germany and Switzerland, like the controls on capital outflow from the United States, were never very effective, their removal no doubt facilitated part of the increased U.S. acquisition of foreign assets in the mid-1970s that shows up in table 9.1.

The United Kingdom maintained controls to discourage capital outflows until 1979. But when Margaret Thatcher came to office, Britain too joined the club of countries with essentially open financial markets, which by then consisted of the United States, Canada, Germany, Switzerland, and the Netherlands.

An interesting case is Japan. Until relatively recently, Japan had very highly regulated capital markets, both domestically and with respect to international transactions. In the period 1975–78, the Japanese controls worked to discourage capital inflow, with the aim of dampening the appreciation of the yen. Foreigners were not allowed to hold gensaki (a three-month repurchase agreement) and other Japanese assets. That the controls worked to discourage capital inflow can be seen by looking at the differential in interest rates between gensaki in Tokyo and three-month Euroyen in London, which averaged 1.84 percentage points:[13] If it were not for the controls, investors would not have been willing to hold Euroyen when a higher interest rate was available in Tokyo.

When the yen began to depreciate rapidly in 1979, the Japanese moved quickly to remove restrictions on foreign purchases of Japanese assets. The differential between the gensaki and Euroyen interest rates dropped sharply. Indeed, the London rate exceeded the Tokyo rate after April 1979, although the differential was relatively small.[14] This is evidence that Japanese controls on capital inflow were liberalized more quickly than controls on capital outflow, with the objective of dampening the depreciation of the yen against the dollar. If some barriers to capital outflow had not remained, Japanese investors would not have been willing to hold assets in Tokyo when a higher interest rate on comparable yen securities was available in London.

A controversy arose in October 1983 when some American businessmen, alarmed by devastating competition from Japanese exporters, convinced top officials in the U.S. Treasury Department, despite the evidence just cited, that the Japanese government was still using some form of capital market restrictions to keep the value of the yen lower than it would otherwise be. There followed a campaign by the U.S. government to induce the Japanese to adopt a whole list of measures further liberalizing their financial markets. This campaign came to fruition in the May 1984 Yen/Dollar Agreement between the U.S. Treasury and the Japanese Ministry of Finance. Measures liberalizing capital inflows included the elimination of the "designated company" system that restricted foreign direct investment in eleven companies. Measures liberalizing capital outflows included relaxation of restrictions on nonresident issue of yen bonds (called samurai bonds when sold in the Japanese market), relaxation of "administrative guidance" on the part of the Ministry of Finance over overseas lending by Japanese banks, and permission to Japanese residents to purchase foreign-issued commercial paper and certificates of deposit. The Ministry of Finance retained ceilings on foreign security holdings by insurance companies and trust banks, equal to 10 percent of total assets, until the ceilings began to become binding in early 1986, at which point they were raised to a much higher level.

The result of the liberalization was an increase in net capital outflows: The Japanese rate of acquisition of long-term assets abroad jumped from $32.459 billion in 1983 to $56.775 billion in 1984,[15] the majority of it in the form of portfolio investment, as shown in table 9.4. The positive offshore-onshore interest differential, which had been fifty basis points (briefly) as recently as November 1983, disappeared altogether in 1984.[16] Furthermore, the yen depreciated another 8 percent against the dollar in 1984. In short, the Yen/Dollar Agreement was successful at increasing Japan's integration into world financial markets, but not at promoting capital inflow into Japan or a short-term appreciation of the yen if that was its goal.

As of early 1986, only France, of the largest industrial countries, maintained capital controls that were clearly binding by the test of interest rate differentials. These are controls on capital outflow that were tightened when the Socialists came to office in 1981. But even the French, like the Italians, are in the process of liberalizing. The offshore-onshore differential, which was 3.88 percent in March 1986,[17] vanished thereafter with the election of Jacques Chirac, at least temporarily.

In the Pacific region, Australia and New Zealand have recently removed their capital controls, and Hong Kong and Singapore have had open financial markets for some time. Elsewhere among developing countries, however, markets remain heavily controlled. Table 9.5 shows onshore-offshore interest differentials for a cross section of twenty-four countries. Many have differentials that are highly variable and significantly negative on average, indicating effective controls on the outflow of capital to the world market.[18]

9.3.3 Taxes

Taxes are a determinant of international capital flows that might be considered a sort of government control. But it is more common that avoiding taxes is an incentive to invest abroad than paying taxes is a barrier to it.

The mere fact that the citizens of one country are taxed at a higher rate than those of another does not necessarily create an incentive for capital flows, assuming both groups of citizens are taxed at the same rate on their foreign interest earnings as on their domestic earnings. But in practice, investors can sometimes evade taxes by keeping their money in tax havens, in the Caribbean and elsewhere. The United States has to an extent played the role of tax haven in recent years. U.S. borrowers have offered bearer bonds, whose ownership depends on physical possession rather than registry, to eager investors in Europe and Latin America.[19]

The requirement that banks hold a certain fraction of their deposits in the form of reserves, rather than lending them out at market interest

Table 9.4 Long-Term Capital Movements in Japan (millions of U.S. dollars)

	1976	1977	1978	1979	1980	1981	1982	1983	1984	1985
Foreign capital[a]	3,575	2,063	2,483	3,318	13,141	13,137	12,449	14,759	7,124	17,273
Direct investment	113	21	8	239	278	189	439	416	-10	642
Portfolio investment[a]	1,595	1,256	1,654	2,072	11,877	11,852	7,579	8,485	-156	3,851
Import credits	-5	-13	-22	-33	-16	-15	-6	8	3	29
Loans	326	-324	-7	-169	-231	-186	-181	-37	-77	-75
Bonds	1,509	1,099	833	2,210	1,236	1,368	4,281	5,663	7,350	12,890
Others	37	24	17	-1,001	-3	-71	337	224	14	-64
Japanese capital	-4,559	-5,257	-14,872	-16,294	-10,817	-22,809	-27,418	-32,459	-56,775	-81,915
Direct investment	-1,991	-1,645	-2,371	-2,898	-2,385	-4,894	-4,540	-3,612	-5,965	-6,452
Portfolio investment	-146	-1,718	-5,300	-5,865	-3,753	-8,777	-9,743	-16,024	-30,795	-59,773
Export credits	-571	-1,388	-142	1,288	-717	-2,731	-3,239	-2,589	-4,937	-2,817
Loans	-1,525	-472	-6,299	-8,102	-2,553	-5,083	-7,902	-8,425	-11,922	-10,427
Others	-326	-24	-760	-717	-1,409	-1,324	-1,994	-1,809	-3,156	-2,346
Net[b]	-984	-3,184	-12,389	-12,967	2,324	-9,672	-14,969	-17,700	-49,651	-64,542
Memorandum:										
Net banking flows	-621	1,684	-2,243	-4,020	-13,144	-6,386	-35	3,570	-17,560	-10,848

Source: Bank of Japan, *Balance of Payments Monthly*, in OECD *Economic Survey, Japan*, August 1985 and November 1986.

Note: Minus sign indicates capital outflow.

[a] Excluding foreign investors' gensaki transactions (bond transactions with agreements to repurchase, usually within three months). Since the liberalization in 1979 up to the end of 1981, although short term in nature, those transactions had been classified as long-term capital movements.

[b] Actual rate.

Table 9.5   **Deviations from Covered Interest Parity, September 1982 to October 1985, in Percentage Points (local interest rate–London Eurodollar interest rate–London forward discount) three-month maturity**

Country	Mean Error	S.D.	Sample S.D.	Root Mean Squared Error	95% Bound
United Kingdom	− .02	.05	.27	.27	.45
West Germany	.50[a]	.03	.20	.54	.84
Netherlands	.25[a]	.02	.13	.28	.50
Canada	− .13[a]	.02	.13	.28	.50
Switzerland	− .06	.05	.73	.73	1.47
Group 1	− .13	.10	.33	.74	
Malaysia	− 1.53[a]	.15	.89	1.77	3.39
Hong Kong	.18[b]	.07	.43	.47	1.01
Singapore	− .47[a]	.08	.50	.68	1.21
Group 2	− .60[a]	.13	.61	1.12	
Mexico	− 17,89[a]	2.00	12.02	21.55	37.83
South Africa	− 1.32[a]	.14	.08	1.55	3.09
Greece	− 9.39[a]	1.17	7.03	11.73	20.45
Saudi Arabia	− 2.21[a]	.20	1.20	2.52	4.23
Group 3	− 7.81[a]	1.44	5.27	12.44	
France	− 2.14[a]	.51	3.06	3.73	7.93
Italy	.56	.60	3.58	3.62	6.21
Belgium	.32	.19	1.12	1.17	2.11
Austria	− 1.80[a]	.30	1.81	2.56	4.52
Denmark	− 4.12[a]	.27	1.62	4.42	7.18
Ireland	− .11	.08	.48	.49	.74
Norway	− .65[a]	.08	.46	.80	1.42
Sweden	− .81[a]	.22	1.30	1.53	3.06
Spain	− 3.71[a]	.67	4.03	5.47	11.79
Group 4	− 1.38[a]	.31	1.94	2.64	
Japan	− 1.78[a]	.16	.93	2.01	2.65
Australia	− .79	.41	2.47	2.59	3.59
New Zealand	− 1.90[a]	.53	3.15	3.68	6.27
Group 5	− 1.49[a]	.24	2.18	2.84	
Total Sample	− 2.13[a]	.32	2.02	5.58	

Source: Barclay's Bank.

[a]Statistically significant at 99 percent level.

[b]Statistically significant at 95 percent level.

rates, might be thought of as another tax. U.S. reserve requirements were one reason for the growth of the Euromarket in the 1960s and 1970s. Banks do not have to hold reserves against their offshore deposits and for that reason are willing to pay a higher interest rate on deposits in the Euromarket than on deposits in the United States. The differential in three-month interest rates between the Eurocurrency market and the U.S. interbank market exceeded one hundred basis points in 1980, as the second column of table 9.6 indicates.

By the early 1980s, discouraging capital ouflow was no longer a goal for the United States, and authorities were concerned that the U.S. banking industry was losing business to Eurobanks. Beginning December 1981, U.S. banks were allowed to participate in a sort of domestic Euromarket by establishing International Banking Facilities (IBFs), which are simply a separate set of deposit accounts without reserve requirements.[20] There followed a large shift in accounts from overseas offices of U.S. banks to the offices at home, the majority in New York. But the change is to be thought of as a shift in the location at which banking services are provided, rather than as a net capital inflow: both claims and liabilities to foreigners were shifted to U.S. banks.

An important factor in determining international capital flows is withholding taxes. Until recently, the United States and most other major countries withheld income taxes on bond interest paid to foreigners, unless the foreign residents fell under bilateral tax treaties, on the theory that the income might otherwise escape taxation altogether. But in July 1984, the United States abolished its withholding tax.[21] This move was an inducement to foreign investment in the United States. West Germany, France, and Japan have since also found it necessary or desirable to abolish their own withholding taxes, in order to "remain competitive" in the eyes of international investors. Now *most* countries are potential tax havens for residents of other countries.

9.3.4 Default Risk and Other "Political Risk"

A corporation or other borrower that has a possibility of defaulting on its obligations has to pay a correspondingly higher interest rate to compensate lenders for that possibility. For example, the reason investors in the early 1980s were willing to hold deposits in U.S. banks at lower interest rates than could be earned in the Euromarket, in the absence of controls on capital outflow from the United States, may be that they thought there was a greater risk of default in the Euromarket. The differential between the Eurodollar and domestic deposit rates cannot be explained solely by the difference created by reserve requirements on the side of banks' costs. Figure 9.1 shows that the differential existed even when the U.S. deposit rate is adjusted for reserve requirements.

While U.S. government debt has always been considered close to free of default risk, the 1980s debt crisis has forcefully established the point that governments can default. Indeed, in many Latin American and other financially troubled countries, government debt has turned out to be no more guaranteed than private debt. Even many European

Table 9.6   Deviations from Closed Interest Parity: Offshore Interest Rate (covered for exchange risk) Minus the U.S. Interest Rate (three-month interest rates in percentage per annum)

Offshore rate	Euro-$		Euro £ + fd	U.K. ib + fd	U.K. T-Bill + fd	Euro-DM + fd	Ger. ib + fd
U.S. rate	T-Bill	Interbank	Interbank	Interbank	T-Bill	Interbank	Interbank
Means							
1978	1.573	0.564	0.618	-0.840	-0.301	0.738	1.075
1979	1.894	0.786	0.886	0.622	1.656	1.047	1.491
1980	2.581	1.016	1.145	0.989	2.070	1.384	1.931
1981	2.190	0.923	1.080	1.085	2.105	1.242	1.778
1982	2.091	0.900	1.074	1.082	2.066	1.208	1.640
1983	0.660	0.546	0.676	0.691	0.577	0.786	1.127
1984	0.878	0.408	0.566	0.558	0.583	0.709	1.008
1985	0.571	0.295	0.414	0.410	0.305	0.396	0.622
Standard Deviations							
1978	0.666	0.262	0.390	0.846	0.975	0.477	0.484
1979	0.690	0.272	0.376	0.498	0.751	0.410	0.549
1980	1.027	0.371	0.785	0.795	1.233	0.526	0.565
1981	0.578	0.280	0.353	0.316	0.742	0.344	0.455
1982	0.736	0.205	0.242	0.223	0.746	0.308	0.357
1983	0.156	0.116	0.201	0.222	0.282	0.140	0.186
1984	0.401	0.078	0.143	0.134	0.418	0.194	0.234
1985	0.176	0.109	0.301	0.275	0.498	0.552	0.555

Notes: ib ≡ interbank rate.
fd ≡ adjustment for the forward exchange discount.

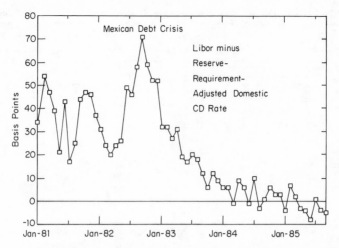

Fig. 9.1   Deviations from closed interest parity offshore less domestic.
                     Source: Federal Reserve Board.

governments have to pay a default risk premium over U.S. government debt, as shown in figure 9.2b below.

One cannot look at interest rates on new bank lending to the troubled debtors after 1982 for a measure of the perceived probability of default. The banks that have large loans already outstanding, knowing that the likely alternative is default on the earlier debt, have "involuntarily" had to put in new money in rescheduling agreements. The new loans have been made at interest rates that—though maintaining positive fig-leaf spreads over LIBOR (London Interbank Offered Rate)—are far lower than would compensate them for the true risk. But one can estimate the perceived default risk from the discount at which loans trade on the secondary market. As of December 1986, bank loans were trading at a discount of 32.9 percent for a weighted average of 15 problem debtors, as reported in table 3.17 (Dornbusch) in this volume. There is also a secondary market in bonds issued by some of these countries. Before August 1982, when the Mexican debt crisis first surfaced, the rate of return on Mexican or Brazilian bonds was below that on World Bank bonds. The prices of the bonds fell to a discount thereafter, so their rate of return rose above that on World Bank bonds. The difference, which should be interpreted as a default risk premium, peaked at 8.14 percent in April 1983 for Mexican bonds and 6.71 percent in January 1985 for Brazilian bonds (Folkerts-Landau 1985; Edwards 1986) (see table 9.7).

Many analysts believe that the perceived increased risk of default in Latin America and elsewhere in the world after August 1982 caused a large flow of capital to the United States, which was considered a safe

Table 9.7 **Default Risk Premiums on Foreign Bonds, 1981–85 (U.S. dollars)**

	Returns on Foreign Bonds[a]			Difference in Rates of Return[a]	
	World Bank (1)	Mexico (2)	Brazil (3)	(2) − (1)	(3) − (1)
1981					
July	14.99	13.66	14.63	−1.33	−0.36
August	15.33	13.71	14.69	−1.62	−0.64
September	16.42	13.18	15.07	−3.24	−1.35
October	16.89	14.15	15.13	−2.74	−1.76
November	16.46	14.21	15.20	−2.25	−1.26
December	14.03	14.30	13.90	0.27	−0.13
1982					
January	15.36	13.29	13.84	−2.07	−1.52
February	15.63	13.33	13.88	−2.31	−1.76
March	14.98	13.41	13.96	−1.57	−1.02
April	14.96	13.51	14.03	−1.45	−0.93
May	14.56	13.55	14.09	−1.01	−0.47
June	15.22	13.62	14.17	−1.60	−1.05
July	15.11	13.69	14.24	−1.42	−0.87
August	14.11	15.86	15.19	1.75	1.08
September	13.30	17.15	15.59	3.85	2.29
October	11.93	18.05	15.24	6.12	3.31
November	11.28	18.43	14.47	7.15	3.19
December	11.26	18.36	12.94	7.10	1.68
1983					
January	10.79	18.43	13.72	7.64	2.93
February	10.79	18.59	13.79	7.80	3.00
March	10.58	18.71	13.87	8.13	3.29
April	10.49	18.63	13.58	8.14	3.09
May	10.31	16.93	13.41	6.62	3.10
June	10.65	17.05	13.59	6.40	2.94
July	11.10	17.17	13.96	6.07	2.86
August	11.88	17.05	14.32	5.17	2.44
September	11.47	17.12	14.42	5.65	2.95
October	11.22	16.77	14.73	5.55	3.51
November	11.40	15.77	14.72	4.37	3.32
December	11.55	13.21	14.73	1.66	3.18
1984					
January	11.44	13.27	14.71	1.83	3.27
February	11.34	13.32	14.54	1.98	3.20
March	11.56	12.51	13.88	0.95	2.32
April	11.55	12.56	13.86	1.01	2.31
May	11.97	12.43	13.96	0.46	1.99
June	12.33	12.77	14.09	0.44	1.76
July	13.54	13.34	16.13	−0.20	2.50
August	13.61	13.71	15.84	0.10	2.23
September	13.03	13.88	16.02	0.85	2.99
October	12.78	13.85	16.40	1.07	3.62

Table 9.7   (continued)

	Returns on Foreign Bonds[a]			Difference in Rates of Return[a]	
	World Bank (1)	Mexico (2)	Brazil (3)	(2) − (1)	(3) − (1)
1985					
November	12.71	14.00	16.58	1.29	3.87
December	11.93	13.92	16.84	1.99	4.91
	11.02	13.28	16.85	2.26	5.83
1985					
January	10.31	12.56	17.02	2.25	6.71
February	10.07	12.42	12.73	2.35	2.56
March	11.09	12.26	12.73	1.17	1.64

Source: International Herald Tribune, various issues, in Folkerts-Landau 1985.

Note: The bonds are medium-term seasoned bonds, January 1982–March I 1984.

[a]Call provisions on the World Bank bonds raise rates of return on these relative Mexican or Brazilian bonds of same risk and maturity. Hence, the changes over time of the differences in the rates of return are of interest.

[b]For the World Bank 10.25, June 1987; for Mexico 8.5, March 1987; for Brazil 8.25, December 1987.

haven, and that this was responsible for the large appreciation of the dollar. That there was massive unrecorded "capital flight" out of Latin America is clear. Comparisons of the current account deficits of countries such as Mexico, Venezuela, and Argentina with the bank debt incurred suggest that there must have been a large increase in unrecorded overseas claims by citizens of those countries. It is less clear that this explains why the demand for U.S. assets should have been increasing over the entire period 1981–85, particularly relative to European or Japanese assets, as would be necessary if it were to explain the appreciation of the dollar. If there was a shift during this period into U.S. assets based on increased perceptions of safety in the United States, relative to assets held in Europe, then one would expect interest rates on U.S. assets to decline relative to comparable dollar assets in Europe. This did not happen in short-term interest rates. Figure 9.1 shows that the Eurodollar rate actually fell relative to the domestic U.S. deposit rate after August 1982. Table 9.6 shows that the offshore-onshore differential also fell by other measures between 1980–82 and 1983–85. The domestic interest rate can be measured by the U.S. Treasury bill rate instead of by the interbank rate (first column), and the offshore rate can be measured in pounds or marks, covered on the forward exchange market, instead of by the Eurodollar rate (last five columns). In every case, the short-term interest differential moves in the opposite direction from what the safe haven hypothesis would predict. (In section 9.5, we consider analogous long-term interest differentials.)

There are other kinds of risk, besides the risk of outright default, that can discourage investors from holding a country's assets. Even if the country does not currently have taxes on interest payments abroad, or on the repatriation of profits, and does not have controls on the removal of principal, there is always the possibility that it will enact such policies in the future. This is particularly relevant for countries that have had capital controls in the past. In the case of direct investment in less developed countries, there is the possibility of nationalization of the industry. This is one of the reasons why investment in these countries prior to 1982 usually took the form of bank lending rather than direct investment. All these forms of "political risk" are less applicable to assets held in the United States than elsewhere, consistent with the view of the country as a safe haven for capital. On the other hand, U.S. authorities have in recent years been ready to freeze assets of unfriendly states Iran and Libya; Soviet fears along these lines thirty years ago may have been behind their decision to hold dollars in London banks—the genesis of the Euromarket.[22]

9.3.5   Exchange Risk

Because of the risk of changes in the exchange rate, assets denominated in dollars are viewed by investors as different from assets denominated in other currencies. This is true even in the absence of transactions costs, capital controls, taxes, political risk, or other barriers to the movement of capital across national boundaries.

There are many ways residents of one country can increase their net investment position in another country without increasing their exposure in its currency. In the first place, even if all assets were denominated in the currency of the country where issued, U.S. residents could, for example, increase their net investment position abroad by buying back previously issued dollar bonds. A net capital outflow can be either an increase in foreign assets or a decrease in liabilities, as the high gross flow numbers in table 9.1 or 9.9 illustrate.

In the second place, an investor can acquire claims on foreigners without the claims being denominated in foreign currency, and can acquire assets denominated in foreign currency without their being claims on foreigners. Many smaller countries issue bonds denominated in dollars, rather than in their own currencies, so that they will be more acceptable to international investors.[23] The majority of bank lending to less developed countries has been denominated in dollars, and the rest in the currencies of other major industrialized countries, not that of the borrower. Even the United States government issued "Carter bonds" denominated in marks in 1978–79. Corporations increasingly borrow abroad in foreign currency, either as a foreign bond issue or in the Euromarket.

At the shorter end of the maturity spectrum, there have been active forward exchange markets for some time; borrowers are able to hedge foreign currency liabilities by buying exchange forward, and lenders to hedge foreign currency assets by selling exchange forward. At the longer end of the maturity spectrum, the rapid growth of currency swaps in the 1980s allows U.S. corporations to issue Euroyen or Euromark bonds to Japanese, Germans, or anyone else wishing to hold these currencies, and then to swap the proceeds into dollars. Finally on the list of ways that currency of denomination can be divorced from the location of the asset, the prices of equities and direct investment are not fixed in any currency, either domestic or foreign (though the dollar price of foreign equities does often seem to move one for one with the exchange rate).

While these ways exist for an investor to buy a foreign asset without taking a position in foreign currency, not all investors should wish to avoid taking such a position. Unless an investor is indifferent to risk, or is certain what the future exchange rate will be, or is tied to his own currency by accounting practices, he should wish to diversify his holdings among dollars, marks, yen, pounds, francs, and so forth so as to reduce the variability in the value of his overall portfolio. It is easy for an investor, particularly an American, to slip into the habit of viewing his own currency as safe and others as risky. This view would assign exchange risk a purely negative role, a cost to be weighed against other factors like expected return in the decision to buy foreign currencies. But the value of domestic currency is not completely safe, even for an American. A firm that imports raw materials, intermediate inputs, or other goods from abroad is vulnerable to an increase in costs from a depreciation of the domestic currency; such a firm would be wise to take an "open" position in foreign currency, that is, to hold some foreign assets or to buy some foreign exchange on the forward market. (The word "open" is in quotations because in this case the firm is reducing overall exposure to currency risk, not increasing it except in the most narrow of accounting senses.) Households also consume some imported goods and thus are partially vulnerable to a depreciation, though there is generally a lag before the depreciation is passed through to retail prices. Furthermore, the possibility of inflation in prices of domestically produced goods, whether associated with a change in the exchange rate or not, provides another reason why the domestic currency should not be viewed as perfectly safe. The point is that even a highly risk-averse American might want to hold some foreign currency assets.

To citizens of smaller, more open, countries, this point is more important. In countries with a past history of hyperinflation, particularly in central Europe and Latin America, the desirability of holding some foreign currency is well understood even by relatively unsophisticated citizens. The role of "asset least likely to lose purchasing power" has been played by various currencies at various times. In the 1970s, marks and Swiss francs, in addition to gold, were popular. But in the 1980s, the U.S. dollar is the currency of choice, in large part due to the firm antiinflation policy of the Federal Reserve Board under Chairman Paul Volcker. In countries that are highly unstable monetarily, residents are willing to give up interest earnings on securities to hold dollars in the form of currency. Dollars are known to circulate freely in such countries as Argentina and Israel. There are no data on foreign holdings of U.S. currency, but Cooper (1986, 7) conjectures that over $20 billion of the roughly $169 billion in dollar currency in circulation at the end of 1984 was held abroad.

Because exchange rates have become more variable since 1973, and even since 1980, the typical international investor should be more diversified among currencies than in the past. Despite this, and despite the low level of transactions costs and capital controls among major industrialized countries, residents everywhere appear to hold far less foreign assets, and far more of their own country's assets, than would be present in a theoretically well-diversified portfolio. For example, table 9.8 suggests that most U.S. assets are still held by U.S. residents. Similarly, most Japanese assets are still held by Japanese residents, and so forth. But investors everywhere are increasing their level of diversification, which explains why U.S. residents are increasing their gross claims on foreigners even at a time when capital is *on net* flowing into the United States (table 9.9). This process can be expected to continue for many years.

9.4   U.S. Capital Inflows in the 1980s

The 1980s have witnessed a historic swing in the U.S. capital account. In 1980, U.S. residents were on net investing overseas, as they had for many decades, at a rate estimated in the last line of table 9.9 at $10.4 billion a year. By 1982, U.S. residents appear to have been on net *borrowing* from abroad, at a rate of $10.5 billion a year. The estimated rate of net borrowing rose very rapidly, to $41.8 billion in 1983 and $106.5 billion in 1984, until it reached an apparent plateau in 1985 of $122.9 billion.[24] During this same period, the dollar appreciated sharply.

The balance of payments statistics in table 9.9 give some (limited) insight into the composition of the net capital inflow. The inflow has primarily taken the form of foreigners increasing their holdings of U.S.

Table 9.8   **Foreign Holdings of U.S. Financial Assets, 1962–85**

	Amount at Year End (billions of dollars)	Total U.S. Market[a] (billions of dollars)	Percentage
1962	45.4	1,457.8	3.1
1970	99.0	2,600.0	3.8
1975	183.4	3,507.9	5.2
1980	399.6	6,256.0	6.3
1981	419.7	6,628.0	6.3
1982	414.8	7,250.5	5.7
1983	502.4	8,219.2	6.1
1984	620.8	9,055.6	6.9
1985	788.4	10,663.4	7.4

Source: Board of Governors of the Federal Reserve System, *Flow of Funds Accounts, Financial Assets and Liabilities,* September 1986, pp. 1–2, 15–16.

[a]Total credit market debt owed by nonfinancial sectors plus security credit, trade credit, mutual fund shares, and other corporate equities.

assets. U.S. residents have not noticeably cashed in their holdings of foreign assets. In fact, U.S. residents have continued to increase their investments abroad.

9.4.1   U.S. Assets Abroad

Some have argued that the sharp fall in the recorded rate of U.S. acquisition of foreign assets, from $110.2 billion in 1982 to $15.0 billion in 1984 and $25.8 billion in 1985, means that actions by U.S. residents are dominating the net capital inflow, not actions by foreign residents.[25] But there are several things to be said against this argument. First, the recorded *stock* of U.S. assets abroad continues to rise; it is only the rate of change that has declined. Second, part of the apparent fall in U.S. investment abroad is an apparent fall in foreign direct investment between 1980 and 1982–84 (line 5 in table 9.9; the recorded figure for 1982 even shows a net decrease in the U.S. foreign direct investment position). But this fall in recorded direct investment is in part due to the problem of U.S. corporations obtaining funds via subsidiaries in the Netherlands Antilles. When these credit items are moved from the direct investment numbers to foreign purchases of U.S. corporate securities where they belong, foreign direct investment shows less of a decline in the early 1980s.[26]

In the third place, and quantitatively much more important, the reported slowdown in the period 1983–85 in U.S. banks' acquisition of claims on foreigners (line 8 in table 9.9) relative to 1981–82 can be traced to exaggeration of the 1981–82 figures by the establishment of IBFs (international banking facilities) in the United States beginning

Table 9.9   Capital Flows in the Balance of Payments, 1980–85 (billions of dollars)

	1980	1981	1982	1983	1984	1985
(1) U.S. assets abroad, net (increase/capital outflow [−])	−86.1	−111.0	−121.3	−50.0	−23.6	−32.4
(2) U.S. official reserve assets	−8.2	−5.2	−5.0	−1.2	−3.1	−3.9
(3) Other U.S. government assets	−5.2	−5.1	−6.1	−5.0	−5.5	−2.8
(4) U.S. private assets abroad	−72.8	−100.8	−110.2	−43.8	−15.0	−25.8
(5) Direct investment	−19.2	−9.6	2.4	−0.4	−3.9	−18.8
(5a) of which Netherlands Antilles capital (decrease/inflow [+])	2.7	3.5	8.7	3.1	1.7	−3.0
(6) Foreign securities	−3.6	−5.8	−8.1	−7.0	−5.1	−8.0
(7) Other claims reported by U.S. nonbanks	−3.2	−1.2	−6.6	−6.5	−5.1	−1.7
(8) Other claims reported by U.S. banks	−46.8	−84.2	−111.1	−29.9	−11.1	−0.7
(9) Foreign assets in the U.S. net (increase/capital inflow [+])	58.1	83.3	94.1	85.5	102.8	127.1
(10) Foreign official assets in the U.S.	15.5	5.0	3.6	6.0	3.0	−1.3
(11) Other foreign assets in the U.S.	42.6	78.4	90.5	79.5	99.7	128.4
(12) Direct investment	16.9	25.2	13.8	11.9	25.4	17.9
(13) U.S. Treasury securities	2.6	2.9	7.1	8.7	23.1	20.5

(14) Other U.S. securities	5.5	7.2	6.4	8.6	12.8	50.9
(15) Other liabilities reported by U.S. nonbanks	6.9	0.9	-2.4	-0.1	4.7	-1.2
(16) Other liabilities reported by U.S. banks	10.07	42.1	65.5	50.3	33.8	40.4
(17) Current account balance	1.9	6.3	-9.1	-46.6	-106.5	-117.7
(18) Recorded nonofficial capital account balance (3)+(4)+(1)	-35.4	-27.5	-25.8	30.7	79.2	99.8
(19) Adjusted direct investment balance (5)+(12)-(5a)	5.0	12.1	7.5	8.4	19.8	2.1
(20) Adjusted securities balance (6)+(13)+(14)+(5a)	7.2	7.8	14.1	13.4	32.5	60.4
(21) Other claims and liabilities (3)+(7)+(8)+(15)+(16)	-37.6	-47.5	47.4	8.8	26.9	37.4
(22) Official reserves (2)+(10)	8.5	0.9	1.4	4.8	-0.1	-5.2
(23) New SDR allocations	1.2	1.1	—	—	—	—
(24) Statistical discrepancy -[(17)+(18)+(22)+(23)]	25.0	20.3	36.3	11.1	27.3	23.0
(25) Estimated private capital account balance (18)+(24)[a]	-10.4	-7.2	10.5	41.8	106.5	122.8

Sources: *Survey of Current Business*, June 1986, table 1; for 5a. 1980–81, *Survey of Current business*, June 1983, table D; 1982, (revised) Department of Commerce; 1983–85, *Survey of Current Business*, June 1986, table D.

[a]Assumes statistical discrepancy is entirely unrecorded capital inflows.

in December 1981. About $44 billion of IBF liabilities to foreigners originated in 1981, and $72 billion in 1982. Since these increased liabilities were matched by increased claims when the accounts were moved from overseas, the acquisition of foreign assets reported by U.S. banks is estimated to have been exaggerated by these amounts.[27] Thus, the decline in acquisition of foreign assets in the subsequent years is exaggerated similarly. More generally in the case of bank-reported flows, the statistics need say nothing about the residence of investors on whose behalf the banks are reporting. In the case of interbank transactions, the distinction between increases in liabilities and decreases in claims is particularly lacking in economic significance.

9.4.2 Foreign Direct Investment in the United States

The side of the balance sheet covering foreign investments in the United States is perhaps the more interesting, as the country is becoming increasingly dependent on the willingness of foreigners to continue to increase their lending. From lines 11 to 16 in table 9.9, foreign acquisition of U.S. assets during 1983–85 consisted of 18 percent direct investment, 17 percent purchases of U.S. Treasury securities, 24 percent purchases of other securities, 1 percent other U.S. liabilities to unaffiliated foreigners reported by U.S. nonbanking concerns, and 40 percent U.S. liabilities reported by U.S. banks not included elsewhere.

Table 9.10 shows the foreign direct investment position in the United States at the end of 1985. The investment is mostly in the hands of Europeans: 66 percent. Nine percent is held by Canada, 10 percent by Japan, 9 percent by Latin America, and only 5 percent by the Middle East and all others. The largest category is in manufacturing (33 percent), followed by trade (18 percent), petroleum (15 percent), real estate (10 percent), banking (6 percent), insurance (6 percent), other finance (3 percent), and other industries (8 percent).

A highly publicized component of foreign direct investment in the United States is the purchase or construction of factories by foreign manufacturers to avoid current or threatened U.S. restrictions against imports, most notably in the Japanese automobile industry. Japanese direct investment is indeed increasing rapidly: $3.1 billion in 1985 on U.S. figures, or $5.4 billion on Japanese accounting. But it is still relatively small, and it is concentrated in trade and in financial services. The Japanese figures show that 68 percent of the (cumulative) direct investment in North America is in nonmanufacturing industries and only 29 percent in manufacturing industries (5 percent in transportation machinery and 8 percent in electrical machinery).[28] This is in contrast to U.S. direct investment in other countries which as of end-1985 was 41 percent in manufacturing, 25 percent in petroleum, and only 16

Table 9.10   Foreign Direct Investment Position in the United States at Year End (millions of dollars)

1984

	All Industries	Petroleum	Manufacturing	Trade	Banking	Finance, Except Banking	Insurance	Real Estate	Other Industries
All countries	164,583	25,400	51,802	31,219	10,326	5,633	8,922	17,761	13,519
Canada	15,286	1,544	4,115	1,734	1,219	608	1,418	2,844	1,804
Europe	108,211	23,142	39,083	16,934	5,740	3,457	6,748	8,255	4,850
European Communities (10)	96,555	22,813	32,990	15,238	5,335	2,879	5,424	7,714	4,163
Belgium	2,548	(d)	471	296	(d)	(d)	(d)	10	(d)
France	6,591	(d)	5,368	728	420	−623	91	66	(d)
Germany	12,300	71	4,389	4,256	272	335	1,295	966	745
Italy	1,438	(d)	333	(d)	298	(d)	(d)	(d)	8
Luxembourg	753	(d)	74	(d)	(d)	121	0	(d)	8
Netherlands	33,728	9,981	12,497	2,787	1,427	1,970	1,445	2,471	1,152
United Kingdom	38,387	10,991	9,719	6,732	2,194	743	2,548	4,135	1,325
Denmark, Greece, and Ireland	779	(d)	139	216	214	2	(d)	42	50
Other Europe	11,655	329	6,093	1,696	405	579	1,325	541	688
Sweden	2,258	307	1,048	650	(d)	(d)	119	0	(d)
Switzerland	8,146	19	4,774	794	(d)	536	1,152	393	(d)
Other	1,251	3	271	252	271	(d)	54	148	(d)
Japan	16,044	−88	2,460	9,941	1,853	513	138	744	482
Australia, New Zealand, and South Africa	2,152	57	362	(d)	51	(d)	(d)	120	(d)
Latin America	16,201	656	5,537	2,027	665	861	580	4,664	1,212
South and Central America	2,859	50	981	44	(d)	115	(d)	372	186
Panama	1,924	45	959	14	(d)	108	(d)	256	6
Other	935	5	22	30	574	7	(d)	116	181

Table 9.10 (continued)

1984

	All Industries	Petroleum	Manufacturing	Trade	Banking	Finance, Except Banking	Insurance	Real Estate	Other Industries
All countries	164,583	25,400	51,802	31,219	10,326	5,633	8,922	17,761	13,519
Other Western Hemisphere	13,343	606	4,555	1,983	(d)	746	(d)	4,292	1,025
Bermuda	1,370	110	306	363	0	7	(d)	151	(d)
Netherlands Antilles	10,935	452	4,092	1,394	(d)	643	(d)	3,715	543
United Kingdom Islands, Caribbean	866	(d)	140	186	16	109	(d)	369	10
Other	172	(d)	18	40	0	−13	0	57	(d)
Middle East	5,336	15	116	(d)	481	(d)	0	709	(d)
Israel	525	6	97	(d)	319	(d)	0	0	−6
Other	4,811	9	20	(d)	162	9	0	709	(d)
Other Africa, Asia, and Pacific	1,353	75	128	291	318	28	(d)	423	(d)
Memorandum,–OPEC[1]	4,892	12	−21	(d)	268	9	0	707	(d)

1985

	All Industries	Petroleum	Manufacturing	Trade	Banking	Finance, Except Banking	Insurance	Real Estate	Other Industries
All countries	182,951	28,123	60,798	34,212	11,503	4,708	11,069	18,557	13,982
Other Western Hemisphere	16,678	1,659	5,130	2,143	1,332	513	1,337	2,580	1,985
Bermuda	120,906	25,437	46,515	17,611	5,963	2,387	8,921	8,821	5,251
Netherlands Antilles	106,004	25,114	37,553	15,738	5,616	1,681	7,497	8,238	4,566
United Kingdom Islands, Caribbean	2,288	(d)	477	340	(d)	(d)	(d)	9	(d)
Other	6,295	(d)	5,485	581	483	−917	92	26	(d)
Middle East	14,417	(d)	6,198	4,726	222	(d)	1,656	1,049	697
Israel	1,401	(d)	273	(d)	300	25	(d)	(d)	(d)
Other	584	(d)	86	(d)	(d)	129	0	24	22
Memorandum,–OPEC[1]	36,124	11,135	12,986	2,544	1,570	2,088	1,975	2,325	1,321

43,766	12,246	11,844	6,847	2,539	262	3,727	4,623	1,638
1,129	(d)	165	404	199	3	(d)	(d)	52
14,902	323	8,961	1,873	347	705	1,424	583	685
2,384	296	1,132	790	3	-46	(d)	0	(d)
11,040	(d)	7,431	778	88	627	1,232	444	(d)
1,478	31	398	305	255	125	122	139	(d)
19,116	101	2,621	11,822	2,176	710	(d)	054	582
2,702	608	747	(d)	63	-19	662	117	(d)
17,050	112	5,558	2,099	1,122	917	(d)	4,808	1,276
3,385	104	803	190	1,041	132	(d)	307	(d)
2,137	8	842	113	(d)	123	4	199	1
1,248	496	-39	78	(d)	8	(d)	108	(d)
13,665	97	4,755	1,909	80	785	(d)	4,501	(d)
1,903	406	955	(d)	(*)	5	24	110	(d)
10,603	(d)	3,717	1,364	66	480	(d)	3,945	602
983	(d)	63	190	14	288	0	399	(d)
177	(d)	19	(d)	(*)	12	0	47	(d)
4,961	(d)	58	(d)	521	186	0	746	(d)
505	(d)	54	(d)	334	(d)	0	1	4
4,455	(d)	3	(d)	188	(d)	0	745	(d)
1,538	(d)	171	231	327	16	(d)	430	(d)
4,560	19	-36	(d)	188	2	0	737	(0)

Source: Survey of Current Business.

*Less than $500,000(+).

(d)Suppressed to avoid disclosure of data of individual companies.

percent in banking, finance, and insurance. (U.S direct investment in Japan is 51 percent in manufacturing, 24 percent in petroleum, and only 8 percent in banking, finance, and insurance.)[29] Japanese direct investment in manufacturing in the United States may be important for redirecting trade flows, or for any transfer of managerial practices that may be taking place, but it is not a quantitatively substantial part of the capital inflow into the United States.[30]

9.4.3   Securities Sales versus Banking Flows

In the past, banking transactions have generally been the largest component of the capital account. But in 1984, foreign purchases of U.S. securities passed bank-reported liabilities as the largest component of the capital inflow, either on a gross or net basis.

This trend, which accelerated in 1985, partly reflects the securitization of international capital markets: the rapidly growing role of direct investor purchases of bonds and equities, at the expense of bank intermediation. Some of the reasons suggested for the decline in banking's share are deregulation and innovation in securities markets, concern over bank exposure to developing countries, the pressure on banks to increase their capital-asset ratio, and concern over the Continental Illinois Bank crisis in 1984.[31] A rapidly growing component of the increased purchases of securities by foreigners consists of issues of Eurobonds by U.S. corporations: $38 billion in 1985 as compared to $7 billion in 1983.[32] Purchases of all non-Treasury U.S. securities reached $50.9 billion in 1985, over nine times higher than the level of five years earlier.

Another large chunk is increased purchases of U.S. government bonds. In 1984 the U.S. Treasury began a new effort to tap foreign savings and help finance the enormous federal budget deficit by issuing "foreign-targeted registered obligations" directly into the Eurobond market. Foreign purchases of all Treasury securities reached $20.5 billion in 1985, almost eight times higher than the level of five years earlier. A remarkable 83 percent of the foreign purchases were by Japanese residents.[33] This reflects the magnitude of the capital inflow from Japan and the relative preference of Japanese investors for U.S. bonds rather than equities. In 1986, however, foreign purchases of U.S. equities picked up sharply, surpassing purchases of U.S. Treasury securities as a component of the capital inflow.

9.4.4   Official Reserve Holdings of Dollars

Until 1973, the holdings of international reserves by central banks were thought of as endogenous, as accommodating the decisions of private residents regarding either investment or current account transactions. With the end of the Bretton Woods system, the obligation for the major central banks to intervene in the foreign exchange market ended. Most continued to intervene as it suited them, the European and Japanese central banks much more so than the U.S. authorities. For example, their purchases of dollars to try to dampen the dollar depreciation of 1977–78 were several times greater than the record U.S. current account deficits. One could think of the major central banks during this period playing to an extent the same role they did under the Bretton Woods system: financing U.S. current account (and private capital account) imbalances.

In the early 1980s, as the dollar swung from a level perceived as too low to a level perceived as too high, the European and Japanese central banks reversed the direction of their intervention, now selling dollars to dampen the depreciation of their own currencies. But even in 1985, when the U.S Treasury under Secretary James Baker abandoned its previous policy of benign neglect and spearheaded a new cooperative effort to get the dollar down, the quantity of intervention was relatively small. Reported U.S. liabilities to official institutions in Western Europe fell by only $7.3 billion between the end of 1980 and the end of 1985.[34] Dollar holdings by most smaller central banks increased steadily over this period (except in 1985): they either were unconcerned about the strength of the dollar or viewed themselves as too small to affect it, and were more interested in the high rates of return they could earn on dollar securities. The result was the positive numbers in line 10 of table 9.9.

The U.S. statistics probably underestimate the dollar holdings of central banks, those in developing countries in particular, because they do not count Eurodollar holdings. Statistics on reserve holdings reported by the central banks themselves show greater increases in quantity terms in 1983–85.[35] It is as if central banks in the aggregate acted like "destabilizing speculators," rather than "leaning into the wind" to resist swings in the dollar.[36] The tendency for central banks to shift their portfolios in the same direction that currency values are already moving is necessarily even stronger when reserves are reported in value terms. As table 9.11 shows, the share of official reserve portfolios allocated to dollars declined rapidly from 1977 to 1980, and then rose from 1980 to 1984, like the value of the dollar itself. Perhaps central banks should be lumped together with other foreign residents in their portfolio behavior.[37]

At the Plaza Accord of September 22, 1985, the five largest central banks agreed to coordinated intervention in order to bring down the dollar. Subsequently, when foreign central banks became convinced that the dollar depreciation threatened to go too far (e.g., at the Louvre Meeting of February 22, 1987), they switched back to purchasing dollars. The magnitude of the intervention in 1986–87 was large. In 1987:I, foreign official purchases of U.S. assets even exceeded private purchases as a component of the capital inflow.

Table 9.11 Share of National Currencies in Total Identified Official Holdings of Foreign Exchange, End of Year 1977–85 (percentage)

	1977	1978	1979	1980	1981	1982	1983	1984	1985	Memorandum: ECUs Treated Separately[a]
All countries										
U.S. dollar	80.03	78.2	75.2	69.0	73.1	71.7	72.2	70.5	65.1	56.4
Pound sterling	1.8	1.8	2.1	3.1	2.2	2.5	2.7	3.1	3.2	2.9
Deutsche mark	9.3	11.2	12.8	15.6	13.4	12.9	12.0	12.8	15.5	14.2
French franc	1.3	1.2	1.4	1.8	1.4	1.3	1.1	1.1	1.2	1.1
Swiss franc	2.3	2.2	2.6	3.3	2.8	2.8	2.4	2.1	2.4	2.2
Netherlands guilder	0.9	0.9	1.1	1.4	1.2	1.2	0.9	0.8	1.0	1.0
Japanese yen	2.5	3.4	3.7	4.5	4.3	4.7	5.0	5.7	7.6	7.0
Unspecified currencies[b]	1.6	1.1	1.2	1.4	1.4	2.8	3.5	3.8	3.9	15.2
Industrial countries										
U.S. dollar	89.4	86.4	83.4	77.6	78.7	76.7	76.0	71.6	63.2	48.9
Pound sterling	0.9	0.7	0.8	0.8	0.7	0.8	0.9	1.6	2.0	1.7
Deutsche mark	5.5	7.9	9.7	14.4	13.1	12.5	12.9	14.7	19.2	16.4
French franc	0.3	0.4	0.6	0.5	0.5	0.4	0.3	0.4	0.5	0.4
Swiss franc	0.8	1.2	1.5	1.8	1.8	1.8	1.8	1.4	1.8	1.5
Netherlands guilder	0.6	0.5	0.6	0.7	0.8	0.7	0.5	0.6	1.0	0.9
Japanese yen	1.8	2.3	2.6	3.5	3.7	4.4	5.1	6.1	8.5	7.3
Unspecified currencies[b]	0.7	0.5	0.7	0.6	0.7	2.8	2.9	3.5	3.9	22.9

Developing countries[c]

U.S. dollar	70.9	66.6	66.3	60.1	67.1	66.5	68.0	69.2	67.5	67.5
Pound sterling	2.8	3.2	3.4	5.4	3.8	4.4	4.8	4.8	4.7	4.7
Deutsche mark	13.3	15.9	16.2	16.7	13.9	13.3	11.1	10.6	10.9	10.9
French franc	2.3	2.3	2.2	3.1	2.5	2.4	2.0	1.9	2.1	2.1
Swiss franc	3.9	3.6	3.8	4.9	3.9	3.9	3.6	3.0	3.1	3.1
Netherlands guilder	1.2	1.5	1.6	2.0	1.6	1.7	1.3	1.0	1.1	1.1
Japanese yen	3.2	4.9	4.8	5.6	5.0	5.1	4.9	5.3	6.5	6.5
Unspecified currencies[b]	2.5	1.9	1.7	2.2	2.2	2.8	4.2	4.1	4.0	4.0

Source: International Monetary Fund, *Annual Report*, 1986.

Notes: Starting with 1979, the SDR value of European currency units (ECUs) issued against U.S. dollars is added to the SDR value of U.S. dollars, but the SDR value of ECUs issued against gold is excluded from the total distributed here. Only selected countries that provide information about the currency composition of their official holdings of foreign exchange are included in this table.

[a]The column is for comparison and indicates the currency composition of reserves when holdings of ECUs are treated as a separate reserve asset, unlike the earlier columns starting with 1979 as is explained in the preceding note. The share of ECUs in total foreign exchange holdings was 10.9 percent for all countries and 20.2 percent for the industrial countries in 1985.

[b]This residual is equal to the difference between total identified reserves and the sum of the reserves between the seven currencies listed in the table.

[c]The calculations here rely to a greater extent on Fund staff estimates than do those provided for the group of industrial countries.

9.5   Rates of Return

What could cause swings in net capital flows of the magnitude seen in the 1980s? From the standpoint of macroeconomic policy, the most important determinants of capital flows between countries are expected rates of return. U.S. interest rates increased sharply after 1980. Interest rates in other major industrialized countries also increased, but not as much. The differential between the U.S. ten-year interest rate and a weighted average of other countries' ten-year interest rates averaged zero in 1976–80, but rose to about 2 percent by 1982, and rose further to about 3 percent in 1984. This increase in the differential rate of return on U.S. assets is widely considered the most important cause of the net capital inflow that began in the early 1980s. But measuring expected rates of return is not as straightforward as might appear. For equities or direct investment, the rate of return is uncertain, and investors treat such assets as different from bonds so that one cannot use the bond interest rate to measure their expected rate of return. Even for deposits, loans, and bonds, where the nominal interest rate is known in terms of domestic currency, the dollar interest rate on U.S. bonds cannot be directly compared with the mark interest rate on German bonds because of the likelihood of future changes in the mark-dollar exchange rate.

9.5.1   Dollar Bond Rates in the Domestic and Euro Markets

If we are interested in the investor's decision whether to invest in bonds issued in the United States versus bonds issued in other political jurisdictions per se, rather than necessarily dollar bonds versus other currencies, then we can get around the problem of exchange rate uncertainty by comparing U.S interest rates to Eurodollar interest rates. This is the same thing we did in table 9.7 for three-month deposit rates. Figure 9.2 shows four series of long-term dollar interest rates, two on each side of the Atlantic. The dominant impression is that the rates move together, suggesting that capital controls or political risk is relatively unimportant and that arbitrage works relatively well. But there is still some variation in the differential.

Figure 9.2a shows the domestic U.S. versus Eurodollar interest rate on bonds issued by U.S. corporations. In the mid-1970s, the rates were essentially the same. The domestic U.S. interest rates began to rise, especially in 1980 and 1981, providing a strong incentive for capital to flow from the Euromarket into the United States. The Eurobond rate also rose, but not by as much. The differential, represented by the solid line in figure 9.2c, reached 3.3 percent in July 1981. Evidently, the capital inflow was not large enough to arbitrage it away. It is unclear why U.S. corporations did not elect to do even more of their borrowing in the Euromarket at the cheaper rate.[38]

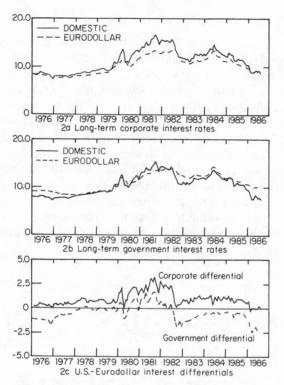

Fig. 9.2   Domestic U.S. and Eurodollar corporate bond rates, government bond rates, and differentials. *Source:* Morgan Guaranty.

Figure 9.2b shows the U.S. and Eurodollar interest rates for government bonds. These Eurodollar bonds are issued by European governments, so the fact that they offered a higher interest rate than the U.S. bonds in the 1970s was presumably compensation for somewhat greater risk of default. But when the U.S. rate rose in 1980–81, the Euromarket rate lagged behind, just as with the corporate bonds; the differential turned positive and reached 1.7 percent in September 1981.

When the U.S. corporate and government interest rates fell in mid-1982, the respective Eurobond rates again lagged behind and the differentials returned to their earlier levels. The drop in the Euro-U.S. long-term differentials in mid-1982 is consistent with the idea that investors sought to shift their portfolios into U.S. assets for "safe haven" reasons associated with the Latin American debt crisis.[39] But the evidence is also consistent with the idea that there was a (short) lag in the time necessary for U.S. borrowers to take full advantage of the lower interest rates in the Euromarket and thus arbitrage away the differential. Swaps, note issuance facilities, and other innovations to facilitate borrowing in the Euromarket were developing at this time.

9.5.2   U.S. versus Nondollar Interest Rates

Figure 9.3a shows the differential between the U.S. long-term government bond rate and a weighted average of six trading partners' long-term government bond rates (solid line).[40] The differential peaked in June 1984 at 3.19 percent, with the differentials against Germany and Japan somewhat higher. It then declined over the subsequent two years, falling below 1.00 percent in 1986, though still 2.0 percent against Germany and 2.8 percent against Japan as of September 1986.

When comparing incentives to invest in U.S.- versus foreign-currency bonds, we must consider exchange rate expectations in addition to interest rates. This is difficult because there are many different views as to how exchange rates move and no way to measure expectations directly. But it is possible to get a rough handle on the exchange rate expectations that investors must have held during this period.

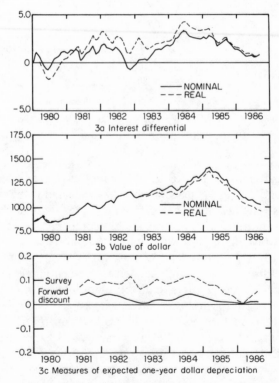

3a Interest differential

3b Value of dollar

3c Measures of expected one-year dollar depreciation

Fig. 9.3   Nominal and real long-term interest rate differentials, nominal and real effective exchange rates, and twelve-month forward discount and twelve-month expected depreciation—U.S. versus trading partners.

There is a historical tendency, albeit very slow and erratic, for the exchange rate eventually to return to a long-run equilibrium in real terms (that is, adjusted for changes in the price level). The large appreciation of the dollar from 1980 to 1984, 35 percent against a weighted average of fifteen trading partners' currencies, was not much offset by higher inflation abroad, and so constituted a similar appreciation in real terms, 32 percent.[41] The result of this loss of competitiveness was the rapidly growing trade deficit, which reached $113 billion in 1984 and $124 billion (on a balance of payments basis) in 1985. It was widely believed at this time that the trade situation was unsustainable, that the dollar was overvalued and would in the future have to depreciate back to levels at which U.S. producers could compete on world markets. Such expectations of future depreciation must have had an effect on investor thinking.

There exist surveys of the forecasts made by participants in the foreign exchange market, and they tend to confirm the idea that the large appreciation of the dollar in the early 1980s generated an anticipation of a future depreciation back to equilibrium. One survey conducted by the *American Express Bank Review* shows that the forecasted depreciation of the dollar one year ahead climbed from approximately zero in the late 1970s (− 0.20 on average in 1976–79) to a peak of 8.47 percent in the year 1984. Another survey conducted by *The Economist Financial Report* (beginning only in 1981) shows the forecasted depreciation of the dollar rising to 10.02 per annum in 1984. A third survey, by Money Market Services, Inc., (beginning in 1983) shows three-month-ahead forecasts of dollar depreciations rising to 7.26 percent (per annum) in 1984.[42] It seems unlikely that investors based their portfolio decisions on the full magnitude of the expectation depreciation numbers reported in the surveys; since the expected depreciation numbers were considerably in excess of the interest differential, there would not be much incentive for investors to hold dollar assets. It is likely that investors at each point assigned a significant probability to the possibility that the forecasted fall in the dollar would not materialize in the coming year, as was reasonable given that such forecasts had turned out wrong for four years. In that case the rising interest differential could have been an adequate offset for expected depreciation, providing adequate incentive for investors to continue to increase their holdings of dollar securities in the 1981–84 period.

Given our argument that investors expect deviations from long-run equilibrium such as the 1984 overvaluation of the dollar to be corrected, investors' expectations of future depreciation should have diminished after March 1985 when the dollar depreciation finally took place. In other words, if one thinks, as of the end of 1986, that much of the return to equilibrium has already taken place, then one should think that less depreciation remains to be accomplished in the future. The survey data confirm this, as can be seen by the dashed line in figure 9.3c. For example, the *Economist* survey showed an expected one-year depreciation of the dollar against the mark of only 4.9 percent as of October 30, 1986, as compared to 9.3 percent on September 5, 1985, just before the Plaza Accord (or 10.7 percent on average between June 1981 and December 1985). The 1985–86 decline in the expected rate of future depreciation explains how foreign residents would have wished to continue increasing their holdings of dollar assets despite the decline in the nominal interest differential shown in figure 9.4a.

A useful alternative way to measure the expected rates of return on different countries' assets is to look at the differential in *real* interest rates, that is, nominal interest rates adjusted for expected inflation.[43] There is no unique way of measuring expected inflation, but the problem is not as difficult as measuring expected exchange rate changes. Alternative possible measures of expected inflation tend to give similar answers.

During the late 1970s, and through 1980, the U.S. real interest rate by the available measures was usually below foreign real interest rates. As figure 9.3a shows, the real interest differential increased in the early 1980s even more than did the nominal interest differential, and peaked in June 1984.[44] Depending on whether expected inflation is measured by a three-year distributed lag on actual inflation, the three-year forecast of Data Resources, or the two-year forecast of the OECD *Economic Outlook,* the average long-term real interest differential rose between 1979–80 and 1983–84 by 4.79 percentage points, 3.88 percentage points, or 3.54 percentage points.[45] This increase in return differentials was a significant inducement to demand for U.S. assets.

9.5.3 U.S. versus Foreign Returns on Equity

To compare countries' rates of return on real capital we can look at the earnings-to-price ratio or dividend-to-price ratio on equity. These numbers are already expressed as real rates of return and need not be corrected for inflation. They are reported for stock markets in Europe, the Far East, and Australia, in addition to the United States, by *Capital International Perspective* of Geneva.[46]

The difference in the rate of return on equity between the United States and abroad is shown in figure 9.4. Like the real interest differentials, the measures of return on equity show a substantial increase from 1980 to 1984, with a dip in-between at 1983. The difference in dividend yields rose from 1.1 in 1980[47] to 2.3 at the first peak in mid-1982, and 2.1 at the second peak in early 1984. The difference in earnings-price ratios followed a similar pattern, but with larger swings, rising from 1.6 on average in 1980 to 5.6 at the first peak in early 1982,

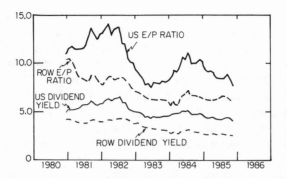

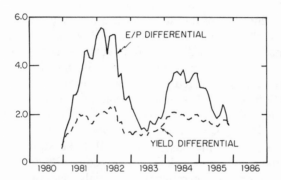

Fig. 9.4   Returns on equity, the United States versus the rest of world (Europe, Far East, and Australia): earnings-price ratios and dividend yields. *Source: Capital International Perspective,* Morgan Stanley.

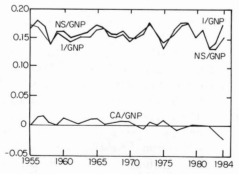

Fig. 9.5   U.S. national saving (NS), investment (I), and current account (CA) as shares of GNP, 1955–84. *Source: Economic Report of the President,* 1985.

and 3.9 in mid-1984. Both the dividend yield and the earnings-price ratio show the differential between the United States and foreign equity markets declining in 1985 and 1986. As of 1987, the rate of return on U.S. equities was still perceived as high, particularly relative to Japanese equities, attracting new foreign money into the U.S. stock market. The same could have been said for U.S. real estate.

To summarize the results on various assets, they generally show that the low or negative differentials in the rates of return between the United States and other countries in the late 1970s turned to substantial positive differentials in the early 1980s. Since the dollar was weak in the late 1970s and strong in the early 1980s, the evidence supports the argument that the change in return differentials induced a shift in investor preferences, away from foreign assets and toward U.S. assets. One dent in the simplicity of this story is the dip in return differentials from mid-1982 to 1983, while the dollar was still appreciating. Some argue that this may have been due to safe haven effects associated with the debt crisis. The other problem of timing is that the second peak in return differentials occurred nine months before the dollar peaked in March 1985. It is possible that a "speculative bubble" was driving the dollar during that short period, with investors increasing their demand for dollars due to short-term expectations of continued appreciation formed by extrapolating past trends.[48] But the subsequent 1985–86 decline in the value of the dollar, simultaneous with continued declines in all of the measures of return differentials, supports the causal relationship between the two.

9.6 Saving, Investment, and U.S. Macroeconomic Policies

If rates of return have been the driving force behind international capital flows and the exchange rate, what is the driving force behind rates of return?

Interest rates and securities prices are determined by many factors. Particularly on a daily or monthly basis, corresponding fluctuations in the market-clearing price will result from whatever unpredictable fluctuations in demand for an asset occur. Interest rate volatility has been even higher in the 1980s than previously. This is partly the result of deregulation and innovation in world financial markets. However, the dominant source of the longer-term swings in the real rates of return discussed in the preceding section appears to be domestic: U.S. macroeconomic politices. So far in the 1980s, international capital markets have worked to dampen swings in U.S. rates of return, rather than working as a source of disturbances. But in the future, U.S. interest rates will increasingly be determined at the mercy of foreign investors.

9.6.1 Monetary Policy

In the latter half of the 1970s, expansionary monetary policy on the part of the Federal Reserve Board drove down U.S. real interest rates. That is, even though nominal interest rates were at high levels by historical standards, the expected inflation rate was also very high, so the difference of the two was low, even negative. Toward the end of the decade, public concern shifted toward the inflation problem and away from employment and growth, which had turned out to be surprisingly steady. The Fed tried to brake the rapid rate of money growth, particularly after Paul Volcker was appointed chairman, but with no success at first. Monetarist economists charged that the problem was the Fed's use of the nominal interest rate as an intermediate target, as opposed to the supply of bank reserves or the monetary base, which was argued to be evidence of a lack of true commitment to the yearly announced target for growth in the aggregate money supply (M1). By October 1979 Volcker had decided that interest rates would have to be allowed to rise much more sharply if money growth and the inflation rate were to be reduced. He went along with the monetarists to the extent of announcing that the Fed would no longer target the interest rate on federal funds, even on a short-term basis, but would instead target reserves. This was a convenient way of tightening monetary policy without taking the political heat for higher interest rates. Interest rates have been significantly more volatile ever since (though the various measures of the money supply have also been more variable than before).

With a small lag, the new policy produced the anticipated reduction in demand for goods when interest rates shot up, particularly after credit controls were imposed in March 1980. After the brief 1980 recession had passed, monetary policy was tightened anew, and interest rates climbed further. The period of dollar appreciation dates from this time. The second, more serious, recession began in mid-1981. A major consequence of the higher degree of international capital mobility in the 1980s compared to earlier decades is that changes in monetary policy operate strongly through the exchange rate and foreign demand for U.S. products, rather than solely through the interest rate and domestic demand.

Although nominal interest rates had reached a plateau, and even dropped discretely in August 1982 when the Federal Reserve responded to the Mexican debt crisis and general macroeconomic conditions by increasing money growth, inflation was coming down. Thus, long-term real interest rates continued their general upward trend through mid-1984, with the further consequences for the behavior of international investors and the appreciation of the dollar that we have seen.

Money growth by the conventional measures has been relatively rapid ever since the recession; M1 grew 10.3 percent per year from 1982: 2 to 1986: 2.[49] For the first four years after the acceleration began, the monetarists warned that inflation would resurge with the customary six- to eighteen-month lag. Volcker publicly justified exceeding the yearly money targets by pointing to exogenous shifts in velocity (defined as the relationship between the money supply and dollar GNP). The exogenous shifts were at first identified as the special factors of maturing All-Savers' Certificates and the nationwide legalizing of interest on checking accounts, then more generally as the environment of deregulation and innovation in the banking industry. An equally important reason for allowing faster growth in the money numbers was the *endogenous* shift in velocity that occurs when people wish to hold more money because expected inflation and nominal interest rates have fallen.

In the event, Volcker was right and the monetarists were wrong. Inflation did not reignite during this period. Even with the recovery of real economic activity that began in 1983, which proceeded rapidly until mid-1984 and then continued at a considerably slower pace through 1986, nominal GNP grew more slowly than the money supply: 8.0 percent per year from 1982:II to 1986:II (*Economic Indicators,* September 1986). Thus velocity grew at 2.3 (= 10.3 − 8.0) percent per year, in contrast to its past historical pattern of *declining* roughly 3 percent per year. If the Federal Reserve had followed the explicit monetarist prescription of rigidly precommitting to a money growth rate lower than that of the preceding period, say 3 percent, and velocity had followed the same path, then nominal GNP would have risen at only 0.7 per year. This is an upper bound, because with even lower inflation than occurred, velocity would almost certainly have fallen even more than it did. The implication seems clear that the 1981−82 recession would have lasted another four years.

9.6.2   Corporate Tax Policy and Investment

If the velocity-adjusted growth rate of money was not unreasonably high after 1982, neither was it low. How do we explain the fact that the long-term real interest rate in mid-1984 was as high as or higher than it was in mid-1982? Or that even in 1987 it was still higher than in 1980?

Think of the real interest rate being determined so that the funds needed for investment do not exceed the funds available from saving, the investment rate depending negatively on the real interest rate, and the national saving rate also depending (presumably positively) on the real interest rate.[50] (Investment is defined as additions to business plant and equipment, the residential housing stock, and inventories. National saving is defined as private saving plus public saving.) Then the increase in real interest rates could be due either to an upward shift in investment, a downward shift in national saving, or some combination of the two.[51] First, we consider investment.

The productivity slowdown of the 1970s convinced many that enhanced incentives to capital formation were called for, and Ronald Reagan was elected in 1980 in part on that platform.[52] The 1981 tax bill granted liberalized depreciation allowances (ACRS, the accelerated cost recovery system) and a liberalized investment tax credit. When investment grew rapidly in 1983–84, some claimed that the tax incentives, together with the more general probusiness climate (a "golden age of capitalism"), was responsible, and that the demand for funds to finance the investment boom in turn explained the increase in real interest rates and the net capital inflow. The argument seemed to fit in well with the safe haven explanation for the strength of the dollar. The main problem with it is that the investment rate always rises in expansions, and the increase in the 1983–84 recovery was no greater than the decrease in the 1981–82 recession.[53] By 1985 the investment rate had merely reattained the approximate level of the 1970s, as table 9.12 shows. A second argument is that calculations of the benefits of the tax incentives suggest that (1) they were smaller than the increase in real interest rates, so that the after-tax real cost of capital to firms was not reduced, and (2) the investment boom was concentrated in sectors like office computers, where the tax incentives were not very relevant and a technological explanation seems to fit instead.[54]

Ironically, the Treasury tax reform plan of December 1984, and the revised tax reform plan actually passed by Congress and signed by the president in 1986, sharply raised corporate taxes. The logic was that raising corporate tax revenue was the only way to change personal income tax brackets and deductions in such a way as to leave a majority of taxpayers feeling that they were better off, and simultaneously maintain overall "revenue neutrality." But the effect was to undo the incentives to investment enacted in 1981.

9.6.3 Budget Deficit

Having found that there has been no increase in the investment rate, relative to the 1970s, to explain by itself the high level of real interest rates and the high capital inflow in the mid-1980s, we now turn to national saving.[55] We begin with the "dissaving" of the government, that is, the budget deficit.

The federal budget has not been in surplus since 1969. In the 1975 recession, the budget deficit reached the then postwar record high of 3.5 percent of GNP. Steady growth in national income over the next

Table 9.12   U.S. Net Savings and Investment as Percentages of GNP, 1951–85

	1951–60	1961–70	1971–80	1981	1982	1983	1984	1985
Total net saving	6.9%	7.5%	6.1%	5.2%	1.6%	1.8%	4.1%	3.0%
Net private saving	7.2	8.0	7.1	6.1	5.4	5.9	7.4	6.5
Personal saving	4.7	4.7	4.9	4.6	4.4	3.6	4.3	3.3
Corporate saving	2.5	3.3	2.2	1.4	1.0	2.3	3.1	3.2
State-local government surplus	−0.2	0.1	0.9	1.3	1.1	1.3	1.4	1.4
Federal government surplus	−0.2	−0.5	−1.9	−2.2	−4.8	−5.4	−4.8	−4.9
Total net investment	7.0	7.5	6.3	5.4	1.6	1.8	3.8	2.8
Net private domestic investment	6.7	7.0	6.2	5.2	1.8	2.9	6.4	5.7
Plant and equipment	2.7	3.5	3.0	3.1	2.0	1.5	4.8	4.9
Residential construction	3.2	2.5	2.5	1.3	0.6	1.8		
Inventory accumulation	0.8	1.1	0.7	0.9	−0.9	−0.4	1.6	0.8
Net foreign investment	0.3	0.5	0.1	0.2	−0.2	−1.0	−2.6	−2.9
Memoranda: Capital consumption	8.9	8.5	9.9	11.2	11.7	11.4	11.0	11.0
Gross private saving	6.1	16.4	17.0	17.2	17.1	17.3	18.4	17.6

Sources: U.S. Department of Commerce, *Survey of Current Business*, various issues; Friedman 1986.

Notes: Data are averages (except for 1981–85) of annual flows. Data for 1985 are through 1985:2 at seasonally adjusted annual rates. Total net saving and total net investment differ by statistical discrepancy. Detail may not add to totals because of rounding.

four years raised tax revenues and reduced the deficit to 1.5 percent of GNP, or $38 billion, by 1979. But this was still considered too high.

The improbable Laffer curve theory, which held that a reduction in personal income tax rates would stimulate production and income so much as to raise total tax revenues rather than lower them, helped convince politicians to enact large tax cuts in 1981, to be installed over three years. At the same time, some categories of domestic spending were cut sharply, but they were a relatively small part of the total. Given the enormous buildup in military expenditure, the exemption of social security benefits from cuts, the runaway increases in some other categories like farm support, and the exogenous fact of enormous interest payments on the national debt, it was inevitable that the federal budget deficit would soar to unprecedented levels. Initially it was possible to blame the increased budget deficit on the reduced tax revenues from the 1981–82 recession. It was claimed that rapid growth in income and therefore in tax revenues would return the budget to balance in a few years. But the tax rate cuts and spending increases were phased in as quickly as income grew. The deficit reached $208 billion in 1983—more than three times the "intolerably high" levels of the late 1970s—and remained in the vicinity of $200 billion for the following three years. The increase in the federal deficit relative to the 1970s was 3.0 percent of GNP, as table 9.12 shows.

State and local governments in the aggregate improved their surplus by about $30 billion between 1980 and 1985 (*Economic Report of the President* 1986, 284), or by 0.5 percent of GNP relative to the 1970s, as table 9.12 shows. Thus the decline in the general government budget balance was not quite as bad as the decline in the federal budget balance.

9.6.4   Private Saving

Table 9.13 reports the total gross national saving rate, including both private and government saving, for the twenty-four countries in the OECD. The figure for the United States in 1984 was 17.0 percent, and the average for the others was 23.1 percent. Even aside from public dissaving in the form of government budget deficits, there are disparities in private saving between the United States and other countries. The U.S. household saving rate, at 5.1 percent of disposable income in 1985, is extremely low by international standards. The United Kingdom's is 11.9, West Germany's 13.0, Japan's 22.5.[56] Japan's especially high rate of household saving has been attributed to, among other things, a prosaving tax and financial system, a shortage of housing, leisure, and consumption goods on which to spend income, and a demographic bulge in the generation of Japanese who will be retiring over the next twenty years.

According to some theories, an increase in the U.S. budget deficit such as has occurred in the 1980s should produce an increase in private

Table 9.13   Gross Saving as Percentage of GDP

Country	1965	1966	1967	1968	1969	1970	1971	1972	1973	1974	1975	1976	1977	1978	1979	1980	1981	1982	1983	1984
United States	21.0	20.3	19.4	19.5	19.8	18.1	18.3	18.6	20.7	19.3	17.4	17.9	18.9	20.2	20.3	18.3	19.0	15.9	15.2	17.0
Japan	31.5	32.1	34.4	35.8	36.7	40.2	38.0	38.3	39.2	36.3	32.3	32.6	32.0	32.3	31.5	31.1	31.1	30.5	29.8	30.6
Germany	27.2	26.8	25.2	26.8	27.6	28.1	27.1	26.4	26.6	24.8	20.9	22.6	21.8	22.6	22.7	21.8	20.2	20.3	21.2	21.9
France	25.7	25.8	25.7	24.6	25.0	26.2	25.6	26.0	26.0	24.5	23.0	23.0	22.7	22.6	22.8	22.2	19.7	18.6	18.1	18.6
United Kingdom	20.1	19.6	18.4	19.0	21.6	22.0	20.1	19.6	21.0	16.3	15.5	16.0	19.6	19.6	20.0	18.5	17.3	18.2	17.9	19.3
Italy	23.6	22.8	22.8	23.6	24.4	24.2	22.7	22.0	22.4	21.9	20.1	22.1	22.6	22.4	23.0	22.5	19.0	18.4	17.9	18.1
Canada	23.0	23.9	22.6	22.1	23.0	21.2	20.5	21.3	23.5	24.8	21.1	21.3	19.7	20.1	22.5	22.9	22.4	19.0	19.2	19.4
Total of above countries	22.9	22.5	22.0	22.4	23.2	23.0	22.5	23.0	24.9	23.2	20.8	21.4	22.1	23.2	23.1	21.8	21.4	19.5	19.1	20.3
Austria	27.5	28.6	26.9	27.0	28.3	30.3	30.2	30.8	30.6	30.2	25.9	25.0	24.3	25.3	25.7	25.8	24.3	23.9	22.6	24.1
Belgium	23.7	23.6	24.2	23.3	24.4	27.1	25.6	25.5	24.6	25.3	21.8	22.4	20.8	20.5	18.8	17.5	13.5	13.9	14.9	15.6
Denmark	24.6	22.9	21.8	22.3	23.0	21.8	22.4	24.4	24.4	22.1	19.4	19.1	18.9	18.8	16.6	14.9	12.4	12.1	13.9	15.3
Finland	23.7	23.5	23.2	25.6	26.8	28.0	27.9	27.2	28.7	30.4	26.5	24.5	23.7	23.8	25.5	26.0	25.1	23.8	23.7	24.5
Greece	20.5	20.3	20.1	19.5	21.9	25.0	26.4	28.3	32.0	26.5	23.3	24.4	24.5	26.3	28.3	28.9	25.3	18.4	16.6	16.1
Iceland	31.0	28.2	23.3	21.7	27.3	25.8	26.3	25.1	28.8	24.2	23.7	26.5	27.3	25.6	23.6	23.8	21.5	19.1	18.8	18.0
Ireland	19.4	19.0	21.0	20.7	20.9	20.4	20.2	22.9	23.4	19.2	21.8	20.1	22.5	22.2	19.6	16.1	13.1	14.6	16.4	17.5
Luxembourg	30.8	30.0	28.3	29.9	35.0	40.8	36.5	39.3	43.2	47.9	39.1	44.0	41.8	44.8	44.9	46.6	46.1	51.8	54.7	57.5
Netherlands	26.9	26.3	26.6	27.5	26.9	26.5	26.2	26.9	28.3	27.3	23.0	23.6	22.4	21.1	20.4	20.0	20.4	20.8	20.8	23.0
Norway	28.0	27.9	27.7	27.3	25.8	28.3	27.5	27.3	28.4	28.9	26.7	25.2	22.3	23.4	25.3	29.6	29.4	27.7	28.3	30.8
Portugal	26.3	26.6	30.3	26.4	27.7	31.7	30.4	37.1	36.9	23.0	12.5	15.3	19.7	24.8	27.8	26.8	23.4	22.3	21.2	20.1
Spain	22.6	22.8	22.1	22.8	24.6	24.6	24.7	24.9	25.4	24.6	23.5	21.4	20.8	21.2	20.4	18.8	18.2	17.5	17.6	19.9

Sweden	26.3	25.2	24.9	23.8	23.8	24.8	24.0	23.4	24.1	22.9	23.8	21.4	17.9	17.6	17.8	17.7	15.7	14.2	16.4	17.9
Switzerland	29.9	30.2	30.6	31.3	31.1	32.6	32.9	32.6	32.1	31.7	27.8	26.8	26.5	27.0	26.6	26.7	28.4	28.1	27.9	28.6
Turkey	14.1	16.8	16.9	16.7	16.5	19.2	17.6	20.9	21.4	19.2	18.0	19.6	18.2	16.0	16.5	16.2	18.4	19.0	17.0	17.2
Total smaller European countries	24.8	24.6	24.5	24.5	25.1	26.3	26.0	26.6	27.2	26.0	23.3	22.7	21.6	21.7	21.3	21.1	20.2	19.7	20.0	21.4
Australia	24.6	23.9	23.5	24.0	25.3	25.2	25.8	26.6	27.3	26.6	23.7	23.0	21.9	20.6	22.5	21.9	21.7	19.8	17.9	20.3
New Zealand	20.9	17.9	19.5	20.3	21.3	21.8	25.6	26.6	27.7	23.3	22.5	25.8	22.0	21.2	24.0	21.6	22.8	21.4	21.6	24.5
Total smaller countries	24.6	24.3	24.2	24.3	25.0	26.0	26.0	26.6	27.2	26.0	23.3	22.8	21.6	21.6	21.5	21.2	20.5	19.8	19.8	21.3
Total OECD	23.1	22.7	22.3	22.6	23.4	23.4	23.0	23.5	25.3	23.7	21.2	21.7	22.0	22.9	22.8	21.7	21.2	19.5	19.2	20.4
Four major European countries	24.3	23.9	23.1	23.8	24.9	25.5	24.4	24.1	24.7	22.6	20.3	21.4	21.8	22.0	22.2	21.3	19.2	19.0	19.1	19.8
OECD Europe	24.4	24.1	23.5	24.0	25.0	25.8	24.9	24.8	25.5	23.7	21.3	21.8	21.7	21.9	21.9	21.2	19.5	19.2	19.4	20.3
EEC	24.3	23.9	23.2	23.8	24.9	25.6	24.6	24.5	25.1	23.2	20.7	21.5	21.7	21.9	21.9	20.9	19.0	18.7	18.8	19.7
Total OECD less the United States	25.2	25.2	25.1	25.8	26.9	28.0	27.0	27.3	28.3	26.5	23.5	24.1	23.9	24.4	24.1	23.4	22.6	21.9	22.0	23.1

Sources: National Accounts (annual OECD publication); table from OECD *Economic Outlook*, May 1986.

Notes: The data in this table are measured according to the standard definitions of the OECD–United Nations system of accounts (see *A System of National Accounts*, Series F, no. 2, rev. 3, *United Nations*, 1968). The percentages for each group of countries are calculated from the total GDP and gross saving for the group, with both aggregates expressed in U.S. dollars at current exchange rates. Percentages for country groups exclude countries for which no data are shown in the table. Gross saving is the sum of national disposable income and consumption of fixed capital *less* consumption expenditure of households and government. It is the surplus available from current transactions to finance gross capital formation and capital transactions with the rest of the world.

saving to offset it. The theoretical argument is that households will think ahead to the day when the government has to raise taxes to pay off the debt, and that they will increase their saving today so that they or their children will have the resources to pay those taxes. The original supply-siders in the administration relied less on that theoretical argument than on the argument that households would respond to a higher after-tax rate of return by saving more. In any case, the predicted increase in the personal saving rate did not materialize. The personal saving rate, as a percentage of disposable personal income, fell from 7.1 percent in 1980 to 5.1 percent in 1985. Corporate saving rose, on the other hand, by 1 percent of GNP in 1985 relative to the 1970s. When personal and corporate saving are added together, total private saving as a share of GNP in 1985 was approximately the same as it was on average in the 1970s.

Thus, there was no upsurge in private saving to offset the increase in the budget deficit. This means that there was less national saving left over to finance investment.

9.6.5 The Relationship between National Saving and Investment

In a closed economy, that is, one cut off from the rest of the world, the fall in national saving would have driven up the cost of capital however much necessary to reduce the level of investment to the level of domestic funds available to finance it.[57] As it was, the cost of capital did rise in the 1980s, whether measured as the real interest rate or the return on equity, as we saw in the previous section. But because the increase in interest rates attracted a large capital inflow ("net foreign investment," in table 9.9), investment in plant and equipment was not crowded out as much as it otherwise would have been. The net capital inflow is precisely the current account deficit, which has generated so much concern, viewed from its more flattering profile. That a decline in national saving must either be offset by a net capital inflow or else reflected as a decline in investment, is a very general proposition; the natural mechanism is the increase in real interest rates, but the proposition must hold, no matter what happens to financial market prices.

An interesting question is how changes in national savings have been divided between changes in capital flow and changes in investment in prior historical episodes. Figure 9.5 shows U.S. national saving, investment, and the current account surplus (capital outflow) over the last three decades, each as shares of GNP. The saving rate and investment rate move closely together; the difference between the two, the current account, moves less. That is, before the 1980s, foreign capital usually played a small role in financing U.S. investment.

It would be wrong to conclude from this correlation alone that a change in national saving resulting from an exogenous change in fiscal policy is necessarily reflected in investment rather than in the current account. The close correlation between saving and investment rates in figure 9.5 could result from the effect of a third factor on both, rather than a causal relationship between the two. The business cycle is the most obvious third factor: saving rates and investment rates are both known to rise in booms and fall in recessions.

There are several ways of attempting to address this problem. One would be to adjust saving and investment cyclically, or to use more sophisticated econometric techniques. A second is to look at saving and investment rates *across countries* rather than over time. Table 9.14 gives the investment rates for twenty-four countries to match the national saving rates in table 9.13. A country like the United States—or Belgium, Denmark, and Sweden—which has a low rate of national saving, also tends to have a low rate of investment; a country like Japan—or Finland, Norway, and Switzerland—which has high saving rates, tends to have high investment rates.

A third way to get around the problem of cyclical variation in saving and investment is to average yearly observations over somewhat longer time intervals to take out some of the cyclical effect. Figure 9.6 shows decade averages of saving, investment, and the current account from the 1870s to the 1970s. The saving and investment rates are still highly correlated. The only time when the two diverged as widely as they have in the mid-1980s was the 1910s. U.S. investment had fallen slightly below national saving, that is, the country had begun to run current account surpluses, in the 1890s. But this capital outflow reached its highest during World War I, as the United States was lending to finance dissaving in Europe. Subsequent divergences between saving and investment were much smaller.

The experience of the 1980s stands out among industrialized countries, even if we look only at the absolute magnitude of the net capital flow (as opposed to the direction). The United States and other economies, which erected barriers to trade and capital flows in the 1930s and 1940s, have become more integrated since. The increasing degree of integration of financial markets in the 1970s and 1980s allows countries to have different saving rates without the differences in investment rates having to be as large; international capital flows make up the difference.

9.6.6   The United States as a Net Debtor

The U.S. current account at present stands out, even more than by virtue of its absolute magnitude, because a wealthy country is running persistent deficits. Through most of the twentieth century the United States has run current account surpluses, as we have seen. Even in the 1970s, when the two oil shocks raised import spending, the current account was on average equal to zero.

Table 9.14 Gross Fixed Capital Formation as Percentage of GDP

	1965	1966	1967	1968	1969	1970	1971	1972	1973	1974	1975	1976	1977	1978	1979	1980	1981	1982	1983	1984
United States	18.7	18.5	17.9	18.1	18.2	17.6	18.1	18.7	19.16	18.4	17.0	17.1	18.3	19.5	19.8	18.5	17.8	16.5	16.8	17.9
Japan	29.8	30.4	32.0	33.2	34.4	35.5	34.2	34.1	36.4	34.8	32.5	31.2	30.2	30.4	31.7	31.6	30.7	29.7	28.3	27.8
Germany	26.1	25.4	23.1	22.4	23.3	25.5	26.1	25.4	23.9	21.6	20.4	20.1	20.2	20.7	21.8	22.7	21.8	20.5	20.6	20.3
France	23.3	23.7	23.8	23.3	23.4	23.4	23.6	23.7	23.8	24.3	23.3	23.3	22.3	21.4	21.5	21.9	21.4	20.8	19.8	18.9
United Kingdom	18.5	18.5	19.1	19.4	18.9	19.0	18.9	18.7	20.0	20.9	19.9	19.4	18.6	18.5	18.8	18.1	16.4	16.4	16.4	17.4
Italy	19.3	18.8	19.5	20.3	21.0	21.4	20.4	19.8	20.8	22.4	20.6	20.0	19.6	18.7	18.8	19.8	20.2	19.0	17.9	18.2
Canada	23.5	24.5	23.2	21.5	21.4	20.8	21.8	21.7	22.4	23.0	24.0	23.1	22.7	22.2	22.6	22.8	23.5	21.5	19.2	18.1
Total of above countries	20.9	20.8	20.5	20.7	21.1	21.3	21.6	22.1	23.0	23.0	21.0	20.8	21.2	21.9	22.3	21.8	21.1	19.9	19.5	19.9
Austria	27.3	27.8	26.6	25.7	25.1	25.9	27.9	30.2	28.5	28.4	26.7	26.0	26.7	25.6	25.1	25.5	25.2	23.0	22.2	21.8
Belgium	22.4	22.9	22.9	21.5	21.3	22.7	22.1	21.3	21.4	22.7	22.5	22.1	21.7	21.7	20.8	21.2	18.1	17.4	16.4	16.1
Denmark	24.1	24.1	24.2	23.4	24.6	24.7	24.2	24.6	24.8	24.0	21.1	23.0	22.1	21.7	20.9	18.8	15.6	16.1	15.9	17.3
Finland	26.3	26.5	25.1	23.1	23.8	26.3	27.5	27.9	28.8	29.8	31.3	27.9	27.0	24.0	23.2	25.3	25.0	24.9	25.1	23.4
Greece	21.6	21.7	20.3	23.2	24.6	23.6	25.2	27.8	28.0	22.2	20.8	21.2	23.0	23.9	25.8	24.2	22.3	20.2	20.3	18.6
Iceland	27.2	28.5	32.1	32.7	25.7	25.0	30.7	29.2	31.6	33.9	33.2	28.7	27.8	24.8	23.7	25.3	24.8	25.1	22.5	22.2
Ireland	21.4	19.8	20.1	20.9	23.3	22.7	23.6	23.7	25.3	24.6	22.7	25.0	24.8	27.7	30.5	28.6	29.1	25.9	22.7	21.0
Luxembourg	28.0	26.6	23.9	22.1	22.2	23.1	28.4	27.8	27.3	24.5	27.8	24.9	25.1	24.1	24.3	27.0	25.4	25.9	23.7	22.2
Netherlands	25.2	26.3	26.4	26.9	24.6	25.9	25.4	23.6	23.1	21.9	21.1	19.4	21.1	21.3	21.0	21.0	19.2	18.2	18.1	18.4
Norway	28.2	28.7	29.7	26.9	24.3	26.5	29.7	27.7	29.3	30.5	34.2	36.3	37.1	31.8	27.7	24.8	28.0	25.5	24.8	25.6
Portugal	22.8	25.1	26.6	22.2	22.6	23.2	24.7	27.1	26.8	26.0	25.9	25.1	26.5	27.9	26.6	28.6	32.2	32.3	30.3	24.7
Spain	21.7	22.0	22.3	22.8	23.2	23.2	21.2	22.2	23.6	24.7	23.3	21.8	21.0	19.9	18.9	19.4	20.3	19.7	18.8	17.8
Sweden	24.7	24.8	24.8	23.9	23.2	22.5	22.0	22.2	21.9	21.5	20.9	21.2	21.1	19.4	19.8	20.2	19.2	18.8	18.7	18.4

Switzerland	28.7	27.4	26.0	25.6	25.8	27.5	29.2	29.7	29.4	27.6	24.0	20.6	20.7	21.4	21.8	23.8	24.1	23.1	23.3	23.3
Turkey	14.6	15.9	16.4	17.3	17.4	18.6	17.0	20.2	20.1	18.6	20.8	23.1	24.4	21.9	20.8	19.9	19.3	19.1	18.9	18.5
Total smaller European countries	24.0	24.3	24.1	23.7	23.4	24.1	24.2	24.5	24.7	24.3	23.5	22.9	23.1	22.2	21.6	21.8	21.4	20.6	20.2	19.7
Australia	27.7	27.3	26.5	26.9	26.7	26.5	26.9	25.2	24.4	23.8	24.2	24.1	23.8	23.8	23.1	23.9	25.6	24.8	22.3	21.8
New Zealand	21.9	21.9	20.3	18.5	19.6	20.8	20.7	22.5	22.7	25.9	27.0	24.8	22.4	20.8	18.2	18.2	21.2	23.0	22.7	21.5
Total smaller countries	24.4	24.6	24.3	24.0	23.7	24.3	24.5	24.5	24.6	24.3	23.6	23.1	23.2	22.4	21.7	22.0	21.9	21.2	20.5	20.1
Total OECD	21.3	21.3	21.0	21.1	21.5	21.7	22.0	22.4	23.2	22.7	21.5	21.2	21.5	22.0	22.2	21.8	21.3	20.1	19.7	19.9
Four major European countries	22.2	22.0	21.6	21.6	21.9	22.7	22.8	22.5	22.6	22.3	21.1	20.9	20.4	20.2	20.6	21.0	20.1	19.4	18.9	18.9
OECD Europe	22.7	22.7	22.4	22.2	22.3	23.2	23.3	23.1	23.3	23.0	21.9	21.6	21.3	20.9	21.0	21.3	20.5	19.8	19.3	19.2
EEC	22.4	22.3	22.0	22.0	22.2	23.0	22.9	22.7	22.8	22.6	21.4	21.0	20.7	20.5	20.7	21.0	20.1	19.4	18.9	18.7
Total OECD less the United States	23.9	24.0	24.0	24.1	24.5	25.3	25.3	25.3	26.0	25.5	24.2	23.8	23.5	23.4	23.5	23.6	23.4	22.4	21.7	21.6

Source: National Accounts (annual OECD publication); table from OECD *Economic Outlook*, May 1986.

Notes: The data in this table are measured according to the standard definitions of the OECD–United Nations system of accounts (see *A System of National Accounts*, Series F, no. 2, rev. 3, United Nations, 1968). The percentages for each group of countries are calculated from the total GDP and gross fixed capital formation for the group, with both aggregates expressed in U.S. dollars at current exchange rates.

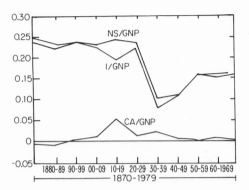

Fig. 9.6   U.S. national saving (private saving plus government budget surplus) (NS), investment (I), and current account (CA) as shares of GNP, 1870–1979. *Sources:* Ransom and Sutch 1983, tables 4 and E1; U.S. Department of Commerce, *Historical Statistics of the United States.*

As the direct implication of the current account surpluses from the 1980s to the 1960s, the United States was accumulating net claims on foreigners. During World War I the country passed from being a net debtor vis-à-vis the rest of the world to being a net creditor. By 1981 the United States had attained a recorded net investment position of $140.7 billion (with 37 percent of the private assets consisting of direct investment and 47 percent consisting of bank-reported claims) (*Economic Report of the President* 1986, 371).

Net interest and other income on this investment position earned $34.1 billion in 1981, more than enough to pay for the deficit in merchandise trade and leave a surplus in goods and services or in the overall current account. But the current account went into deficit in 1982, as we have seen, as a result of the pattern of high U.S. real interest rates, capital inflow from abroad, strong dollar, and U.S. trade deficit. The situation deteriorated rapidly. By 1985 the current account deficit reached $117.7 billion. (Despite the depreciation of the dollar that began in March 1985, the current account deficit in 1986 was in the neighborhood of $140 billion.) It took only three years of current account deficit to undo a century of accumulation of foreign assets. Sometime in early 1985[58] the country on the books returned to net-debtor from net-creditor status, as table 9.15 shows. By the end of 1986 the U.S. recorded position was approximately −$225 billion, a debt far higher than the creditor position was at its peak. Even if the depreciated dollar leads to an improved trade balance by 1988, as it is expected to in line with the customary lags, the United States will probably continue to run substantial trade deficits for quite a few years, and the net debt will continue to mount rapidly.

Even if the 1985–86 depreciation of the dollar soon reduces the trade deficit to a plateau of $100 billion, the net debt position would reach the vicinity of $600 billion by the end of 1989. Simply multiplying by an interest rate would suggest that the annual cost of interest and dividends to investors in other countries would then run on the order of $40 billion to $50 billion. In other words, to eliminate the overall current account deficit in the 1990s would then require not just an elimination of the remaining $100 billion trade deficit, but a reversal to a trade *surplus* of $40 billion to $50 billion in order to earn the money to service the debt that has been incurred in the meantime.

Calculation of the interest and dividend payments is more complicated than this, however, because different assets pay different rates of return and the composition of U.S. overseas assets is different from the composition of U.S. liabilities. Foreign investments in the United States are somewhat more concentrated in Treasury and other bonds (19.3 percent of privately held assets) as opposed to direct investment (21.3 percent) and bank-reported liabilities (41.3 percent). (Corporate stocks are 14.7 percent, and other U.S. liabilities are 3.4 percent.) This is as compared to U.S. investments abroad which are relatively less concentrated in bonds (8.9 percent of private assets) and relatively more in direct investment (28.3 percent) and bank-reported assets (54.4 percent). (Corporate stocks are 5.0 percent, and other U.S. assets are 3.4 percent.) Earnings on direct investment and bank loans tend to be greater than interest earned on bonds; as a result, recorded earnings on U.S. assets abroad still exceed recorded payments on foreign investments in the United States, even a year after its return to net debtor status. In 1986 (first three quarters), the recorded return on all U.S. investments abroad ran at an average 9.7 percent, the payment rate on U.S. liabilities at only 6.5 percent. If this differential holds up, the recorded balance on overseas investment income will decline more slowly than one would otherwise think. But an unprecedented decline will nevertheless take place. Estimates by the Institute of International Economics place the likely 1990 investment income balance in the range of −$15 billion to −$25 billion (Islam 1987).

If the funds borrowed from abroad in the 1980s were being used to finance productive investment in plant and equipment, then the additional output would be available in future decades to service the debt. Unfortunately, as we have seen, the funds have been going to finance the federal budget deficit (or, equivalently, to offset crowding out of private investment). As many less developed debtor countries have discovered over the last five years, military arms or consumer goods do not generate the foreign exchange earnings needed to service the debt incurred when they were earlier purchased.

All of the above figures on the U.S. net indebtedness position are subject to more than the usual amount of measurement error. The two

Table 9.15 **International Investment Position of the United States at Year End, 1984 and 1985 (millions of dollars)**

Line	Type of Investment	Posi-tion 1984^r	Changes in Position in 1985 (decrease [−])					
			Attributable to:					
			Capital Flows (a)	Price Changes (b)	Ex-change^a Rate (c)	Other Changes^b (d) Changes	Total (a + b + c + d)	Position 1985^p
1	Net international investment position of the United States (line 2 less line 20)	4,384	−94,670	−24,335	7,007	174	−111,824	−107,440
2	U.S. assets abroad	898,187	32,436	11,991	8,540	1,212	54,180	952,367
3	U.S. official reserve assets	34,187	3,436	—	4,400	−6	8,252	43,185
4	Gold	11,096	—	—	—	−6^c	−6	11,090
5	Special drawing rights	5,641	897	—	755	—	1,652	7,293
6	Reserve position in the International Monetary Fund	11,541	−908	—	1,314	—	406	11,947
7	Foreign currencies	6,656	3,869	—	2,331	—	6,200	12,856
8	U.S. government assets, other than official reserve assets	84,636	2,824	—	−42	—	2,782	87,418
9	U.S. loans and other long-term assets^d	82,657	2,935	—	−7	2	2,930	85,587
10	Repayable in dollars	80,487	2,961	—	1	2	2,964	83,811
11	Other^e	1,810	−26	—	−8	—	−34	1,776
12	U.S. foreign currency holdings and U.S. short-term assets	1,979	−111	—	−35	−2	−148	1,831
13	U.S. private assets	778,618	25,754	11,991	4,182	1,218	43,146	821,764
14	Direct investment abroad	212,994	18,752	—	—	921	19,673	232,667
15	Foreign securities	89,997	7,977	11,991	4,182	—	24,150	114,147
16	Bonds	62,071	4,018	5,688	1,648	—	11,354	73,425
17	Corporate stocks	27,926	3,959	6,303	2,534	—	12,796	40,722

Source: Survey of Current Business, June 1986.

Notes: r = revised; *p* = preliminary.

*Less than $500,000 (+ or −).

^{a}Represents gains or losses on foreign currency-denominated assets due to their revaluation at current exchange rates.

^{b}Includes changes in coverage, statistical discrepancies, and other adjustments to the value of assets.

^{c}Reflects U.S. Treasury sales of gold medallions and comemorative and bullion coins; these demonetizations are not included in international transactions capital flows.

| | Position by Area | | | | | | Position by Area | | | |
| | Western Europe | | Canada | | Japan | | Latin American Republics and Other Western Hemisphere | | Other Countries, International Organizations and Unallocated | |
	1984	1985	1984	1985	1984	1985	1984	1985	1984	1985
	−150,522	−198,480	56,511	52,926	−19,269	−45,531	78,311	54,048	39,350	29,597
	272,148	316,552	115,006	118,670	48,362	56,288	267,040	266,102	195,630	194,755
	4,119	8,491	*	*	2,037	4,365	500	—	28,277	30,330
	—	—	—	—	—	—	—	—	11,096	11,090
	—	—	—	—	—	—	—	—	5,641	7,293
	—	—	—	—	—	—	—	—	11,541	11,947
	4,119	8,491	*	*	2,037	4,365	500	—	—	—
	10,511	10,179	709	619	443	361	15,510	16,535	57,462	59,723
	10,419	10,036	676	589	425	339	15,154	16,245	55,983	58,377
	10,172	9,815	676	589	425	339	14,730	15,854	54,844	57,213
	247	221	—	—	—	—	424	391	1,139	1,164
	92	143	33	30	18	22	356	290	1,479	1,346
	257,518	297,282	114,297	118,051	45,882	51,562	251,030	249,567	109,891	104,702
	92,017	106,762	46,830	46,435	7,920	9,095	25,229	29,479f	40,998f	40,896
	31,414	50,063	40,662	46,806	3,508	5,383	2,689	2,225	11,724	9,670
	19,667	29,748	29,671	33,297	659	1,532	2,087	1,548	9,987	7,300
	11,747	20,315	10,991	13,509	2,849	3,851	602	677	1,737	2,370

dAlso includes paid-in capital subscriptions to international financial institutions and outstanding amounts of miscellaneous claims that have been settled through international agreements to be payable to the U.S. government over periods in excess of one year. Excludes World War I debts that are not being serviced.

eIncludes indebtedness that the borrower may contractually, or at its option, repay with its currency, with a third country's currency, or by delivery of materials or transfer of services.

fIncludes, as part of international and unallocated, the estimated direct investment in international shipping companies, in operating oil and gas drilling equipment that is moved from country to country during the year, and in petroleum trading companies.

Table 9.15   (continued)

			Changes in Position in 1985 (decrease [−])					
			Attributable to:					
Line	Type of Investment	Position 1984^r	Capital Flows (a)	Price Changes (b)	Exchange^a Rate (c)	Other Changes^b (d) Changes	Total (a+b+ c+d)	Position 1985^p
18	U.S. claims on unaffiliated foreigners reported by U.S. nonbanking concerns	29,996	−1,665	—	—	−111	−1,776	28,220
19	U.S. claims reported by U.S. banks, not included elsewhere	445,631	691	—	—	408	1,099	446,730
20	Foreign assets in the United States	893,803	127,106	36,326	1,533	1,038	166,004	1,059,807
21	Foreign official assets in the U.S.	199,127	−1,324	4,507	—	−2	3,181	202,308
22	U.S. government securities	143,014	−841	1,563	—	—	722	143,736
23	U.S. Treasury securities	135,510	−546	1,072	—	—	526	136,036
24	Other	7,504	−295	491	—	—	196	7,700
25	Other U.S. government liabilities^i	14,798	483	—	—	−1	482	15,280
26	U.S. liabilities reported by U.S. banks	26,090	522	—	—	−1	521	26,611
27	Other foreign official assets	15,225	−1,488	2,944	—	—	1,456	16,681
28	Other foreign assets in the United States	694,676	128,430	31,819	1,533	1,040	162,823	857,499
29	Direct investment in the United States	164,583	17,856	—	—	512	18,368	182,951
30	U.S. Treasury securities	58,330	20,500	5,002	—	—	25,502	83,832
31	U.S. securities other than U.S. Treasury securities	128,560	50,859	26,817	1,533	—	79,210	207,770
32	Corporate and other bonds	32,724	46,004	1,569	1,533	—	49,107	81,831
33	Corporate stocks	95,836	4,855	25,248	—	—	30,103	125,939
34	U.S. liabilities to unaffiliated foreigners reported by U.S. nonbanking concerns	31,024	−1,172	—	—	−750	−1,922	29,102
35	U.S. liabilities reported by U.S. banks	312,179	40,387	—	—	1,278	41,665	353,844

^{g}Details not shown separately are included in totals in lines 21 and 28.

^{h}Details not shown separately are included in line 20.

| Position by Area | | | | | | | | | |
| Western Europe | | Canada | | Japan | | Latin American Republics and Other Western Hemisphere | | Other Countries, International Organizations and Unallocated | |
1984	1985	1984	1985	1984	1985	1984	1985	1984	1985
9,479	9,796	5,158	4,429	1,544	1,491	10,237	9,457	3,578	3,047
124,608	131,261	21,647	20,381	32,910	35,593	212,875	208,406	53,591	51,089
422,670	515,032	58,485	65,744	101,819	188,729	188,729	212,054	156,280	165,158
72,322	77,862	1,686	1,473	h	h	9,359	11,781	h	h
g	g	g	g	h	h	g	g	h	h
g	g	g	g	h	h	g	g	h	h
g	g	g	g	h	h	g	g	h	h
2,684	3,098	157	156	1,564	1,361	908	766	9,487	9,899
g	g	g	g	h	h	g	g	h	h
g	g	g	g	h	h	g	g	h	h
350,348	437,170	56,809	64,271	h	h	179,370	200,273	h	h
108,211	120,906	15,286	16,678	16,044	19,116	16,201	17,050	8,841	9,201
g	g	g	g	h	h	g	g	h	h
89,519	150,117	19,718	25,317	4,193	10,542	8,107	12,314	7,023	9,480
25,585	67,453	1,290	1,579	2,910	8,628	1,236	1,826	1,703	2,345
63,934	82,664	18,428	23,738	1,283	1,914	6,871	10,488	5,320	7,135
11,412	11,986	3,022	2,388	2,475	2,969	7,190	4,654	6,925	7,105
g	g	g	g	h	h	g	g	h	h

[i]Primarily included U.S. government liabilities associated with military sales contracts and other transactions arranged with or through foreign official agencies.

major sources of error go in opposite directions. On the one hand, if most of the statistical discrepancy in the balance of payments, which has run at roughly $25 billion a year from 1979 to 1986, is unreported capital inflows, then the true net indebtedness is *worse* by some $200 billion.[59] On the other hand, some of the foreign assets acquired in the past, particularly direct investment, have undergone increases in value that are not reflected in the figures, suggesting that the true position may be better than recorded. It seems likely that the first effect is at least as important as the second. The Federal Reserve Board estimates that the country may have become a net debtor in 1983 rather than 1985, with net indebtedness reaching $235 billion in 1985.[60] In any case, the sheer magnitude of the current account deficits guarantees that the net indebtedness position is deteriorating very rapidly.

9.7   Conclusion

Massive U.S. borrowing from the rest of the world in the 1980s is the result of massive borrowing by the U.S. government. By 1980, the U.S. government had accumulated a debt of $914 billion over two centuries. This debt precisely doubled by 1985 and is estimated to have reached $2,130 billion by the end of 1986 (*Economic Indicators,* October 1986). The role of foreigners in financing the U.S. budget deficit is dramatized by the fact that foreign ownership of Treasury securities is rising rapidly; recorded private holdings stood at $84 billion as of the end of 1985, and official holdings at $136 billion. But from an economic viewpoint, it is immaterial whether foreign residents buy U.S. government debt directly or whether they lend the money to private U.S. residents who use it to buy government debt.

The big increase in government borrowing after 1980 was not on the whole accommodated by monetary policy. While the total federal debt doubled, the debt held by the Federal Reserve went up by somewhat less and consequently the debt held by the public went up somewhat more. The borrowing drove up real interest rates in the United States, attracting capital inflows from all parts of the world and in all forms. This capital inflow has been made easier by reduced taxes and controls on international capital movements and a general trend of liberalization and innovation. The favorable aspect of the inflow is that by helping to finance the federal deficit it has kept U.S. real interest rates lower than they would otherwise be. The unfavorable aspect is that the counterpart to the record capital account surpluses is the record trade and current account deficits.[61]

The widespread feeling is that these imbalances are unsustainable. The U.S. trade deficit may be politically unsustainable, in the sense that congressmen will be pushed, by those of their constitutents that suffer from the international competition, into enacting protectionist barriers. This would be very costly for both the country as a whole and the world trading system as a whole.

It is also possible that the borrowing from abroad is unsustainable in the sense that at some point foreigners will tire of accepting ever-larger quantities of U.S. assets into their portfolios. The consequence then could be a sharp fall in the value of the dollar combined with a sharp increase in U.S. interest rates. For the dollar by itself to accomplish enough trade improvement to return the country to current account equilibrium, the depreciation would have to be considerably larger than what we have already seen in 1985 and 1986.

The unpleasant alternative is that the same improvement in the trade balance would at some point instead be accomplished by a recession, reducing imports. The large stock of debt already outstanding means that U.S. policy-making will from now on find itself much more restricted in its ability to respond to adverse developments. Because the federal deficit is already large despite four years of economic expansion, the government will not be able to respond to any future recession by reducing taxes or raising expenditure. Still less will the Federal Reserve be able to respond to a recession by lowering interest rates, if the source of the recession is a reduction in the willingness of foreign investors to keep supplying the United States with capital. Indeed, the outstanding debt to foreigners means that a likely scenario is the one in which investors' fears that the United States will have difficulty maintaining the future value of those assets will cause the depreciation of the dollar to accelerate and interest rates to rise. In such a scenario the Federal Reserve would be reluctant to expand monetary policy because that might further enhance fears of inflation and dollar depreciation. At that point there might be no alternative to a combination of sharply higher interest rates and recession in order to reduce imports and restore the confidence of financial markets. This position, a familiar one to many debtors, would be a new one for Americans.

As of the beginning of 1987, the financial markets are still absorbing the imbalances with little difficulty. The decline of the dollar has been a "soft landing" rather than a "hard landing" in the sense that interest rates have come down since 1984 rather than gone up. This is probably because the dollar depreciation has been the result of a combination of (1) easier monetary policy, (2) perceptions of reduced future budget deficits under the Gramm-Rudman legislation, and (3) a confidence-inspiring process of consultation and coordination between U.S. and other authorities, most dramatically represented by the September 1985 Plaza Accord. The federal budget deficit will decline somewhat in 1987, and probably the trade deficit soon thereafter. But the policies now in place imply continued massive federal deficits, and as a result continued capital inflows and trade deficits, into the indefinite future.

Notes

The author would like to thank Morgan Guaranty, *The Economist Financial Report*, and the Japan Center for International Finance for data; Dan Dorrow, Ken Froot, David Hicks, and Alan MacArthur for some calculations; and Martin Feldstein, Peter Kenen, Richard Levich, and Alan MacArthur for many valuable comments on an earlier draft. Views expressed are those of the author.

1. In table 9.1, the private capital outflow is measured as increases in U.S. "private assets abroad" (which appear with negative signs because they are accounting debits) less increases in other foreign assets in the United States (which appear with positive signs because they are accounting credits).

2. Under the floating exchange rate system, an investor's increase in demand for dollar assets can take the form of an increase in the exchange value of the dollar and does not need to show up as an actual inflow of capital.

3. This figure is arrived at by assuming that the statistical discrepancy represents primarily unreported capital flows.

4. If the statistical discrepancy is interpreted as unrecorded private capital inflows, then the true private capital account was approximately in balance in 1979–80 (a surplus in 1979 for the first time in decades, and a deficit in 1980). The recorded private capital account continued to show a deficit in 1979 and for several years thereafter.

5. See Levich 1985 for a survey of empirical evidence on efficiency in international financial markets.

6. See Levich in this volume, chap. 4, for elaboration on such innovations.

7. Press release, August 20, 1986. The figures have been adjusted to eliminated double counting of transactions between institutions.

8. Press release, Bank of England, August 20, 1986. Tokyo was counted as $48 billion, other Pacific centers have been estimated at $30 billion, and Zurich and Frankfurt together have been estimated as big as New York.

9. The calculation is the average of the bid-ask spread as a percentage of the rate, quoted at 3:00 P.M. daily by Barclay's Bank in London. A Bank of Canada study shows the pound ahead of the mark and yen in bid-ask spreads for 1973–81 (Longworth, Boothe and Clinton 1983, 63).

10. In the London foreign exchange market, the ranking by volume is pound, mark, yen, Swiss franc, French franc, lira, and Canadian dollar. (The sources on 1986 trading volume are the press releases cited above.)

11. Frankel 1984 reports figures on how much of Japanese trade is invoiced in yen. Table 9.11 in this chapter gives the figures for shares of dollars, yen, and other currencies in the foreign exchange reserve holdings of central banks.

12. For a description of Germany's controls, see Dooley and Isard 1980.

13. January 1975–April 1979. The variance of the differential was 3.29. The source is Frankel 1984, 23.

14. The mean differential was 0.26 and the variance 0.22 for the period May 1979 to November 1983 (Frankel 1984).

15. Also, the rate of increase in long-term liabilities abroad fell from $14.759 billion to $7.124 billion. The source is the Bank of Japan, *Balance of Payments Monthly*, as reported in the OECD *Economic Survey* on Japan, August 1985, p. 21.

16. Eurodollar rate, covered, relative to yen gensaki (Ito 1986, 240).

17. Morgan Guaranty, *World Financial Markets*, September 1986.

18. When there is a large and variable differential (even with the offshore interest rate measured in domestic currency) it means that barriers must exist, in the form of either capital controls or the sort of political risk discussed

below. Although there is no surefire way of telling which sort of barrier is operating just by looking at the interest rates, there is a useful rule of thumb. When a country is seen to experience an increase in perceived riskiness, due to high budget or balance of payments deficits or political instability, if the offshore rate rises relative to the onshore rate it signifies that controls are preventing the free outflow of capital; if the onshore rate rises relative to the offshore rate, it signifies that political risk is scaring off investors and so a higher return is needed to clear the market.

19. U.S. corporations issue bearer bonds in the Euromarket. In October 1984, the U.S. government began to do the same, in the form of "specially targeted Treasury notes." The premium that investors were willing to pay to hold these securities, relative to regular registered Treasury notes, fluctuated from around forty basis points to zero, apparently as foreign perceptions fluctuated as to how onerous was a requirement that bond dealers certify that the beneficial owners are not U.S. citizens or residents (Merrill Lynch 1985, 14).

20. However, IBFs remain subject to several important restrictions that do not apply to Eurobanking (Chrystal 1984, 6).

21. One (intended) result of the abolition of the U.S. withholding tax was the demise of large-scale Eurobond issues by U.S. corporations through subsidiaries in the Netherlands Antilles to avoid the tax. This corporate borrowing, which previously showed up in the balance of payments accounts as reductions in U.S. direct investment claims on foreigners, now takes its true form—foreign purchases of U.S. securities.

22. Interestingly, U.S. Treasury securities issued in the Euromarket often must pay a higher yield than Eurobonds issued by top-rated U.S. corporations, suggesting some perceived default risk (Gonzales 1985, table 14).

23. Golub (1986, 8a) estimates that net borrowing in dollars by eighteen OECD governments alone rose from $2.619 billion in 1972 to a peak of $25.852 billion in 1982. Dollar borrowing by developing countries was much greater, at least until recent years.

24. The recorded capital inflow (change in foreign assets in the United States less U.S. assets abroad, not counting official reserve assets) did not turn positive until 1983 and climbed to $99.852 billion in 1985. Most of the statistical discrepancy is thought to be unrecorded capital inflows, hence the higher capital inflow numbers in the text. But some fraction of the discrepancy is probably unreported service exports, particularly interest earnings, so the capital inflow numbers in the text may be a little overstated.

25. The subsequent discussion draws on Isard and Stekler 1985.

26. The borrowing via Netherlands Antilles subsidiaries was reversed, following the abolition in 1984 of the U.S. withholding tax; in 1985, U.S. corporations began retiring the past debt issued through the subsidiaries.

27. The source is the *Survey of Current Business,* e.g., table 1, p. 35, and table 8, p. 50, in the March 1985 issue. Isard and Stekler (1985, 222–23) admit that decisions on how to adjust the data are necessarily somewhat arbitrary.

28. The U.S. figures are from *Survey of Current Business,* June 1986, table 10, p. 65. The Japanese figures are from the Japan Center for International Finance.

29. *Survey of Current Business,* June 1986, table 3, p. 31.

30. For more on foreign direct investment, see Lipsey in this volume, chap. 8.

31. *Federal Reserve Bulletin,* May 1985, p. 279.

32. Ibid., and *Federal Reserve Bulletin,* May 1986, p. 295.

33. Ibid.

34. *Federal Reserve Bulletin,* table 3.15, August 1982 and June 1986. More than 100 percent of this decline in dollar holdings occurred in 1981. Liabilities

to foreign official institutions actually rose from then until 1985. However this rise in dollar holdings can be completely accounted for by interest earnings.

35. *IMF Annual Report,* 1986, table 1.3, p. 61.

36. Central banks make the decision to trade their own currencies for foreign reserve currencies on the basis of macroeconomic considerations. But the decision how to allocate a given portfolio of foreign currency reserves is influenced by expected returns on the various currencies. Admittedly the distinction can be blurred because some countries habitually do their foreign exchange intervention in dollars, perhaps for the sake of convenience. The argument that central bank portfolio behavior is destabilizing is due to Bergsten and Williamson, forthcoming.

37. The argument that official reserve transactions should be classified together with the private capital account validates the decision made by the Department of Commerce ten years ago to cease reporting the "official settlements balance" in the balance of payments statistics, to force readers to look at the trade or current account balances in its place. See Stern 1977. Table 9.9 here compromises, by reporting some net balances within the capital account, both private and official.

38. Kidwell, Marr, and Trimble (1986) document this differential in more detail. But it is possible that the apparent differential is simply due to different composition of the corporations issuing the bonds in the two markets. Maharajan and Fraser (1986), by examining ninety-two pairs of bond offerings that are closely matched with respect to corporate parent, rating, maturity, and other characteristics between 1975 and 1983, test the widespread perception that U.S. corporations can borrow more cheaply in the Euromarket than at home. They find, to the contrary, no differential.

39. For the periods 1980–81 and 1983–84, increases in the interest differentials do not support the safe haven explanation of the dollar appreciation. Similarly, the period when the differentials resumed their decline, 1985–86, is the period when the dollar was finally depreciating, not continuing to appreciate as one would expect under the safe haven hypothesis. Even in 1982, the one year in which movement in the long-term interest differential supports the hypothesis, the evidence from short-term differentials goes the other way, as we saw in section 9.3.

40. The United Kingdom, France, Germany, Italy, Canada, and Japan. The interest rates are yields on government bonds, in their own currencies, with maturities ranging from ten years or more for Japan and Canada to twenty years for the United States and Canada. The weights are moving averages of GNP shares. The source is the International Monetary Fund.

41. Morgan Guaranty's index. The weights are based on 1980 U.S. bilateral trade in manufactures, and the price levels are wholesale prices of nonfood manufactures.

42. The three statistics are simple averages of dollar depreciation against other currencies: the mark, yen, pound, French franc, and Swiss franc in the case of the American Express and *Economist* surveys, and the first four currencies in the case of the Money Market Services survey. For further description and analysis of the survey data, see Frankel and Froot 1986.

43. If arbitrage equates the nominal interest differential to investors' expected nominal depreciation, then the real interest differential will equal expected real depreciation.

44. The peak real interest differential by this measure was 4.2 percent. The expected inflation rates in the figure are calculated by the International Monetary Fund from distributed lags on actual inflation rates.

45. The interest rates are on ten-year bonds from Morgan Guaranty. The trading partners are the United Kingdom, France, Germany, and Japan, weighted by GNP shares. Following the logic of note 43, one might infer from a 1984 ten-year real interest differential of 3 percent that investors must have expected the dollar to depreciate in real terms over the next ten years at an average rate of 3 percent a year, or approximately 30 percent cumulatively. If ten years is thought to be a long enough time to guarantee a return to long-run equilibrium, this rough calculation suggests that in 1984 the market considered the dollar to be about 30 percent above its equilibrium. (Note that investors do not respond directly to real interest differentials, but rather to nominal interest differentials and expected exchange rate changes; Frankel 1986.)

46. Now owned by Morgan Stanley.

47. The average of the four end-of-quarter figures (Frankel 1986, table 2-1).

48. Such bandwagon expectations are supported by survey data at horizons of one week to one month, shorter-term than the survey data shown in figure 9.3c.

49. *Economic Indicators,* September 1986. The Federal Reserve Bank of St. Louis, September 12, 1986, reports 9.9 percent at a compounded annual rate of change.

50. The identity is that investment is equal to national saving plus the net capital inflow from abroad.

51. In this framework, how would we interpret an increase in real interest rates caused by a monetary contraction as in 1980–82? One could think of it as a fall in the private saving rate associated with the recession.

52. Reductions in personal income taxes were more important to the supply-siders in the Reagan camp than the corporate investment tax incentives.

53. Investment net of depreciation shows more of a decline after 1980 than gross investment because the capital consumption allowance is higher in the 1980s than in the 1970s.

54. Bosworth 1985. Feldstein (1986) finds no evidence of an effect of changes in corporate tax rates and investment incentives on interest rates. He estimates that the increase in projected budget deficits was responsible for about two-thirds of the rise in interest rates between 1977–78 and 1983–84.

55. An upward shift in firms' desire to invest could lead to an increase in real interest rates, without an increase in the *quantity* of investment actually undertaken, if the sources of saving available to finance investment were completely unresponsive to interest rates. But even if domestic U.S. saving, both private and public, is indeed unresponsive to interest rates, the available supply of *foreign* saving is to the contrary highly responsive to the U.S. interest rate. Thus the failure of the observed investment rate to rise in the 1980s is valid evidence against the claim that enhanced investment incentives can alone explain the increase in the U.S. interest rate and the capital inflow.

56. U.S. Department of Commerce, British Central Statistical Office, West German Bundesbank, and Japanese Economic Planning Agency.

57. Changes in private or public saving also tend to affect the level of income, when the economy is operating at less than full employment. To focus on the relationship among saving, investment, and overseas borrowing as percentages of aggregate income, it helps to think of monetary policy in the background, holding income constant. It is, in fact, not unrealistic to think of the Federal Reserve as having targeted nominal GNP in recent years.

58. The 1982–84 figures were revised in 1985 to incorporate the results of a 1982 benchmark survey of U.S. direct investment abroad. On the revised figures, the United States passed into net-debtor status in January 1985.

59. The uncertainties are particularly large vis-à-vis Latin America. Much capital flight to the United States is unreported. Furthermore, one might not wish to count the loans of U.S. banks to troubled debtors at full value as they now appear on the books. A 50 percent write-down, for example, would wipe out over $100 billion of claims on Latin America alone.

60. *Federal Reserve Bulletin,* May 1986, p. 294. A separate point is that a precise definition of the term *net debtor* would include only loans and bonds, excluding corporate stock and direct investment. See Van der Ven and Wilson 1986, 11. However, investment income has to be paid to foreign residents not just in the form of interest on the debt, but equally in the form of dividends and repatriated earnings on the rest.

61. From the viewpoint of other countries, the favorable aspect of the capital flow is their trade *surpluses* vis-à-vis the United States, and the unfavorable aspect is that their real interest rates are *higher* than they would otherwise be. Both points are particularly relevant for troubled debtors who must compete with the United States for funds.

References

Bergsten, C. Fred, and John Williamson. Forthcoming. *The multiple reserve currency system.* Institute for International Economics, Washington, D.C.

Bosworth, Barry. 1985. Taxes and the investment recovery. *Brookings Papers on Economic Activity* 1:1–45.

Chrystal, D. Alec. 1984. International banking facilities. Federal Reserve Bank of St. Louis. *Review* (April): 5–11.

Cooper, Richard. 1986. The United States as an open economy. In R. Hafer, ed., *How open is the U.S. economy?*, 3–24. Lexington, Mass.: D. C. Heath.

Dooley, Michael, and Peter Isard. 1980. Capital controls, political risk and deviations from interest-rate parity. *Journal of Political Economy* 88 (April): 370–84.

Edwards, Sebastian. 1986. Country risk and developing countries' foreign borrowing: An empirical analysis of the bank loan and bond markets. *European Economic Review.*

Feldstein, Martin. 1986. Budget deficits, tax rules, and real interest rules. NBER Working Paper No. 1970. July.

Folkerts-Landau, David. 1985. The changing role of international bank lending in development finance. IMF *Staff Papers* 32 (June): 317–63.

Frankel, Jeffrey. 1984. *The Yen/Dollar Agreement: Liberalizing Japanese capital markets.* Institute for International Economics Policy Analyses in International Economics, no. 9. Cambridge, Mass.: MIT Press.

———. 1986. International capital mobility and crowding-out in the U.S. economy: Imperfect integration of financial markets or of goods markets? In R. Hafer, ed., *How open is the U.S. economy?*, 33–68. Lexington, Mass.: D. C. Heath.

Frankel, Jeffrey, and Kenneth Froot. 1986. Using survey data to test standard propositions regarding exchange rate expectations. *American Economic Review* 77 (March): 133–53.

Friedman, Benjamin. 1986. Implications of the U.S. net capital inflow. In R. Hafer, ed., *How open is the U.S. economy?*, 137–62. Lexington, Mass.: D. C. Heath.

Giordano, Robert. 1986. Myth and reality of Japanese influence on the U.S. Treasury securities market. *Economic Research,* September/October.

Golub, Stephen. 1986. Foreign-currency government debt, asset-market equilibrium and balance-of-payments equilibrium. Swarthmore College. September.

Gonzales, Ernesto. 1985. The international dollar bond market. Applied Business Project, New York University. May.

Isard, Peter, and Lois Stekler. 1985. U.S. international capital flows and the dollar. *Brookings Papers on Economic Activity* 1:219–36.

Islam, Shafiqul. 1987. America's foreign debt: Is the debt crisis moving north? Institute for International Economics, Washington, D.C. February.

Ito, Takatoshi. 1986. Capital controls and covered interest parity between the yen and the dollar. *Economic Studies Quarterly* 37 (September): 223–41.

Kidwell, David, M. Wayne Marr, and John Trimble. 1986. Domestic versus Euromarket bond sales: A case of issuing arbitrage. Tulane University. August.

Levich, Richard. 1985. Empirical studies of exchange rates: Price behavior, rate determination and market efficiency. In R. Jones and P. Kenen, eds., *Handbook of international economics,* 2:979–1040. Amsterdam: Elsevier Science Publishers.

Longworth, David, Paul Boothe, and Kevin Clinton. 1983. *A study of the efficiency of foreign exchange markets.* Ottawa: Bank of Canada.

Maharajan, Arvind, and Donald Fraser. 1986. Dollar eurobonds and U.S. bond pricing. *Journal of International Business Studies* (Summer): 21–36.

Merrill Lynch. 1985. Specially targeted treasury notes revisited. *International Fixed Income Strategy* 1 (May 28): 14.

Ransom, Roger, and Richard Sutch. 1983. Domestic saving as an active constraint on capital formation in the American economy, 1839–1928: A provisional theory. University of California Project on the History of Saving, working paper no. 1. University of California, Berkeley.

Stern, Robert. 1977. The presentation of U.S. balance of payments: A symposium. Princeton Essays in International Finance, no. 123.

Van der Ven, Guido, and John Wilson. 1986. The United States international asset and liability position: A comparison of flow of funds and Commerce Department presentations. International Finance Discussion Papers, no. 295. Washington, D.C.: Federal Reserve Board.

2. *Saburo Okita*
Domestic Economic Policy and International Capital Flows

In the twenty years from 1961 through 1980, Japan's international balance of payments current account was in the red about as many years as it was in the black—eight years in the red and twelve in the black. Our trade statistics were in the red for eleven yers and in the black for nine. Yet since the early 1970s, the tendency has been for the current account balance to run consistently in the black, as pointed out by Hendrik Houthakker, then a member of the President's Council of

Economic Advisers. Nevertheless, the oil crises of 1973 and 1979 sharply increased Japan's oil import bill and broke the string of consecutive surplus years. Since then, the Japanese economy has recovered from the oil crises and, with the help of the recent slippage in oil prices, recorded annually increasing surpluses in its current account. Still, surpluses are a very new situation for Japan, and one that we are unaccustomed to dealing with.

In 1981, Japan's current account surplus was $4.8 billion. In 1985, this had risen tenfold to $49.2 billion, and in 1986 it was $86.0 billion. United States economic policy must be cited as one of the causes of this surplus. Whereas the United States achieved a real economic growth rate of 6.5 percent in 1984 through running massive fiscal deficits and spurring domestic consumption, the combination of this stimulative policy and a policy of maintaining the dollar's exchange strength meant that the United States drew increasing imports from Japan and the rest of the world.

On the other side of the Pacific, the Japanese savings rate has been high for a long time, approximately 20 percent of personal disposable income going to savings for many years now. In the period of rapid growth from 1960 through the early 1970s, this high Japanese savings rate was absorbed by an equally high rate of investment, and the balance between savings and investment was maintained. Yet in the early 1970s, notably in the wake of the 1973 oil crisis, the Japanese economic growth rate fell from 10 percent to only 5 percent on average for the 1970s and 3 percent to 4 percent in recent years, while the savings rate showed little if any decline, with the result that Japan has run chronic savings surpluses.

Going into the 1980s, this savings surplus contributed to a sharp increase in the outflow of capital from Japan, and Japan has been the world's largest capital-exporting nation since 1985. According to Bank of International Settlements statistics, the total overseas assets of Japanese banks were $1,019.4 billion as of the end of September 1986, easily outpacing the United States, the United Kingdom, and West Germany to account for 31.5 percent of the balance outstanding in international financial markets.

Anticipating this, *The Economist* published an article titled "A New Japan" on October 13, 1983, saying that "the third western muddle over Japan's current-account surplus is mirrored in a deficit on the capital account, which means that more Japanese savings are being invested abroad than foreigners are investing in Japan. Excellent. The second biggest capitalist economy ought to be a capital exporter. Since countries first learned how to help each other grow, the rich have been lending to the poor. Nineteenth-century Britain ran a huge current surplus every year, had nil inflation (indeed, a 10 percent fall in retail prices over the period 1860–1913), and thus invested at cheap interest rates in backward places like California and Canada.''

The United States was also an important capital-exporting nation from the end of World War II until recently. Such programs as the postwar Marshall Plan (the European Recovery Plan) and capital exports to countries throughout the world were a major pillar of support for global economic development after the war. Although Japan's current account surplus is expected to decline with the yen's appreciation since early 1985, the high Japanese savings rate and the decline in domestic investment opportunities suggest that Japan will continue to be a major capital exporting nation for some time to come.

Japanese domestic economic policy since the war has been one of promoting recovery and economic growth. In 1960, a plan for doubling national income was drafted, with myself directly responsible as head of the Planning Bureau in the Economic Planning Agency. We proposed five main tenets underlying this plan. As MIT's Lester Thurow wrote on this plan in 1982 in the proceedings of a symposium, The Management Challenge: Japan's Views, convened to assess Japan's postwar economic performance, ''Consider the five elements in the Japanese economic strategy at the beginning of the income-doubling decade: strengthen social overhead capital, push growth industries, promote exports, develop human ability and technology, and secure social stability by mitigating the dual structure of the economy. This list could easily serve as strategic objectives for the American economy by the year 2000.''

On the fourth objective, that of developing our human resources and promoting science and technology, the Ministry of Education initiated a project to sharply expand technological education in Japan in line with this income-doubling plan. In the past, plans for upgrading the industrial structure had focused on promoting heavy industry. In steel, for example, crude steel production went from 22 million tons in 1960 to 118 million tons in 1973. Yet with the oil crisis, there was a shift to energy conservation, and the Japanese industrial structure shifted from one centered on heavy industry to one centered on science and technology, with particular emphasis on electronics and other precision industries. In Japan, this is termed the shift from ju-ko-cho-dai (heavy, thick, long, and big) to kei-haku-tan-sho (light, thin, short, and small). Looking again at steel production, output was down to 98 million tons in 1986 and is still declining with the yen's appreciation.

Fiscal policy has also undergone a change. Until the early 1970s, policy was to keep the budget balanced. Yet with the 1973 oil crisis, the Japanese economy recorded its first negative growth since the war. Prime Minister Fukuda's administration responded by issuing deficit-financing national bonds to avert a recession. Since then, the fiscal deficit grew steadily, reaching one-third of general budget expenditures in 1977. Alarmed at this trend, the Japanese government turned to budget austerity, and the belt-tightening efforts have brought the general budget's dependency on deficit financing down to 21.4 percent in 1986. While the fiscal policy of deficit spending did serve to alleviate the domestic economic impact of the oil crises, it also burdened the nation with massive debt service payments. As of the end of March 1986, the ratio of national bonds outstanding to GNP was 41.9 percent, and national debt service has topped 20 percent of general account expenditures for 1986.

On monetary policy, the emphasis has been on holding interest rates down, in part because of the potential exchange rate impact of capital flow responding to interest rate differentials, with the result that the official discount rate has been lowered several times in recent years. The latest cut, on February 23, 1987, has brought it down to a record low 2.5 percent.

Looking at recent trade trends, Japan recorded a $86.0 billion current account surplus and a $92.7 billion trade surplus, and had a net long-term capital outflow of $131.8 billion in 1986, despite the yen's rapid appreciation against the dollar. Most of these increases were due to the fall in oil prices and the J-curve effect as the yen appreciated. While dollar-denominated exports were up 19.1 percent over the previous year, yen-denominated exports were down 15.9 percent and export volume was down 1.2 percent. There has not only been a drop in the value of exports with all of the deflationary consequences that entails; there has even been a decline in export volume. On the import side, imports were down 2.3 percent in dollar-denominated terms and down 30.6 percent in yen-denominated terms but up 12.5 percent in volume terms. These figures are largely explained by the fact that the collapse in oil prices has resulted in a savings of over $30 billion in Japan's oil import bill.

According to U.S. statistics, the United States' trade deficit with Japan went from $49.7 billion in 1985 to $58.6 billion in 1986. Yet during the same period, the United States' global trade deficit went from $148.5 billion in 1985 to $169.8 billion in 1986, the deficit with Japan continuing to account for approximately one-third of the total. In the bilateral trade between Japan and the United States, even as total U.S. exports were declining from $233.7 billion in 1981 to $217.3 billion in 1986, exports to Japan rose from $21.8 billion in 1981 to $26.9 billion in 1986. Likewise, the ratio of manufactures to Japan's total imports from the United States also rose, from 45.3 percent in 1981 to 60.7 percent in 1986. During the same period, manufactures' share of total Japanese imports rose from 24.3 percent in 1981 to 41.7 percent in 1986. It would thus appear that there is a very good chance that the impact of currency exchange rate adjustments will result in shrinking both Japan's surplus in its trade with the United States and its overall current account surplus in 1987 and beyond. Government estimates predict an $11 billion smaller current account surplus in fiscal 1987.

The Maekawa report (formerly the Report of the Advisory Group on Economic Structural Adjustment for International Harmony) of April 1986 argued that Japan needs to restructure its economy from growth dependent on external demand to growth dependent on domestic demand. Already the estimate for fiscal 1986 (the year ending March 31, 1987) is for real economic growth of 3.0 percent, of which domestic demand is expected to contribute 4.2 percent and net exports minus 1.3 percent. In the forecast for fiscal 1987 too, the prospects are for 3.5 percent real growth, with domestic demand contributing 4.0 percent and exports minus 0.5 percent. The Japanese economy is clearly shifting to growth powered by domestic demand rather than by exports. Among the factors contributing to this shift are the fact that fiscal policy has made an effort to expand public works, including those by local governments and those under the government's fiscal investment and loan program, and the fact that lower interest rates have stimulated housing investment and capital investment in the nonmanufacturing sector.

Even with all the best efforts that can be made to promote imports and to spur domestic demand, however, Japan will continue to record substantial current account surpluses for some years to come. And while currency exchange rate adjustments are important, there is a limit, economically and politically, to what they can achieve. According to the *Nihon Keizai Shinbun*'s world economic model, Japan's net overseas assets will top $1 trillion by 1997, while the United States' accumulated debt will also approach the $1 trillion mark. As David Hale summarized in the December 5, 1986, *Times* of London, "The U.S. is a debtor nation with the habits of a creditor nation: Germany and Japan are creditor nations with the habits of debtor nations."

The questions for the future of the Japan–United States relationship are therefore what political and economic impact these economic imbalances and outdated perceptions will have on the relationship and whether or not there might be some poliical means of braking the imbalance before it gets out of hand. One question here is whether the U.S. effort to turn its trade deficit into a surplus as described by Martin Feldstein should depend solely on exchange rate adjustments or whether more direct quantitative controls over imports, such as voluntary export restraints or import quotas, for example, should be used alongside these exchange rate adjustments.

As seen, there is a very strong likelihood that Japan will continue to be a major capital exporter. The United States, formerly a major source of development capital, is now a major debtor nation, a black hole draining savings from Japan, Europe, and the rest of the world. If we leave the flow of capital to laissez-faire market mechanisms, the bulk of the capital will be drawn to the United States in search of investment security and high interest rates. Conscious policy measures, including risk insurance and interest subsidies to offset the low-interest and long-term nature of the return, are needed if we are to divert at least some of this capital flow to the developing countries. Responding to this need, the World Institute for Development Economics Research (WIDER), established in Helsinki under the auspices of the United Nations University, released a report in April 1986 titled "The Potential of the Japanese Surplus for World Economic Development" and drawn up by WIDER director Lal Jayawardena, WIDER adviser on international economic issues and IMF executive director Arjun Sengupta, and myself as chairman of the WIDER governing board. Subsequently, I sought to give these ideas wider currency with a July 2 contribution to the *Nihon Keizai Shinbun* titled "Using Its Surpluses to Advantage: A Proposal for Enhancing Japanese and World Security." The thrust of this proposal is that "given (i) the imperative that Japan find ways to utilize its high savings rate and massive trade surplus effectively for Japanese and world economic development and (ii) the fact that a serious effort by the United States to reduce its fiscal and trade deficits would have a deflationary impact on the world economy, the author proposes that Japan use its surplus one third each for stimulating domestic demand, providing development capital for the developing countries, and supplying capital to the United States and the other industrialized countries."

In November, as follow-up to this first WIDER report, a second report was released simultaneously in Tokyo and London titled "Japan Urged to Lead in Tackling International Economic Problems."

Among the main problems facing the world economy today are the major current account surpluses in Japan and West Germany, the twin fiscal and trade deficits in the United States, the developing countries' external indebtedness, and stagnating commodity prices. Although there are a number of issues outstanding among and between the United States, Europe, and Japan, these should be solved not only with bilateral negotiations but with active policies to revitalize the world economy, including the developing countries. These issues are all interrelated. For example, one of the causes of the United States' trade deficit is that the Latin American countries, long a major market for the United States, have had to cut back on imports because of their burgeoning debts. Most of the countries of Asia, with a few notable exceptions such as the Republic of Korea and Taiwan, are finding it very hard going in the face of slow growth in the industrial countries, protectionism, and lackluster commodity prices.

It is to be hoped that these problems will be solved with the emphasis on growth. In so doing, it may be necessary for Japan to formulate its own "Marshall Plan" for the developing countries. One problem here is that the surpluses are entirely in the hands of the private sector. The government of Japan is moving to recycle its current account surplus to the developing countries with subscriptions to the Asian Development Bank, the IMF, the World Bank, and the IDA, but these efforts should be stepped up. Although the present state of Japanese government finances does not leave much leeway for increased expenditures on top of its plan to double official development assistance (ODA) in the seven years 1987 through 1993, there is growing support in Japan for having the government provide incentives to encourage the outflow of private sector capital to the developing countries.

There must be a global approach to these issues, and it must include effective utilization of our financial resources and the full mobilization of our intellectual resources. One first step might be for the World Bank, for example, to take the initiative in appointing a World Commission for the Revitalization of the World Economy to write a prescription for world growth. Another possibility is for the group of economists to look into the impact on the global economy of U.S. adjustments for turning the trade deficit into a surplus as prescribed by Feldstein and to make the necessary policy recommendations. The urgency of the issue allows no delay. It is imperative that we act today to fend off a tomorrow of bilateral protectionism, spreading recession, and impoverishment for all.

3. Peter G. Peterson
Deficit, Debt, and Demographics: Some International Aspects

Let me go back to August 15, 1971, when a bunch of us were out at Camp David closing the gold window, among other things. The view of exchange rates at that time as I look back on it was a bit simplistic, in terms of what has happened since. We had the view that, if we could just have flexible exchange rates, that somehow the balance of payments, by which I think we really meant the balance of trade, because that is what was politically hot, would get equilibrated painlessly. Now ten to fifteen years later, we are confronted with the largest trade deficit in the history of the United States, the largest current balance of payments deficits in the history of the United States, and the strongest dollar in the history of the United States, all of these events happening simultaneously. I can tell you almost with certainty that no one at Camp David in 1971 could have even imagined those events happening simultaneously.

What we had not predicted was the magnitude and speed of the capital flows that now, various estimates tell me, are forty times the trade flow. We were a group of people who were more or less dominated by the relationships between exchange rates and trade, not between exchange rates and capital movements.

Now we are confronted with the situation in which foreign capital flows are interacting in a very interesting way with our own economy and are financing about 60–65 percent of our deficit. If they had not been available, the results, I am persuaded, would have been totally different.

We just were not thinking, fifteen or twenty years ago, about anything like this level of fiscal imbalance, or international imbalance. Now, I am not going to talk about domestic deficits. I have been railing about them for about five years; I am persuaded they are near the center vortex of many of our other problems. Rather than being "Peter One Note" again, I thought I might focus more on the foreign aspect of the deficits.

Table 9.16 presents one scenario of foreign debt and interest projections. In 1971, U.S. investment income, interest income, and so on would have been much higher than now in real terms. Therefore, while we may have gotten upset about a $7 billion trade deficit, we had all the means in the world to finance it.

Look out to 1990 and notice that with a $600 billion foreign debt, our net U.S. investment income is estimated at about $20 billion. And we might have interest costs of about $40–50 billion. And that is only

Table 9.16   Foreign Debt and Interest Projections (billions of dollars)

	1980	1985	1990
U.S. net foreign debt (net investment position)	$ + 106.1	$ − 93.5	$ − 600
(1) Net U.S. investment income	+ 28.5	+ 12.9	+ 20
(2) Interest income or cost	+ 1.9	− 2.7	− 48
Total net "income"	+ 30.4	+ 10.2	− 28

Source: Institute for International Economics.

Notes: U.S. and OECD growth: 3.0 percent; LDC growth: 3.75 percent; dollar at level of September 27, 1985.

1990. We are left with the unpleasant question now of how we are going to finance those debt service costs.

I have also studied projections that go out further. If we reduce our current account deficits to only $75 billion for another five or ten years, we hit a trillion dollars of debt before long, and interest payments get even higher. So in Herbert Stein's immortal words, if something's unsustainable, it tends to stop. One of the important questions is how it is going to stop, not whether it is going to stop.

Look at the trade account, because clearly that is the place we must look to finance these debt service costs. I remind you of two or three obvious sectoral points. First on the question of oil. Remember that about 38 percent of our domestic consumption comes from foreign sources; the estimates for the next decade range from 50 percent to 70 percent of our domestic consumption. The odds certainly favor that prices will likely go up with demand. So, in the oil sector of our trade account, I do not see how any prudent person can do anything but assume that the oil import bill will go up substantially.

I look with embarrassment at Bruce Atwater and John Block, as I try to predict the agricultural aspect of things, but clearly there has been something approaching a systemic or structural change in the production of grains around the world. Other people have learned how to produce them far more efficiently and quickly than we thought they could. A number of us just came back from the Soviet Union, where we visited at length with General Secretary Gorbachev, among other people, and even he had the courage, or chutzpah, to announce that it was his objective to become a net exporter of food. So et tu, Brute, I said, as I listened to that.

So that leads, with all due respect to what Lionel Olmer and Hank Greenberg were saying this morning about services, to the manufacturing sector (and I do not know how much nourishment we might get there) as being the principal place we might look. To give you an idea of what the historians will call a wrenching distortion to our industrial structure: It was five years or so ago that we had a surplus in our manufactured trade accounts of probably $20 billion, and this past year we probably have a deficit of around $140 billion in our manufactured accounts.

We have had a swing that amounts to 15–20 percent of our entire capacity, probably 4 percent of the GNP. Now we are about to say that we must move into a trade surplus in the face of the oil situation I mentioned. If you look at it numerically, you could get to a number that might achieve some balance, probably a swing in the manufactured accounts of something like $200 billion.

That $200 billion swing is what occasioned my comment on the first morning as to why there is an essential asymmetry between hearing other important nations in the world economy saying that they must increase exports very rapidly while at the same time we, the world's leading industrial power, are making exactly the same observation. The case therefore for Germany and Japan and others stimulating domestic demand, while it is presented often as helping us in the world economy, can be easily rationalized in terms of "they better do it for the sake of their own economies, given the inevitable drop in our trade deficit."

I have heard at least as many scenarios as there are people in this room, and I am not going to get into the projection business. For the benefit of some of you who do not follow this too carefully, there are roughly three categories of scenarios: One is the so-called crash landing, in which there is a sudden loss of foreign confidence and a sudden drop in the dollar. There is then a combination of rapid inflation as the dollar plunges and recession or worse as interest rates soar. This in turn detonates the third world bomb, because you have got the combination of slow growth and very high interest rates. And if that is not enough to cheer you, a protectionist America responds to that series of phenomena. That is the crash scenario.

Another scenario that is worth looking at is the so-called stop-and-go British scenario in which one looks at the British economy not so much from the vantage point of the slow gradual decline in productivity that began in the late 1800s, but in the more recent response of the economy that was constrained by balance of payments problems. Britain in the post–World War II period was endlessly subjected to the whims of foreign confidence and foreign inflows. Their industrial structure was subjected to the yo-yo effects of the pound and surges of imports. Michael Stuart, a British economist, recently said, "anyone who has lived through our forty years of balance of payments crises and seen the constraints they have imposed on domestic policies must stand amazed at the insouciance with which the United States is piling up foreign debt."

Finally, there's the muddling-through, gradual-decline scenario which leaves us poorer than we could have been.

All of them are rude scenarios that are not very happy. All of them confront the fact that we must repay our debts in one way or another, that we have been consuming far more than we have been producing, and that we are going to have to start producing far more than we consume. That is a rude fact that the American people are really not prepared to confront at the present time.

I now want to say a word or two about foreign policy implications, which we have only alluded to until now. We are facing a country that for the first time is going to be seriously constrained by a lack of resources. I will give you three or four quick things to reflect on if you have not already done so.

I guess Corazon Aquino is as close to the counterpart of Ronald Reagan at the height of his popularity as anybody. The Philippines is about as bipartisan a foreign country as we have in terms of support and its relationship to our national security. Aquino gives what some senators and congressmen have told me is the best speech that has been given in quite a few years in terms of its response. Yet the way we had to grovel around to find $50 million for such a high priority foreign policy objective as that is significant.

As to our friend Mexico, one could make an elegant case that our true national security interests could be very much enhanced by some kind of substantial program with Mexico that would include bilateral aspects in many areas—investment, trade, and so forth. But I am not sure there are many politicians around in the context of Gramm-Rudman who are going to be engaging in innovative new ventures, however important, in foreign policy.

Look at the third world debt problem. I am deeply impressed with James Baker in every way and with his program. But the issue of how we are going to fund any level of program has not yet really touched our consciousness. I chaired a commission for Gerald Ford on federal pay. I recall with great interest seeing a survey of American opinion on "where do you want to spend more money and where do you want to spend less money." The only one that ranked below paying public officials more was foreign aid. And that was in a different context than the current one.

Let's take foreign military forces in Europe. After the (adventure or misadventure, as you see it) in Rejkjavík, when it was pointed out to some of our officials that, in the zero nuclear world they were hypothesizing, we would have substantial vulnerability to the Soviet conventional forces that were far superior to ours, I was amazed to see one of our senior government officials allege that we can afford to spend in a $4 trillion economy whatever we need to spend on defense. I am sure in a rational sense that is true. But as a practical political matter, I wonder what would happen if after that negotiation someone suggested that the United States should spend another $25 billion, or $30 billion, or $40 billion in Europe because it enhances Europe's security. I think that is a nonevent, as we say.

So the overwhelming question in the next decade is where do we find the resources, not simply the resources to pay back this debt service, but the resources to invest in our economic future, because any view of the future that I have been able to think about involves a desperate need to invest much more in human resources and infrastructure. We must rely heavily on our own domestic savings, in view of what I said earlier about the inevitable fall of the trade deficit, and the capital flows that are going to go with it. The reason some of us have been so concerned about the budget deficit is that it is clearly the biggest source of negative savings around, and it is the surest place to get increased savings. Because as I look at all of the studies on the effect of taxes on increased savings, I find the results fairly uncertain and hard to predict. So deficit reduction is a big source of savings and a sure source.

Where then do you look for these resources? It seems to me you look abroad and then you look at home. Let's start abroad. That is going to require a level of macroeconomic coordination and burden sharing that is utterly unprecedented and probably very difficult.

Let's start with NATO. It is impossible for me to visualize the next ten years, with the kinds of constraints we are talking about, where the subject of what we are going to do to reduce the NATO burden does not become a very high priority item. How we maintain the alliance while doing that is an important issue.

I recently came back from the Soviet Union. We talked to their top military officials, their top arms control officials, and so forth. In addition to having some fascinating discussions about SDI and how it looks to them and so forth, there were intensive discussions about their possible interest in reducing 25 percent of their conventional troops from the Urals to the Atlantic, and when General Jones and Harold Brown pressed them on whether they would destroy equipment, whether they would demobilize, whether they would be willing to verify, the answers to those questions were yes. Now whether they actually would or not is another question. But the point I am trying to make is that I find when talking to foreign policy people about the role of resource constraints on foreign policy that we are treated in a very unhappy way, as though Why would you ever want to play around with troops in Europe? Why would you ever want to upset a balance of that sort that has worked pretty well? Why would you ever want to seriously discuss negotiations with the Soviet Union in which you might be talking about one of your objectives being to reduce the resources that are allocated to that purpose?

And my response to that is threefold: In the first place, we need resources. The resources we have allocated there are not going to be available to be invested in other areas that are going to be of great importance to the future of this country. Second, we can either reduce these resources on a planned reciprocal basis, keeping in mind our national security interests, or it can be done because of some external event like a financial crisis, in which our security interests are not protected and in which the reductions are not on a reciprocal basis.

I just wanted to make the point that I think the foreign policy aspects of this deserve a lot of thought, and I am not sure they are getting that thought.

On the economic peace-keeping side, James Schlesinger has pointed out that post–World War II, we were the biggest supplier of capital, the guys who financed the multilateral institutions. I think this was one of our proudest moments because it helped with the peace as well as the war.

Where are we today? Japan talks magnificently about how they have made commitments of another $2 billion or $3 billion, spread over some period of time, and we should accept that with gratitude. But in an area of limited resources, if we aggregate what we might call the military and economic peace-keeping burden together, and they are both burdens, we would hit about 7 percent or thereabouts, if we added aid plus the military. If we take Japan's military plus aid, it is about 1.5 percent of GNP. That spread of 5.5 percent of GNP happens to be about 50 percent more than our total investment, net, in business-productivity-enhancing equipment, just to take one number.

We ought to be talking about some kind of division of labor, or division of burden, on a much larger scale than we have been.

Now as far as the United States is concerned, we have heard a lot at this conference about the third world debt, how it is going to require resources. I am not sure the United States will participate in a big way in that; I am not even sure it should, given its burdens; Japan (it seems to me to some extent) and Europe must step in to this. Saburo Okita has always been ahead of me, and he certainly was today; I was going to timidly suggest that instead of talking about 1 percent or 2 percent, we ought to sit down with Japan and talk to them in larger terms, like perhaps adding another 1 percent or 2 percent of the GNP at least over this period of time. But as I calculate the number, Okita suggests one-third of the $75 billion being contributed to multilateral institutions. That is an order of magnitude beyond anything that is being discussed, and it is the appropriate order of magnitude.

That is going to raise some interesting questions in Washington because we are highly ambivalent. We want all the perquisites and all the appearances of being a post–World War II superpower. But alas we are not quite willing, nor do we have the resources, to step up to it.

The other place we can get resources is obviously at home; we should look at consumption generally, and subsidized consumption in particular. Let us look at four charts that focus on the entitlement programs, the transfer payment programs that go to the unpoor, that account for about 40 percent of the budget. They have been going up 10–15 percent a year. Figure 9.7 shows that during the seventies the real dollars going to defense went down. That made it possible for domestic spending to go up painlessly without having to increase taxes. Now we are confronted with making up for that, and the crunch is on.

We continue to insist that Social Security is not part of our problem, but figure 9.8 gives an idea of the dominance of Social Security as a

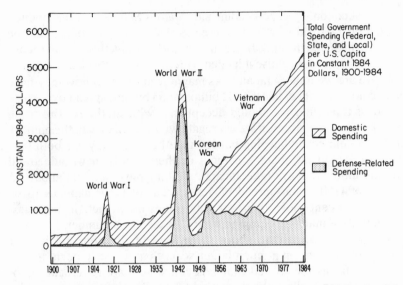

Fig. 9.7   Real public spending per capita: Are we mobilizing for "domestic" warfare?

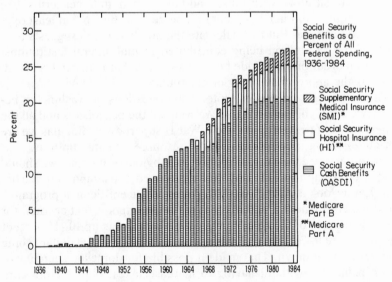

Fig. 9.8   Forty years of Social Security: How much more growth is yet to come?

source of our spending in this country. Now look at figure 9.9, because as they say these days, "you ain't seen nothing yet."

I do not know how many of you are aware, many of the economists are, that the Social Security department has three estimates they use to project future costs of Social Security. One is called optimistic, case one, which I would call hysterical. The second is called—they are now using something called II-B—intermediate pessimistic, and who could object to that! And then finally, there is something called pessimistic. In here I have put all of the estimates that are being used. For those of you who wish to look at them, they are enormously important for predicting the future.

In the so-called intermediate case, the number of babies being born per woman is projected to go up about 10 percent to 12 percent. This is in the face of the fact that there are eleven industrial countries that have a lower birth rate than we do, and a number that are even below 1.6, which is the pessimistic case. I have shown these estimates to a group of people without telling them what they are, and typically most people look at the pessimistic case and say that sounds about right for planning purposes.

Figure 9.10 shows what the pessimistic case forecasts, given the demographic explosion, and in particular the explosion of the over-eighty-five-year-olds. It shows the modest result that our children would have to pay 42 percent of their pay just to finance the Social Security system. This is a projection that could never happen in terms of the

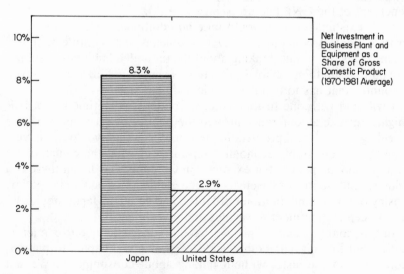

Fig. 9.9   Business investment—the fundamental disparity.

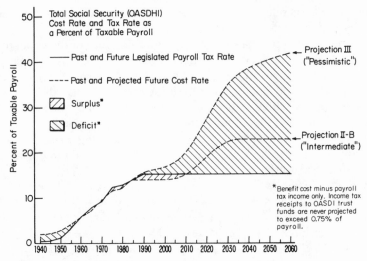

Fig. 9.10   Social Security: both the "likely" and "pessimistic" scenarios are terrifying.

economy and in terms of policy. But this is where this so-called untouchable program might be leading us.

The so-called intermediate case calls for 22 percent of payroll. James Capra has done some projections using the pessimistic case and leaving defense spending where it is. It is clear this case cannot work because by the year 2025, interest costs get hysterical when you let deficits of 5 percent of the GNP pile up (see table 9.17).

With existing rules, it would take an additional 7.5 percent of the gross national product just to cover non-means-tested entitlement programs. This is without thinking about the unfunded liabilities. I submit to you that anything remotely like that is simply not affordable, given a country that has to focus on the investment side.

I will end with one further note. I wonder if sometime the NBER might organize a conference around the politics of economics. I have a feeling that the real problem in our country is that we do not have a long-term deep, stable economic consensus of what the elements are of an economic policy. For example, in Germany and Japan there is a wide-spread political consensus on the elements of economic policy, arising out of the inflation, out of Hitler, and so forth. Japan obviously has a deep commitment to savings and investment.

In our country, people say we have a consensus about economic policy, but I find it remarkably fickle. We talk about capital formation, both sides of the aisle, without talking about consumption. We had supply-side economics in 1980, but by 1986 we ended up with demand-

Table 9.17   **Federal Revenues and Outlays as a Percentage of GNP, by Fiscal Year**

	1988	2000		2025	
		II-B	III	II-B	III
Revenues					
Individual	8.6	10.0	9.8	13.9	13.0
Corporate	2.0	2.0	2.0	2.0	2.0
Social Security					
Retirement and disability	4.9	4.9	4.9	4.7	4.6
Hospital insurance	1.3	1.3	1.3	1.2	1.2
Other	2.3	1.6	1.4	.8	.7
Total Revenue	19.1	19.7	19.4	22.4	2.13
Outlays					
Defense	6.6	6.6	6.6	6.6	6.6
Means-tested benefits	2.1	1.9	2.0	1.6	2.2
Medicaid	0.6	0.6	0.7	0.8	1.2
Other means-					
tested benefits	1.5	1.2	1.3	0.9	1.0
No-mean-tested benefits	9.2	9.2	10.2	12.0	16.7
Social Security	6.3	6.3	7.0	9.1	12.3
Retirement and disability	5.0	4.5	4.8	6.3	7.3
Hospital insurance	1.3	1.8	2.2	2.8	5.0
All other	3.1	2.8	3.3	2.9	4.5
Grants, operations,					
and subsidies	2.5	2.4	2.4	2.3	2.5
Interest	4.2	7.6	8.4	20.4	35.5
Total Outlays	24.7	27.7	29.7	42.9	63.5
Deficit	5.6	8.0	10.3	20.5	42.2

Source: James Capra, Senior Economist, Shearson Lehman Brothers; Consultant, Bi-Partisan Budget Appeal.

Notes: II-B and III with current nominal interest rates (8 percent); defense constant as percentage of GNP; "prudent case" starting point in 1988.

side economics. We are now talking about competitiveness; the only question is How big is the grab bag and how long is the list?

The one thing these policies all have in common is that they all avoid the underlying fundamental of what I am talking about, which is essentially the consumption, savings, investment choice. And we talk about how we can solve this problem by ignoring the main element of the problem.

What to do about it, I do not know. There are two approaches that have been used in the past politically. I went to a diet doctor a number of years ago. He said, "you've been on a lot of diets." And I said, "yeah, I've been on a lot of diets," and I weighed about thirty pounds more then than I do even now. He said, "Mr. Peterson, I can tell you that people have trouble sustaining denial, sustaining negative visions. And what you need is a positive vision that you have become committed to." So I said, "well fine, what does that mean exactly?" He said, "well, until you decide what you want to weigh and what you want to look like, we aren't going to be successful." So he walks me over to a mirror that was like one of those mirrors you see in county fairs, and he has a dial in it. He says, "you weigh 211 pounds now and you said you want to weigh 175." So he dials in 175 pounds, and there is this magnificent lean vision. He says, "I want you to look at that for about 5 or 10 minutes, and then I want that image in your head. Every time you sit down and eat I want that positive vision. And then you'll say that's what I've decided to look like."

So that is one way we can do it, I guess. If we could sell the American people some positive vision.

The other is the fear of a crisis, which seems to have energized Japan and Germany. I do not know which of those it is going to take, but I suspect that we can spend days looking at numbers and agreeing on the seriousness of the problem, but until we put equivalent time into changing the politics of this country, we are going to be sitting here having conferences for years.

4. James R. Schlesinger
Domestic Policies and International Capital Flows

I intend to put forward certain propositions that some of you may regard as heretical. In uttering these mild heresies I shall be following in the path of my own great mentor of nearly forty years ago, J. H. Williams of Harvard. Williams entitled his AEA presidential address "An Economist's Confessions." In it Williams indulged in those doubts and heresies that were his hallmark. My own remarks will be not so much the confessions of an economist as those of a sometime government official.

At the outset I wish to make three preliminary points. The first point is a trite one, what has become a commonplace observation: the international economic system has in recent decades become dominated by capital flows. In this there is a deep irony. The theory of international trade (and even more clearly the policy reflexes about international trade), as it has come down to us, is erected on Ricardian foundations. But Ricardo scarcely acknowledged the existence of capital flows. Thus, we face the paradoxical situation that what became first the major equilibrating mechanism and then the dominant element in international trade was itself not incorporated in the original theory in international trade.

Ricardo himself thought of the factors of production (land and labor, rather than capital) as relatively fixed among nations. Trade, reflecting comparative advantage, was based on these more or less permanent endowments. Thus, comparative advantage itself was more or less permanent. By contrast, when we introduce capital mobility as the major element in determining the evolution of the international economy (and even more so when capital flows become the dominant element in international transactions), then the basis for the Ricardian formulation disappears. Comparative advantage is no longer permanent, but is strongly influenced by the flow of capital. Comparative advantage—and thus both the composition and the level of a nation's trade—may be highly transitory.

The new equilibrating mechanism, international capital flows, can be and intermittently will be highly disruptive. From time to time we see the torrential movement of capital, reminiscent of the "hot money flows" of the thirties. In its extreme form we see that torrential movement of capital known as capital fight. Need one observe how disruptive such capital flight will be, how little related to a useful equilibrating mechanism?

All of this implies to me that major elements in the actual functioning of the internatinal economy are no longer captured within the theory of international trade. That implies we should be engaged in the reconsideration and the radical restructuring of the contemporary meaning of comparative advantage. Comparative advantage is now a reflection of the unanticipated mobility and the movement of capital. Sometimes such movements are torrential. Such movement of capital, as opposed to the relatively fixed endowments that Ricardo discussed, brings about the volatile movement of exchange rates. That exchange rate volatility in turn will suddenly and substantially alter the position of domestic industries. Thus, we are immediately faced with a dilemma, for here in the American democracy we expect the farmer, the steelworker, the autoworker, the shoe worker, and the textile worker—in short, the voters and those who represent these voters—to accept the higher wisdom that makes them the playthings of these larger economic forces—and most particularly the movement of capital.

Let me turn to my second point: to make the international economic system work *well* there must be recognized rules of the game, accepted by the principal parties. To be sure, some sort of equilibrium will come about as a result of unfettered market forces, but few governments will for long tolerate such a system. All of the principal nation-players will be obliged to cooperate in order to obtain the benefits of international trade, while not too adversely affecting the interests of the major participants that must be induced to cooperate.

The rules of the game, generally recognized and accepted, for governing international economic activity will not come about automatically. In times past we had such recognized rules for the game—the gold standard especially before World War I and the Bretton Woods system after World War II. To some extent the Bretton Woods framework depended on the United States, as the dominant player, to make it work. It has now broken down. For a system of rules of the game to be effective presupposes not only a framework in which trade and capital flows take place, but also the willingness of national governments to take actions to make the system work.

Such a framework, especially the willingness of national states to take those actions necessary to make the system work, has largely disappeared. Today we see instead behavior that is typically self-centered and ad hoc, designed in response to short-term pressures and having long-term consequences that are pernicious. There was a far deeper wisdom in what emerged after World War II, in which each nation accepted the obligation to take self-correcting actions to correct a long-term disequilibrium in its balance of payments. In the view of those who put together the Bretton Woods system, such action was particularly necessary for the great creditor nations.

Let me point out that in the world today we have only one "great creditor nation." No longer is it the Land of the Free. Rather it is now Japan. Japan has been the chief beneficiary of the relatively free system of international trade. Yet Japan has been singularly insensitive to the obligations imposed upon her by participation in that world trading system from which she has so notably benefited. Today, in addition to that one great creditor nation, there is also a notable has-been creditor nation. It is, indeed, the Land of the Free, our United States, which has lately been transformed into the world's great debtor nation. The United States too, for reasons quite different from Japan, is failing to fulfill its obligations to make the system work.

The third point I wish to make is the decline in the role of conscious policy-making. In its place is a corresponding rise in reliance upon impersonal market forces. I point to this phenomenon simply as a datum. Some will regard this change as unfortunate—or even tragic. Many today will welcome such a change—as reflecting diminished reliance on the presumed clumsiness of government policy and greater reliance on supposedly "superior" market forces. For my purpose at the moment I present it simply as a fact of life.

No doubt, this trend reflects in considerable degree the disappearance of the preponderant economic position of the United States, as it had emerged at the close of World War II. There has been a loss of real power and of influence on the part of the United States that has become increasingly (and painfully) obvious during the last two decades. The United States faces far greater competition, not only in product markets but in critical technologies as well. The United States thus has lost the luxury of a position of deciding upon the best course of international action relatively free of external pressures upon its own interests. In brief, the possibility has now disappeared that the United States, based upon its own judgments, can be the preponderant influence in achieving needed adjustments in international trade and capital flow.

But there is more to it than that. In addition to the decline in real power, there has been a significant decline in U.S. eagerness to make the system work. In one of his ironical asides, Sir Dennis Robertson referred to the United States after World War I as "the Great Sir Galahad of the West, . . . whose bills were no smaller because his heart was pure." That was a transitory judgment! No such statement would have been made after World II. No other nation could have achieved the same missionary zeal, the same Puritan impulse to labor in the Lord's vineyard, above all to make the system work, that the United States displayed in the two decades after Bretton Woods.

Such altruistic behavior or missionary zeal has not marked the actions of Japan, Germany, or other countries that have emerged in the subsequent period. As Charles Kindleberger has observed, the United States has now lost much of its appetite for providing what he described as "international economic public goods." These are the actions or the institutions that provide spillover benefits for the entire international community, benefits exceeding those accruing to the direct provider.

There has been a contraction of focus, most notably here in the United States, from looking at the world as a whole to concentrating on the interests of the individual nation. The problem is (and here I turn from pointing to a datum of expressing a policy judgment) that the proper functioning of the international economy can only be *satisfactorily* attacked on a systematic worldwide basis. The pity (or the irony) is that as international economic problems have become more urgent and as the need for systemic attack has grown, the motivation that might give force to such a systemic attack has simultaneously decreased.

We are not going to be able to solve the problems that afflict the international trade and financial system unless and until we recognize that it must be a common attack by all the key players, which would accept their separate obligations to make the overall system work well.

Now that I have spelled out my three preliminary points, let me turn to a summary of the present scene. What do we see today? As I have indicated, we have a decline in the role of policy—and a corresponding rise in the role of economics in the sense of impersonal market forces. We discern both a weakening of the instruments of policy and a weakened desire to define *and achieve* policy goals. The world's largest, and in a limited sense, strongest economy has now become a sink for foreign capital. Once it was regarded as the moral obligation of the United States to serve as a provider of capital to poorer countries. Now the United States has become the sponge that sucks in capital from abroad—at the astonishing rate of over a $100 billion a year.

We also observe an international economy marked by massive shifts in capital, whose direction of flow changes from time to time. Sometimes for reasons apparently economic or for political reasons, such capital movements may become torrential. In general, the capital flows from nations with excessive savings (or insufficient consumption) to those, like the United States, that are marked by excessive consumption and insufficient savings.

These capital movements, subject to reversal, also cause the volatile movements of exchange rates. Such volatility undermines what is indispensable in the modern capitalist system: the reliable calculations essential for making long-lived investments, which depend upon an extended planning horizon.

All in all, the international economy is marked today by ex post balancing of the books—a simple variant of source-and-use analysis. To be sure, there is an examination of how some items move to compensate for other items. All this takes place in a sort of policy void. Not only has there been diminished attention to the policy implications, but there has been remarkably little public consideration of what it all means—for the country and the world.

All of this might be tolerable except for one ineluctable point. *It is unsustainable.* Something that is unsustainable tends to come to an end. What we see today is a system akin to water building up behind a barrage. The water continues to collect behind the barrage until the barrage ultimately collapses.

Where do we want the country to go—politically, strategically, morally, ethically? Are we satisfied to be a sink for international capital. Is self-concern sufficient? Are we content to be the playthings of "impersonal forces"? Are we indifferent to the problems that we create for future generations of Americans, indifferent to the call to aid the less fortunate, indifferent to the need for international stability?

Let me turn now to the critical question: how these broader international developments affect—and in turn are affected by—domestic policies. Domestic *policies* are themselves largely a reflection of domestic *politics,* domestic perceptions and preoccupations, and, if you will, domestic fixations.

I have already more than hinted at my belief that international stability requires intelligent international policy-making. In a sense this sounds like a call for a Kantian Imperative. But how to achieve it in a world of self-centered, economic policies is, of course, the difficult question. Nonetheless, international stability will require at a minimum a harmonization of policies among the principal players in the game.

Such action is, to be sure, in the long-term self-interest of the major nations. Adjustment of the international imbalances is coming. It is unavoidable. The adjustment brought about by "impersonal forces" will prove highly distressing, if not devastating, to some nations. Neither the current American payments deficit nor the trade deficit is sustainable over the intermediate term. But that implies that nations that have become dependent upon export surpluses must seek other means of sustaining levels of employment and output, to say nothing of further economic growth. It also implies a revival of the American manufacturing base. Quite clearly, the decline of the dollar required to bring about a "market adjustment" under these conditions will be as painful to us as it will be to others. The question is not whether existing imbalances will be eliminated, but how.

It seems self-evident that rather than have painful adjustment forced upon individual nations by external conditions, they should seek gradual improvement through deliberate adjustment. I am not particularly optimistic. Over the years I have observed that national policies tend to reflect deep-seated urges rather than rational calculation. The dismal science is perhaps sufficiently dismal that it ought not be additionally burdened with Freudian psychology. But to borrow a Freudian metaphor (for those of you who might welcome it), characteristically national policies are driven more by the Id than by the Ego.

If national policies are not driven by neuroses reflecting overreaction to prior national traumas, such policies at least reflect national habits that are very deeply ingrained. Consider, for example, the quotation cited earlier by David Hale in the *Times:* "the U.S. is a debtor nation with the habits of a creditor nation. Germany and Japan are creditor nations with the habits of debtor nations." Such ingrained national habits prolong the imbalances in the international system. But the new volatility in the international economy, in particular the more rapid movements and the interruptions of capital flows, implies that the slow-paced adjustment based on the alterations of ingrained national habits is no longer adequate. At the moment each of the key nations not only has these deep-seated urges, but appears to have enshrined them. It requires conscious policies successfully carried out to facilitate adjustments. But policy remains dominated by these ingrained habits.

Quite clearly, on the international scene we do not have what economists have regularly presupposed: a rational policy-making model.

Consider the case of the United States. In recent years fiscal policy has been dominated, if not crippled, bu an antitax mood on the part of the public that has precluded revenues even remotely approaching the level of public expenditures on which the public insists. American fiscal policy has become a scandal—in relation either to our prior fiscal standards or to expectations about the behavior of the world's leading power. The public's antitax mood, perhaps now fading, was driven by a belief that we had been conned by government ("fraud, waste, and abuse"), and consequently we came to resent the personal sacrifices that we had borne willingly in the past.

The erosion of the revenue base is driven by two elements. The first is Lafferism. Lafferism propounds the simple rule of thumb or, more precisely, the illusion that if tax rates are cut, somehow, through the release of pent-up energies, there will be an immense gusher of revenues that will more than offset the decline in tax rates and thus bring about fiscal balance. Lafferism provided us with a rationale, however flimsy, for doing what we apparently wanted to do anyhow.

The second element was the antitax revolt. In its more civilized form it is provided a certain respectability in the editorial pages of the *Wall Street Journal* and other publications. In its more dramatic—and certainly more primitive form—it is embodied in Proposition 13, passed in California in the mid-1970s. It is based upon the belief that if one cuts revenues, that one will be obliged to reduce expenditures. In that fashion it has worked in California with its ever-growing population and revenue base and somewhat luxuriant levels of expenditures, as well as its balanced budget requirement. Its imitations elsewhere have been less successful.

At the federal level the conviction took hold, after the Lafferist hope that we could have our fiscal cake and eat it too proved illusionary and ephemeral, that the reduction and revenues would "force" the Congress sharply to reduce domestic programs, presumably unwanted and wasteful.

Curiously, this conviction existed in parallel with another conviction—that the Congress would be prepared to accept an extended military buildup over the years in which military outlays would ultimately reach about 9 percent of the Gross National Product.

As might be expected, the device of revenue-denial-to-limit-expenditures has proved to be a half truth. Congress has not been "forced" sharply to reduce domestic programs. It has imposed restraints, but the radical shrinkage in projected appropriations has occurred in President Reagan's proposed military buildup. Congress imposed limits as early as 1982. By 1985 it had begun to impose real annual reductions in defense expenditures. Rather than rising toward the 9 percent of the Gross National Product as intended, defense appropriations are now shrinking back toward the 6 percent level. While limiting revenues clearly does reduce expenditures, only one with ideological blinders could have expected a different outcome.

To sustain the now-ingrained habits and the expectations of Americans would require an immense and continuing inflow of foreign capital resulting in a steadily burgeoning level of American indebtedness to foreigners. Americans have come to like high consumption, low or zero savings, low tax rates. Americans have also liked the high dollar (a demand now rapidly being eroded). That high dollar not only satisfies personal needs when one travels abroad; it has also been a major element in national security and in our international role. One consequence of the fall of the dollar will be a deterioration in the international security position of the United States. We shall find it both increasingly costly and increasingly difficult to sustain our commitments. In an earlier period in which the dollar declined, we saw the pressures for the Mansfield amendment and similar difficulties. As the living standards and the treatment of our forces overseas deteriorate, domestic political pressures build within the United States to reduce the level of forces. The high dollar may be our historic preference; it may be in our own national security interest and clearly even more in the national security interest of our allies. Nonetheless, the high dollar is a thing of the past. It can no longer be sustained—even by immense inflows of foreign capital.

A debtor nation will find it difficult to sustain the international security obligations that the United States has borne. This points to a larger truth. If Americans are to sustain their present habits—low domestic savings, large capital imports, the center of the free world's security system—ultimately it would require that foreigners be prepared periodically to wipe out their claims against the United States. This is not a likely development.

Let me cite one other national habit that may no longer be a luxury we can afford. In the United States we tend to confuse the free economy with laissez-faire. But nothing about the free market implies that anything goes. That results in the misdirection, indeed the waste, of the energies of our senior executives. Many of our senior executives, who are not investing their time searching for new takeover targets, are spending much of their time either fending off corporate raiders or searching for the white knights who contingently will help them fend off corporate raiders. From a national standpoint, much of such activity represents sheer waste. It contributes little to the more efficient production of goods and services or to the improvement of American "competitiveness." I suspect that this point may lie behind Secretary

Darrman's stringent comments regarding the inefficiencies and misdirected efforts of American executives.

Let us turn to the deep-seated urges and their effects in places other than the United States. Consider what might be the polar contrast to the United States: the case of Japan. Japan is the archetype of the creditor nation with the ingrained habits of a debtor. Among the market economies, Japan has achieved a persistent and remarkable performance as a savings-generating machine. But Japan has no effective way of absorbing such high savings into domestic investment. Consequently, in flagrant violation of the spirit of Bretton Woods, its economic performance has become vulnerably dependent upon the maintenance of a large export surplus. If the Japanese wish to sustain a high-savings, low-consumption, high-employment economy driven by an export surplus, it must accept periodic extinction of the claims against foreigners, notably the extinction of claims against the United States. Otherwise, the Japanese economic "style" is unsustainable. Only the American market could absorb over many years the outflow of goods that the Japanese produce. Ultimately, even the American capacity for the absorption of Japanese exports is becoming satiated.

While Japan may be the polar case, what is true for Japan is also true for others. Ultimately it is true for the Federal Republic, even though German membership in the European economic community provides a cushion for sustaining German exports. Ultimately it will also be true for Korea, a kind of post-Japan Japan. The Koreans possess a cushion in their margin for raising their very low living standards. But in the long run it too must change. The simple truth is that no great trading nation can over a long period of time be dependent for its economic health on the maintenance on a very large trade surplus.

Just as the American trade deficit cannot be indefinitely sustained, so those economies dependent upon export surpluses will ultimately find that neither can they be sustained. The question is not whether these balance of payments anomalies, which over recent years we have observed with increasing clarity and concern, will be eliminated; the only questions are when and how. Will the return to a sustainable long-term equilibrium be based on gradual adjustment reflecting conscious policy—or, conversely, will it reflect a sudden so-called market adjustment or an angry political reaction?

Economists sometimes refer either mysteriously or hopefully to self-correcting forces. The normal inference is that such self-correcting forces imply smooth transitions. Indeed, there are such self-correcting forces. But they need not convey a smooth adjustment to a new equilibrium. Rather those self-correcting forces will appear, as in Greek mythology, as Nemeses.

The U.S. trade deficit, which has swollen to bizarre levels, inevitably will disappear. That is not a guess: that is an inevitability (Feldstein

1987). And, in terms of economic time, it will end relatively soon—not necessarily in the next few years, but clearly within the next decade. When the decline sets in, it will proceed rapidly. The ability of the rest of the world to absorb either dollars or dollar claims against the United States is not unlimited.

Thus the activity on Capitol Hill represents a belated reaction. As is so frequently the case, it represents an attempt to lock the barn door after the horse has been stolen. (It might also be observed that a good deal of the handwringing about "protectionism," given U.S. trade deficits in excess of $150 billion dollars a year, is also exaggerated.) It is not wise to invest too much energy in protesting against inevitability. Other nations in the world should prepare for the day that the U.S. trade deficit will be eliminated.

Economists sometimes have a rather naïve faith in the role of the price mechanism and therefore in the likelihood of smooth adjustments. But if decisions, as is so regularly the case, are not based on the presupposed economic rationality, adjustments, rather than being smooth, may come in the form of an earthquake. Far more frequently than contemplated in economic models, real-world decisions are based on ingrained habits, bilateral relations, or sheer national prejudice or self-centeredness. Consequently, the likelihood is high that real-world adjustment will be traumatic.

Curiously enough it is not the United States that will suffer most from the elimination of the American trade deficit. To be sure, the rate growth of U.S. living standards will be squeezed, even if there is not an actual reduction for a few years. But that pain should be partially relieved by the revivification of the American manufacturing base and an employment boom.

It is the export-oriented, export-dependent nations that ultimately will suffer the most from the elimination of these unsustainable trade imbalances. The most obvious sufferer will be Japan, but others will suffer as well. As the American trade deficit is sharply reduced, those overseas suppliers will experience the painful loss of foreign markets. They will also experience the high cost embodied in the wastage of invested capital which we so dramatically saw at the time of the oil shocks. There will be a rise in unemployment, concentrated in the export-oriented nations but spreading beyond them.

The conclusion that one is led to is rather pessimistic—a dismal note going beyond the dismal science. It reflects psychological considerations—those deep-seated national impulses to which I referred earlier. Economists find it easy to paint a smooth transition from one static equilibrium to another. One can, of course, theorize about Japan adjusting rapidly, or Germany adjusting rapidly, to changes in the external market. But both countries are marked by those deeply ingrained national habits. I do not think—as a practical as opposed to a theoretical matter—that Japan can rapidly make the kind of adjustments outlined in the Maekawa report. Consequently, as the American trade deficit recedes, the Japanese will be unable to avoid the lengthy period of economic difficulty.

Despite some notable differences, the conclusion regarding Germany is similar. While Germany's positions may be eased by its membership in the European economic community, its "neurosis" regarding anything that smacks of inflation is even more deep-seated. Thus, government policies designed to stimulate domestic demand, as the export surplus shrinks, will face substantial psychological and political obstacles. Both the demographic structure of its population with the high proportion of the aging and the prospective shrinkage of the population add to the difficulty of justifying expenditures on domestic infrastructure in stimulating additional consumption.

Earlier I emphasized the desirability of conscious policy-making within the international community as the preferred way to achieve adjustment. I strongly believe that such action, akin to the enlightened institution-building after World War II, is the proper way to deal with the imbalances and distortions in the international economy. But later I have conceded that the psychological obstacles, those deep-seated national impulses, will make exceedingly difficult the acceptance by individual nations of the required actions. I began by stating my intention to present certain propositions that some of you might regard as heretical. I believe I have done just that. If in the academic world there is the equivalent of a defrocked priest, it may apply to a sometime economist who will have his Ph.D. rescinded.

Reference

Feldstein, Martin. 1987. Correcting the trade deficit. *Foreign Affairs,* Spring.

Summary of Discussion

Several people commented on the shape that the world economy will take when the imbalance in the U.S. current account is eliminated. James Schlesinger suggested that eventually the United States should run a current account surplus, as befits the biggest economy in the world. This implies a substantial revival of manufacturing, as the public relearns to purchase American goods. One of the implications of this, he noted, is that a lot of capital investment is needed in electric power generating capacity.

Peter Peterson remarked that he would be interested in investigating the compatibility, in the context of a global model, of a balanced U.S. current account, given that the United States now imports 60 percent of the manufacturing exports of the third world. Martin Feldstein thought it could be compatible, and Anne Krueger agreed, suggesting that an American current account balance would be compatible with third world needs due to the corresponding shift in the capital flows toward LDCs, allowing their imports to rise.

Lionel Olmer was impressed with the prediction of an elimination of the trade deficit in the near future. There is no sign of this reduction now nor of any resurgence in manufacturing. Schlesinger responded that the prediction of a recovery in manufacturing follows from the projected elimination of the trade deficit. This will presumably happen, he reasoned, with some increase in quality but primarily through an increase in price competitiveness. When foreigners no longer want to to accept U.S. obligations, the transformation of the balance of payments will occur. When this happens depends on political psychology, but Schlesinger predicted it within five or seven years. Several people pointed out that the satiation of foreign borrowers is happening faster than it might seem since recently foreign governments have been filling in for falling private demand for U.S. obligations.

Martin Feldstein remarked that a large fraction of the adjustment in the real exchange from its peak may already have taken place, and agreed with Rudiger Dornbusch and Jeffrey Frankel, who both claimed that the trade deficit would decrease to about $100 billion per year as a result of the recent fall of the dollar to its current level.

Several participants raised some doubts about the prospects for a smooth adjustment process. Anne Krueger suggested that without a decrease in excess demand in the United States, there will be little change in the situation and then a sudden crash. Charles Parry summarized the problem by observing that our consumption is greater than our income and worried that, since Americans seem to respond primarily to crises, it would be difficult to solve the aggregate problems without some real economic conflagration.

Schlesinger feared the effects of a large fall in the dollar, noting the impact of a low dollar-mark exchange rate on the real wages of American soldiers and their families in Germany and hence on the willingness of Americans to support the U.S. troop commitment to NATO. He echoed the fears of an economic crisis, suggesting that sustained inflation is a real possibility given the low tolerance in the United States for high unemployment and the likelihood that the fall in the dollar and the weakening of foreign competition will also lead to the restoration of union bargaining power.

Feldstein asked why the Japanese in particular focus on protecting imports at the cost of an even stronger yen and greater loss of exports instead of letting the market allocate the pain. Saburo Okita replied that there is a trade-off between voluntary export restraint and letting the yen appreciate. In this context, Okita recalled an occasion about seven or eight years ago in London when several British economists said that the British government needed to establish import penetration ratios in twenty major industries and noted a similar trend currently in the United States. Quantitative limits may be better than allowing full exchange rate adjustment because with only price adjustment the dollar may fall too low, leading to low growth in Japan and Germany, decreased demand for American exports, and a vicious circle.

Schlesinger's fears about a pure exchange rate adjustment, which he noted would happen if nothing else does, were about its effects on foreign policy. A radical political change in the world could result from a drastic fall in the dollar. American strategic objectives would change, and the ethical obligation to provide for the poor would not be likely to revive. Grand policy aspirations, he suggested, are the luxury of a creditor nation.

In conclusion Schlesinger outlined three political-economic scenarios, in order of decreasing likelihood. First, a steep fall in the value of the dollar could lead to an increase in inflation and interest rates, while a failure to deal with the budget deficit could cause aggregate demand to remain high, leading to high interest rates and stagflation.

In a second and perhaps overly optimistic scenario, in Febraury 1989 a new president oversees an attack on the new problems facing the country and a sixty-day campaign is waged on incorrect domestic policies, based on some of the principles we have discussed today. The third possibility is an external shock, probably caused by an adventuresome third world country.

Robert Bartley explained that he had a different model from most of the people at the conference. He never believed in the Club of Rome predictions, never thought that James Schlesinger's 50 cent/gallon gasoline tax was the answer to the energy crisis, and disagrees with much that has been said at this conference.

He argued that the balance of trade numbers themselves should be of little concern. Next to M1, the balance of trade is the most misleading economic statistic reported. We had a trade deficit for our first one hundred years as a nation, and the only time we have had a surplus was during the Great Depression. The trade deficit is not a problem: to straighten it out we need only a recession, and protectionism would lead to this recession.

Bartley recalled that Alan Reynolds in the *Wall Street Journal* recently collected quotations from many years ago asking how long Japan could continue to buy from the rest of the world twice what it sells. Well, it turned out that the answer was twenty years.

The trade debate is a mercantilist debate, and the best solution to the problem would be to stop collecting figures, but since this is not good for the economics profession it would be better to publish five trade balances as was done until 1976. The problem with analysis based on this number is Where is the bottom line? The deficit is not a sign of weakness. Americans buy Japanese cars; Japanese buy U.S. asets; we are all consenting adults, so who cares? We are recycling excess Japanese savings into the world economy, which is a good thing for all concerned.

We have overcome a great inflation without a great depression, so far, and this is remarkable. There has been rapid job creation and a five-year expansion, and the U.S. trade deficit has kept it going. We need some aggregate demand in the world.

In the process, foreigners have acquired debt, but what is the significance of who holds the debt? Does it really matter if it is in a safe in Zurich or a safe in New York, and which citizen holds it?

The dollar will not go to 120 yen. If it did, it would be inflationary in the United States and contractionary in Japan, and the Fed would tighten as the Japanese loosened, and the dollar would arrest its fall. This would lead to what we need, faster Japanese growth and slower U.S. growth, and the trade balance will straighten out. The problem has been that for a long time Japanese and German monetary policy has been too tight. As they recognize this too, the deficit will correct itself, Bartley concluded.

Schlesinger suggested that Bartley's strategic model is entirely different from his economic model, and he acknowledged that though Bartley's remarks were generally true, the implication is that the United States will decline relative to Japan and Germany, and the strategic and political implications of this would be serious. Bartley rejected a dichotomy between his models, proposing that he and Schlesinger agreed that a strong economy was important and disagreed only about what makes a strong economy. He added that usually a strategic power with a strong economy also has a fixed exchange rate and a convertible currency.

Rudiger Dornbusch suggested that the U.S. budget deficit might belong in Bartley's model. He also subscribed to the idea that there is a difference between a trade deficit in capital goods and a trade deficit in consumer goods, so the comparison with Korea and Japan might be specious. He asked Bartley about the difference between the U.S. situation now and that of Chile and Argentina in the 1970s. He proposed that a distinction would have to be based on the ability of the United States to raise a lot of tax revenue at the end of the consumption spree. Bartley answered that the difference is that their foreign debt is denominated in dollars while our debt is in dollars, so we have greater leverage.

Martin Feldstein argued that the income elasticities of import demand demonstrate that the trade balance effects of faster growth abroad and slower growth here will not redress the trade balance. For example, an increase of two percentage points in non-U.S. growth in the entire world would lead to only a $15 billion or $20 billion decrease in the U.S. trade deficit over two or three years. Something else has to give, he concluded. Bartley said that he had seen other figures and in any case it will be an interesting test.

Thomas Enders emphasized the impact of running trade deficits on the ability of the country to lead and to sustain a consensus for defense. As foreign central banks substitute for private foreign investors in holding U.S. assets, the United States loses the ability to decide on its own reserves and exchange rate. Bartley interpreted the large amount of official financing of the U.S. deficit by foreign central banks in 1986 to mean that these banks are already feeling the pinch of the lower dollar. Up to now they have been intervening in a sterilized fashion, without affecting their domestic money supply. This is stupid and ineffectual and soon they will have to change their money supply, which will stabilize exchange rates.

Biographies

H. B. Atwater, Jr., is currently chairman and chief executive officer of General Mills. He is a member of the Business Roundtable, the Business Council, and the International Council of Morgan Guaranty Trust Company.

Robert E. Baldwin is Hilldale Professor of Economics at the University of Wisconsin–Madison and is a research associate at the National Bureau of Economic Research. He was chief economist in the Office of the U.S. Trade Representative and has served as a consultant on trade matters for the U.S. Department of Labor, the United Nations, and the World Bank.

Robert L. Bartley is editor of the *Wall Street Journal* with primary responsibility for the editorial page. He is a vice-president of the *Wall Street Journal* and a member of the Dow Jones management committee, the body of senior executives who advise on and formulate corporatewide policy.

Andrew Berg is a graduate student in economics at the Massachusetts Institute of Technology. He spent a year at the Council of Economic Advisers and has worked at the Bolivian Ministry of Finance and for the OECD in Senegal and Mali.

John R. Block was U.S. secretary of agriculture from 1981 to 1986. He currently is the president of the National-American Wholesale Grocers' Association, a trade association representing 350 wholesale grocers and food service distributors.

Philip Caldwell is senior managing director of Shearson Lehman Brothers Inc. and chairman of its Investment Banking Group Policy Committee. He is a member of the President's Export Council, the Business Council, the Conference Board, and the Council on Foreign Relations and a trustee for the Committee for Economic Development. He was the former chairman of the board and chief executive officer for the Ford Motor Company.

Geoffrey Carliner is executive director of the National Bureau of Economic Research. Prior to coming to the NBER, he was a senior staff economist at the Council of Economic Advisers working on labor issues and international trade policy.

E. Gerald Corrigan is president of the Federal Reserve Bank of New York. He is also vice-chairman of the Federal Market Open Committee, the Fed's principle body for establishing national money and credit policies. He is a member of the Council on Foreign Relations and the Trilateral Commission.

Rudiger Dornbusch is the Ford International Professor of Economics at the Massachusetts Institute of Technology and a research associate at the National Bureau of Economic Research.

Sebastian Edwards is associate professor of economics at the University of California, Los Angeles, and a faculty research fellow at the National Bureau of Economic Research. He has been a consultant to the World Bank, the International Monetary Fund, and the governments of Costa Rica and Indonesia.

Barry Eichengreen is professor of economics at the University of California, Berkeley, and a research associate of the National Bureau of Economic Research. He has served as a consultant to the World Bank and the International Monetary Fund.

Thomas O. Enders is a managing director of Salomon Brothers in International Corporate Finance. He has served as U.S. ambassador to Canada, to the European communities, and to Spain. He was also deputy secretary of state for economic and business affairs and international monetary affairs.

Martin Feldstein is the George F. Baker Professor of Economics at Harvard University and president of the National Bureau of Economic Research. He was chairman of the Council of Economic Advisers from 1982 through 1984. He is a member of the Trilateral Commission, the Council on Foreign Relations, and the International Council of the Morgan Guaranty Company.

Jeffrey A. Frankel is professor of economics at the University of California, Berkeley, and a research associate of the National Bureau of Economic Research. He has served as a senior staff economist at the Council of Economic Advisers and has held visiting appointments with the International Monetary Fund, the Federal Reserve Board, and the World Bank.

Bruce L. Gardner is professor in the Department of Agricultural and Resource Economics at the University of Maryland. He was the senior staff economist covering agricultural issues on the Council of Economic Advisers between 1975 and 1977.

Maurice R. Greenberg is president and chief executive officer of American International Group. He is a member of the President's Advisory Committee on Trade Negotiations and vice-chairman of the ASEAN-U.S. Business Advisory Council.

Robert S. Ingersoll is a former U.S. ambassador to Japan and deputy secretary of state. Prior to his appointment as ambassador, he was chairman and chief executive officer of Borg-Warner Corporation. He is a member of the Business Council and the Trilateral Commission.

Thomas S. Johnson is president of Chemical Bank Corporation with primary responsibility for managing Chemical's Capital Markets Group. He is a member of the Council on Foreign Relations.

Woo-choong Kim is chairman of the Daewoo group based in Korea. He is currently vice-chairman of the Federation of Korean Industries, the Korea Traders Association, and the Korea-Japan Economic Association.

Anne O. Krueger is Arts and Science Professor of Economics at Duke University and a research associate of the National Bureau of Economic Research. Prior to coming to Duke, she was vice-president of economics and research at the World Bank.

Richard M. Levich is professor of finance and international business and chairman of the International Business Program at New York University. He is also a research associate of the National Bureau of Economic Research.

Robert V. Lindsay is former president of J. P. Morgan & Co. and its principal subsidiary, Morgan Guaranty Trust Company. He is currently chairman of the Bank's International Council. He is also chairman of the Foreign Policy Association and a member of the Council on Foreign Relations.

Robert E. Lipsey is professor of economics at Queens College and the Graduate Center of the City University of New York and a research associate of the National Bureau of Economic Research.

Rachel McCulloch is professor of economics at the University of Wisconsin–Madison and a research associate of the National Bureau of Economic Research. She is a member of the Advisory Committee of the Institute for International Economics and of the Committee on International Relations Studies with the People's Republic of China.

Saburo Okita was former foreign minister of Japan. He is president of International University of Japan and chairman of the Institute for Domestic and International Policy Studies. He is also adviser to the minister of foreign affairs, the Economic Planning Agency, the Science Technology Agency, and the Environmental Agency.

Lionel H. Olmer has served as under secretary of commerce for international trade and is currently a partner with the law firm of Paul, Weiss, Rifkind, Wharton and Garrison. As under secretary, he was head of the International Trade Administration.

Charles W. Parry is chairman and chief executive officer of the Aluminum Company of America.

Peter G. Peterson is chairman of the Blackstone Group and chairman of the board of the Council on Foreign Relations and the Institute for International Economics. He was former chairman and chief executive officer of Lehman Brothers and served as secretary of commerce in the Nixon administration.

Charles S. Sanford, Jr., is deputy chairman of Bankers Trust Company. He is a member of the Conference Board, the Council on Foreign Relations, and the Brookings Institution.

John E. Sawyer is currently president of the Andrew W. Mellon Foundation. Prior to going to the Mellon Foundation, he was president of Williams College.

Mario Schimberni is chairman, president, and chief executive officer of Montedison S.p.A. He is a member of the Trilateral Commission, Bilderberg, InterAction Council, Alpha Alpha, and AEI World Forum.

James R. Schlesinger has held numerous positions in government, including assistant director of the Bureau of the Budget, chairman of the Atomic Energy Commission, director of the CIA, secretary of defense, and secretary of energy. He is currently counselor to Georgetown University's Center for Strategic and International Studies and senior adviser to Shearson Lehman Brothers Inc.

Jesus Silva-Herzog is currently a professor at the University of Mexico and El Colegio de Mexico. He was formerly finance minister of Mexico.

George J. Votja is executive vice-president in charge of development and administration at Bankers Trust Company. He is a member of the Council on Foreign Relations and the North-South Roundtable.

Contributors

H. B. Atwater, Jr.
Chairman
General Mills, Inc.
P.O. Box 1113
Minneapolis, MN 55440

Robert E. Baldwin
Department of Economics
University of Wisconsin
Madison, WI 53706

Robert L. Bartley
Editor
Wall Street Journal
22 Cortlandt Street
New York, NY 10007

Andrew Berg
National Bureau of Economic
  Research
1050 Massachusetts Avenue
Cambridge, MA 02138

John R. Block
President
NAWGA
201 Park Washington Court
Falls Church, VA 22406

P. Daniel Borge
Bankers Trust Company
280 Park Avenue
New York, NY 10017

Philip Caldwell
Senior Managing Director
Shearson Lehman Brothers
200 Vesey Street
19th Floor
New York, NY 10285-1900

Geoffrey Carliner
Executive Director
National Bureau of Economic
  Research
1050 Massachusetts Avenue
Cambridge, MA 02138

E. Gerald Corrigan
President
Federal Reserve Bank of New York
33 Liberty Street
New York, NY 10045

Rudiger Dornbusch
Department of Economics
Massachusetts Institute of
  Technology
E52-357
Cambridge, MA 02139

Sebastian Edwards
Department of Economics
University of California at Los
  Angeles
Bunche Hall, Room 8283
405 Hilgard Avenue
Los Angeles, CA 90024

Barry Eichengreen
Department of Economics
Harvard University
Littauer Center 232
Cambridge, MA 02138

Thomas O. Enders
Salomon Brothers
One New York Plaza
New York, NY 10004

Martin Feldstein
President
National Bureau of Economic
    Research
1050 Massachusetts Avenue
Cambridge, MA 02138

Jeffrey A. Frankel
Department of Economics
University of California
250 Barrows Hall
Berkeley, CA 94720

Bruce L. Gardner
Department of Agricultural
    Economics
University of Maryland
College Park, MD 20742

Maurice R. Greenberg
Chairman of the Board
American International Group, Inc.
70 Pine Street
New York, NY 10270

Robert S. Ingersoll
Suite 2530
One First National Plaza
Chicago, IL 60603

Thomas S. Johnson
President
Chemical Bank
20 Pine Street
New York, NY 10005

Woo-choong Kim
Chairman and Chief Executive
    Officer
Daewoo Group
1120 19th Street, N.W.
Washington, DC

Anne O. Krueger
Department of Economics
Duke University
Durham, NC 27706

Richard M. Levich
Graduate School of Business
    Administration
New York University
100 Trinity Place
New York, NY 10006

Robert V. Lindsay
Retired President
Morgan Guaranty Trust Co.
23 Wall Street
New York, NY 10015

Robert E. Lipsey
National Bureau of Economic
    Research
269 Mercer Street
8th Floor
New York, NY 10003

Rachel McCulloch
Department of Economics
University of Wisconsin
Madison, WI 53706

Saburo Okita
Chairman
Institute for Domestic and
    International Policy Studies
Fukoku Seimei Building
2-2-1. Kasumigaseki
Chiyoda-ku, Tokyo
Japan

Lionel H. Olmer
Paul, Weiss, Rikfind, Wharton and
    Garrison
1615 L Street, N.W.
Washington, DC 20036

Charles W. Parry
Chairman and Chief Executive
    Officer
Aluminum Company of America
1501 Alcoa Building
Pittsburgh, PA 15219

Peter G. Peterson
Chairman
Blackstone Group
375 Park Avenue
Suite 3401
New York, NY 10152

Charles S. Sanford, Jr.
Bankers Trust Company
280 Park Avenue
New York, NY 10017

John E. Sawyer
President
Andrew W. Mellon Foundation
140 East 62d Street
New York, NY 10021

Mario Schimberni
Chairman and Chief Executive
    Officer
Montedison S.p.A.
Foro Bonaparte 31
20121 Milano
Italy

James R. Schlesinger
1800 K Street, N.W.
Suite 400
Washington, DC 20006

Jesus Silva-Herzog
Cerro ve Xico #44
Delegacion
Coyoacan 04310
Mexico, D.S.

George J. Votja
Bankers Trust Company
280 Park Avenue
New York, NY 10017

Author Index

Adams, Walter, 349n.34
Ahamed, L., 61n.30
Ahearn, Raymond J., 138n.14
Aho, C. Michael, 400
Ajanant, Juanjai, 138n.12
Akrasanee, Narongchai, 138n.12
Alburo, Florian, 103, 138n.8
Alexander, Gordon J., 246
Aliber, Robert Z., 255n.27
Alston, Julian M., 458
Altshuler, Alan, 338
Anderson, Kym, 440, 455
Ando, Albert, 298, 347n.7
Anwar, M. Arsjad, 138n.13
Ariff, Mohamed, 138n.10
Aronson, Jonathan David, 400
Arpan, Jeffrey S., 328
Atwater, H. B., Jr., 76, 460–68, 473, 558
Auerbach, Alan, 298, 347n.7
Avery, Dennis, 455

Balassa, Bela, 23, 26, 57, 60nn.19, 23,
    61n.32, 138nn.6–7
Balassa, C., 60n.23
Baldridge, Malcolm, 411
Baldwin, Robert E., 79–141, 138n.8,
    159, 402, 421, 498
Barnett, Donald F., 313, 318, 323,
    347n.13, 349n.35
Bartley, Robert, 656, 657
Batten, D. S., 436
Bautista, Romero M., 138n.8

Belongia, M. T., 436
Berliner, Diane, 322, 325, 349n.40,
    350n.45
Bhagwati, Jagdish, 377
Black, Deborah G., 233, 239, 254n.19,
    255n.23
Black, John, 76
Blejer, M., 14
Block, John R., 468–73
Bluestone, Barry, 279
Boone, Jean, 138n.14
Boothe, Paul, 622n.9
Borge, P. Daniel, 264
Bradley, Bill, 191
Brandis, R. Buford, 349n.39
Branson, William, 342
Brereton, Barbara F., 491
Brock, William, 410
Burt, Oscar, 458
Butler, Charles, 346
Butz, Earl, 442, 469

Caldwell, Philip, 74, 75, 358–64
Calvo, G., 59n.4
Cantor, David, 315, 325
Capra, James, 642
Cardoso, Eliana, 169, 192, 193n.7
Carliner, Geoffrey, 276, 366
Carroll, John C., 402
Carvalho, J., 46
Cavallo, D., 46
Caves, Richard E., 498

Chambers, Robert G., 435–36
Chen, Edward K. Y., 138n.4
Choksi, A., 47
Chrystal, K. Alec, 253n.4, 623n.20
Cline, W., 60n.23
Clinton, Kevin, 622n.9
Cohen, Stephen S., 361
Collins, James F., 338
Cooper, Ian, 240, 243
Cooper, William H., 138nn.4–7, 569
Corbo, V., 59nn.2, 4
Corrigan, E. Gerald, 76, 213, 257–64,
    276
Cox, John C., 254n.21
Crandall, Robert W., 314, 349n.35, 346
Cuddington, J., 61n.30, 40, 46

Deardorff, Alan V., 377
de Hoz, Martinez, 167, 193n.5
de la Torre, José, 328
de Melo, J., 59n.4
Diaz-Alejandro, C. F., 14, 59n.2, 60n.27
Dirlam, Joel, 349n.34
Dixit, P. V., 437
Dooley, Michael, 253, 255n.28, 622n.12
Dornbusch, Rudiger, 61nn.34–36, 75, 76,
    161–96, 213, 277, 422, 655, 656
Dorosh, Paul A., 454
Dufey, Gunter, 231–34
Dunmore, John, 438
Dutton, John, 434–36, 439

Edwards, Alejandra Cox, 45, 46, 59,
    193n.6
Edwards, Sebastian, 9–64, 71, 74, 146,
    193n.6, 422
Eichengreen, Barry, 279–346, 350n.48,
    354, 365
Elliott, Kimberly Ann, 322, 325, 349n.40,
    350n.4
Enders, Thomas, 64–68, 73–74, 77, 213–
    14, 421, 557
Eun, Cheol So, 246
Evans, P. B., 61n.37

Fama, Eugene F., 254n.20
Favaro, E., 46
Feenstra, Robert, 327
Fei, John C. H., 138n.7
Feketekuty, Geza, 378
Feldman, Robert Alan, 245–47, 255n.29
Feldstein, Martin, 1–8, 192, 213, 253,
    276, 359–60, 363, 458, 556, 622, 634,
    655, 657

Ferguson, Ronald, 337
Figlewski, Stephen, 254n.12
Fischer, Stanley, 176, 192
Frank, Charles R., Jr., 138n.6
Frankel, Jeffrey A., 329, 552, 556, 559–
    626, 655
Fraser, Donald K., 246
Frenkel, Jacob A., 255nn.27–28
Friedman, Martin, 607
Friedman, Milton, 192
Froot, Ken, 622
Furtado, C., 44, 559nn.2–3
Fuss, Melvyn, 311

Galston, W. A., 434
Gardiner, W. H., 437
Gardner, Bruce L., 423–60, 469, 470, 474
Gerschenkron, Alexander, 280, 346n.1
Giddy, Ian, 231–34, 254n.14, 273
Golub, Stephen, 623n.23
Gomez-Ibanez, José, 302
Gonzales, Ernesto, 623n.22
Gould, David, 59
Grabbe, J. Orlin, 254n.10
Graham, Frank, 403
Greenberg, H., 635
Greenberg, Maurice R., 74, 407–13, 421,
    422
Grennes, T. J., 434–36, 439
Grossman, Gene M., 319, 325

Haddad, C., 46
Hale, David, 649
Haley, S. L., 438
Hamilton, Carl, 346
Hanson, J., 59n.4
Hardt, John P., 138n.14
Harrison, Bennett, 279
Harrison, David, 302
Haves, James, 543
Hekman, Christine, 254n.14
Hicks, David, 622
Hillman, Arye, 59
Hilton, R. Spencer, 126
Ho, Yin Ping, 138n.4
Hogan, William, 347n.6
Hong, Wontack 138n.6
Hood, Neil, 489, 502
Hufbauer, Gary Clyde, 322, 325, 349n.40,
    350n.45

Ingersoll, Robert S., 75, 141–51, 160,
    363–64, 366, 558
Insel, Barbara, 434
Isard, Peter, 255n.28, 622n.12

Jayawardena, Lal, 632
Johnson, P. R., 434–36
Johnson, Simon, 192
Johnson, Thomas S., 76, 192, 196–201, 213, 421
Johnston, B. F., 433
Jones, C. D., 60n.23
Just, R. E., 435–36

Kalt, Joseph P., 332–33, 346
Karlson, Stephen H., 318, 349n.34
Katz, Harry, 340
Keeling B., 300
Kenen, Peter, 622
Kidwell, David S., 246
Kim, Woo-choong, 152–60, 162
Kindleberger, Charles, 647
Kiyoshi Kawahito, 298, 302, 349n.36
Kraft, J., 169
Krause, Lawrence B., 123, 378
Kravis, Irving B., 402, 492
Kreinen, Mordechai, 279, 302, 348n.22
Kreiner, Irene J., 254n.16
Krishna, Kala, 346
Krissoff, B., 438
Krueger, Alan, 305
Krueger, Anne O., 14, 43, 201–13, 364, 473–74, 655
Krugman, Paul, 295, 297–98
Kuo, Shirley W., 138n.7
Kvasnicka, Joseph G., 253n.4

Ladd, Helen, 337
Lappe, Frances Moore, 461
Lawrence, Colin, 307
Lawrence, Robert, 307
Leamer, E. E., 30n.15, 59n.9
Leonard, James H., 338
Lessard, D., 193n.12
Lever, Lord, 191
Levich, Richard M., 215–53, 253n.2, 255nn.27–28, 265, 543, 554–55, 622
Levy, S., 193n.7
Liang, Chung-ing, H., 138n.7
Liang, Kuo-shu, 138n.7
Lim, Chee-peng, 138n.10
Lin, Tzong-biau, 138n.4
Lin, William, 446
Lindert, Peter, 346
Lindsey, Robert V., 550–57
Lipsey, Robert E., 402, 475–545, 550–51
Lodge, George, 360
Longmire, James, 438

Longworth, David, 622n.9
Love, James P., 342, 346

MacArthur, Alan, 622
McCulloch, Rachel, 367–402, 557
Mahajan, Arvind, 246
Marr, M. Wayne, 246
Marsden, David, 350n.49
Martin, Randolph, 322
Maskus, Keith E., 498
Mathia, G., 433, 434
Melichar, E., 458
Mellor, J. W., 433
Meltzer, A., 192
Michaely, M., 47
Michiya Matsukawa, 555
Miller, Merton H., 254nn.9, 20
Mills, R. H., 192n.1
Mok, Victor, 138n.4
Molinari, Linda, 543
Moscheni, Marinella, 543
Meuller, Hans, 298, 302, 346, 349n.36

Nam, Chong-hyun, 138n.6
Neiheisel, Gary L., 338
Ng, F., 61n.33
Niksch, Larry A., 138nn.8, 10, 12
Nogues, J., 40–42, 46, 60nn.23, 25

Obey, David, 193n.16
O'Boyle, Thomas F., 279
Olechowski, A., 40–42, 60nn.23, 25
Olmer, Lionel H., 366, 413–20, 557, 635, 655
Orden, David, 435–37
Oswald, Andrew, 306
Overton, E., 433, 434

Papageorgiou, D., 47
Parry, Charles W., 354–58, 365–66, 420, 558, 655
Pearson, S. R., 454
Pelzman, Joseph, 322
Peterson, Peter G., 73, 474, 558, 633–44, 655
Pfefferman, G., 61n.30
Pinera, J., 61n.38
Pitt, Mark M., 138n.13
Prebisch R., 43

Ramos, J., 193n.6
Ranis, Gustav, 138n.7
Reboul, Jean, 254n.8
Regan, Donald, 411

Reynolds, Alan, 656
Richardson, J. David, 402, 543
Roberts, Bee-yan, 138n.5
Robinson, Jim, 193n.16
Rodriguez-Mendoza, M., 60
Rosendale, Phillis, 138n.13
Rostenkowski, Dan, 411
Rubenstein, Mark, 254n.21
Rungkasiri, Lulapa, 253

Saburo Okita, 74, 160, 363, 627–33, 656
Sampson, Gary P., 377
Sanchez, Rolando, 59
Sandor, Richard 254n.6
Sanford, Charles S., Jr., 264–77
Sarbanes, Paul, 193n.16
Sawyer, Jack, 474
Saxonhouse, Gary, 347n.7
Schenk, W., 348n.30
Schimberni, Mario, 557
Schive, Chi, 138n.7
Schlesinger, James R., 365–66, 473, 639,
    644–54
Schorsch, Louis, 313, 318, 323, 347n.13,
    349n.41
Schuh, G. Edward, 435, 437
Schumpeter, Joseph, 279
Schupbach, Rosa, 543
Scott, Bruce, 360
Sengupta, Arjun, 632
Shepherd, Geoffrey, 103, 138n.8
Silva-Herzog, Jesus, 69–77
Smith, Adam, 413
Snape, Richard H., 377
Sommariva, Andrea, 253n.2

Spiler, P., 46
Stalson, Helena, 395, 402
Stein, Herbert, 635
Stern, Robert M., 59n.9, 498
Summers, Lawrence, 305

Tatom, J. A., 436
Thatcher, Margaret, 572
Thomas, V., 61n.27
Thurow, Lester, 629
Torre, José de la, 328
Toyne, Brian, 328, 348n.27, 350n.50
Trimble, John L., 246
Tsao, James T. H., 325
Tyers, Rod, 440, 455

van der Ven, Hans, 323, 350n.48
Vernon, Raymond, 346n.1
Vojta, George, 74, 264–77, 365, 558
Volcker, Paul, 584

Watkins, A. J., 434
Waverman, Leonard, 311
White, T. K., 433, 434
Wilkins, Mira, 480
Williams, J. H., 644
Williamson, J., 193n.12
Winters, L. A., 40–42, 60nn.23, 25
Wong, Kum-poh, 138n.5

Yeutter, Clayton, 410
Young, Stephen, 489, 502
Yue, Chia-siou, 138n.5

Zysman, John, 361

Subject Index

Accelerated cost recovery system (ACRS), 605
Accounting, globalization of, 374–80
Acreage reduction programs, U.S., 444–46
ADCs. *See* Advanced developing countries
Adjustment assistance, 328
Advanced developing countries (ADCs): category of imports from, 137; export-oriented economic policies, 136; investment and savings rate, 85; per capita income, 84; trade and development policies of, 89–102. *See also* Developing countries; specific country
Advertising: multinational firms advantage in, 497–98; rapid U.S. growth, 387
Affiliates, foreign, 391; export orientation, 499; majority-owned sales, 502, 527-29; ownership of, 501; sales to host countries, 498; service sectors and, 374, 378, 401; in U.S., 505–7
Afghanistan, debt ratios, 163
Africa: debt-GDP ratios, 163; debt service, 164–65; food export declines, 435; food productivity in, 464; grain imports, 432–33; Gross National Product growth, 434; increase in official credit, 164; sub-Saharan countries, 204. *See also* specific country

Aggregate money supply (M1), U.S., 603–4; food exports and, 436; as misleading statistic, 656
Agriculture: dramatic reversal in world trade, 460–68; exchange rate overvaluation and, 435; food subsidies, 193n.9; global labor force, 389; global policies, 439–42; international competition in, 423–74; as labor-intensive, 463; liberalization of trade issues, 454–55; macroeconomic variables, 435–37; output per capita indexes, 431–32, 441; production by major sector, 390; real price trends, 431; technology transfer, 471; total factor productivity index, 428–29; world food demand, 431–35; world output, 423, 425–431. *See also* Agriculture, U.S.; Commodity markets; specific products
Agriculture, U.S: Agriculture and Food Act (1981), 446; CCC price support programs, 448–52; competitiveness of, 428–31, 466; consumer boycotts, 462; efficiency of, 430; elasticity of demand for, 437; embargoes (1973–80), 451–52; employment in, 382, 389; exports of, 5, 123, 424, 437–41; farm lobby, 465; farm support policy, 442–55, 469–70, 607; financial policies and, 435–37; Food Security Act (1985), 447–50; foreign investment in, 518; GATT issues, 451–55; government-assisted

Agriculture, U.S. (*continued*)
exports (1956–85), 452; Gramm-
Rudman-Hollings legislation and, 447;
market incentives, 467; multinational
export share, 496; PIK program, 425,
443; productivity decline, 428; P. L.
480 program, 452; tariffs, 453. *See also*
U.S. Department of Agriculture;
specific commodities
Agriculture and Food Act (1981), 446
AIG Company, 407
Air transport, regulation of, 402n.1
ALADI, 46
Alcoa, 354–58, 365
Allied Irish Banks, 556
All-Savers' Certificates, 604
Aluminum industry, 354–58, 365, 420
American depositary receipt (ADR)
accounts, 555
American Express Bank Review, 599
American Soybean Association, 451
Amortization, 164
Andean Pact, 14, 52, 74, 501
Antidumping laws, 41, 159, 322–23
Antitrust laws, 274
Apparel industry, U.S.: female labor
force and, 305; foreign competition in,
279–366; global production changes
(1974–83), 290; government policies
and, 295–99; imports of, 137; product
cycle, 293–95; regional location of,
334; stability of, 282
Apple Company, 75
APR countries. *See* Asian Pacific Rim
countries
Arbitrage, 245
Argentina: Austral Plan, 65–66, 68;
capital flight (1978–82), 168, 188;
current accounts deficits, 581; cut in
grain export tax, 425; debt
mismanagement, 65, 167–168, 181,
192; devaluation schedules, 48; dollar
value and, 439; economic reforms, 14,
44–45, 65–66, 68; exports to industrial
nations, 42; food export markets, 17,
435, 440, 466; imports, 16, 21, 25–26,
31, 33; inflation rates in, 175; massive
reforms, 14; monetary and fiscal
policies, 48; multiple exchange rates,
51; overvaluation, 167; per capita debt
figures, 165; protectionism in, 42, 45;
real exchange rate, 167; relaxation of

capital controls in, 48; trade surpluses,
19; value of exports, 15, 33–43. *See
also* Latin America; Southern Cone
countries
Artificial intelligence, 267
ASEAN. *See* Association of Southeast
Asian Nations
Asia, 160; agricultural imports, 434;
debt-GDP ratios, 163; farm economy,
461; GNP growth (1980–85), 435; grain
imports, 432–33, 440; increased price
incentives in, 434; interest as fraction
of GDP, 164–65; Latin American
exports, 37; purchases of U.S.
Treasury securities, 512; U.S. bank
loans to, 513. *See also* Asian Pacific
Rim countries; Developing countries;
specific nations
Asian Development Bank, 633
Asian Pacific Rim (APR) countries: basic
economic indicators, 82; commodity
structure of, 87; debt service of, 85,
87; development policy, 89–116; direct
investment in, 130–32; distribution of
exports, 130; diversity among, 83–85;
economic performance of, 80–88;
export product mix, 137; export rates,
86, 129, 153; factor-intensity
breakdowns of exports to, 126; FDI in,
130–32, 134–35; GDP growth rates,
81, 86; GNP, 80-81, 143; import rates,
86; investments in U.S., 590;
merchandise trade of, 88; natural
resources of, 155, 158; NICs, 143;
population, 143; outputs and imports,
81; per capita income, 81, 143;
population of, 80, 143; RRCs in, 84;
savings rates, 83; U.S. exports to, 4,
120–22, 124–25; U.S. imports from,
124–25; U.S. investments in, 134–35,
152; U.S. market competition, 116–28.
See also specific countries
Association of American Iron and Steel
Engineers, 315
Association of Southeast Asian Nations
(ASEAN): establishment of, 104;
export shares, 104; natural resources,
155, 158; RRCs in, 84; stake in
services, 411. *See also* Asian Pacific
Rim countries
Australia: dollar value and, 439; exports
from APR countries, 129; exports to

APR countries, 80, 119–23; grain export-imports, 440–41; imports from APR countries, 129; natural resources, 155; open financial markets, 574; output of, 142; per capita income, 143; trade with U.S., 147; wheat prices, 429
Austral Plan, 65–66, 68
Automobiles. *See* Motor vehicles and parts industries

Baker Plan, 65, 197
Balance of payments, Japanese, 627
Balance of payments, LDCs, 202; debt-equity swaps, 187; multilateral approach to, 198. *See also* Debt crisis, global; specific nations
Balance of payments, U.S.: APR nations and, 137, 148; capital account deficit (1960s), 561–66; capital inflows (1980–85), 585–95; economic policy and, 652; flexible exchange rates and, 633; 1946–85, 562–65; 1970–86, 147; omnibus plan for, 157–58; statistical discrepancy in, 620; surplus, 561; as trade problem, 566. *See also* Budget deficit, U.S.; Current account, U.S.; Trade deficit, U.S.
Banco Central do Brasil, 186
Bangladesh, debt ratios, 163
Bank for International Settlements (BIS), 171, 181, 221, 257, 628
Banking industry, 219–23, 394; capital-reserve surpluses, 197; central. *See* Central banks; commercial, 215, 554; debt-equity swaps, 185–88; debt quality and, 179–82; deregulation, 264–65, 569; double standards in, 76; Eurocurrency markets and, 219–22; failures, 175; FDI, in U.S., 589–91; FDIC and, 264–65; financial innovations risks, 248; foreign exchange market, 219–22; foreign lending by, 180, 511, 514, 542; IBFs, 222, 585, 588; insurance reform for, 270–72; Japanese and, 421, 573, 628; lending boom, 1979–81, 171; loan discount rate, 579; location, 577; multilateral lending, 201; offshore, 262, 574, 576; regulation, 220, 271–72; securitization and, 223–25, 273; underwriting losses, 67, 180, 273–74;

U.S. vs. European, 181, 265. *See also* Capital markets, global; Financial services industry
Barley, price supports, 446
Basic industries, U.S.: commodity market integration, 298–99; defined, 281; diversification in, 340–41; earnings differentials, 303–5; economies of scale changes, 355; employment trends, 344–45; energy prices, 319; future prospects, 341–42; government policies and, 295–99; hourly earnings, 303; import penetration (1973–85), 283–84; industrial policies and, 327–38; joint ventures, 339–40; labor vs. capital-intensive, 293–94; labor competitiveness of, 302–12; lagging domestic demand, 299–302; macroeconomic policies and, 329–30, 354; new product development, 337–39; overcapacity, 355–56; pollution abatement programs, 330–33; process innovations, 355; product cycle, 293–95; production costs, 314–19; regional location of, 333–37; share of manufacturing investment, 312–14; supply competition, 287–99; technology transfer, 359; trade policies and, 319–27; trends in, 281–87. *See also* specific industry
Basle Concordant, 221, 260
Beef: competition for markets, 470; supply-demand equations, 440–41
Belgium, textile industry, 297
Bid-ask spread, 569
Bilateral trade negotiations. *See* specific nations
Birth rate, U.S., 641
BIS. *See* Bank for International Settlements
Black-Scholes option-pricing model, 233
Bolivia: debt-GDP ratio, 165; exports, 17; imports from industrialized countries, 16, 23, 25, 33; imports to GDP ratio, 20; openness index, 19
Bond markets: denominated in dollars, 582; direct investor purchase of, 592; futures trading, 229; international (1982–86), 570–71; LCDs, 193n.10; rate differentials, 596–97; secondary markets, 579; swap-driven issues, 230;

Bond markets (*continued*)
value of-GDP ratio, 223–24; World
Bank call provisions, 580–81; yen-
dominated issues in, 571, 573, 629. *See
also* Capital markets, global;
Eurobonds; U.S. Department of the
Treasury
Bonds, U.S.: defaults, 485; Euromarket-
issued, 223, 583, 623nn.19, 22; FDI
earnings vs., 556; foreign purchases of,
223, 511–13, 539, 588–92, 620; interest
paid to foreigners, 577; vs. nondollar
rates, 598–600; zero-coupon, 234–35,
569. *See also* U.S. Department of the
Treasury
Botswana, food production decline, 434
Bradley Plan, 65–66, 191, 212–13
Brandt Commission (1980), 425
Brazil: auto production, 287, 295; bonds,
579; budget crisis, 64, 66, 163, 167,
169, 178, 181–82; economic changes
in, 71, 361; exports of, 15, 17, 33–43,
435, 440, 464, 466; FDI in, 52–54;
government bonds of, 186; imports of,
16, 21, 25, 27, 31; inflation rates in,
175; macroeconomic indicators, 179;
protectionism in, 42; real exchange
rate, 48-51, 167; steel industry, 294;
telecommunications exclusions, 398;
trade surpluses, 19
Bretton Woods system, 561, 566, 646–47
British Gas, 555
British Telecom, 555
Brokerage fees, 569
Brunei, trade with United States, 147
Budget deficit, LDCs, 161–214. *See also*
specific nation
Budget deficit, U.S., 2, 611, 613–20;
basic industry decline and, 354; change
in, 475; debt service costs and, 607,
634–35; entitlement programs and,
639–40; Eurobonds and, 592; external
debt, 196–201, 511; food imports and,
434–35; foreign exchange earnings
and, 615; foreign policy and, 636–37;
Gramm-Rudman-Hollings and, 200;
1914–19, 480–81; 1986, 614; private
savings and, 607, 610; third world
growth and, 467; true net
indebtedness, 620. *See also* Current
account, U.S.; Debt crisis, global;
Trade deficit, U.S.

Building services, 387
Bureau of Labor Statistics, services
defined, 403n.19
Burma, per capita income, 143
Business cycle, basic industries and, 300,
343
Business plant/equipment investment,
U.S.-Japan (1970–81), 641
Business services sector, U.S.: current
account (1977–86), 372, 416–17;
defined, 402n.3, 403n.18; employment,
380–83, 386–87; foreign markets, 374–
80; information-based, 265–68, 368,
375–80, 414; major industries, 387;
trade by component, 373; trade
decline, 408–9
Business Week, 552

California: automobile production, 339;
steel industry employment, 335
Cameroon, food production decline, 434
Canada: corn tariff, 453; dollar value
and, 439, 570–71; exports to APR
countries, 80, 116–28; grain exports
share, 441; imports, 129, 440–41;
investments in U.S., 512, 552, 589;
labor force by industry, 389; metal
fabrication in, 287; minimills, 318;
motor vehicle industry, 287; open
financial markets, 572; production by
major sector, 390; services
negotiations, 400, 421; U.S. FDI in,
480, 483; wheat prices, 429
Capital account, U.S., 510; banking
transactions, 592; inflows (1980–85),
585–95; private capital on net, 568;
securities liabilities, 592; surplus in,
620. *See also* Current account, U.S.
Capital flight, LDCs and, 168, 188–89,
192, 202, 219; real interest rates and,
176
Capital International Perspective, 600
Capital markets, global, 6–8, 188, 201,
371, 559–60, 644; barriers, 242–44;
capital-exporting nations, 628–29; debt
and, 202, 219; dollar decline and, 4;
economies of scale, 569; equity inflows
into U.S., 552; expected rates of
return, 568, 596–602; financial
innovations in, 215–53; foreign vs.
domestic holdings, 572; government
controls on, 571–74, 582; imperfect,

241–42; information technology effects on, 265–70; integration of; 407; Latin America and, 65, 75–76; official, *see* Foreign aid; offshore, 262, 509, 511, 556, 574, 582; open, 572; perfect, 240–44; regulatory arbitrage, 251; safe haven hypothesis, 577–82, 596–97; securitization of, 592; trade deficit and, 559; transaction costs, 245, 569–71; U.S. transactions, 200, 475, 480, 486–87, 552, 534–38, 560–68, 585–95; World War II effects, 487; worldwide liquidity growth, 199. *See also* Banking industry; Bond markets; Financial services industry; Interest rates; Loans; specific instruments

Caribbean: banking in, 262, 509, 511, 582, 585; GDP, 81; purchases of U.S. Treasury securities, 512; sugar dumping by, 470

Cartegena Agreement, 52

Cartelization, service activities, 402n.1

Carter administration: Carter bonds, 582–83; trade deficits, 567

Cedel systems, 233

Central America, 14; GDP, 81; investments in U.S., 589; U.S. interests in, 73. *See also* Latin America; specific countries

Central American Common Market, 14

Central banks, 566; Basle meetings, 221, 260; dollar reserves, 592–95; U.S. fiscal policy and, 658. *See also* Banking industry; Eurocurrency market; Financial services industry; Foreign exchange market

CEPAL/ECLA projections, 56

Cereals. *See* Grain

Certificates of deposit (CDs), 573

Certificates on automobile receivables (CARS), 233

Chase Manhattan Bank, 556

Checking accounts, interest on, 604

Chemical industry: global distribution of exports, 522–25; U.S. multinational export shares, 496

Chicago Mercantile Exchange (CME), 246

Chicken, supply-demand equations, 440

Chile: cost of debt, 68; deals with creditors, 65; debt-GDP ratio, 165; debt mismanagement, 168–69;

economic reforms, 14, 44–45, 48, 168; exports, 17; imports, 16, 21, 23, 25, 27, 31, 33; Mining Law (1979), 61n.36; multiple exchange rates, 51; new money, 65; non-oil exports, 68; overvaluation, 167; per capita debt figures, 165; protectionism in, 43, 45; real exchange rate, 48–51, 167; relaxation of capital controls in, 48; trade surpluses, 19; wage indexation in, 48. *See also* Latin America; Southern Cone countries

China: agricultural output, 142, 425, 428; economy of, 84–85, 141–42, 152; exports, 117, 137; foreign investment, 146; Hong Kong exports and, 92; imports, 117, 322; industrial sector and, 150, 158; investment and savings rate, 85; merchandise trade, 115; modernization reforms, 115: natural resources, 155, 158; per capita income, 85, 143; production incentives in, 5; rate of growth, 144; Special Export Zones, 115; steel industry, 294; trade and development policies, 115–16; trends in production, 284; U.K. agreement, 92; U.S. exports to, 116–18, 147, 440, 470

CHIPS, 271

Chrysler Corporation, 307, 328, 364

Clark Air Force Base, 105–6

Club of Rome, 213, 460–61, 656

Coalition of Service Industries, 410

Coffee, boom in trade, 61n.27

Colombia: exports, 14, 16; illegal drug trade in, 61n.27; imports of, 16, 22, 25, 28, 31, 44; multiple exchange rates, 51; nontariff barriers, 45; protectionism in, 43–45

Commerce Department. *See* U.S. Department of Commerce

Commercial bank creditors. *See* Banking industry; Debt crisis, global; Loans

Commercial paper market, 237–39; banking and, 264–65; bridges, 555

Commodity Credit Corporation (CCC): disposal of stocks, 448, 452; loan rate, 442–43, 446; price support cuts, 450

Commodity Futures Trading Commission, 239

Commodity markets: agricultural, U.S., 423–74; APR countries and, 87, 136;

Commodity markets (*continued*)
categories of, 30–31; dramatic
reversals in, 460–68; export price
comparisons, 429–31; global
integration of, 298; liberalization of,
441; price shocks and, 436; rapid
demand growth categories, 123;
relative factor-price differences model,
126–28; speculation in, 431; stagnated
prices, 632–33; supply-demand
equations, 440–41; surplus disposal
programs, 448, 452; U.S. price
policies, 448; U.S. trade share, 440;
world output trends, 425–26. *See also*
specific products, sectors
Common markets: Central American, 14.
See also European Economic
Community
Communications Workers of America,
402n.4
Communication technologies. *See*
Telecommunications
Comparative advantage theory, 60n.17,
403n.15; capital flows and, 645;
national boundaries and, 507; service
sectors and, 379–80; swaps and, 235–
37; U.S.-APR countries and, 128
Competition, international, 153; constant
market share criterion, 59n.9;
indicators of, 55, 430, 493–502; labor
cost differentials and, 308–12; new
financial instruments and, 250–51;
theories of, 361; U.S. decline and,
428–31. *See also* specific sectors
Computer software, 414; market access,
373; proprietary, 376
Conditional import authorizations, 41
Construction industry: foreign affiliate
jobs in U.S., 506–8; market access,
373
Consulting services, 387
Consumer(s), U.S., 559; demand
expansion, 198; income and food
prices, 431, 433, 462, 465
Consumer credit reporting, 387
Consumer Price Index (CPI), real wages
and, 342
Contracts: cross-border regulation,
254n.22; futures market and, 239;
option-like features, 233–34;
replicating porfolio approach, 239
Copyright protections, 403n.8

Corn, 430–31; export-exchange rate
relation, 435; price support programs,
442–51;
Corporate bonds: domestic U.S. vs.
Eurodollar rates, 585, 596–97; foreign
vs. domestic holdings (1984), 572. *See
also* Bond markets; Eurobonds
Corporations, U.S.: capital costs for,
685; collaboration agreements, 546–47;
competitiveness of, 491–502; foreign
affiliates, *see* Affiliates, foreign; foreign
borrowing by, 225, 560, 572, 583, 585,
596–97; FDI and, 480, 502–10;
innovative, 475; internationalization of,
488–502; raids on, 651–52;
securitization and, 225; stock market
values, 227; tax policy and investment,
604–05. *See also* Basic industries,
U.S.; Corporate bonds; Multinational
firms
Costa Rica: debt crisis, 466; exports, 17;
imports of, 16, 22, 25; imports-to-GDP
ratio, 20; openness index, 19
Cotton, price supports, 446–47
Countervailing duties, 41, 159
Credit, 415; consumer reports, 266, 387;
new sources of, 215–18; rationing,
171; U.S. banks, 513–14. *See also*
Capital markets, global; Financial
services industry; Loans
Crops. *See* Agriculture; Commodity
markets
Cruzado Price Freeze Plan, 65, 68
Culture, comparative, 154
Currency: devaluation as source of
inflation, 176; dual issues, 569; foreign
liabilities, 583; forward exchange
markets, 583; options, 215;
overvaluation, 166–69; ranking of, 571;
swaps, 215, 230–31, 233, 236–37, 240,
583. *See also* Eurocurrency market;
Foreign exchange market; specific
currency
Current account, LDCs, 18–19, 161–214.
See also specific country
Current account, U.S., 614; basic
industry decline and, 333–37; bonds
vs. FDI, 556; component parts, 416–
17; deficits, 567; dollar depreciation
and, 621; 1946–85, 562–65, 567; in
1980s, 611, 613–20; as shares of GNP,
601; surpluses (1973–76), 567. *See also*

Budget deficit, U.S.; Trade deficit, U.S.

Dairy products: price supports, 447; supply-demand equations, 440–41
Data processing services, 374–80, 387
Data Resources, 600
Debt crisis, global, 64–68, 423, 577, 597; agriculture and, 465–68; APR countries and, 84–85, 87; Baker Plan, 65, 197; bank write-offs, 67, 273–74; Bradley Plan, 65–66; budget problems and, 165–66, 174–76; case-by-case approach, 196–97; commercial vs. concessional, 165; debt-equity swaps, 76, 185–88; debt service fatigue, 72, 172–78; declining cost of, 67–68; defaults, 66, 201, 249–50, 485–86, 577, 579–82; dollar and, 165, 173–74; export unit value and, 162; international cooperation, 259; Latin American, 14, 26, 57, 64–68; LDCs, 161–214; major problem debtors, 165–66; market price of problem debt (1986), 181; overview of, 161–66, 202–4; political approach to, 190–92; savings-investments imbalances, 198–99; scale variables, 162; servicing problems, *see* Interest payments; share of long-term debt in total, 163; solutions to, 184–92; trade credits and, 213; transfer problem and, 172–78; U.S. debt relaxation, 196–201; Western nations' debt-GDP ratios, 163; world economy downturn and, 169–70. *See also* Budget deficit, U.S.
Debt service. *See* Interest payments
Defense spending, U.S., 7; budget crisis and, 637; current account and, 562–63; decline in, 650–51; Vietnam War and, 566
Deficits, fiscal. *See* Budget deficit, U.S.; Debt crisis, global
Deindustrialization, of American economy, 374
Demander-located services, 377
Department of Trade, U.S., 411
Deposits, 574; ADR accounts, 555; foreign vs. domestic holdings (1984), 572; insurance, 220, 271–72, 275; offshore, 253n.4, 262, 509, 511, 556, 582, 585; reserve requirements, 220–

21, 574, 577. *See also* Banking industry
Depreciation allowances (ACRS), 605
Deregulation, banking, 76, 215, 220–21, 271–72, 569
Deutsche mark, 557; Carter bonds and, 583; synthetic securities, 237–39; trading in, 570–71
Developed countries. *See* specific country
Developing countries: affiliate sales, 502; agricultural export demand, 423; agricultural output, 425–26, 432; capital flow needs of, 632; dollar and, 439, 593–95; export performance of, 129, 137; food import increases, 431–35; GATT service sector talks, 400; inadequate policy reforms, 205; investment incentives, 201; labor advantage, 341, 404n.24; metals production, 284–85; NTBs in, 41–43, 46; real exchange rate, 61n.30; real income per capita, 433; U.S. import share, 118–19. *See also* Debt crisis, global; specific country, region
Diet for a Small Planet (Lappe), 461
Discretionary import authorizations, 41
Displaced workers, 150–51
Distribution: employment changes and, 386–87; market access, 373. *See also* Transport industry; specific country, product
Diversification, 340–41
Dollar: appreciation of, 423, 599; basic industry competition and, 354; bond rates and, 596–97; Bretton Woods system and, 561, 566, 646–47; commercial paper rate and, 237; current account and, 621; depreciation of, 2, 165, 567–68, 593, 599–600; devalued, 566; European shortage, 561; exchange risk, 582–83; food exports and, 435–39; foreign direct investment in U.S. and, 7; foreign reserves of, 561, 566, 584–85, 592–95; FRB trade-weighted index, 1, 436, 438; inflation and, 185; market export competitors and, 439, 649; national security and, 651; real exchange rates and, 48–52; speculation in, 566; standard, 561, 566; trade deficit and, 359–60, 615; transactions balances, 57;

Dollar (*continued*)
  yen and, 149, 573–74. *See also*
  Exchange rates; Eurocurrency market
Domestic International Sales Corporation
  (DISC), GATT and, 405n.33
Dominican Republic: exports, 17;
  imports, 16; multiple exchange rates, 51
Dreams, Inc., 186
Drugs, illegal trade in, 61n.27
Dumping practices, 10, 41, 159, 322–23
Dutch trading houses, 112
Duties, NTBs, 41

East Asia: access to markets, 81, 154; as
  competitor, 142; description of region,
  142–44; economic policy, 151–52;
  export dependence of, 144; foreign
  investment, 146; GNP, 143; industrial
  development, 150, 154; Japan as model
  for, 149; output of, 142; per capita
  income, 143; trade deficit with U.S.,
  141, 147–50. *See also* Asian Pacific
  Rim countries; specific nations
Eastern Europe: CAME, 30; capitalism
  and, 152; farm economy of, 461; grain
  imports, 433; labor force by industry,
  389
ECLA. *See* Economic Commission for
  Latin America, U.N.
Econometric techniques, 611
Economic Commission for Latin
  America (ECLA), U.N., 14, 29–30,
  56, 71
Economic Outlook (OECD), 600
Economies of scale, trade flow and, 380
Economist Financial Report, The, 599–
  600, 628
Ecuador: exports, 15, 17, 33–34;
  imports, 16, 20, 22, 25, 33; multiple
  exchange rates, 51
Education, foreign revenues, 395
EEC. *See* European Economic
  Community
Efficiency, numerical indicator
  limitations, 430
Elasticity of demand, U.S. food exports,
  437
Electrical machinery industry, 496–97,
  522–25
Electric power, capital needs, 654. *See
  also* Energy costs

Electronics industry, collaboration
  agreements, 546–47
El Salvador: imports, 23, 25, 31, 33; real
  exchange rate, 48–51
Employment, 174; agencies, 387;
  agricultural, 382; basic industry trends,
  279, 282–83, 333–37; benefits, 388;
  displaced workers, 150–51; foreign
  affiliates by industry, 532; by foreign-
  owned firms, 490–91, 505–7, 516;
  long-term shifts, 386–88;
  nonagricultural payrolls, 380–83;
  regression analysis and, 342–46;
  sectoral, 380–84; service sector, 367–
  402, 403n.7, 413–14; wage freezes, 175
EMS. *See* European monetary system
Energy costs, 343; basic industries and,
  319; Japanese energy conservation,
  629. *See also* Oil crisis shocks
England. *See* United Kingdom
Entitlement programs, U.S., 639–40
Environmental regulations, 425. *See also*
  specific industry, regulation
Equities. *See* Stock markets
Eurobonds, 216, 238, 577; bond rates,
  592, 596–97; bonds swaps, 230, 238;
  Cedel system, 233; dimensions of,
  222–23; Euro-clear system, 233; Euro-
  DM bond, 238; futures contracts, 228;
  grey market, 233; 1982–86, 570–73;
  rates, 592, 596–97; risks of, 250;
  swaps, 230, 238. *See also* Eurocurrency market; Eurodollar market
Eurocurrency market, 569, 577;
  commercial paper, 215–16, 569;
  foreign exchange and, 219–22; genesis
  of, 220, 566, 582; higher interest rates
  and, 576–77; 1973–86, 221; risk of
  default in, 577–82; as source of global
  instability, 221. *See also* Exchange
  rates
Eurodollar market, 220–22, 570–73, 577;
  futures contracts, 228; rates, 596–97;
  swaps, 238
Euromarkets. *See* Eurobonds;
  Eurocurrency market
European Economic Community (EEC):
  APR countries and, 80, 116–29; bank
  write-offs, 67; basic industries, 297,
  354, 359; Common Agricultural
  Program (CAP), 466, 474; currency
  markets. *See* Eurocurrency market;
  debt-GDP ratios, 163, 165; dollar value

effects, 439; EEP, 448–50, 453; EMS, 253; export shares, 92; export subsidies, 5, 438, 469, 473; footwear production, 287; GATT and, 419; grain surpluses, 439, 462; investments in U.S., 589; Latin American trade balance, 183; metal fabrication, 287, 354, 359; motor vehicle industry, 287; production incentives, 465; service exports and, 411; textile policy, 297; U.S. trade war, 453, 467; U.S. Treasury purchases, 512

European monetary system (EMS), 233

European Recovery Plan, 629

Euroyen, gensaki rate differential, 573–74

Exchange rates: adjustments, 631, 656; black market, 47, 51; bond rates and, 598; Columbian crisis, 44; crawling peg system, 44; domestic controls, 218; fixed, 566–67; floating, 567, 569, 622; flows of capital and, 560; food exports and, 435–39; Latin American policies, 71; long-dated forward contracts, 555; multiple, 12, 46–47, 51–52; protectionist role, 51, 553; real exchange rates, risk of changes in, 582–84. See also Eurocurrency market; Foreign exchange market

Export(s): categories of, 120–27; East Asian growth, 144; embargoes, 451; financing of, 415; GATT focus, 396; multinational shares in, 493–502; price indexes, 59n.5, 165; real value of, 34–35, 55; relative factor-price differences model, 126–28. See also Exports, Latin American; Exports, U.S.; specific countries, products, regions

Export(s), Latin American, 11, 15, 17; to Asia, 37; destination of, 35–37; manufactured goods, 40; primary products, 39; protectionism and, 33–43; sectoral composition of, 38–39; to Soviet bloc, 37; to U.S., 41. See also specific countries

Export(s), U.S.: dollar depreciation and, 568; 1946–85, 562–63; distribution of, 80, 90–94, 124–25, 127, 129, 134; real dollar value, 55; world market share, 226. See also specific commodities, industries, services

Export Enhancement Program (EEP), 448–50, 453

Export Promotion Act (1972), 109

Exterminating services, 387

Factor-proportion theory of international trade, 123, 136

Fair trade laws, 159

FAO. See Food and Agricultural Organization, U.N.

Farm commodities. See Agriculture

Farmland, U.S.: acreage idling program, 425, 467; prices of, 423, 431, 456, 458n.2; shrinkage of, 456

Farm policy, U.S., 423–474. See also Agriculture, U.S.

Fast-food outlets, 387, 407

Federal Deposit Insurance Corporation (FDIC), 181–82, 265, 271–72, 275

Federal Reserve Board: antiinflation policies, 584; banking and, 7, 264, 569; expansionary monetary policy, 603; recession response of, 621; trade-weighted dollar index, 436, 438

Fedwire, regulation of, 271

Feed grains. See Grain

Financial assets, foreign vs. domestic holdings (1984), 572

Financial instruments, 215–53; competition among, 268–70; design and evolution of, 239–40; innovation effects, 257–64. See also Financial services industry

Financial services industry, 219–21; capital flow effects, 559; competition in, 369; debt-equity swaps, 187; dimensions of, 218–30; expert systems and, 267–68; exports of, 559–60; funding vehicles, 226–30, 239–70; globalization of, 6–8, 559–60; information costs, 250, 265–68; innovation effects, 240–52, 258; Japan and, 555–57; mergers and acquisitions, 554; overseas investment, 489–90; policy implications, 247–52; regulation of, 262, 264–77, 602; replicating portfolio approach, 239–40; risk management tools, 226–30; transaction costs, 569–71; U.S. employment in, 380–83. See also Banking industry; Capital markets, global; specific type of market

First National Bank of Maryland, 556

First Regional Bank, 186

Fiscal deficit. See Budget deficit, U.S.

Fiscal policy, U.S., 567, 603–20, 629–30; agricultural exports and, 435–37; basic industries and, 295–99; domestic demand and, 199; domestic vs. global, 648–49; rational model, 650; service sector, 412; timing of, 3. *See also* Budget deficit, U.S.; Current account, U.S.

Floating rate notes, 221; global comparisons, 268; mismatched, 569; risks of, 250

Florida, export-related industry, 415

Food. *See* Agriculture

Food and Agricultural Organization (FAO), U.N., 425

Food Security Act (1985), 447–50

Footwear industry, 287, 291

Ford Motor Company, 294–95, 299, 307, 366

Foreign affiliates. *See* Affiliates, foreign

Foreign aid, 189, 203, 561, 629, 637

Foreign central banks. *See* Central banks

Foreign debt. *See* Debt crisis, global

Foreign direct investment (FDI): bilateral treaties, 74; budget cuts vs., 176; controls on, 582; cycles in, 514; debt-equity swaps and, 184–88; by Japan, 146, 552, 573–75, 631; in Latin America, 52–55; trade links, 401. *See also* Foreign direct investment, by U.S.; Foreign direct investment, in U.S.

Foreign direct investment (FDI), by U.S., 475–558; decline in, 486; defaults and liquidations (1929–35), 485–86; in East Asia, 131–34, 137, 145–46; by industry of affiliate, 518–21; in Latin America, 53; 1919–29, 481–85; 1962–87, 585–88, 616–17; Post-WWI, 487–502; rates of return on, 615; type of industry, 492

Foreign direct investment (FDI), in U.S., 2, 502–17, 550–57; ADR accounts, 555; basic industries, 339–40; fast growth of, 86–87; by industry and country, 533; by industry of affiliate, 530–31; by Japan, 631; 1790–1914, 476; 1984–85, 588–92; politics and, 7, 577–82, 596–97; shared ownership, 501; sources of, 509–10; stock value of, 503–4

Foreign exchange market: bid-ask spread, 569, 571; central banks and, 221, 260, 566, 592–95, 658; debt service and, 70–71, 88; delta hedging procedure, 234; dollar depreciation and, 599–600; Euromarkets and, 219–22; futures contracts, 233; LDCs'problem, 173–74; macroeconomics of, 172; official share of national currency, 594–95; oil and, 10; parallel markets for, 12, 47, 51; trading in, 219, 567–71. *See also* Exchange rates

Foreign investment. *See* Foreign direct investment

Foreign policy, U.S.: exchange rate adjustment and, 656; foreign aid, 189, 203, 561, 629, 637; resource constraints, 638

Forward rate agreements, risks of, 250

Franc: offshore-onshore differential, 574; Swiss, 584; trading in, 570–71

France: capital controls, 574; as exporter of services, 411; farmer's lobby, 466; labor force by industry, 389; land value declines, 471; production by major sector, 390; securitization of, 226; stake in services, 411; steel industry, 297; telecommunications, 418; textile industry, 297

Free trade policy: capital liberalization and, 218; Chile and, 168; GATT and, 151, 156; Pacific economic community and, 157

Futures contracts, 226–30; aggregate open interest in, 228; commodity-contract characteristics, 239; daily trading volumes, 229; exchange-traded, 233; hedging risk and, 255n.23

GATT. *See* General Agreement on Tariffs and Trade

Gaz de France, 254n.8

GDP. *See* specific country

General Agreement on Tariffs and Trade (GATT), 5; agricultural negotiations, 451–55, 472; bilateral pressure and, 159; Congress and, 421; East Asia and, 151; financial services and, 559–60; free trade issues, 151, 156; Japan's admission to, 320; mercantilistic view of gains, 396; Mexico and, 75, 167;

NICs and, 156, 159; nontariff measures, 40, 417; service issues, 5, 368–75, 395–401, 415, 417–19; tariff rates, 396; trade sanctions, 10

Generalized System of Preferences, U.S., 106

General Motors Company, 294–95, 299, 307, 366

Gensaki rate differential, 573–74

Georgia, textile industry employment, 335

Germany: capital inflow control, 572; as creditor nation, 652; current account surpluses, 631–32; decline in earnings, 329; decline in growth rates, 81–82; direct investment in U.S., 552; food price increases, 473; GDP, 81; inflation fears of, 654; labor force by industry, 389; open financial markets, 572; per capita income, 81; production by major sector, 390; steel industry of, 294; telecommunications in, 418

Ghana: food export markets, 435; food production decline, 434

Glass-Steagall Act, 242, 265–66, 273, 421

GNMA. *See* Government National Mortgage Association

GNP. *See* Gross national product

Gold: purchasing power of, 584; standard, 561, 566, 646–47

Goldman Sachs, 556

Goods-producing sectors, employment in, 382–83, 388–89

Government National Mortgage Association (GNMA), 226

Government procurement policies, services sector, 400, 412

Government securities. *See* Bonds; Eurobonds; U.S. Department of the Treasury

Grain: CCC loan rates, 442–43; embargoes, 451–52, 466; export decline, 424, 437–38; exports-dollar value ratios, 437–39; exports-exchange rate models, 436; foreign policy and, 439–42; imports in, 432–33; international trading companies, 429; lost markets, 435–54; market price drop, 423; price ratios of, 429–31; production outside U.S., 426–27; productivity decline, 428–29; supply-demand equations, 440–41; support

programs, 442–55; surpluses, 462; taxes and, 425; value of exports, 423; world sales, 441, 469

Gramm-Rudman-Hollings Act, 185, 200, 447, 621

Great Britain. *See* United Kingdom

Great Depression: Latin America and, 12, 75; U.S. defaults and, 485–86

Great Lakes states, steel industry employment, 335

Great Society program, 566

Green field start-ups, 555

Green Revolution, 424, 427, 432

Gross national product (GNP), developing countries, 433–34, 436. *See also* Gross national product, U.S.; specific country

Gross national product (GNP), U.S.: budget deficit and, 605; corporate saving, 610; defense spending, 650; 1870–1979, 614; federal outlays-revenues, 643; gross fixed capital formation and, 612–13; by industry (1947–85), 385; investments (1951–85) and, 606; labor's share of, 334; monetary policy and, 3; net savings (1951–85) and, 606; non-means-tested entitlement programs and, 642; pollution control and, 330–31; services sector and, 383–86; state/local government surpluses and, 606–07; steel demand and, 300

Group of Five agreement, 199, 259

Group of Seven agreement, 199, 259

Group of Six agreement, 199–200

Group of Ten agreement, 221

Group of Thirty agreement, 171, 555

Guatemala: exports, 17; imports, 16, 22, 33

Guilder, trading in, 570–71

Harvard Business School, 360

Health services, U.S.: employment, 380–83; foreign markets, 376–77, 395

Heckscher-Ohlin theory of trade, 30, 60n.15

Hewlett-Packard Company, 75

High-technology industries: basic industries and, 342; emphasis on, 159; trade deficit and, 415; U.S. dominance in, 371, 379–80

Honduras, imports, 23, 25, 31, 33

Hong Kong: Communists and, 89; domestic savings, 85; export quotas, 321; exports to Japan, 129; growth rate of, 83, 141, 143; immigration from China, 89; income levels in, 84; limits on textile imports, 321; long-term economic outlook, 92; merchandise trade, 90–92; MFA and, 320; open financial markets, 574; trade and development policy, 89–90; trade performance, 90–92; U.N. embargo, 89; U.S. export share, 116–18

Household saving rate, 607

Housing services, 403n.18

Human-capital-intensive imports, 120–27. See also Labor force

Hungary, agricultural experiments in, 471

Hyperinflation, 176, 584

IBM: Mexico and, 75; World Bank and, 237

IET. See Interest equalization tax

Illinois, automobile production, 339

IMF. See International Monetary Fund

Immigration, labor force and, 479

Imports: constant market-share criterion, 11; external price indexes and, 59n5; market shares, 55, 58; nontrade barriers, 40–47; prior licences, 46; relative factor-price differences model, 126–28. See also specific country; SITC classification, 29; substitution strategies, 43–45; unskilled-labor intensive, 120–27. See also specific commodity, service

Imports, Latin American, 11, 15–33; agriculture, 432–33; composition of, 20–33; distribution by origin, 21–23; substitution strategies, 15, 43–45, 71; trend regressions, 13, 25; U. S. share in, 23–25. See also specific commodity, country

Imports, U.S.: 1946–85, 562–63; as percentage of world exports, 198; textiles, 320–22. See also specific commodity

Income. See Current account, U.S.; specific country

Income tax: corporate tax and, 605; withholding tax, 577

India: agricultural policies, 425; GATT negotiations, 368, 419, 421; GDP growth rate, 83; Green Revolution, 464

Indiana, automobile production, 339

Indonesia: debt-servicing problems, 85–88; export shares, 92, 114; exports to Japan, 129; factor-price advantage, 128; FDI in, 112; growth rate, 137, 142–44; imports, 114, 116, 440; liberalization in, 112; merchandise trade of, 113; rice harvest of, 428; subsidized farms in, 454; trade and development policies, 110–12; trade balance of, 88, 113–15; U.S. export share, 116, 440

Industrial nations. See specific country

Industrial patents, 376

Industrial policies, U.S., 327–28

Industrial technology, U.S. superiority in, 150, 159, 379–80

Industry. See Basic industries, U.S.; specific industry

Inflation: Brazil and, 179; corporate asset measures and, 490; currency valuation and, 166–69, 176; expected, 600, 654–55; heterodox approach to, 70; Mexico and, 177; M1 and, 199; real interest rates and, 603; U.S. and, 3, 169–70, 566

Informatics, software vs. hardware values, 414

Information-based services, 368, 375–80

Information costs, 571

Information technology, international finance and, 265–68

Institute of International Economics, 615

Insurance industry: direct investment by U.S., 520; exported, 379, 395; foreign brokers, 379; foreign investment in U.S., 589–91; globalization of, 374–80, 407–13; in Japan, 573

Intellectual property, protection of, 403n.8

Interamerican Development Bank, 54

Interest earnings: onshore-offshore differentials, 573–74; taxed, 574. See also Interest rates

Interest equalization tax (IET), U.S., 222

Interest payments, 164–65; debt-equity swaps, 185–88; debt service fatigue, 172–78; dollar-denominated, 261–62; economic growth and, 204–20; external vs. domestic, 186–87; GDP ratio of major debtors, 166, 207–8; national income and, 65; official vs. private debt, 164; as political issue,

190–92; special taxes on, 572; U.S. foreign debt, 420n.1, 624

Interest rates, 204: availability of capital and, 7, 560, 632; bonds, 596–602; budget deficits and, 3; checking accounts and, 604; default risk, 577–82; deviations from interest parity, 576, 578–79; foreign investors and, 7, 566; futures contracts, 226–30, 234; global changes in, 10, 371; LIBOR, 579; market-determined, 215; official vs. private debt, 164; offshore-onshore differences, 578, 581–82; options contracts, 215, 226–30; real, *see* Interest rates, real; short-term, 581; swaps, 215, 230–31, 235–37, 240, 555, 569, 581; trade and, 436; U.S. vs. nondollar, 598–600

International Banking Facilities (IBFs), 222, 577, 585, 588

International investment income account, U.S., 416–17, 562–63, 634. *See also* Current account, U.S.

Internationalization. *See* Multinational firms

International Monetary Fund (IMF), 633; debt collection process, 192; stabilization programs, 202; stringent criteria, 211

International Trade Commission (ITC): Canadian timber sales and, 453; international service survey, 397

Investment, global. *See* Foreign direct investment; specific markets

Investment, U.S. *See* Current account, U.S.; Foreign direct investment, by U.S.

Investment Incentive Act (1968), 106, 201. *See also* Tax policy

Iran, frozen assets of, 582

Iron: global production of, 285; unit labor costs, 311

Italy: labor force by industry, 389; production by major sector, 390; telecommunications, 418; textile industry, 297

Janitorial services, 387

Japan: ADCs and, 135; agricultural subsidies in, 5; aluminum production, 354; APR countries and, 80, 94, 116–18, 129, 137, 144; auto industry, 287, 294–96, 325, 327, 588; banking and, 421, 573, 628; basic industry policies, 296–99; business investment (1970–81), 641; clothing output, 287; cost-of-capital advantage, 299; as creditor nation, 67, 646, 649, 652; current account surplus, 627–28; decline in growth rates, 81–82; direct investment by, 130–31, 137, 144, 146, 552, 573–75, 588–91, 631; dollar value effects, 439; domestic savings, 85; economic goals of, 361, 629, 631, 654; export shares, 11, 80, 90–92, 116–28, 135, 137, 144; finance services, 245, 417; food imports, 474; footwear production, 287; gross domestic product, 81; growth of, 141, 143, 631; high-technology and, 136, 398, 418; household saving rate, 607; industrial sector and, 158; labor force by industry, 389; labor productivity, 308–09, 311–12, 329; Latin America and, 9, 56–57, 67, 183; long-term capital movements in, 573–75; Maekawa report, 631, 654; manufactured imports, 32–33; manufacturing affiliate sales, 502; metal production declines, 284–85; official development assistance, 633; per capita income, 81, 142; production by major sector, 390; production costs in, 311, 339; regulated capital markets, 573; saving-investment ratio, 628; self-sufficiency in rice, 439; stake in services, 411; steel and iron industry, 284, 294, 318, 332, 340; targeting-industry strategy, 153; technological development capabilities, 153–54; telecommunications and, 398, 418; textile industry, 293, 296; third world debt and, 67, 639; trade barriers of, 148–50, 156, 159; U.S. bond preference, 592; U.S. investments in, 144–45, 421, 555–56; U.S. trade and, 4, 146–47, 509, 630–33, 653–54; voluntary export restraints, 320, 325, 327

Japan Center for International Finance, 623n.28

Joint ventures, U.S., 339–40, 378, 546, 555

Kawasaki, 299

Kennedy administration, capital outflow and, 566

Kenya, food production decline, 434
Knowledge-based industries, 375–80, 547
Korea, North, 89, 96, 99
Korea, South: auto industry, 287, 295–96, 327; bilateral U.S. trade treaty, 160; commodity price developments, 170; construction projects, 417; debt service of, 64, 85–88; distribution of exports, 99; domestic savings, 85; economic goals of, 361; exchange rate, 159, 167; exports, 92, 97–98, 129, 144; foreign investments, 146; growth rate of, 141; imports, 98, 129, 474; income levels of, 81, 84; industrial sector and, 158; intraregional trade, 56; Japan and, 129, 158; merchandise trade, 97; MFA and, 320; restrictive trade policies, 96–97, 159, 321; steel industry of, 294; technology and, 359; trade balance of, 88, 97–99, 158; U.S. export share, 116–18; voluntary restraint agreements, 295
Korean War, 89, 96
Kravis index of price competiveness, 429

Labor adjustment assistance, U.S., 328
Labor costs: global economy and, 308–12, 356–57; real exchange rate and, 329–30, 342
Labor force, 370; comparative advantages in, 295, 308–12; earnings differentials, 303–5; elasticity of demand, 306–7; employee involvement programs, 312; employment by sector, 382; foreign affiliate firms and, 490–91; global, by industry, 389; immigration and, 479; international division of, 158–59; national income decline and, 334; retraining of, 150–51, 328; service-producing sectors, 370–75; U.S. vs. European practices, 553; women in, 386–87. See also Employment; Unions; specific sectors
Laffer curve theory, 607, 650
Latin America: basic indicators for, 13; bilteral trade balance, 183, 415; capital controls, 236; capital flights from, 65, 75–76; Central America, 73; commercial trade policies, 43–47; commodity price developments, 170; currency overvaluation in, 48; current

account balances, 18–19, 171, 581; debt crisis in, 5–6, 64–73, 162, 180–81, 190–92; defaults on debt, 577; development policies, 12; direct foreign investment in, 52–55; economic policy changes in, 70–73; economies of, 10–15; exchange rate policies, 47–52; exports, see Exports, Latin American; external sector policies, 11, 13–15, 47–52; FDI in, 52–55, 483; GDP-export ratio, 165; gross investment (1977–85), 173; imports, see Imports, Latin American; import substitution strategy, 14, 43–45, 71; income per capita, 68; increase in official credit, 164; industrialization programs, 14; inflation in, 65, 70; interest as fraction of GDP, 165; investments in U.S., 509; manufacturing wages, 54; minority ownership trend, 501; NIC trade, 9–64; noninterest external surplus (1977–85), 173; NTBs in, 41–43, 47; openness index, 19; overlending to, 171; production incentives in, 5; protectionism in, 43–47; purchases of U.S. securities, 512; sectoral composition of exports, 38–41; terms of trade index, 35; trade surpluses, 64–68; value of imports, 20–33 U.S. bank lending to, 513; U.S. public utility investments in, 483; U.S. trade with, 9, 24–29, 58, 182–83, 415. See also Debt crisis, global; specific countries
Law, globalization of, 374–80
Law firms, FDI and, 554
Law of one price, 242
LDCs. See Less-developed countries
Leasing, market access to, 373
Lesotho, food production decline, 434
Less-developed countries (LDCs): affiliate sales, 501–02; agricultural trade, 460–68; auto industry in, 295; capital flow needs, 655; debts of, 162, 165, 172–73, 182, 184–92, 259; dollar needs, 173–74; equity-debt swaps, 185–88; import competition, 339; interest payments, 164, 166; Latin America and, 21–23; R&D in, 502; services sector, 422; systemic reform in, 197; U.S. and, 180, 182. See also specific country

Liberalization indexes, 47
LIBOR. *See* London Interbank Offer Rate
Libya, frozen assets of, 582
Lipsey index of price competitiveness, 429
Livestock disease, 425
Living standards, real adjustment of, 198
Loans, 202; Baker Plan, 197; corporate cost of, 298–99; credit rationing, 171–72; currency denomination, 165, 582; default risks, 577, 579–82; discount rate, 213, 579; FDI risks vs., 582; marketable financial instruments vs., 215; multilateral lending, 201; private vs. governmental, 203; risk premiums, 190; secondary market, 186, 213, 579; securities and, 223, 225, 273; short vs. long-term, 273–74; by U.S. banks, 179–83; U.S. vs. European, 181, 221. *See also* Debt crisis, global; Interest rates
Local government: spending (1900–1984), 640; surpluses, 606–7
London Economic Summit (1984), 410–11
London Interbank Offer Rate (LIBOR), 164–65, 579; Eurocurrency market and, 219, 221; hedging and, 228; interest rate exposure, 228
Long-dated forward exchange contracts, 555
Long-distance services, 377
Long-Term Arrangement on Cotton Textile Trade (1962–73), 320

Machinery: Latin American imports, 29; multinational share in exports, 496
Macroeconomic policies: budget deficit and, 605–6; determinants of capital flow, 596–602; financial innovation impact, 218; Japan-U.S. trade imbalance and, 628; key variables in, 170; LDCs debt and, 184–85, 209; U.S. monetary policy and, 603–5
Maekawa report, 631, 654
Malaysia: auto production, 296; common market, 93; debt-servicing, 88; exports, 92, 108, 129, 137; factor-price advantage, 128; imports, 106, 108, 116–18; investment ratio in, 85; merchandise trade, 107; MFA and,

320; per capita income, 106; rate of growth, 83, 143–44; trade and development policies, 106, 137; trade performance, 106–7; U.S. import market share, 106, 116–18
Management, 387, 408; cost competitiveness and, 306; consulting, 376; cultural mergers, 154–55; financial. *See* Financial services industry; five-year plans, 554–55; U.S. exports of, 475
Manufacturing industries, 119; affiliate exports to U.S., 500; direct investment in U.S., 589–91; FDI by U.S., 518, 552; foreign employment in, U.S., 505–6; global distribution of, 522–25; high-technology, 374; Latin American exports-imports of, 29–30, 33–34, 40, 71; multinational export share, 494; production by major sector, 390; R&D by parent firm, 526. *See also* Basic industries, U.S.; Manufacturing industries, U.S.
Manufacturing industries, U.S.: current account and, 420n.1; employment, 382–83; imports, 655; revival of, 654
Marathon Oil, 340
Mark. *See* Deutschmark
Marketing, U.S. competitive advantage, 341
Marshall Plan, 189, 629
Massachusetts, decline in basic industry employment, 335–37
Mauritius, import growth, 322
Meat, indirect price supports, 470
Medicare, costs of, 639–43
Merchandise trade: barriers to, 395–96; GATT and, 368, 402n.1; services and, 373; U.S. current account, 371–72
Mergers and acquisitions, FDI, 554
Merrill Lynch Company, 556
MESA network, 233
Metal industries: exchange rates and, 365; export distribution, 496, 522–25; global production in, 288; U.S., 284–86. *See also* specific industry
Mexico: auto production, 287, 295; budget deficit, 177–78, 581; capital flight from, 75, 188–89; changes in government, 71; cost of debt, 68, 190; creditors and, 65, 67, 169, 172, 182, 192; debt ratios, 163, 165; economic

Mexico (*continued*)
goals of, 66, 361; export market, 15, 17, 33–43, 67, 464; foreign investment in, 52, 75, 501; imports, 16, 21, 25, 28, 31, 33, 75; macroeconomic indicators, 177; monetary and fiscal policies, 48, 65–66; noninterest budget, 177; non-oil export growth, 68, 178–79, 464; overvaluation in, 167; real exchange rate, 48–51, 167; trade surpluses, 19. *See also* Latin America

MFN. *See* Most favored nations

Michigan, automobile production, 339

Mid-Atlantic states: apparel industry 334; steel industry, 335

Middle East: as debtor countries, 162; non-oil debt-GDD ratios, 163, 165; OPEC, 400, 512–13, 567

Midwest states, steel industries, 335

Milk production, 425

Minimills, steel, 318–19, 339

Minimum price systems, 41

Mining: direct investment by U.S., 518; foreign affiliate jobs in U.S., 506–8

Minority shareholdings, 546

MITI, 325, 552

Monetary policy, U.S.: agriculture exports and, 435–37; Bretton Woods system, 561, 566, 646–47; capital market barriers, 220–22, 242–44; expansionist, 3, 199; financial innovation and, 218, 251; food exports and, 436; foreign investors and, 566; inflation and, 175; G-5 policies, 198; in mid-1970s, 567; MI supply, 656; real exchange rates and, 436; telecommunications and, 362

Money market accounts: functional regulation of, 272–73; mutual funds, 234

Money Market Services, Inc., 599

Morgan Guaranty, 554–55

Morocco, as problem debtor, 165, 180–81; wheat sales to, 449

Mortgages, 571–72. *See also* Banking industry

Most favored nations (MFN), 400, 418

Motor vehicles and parts industries: country of origin imports, 326; cyclical volatility of, 282; domestic demand, 301–2; earnings vs. productivity, 303–4; employee involvement programs, 312; employment decline,

358–59; foreign dealer network, 378; global production of, 292; government policies and, 295–99; investment in, 313; Japanese, 311, 588; joint ventures, 339–40; location of, 336; process innovation, 338; product cycle, 293–95; technology transfer, 294–95; trade deficit and, 333; VERs, 325–26; wage concessions, 307

Mozambique, food production decline, 434

Multifiber Agreement (MFA), 320

Multilateral trade negotiations. *See* General Agreement on Tariffs and Trade

Multinational firms: advantage of, 491–502; debt-equity swaps and, 187; distribution of exports, 523–25; export shares, 493–502; foreign asset equilibrium, 505; host country sales, 498; OTA review of service firms, 394; overseas production basis, 153, 497; rise in, 154; service-oriented, 370, 378, 391–95; share in export of manufactures, 524. *See also* specific industries, sectors

Multiple exchange rates, 47, 51–52, 61n.34

Mutual funds, 234

National Bureau of Economics Research (NBER), 642

Nationalization, of industry, 582

National Planning Association, 402n.4

National saving: capital flow changes and, 610; deficit reduction and, 605, 637–38; defined, 605; global comparisons, 608–9, 611; investment and, 610–11; Japanese, 628; total gross rate, 607–10; U.S. percentages of GNP, 601, 606; U.S. private, 607–10

National security: basic industries and, 365–66; dollar decline and, 7; U.S. budget deficit and, 637

National Study on Services, U.S., 411

Natural-resource-intensive imports, 120–27

Netherlands: FDI in U.S., 508–9; open financial markets, 572; textile industry, 297

Netherlands Antilles: corporate bond tax and, 585, 623nn.21, 26; FDI in U.S., 509, 590

Newly industrialized countries (NICs): basic industry cycle, 293–95; exports, 57, 153, 322, 339; foreign investment by, 146; import growth, 322, 339; industrial technology, 150; Latin American trade, 57; nations included in, 142–43; restrictive trade policies, 156, 159; textiles, 293; U.S. market access to, 4. *See also* specific country

New York, as trading center, 220

New Zealand: APR import-export shares, 80, 116–29; open financial markets, 574; per capita income, 143

Nicaragua: imports, 23, 25, 31, 33; industrial technology and, 150; U.S. trade, 25

NICs. *See* Newly industrialized countries

Nigeria: food export markets, 435; as OPEC country, 179; problem debts, 180–81; wheat import bans, 465

Nihon Keizai Shinbun, 631–32

Nikko Securities, 555

Nippon Steel, 294, 299

Nominal exchange rates, 12, 44

Nomura Securities, 555

Nonelectrical machinery, global distribution of exports, 522–25

Nonequity collaboration agreements, 546

Nonferrous metals, production trends, 284–87

Nontariff barriers (NTBs), 41–43, 396–97; codes of conduct for, 404n.31; Japanese, 148–49; real exchange rates and, 329; textiles and, 320–21

North Atlantic Treaty Organization (NATO), 638

North Carolina, textile industry employment, 335

Norway: domestic savings, 85; textile industry, 297

Note issuance facilities, 226, 250. *See also* Capital markets, global

NTBs. *See* Nontariff barriers

Ocean shipping, regulation of, 402n.1

OECD. *See* Organization of Economic Cooperation and Development

Office of Technology Assessment (OTA), 394; agriculture and, 464; services exports and, 368–69, 394, 402n.6

Offshore banking, 262, 509, 511, 566, 574, 576, 582, 585

Ohio, automobile production, 339

Oil industry: FDI in U.S., 508–9, 589–91; Japanese investments in, 552; U.S. FDI, 518, 552; U.S. imports, 635

Oil crisis shocks, 10, 169, 567; FDI and, 511, 513; Japan and, 628–29; Mexico and, 191; U.S. current account and, 611

Oilseeds, U.S. export decline, 438

Omnibus Trade Act (1984), 410–12

OPEC. *See* Organization of Petroleum Exporting Countries

Open interest contracts, 226–30

Openness index, Latin American countries, 19

Operation Twist, 566

Option contracts, 226–30; aggregate open interest in, 228; daily trading volumes, 229; delta hedging and, 233

OTA. *See* Office of Technology Assessment

Organization of Economic Cooperation and Development (OECD), 209–10; automobile industry demand, 302; clothing output, 287; exports of primary products to, 37; footwear production, 287; GATT service negotiations and, 400; grain import policies, 440; Latin American imports to, 37; manufactured imports, 32–33;

Organization of Petroleum Exporting Countries (OPEC): transfer of wealth to, 567; U.S. reserve holdings and, 512–13. *See also* specific country

Other goods and services account, 416

Outsourcing, of manufacturing, 555

Pacific Theater: democracy and, 155; economic community proposal, 157; future of, 154–155; growth in trade, 152, 154–55; industrial development, 154; nations included in, 152. *See also* Asian Pacific Rim countries; East Asia

Panama, exports-imports, 16–17

Paraguay: manufactured imports, 33; multiple exchange rates, 51; origin of imports, 22; real exchange rate, 48–51; U.S. export share, 25

Passenger cars, U.S., imports, 326. *See also* Motor vehicles and parts industries

Passenger fares, 373

Patents, U.S. decline in, 417

Payment-in-Kind (PIK) program, 443

Pennsylvania, steel industry employment, 335

People's Republic of China. *See* China

Personal consumption, U.S. (1929–86), 386

Peru: debt-GDP ratio, 165; debt service, 66, 190; exports, 17; imports, 16, 22, 25; monetary and fiscal policies, 48; protectionism in, 45; real exchange rate, 48–51

Petroleum industry. *See* Oil industry

Pharmaceutical industries, collaboration agreements, 546–47

Philippines: debt-servicing problems, 85–88, 180–81; development strategy, 104; exports, 103–4, 129; factor-price advantage, 128; growth rate, 137, 144; import market, 103–4, 116–18; Japan and, 129; merchandise trade, 104; per capita income, 81; political uncertainty in, 136–37; trade performance, 88, 102–3, 116–18; U. S. trade share, 103–4, 116–18

P.I.K. *See* Payment-in-Kind program

Pioneer Industries Ordinance (1958), 106

Plaza Accord (1985), 199, 593, 600, 621

Political factors, of trade: FDI and, 155–56, 553; ideal reform and, 206–7; ideological amalgamation, 155; U.S. advantage, 128, 155–56

Pollution abatement programs, 330–33

Population, U.S.: age composition changes, 386–87; migration and, 153; real food price decline and, 431

Pork, supply-demand equations, 440–41

Portfolio investment. *See* Foreign direct investment

Postindustrial economy, 380–83

President's Council of Economic Advisors, 469, 627–28

Price: competitiveness indexes of, 429; export unit value, 162; investigations, 41; law of one price, 242; NTBs, 41–43, 320–21, 396–97; subsidy elimination, 175; TPM, 323; U.S. supports, 442–51

Private saving: Japanese, 85, 607–10

Private sector: determinants of competitiveness, 302–19; savings, 85, 607–10

Production: capital-intensive, 281; costs, 314–19, 337–39. *See also* specific industry

Productivity: labor investment and, 312–14; service economy and, 386–88; U.S. labor force, 303–12

Professional services. *See* specific service industry

Prohibitions, trade, 41–43. *See also* specific barriers

Proposition 13, California, 650

Proprietary rights, 373

Protectionism: EEC, 11; FDI and, 553; industrialized nations, 37–43, 71; Latin American, 11–12, 15, 33, 43–45, 51–52, 71, 205; NTBs and, 42; openness index and, 19. *See also* Protectionism, U.S.

Protectionism, U.S., 1, 9–11, 653; agricultural sector, 424, 439–42; basic industries, 322–28; dollar decline and, 4; service sector, 391, 410; trade deficit and, 621

Protective services, 387

Provider-located services, 377

Public sector: debt crisis cuts and, 175; deficits and, 203, 205; employment in, 380–83

Public utilities: FDI by U.S., 376, 481, 483–85, 519; foreign affiliate jobs in U.S., 506–8

Public Works and Economic Development Act (EDA) (1965), 328

Quotas, 4, 41, 322. *See also* Protectionism

Radio industry: foreign ownership of, 398

Rates of return, determinants of, 602. *See also* Foreign direct investment

Reagan administration: GATT agenda on services and, 410; target price cuts, 451

Real estate, U.S.: FDI in, 509, 552, 589–91; U.S. employment, 380–83, 414

Real exchange rates (RER): basic industries and, 329–30; debt service and, 164, 166–67; IMF index of relative unit labor costs and, 342; Mexican, 178; misaligned, 47; overvalued, 48

Real interest rate: budget deficits and, 200, 614, 620; capital flight and, 176; in debtor countries, 166–67, 187; differential in, 598, 600; investment-saving ratios and, 604–5; macroeconomic policy and, 602; net foreign investment and, 610; tax incentives and, 605. *See also* Interest rates

Recent Innovations in International Banking (BIS), 257

Recession: FDI and, 511, 611; Latin American, 10; 1975 global, 567; U.S., 3, 603, 621

Reforms, credit worthiness and, 204–12

Regional trade. *See* specific areas

Regulation: capital markets, 220–22, 242–52, 264–65, 271–72, 569; cross-border, 254n.22; environmental, 330–33, 365; financial innovations and, 233, 240; information technology and, 270; international standards, 259–61; local trade barrier effect, 398; services, 410. *See also* specific acts, barriers, regulations

Repair market, access to, 373

Reproduction services, 387

Republic of China. *See* Taiwan

Republic of Korea. *See* Korea, South

Research and development (R&D) 387, 526; collaboration agreements, 546–47; global centers for, 546; high technology, 371; intergovernmental, 158; monetary policy and, 362; multinational advantage and, 492, 497–98; service sectors, 376

Resource-rich countries (RRCs), 84; investment and savings rate, 85; pattern of exports, 137; trade and development policies of, 102–16. *See also* specific country

Retail trade sector: employment in, 380–83, 387, 413–14; foreign affiliate jobs in U.S., 506–08; foreign markets, 376; restaurants, 387

Reuters, ADR facility, 555

Revealed comparative advantage. *See* Comparative advantage theory

Rice: Asian self-sufficiency in, 434, 439; price fall, 453; price supports, 446–47

Rich Inc., 555

Risk management, of investments, 226–30, 233; delta hedging procedure, 234; transfer of risk, 248–52. *See also* Financial services industry

Romania, trends in production, 284

RRCs. *See* Resource-rich countries

Safe haven hypothesis, 577–82, 596–97, 632

Salomon Brothers, 223

Samurai bonds, 573

Saudi Arabia, grain exports, 454, 470

Saving, national: APR countries, 83; capital flows and, 202–3, 567; debt service ratio, 207; investment and, 199; Latin American, 70, 72. *See also* specific country

Scandinavia: motor vehicle industry, 287; offshore companies in, 553

Seasonal tariffs, 41

Securities, 215, 511–13; banking and, 219–22, 264–65, 273–74, 569; brokerage fees, 569; foreign purchase of U.S., 592; growth of, 222–30; market profits of, 273–74; mortgage-backed, 234; risks of, 250; U.S. holdings, 511–13, 572; welfare losses, 217–18. *See also* Financial services industry; specific markets

Securities and Exchange Commission (SEC), 223, 266

Separated services, 377

Separate trading of registered interest and principal securities (STRIPS), 235

Service industries: analytical issues, 375–80; barriers to global competition, 395–399; classification of, 370, 377–79, 393; domestic economy and, 380–89; exchange rate and, 422; financial institutions, *see* Banking industry; Financial services industry; foreign affiliate employment in U.S., 506–8; GATT and, 368–75, 395–401; global labor force, 387–89; growth in, 371, 386–87; information-based, 375–80; international competition in, 369–70, 388–89, 391–92, 395–401; international transactions, 389–395; local regulation of, 398; manufactures income vs., 361; measurement of, 404n.25, 409; NTBs, 397; policy and, 370–75; production by major sector, 390; production process, 376–77; productivity and, 387–88; role of, 413–19; speciality firm contracts, 414; U.S. employment in, 380–83, 559; U.S. surplus, 371; world trade percentages, 389–95, 408. *See also* specific service industry

Shipping industries, 369, 373, 402n.1

Short-Term Arrangement on Cotton Textile Trade (1961–62), 320

Singapore: debt-servicing, 88; domestic savings, 85; exports, 91–96, 116–18, 129; growth rate of, 141, 143; imports, 91, 94–96; income levels in, 84; investment ratio in, 85; merchandise trade, 94; open financial markets, 574; reliance on foreign investment, 93; SIMEX, 246; trade and development policies, 92; U.S. trade share, 116–18

Singapore International Monetary Exchange (SIMEX), 246

SITC, Latin American exports and, 37

Small Business Administration Program, 328

Socialist countries, agricultural output, 427–28

Social Security, U.S.: budget deficit and, 639–40; projected cost rate of income, 635–42

Society for Worldwide Interbank Financial Transfers (SWIFT), 233

Somalia, food production decline, 434

Sorghum, price supports, 446

South Africa: food production decline, 434; grain export shares, 441; VERs, 324

South America: GDP, 81; investments in U.S., 483–84, 589; U.S. trade with, 183. See also Latin America; Southern Cone countries

South Atlantic states, motor vehicle industry employment, 335; textile industry employment, 335

South Carolina, textile industry employment, 335

Southeast Asia: GDP, 81; Latin American trade, 9; population of, 80; as potential market, 81. See also Asia; specific country

Southern Cone countries: import substitution strategy, 12; liberalization in, 44–45, 56; NTBs in, 47; real value of imports, 59n.6; tariffs, 45–46. See also Latin America; South America; specific country

South Korea. See Korea, South

Soviet bloc (CAME), 30. See also specific country

Soviet Union: agricultural output, 428, 635; asset freezes and, 220, 582; CAME, 30; capitalist system and, 152;

food exports, 635; grain agreements with U.S., 438, 453, 468; steel industry, 294; U.S. embargoes, 451, 466

Soybeans, price supports, 447

Spain, EEC membership, 473

Special Export Zones, China, 115

Sri Lanka, import growth, 322

State government: securities, 572; spending (1900–1984), 640; surpluses, 606–7

Steel industry: capital-intensiveness of, 281; cyclical volatility of, 282; deinvestment, 313–14; demand decline, 299–300; global production changes, 284–85; government policies and, 295–99; Japanese, 316–19, 629; labor costs in, 307–08; location of, 336; minimill firms, 318–19; pollution abatement costs, 331–33; product and process innovation, 316–19, 333–38; product cycle, 293–95; productivity problems, 303–5; protectionism and, 322–27; substitutes for, 300; technology choices, 314–19; unit labor costs, 311; VERs, 323–27

Stenographic services, 387

Stock markets, 222–30; direct investor purchases in, 592; dividend-to-price earnings ratio, 600; dual listings, 233; foreign investment in, 484, 511–13, 539, 555; gross new issues (1980–87), 228; interest rate contracts, 226–30; U.S. vs. foreign returns in, 600–02; value of domestic companies, 227. See also Capital markets, global; Financial services industry

Strategic planning, 555

Subic Bay Naval Base, 105–6

Subsidies. See specific industries, sectors

Sugar: Caribbean dumping of, 470; GATT price waiver, 454; market competition, 470; price supports for, 447; real price decline in, 431; supply-demand equations, 440–41

Supply-side economics, 607, 642, 650

Swaps, financial, 230–31, 235–37. See also specific type

Sweden, investments in U.S., 557, 589

SWIFT. See Society for Worldwide Interbank Financial Transfer

Switzerland: capital inflow controls, 572; FDI in U.S., 552, 589; franc trading,

570–71; GATT negotiations, 419; open financial markets, 572; securitization of, 226

Synthetic securities, 237–39, 245

Taiwan: automobile industry, 287; debt-servicing, 88; development strategy, 100; domestic savings, 85; economic goals of, 361; exports, 92, 101, 129, 144; feed use of cereals, 433; growth rate of, 141; imports of, 74, 101; income levels in, 84; intraregional trade, 56; limits on textile imports, 321; MFA and, 320; output of, 142; political future of, 102; technology and, 359; trade and development policies, 99–100; trade performance, 92, 100–102, 116–18, 129, 144, 146–47

Tariffs, 395–96; NTBs and, 45; quotas, 4, 41, 322; true protection and, 45–47

Tax havens, 574, 577

Tax policy: antitax revolt, 650; basic industries and, 299; bilateral treaties and, 577; bond interest and, 577; capital gains, 235; capital flight and, 189; corporate, 604–5; debt crisis and, 175; domestic demand and, 199; financial innovation and, 233; global capital flows and, 7, 106, 201, 574, 576–77, 604–6; IET, 222; job mobility and, 556; reform plans, 354, 605; service economy and, 388, 412; stimulation of savings and, 72; tax amnesty, 193n.17. *See also* Fiscal policy, U.S.

Tax Reform Act (1986), 354

Technology: Asian competition in, 153–54; imported, 294, 475; Japanese, 629; production costs and, 314–19; transfer, 359, 546–47; U.S. exports, 475

Technology-intensive exports, 120–27

Telecommunications: costs, 569; globalization of, 374–80; infrastructure, 407; switching software for, 414; trade barriers, 373, 398

Temporary-help suppliers, 387

Tennessee, automobile production, 339

Terms of trade changes (1980–82), 170

Texas Oil and Gas, 340

Textile industry: domestic demand for, 301; global production changes (1974–83), 289; industrial policies, 327–28; investments in, 313; process

innovation, 338; product cycle forces, 293–95; protectionism and, 322–27; regional location of, 334–35; stability of, 282; trade agreements, 320–21; U.S. foreign competition, 137, 279–366

Thailand: auto production, 295; debt-servicing problems, 85–88; export shares and, 92, 111, 116–18, 129; factor-price advantage, 128; grain export shares, 441, 448; Japan and, 129; trade balance, 88; trade policies, 107–9, 127; United States and, 109–10, 116–18, 440

Tobin's q, 314

Tourism industry, 377, 404n.25

TPM. *See* Trigger price mechanism

Trade Act (1962), 328

Trade Act (1974), 328

Trade and Tariff Act (1984), 61n.26

Trade balance. *See* Trade deficit, U.S.; specific countries

Trade barriers, 205, 395–401; APR countries, 136; Brazil, 169; Japanese, 148–49, 296; nontariff measures, 40–47; trade deficit and, 4. *See also* specific country, type

Trade credits, 213

Trade deficit, U.S., 1–3, 415, 566, 559; basic industry decline and, 354, 359; capital vs. consumer goods, 657; current account and. *See* Current account, U.S.; debt service and, 161; dollar role in, 2, 359–60, 599; East Asia and, 147, 630; end of, 652–53; exchange rate adjustments and, 631; goods to service shift and, 371; manufactured goods, 635; merchandising industries and, 333, 408

Trade in services, definition, 370

Trade legislation, 1, 61n.26, 328. *See also* Protectionism

Trade policy, U.S., 9, 11, 341, 653; agricultural, 424, 439–42; basic industries, 319–27, 357; service industries, 391, 410; trade deficit and, 621; U.S. Trade Department, 411

Trade secrets, 376

Trade surpluses, U.S., 2, 561, 652–53

Training services, market access and, 373

Transnational documentation, 554

Transport industry: employment changes and, 386–87; foreign affiliate jobs in

Transport industry (*continued*)
U.S., 506–8; global export
distribution, 369, 375–76, 522–25;
U.S. multinational shares, 496
Travel industry, 373, 376, 404n.25
Treasury securities. *See* U.S.
Department of the Treasury
Trigger price mechanism (TPM), 323
Turkey, macroeconomic policy, 204

Unemployment, 10; in basic industries,
333–37; export-oriented nations and,
653; spending cuts and, 174
Unfair trade practices, 156–57, 159. *See
also* Protectionism
Unilateral transfers account (1986), 416–
17
Unions: global economy effects on, 356–
57; voluntary restraint agreements,
307; wage differentials and, 305–6
United Autoworkers Union, 306–7
United Kingdom: bank supervision, 259;
Big Bang, 265; capital control, 572;
China agreement, 92; food price
increases, 473; investment in U.S.,
508–9, 552; labor force by industry,
389; production by major sector, 390;
stake in services, 411; sterling market,
236; textile industry, 293, 297; U.S.
trade agreements, 259–61
United Nations (U.N.): ECLA, 14, 29–
30, 56, 71; FAO, 425
UNCTAD trade data, 100–01; WIDER,
632
United States: agriculture in. *See*
Agriculture, U.S.; aluminum
production, 356; APR competition,
116–28, 134, 148; bank claims of, 179–
80; *see also* Banking industry; basic
industries, 279–366; bilateral trade
agreements, 259–61, 559; *see also*
specific country, type; as capital
importer, 510–17; capital outflow, 560–
68; *see also* Foreign direct investment,
by U.S.; competitiveness in global
environment, 358–62; decline in
growth rates, 81–82; decline in
productivity, 284, 311, 428–29; defense
costs, 7, 562–63, 566, 637, 650–51;
economic power loss, 647; equity
market shares, 226–27; expansionary

policies, 566; foreign debt (1914–19),
480–81; *see also* Budget deficit, U.S.;
FDI in, *see* Foreign direct investment,
in U.S.; GNP deflator, 162; high
technology, 159, 342, 371, 379–80, 415;
income growth, 566; inflation, 169–70,
600, 603, 654–55; interest equalization
tax (IET), 222; international capital
transactions (1946–85), 534–38, 562–
65; international investment position,
475–558, 616–17; ITC, 397, 453; labor
costs, 54, 308, 311; labor force by
industry, 389; Latin American trade
and, 9–64, 183; merchandise trade
deficit, 371; natural resources, 155; net
liabilities, 477, 479, 634; per capita
income, 81, 142–43; policy needs of,
141–42, 341, 642; production by major
sector, 390; production costs in, 339;
relative factor-price advantages, 128;
as service economy, 370–83, 409; steel
industry, 307–32; technology exports,
371, 379–80, 414, 475; textile market,
293, 320; total government spending
(1900–1984), 640; trade deficit, *see*
Trade deficit, U.S.; wheat sales, 429,
453, 468; world debt and, *see* Debt
crisis, global; world market share, 226,
440
U.S. Council on Environmental Quality
(1980), 425
U.S. Department of Agriculture (USDA):
agriculture production index, 425–26;
Economic Research Service, 433; farm
real estate price index, 431; index of
food output per capita, 431, 441; price
exports projections, 450; total factor
productivity index, 428–29
U.S. Department of Commerce:
automobile industry demand and, 302;
breakdown of goods, 123–27; textile
barriers and, 328
U.S. Department of the Treasury,
securities of, 235; bond futures trading,
229; Canadian purchases of, 512;
defaults, 485; Euromarket-issued
securities, 583, 623nn.19, 23; FDI
earnings vs., 556; foreign investment
in, 511–13, 539–41, 571, 588–92, 620;
interest paid to foreigners, 577;
Japanese dealers in, 421; STRIPS, 235;

U.S. vs. nondollar rates, 597–600; zero-coupon securities, 234–35, 569. *See also* Capital markets, global

U.S. Steel Corporation (USX), 340, 355

United Steelworkers of America (USWA), 306, 318

Universities, science research in, 547

Unskilled-labor-intensive imports, 120–27

Uruguay: as debtor, 182; devaluation schedules, 48; economic reforms, 14, 44–45; exports, 17; imports, 16, 21, 24–25, 31, 33; protectionism in, 43, 45; relaxation of capital controls in, 48; services issue, 371; trade surpluses, 19

Variable levies, 41

Venezuela: current account deficit, 581; cost of debt, 65, 68; exports, 17; imports, 16, 21, 25, 29, 33; net disinvestment, 52–53; as OPEC country, 179; overvaluation, 167; real exchange rate, 167

VERs. *See* Voluntary export restraints

Voluntary export restraints (VERs), 41, 320; basic industries, 323–27; GATT dissatifaction and, 396

Voluntary price restraints, 41

Wages: competitiveness and, 174–76; concessions, 307; CPI and, 343; cost-of-living escalators, 306; downward rigidity, 388; female, 305, 307; freeze of public sector, 175; international comparisons, 308–12; in manufacturing sector, 54; regression analysis and, 346; service industries, 404n.22

Wall Street Journal, 469, 473

West Germany. *See* Germany

Wheat: dollar value-export ratios, 438; EEP and, 449; global price comparisons of, 429; price supports, 446–47; quality of, 430; real price declines, 431; supply-demand equations, 440–41

Winrock International, 433

Withholding taxes, 577

Women: apparel industry wages, 305; service economy and, 387

Work rules, 388

World Bank, 54, 189, 211; bonds, 579–81; currency swaps, 237; environmental regulations and, 365; exchange rate overvaluation and, 435; GDP per capita estimates, 433–34; IBM swap, 236-37; Japan and, 633; LDCs debt buying, 189; liberalization indexes, 47; *World Development Report* (1986), 463

World Commission for the Revitalization of the World Economy, 633

World Institute for Development Economics Research, U.N., 632

World War II: capital outflows after, 639; European Recovery Plan, 629

Yen, 557; appreciation of, 573; dollar exchange rate (1970–86), 149, 630; expected decline in, 629; trade invoice currency, 571; Yen/Dollar Agreement (May 1984), 573–74

Young Commission on Competitiveness, 362

Yugoslavia: auto industry 296, 327; as problem debtor, 180–81

Zambia, food production decline, 434

Zero coupon bonds, 234–35, 569

Zimbabwe, food production decline, 434